BAA plc

A report on the economic regulation of
the London airports companies
(Heathrow Airport Ltd, Gatwick Airport
Ltd and Stansted Airport Ltd)

Volume 1: Chapters

Presented to the Civil Aviation Authority
October 2002

Web site: www.Competition-Commission.org.uk

Members of the Competition Commission as at 31 October 2002

Dr D J Morris[1] *(Chairman)*
Professor P A Geroski *(Deputy Chairman)*
Mrs D P B Kingsmill CBE *(Deputy Chairman)*
Professor J Baillie
Mr R D D Bertram
Mrs S E Brown
Mr C Clarke
Dr J Collings
Dr D Coyle
Mr C Darke
Mr L Elks
Dr G G Flower
Mr N Garthwaite
Mr C Goodall
Professor C Graham
Professor A Gregory
Mrs D Guy
Mr G H Hadley
Professor A Hamlin
Miss J C Hanratty
Professor J E Haskel
Mr P F Hazell
Mr C E Henderson CB
Mr R Holroyd[1]
Professor B Lyons
Professor P Klemperer
Dame Barbara Mills QC
Professor P Moizer[1]
Dr E M Monck
Mr R J Munson
Professor D Parker
Mr A J Pryor CB
Mr R A Rawlinson
Professor J A Rees[1]
Mr T S Richmond MBE
Mr J B K Rickford[1]
Mr E J Seddon
Dame Helena Shovelton DBE
Mr C R Smallwood
Mr J D S Stark
Professor A Steele
Mr P Stoddart
Mr R Turgoose
Professor C Waddams
Mr S Walzer
Mr M R Webster
Professor S Wilks
Mr A M Young

Mr R Foster *(Secretary)*

---

[1] These members formed the Group which was responsible for this report under the Chairmanship of Dr D J Morris.

Note by the Civil Aviation Authority

In accordance with section 45(7) and (3A) of the Airports Act 1986, the Secretary of State for Transport has directed the CAA to exclude from the published report certain matters, publication of which appear to the Secretary of State to be against the public interest or the commercial interests of a person. Accordingly certain figures and text have been omitted. The omissions are indicated by a note in the text.

Volume 1 contents

Part I

Summary and Conclusions

1 Summary

1.1. Under the references made by the Civil Aviation Authority (CAA) on 28 February 2002 (see Appendix 1.1), we are required to recommend the maximum levels of airport charges at Heathrow Airport Ltd (HAL), Gatwick Airport Ltd (GAL) and Stansted Airport Ltd (STAL), for the period of five years beginning on 1 April 2003. (This is the fourth regulatory period since privatization of the airports, referred to as Q4.) HAL, GAL and STAL are all subsidiaries of BAA PLC (BAA). We are also required to consider whether any of the three airport companies have, at any time from the date of the last references to us in December 1995 up to the date of the current references, pursued a course of conduct (in relation to matters specified in the references) which has operated, or might be expected to operate, against the public interest.

1.2. During the current regulatory period (Q3), airport charges per passenger at Heathrow and Gatwick combined have been required to increase by no more than RPI–3 and at Stansted by no more than RPI+1. The current reference follows a substantial review by the CAA of the appropriate basis on which to set the maximum level of airport charges. In the references to us, the CAA recommended a formula of RPI+6 at Heathrow, RPI+5 at Gatwick, and slightly above RPI+6 at Stansted (but did not expect STAL to be able fully to recover the price cap set). This represented increases in airport charges per passenger (in 2000/01 prices) between 2002/03 and 2007/08 from £5.37 to £7.25 at Heathrow; from £4.03 to £5.09 at Gatwick; and from £4.47 to £6.10 at Stansted.

1.3. During the inquiry, we had to consider a number of general issues relevant to setting the maximum level of charges, as well as a number of more specific issues relating to the future costs and revenues of the three airports.

1.4. The most controversial aspect of the CAA's recommendations was its proposal for a 'dual-till' approach. Currently, airport charges are set on a 'single-till' basis, which takes into account the revenues and costs of BAA's highly profitable commercial activities (primarily rental income from retail and other concessionaires). The CAA proposed that they should instead be set to cover the costs of aeronautical activities, ie those regarded as essential for the operation of the airport, and monopolizable by the airport, users therefore having little choice but to use them. This would exclude not only activities such as retail and catering outlets, but also surface access to the airports (such as the existing Heathrow Express) unless required as a condition for planning permission of new facilities (for example, the extensions to Heathrow Express and Piccadilly lines). Other things being equal, the dual till would lead to significantly higher airport charges over the longer term, but in practice the CAA proposed to set charges for Heathrow in Q4 at a level that was consistent with a single-till approach, since it regarded that as the reasonable upper limit for price increases in this period. The CAA proposed that the maximum level of charges at Gatwick and Stansted in Q4 would, however, be on a dual-till basis, and that Heathrow should recover in subsequent regulatory periods the difference between the single-till and dual-till approach at Heathrow in Q4.

1.5. Airlines all objected strongly to the dual-till approach, regarding it as unnecessarily increasing charges, to the benefit of BAA at the expense of airlines and, through the higher fares that would result, at the expense of passengers. Among their other arguments, they regarded commercial activities as an inseparable part of the aeronautical business; and there were also concerns that it gave BAA the incentive to favour commercial development at the expense of aeronautical development.

1.6. The main benefits claimed by the CAA and BAA for the dual-till approach related to effects on investment incentives, efficient utilization of scarce runway capacity, and deregulation of non-monopoly activities. BAA's investment programme—about £8 billion from 2002/03 to 2012/13 including about £3.5 billion on Terminal 5 (T5) at Heathrow—is important to the airlines. However, we found no evidence that the single till had led to any general under-investment, nor in current or foreseeable circumstances, any basis for an expectation that it would do so over the next five years; nor was it clear that the dual till would lead to better aeronautical investment in future. The dual till could improve the efficient utilization of capacity, but the benefits are unlikely to be more than marginal, even at Heathrow, where there is significant excess demand. The case for the dual till is, indeed, even weaker in Q4, where the CAA proposed to apply it only to the less congested airports: GAL and STAL.

1.7. Nor do we see significant benefits from any deregulation of BAA's commercial activities, most of which relates to the leasing of space for retail and other commercial activities. In so far as airport charges affect fares, BAA's current relatively high profits from its commercial activities are mitigated by the fact that they are applied to the benefit of passengers. The dual-till approach would break this link and may therefore require increased regulation of such activities. The dual till could also risk unduly benefiting commercial activities at the expense of aeronautical activities, which may not attract sufficient funds or management priority.

1.8. Against those, at most, limited benefits, we see significant disadvantages from the dual-till approach. We believe it is difficult sensibly to separate commercial and aeronautical activities. BAA's rental and other commercial revenues at the three London airports would not be generated without aeronautical facilities—commercial and aeronautical facilities are better, therefore, in our view, and more realistically regarded as one business. Since the successful development of commercial revenues requires airlines to attract passengers to the airport, the benefits of commercial activities should also in our view be shared with airlines and airline users.

1.9. The increase in airport charges resulting from the dual till could, on the basis of some figures we saw, increase the net present value of revenues to BAA over the longer term by between £3.2 billion and £3.7 billion. The CAA argued that this would merely be a shift of economic rents from airlines to the airports, but was unlikely at congested airports to make a material difference to airfares or passengers: it did not therefore see such a transfer of rent as of concern to the regulator in this case. We do not believe average fares would be unaffected at either congested or uncongested airports. We cannot, however, be indifferent to such a transfer of resources to a regulated utility whether the effect was on airlines or their passengers, potentially undermining regulatory credibility and creating regulatory uncertainty.

1.10. It is also difficult, in practice, to allocate either investments or operating costs between aeronautical and commercial activities. To the extent that some of the judgements that have to be made are arbitrary, future disputes about cost allocation could also harm relations between the airport and its users.

1.11. We recognize that the current level of prices particularly at Heathrow are very substantially below market-clearing prices or the long-run incremental cost (LRIC) associated with new capacity. But setting market-clearing prices is not consistent with international obligations, and the net effect of setting charges equal to LRIC (which would transfer some £10 billion of value from airlines and passengers to BAA) would be very detrimental to users. Our approach does, however, capture some important elements of a modified LRIC approach.

1.12. One argument put to us for the dual till was that it would raise prices towards market-clearing or LRIC-based levels. However, in the circumstances which Heathrow faces for the foreseeable future, the overall balance of effects on users would remain adverse, and the approach significantly less acceptable than the one we recommend. We do not therefore share the view of the CAA that the dual till is best calculated to meet the objectives of the Airports Act 1986 (Airports Act); in our view, with these objectives in mind, the single till approach should be retained for Q4.

1.13.   Among other aspects of the general approach we had to consider:

(a) In principle we believe that the 'system approach' to setting the maximum level of airport charges—with respect to the rate of return of the system as a whole rather than that of each airport—should be retained under current conditions. However, on the basis of our forecasts this makes no difference in the period we have to consider due to STAL's increasing profitability and the current projections of investment requirements of the airports.

(b) The CAA proposed a price path commitment for future quinquennia. One element of that commitment would be a significant increase in prices when T5 came on stream to reflect the high costs of T5, that element of prices being maintained in future quinquennia. There would also be a commitment to fix the element of charges relating to the current capital base. Such a commitment is intended to improve incentives to invest, and reduce the uncertainty as to the future return on projects which depend on the outcome of future reviews. In our view, however, there can be no meaningful commitment, since neither we nor the CAA can prejudge the outcome of future reviews; we also believe that, even if such a commitment could be given, it may be undesirable since it would prevent users sharing in the benefits of future cost reductions. In our view, a preferable, alternative approach to promoting adequate incentive to invest is to allow for assets in the course of construction (AICC) subject to a series of triggers relating charges to progress particularly of T5, but together, where necessary, with an element of smoothing of return between quinquennia, reducing reliance on future large increases in charges.

(c) During Q3 there was also allowance for AICC on T5. That investment could not proceed due to delay in the planning inquiry for T5. There was also a significant advancement of revenue for such smoothing purposes. We believe recovery of these revenues and of the effects of under-investment in Q3 should in principle be allowed for in Q4.

(d) Among more detailed aspects of the formulae, we believe BAA should still be permitted to pass on 95 per cent of the costs of additional security requirements given the uncertainty as to the future level of such requirements. As proposed by the CAA, we recommend that the formulae should apply to charges as if users pay the full price before discounts; and that revenues from non-passenger flights should be removed from the cap (subject to a condition that charges should be no more than for passenger flights).

1.14.   We have estimated a cost of capital for the three airports of 7.75 per cent. This reflects in part the extra risk to BAA of the investment in T5, but which also in our view equally affects the cost of capital of all three airports. We have also taken into account scope for savings in operating costs through higher productivity, and lower pension costs. We have not adjusted BAA's forecasts for capital expenditure: even if there is scope for lower costs on some projects, there is in our view likely to be a demand for any cost savings to be spent on additional projects. We have, however, recommended a number of triggers relating airport charges to progress particularly on T5.

1.15.   We have recommended formulae of RPI+6.5 at Heathrow and RPI+0 at Gatwick. We have based Stansted's cap on its current yield gross of marketing expenditure of £4.20 at

2000/01 prices throughout Q3, but, for the purposes of the projections, STAL is assumed to be unable to increase its net charges to that level within Q4. On this basis, however, each airport earns almost exactly its cost of capital over the ten years as a whole. The effect of our recommendation is to result in charges by 2007/08 of £7.82 at HAL and £4.08 at GAL (both in 2000/01 prices). STAL's net charges are expected to remain below the cap of £4.20. (Our figures are not directly comparable with the CAA's proposals, however, since they include the currently separate charge for transfer baggage infrastructure at Heathrow, and exclude cargo flights at Stansted.)

1.16. A wide range of public interest issues were raised with us. Some airlines were critical about aspects of BAA's investment performance, including its not promoting additional runway development at Heathrow and delays to additional pier developments. However, there were in our view good reasons for BAA's approach, in particular in relation to planning constraints and uncertainty following the events of 11 September. Underlying the complaints to us, however, is a perception of inadequate consultation between BAA and the airlines. The consultation process in Q3 has been hindered by uncertainty as to the outcome of the T5 inquiry and as to additional runway developments at one or more of the airports. We nonetheless have significant reservations about the process of consultation and as those uncertainties are resolved believe improvements both to consultation and complaints procedures (which BAA itself proposes to bring about) should be put into operation.

1.17. We also regarded it, however, as unsatisfactory that airlines appear to have to use five-yearly reviews as the main means to pursue complaints, many of which should, more properly, in our view, have been addressed when they arose. We acknowledge the significant constraints on the CAA resulting from the Airports Act, which hopefully can be resolved when that Act is brought into line with other legislation. But we also suggest that the CAA examine whether current procedures under section 41 of the Airports Act can be made more effective in resolving disputes between airports and users and whether it has more scope to be involved in relationships between airlines and users aside from its formal role under that section of the Airports Act. On one detailed issue, we have found aspects of the imposition of a levy on taxi drivers at Heathrow to be against the public interest, and we have put forward an appropriate remedy.

1.18. A further main issue related to BAA's quality of service. The CAA had been concerned with this and believed that BAA's revenue from airport charges should reflect the quality of service provided. To achieve this it proposed adding a term in the RPI–X formula which would partly relate charges to quality of service. We do not believe the average level of service in Q3 has been poor. We have, however, noted a variability of quality of service provided; that although service standards were agreed, they were not comprehensive; that variability in standards has been reflected in variability of charges in only a few areas; and that users have not known what quality of service they were entitled to expect. We are in no doubt that, in a fully competitive market, airport charges would vary according to the level of service provided, but as regards Heathrow and Gatwick, during the last quinquennium, this occurred only to a minimal extent. We find that in failing to conduct themselves so as to make prices paid sufficiently reflect the levels of service provided, HAL and GAL have pursued a course of conduct which may be expected to operate against the public interest. The adverse effect of this conduct is that charges do not adequately reflect the quality of service provided to the extent that would occur in a competitive market and in consequence that there is an absence of the financial incentive to provide the combination of price and quality of service that would obtain in a competitive market.

1.19. We have recommended that HAL and GAL be required to pay specified rebates to the airlines whenever their quality of service fails to meet such performance standards as may from time to time be specified by the CAA (guidelines for which we have set out in our report) together with other requirements relating to the operation of its Quality of Service Monitor, which we regard as an important part of monitoring of quality of service.

2 Conclusions

Contents

Introduction

2.1. Under the references, made by the CAA on 28 February 2002 (see Appendix 1.1), we are required to investigate and report on and to recommend the maximum amounts that may be levied by way of airport charges (referred to hereafter as the 'maximum level of airport charges') by HAL, GAL and STAL for the period of five years beginning on 1 April 2003.[1] We are also required to consider whether any of these three airport companies (and, in the case of HAL, any associated company) have at any time during the period beginning 11 December 1995 (the date of the last reference) and ending with the date of this reference pursued a course of conduct which has operated, or might be expected to operate, against the public interest, in relation to any airport charges levied by it at the airport, to any operational activities carried on by it in relation to the airport, or to the granting of a right to carry out operational activities at the airport.

2.2. 'Airport charges' are defined in the Airports Act broadly as charges levied on operators of aircraft in connection with the landing, parking or taking-off of aircraft at the airport and charges levied on airport passengers. 'Operational activities' are defined broadly as any activities carried on wholly or mainly for the benefit of users of the airport (which include airlines and passengers) or the revenues from which are wholly or mainly attributable to payments by such users: in addition to activities for which airport charges are levied, it includes commercial activities carried out at the airport, by the airport companies themselves and by concessionaires, licensees and tenants.

2.3. The reference followed a substantial review by the CAA of the appropriate basis of airport charging at the three airports. As part of the reference, the CAA provided extensive documentation setting out its recommendations on the principles to be adopted; on the structure of the formula; and on the resulting increase in charges. The CAA proposed that average income per passenger from airport charges should not increase at Heathrow by more than 6 per cent above RPI in each year (an RPI+6 formula), with RPI+5 for Gatwick and slightly higher for Stansted, although in the case of Stansted the CAA believed that STAL would not be able to increase charges by that amount. We give the details of the CAA approach below and in the supporting chapters. We have taken full account of the information provided by the CAA in carrying out our investigation, and considered each of the issues raised by the CAA in its recommendations as well as many other issues raised with us by other parties to the inquiry.

2.4. The Airports Act specifies that the CAA must perform its functions relating to the economic regulation of airports, in the manner which it considers best calculated:

(a) to further the reasonable interest of users of airports within the UK;

(b) to promote the efficient, economic and profitable operation of such airports;

(c) to encourage investment in new facilities at airports in time to satisfy anticipated demands by the users of such airports; and

---

[1]This is the fourth regulatory period, or fourth quinquennium. In our report, we refer to the different regulatory periods as follows:

First quinquennium (Q1)	1987/88–1991/92
Second quinquennium (Q2)	1992/93–1996/97
Third quinquennium (Q3)	1997/98–2002/03
Fourth quinquennium (Q4)	2003/04–2007/08
Fifth quinquennium (Q5)	2008/09–2012/13

Following a decision by the CAA in May 1999 to extend the current price caps at the BAA London airports into a sixth year, the price caps due to expire on 31 March 2002 will expire on 31 March 2003: we nonetheless refer to the period 1997/98 to 2002/03 as the 'third quinquennium'.

(d) to impose the minimum restrictions that are consistent with the performance by the CAA of these functions.

In performing these functions the CAA is also required to take into account such of the international obligations of the UK as may be notified to it by the Secretary of State for Transport (the Secretary of State).

2.5. We are explicitly required to have regard to the above objectives in considering the public interest. In considering any matter relating to the granting of a right by virtue of which any operational activities may be carried on, we are also required to have regard to those objectives and to an additional objective, namely the furtherance of the reasonable interests of persons granted such rights. The Airports Act does not explicitly require the Competition Commission (CC) to have regard to those objectives in recommending the maximum level of airport charges. However, such a recommendation is a recommendation as to how the CAA should perform its functions and, accordingly, we need to have regard to the CAA's duty to act in the manner which it considers best calculated to achieve its objectives, and to its duty to take account of notified international obligations (see paragraph 3.74). The CAA disagreed, arguing we were only required to recommend what the maximum amounts should be in the five years in question. We disagree with its view, but in any event our conclusions would be the same irrespective of this point.

The airport companies

2.6. The holding company of HAL is London Airports 1992 Ltd and of GAL and STAL London Airports Ltd, both holding companies being subsidiaries of BAA and which we refer to collectively as LAL: we use BAA to refer to the group and any company in the group as appropriate. Although we are required to consider HAL, GAL and STAL separately, BAA regards the three airports to some extent as a system and applies similar policies to each of the companies, and gave evidence on behalf of them. We refer in this report to various policies and statements as being those of BAA when applied by or stated on behalf of the separate airport companies.

2.7. Airport charges at the three London airports amounted to some £531 million in 2001/02; other operational income (income that does not fall within the definition of airport charges but is derived from operational activities, ie activities that can be included in the public interest investigation) accounted for a further £794 million; and non-operational income (income that is derived from activities that are not operational activities and excluded from our investigation of public interest, consisting primarily of advertising) for some £39 million. The total income of the three London airports, some £1,364 million, represented about 59 per cent of the total income of BAA in 2001/02. The remainder was generated from the other four UK airports under its ownership (Southampton, Glasgow, Edinburgh and Aberdeen), from management of other airports and non-airport property and other activities, in particular World Duty Free Europe Ltd (WDFE), formed by BAA in 1996 which carries out retail operations at BAA's UK airports.

2.8. The figures in Table 2.1 therefore include payments by WDFE to BAA, but exclude revenue of WDFE at the three airports—£317.2 million in 2001—and WDFE's operating profits: £41.9 million in 2001/02 (but after allocating central costs pro rata to revenue, profit would be some £18 million). A summary of the revenue and profits of the three BAA London airports for the last three years is given in Table 2.1. We discuss in paragraph 2.366 whether under the single-till approach allowance should be made in setting airport charges for the separate profits of WDFE; they are, however, small in comparison with the profits of the three airports and do not significantly affect the general trends. We have therefore excluded WDFE from the historical analyses of the accounting figures for the three airports.

TABLE 2.1 **Revenue and profitability of BAA London Airports**

£ million

	Revenue				Operating profit			
	Airport charges	Other operational activities	Non-operational	Total	Airport and other traffic charges	Other operational activities	Non-operational	Total
1999/2000								
HAL	309	505	20	834	84	228	12	324
GAL	125	189	3	317	6	104	2	112
STAL	39	55	1	95	−13	33	1	21
Total	473	749	24	1,246	77	365	15	457
2000/01								
HAL	337	525	32	894	116	214	19	349
GAL	130	190	5	325	3	113	3	119
STAL	54	62	2	118	−12	39	1	28
Total	521	777	39	1,337	107	366	23	496
2001/02								
HAL	338	534	32	904	94	210	21	325
GAL	130	187	5	322	−5	103	3	101
STAL	63	73	2	138	−13	48	1	36
Total	531	794	39	1,364	76	361	25	462

Source: BAA and airport report and accounts excluding WDFE profits.

2.9. Some 39 per cent of the airports' revenue in 2001/02 was accounted for by airport charges, compared with some 33 per cent in 1994/95 due to the loss of intra-EC duty- and tax-free sales in 1999. Moreover, 78 per cent of the overall profitability of the three companies in 2001/02 was generated by their other operational activities. On the basis of these accounts STAL and GAL made losses on airport charges in 2001/02. These figures, however, treat operational activities as bearing none of the cost of bringing customers to the airports: an approach we consider further below.

2.10. As noted in Chapter 8, other operational income includes both services to airlines and services to passengers. In 2000/01, services to airlines, additional to those for which airport charges are levied, accounted for about £210 million of income at Heathrow, £65 million at Gatwick and £24 million at Stansted. The main sources of such income were property, check-in desks, transfer management (at Heathrow), staff car parks and electricity, but hydrant refuelling was also a significant source of income at Gatwick and Stansted. Airport charges (including passenger charges collected by airlines) therefore represent only some 60 per cent of total charges to airlines at Heathrow, a little higher at Gatwick and Stansted.

2.11. Services to passengers accounted in 2000/01 for about £300 million income at Heathrow, £125 million at Gatwick and almost £40 million at Stansted. Table 2.2 gives figures for both 1999/2000 and 2000/01 on the main sources of operating profit from services to passengers (the figures are different from those for commercial activities in Table 2.1 since services to passengers are only one part of commercial activities); the profit centre reporting system of BAA has not separately distinguished the profits of the separate sources of retail income since 1999/2000 because BAA did not regard such figures as relevant to management.

TABLE 2.2 **Profits from services to passengers**

£ million

	Heathrow		Gatwick		Stansted	
	1999/2000	*2000/01*	*1999/2000*	*2000/01*	*1999/2000*	*2000/01*
Duty/tax free	85	N/A	34	N/A	6	3
Duty paid and other shops	19	N/A	24	N/A	4	5
Catering	6	N/A	5	N/A	2	3
Banks	20	N/A	11	N/A	3	3
Total retail	130	122	74	72	15	14
ST car parks	16	19	7	8	5	6
LT car parks	20	23	12	17	8	12
Car rentals	12	12	2	3	1	1
Others	−3	0	−2	−1	0	0
Total	175	176	93	99	29	33

Source: CC study. Figures exclude WDFE.

Note: N/A = not available.

Figures for 1999/2000 include three months in which there was sale of intra-EC duty- and tax-free goods, which would have increased operating profit for that year compared with subsequent years by about £25 million. Even allowing for that, however, sales of duty- and tax-free goods are likely to remain the main source of profits from service to passengers, still accounting for about one-third of such profits. Car parking is the second main source of operating profits, accounting for a little over one-quarter, but with a higher requirement for capital expenditure (capex).

2.12. Table 2.1 shows that HAL accounts for 64 per cent of airport charges of the three BAA London airports, and 68 per cent of other operational income. The importance of Heathrow in terms of number of passengers handled is shown in Table 2.3.

TABLE 2.3 **Number of terminal passengers and air transport movements, 2001**

	Terminal passengers (m)*			Air transport movements ('000)		
	Scheduled	*Charter*	*Total*	*Scheduled*	*Charter*	*Total*
Heathrow	60.3	0.1	60.4	456.1	2.1	458.2
Gatwick	20.0	11.1	31.1	189.5	56.3	245.8
Stansted	12.5	1.2	13.7	135.6	17.2	152.8
Total	92.8	12.4	105.2	781.2	75.6	856.8
Other UK airports	50.0	26.0	76.0	926.4	311.7	1,238.1
All UK airports	142.8	38.4	181.2	1,707.6	387.3	2,094.9

Source: CAA.

*Excludes transit passengers (those who arrive at and depart from the airport on the same plane), but includes transfer passengers (those changing planes).

2.13. Table 2.3 shows that in 2001 the BAA London area airports accounted for about 65 per cent of UK scheduled terminal passengers, and for about 32 per cent of charter passengers. Since the time of our last report, the total number of terminal passengers has grown by some 12 per cent at Heathrow, 39 per cent at Gatwick and 250 per cent at Stansted: an overall growth over the six-year period of 31 per cent compared with 40 per cent at all UK airports. The growth at Stansted results almost entirely from growth in the operation of 'low-fares' carriers (LFCs) there and there being significant spare capacity at Stansted in the mid-1990s; in contrast, growth at Heathrow has been significantly constrained by lack of capacity. These figures also, however, reflect a sharp downturn in air traffic following the events of 11 September 2001. Total UK passenger traffic fell 6 per cent during September to December, with a 1 per cent increase over the year as a whole reflecting not only that decline, but also a historically slow rate of growth in the preceding part of the year. At Heathrow, traffic levels in 2001 fell by 6 per cent, and at Gatwick by 3 per cent, but at Stansted rose by 15 per cent.

2.14. The characteristics of the airports vary widely. Heathrow is the fourth largest airport in the world,[1] and the busiest international airport. A greater share of its passengers travel on business than at the other BAA London airports (37 per cent, compared with 19 per cent at Gatwick, and 20 per cent at Stansted); a greater proportion of its passengers also transfer between flights (some 30 per cent, compared with 20 per cent at Gatwick and 6 per cent at Stansted). Its advantages derive partly from its more convenient location for many of its passengers, but also from the number of destinations served and the frequency of service, which provide significant benefits both to passengers starting or finishing their journeys at the airport and to passengers transferring between flights. Airlines operating there therefore regard the other two airports as not providing a realistic alternative to Heathrow. The CAA estimated that the advantages of Heathrow result in a premium—ie higher profit per passenger—of about £20 per passenger on short-haul routes and of up to £110 per passenger on long-haul services compared with services from the other London area airports. The CAA, in its submission to us, quoted transactions between airlines for slot rights—rights to a slot to arrive or depart at a congested airport at a particular time—implying a valuation of £16 million in one case in 1998 for four pairs of slots, equivalent to an annual valuation of £400,000 a slot; a more recent transaction implied a slightly higher valuation. We also noted that British Airways plc (BA) includes in its accounts a value of £42 million for landing rights acquired for cash. Hence, there is significant excess demand by airlines to use Heathrow given constraints on capacity. Construction of T5, given outline planning permission in autumn 2001, accounts for a substantial majority of BAA's proposed investment programme in Q4.

2.15. Scheduled services account for almost two-thirds of passengers at Gatwick, but these have developed at Gatwick partly because of the difficulty in increasing scheduled services at Heathrow. These difficulties include not only shortage of capacity at Heathrow but in some cases constraints in certain international agreements on the number of operators allowed to operate from Heathrow. We referred in our previous report to BA's attempting to build a second hub at Gatwick because of shortage of capacity at Heathrow. It told us it now realized a second hub was not feasible. Since it was reducing other flights from Heathrow for various reasons, it was moving a number of its international services (critical to its hubbing operation) from Gatwick back to Heathrow. As evident from Table 2.3, charter services account for a significantly higher proportion of passengers (some 36 per cent) at Gatwick than the other two airports (9 per cent at Stansted, virtually zero at Heathrow). Some 80 per cent of Stansted passengers, on the other hand, use LFCs (sometimes referred to as low-cost carriers or no-frills airlines), compared with 2 per cent at Gatwick in 2001 and none at Heathrow.

2.16. As we noted in our previous report the scope for effective competition between airports for originating traffic tends to be limited to that between nearby airports such as between Stansted and London Luton Airport (Luton). Potential competition between airports is greater for transfer traffic (notably from hub airports such as Schiphol and Frankfurt, which are currently growing faster than Heathrow), but reflects a range of factors such as the performance of the user airlines and the scale of the national carrier located at the airport, as well as the price and quality of the airport facilities provided. As we also noted in our previous report, the airports provide an infrastructure essential to the successful operation of the user airlines: hence airlines are concerned as much about the quality of the airports' facilities, which can significantly affect their competitive position, as about the airport charges they pay.

---

[1]Ranking after Atlanta Hartsfield, Chicago O'Hare and Los Angeles International for total passengers in 2001.

2.17. We have noted above the shortage of capacity at Heathrow—both of terminal capacity, although this would be alleviated by T5, and of runway capacity. There is also no spare runway capacity at Gatwick in peak periods. During the course of our inquiry, the Government published a consultation document on the *Future Development of Air Transport in the United Kingdom in the South East* (one of a number of regional consultation documents), based on a South East and East of England Regional Air Services Study (SERAS). The main options it put forward (not necessarily alternatives) were:

(a) for an additional short runway, capable of handling short-haul services at Heathrow;

(b) for up to three additional runways at Stansted; and

(c) for a new airport at Cliffe in Kent.

The Government has decided not to overturn a 1979 agreement between the British Airports Authority (the forerunner of BAA) and West Sussex County Council not to construct a second runway at Gatwick before 2019. No decision would be taken as to which of the above options would be preferred until some time after our inquiry was completed. Given the uncertainty of where any new runways are to be located, it is not feasible to make a specific allowance for the cost of any new runway in our recommendations. Should work start on a new runway at any of the BAA airports during Q4, however, it would be open to the CAA under the Airports Act to revise the charge cap (with the consent of the airport company) in Q4 to finance it.

Current structure of BAA

2.18. During the course of our inquiry some airlines argued there should be further consideration of separate ownership of airports. Virgin, for example, said 'serious consideration should be given to breaking up BAA', although acknowledging that the three airports would only compete with each other to a certain extent since they were not effective substitutes for each other—and hence would still need to be regulated. (This was also acknowledged by other airlines in favour of separation.) Virgin argued, however, that where jointly owned, airports had the option of allocating funds to different airports, investing where returns, rather than benefits to users or the economy, were highest. Among others, the British Air Transport Association (BATA), Qantas, and the Adam Smith Institute were in favour of separate ownership. Among possible grounds for such an approach put to us were the bias/incentive on BAA not to invest where consumers want; failing to push against external constraints on growth; plus processes that limit airlines ability to respond to the market. Some academic commentators also argued separate ownership could allow competition through alternative combination of price and quality. On the other hand, some parties argued against 'enforced competition'. BA suggested separation was irrelevant to solving the problems it had identified. BAA said the question of ownership had been reviewed many times by third parties who had all concluded in favour of the current system framework.

2.19. During Q3, separate ownership of airports was considered by the then Department of Environment, Transport and the regions, now the Department for Transport (DfT) and HM Treasury, which concluded it would not be desirable to break up the south-east airports. The lack of spare capacity to provide a basis for competing for extra business and the risk of reducing operational efficiency were both main factors underlying this conclusion. The CAA also told us that while this could be a remedy under the Airports Act, it was hard to put evidence on the table of detriment or loss of efficiency on a scale sufficient to justify such divestment.

2.20. As we noted in our previous report, separate ownership of airports could only be put forward by ourselves as a remedy if it were relevant and proportionate to any adverse effects identified, for example, if BAA should fail on a significant scale to invest adequately or achieve appropriate service standards. However, given that in most circumstances competition is likely to have important benefits for consumers, this may, nonetheless, be an issue for further consideration by Government at some point in the future once plans have been settled for runway capacity in south-east England, or should there be any other significant change in the circumstances of the air transport industry.

The current regulatory formulae

2.21. Section 40(5) of the Airports Act states that conditions as to airport charges levied in relation to designated airports (HAL, GAL, STAL and Manchester Airport PLC (Manchester)):

(a) may provide:

    (i)   for an overall limit on the amount that may be levied by the airport operator by way of all airport charges at the airport; or

    (ii) for limits to apply to particular categories of charges; or

    (iii) for a combination of any such limits;

(b) may operate to restrict increases in any such charges or to require reductions in them whether by reference to any formula or otherwise; and

(c) may provide for different limits to apply in relation to different periods of time falling within the period of five years for which the conditions are in force.

The Airports Act also makes provision for 'groups of airports': the charges of one airport may be prescribed by reference to the aggregate amounts levied in the group as a whole or regulated separately.

2.22. During Q3, and broadly following the main recommendation of our previous report, the main elements of the airport charging formula have been as follows:[1]

(a) Airport charges per passenger should not increase by more than RPI–3 at Heathrow and Gatwick combined for each of the five years, with a formula of RPI+1 for Stansted. (Regulation by reference to airport charges per passenger is sometimes referred to as a 'revenue yield' approach.)

(b) Within the overall formula for Heathrow and Gatwick charges at Heathrow should increase by at least 1 per cent in each year more than at Gatwick.

(c) The airports should continue to be allowed to recover 95 per cent of additional security costs in the year after they were first incurred (referred to as the 'S factor').

(d) The maximum level of airport charges for Heathrow and Gatwick combined and for Stansted should increase by £0.70 per passenger partly in the year when the concession on intra-EC sales of duty- and tax-free goods was withdrawn and partly in the following year (referred to as the 'D factor'). The concession having been withdrawn in 1999, and the maximum level of charges increased, the D factor is now in effect subsumed in the current level of charges.

---

[1]CAP 664, Economic Regulation of BAA London Airports 1998–2002.

2.23. The cap operates by requiring the airport company to set airport charges in a particular year at the levels best calculated to secure that the average charges per passenger over the year do not exceed the cap in the previous year by more than the amount given in the formulae. The formulae also contain a correction factor where actual average yield per passenger in a year differs from the cap for that year. The correction factor in the formula for a particular year is based on the difference that arose, not in the previous year, but the year before that.

2.24. The CAA said that there should be a mid-term review in the event that T5 did not go ahead or, for reasons connected to planning permission, proceeded on a significantly different scale (paragraph 187(c), CAP 664, summarizing the CAA's decision). In Appendix 1 of CAP 664 it was stated that BAA would cooperate in a mid-term review in the circumstances of planning permission being refused for T5, or granted subject to conditions which would significantly reduce the scale of T5, or BAA voluntarily reducing significantly the scale of T5 to secure planning permission which was subsequently granted, or if it was granted subject to conditions which rendered BAA unwilling to proceed with the project.

2.25. In the previous report, the Monopolies and Mergers Commission (MMC) (now known as the Competition Commission) found various practices to be against the public interest:

(a) the basis of charging for airside licences at all three airports;

(b) restrictions on the use of employment agency staff at Heathrow;

(c) the provision of travel outlets at Gatwick; and

(d) a refusal by HAL to allow information desks in airside departure lounges.

The CAA imposed conditions in each case. Additionally, the MMC referred to a number of ongoing developments—notably on service standards, facilities for transfer baggage, consultation on investment, and rents—the continuation of which it regarded as essential, but without having found evidence that warranted the finding of a course of conduct against the public interest.

2.26. Among the significant general principles underlying the current regulation of airport charges are:

(a) There is some variation in the formulae applied to the three airports. However, in assessing the appropriate level of airport charges, regard was had to generating a reasonable rate of return across the three London area airports as a whole, rather than at each airport separately—in effect a 'system approach'.

(b) As is apparent from Table 2.1, the airport charging formulae directly apply only to a minority of airport revenues, and airports' profits are generated primarily from those operational activities the charges for which are not airport charges (sometimes referred to, for example in previous reports, as commercial activities), in particular—as apparent in Table 2.2—from the sale of duty-free and tax-free goods. The use of profits generated by other operational activities to offset the level of airport charges is referred to as the single-till mechanism.

(c) In setting the asset base for regulatory purposes on which a return would be allowed, there was allowance for AICC—particularly BAA's key investment in T5 at Heathrow. There was also, to avoid a sudden price increase, a further element of advancement of revenue for 'smoothing' of prices and returns between Q3 with a relatively high return, and lower rates of return in Q4 (although with a suggestion that price increases of RPI+2 would still be necessary in Q4, reflecting the increasing marginal cost of new investment, particularly of T5). In its final decision on charges for Q3, the CAA referred to this advancement of revenue as the difference between the price cap of RPI–3 that was actually adopted and

16

one of RPI–8 that would otherwise have been adopted: hence also the provision for interim review if T5 did not go ahead, or did so on a reduced scale, to which we referred above. However, the length of the planning inquiry meant that construction of T5 was not begun in the original five-year period of Q3, although BAA did spend more than expected on other projects. Nor, however, was there any interim review—an issue to which we return below.

2.27. A number of aspects of performance in Q3 differed from that expected when the charging formula was set including:

(a) Passenger numbers were significantly above forecast, even after allowing for the effects of 11 September. We have noted in Table 2.3 that there were 105 million passengers handled at the three London airports in 2001: this compared to 96 million assumed in the financial projections in our previous report (for the financial year 2001/02), which were broadly similar to the forecasts of BAA, the CAA and the DfT at the time. The difference between actual and forecast number of passengers was greatest at Stansted (almost 14 million passengers compared with BAA's forecast of 7 million for that year) due to the success of the LFCs. Before the decline in number of passengers in 2001, Heathrow had also handled more passengers than forecast (64 million in 2000, compared with 60 million previously assumed), capacity constraints being less binding than expected. Expenditure, as well as income, was also higher partly as a result of higher passenger numbers.

(b) Retail income was significantly lower, despite higher passenger numbers, partly reflecting greater than expected effect of loss of intra-EC tax- and duty-free sales. (This is, as we discuss below, partly accounted for by the reduction in the concession fee from WDFE to BAA.)

(c) Rental income from property was significantly higher than expected: considered separately below.

(d) The level of airport charges per passenger was lower than permitted. BAA told us it voluntarily set airport charges 3 per cent below the allowable level for the three years 2000/01 to 2002/03 in recognition of the lower capex. However, the intended under-recovery in 2001/02 was offset by the 'concentration' of revenue in that year—ie in effect actual revenue per passenger proved greater than had initially been expected when charges were set (see also Chapter 5). This occurred in 2001/02 as a result of a reduction in passengers per air transport movement (ATM) following the events of 11 September 2001.

(e) As noted above, there was significantly lower investment, in particular on T5 due to the delay in receiving planning permission, but with an increase in non-T5 investment, the implications of which are also considered further below.

(f) There was a higher depreciation cost in the accounts than projected in the last report, which, other things being equal, has the effect of reducing operating profit. (This would also affect the value of BAA's capital, reducing the capital base on which future returns are set.) BAA has attributed the higher figure to depreciation of investment properties not allowed for in projections, and increased investment on non-T5 projects which have borne a depreciation charge since they have come into use earlier: T5 would not have done so in Q3.

2.28. The effect of the above is summarized in Table 2.4.

TABLE 2.4 **Comparison of actual with projected performance, BAA 1997/98 to 2001/02**

£ million, 2000/01 prices

	Actual	Projected	Difference
Revenue	6,338.6	6,111.5	227.1
Adjustment for property transfers		−68.0	68.0
Opex	−3,115.0	−2,987.5	−127.4
Pension adjustment	49.4		49.4
Total	3,273.0	3,056.0	217.0
Depreciation	−856.2	−775.9	−80.3
Total	2,416.8	2,280.1	136.7
Cost of capital	−1,898.5	−2,003.8	105.3
Surplus after cost of capital	517.9	276.3	241.6
Return on capital %	9.6	8.6	

Source: CC study.

Note: Return on capital is calculated at 7.5 per cent of average actual RAB/projected RCV. Projected revenue and RCV are adjusted for actual transfers out of the regulated till. Figures exclude WDFE.

2.29. Additional revenues were £227 million at 2000/01 prices (plus £68 million effect of property transfers). Additional expenditure was £127 million, but allowance is also necessary for the pension holiday which reduced costs by £49 million. Depreciation was £80 million higher, excluding effects of depreciation of investment properties, not allowed for in our previous report. Operating profit therefore was £137 million greater than projected over the period. However, less capital was employed in the business, as a result of which the cost of capital was some £103 million lower, so BAA's surplus over the cost of capital was some £240 million greater than projected. BAA, on the other hand, estimated that its overall return on capital value (ROCV) was similar to that projected at the time of the MMC's report. In the four years to 2000/01, it estimated that ROCV averaged 8.85 per cent (excluding the effects of the windfall tax in 1997/98) compared with 8.75 per cent in the projections on which the current formula was based. As we discuss further below, however, BAA estimated capital value on a basis different to that used in our previous report, although similar to that in its regulatory accounts, and which it said the CAA had never queried. We do not regard it as appropriate for the purposes of comparison to change the basis of calculation. If our previous methodology is used, BAA's actual rate of return is approximately 1 per cent above that projected.

2.30. We consider below whether these or other aspects of performance in Q3, for example quality of service, are relevant to the setting of charges for Q4.

The CAA's approach

2.31. We noted in paragraph 2.3 that, prior to the reference to ourselves, the CAA undertook a substantial review of the appropriate basis on which to set the maximum level of airport charges. The CAA summarized the basis of its recommendations, which it believed would best meet its statutory objectives, as follows:

(a) regulation should focus on the monopoly services provided by the airport to users;

(b) increased contracting and competition, recognizing the strategic and operational inter-dependency between users and airports, assisted by improved information disclosure, could allow less intrusive economic regulation;

18

(c) congestion on Heathrow and Gatwick runways meant that increases in permitted airport charges were likely to result in better use of those airports with consequent benefits for passengers;

(d) users' high valuation of additional capacity, particularly at Heathrow, indicated that incentives to invest in new capacity were central;

(e) major investments had long lead times and long pay-back periods, both of which could be well beyond the statutory five yearly reviews emphasizing the importance of long-term regulatory commitment;

(f) a greater focus on service quality was a core part of the regulatory framework at Heathrow and Gatwick; and

(g) Stansted would have more limited market power than Heathrow and Gatwick over the 2003 to 2008 period and would remain dependent on the success of LFCs, pointing to a continuation of light-handed regulation.

2.32. It recommended for all three airports:

(a) price caps set in relation to the assets and costs of each airport on a stand-alone basis;

(b) a revised regulatory cost base (RRCB), which should comprise only the costs of what the CAA regarded as services essential to aeronautical activities and monopolizable by the airport—see paragraph 2.59. This excluded not only commercial costs and revenues but also surface access infrastructure or activities (except where, on a case-by-case basis, these are mandated as conditions of planning permission and to do so would be consistent with statutory objectives). This is also referred to as a dual-till approach, compared with the single-till approach adopted to date. Other things beings equal, and as we discuss in more detail below, the dual-till approach is likely over time to result in significantly higher airport charges, revenue and profits to BAA than the single-till approach;

(c) enhanced information disclosure and consultation;

(d) facilitating more direct contracting between airports and users;

(e) no automatic cost pass-throughs (the current formula allowing 95 per cent of costs of new security requirements to be passed on in airport charges);

(f) retention of the revenue yield approach to setting the cap;

(g) removing revenue from non-passenger flights from the yield calculation and setting a separate condition for these flights; and

(h) calculating the revenue yield as if airlines which receive unpublished discounts pay the published tariff (as is the case at Manchester).

In addition for Heathrow it recommended:

(i) a long-term price path commitment (PPC) under which the real price cap for outputs delivered from current capacity and through T5 would be pre-set in real terms for a 20-year period, with a commitment not to reset the cap at future reviews;

(j) average revenue per passenger handled by existing capacity (passengers up to 60 million once T5 is opened) to be set on a RRCB;

(k) average revenue per passenger from T5, to be set at the estimated incremental costs of T5 of £18 per passenger. This was to be triggered by the opening of T5, but applied to the number of passengers at Heathrow as a whole above 60 million passengers per annum (mppa), irrespective of how many may use T5 in any year;

(l) an incentive linked to the opening of aircraft parking stands at the T5 site (expected in 2006/07) that would generate additional revenues of £10 million a year (in real terms) once the stands were operational;

(m) an incentive to deliver additional air transport movements in peak periods;

(n) a service quality term (the so-called Q term) as part of the cap including an element related to airport delays; and

(o) a reduction of the starting regulatory asset base (RAB) to reflect T5 prefinancing and prefunding in Q3.

In addition for Gatwick it recommended:

(p) as for Heathrow, but with no reliance on incremental cost-based incentives for additional outputs from 2003 to 2008 (*(j)* to *(l)* above) given that no major capacity enhancements were planned, nor any additional incentive linked to ATMs.

2.33. Underlying the CAA's approach was an emphasis on economic efficiency—ie that the aim should be to maximize net gains to users and airports combined—reflecting its interpretation of its statutory duties. This meant encouraging the best use of scarce airport capacity, improved incentives to expand capacity to meet demand where it was warranted, incentives to meet the volume of demand at desired level of service quality, and restricting the scope of regulation to monopoly activities.

2.34. The CAA said it was likely that its approach would result in a shift of economic rents from airlines to the airports, but that this was unlikely at congested airports to make a material difference to airfares or passengers. Since it believed there would be no effect on fares, it regarded such a shift in rents as of no concern to the regulator: although rent transfers between consumers and monopoly utilities may be a legitimate concern for other regulators, this did not apply to the distribution of rents between airports and airlines. This general approach underlies some of the individual issues spelt out below. In similar vein is the comment of the Air Transport Users Council (ATUC) to us: 'the passenger interest lies primarily in the timely investment in additional facilities at the airports in line with increasing demand'. The ATUC, like the CAA, assumed that increases in airport charges would not be reflected in fares.

2.35. However, the CAA also argued that the extent of any windfall gains from the shift in economic rents would be limited by its profiling of the proposed level of charges between Q4 and subsequent quinquennia. It said that other instruments, such as a windfall tax, were available to address any appropriate windfall gains that may arise. It regarded the price increases that would result as relatively limited compared with, for example, adopting market-clearing prices at Heathrow. It was essentially proposing (see paragraph 2.64 and Table 2.6) a level of charges at Heathrow for Q4 in line with what would be justified under single-till regulation, and very significantly below what would be allowed if the dual-till approach was applied, believing that the RPI+6 increases implied by the single till were a reasonable limit for Q4. The Stansted cap was likely to be non-binding, and the increase for Gatwick was limited. Prices would, however, be above the dual-till levels at Heathrow in subsequent quinquennia to recover the shortfall from the dual till in Q4.

2.36. A number of airlines argued that the CAA proposals were inconsistent with the requirements of the Airports Act to further the reasonable interests of users. They suggested to us that the regulator could not be indifferent to the distribution of benefits between the regulated party and its customers, as opposed to the CAA's view that 'reasonable interests of users' did not include the allocation of any rents. They also argued that higher airport charges would lead to higher fares, hence affect passengers. The airlines also argued that the Airports Act did not require the CAA to promote the efficient 'use' of airports, but the efficient, economic and profitable 'operation' of airports.

2.37. BA, for example, argued that the objective of using regulation of airport charges to promote efficient operation of airports was intended only to promote greater cost efficiency of the airport operation and to give a stronger incentive to innovate by the airport operator than might otherwise be pursued by a monopoly service provider. The CAA, however, was using airport charges to promote the best use of the airport by users—ie encourage slots to be used more efficiently, for example by a more efficient airline or for a more profitable service. BA regarded the setting of airport charges as an inefficient mechanism for securing the best 'use' of slots, which it regarded as more a matter for slot allocation mechanisms, and believed the CAA did not have the statutory powers to pursue such an objective. We return to these points below.

2.38. This inquiry therefore required us to consider a wide range of issues relating to the general approach to be adopted; on the basis of that general approach, the specific factors relating to financial forecasts such as capex and operating costs which affect the value of X; and finally an extensive range of public interest issues raised with us (some of which may also, however, potentially affect airport charges). In Appendix 2.1, we reproduce the published summary of the range of issues raised with BAA and on which other parties were given the opportunity to comment and which we now discuss.

The general approach—main issues

RPI–X form of control

2.39. On balance, all parties accepted the RPI–X form of control (rather than, for example, limiting the rate of return in any one year), and we also believe this approach provides an incentive to efficiency, has worked effectively and should be retained. Some airlines, however, referred to this system of regulation as more effective in 'sweating' existing assets (including increasing operational efficiency), but were concerned about its effect on investment incentives or quality of service. This concern partly explains the investment and quality of service issues raised by the airlines and the CAA which we consider below.

Regulation of system or individual airports

2.40. As noted above, the current airport charges formula, although effectively applying different price limits to the three different London airports, did so with reference to the overall return on the BAA London airports as a whole—referred to as a system approach. The CAA proposed that each London airport should now be considered separately. This has generally been supported by airlines operating at Heathrow and Gatwick to avoid any risk of subsidizing developments elsewhere; but was opposed particularly by the LFCs at Stansted and by BAA.

2.41. Among the main arguments in favour of such an individual airport approach were that the three airports could be regarded as largely serving separate markets, and should be regarded separately for pricing and/or investment. On the other hand, several airlines argued that the other airports were no substitute for Heathrow, and that the three airports had come to serve specialized markets, the characteristics of traffic at the three airports varying significantly: for example, scheduled, business and transfer traffic primarily at Heathrow; charter primarily at Gatwick; and LFCs primarily at Stansted.

2.42. The CAA and a number of airlines also argued that the system approach allowed undesirable cross-subsidy of airports, in particular of Stansted. The CAA commented that, had Stansted been regulated on a stand-alone basis, investment would have been less given the need to achieve a return on very substantial capital investment from a small initial number of users.

2.43. Some Heathrow airlines also believed that during Q3 they had in effect paid for the increased investment at Stansted, to the benefit of their competitors. LFCs, however, argued that there is currently no cross-subsidy of Stansted, its current relatively low returns merely reflecting its earlier stage of development.

2.44. Finally, it was argued that the system approach distorted the pattern of investment. As a result of the system approach, BAA could earn the same return on investment by taking its profits in any of the three airports. Separate regulation of individual airports, it was argued, particularly if combined with improved consultation on capex and commitment to achieve service and planning standards at each airport, would help to ensure investment was where users wanted it. It was claimed that BAA's failure to push for a new runway development at Heathrow (indeed it appeared during the T5 inquiry to have asked the Government to rule out the possibility of a third runway at Heathrow once and for all) was an example of the distortion in investment that resulted.

2.45. On the other hand, BAA argued there was interdependence of demand between the London area airports. Even though the characteristics of traffic at the three airports differed, this did not necessarily show the markets they served were separate: some of the development of low-fare traffic at Stansted, for example, could be attributed to lack of capacity elsewhere, and to the strategy of the scheduled airlines at the other airports of reducing their share of lower-yield passengers. BAA said that airlines mainly operated at Stansted because they were unable to operate from Heathrow. Because of grandfather rights,[1] airlines at Heathrow had huge incumbent advantages and if they regarded Stansted as unreasonably cross-subsidized they could at any time switch their operation there given its spare capacity. Regulation on a stand-alone basis, if it allowed each airport to earn an adequate rate of return, could lead to higher charges at Stansted than at Gatwick or Heathrow, but it would be inequitable to charge Stansted users more for being forced to operate at Stansted than if they operated at Heathrow.

2.46. Hence, BAA argued that given the capacity constraints at particular airports (in part a result of government decisions and planning limitations), investment in any individual airport could be attributable not just to growth in demand at that airport but also elsewhere in the system: investment at Stansted thus relieved congestion at Heathrow. (LFCs also mentioned diversion/hijack facilities of Stansted that benefit Heathrow and Gatwick airlines.)

2.47. BAA also suggested that relative charges should reflect relative pressure of demand: hence, since excess demand was greater at Heathrow than at Gatwick, and at Gatwick than at Stansted, charges should be highest at Heathrow, lower at Gatwick, and lower still at Stansted. As noted above, individual airport regulation could lead to the highest charges at Stansted, although there was more spare capacity there. The CAA itself acknowledged partial interdependence of demand at the three airports, and that there would be a distortion if prices at Heathrow were below market level but closer to market level at Stansted—but argued that Stansted would not fully recover the proposed price limits anyway.

2.48. There was also concern that in the longer-term requirements for new investment and constraints at particular airports could change the relative desirability of a system and individual airport approach. LFCs were particularly concerned that if regulation was to be on a

---

[1]Airlines that hold a slot in one summer or winter season have the right to the same slot in the following season provided they have used it for at least 80 per cent of the time. These rights of airlines are known as 'grandfather rights' and are set out in the EC slot regulation.

stand-alone basis and investment at Stansted resulted from the SERAS exercise, its users might in effect have to pay for the costs of accommodating increasing demand for access to the south-east market. In its evidence to us, the DfT also suggested that some investments may be economically justified but fail to meet financial viability criteria because of the difficulties in capturing all the benefits for which users were willing to pay: it would not want to see economically justified investment inhibited, and in such circumstances there may be a case for cross-subsidy, albeit more transparent than was currently the case.

2.49. Heathrow airlines, on the other hand, took an opposing view. They argued that investment at Stansted did nothing to relieve congestion at Heathrow, since Heathrow airlines would not move to Stansted, and it would be unacceptable for runway development not to be allowed where demand was greatest: runway expansion at any airport should be based on the business case at that airport.

Assessment

2.50. On balance, we believe the system approach should be retained. We believe the three airports to some extent serve the same market. We do not accept that because airlines are not prepared to switch, investment at Stansted does not reduce excess demand at Heathrow: some of the growth in demand at Stansted is for passengers who would otherwise use Heathrow or Gatwick, albeit that passengers may need lower fares to compensate for Stansted's less attractive location. There is clear evidence that Heathrow airlines are moving to respond to this interdependence of demand, and the business models at the separate airports may indeed already be converging to some extent.

2.51. The impact of separate airport regulation would depend to a large extent on whether BAA would be able to price up to whatever cap is set or whether, as the CAA asserted, prices at Stansted would be similar under either stand-alone or system regulation. Were Stansted to be allowed to earn a return on its assets equivalent to its cost of capital and if, due to steadily increasing pressure of demand on capacity throughout the south-east market, it were to price up its cap, its charges could be higher than at Gatwick or Heathrow even though it was the only one of the three airports to have spare capacity, particularly for use of its runway. Under separate airport regulation, Stansted prices could be above its incremental cost (ie the change in cost resulting from any change in numbers of passengers, rather than the current average cost per passenger). Given the particular nature of traffic at Stansted, with lower fares and demand therefore more sensitive to the level of airport charges, this would be likely to reduce use of Stansted by traffic that could afford to pay its incremental cost. If, however, under a separate airport approach Stansted were unable to price up to its cap, the return of the three airports as a whole could fall short of BAA's cost of capital. This would be inconsistent with the previous basis of regulation of the BAA, and put at risk its ability to finance its investment.

2.52. In contrast, under a system cap, with Stansted unable to price up to its cap, BAA would still be able to earn its cost of capital and maintain its investment programme. Prices would in comparison be somewhat above average cost at Heathrow, but this would be unlikely to have much impact on effective demand, given that prices at Heathrow are (as we discuss below) significantly below incremental cost and any estimate of market-clearing prices. It follows that the structure of prices under a separate airport approach could therefore be somewhat less efficient than under a system approach.

2.53. Following the rapid growth of traffic at Stansted, these concerns, as is apparent from our financial projections, may not apply in Q4, although they had been relevant to Q3. Stansted, now being at a much higher level of capacity utilization, may over Q4 and Q5 together be in a position to earn its cost of capital at charges similar to those of Gatwick, and much below those of Heathrow given the increasing incremental cost of new capacity at Heathrow. Nonetheless, there is greater uncertainty about traffic growth at Stansted, the growth in charges it may be able to achieve, and its requirement for new investment, particularly in any new runway. Hence, the above considerations remain relevant to our assessment.

2.54. As to whether the system approach has encouraged inefficient investment, the initial under-utilization of Stansted reflected the unavoidable uncertainties of such a project inherent in factors such as changes in government policies (in particular, the removal of the 275,000 ATM limit at Heathrow, shortly after Stansted opened, with growth subsequently at Heathrow rather than Stansted). There is also little doubt that the public interest subsequently benefited from the growth in LFCs competing from Stansted. Despite all the investment more recently made at Stansted, there is also little doubt that the expansion of the terminal was, with the benefit of hindsight, if anything 'just too late'. We see therefore no evidence of undue investment at Stansted but more importantly no evidence that investment at Stansted was predictably excessive nor, therefore, that a system cap was driving such an outcome. Stansted now has permission to increase terminal capacity to 25 mppa, current terminal capacity being already heavily utilized despite recent expansion.

2.55. As to whether the system approach could encourage over-investment in future, further investment at Stansted is subject to review by airlines and by the CAA and ourselves in considering whether it should be included in the RAB: projections that it is likely to approach its cost of capital over Q4 and Q5 combined also suggests that new investment cannot be regarded as excessive.

2.56. We also share the concern of the DfT that a separate airport approach could inhibit the financing of additional runways at Stansted, the need for which may arise because of constraints on runway developments elsewhere. The government consultation paper (based on the SERAS study) appears to have confirmed the need for very heavy investment in one or more new runways and associated terminal developments somewhere in the South-East. Given that the current options include Heathrow, Stansted, or a new site, the new capacity could, in effect, be seen as meeting growth in demand for the system as a whole, not just at a particular airport. If the development were to be concentrated at Stansted, Stansted's role would also significantly change. The unpredicted success of LFCs at Stansted over the last five years itself shows the uncertain role of individual airports.

2.57. We regard it as preferable, therefore, to have regard to the rate of return of the system rather than individual airports. This does not, however, necessarily imply significant differences in their rates of return or that there should be one cap for the system as a whole—to which we return below.

The single-till or dual-till approach

Introduction

2.58. As evident in Table 2.1, on the basis of BAA's existing accounting system, almost 80 per cent of its profits in the last two years have been generated by non-airport charges (profits being calculated with reference to costs allocated on the basis of factors such as proportion of space utilized by the various activities). The maximum level of airport charges has to date been calculated so as to provide a reasonable rate of return on regulatory capital value (RCV)[1] of the airports as a whole, including the revenues and profits generated by commercial activities—referred to as a single-till approach. Such airport charges are considerably lower than if they had to cover the costs and generate a return on the assets currently allocated to the activities remunerated by them.

---

[1] Also known as the regulatory asset base (RAB).

2.59. We have noted above that the CAA has proposed a dual-till basis (subsequently referred to by the CAA as RRCB) whereby the maximum level of airport charges is set to cover the operating costs and rate of return on a more limited set of assets deemed by the CAA to be essential to aeronautical activities and monopolizable by the airports. This aeronautical till would include:

(a) facilities on the airfield necessary for arriving and departing airplanes;

(b) facilities within terminals piers and satellites necessary for processing passengers;

(c) baggage handling facilities;

(d) refuelling facilities;

(e) aircraft maintenance infrastructure;

(f) terminal accommodation excluding lounges for commercially important passengers (CIP lounges);

(g) airfield accommodation;

(h) buildings within the airfield perimeter entirely occupied by BAA;

(i) utilities devoted to airfield facilities and some utilities for terminals; and

(j) all airside and a share of landside transit systems and airport-wide systems.

It would therefore include all activities paid for out of airport charges; but also services to airlines regarded as essential for their operation at the airport but not included within airport charges (such as charges for use of check-in desks, terminal offices and airside licences, ie licences required to operate vehicles airside).

2.60. The commercial till would include not only commercial services to passengers (such as tax- and duty-free sales, other retail outlets, catering and car parking), but also the existing Heathrow Express and what the CAA regarded as some non-essential services to airlines such as CIP lounges, non-terminal offices, flight catering facilities, cargo buildings and off-site check-in.

2.61. The estimated relative rate of return of the aeronautical and commercial tills is shown in Table 2.5, which also gives a separate estimate of the profitability of surface access. (These estimated rates of return for individual activities should only be regarded as approximate, given the assumptions that have had to be made in deriving them.)

TABLE 2.5 **Approximate allocation of airport profit across activities, 2000/01**

£ million

	Revenue	Operating expenditure	Depreciation*	Operating profit	RCV	Rate of return* %
Heathrow						
Total	893.6	429.6	142.8	321.2	3,378	9.5
Aeronautical	478.0	288.6	69.4	119.9	1,642	7.3
Commercial	261.4	67.8	23.8	169.8	562	30.2
Road etc†	90.4	28.7	22.2	39.5	525	7.5
Rail	63.9	44.5	27.4	−8.0	649	−1.2
Commercial plus surface access	415.7	141.0	73.4	201.3	1,736	11.6
Gatwick						
Total	325.5	165.9	54.0	105.6	1,153	9.2
Aeronautical	170.4	123.6	33.5	13.3	715	1.9
Commercial	114.3	31.4	9.3	73.6	198	37.3
Road etc†	40.8	10.9	11.2	18.7	240	7.8
Commercial plus surface access	155.1	42.3	20.5	92.3	438	21.1
Stansted						
Total	118.4	72.3	22.1	24.0	703	3.4
Aeronautical	66.9	57.6	18.0	−8.7	573	−1.5
Commercial	29.8	12.8	2.4	14.6	76	19.3
Road etc†	21.7	1.9	1.7	18.1	54	33.7
Commercial plus surface access	51.5	14.7	4.1	32.7	130	25.3
All three airports						
Total	1,337.5	667.8	218.9	450.8	5,235	8.6
Aeronautical	715.3	469.9	120.9	124.5	2,931	4.2
Commercial	405.4	112.0	35.4	258.1	836	30.8
Road etc†	152.9	41.5	35.1	76.3	819	9.3
Rail	63.9	44.5	27.4	−8.1	649	−1.2
Commercial plus surface access	622.2	198.0	97.9	326.3	2,304	14.2

Source: CC calculations based on regulated accounts and RRCB annexes to the CAA submission and the CAA's November 2001 preliminary proposals. See notes to Table 8.2.

---

*Depreciation is allocated to activities pro rata with net book value of fixed assets at 31.3.2001. Hence for figures for depreciation and rate of return should only be regarded as approximate.
†Includes all car parking (short term, long term and staff), car rental, buses, coaches and taxis.

2.62. Under the dual-till approach there would be no 'subsidy', as the CAA sees it, of aeronautical revenues from commercial revenues, without which aeronautical revenues would need to be much increased, as would profitability to BAA. On the basis of the figures in Table 2.5, for example, rate of return of the three airports in 2000/01 was 8.6 per cent (due in part to the advancement of revenue for smoothing purposes, and delay in constructing T5 to which we refer above). The aeronautical rate of return was 4.2 per cent, and that of other activities 14.2 per cent. If aeronautical revenues alone had earned a return of 8.6 per cent, airport charges would have needed to be about £130 million, or almost 20 per cent higher;

BAA's profitability would correspondingly have been about £130 million, or almost 30 per cent higher, with a return of 11.1 per cent of assets.

2.63. BAA, some other airport operators, environmental organizations and some individuals also favoured a dual-till approach. However, BAA told us that it was not seeking an immediate move to full dual-till prices, but a lifting of the strict single-till price cap, and a clear signal of a move towards a dual till over a period of time; it also raised a further option of confining the dual-till approach to new investment rather than existing assets. Airlines were universally opposed to the dual till.

Application of the dual till in Q4

2.64. Application of the dual till in Q4 would require an increase in airport charges of about RPI+12 per annum, equivalent to a 75 per cent increase in Q4. In practice, however, the CAA proposed a formula which was roughly equivalent to the single till for Heathrow in Q4—about RPI+6, but with higher charges in Q5 and, even more so, subsequent quinquennia to recover the difference: there would be a full adjustment to the dual till only after 2012/13. As we have noted above, the CAA regarded RPI+6 as the reasonable upper limit to the increase in airport charges for Q4. The implications of the dual till for Q4 could therefore be regarded as limited.

2.65. Nonetheless, the dual till remains important to the CAA's proposals, not only for Gatwick and Stansted in Q4 (although it believed Stansted would be unlikely to price up to the maximum permitted—a point we consider below) but also for Heathrow in the longer term, given the CAA's further proposals for a PPC extending beyond Q4. Even though, as the CAA acknowledged, it could not bind itself for future reviews, to establish the principle of the dual till now and the precedent of applying it to Gatwick would be of importance to future reviews.

2.66. The differences between the dual till (RRCB in the table) and single till on the CAA's proposals (based also therefore on an individual airport approach rather than the system approach discussed above) in Q4 and Q5 are shown in Table 2.6 (the CAA proposals give the same net present value (NPV) of revenues under the dual till over 20 years, but with a different profiling for the reasons set out above).

TABLE 2.6 **CAA calculation of revenue yield**

£ (2000/01 prices)

Airport charges per passenger

	2002/03	Average Q4	2007/08	Average Q5	2012/13
Heathrow					
Single till	5.37	6.37	7.86	8.32	7.99
RRCB	5.37	7.51	8.83	9.50	9.26
CAA proposal	5.37	6.36	7.25	9.93	10.19
Gatwick					
Single till	4.03	3.57	3.63	3.84	3.84
RRCB	4.03	5.33	5.36	5.55	5.57
CAA proposal	4.03	4.63	5.09	5.59	5.69
Stansted					
Single till	4.47	4.59	3.93	3.79	3.63
RRCB	4.47	6.73	6.10	5.94	5.77
CAA proposal	4.47	5.41	6.10	7.37	8.36

Source: CAA.

Note: The RRCB and the CAA proposal cases still exclude existing surface access from aeronautical till.

2.67. Average charges at Heathrow as proposed by the CAA are the same as under the single till in Q4, but 20 per cent higher in Q5. This is, however, dependent on the allocation of activities between the commercial and aeronautical tills: in particular if the Heathrow Express were allocated to the aeronautical till, the appropriate level of airport charges would need to be between 5 and 10 per cent higher still. Gatwick charges would be 30 per cent higher in Q4 under the CAA proposals than under the single till and 46 per cent higher in Q5 (although BAA was doubtful whether it could recover such charges). Stansted charges would be 18 per cent higher in Q4 under the CAA proposals than under the single till and 94 per cent higher in Q5, although both BAA and the CAA assumed that Stansted would not be able fully to recover such a level of charges. Over a 20-year period, the CAA's financial model showed there would be an increase of between £3.2 billion and £3.7 billion in BAA investor value (compared with BAA's current market value of about £6 billion) as a result of the dual-till approach (the lower figure assuming permitted charges at Stansted are not fully recovered but only increase in line with RPI). Clearly, this figure is subject to some uncertainty: but it is sizeable, and, even if significantly lower, we could not disregard it.

2.68. The arguments for departing from the single-till approach were considered in paragraphs 2.21 and 2.22 of our previous (1996) report. This noted three drawbacks of the single-till ideal approach—that it results in airport charges being below the cost of operating purely aeronautical facilities; contributes to relatively low charges at Heathrow, one of the most congested airports in the world; and could increase demand, exacerbating environmental problems. The report nonetheless endorsed its continuation. It was noted that the single-till approach was the normal way in which airport charges were set around the world; that any higher charges at Heathrow resulting from moving away from the single till would have very little effect on demand; but BAA would receive a very significant increase in the profits which it could earn as a result of its monopoly position. This might then require commercial activities to be regulated, rather than, as at present, the airlines receiving some of the benefits while ensuring BAA did not make excessive profits overall. We have, however, in the light of the CAA's proposals now considered the issue afresh and in much more detail than in the previous report.

International obligations, guidelines and practice

2.69. We received divergent views on whether the dual-till approach could be regarded as consistent with international obligations, guidelines and practice. BAA and the CAA believed this was the case; many airlines challenged this. The position has changed over time. Following a dispute in the 1970s and 1980s, the UK Government appeared to agree in a Memorandum of Understanding with the US Government to retain the single till. This was replaced, however, by a side letter to the original 1977 Bermuda 2 agreement in 1994 that the UK only had 'no current intention' to depart from a single-till approach. The UK Government was therefore free to change its view in future—and the DfT argued in favour of the dual-till approach at least at congested airports during our inquiry. (There remain obligations under Bermuda 2 that charges be just and reasonable and related to cost, which are likely to preclude, for example, setting of market-clearing prices.) We were told that the US Government had been informed, and although US airlines raised objections with us about the dual till, they did not question its legality. It was also suggested to us (see Chapter 14) that the extent of use of the dual till by US airports was a further reason why the US Government is now unlikely successfully to take action against any use of the dual till within the UK. One airline, however, said it was concerned there could be 'retaliation' by overseas governments (see Chapter 12).

2.70. Previous CC reports have also referred to policies and guidelines of the International Civil Aviation Organisation (ICAO). At the time of our previous report, these suggested that the cost basis for airport charges should be after allowing for all revenues, aeronautical or non-aeronautical, accruing from the operation of the airport to its operators. Current policies, however, suggest that commercial revenues should 'contribute' to meeting the costs of aeronautical facilities; and the ICAO has said that there should be flexibility in applying either the single-till or dual-till approach. The CAA is required to take into account such of the international obligations of the UK that may be notified to it by the Secretary of State. While the CAA has been advised to take into account Bermuda 2, we understand the Secretary of State has not given notice of the ICAO guidelines under section 39(3); but the DfT told us that it would be concerned if we disregarded the ICAO guidelines. It also suggested to us that where appropriate different treatment at different airports—for example, dual till at congested airports, single till at uncongested airports—would be more consistent with the ICAO's principle of flexibility.

2.71. Introducing the dual till at all three airports purely on the grounds of regulatory consistency may not be compatible with the ICAO guidelines that each airport should be looked at on its merits, but there may be other reasons to do so if the dual till is to be adopted at all. Excess demand to use the Stansted terminal may be less likely given the planning permission to expand it to take 25 mppa; but excess demand to use the runway could develop at Stansted over the next few years, and towards the end of Q4 or beginning of Q5, there may also be a significant investment requirement if the Government's options for runway development at Stansted are pursued. To apply the single till at uncongested airports and the dual till at congested airports could also, as the CAA pointed out, have adverse effects on incentives, encouraging airports to become congested. Hence, in our view the CAA's recommendation that the dual till should be applied at all three airports could not necessarily be regarded as inconsistent with the ICAO guidelines (although, as we discuss further below, there may be other reasons to query its application in practice in Q4 to Stansted and Gatwick, but not Heathrow, as proposed by the CAA). In the light of these considerations, we do not view these guidelines as either precluding or encouraging the dual till at any of the three airports.

2.72. It was also suggested to us that custom and practice have swung sharply towards the dual till. BAA and the CAA told us that many other international airports—for example, Sydney, some US airports and certain European airports (Frankfurt, Zurich, Hamburg)—have also now gone down versions of the dual-till route, confirming the lack of international obligation to maintain the single-till approach. The relevance of such cases has, however, been disputed. Airlines have said that the Sydney case arose because of the wish to boost profits prior to privatization, the lack of funds for investment, and a very low starting level of charges—equivalent to half those at Heathrow prior to the introduction of the dual till. We accept that Sydney Airport cannot be regarded as providing guidance for these reasons. We also noted that the Australian authorities based their decision in part on the analysis of the CAA in the UK; but that subsequently, in May 2002 the Australian Government chose not to institute formal price regulation of Sydney at all, and also discontinued price regulation of other airports, replacing price regulation by monitoring of pricing. The effectiveness of that approach is still to be established.

2.73. As to US airports, one airline representative body told us that airlines often owned the terminal buildings in the US (as was also the case with domestic terminals in Sydney) and, we were told, some commercial revenues accrued to the airlines as a result, depending on the terms negotiated. Another told us that US airports were required to retain all revenues—aeronautical and non-aeronautical alike—for reinvestment on the airport, and we also understand the Government provides funds for infrastructure investment. As to airports elsewhere in Europe, we understand that public authorities also still play a significant role in many of those referred to; assistance to privatization (partial privatization in some cases) was also a factor in introducing the dual till in some of those cases. Commercial revenues are also relatively limited in airports such as Hamburg. Hence, we were not presented with a single example of a comparable type of private sector airport operating a full dual till in the way and for the reasons envisaged by the CAA. Its application to the BAA airports, which are in many respects unique, including the scale of international traffic and commercial revenues generated, would therefore be the first rigorous application of the dual till.

2.74. In our view, no useful inferences can be drawn at this time from overseas airports which use the dual till in whole or in part, as their circumstances are different from those of the three BAA London airports for the reasons given in the preceding paragraphs. Most airports continue to adopt a single-till approach. As with our assessment of international obligations and guidelines, consideration of international practice neither suggests, nor precludes a dual-till approach. The choice between single and dual till therefore has to be considered on its merits, which we now do.

Arguments for the dual till

2.75. We first consider the arguments put forward for the dual till, and then the arguments against. The arguments for the dual till put forward by the CAA and supported by BAA related to the effect on incentives to invest, utilization of scarce runway resources, and deregulation of commercial activities.

2.76. The CAA's basis for proposing the dual till was largely a theoretical one. In addition, during the inquiry we were shown a number of papers by academic authors submitted either on behalf of parties to the inquiry, or by the individuals concerned regarding the choice between the single- and dual-till methods of economic regulation. All were largely theoretical in nature though different in their approach and focus, but in each case the authors concerned were critical of the single-till mechanism mainly because it led to inefficient use of airport capacity at congested airports such as Heathrow and Gatwick. Instead they favoured the dual-till approach, although there were differences of view as to whether it should be applied on an airport-by-airport or system basis and whether fares could or should rise.

2.77. In the following sections, based on the CAA's three main considerations we include what we see as the main points in these papers of relevance to the single/dual-till debate.

Effect on investment

2.78. The CAA's main argument put to us for the dual till was that it would increase incentives to invest in airport facilities, and thereby encourage investment and increase in capacity. We have noted above that one user group also believed a transfer of rents from airlines to airport would be in passengers' interests if invested in additional facilities and fares did not rise. In order to examine this, we first look at the broader context of economically efficient airport charging, within which a number of the submissions were placed.

- *Efficient airport charging: the theoretical background*

2.79. One basis for setting landing charges at a congested airport is rationing of demand, ie setting price such that demand comes into line with the scarce supply available (market-clearing prices). According to economic theory, this would tend to lead to an efficient overall allocation of resources (in the sense that, compared with other price levels, the benefits to the gainers from market-clearing prices would exceed the costs to the losers). This is likely to be the strategy employed by an unregulated but congested airport, and there is evidently concern if a heavily congested airport like Heathrow has low landing charges. But raising charges to the rationing level, or indeed to a level anywhere close to this, would, as noted by the CAA in 1996, be clearly contrary to international convention and to some of the UK's treaty obligations. It would also involve a very large transfer from users to BAA and, even if permitted, would entail a very major change in the regulatory regime established in the UK in relation to airport charges. Capacity at airports is currently allocated through administrative means (slot allocation etc). Although we accept that rationing by price would in principle be likely to be more efficient, this is a matter for governments and international agreement on slot allocation, trading and pricing.

2.80. An alternative basis could be LRIC. This is justified on the grounds that if price equals LRIC then a supplier will only carry out the investments which customers value at least as highly as the value of the resources used up in supplying them. In industries with economies of scale, LRIC will be below long-run average cost; hence a price based on LRIC will not be profitable, and the usual 'second best' solution is to set price equal to long-run average cost (LRAC), including the cost of capital. In the present case that applies at Stansted and may well do so at Gatwick as well.

2.81. It is clear, however, that LRACs are rising at Heathrow, with LRIC above LRAC. This means that prices based on LRIC are certainly feasible in the sense that they will not result in losses. In fact, on the basis of estimates of LRIC provided by the CAA, a LRIC-based landing charge at Heathrow might well exceed £18 per passenger on a dual-till basis, £15 on a single-till basis. In broad terms, on a dual-till basis this would be likely to increase BAA's current profits by over £800 million or 133 per cent creating a windfall gain to BAA's shareholders of at least £10 billion as against current market value of £6 billion. Even so, LRIC-based charges would fall well short of rationing prices. An alternative which would substantially mitigate these effects but still provide optimal investment incentives to BAA, would be to apply LRIC-based charges to the additional passengers permitted by new investment but adopt the conventional approach for existing passengers or capital. We note that the CAA investigated concepts of LRIC pricing at length through a series of consultation documents. It eventually proposed (for Heathrow and Gatwick) a formula that remunerates major projects (such as T5) via a separate term in the price formula but requires a 20-year commitment by the regulator (see Appendix 5.1). We consider this proposal below (see paragraph 2.226 et seq). However, we note here that the CAA's specific proposal is similar to our current approach in that it requires major projects to be considered by the regulator before they are incorporated in the formula and that, for good reasons, it does not give the company an automatic incentive to carry out all projects costing less than some arbitrary 'LRIC' figure. We return to this below.

2.82. Leaving aside any question of the impact of such a change on airlines and passengers, or its implications for regulatory consistency, there is the theoretical issue of whether LRIC-based pricing would, in the actual circumstances of, in particular Heathrow, be optimal in the manner attributed to it. As noted above, the case for it being optimal is that all those investments which are sufficiently valued by users will occur but no more than that. This, however, assumes that the level of investment is fully flexible, is capable of being set at the level determined by LRIC-based charges, and is not, therefore, constrained, financially, by planning regulations or due to physical or operational limits. In the case of BAA, it is quite likely that such investment would be unconstrained financially, because of the huge increase in profitability that LRIC pricing would engender. However, an assumption that new investment at Heathrow is physically or operationally unconstrained and could readily be set much higher if LRIC-based charges were introduced is unlikely to be valid. With T5 going ahead, the main additional investments wanted by airlines are a new runway, which is constrained by planning considerations, and development of the central terminal area (CTA), which we accept cannot be done while it is under heavy pressure in the period prior to T5 becoming operational. More generally, there has been little evidence that airlines would regard significantly more investment than is already included in BAA's £8 billion programme as a realistic demand. The only significant exceptions are those noted above, or projects such as the tracked transit system (TTS) which BAA said primarily concern individual airline advantage, and which it would not then be appropriate to finance from general landing charges.

2.83. If investment is in fact at or around the maximum feasible, then the theoretical case for LRIC pricing must be reconsidered. Normally, raising prices to this level would be regarded as economically efficient, but if the level of capital investment is not sufficiently flexible, this argument no longer holds. Within current constraints the optimum level of investment can be very largely if not entirely achieved and profitably financed at prices far below LRIC. This does not preclude the possibility that LRIC-based prices would bring forth some extra projects, a point which we develop below; but in the present circumstances we saw no evidence that the huge increases in landing charges consequent upon LRIC-based charging would have a significant effect on investment in the period covered in our price control modelling. (There may, however, be a further disadvantage that LRIC prices—being applied to all passengers—may act as a powerful incentive to excessive cost of investment: the higher the cost of new investment, the greater is the profit generated from existing assets.)

2.84. Given the scale of investment proposed by BAA, the main question is whether within the constraints described, this is broadly optimal from an airline perspective. Ideally, to achieve this, airlines should be given information on the pricing consequences of alternative scales of investment, up to the maximum possible, to see whether the maximum is in their view the preferred outcome, as opposed to some lower level of investment with lower charges.

2.85. This has not happened in any formal way to date, and we believe that there should be significant improvements in the procedure for carrying this through, to which we refer later (see paragraph 2.414 et seq). As a result, some airlines have said that they have found it difficult to comment on the investment programme put forward by BAA, and understandably airlines wish to be assured that capital costs are kept to the minimum necessary to provide the facilities concerned. But the shortage of capacity and the pressures on facilities and, therefore, quality of service, are such that very little evidence was put to us that airlines wanted to see the scale of BAA's proposed investment reduced. To the extent that there was such comment, it reflected concerns on the part of airlines remaining in the CTA that they would be paying more as a result of T5, which BA was likely to occupy; but the fact that some airlines may temporarily gain from expansion, ie until the CTA can be redeveloped, is not in our view an argument for not proceeding with the expansion. But equally the dramatically higher charges resulting from LRIC pricing would not in our view increase the planned investment at Heathrow sufficiently to justify the change. This does not contradict standard economic theory on the advantages of LRIC pricing, but suggests that there are few if any advantages for users in applying it at Heathrow at the present time, as against a very large increase in charges.

2.86. In the light of these considerations, we believe it is preferable for airlines to be able to assess and comment on BAA's rolling investment programme as a means of optimizing the programme, as opposed to the regulator setting very much higher charges and then leaving it to BAA to determine what projects it considers viable at that level of charges. Indeed, given the complex interaction of airline operations with the facilities on which they depend at Heathrow and Gatwick, we doubt that the latter approach is a practical alternative.

2.87. As noted above, however, an alternative which would greatly reduce the adverse impact would be to charge a weighted average of, on the one hand, LRIC charges in relation to costs associated with incremental expansion and, on the other, LRAC-based charges in relation to existing activity. Moreover, it is relevant to consider what might constitute an appropriate pricing regime in the longer term, when the specific circumstances currently pertaining at Heathrow may be rather different.

2.88. We note first that, with certain caveats examined below, this is very similar in character to our general approach described and explained later. To illustrate this, there is a level of charges which would, on the basis of the usual approach, provide BAA with a return equal to its cost of capital but assuming no new investment. (This might well involve a substantial fall in airport charges and a large negative value for X in the pricing formula.) In fact of course, the price control is set to provide the same overall return but with all of the incremental capital, ie the investment programme, included. The resulting charges will in practice approximate a weighted average of the 'no investment' charges for existing capital and an average value of the LRIC charge across all the new investment. The outcome is therefore likely to be rather similar to that which would result from the explicit application of LRIC-based charges for incremental activity.

2.89. There are nonetheless some differences. First, this characterization of the approach we recommend below interprets LRIC in relation to the additional investment, rather than the additional costs of an additional passenger. Proper application of LRIC would result in charges rising only as and when the incremental passengers emerged; in other words, LRIC should be output rather than input based. However, this faces a number of different objections. In particular, applying LRIC to the extra passengers resulting from, for example T5, would shift any such charge increase to Q5, to which no one can credibly commit in Q4. This in turn would prevent any financing of T5 through either AICC or revenue advancement in Q4, which could seriously damage BAA's financing capacity for T5. In these circumstances, an approach which funds the investment programme directly, as the incremental activity, through charges which combine, in the form of a weighted average, the cost of the incremental activity with the charges which would apply if there were no such expansion, in our view gives the best outcome.

2.90. Second, this raises the question of what should constitute the incremental capital. Is it all new investment; only 'non-replacement' investment; only capacity enhancing investment; or should it be thought of in more specific terms, such as the T5 project? In one respect this does not seem critical. If we regard the incremental activity as the whole investment programme, then the implied incremental charge will in broad terms represent an average value of the different values of LRIC for each component part of the programme. This will not, of course, correspond to the actual LRIC at any given point in the expansion programme, ie the actual cost at that time of increasing throughput by one extra passenger, but even a pure and explicit LRIC charge would need to average across, in all likelihood, an increment of many millions of extra passengers.

2.91. The more critical objection is that, despite the apparent broad equivalence of the two approaches, if at some future date BAA is considering a new investment not previously contemplated, then an output-based LRIC would provide an appropriate incentive, whereas our preferred alternative being based on previously agreed capital input would not. This, we accept, could in time be a significant advantage of an explicit LRIC-based approach in relation to incremental passengers. It nevertheless faces a number of practical disadvantages. These arise, first, because of the investment constraints noted earlier which we believe currently exist; but second, even if they did not, in the current circumstances of Heathrow and Gatwick it would have been very difficult to determine reliably the LRIC for either the airport as a whole or for individual projects within the investment programme, and also very difficult to integrate this into the five-year pricing formula laid down by the Airports Act in 1986; and third because there is currently no way in which a commitment to such a charging regime can credibly be made, whereas our approach allows a very considerable degree of commitment via the effects on charges in Q4. It is also difficult to see how the LRIC of investments currently not contemplated could be incorporated in any pricing formulae; or, given the time required to carry out such investment, whether there are likely to be many such investments within the next five years. For all these reasons, we do not currently think it would be the right approach: but it is one which the CAA could keep under review.

2.92. None of this relates directly to the single-till versus dual-till issue, which we address directly below. But some of the submissions put to us were, explicitly or otherwise, based on the idea that single-till regulation means that charges are set to generate an overall return equal to the cost of capital but the dual till implies LRIC-based pricing. While there is a link in that if it is aeronautical investment which is to be optimized then it is the LRIC of aeronautical assets which is relevant, nonetheless, in the constrained investment situation faced by BAA, where the optimal investment has in broad terms been identified as described above, it is a separate question whether the dual till will improve on or detract from the investment being financed and carried out.

2.93. In addition it was apparent in some of the evidence we received that the dual till was supported largely because it raised prices and was regarded as a step in the right direction towards either market-clearing prices, as a way of rationing demand particularly at Heathrow, or long-run marginal (incremental) cost pricing, as a way of ensuring users were willing to pay the full economic costs of investment and that its benefits exceeded the costs. (In fact, the CAA argued that the economic benefits were likely to be much higher than could ever be internalized by BAA, given that charges can only be based on costs.) However, as noted above, the former rationale is not likely to be compatible with the requirement in international agreements that prices reflect cost[1] while the latter would be even less likely than full marginal cost pricing to have any discernible effect on investment. More generally, the dual till still produces airport charges far lower than would result from either long-run marginal cost pricing or market-clearing prices. It is therefore only a very limited move in that direction, any benefits of which would have to be offset against the effects of substantially higher charges, significant excess profits for BAA, and the consequent transfer of resources from airline and passengers that would result, which we consider below.

2.94. The same considerations arise in the context of BAA's argument that a move progressively towards dual-till based charges is now required by the rising marginal cost of investment, in order to discharge the regulatory duty to encourage investment. We noted that BAA's traditional approach to investment to increase capacity, for example, has been to identify the additional throughput (ie passengers) that would result, and the additional income (both airport charges, at an assumed future level, and the commercial income generated by the additional number of passengers), to be evaluated against the capital and operating costs. In a situation of increasing marginal costs, unless future charges are based on those marginal costs (in effect the LRIC approach) BAA cannot generate an adequate return merely on the cash flows resulting from, for example, the additional passengers handled. As we noted above, however, the problem of rising incremental cost can be dealt with under the single till by averaging the costs of new and existing capacity, ensuring an adequate return on investment. This approach would also be necessary even under the dual till (this is in effect the CAA's incremental cost/PPC approach we discuss below). Overall, therefore, we do not consider either market-clearing or LRIC-based charges to be feasible. But our more conventional approach nonetheless effectively remunerates BAA for the additional investment it proposes at a level which would reflect its incremental cost.

- *Historical evidence on investment incentives*

2.95. In order to consider the effect of a switch to the dual till on investment incentives, we first looked at the historical period.

2.96. The CAA argued that historically there was some evidence of under-investment which indicated a need for improved incentives. It suggested that BAA had not tried hard enough to overcome planning constraints as regards lack of both terminal and runway development. The CAA also compared the BAA London airports unfavourably with Continental European ones and criticized aspects of the quality of investments. Some airlines—as summarized in more detail below—also criticized BAA for not doing enough to keep options open as to runway developments at Heathrow. Among their criticisms was that BAA had not pushed more strongly for mixed mode to be permitted at Heathrow. (Mixed mode would allow use of each of the two runways for both arrivals and departures whereas they are currently used, for environmental reasons, for either arrivals or departures for half of the day, and then switch use for the rest of the day. Mixed mode would significantly increase runway capacity.) Airlines also (as referred to below) criticized BAA's calling on the Government (in response to the T5 Inquiry Inspector) to rule out a third runway at Heathrow once and for all. However, the airlines also said that inadequacies of investment could be blamed on planning considerations,

---

[1]One suggestion put to us is that 'cost' should include 'opportunity cost' as reflected, for example, in the apparent value of slots, but we are doubtful that would be an acceptable interpretation.

or other factors unrelated to the single/dual till (BA, for example, believed they resulted from BAA's market power which meant it need not and did not respond to incentives to invest, and the absence of statutory or other requirements on it to invest). They also argued that since the main constraints on investments (both terminal and runway development) were political or from planning consideration, greater incentives could have little effect. For example, one argued that since the planning restriction at Gatwick prevents runway development, it could not be argued that higher prices could give an additional incentive to develop a new runway at Gatwick.

2.97. BAA argued there had been no systematic under-investment. At Heathrow its objective had been to get T5 agreed, and it had not wanted to do anything to undermine this (this argument appears to be supported by the Inspector's recommendation that ATMs should not exceed the current figure). BAA also told us that mixed mode would require approval by the Secretary of State and planning approval for associated developments. The ATM limit to be introduced on opening of T5 would also much reduce the benefits of mixed mode.

2.98. BAA's investment programme has been, and continues to be substantial relative to the size of its equity. As we discuss below, its under-investment to date has been only on T5—its non-T5 investment in Q3 was significantly above its original forecasts. Claimed under-investment (which we discuss in more detail in the context of public interest below) appears to fall into two categories. The first is investment prevented or delayed by external planning constraints. We are aware of no evidence that the length of the T5 inquiry could be attributed to BAA. BAA's main concern has, in our view, been to avoid jeopardizing the outcome of the T5 inquiry: hence its reluctance to promote runway development at Heathrow which we accept might well have impacted adversely on the T5 planning inquiry. We have also referred to criticisms of failing to develop runway capacity at Gatwick, but this follows an agreement before privatization not to build an additional runway. (Indeed, the CAA acknowledged that BAA has dealt with planning constraints at Gatwick quite well, as has also been the case at Stansted.) At Stansted, moreover, BAA has been increasing capacity substantially.

2.99. The second is investment held back for perfectly sensible reasons. Under-investment in some facilities to which airlines drew our attention can to a large extent be attributed to the uncertainty facing the airline industry, particularly after the events of 11 September, or factors specific to particular projects (for example, delay in moving an existing tenant preventing use of a site for another purpose). As we discuss below, the pausing of parts of the investment programme following 11 September appears quite reasonable in the light of the uncertainties then facing the industry.

2.100. It is of course true that airlines and their passengers would like far more investment than has occurred. But there are severe inherent constraints on the rate and scale of investment. These primarily arise from the greater congestion of the London area airports compared with most other airports, both the existing shortage of space and planning problems that go far wider than airports, but which in BAA's case are exacerbated by the location of the airports, particularly Heathrow, close to heavily populated areas. The age of the facilities, and the limited scope to undertake major refurbishment until T5 opens, when some traffic can be switched out of the CTA at Heathrow, also have to be taken into account. Given those constraints, we believe that, overall, BAA has a good record on investment.

2.101. We have, therefore, seen no evidence of under-investment as a result of the single till: main examples of under-investment quoted to us primarily reflect planning constraints or would not be affected by the dual till. BAA have never previously argued that the dual till is necessary for adequate investment, and we accept its arguments that it has invested adequately to date, subject only to the constraint of the T5 planning inquiry. We consider below the more critical issue of future investment, but it should be stressed that the main objective of the dual till is to solve a problem which to date has not materialized.

2.102.   We now consider how the dual till may be expected to affect investment incentives.

2.103.   A first possible effect of the dual till is that it gives greater incentive to investment if it offers returns on some projects above the cost of capital whereas the single till only offers returns equal to the cost of capital. In our view, however, this is no justification for the dual till. The notion that returns in excess of the cost of capital are a stronger incentive than returns equal to the cost of capital is obviously correct, but has never played any significant part in any regulatory regime in the UK. Indeed, any suggestion that returns significantly in excess of the cost of capital are necessary to get required investment would represent a major rebalancing of the interests of users and the regulated monopoly supplier. We also note this could have major implications for the regulatory regime of other utilities.

2.104.   BAA argued that there was considerable uncertainty about the cost of capital—any estimate of it was as likely to be too low as too high—hence the dual till, by increasing returns, provided greater assurance that BAA could earn its cost of capital, if it was higher than we assumed. However, we have seen no evidence that the cost of capital we have assumed for BAA in the past has been inadequate to support an appropriate level of investment: nor do we believe the figure we put forward below is likely to prove inadequate. Indeed, in the longer term there is often concern that over-investment rather than under-investment could result from allowing returns equal to the cost of capital: often referred to as the Averch Johnson effect.[1]

2.105.   The situation is rather different where there is a risk of the single-till regime not providing returns at least equal to the cost of capital in situations where the dual till would do so. In order to consider this possible effect we distinguished between purely aeronautical, purely commercial or mixed investment (ie having both aeronautical and commercial aspects); and within each of those three categories, between investment included in a five-year price control projections, substitute investments, or investment in excess of that which is included in the projections—nine possible categories of investment in total:

(a) any investment included in a five-year projection (be it aeronautical, commercial or mixed, accounting therefore for three of the above nine categories) obtains the cost of capital throughout its life under either the single or dual till (assuming, realistically, that the regulator at some future date does not disallow the investment in the RAB);

(b) any investment which substitutes for investment in the projection (again, be it aeronautical, commercial or mixed, a further three of the nine categories) also obtains the cost of capital throughout its life under either the single or dual till, provided it is not so undesirable that the regulator subsequently excludes it from the RAB. Such a scenario is highly unlikely and, as far as we are aware, without precedent in relation to BAA;

(c) any purely aeronautical investment (for example, service-related) over and above the level incorporated in the five-year projection will not, under the single till, earn the cost of capital in the quinquennium in which it occurs (Q_o) but, assuming it is a reasonable investment, will do so thereafter (Q_1, etc). However, exactly the same is true under the dual till; and

---

[1] Averch and Johnsen, American Economic Review, December 1962.

(d) any purely commercial investment in excess of the level projected is likely at least to earn the cost of capital under either the single or dual till; otherwise it would not be undertaken.[1]

2.106. Thus, for eight of the nine categories there is no theoretical reason for believing that the dual till will lead to superior investment, but particularly so in relation to aeronautical investment. It is only in the ninth category that a case can in theory be made. If an investment is over and above the level envisaged in the Q_0 projections, and has both aeronautical and commercial elements (for example, capacity enhancing) then it could be that the lower long-term commercial revenues associated with the single till are insufficient to offset inadequate remuneration within Q_0, whereas the dual till would have allowed this.

2.107. There are, however, two major caveats to even this case. First, it would only apply to a level of investment which is currently unforeseen, but nonetheless completed within the quinquennium, increasing both capex and capacity beyond that envisaged. Given the scale of BAA's programme—an expenditure of £8.1 billion over ten years, as against the current value of BAA's capital of £6 billion—the scope for such additional projects would appear limited.

2.108. Second, to the extent that BAA had the space, physical and management resources and the finance to contemplate this, there would almost certainly be a stronger incentive under the dual till to devote these resources to purely commercial investment, where all of the return over the indefinite future is retained, rather than a partly aeronautical investment, where part of the investment is unremunerated within the quinquennium and only remunerated at the cost of capital thereafter.

2.109. If these largely theoretical arguments are correct, there appears little if any reason to believe that the dual till will have any significantly positive effect on investment other than in the sense that offering ever higher returns above the cost of capital will increase incentives to investment. There is, however, no reason to believe that this is necessary, desirable or efficient.

2.110. That theoretical position seems very much reinforced by the evidence, of three sorts. First, as noted above, there has been no credible evidence to date of under-investment arising from BAA having insufficient incentive to invest under the single till (although we have noted criticisms of delays to some projects in Q3, largely related to the uncertainty following 11 September and which are now in the CIP).

2.111. Second, there is little evidence that BAA's forward plans reflect systematic under-investment arising from inadequate incentives. This is not just an inference from the scale of the capital investment plan (CIP). It also reflects the absence of complaint by airlines of such problems. As noted earlier, the only two candidates, of any size, are BA's demand for a TTS, and other airline demands for upgrading the CTA. But we recognize BAA's argument for not undertaking the TTS at this time and redevelopment of the CTA is inevitably constrained until T5 relieves pressure on the CTA.

2.112. Third, we see no reason to believe that the CIP is dependent on the single/dual-till decision: BAA's investment programme is fully funded by the single-till approach we adopt below. Indeed, even though no price control has been set for Q4, BAA is already investing substantial sums in T5, showing the adequacy of current investment incentives.

---

[1]The CAA have argued that the single till biases such expenditure to short-term investment, because excess profits in future quinquennia will be removed, but even this seems unlikely. It would only apply where two commercial investments were mutually exclusive, not envisaged at the beginning of the Q_0, able to be brought into operation within Q_0 but where the higher NPV commercial investment alone could not meet the cost of capital within Q_0. If this were a frequent occurrence, we would expect to see Heathrow characterized by poor or inadequate commercial investment which, if anything, is the reverse of the usual concerns expressed.

2.113. Hence, there is neither strong theory nor evidence to suggest that the dual till would have any significant impact on investment in aeronautical assets at Heathrow.

2.114. The dual till could indeed more generally distort investment. Long-term anticipated returns to any aeronautical investment considered for inclusion in either a single- or dual-till investment programme equal the cost of capital. For commercial investment anticipated long-term returns will also equal the cost of capital under the single till, but may be considerably higher under the dual till. Hence aeronautical investments, particularly if they do not enhance capacity and thereby generate additional commercial returns, could lose out if there are funding or space constraints despite offering greater benefits to users. Aside from the delay to T5, attributable to planning delays, it is primarily investment to enhance service rather than increase throughput which airlines criticized BAA for not undertaking in Q3 (for example, lack of investment to improve pier service at North Terminal in Gatwick and Terminal 4 (T4) at Heathrow, lack of investment in transfer baggage facilities, or investment in long haul capacity at Terminal 1 (T1) which BAA initially believed would not increase capacity), which we have noted are primarily due to 11 September and whose rate of return would be unaffected by the dual till. The dual till would result in aeronautical investments being ranked according to the additional commercial profits they generate rather than their benefits to airport users, with purely service-related investment likely to lose out as a result.

- *Other effects on investment*

2.115. BAA argued that the dual till would allow an improved focus on aeronautical investments, in so far as the single till biases managers to invest in projects with an element of commercial returns. We noted above that for a capacity generating project, commercial revenues are taken into account in investment appraisal: the greater the commercial revenues, the greater the apparent rate of return may be on such an approach. Such greater return arises, however, only in the sense of the cashflows directly attributable to the project, without taking into account its inclusion in the RAB and effect on airport charges in subsequent quinquennia. Moreover, purely aeronautical investment, for example in safety or quality of service, may appear not to generate any additional profit, since the bulk of profit is generated by commercial activities.

2.116. Some of the BAA evidence suggested that it decided on individual investments purely on the basis of discounted cash flows, primarily by internal rates of return as opposed to cost benefit analysis (as discussed below, however, other evidence suggested that in practice this was not the case), although such investments were included in the investment programme and taken into account in setting X because the benefits exceed the costs. There would be an artificiality in attributing cash flows to individual projects in this way. The CC and the CAA in setting prices takes into account the volume of investment, thus providing a return on that investment. That return may not be from specific users of a project, but users more generally. We acknowledge that regulation much complicates the process of investment appraisal for an organization such as BAA, and that BAA takes great efforts to ensure that return on investment is not regarded as merely an automatic consequence of allowing a return on the regulatory asset base. While it is clearly appropriate for BAA to try to ensure that the benefit to users of investment exceeds the costs and that the investment meets the needs of airlines, it would be inconsistent for BAA to assume, as it told us was the case, that an aeronautical investment does not generate a specific return, since we have in effect allowed for that return in setting charges; if it does not undertake the investment or equivalent investment, it undermines the basis on which charges were set. Any problems that may currently be faced by BAA are better resolved by reconsideration of BAA's process of investment appraisal, rather than increased charges to users.

2.117. However, there appears to be little evidence of distorted investment priorities in practice. BAA quoted projects to us, such as the provision of long-haul capacity in T1 at

Heathrow (a project named 'Iceberg' to which we refer in more detail below), which it carried out despite initially believing they were uneconomic on the basis of the associated cash flows. This shows BAA is already well able to recognize the benefits of such projects and to resolve the problems they identified while retaining the single till.

2.118. We have also noted above the CAA's proposal to include existing surface access in the commercial rather than aeronautical till. BAA believed this would discourage it from pursuing worthwhile but unprofitable public transport investments: the CAA thought this aspect of its proposals would be advantageous for this reason. In our view the CAA's approach—which would require new surface access projects (unless a condition of planning approval) to be financed out of commercial activities or to be self-standing—would prove less flexible than retention of the single till in this respect, acting as a disincentive to undertake surface access projects which may be regarded as desirable, but which are unlikely to be profitable.

2.119. We also considered whether the dual till would encourage investment in other ways, for example through providing up-front revenues to finance T5, or, as BAA have suggested, provide increased assurance as to future price paths necessary for investment in T5 etc. However, the CAA's proposals themselves do neither: the proposals for Q4 at Heathrow are broadly on a single-till basis, and the PPC for subsequent quinquennia—as we discuss below— has little credibility since it depends on the view of the regulators in the future, nor is it dependent on the specific features of the dual till. To the extent that the single till does give rise to problems, these are areas that should be more directly and more effectively addressed by alternative means—for example, profiling of prices and revenues which we consider below, or, if appropriate, adjustment of rate of return.

2.120. The CAA saw increased levels of information disclosure and more effective consultation as a key part of the framework of their proposals to encourage investment (although they do not propose these be an element of the price cap or charging conditions). Under the single till or dual till, there would be no requirement on the airports to invest (other than the prospect that any previous failure to invest could be found against the public interest): a main source of complaint from airlines who have suggested a mandatory investment requirement. Hence, again issues of investment and consultation arise irrespective of whether the dual till is adopted, and are also relevant to public interest issues below.

2.121. The CAA also raised the possibility of reverting to a single till in future as an effective threat to ensure that BAA improves performance. All airlines were sceptical as to the value of such a threat—for example, on grounds that the CAA cannot bind its successors. To revert to a single till, reducing the rate of return on investment, would be an unlikely and hence non-credible means of addressing any under-investment. Hence, we do not believe that the dual-till approach would act as an effective incentive on BAA to maintain or improve performance by providing 'something to lose' at future regulatory reviews should it fail to do so.

● *Conclusion*

2.122. To conclude on investment incentives, there is therefore no evidence that the single till has led to any general under-investment in aeronautical assets at the three BAA London airports in the past, nor in our view any expectation that it will do so over the next five years. Nor is it clear that the dual till, as opposed to the single till, in the circumstances which BAA faces provides a necessary or acceptable means of encouraging investment in aeronautical facilities, or would be likely to lead to better aeronautical investment in the future; in some respects the dual till is likely to be worse, unduly favouring commercial investment if there are financial or other constraints.

2.123. As evident therefore from the discussion above, in so far as the current regulatory regime may give rise to problems in ensuring adequate investment, these can in our view be resolved through the single till. BAA indeed, in response to our statement of current thinking on the dual till, accepted that adequate incentives can be provided under the single till, if implemented in such a way as to produce the right level of price in a sustainable way, even though it regarded this as more difficult under the single till. The points it believed would meet these criteria were:

(a) continued application of the system approach;

(b) a cost of capital which reflected BAA's growing riskiness;

(c) incorporation of AICC in the asset base;

(d) acceptance of the importance of providing a margin or cushion to avoid a crisis in the event of major disruption; and

(e) resisting the temptation to clawback under-spend indiscrimately.

Each of these points is considered below.

Effect on utilization of aeronautical facilities

2.124. The second main benefit the CAA claimed for the dual-till approach is that it would improve efficient utilization of limited runway capacity because users who value use of the scarce capacity relatively highly displace those who give it a lower valuation. We referred in paragraph 2.76 to the support of academic authors for the dual till partly on the grounds that the single till led to inefficient use of existing capacity at congested airport. However, none of the authors cited any empirical evidence on the actual extent of the inefficiency of airport facilities under the single till. Nor did they refer to the possibilities—to which we refer below—for airlines or groups of airlines either to achieve efficient use of their slot portfolios by operating internal markets or to adjust slot holdings by monetized trading of slots. Finally, the papers generally took little account of the various impediments to achieving a significant improvement in allocative efficiency arising from factors such as international air service agreements.

2.125. We first considered legal arguments put to us against the CAA approach. A number of airlines argued that the use of airport charges to improve the allocation of resources is beyond the remit of the regulator (given, for example, Council Regulations (EEC) No 95/93). Airport resources are allocated by an independent coordinator under a clearly defined administrative slot allocation regulation which falls within the competence of the EC, and has broader objectives than simply ensuring the efficient use of slots. A proportion of slots returned to the pool, for example, have to be allocated to new entrants rather than existing carriers, irrespective of the relative valuations they may put on them. BA said that it did not believe the CAA was entitled to try to pre-empt a change to the regulation unilaterally by using airport charges as an allocation mechanism, and in any case this was likely to create conflicting regulatory objectives between those of the CAA and those of the EC. As noted in paragraph 2.37, BA also argued that the CAA's statutory duty under section 39 of the Airports Act was to ensure the efficient and profitable operation of the airport, as opposed to the efficient use of the airport. Section 39 also expressly provided that the CAA's general objectives under section 4 of the 1982 Civil Aviation Act, which refer to the CAA's objectives to look after passengers' interests in the way that air transport services are provided, do not apply in relation to performance by the CAA of its functions under Part IV of the Airports Act. Hence, it argued that both the Council Regulation (EEC) No 95/93/EEC and section 39 of the Airports Act prevented the CAA from using its powers as an economic regulator of airports to deal with allocation of slots between airlines. We are not persuaded by the arguments that the CAA's approach is necessarily inconsistent with EC or UK legislation: efficient operation of the airport arguably includes its use. It is also arguable that efficient slot allocation would fall within the objective of furthering the reasonable interests of users of the airports within the UK, in that it would be in the interests of passengers as a whole for airlines to make the most profitable use of the slots.

2.126. We need, therefore, to consider whether the CAA's proposals would have any significant benefits on slot allocation. Airlines argued that such benefits were purely theoretical. They quoted, for example, the very efficient use already made of Heathrow's and Gatwick's runways (more ATMs per runway and passengers per ATM than anywhere else in the world) given existing allocation mechanisms. These included optimizing use of slots within airlines and slot exchanges between airlines, including those between alliance parties, to improve use of capacity. They regarded it as questionable whether the higher charges which would result from the dual till would make a difference compared with the present situation.

2.127. The CAA's concern about efficient utilization of facilities goes beyond the number of passengers handled, to include the value put by airlines and passengers on their use of the runway. One aspect of that could be an inefficient mix of traffic—for example, too much domestic or short-haul and insufficient long-haul traffic. Nonetheless, the figures quoted by the airlines do show that the airports start from a position of very high utilization of capacity based on the number of passengers and ATMs that use them; and there clearly are already pressures on airlines to seek continuous improvement in the efficient use of slots and to utilize fully existing mechanisms, even if crude and non-transparent, to assist that process, as shown by the number of domestic routes that have been withdrawn over the last few years. The scope for improvements is correspondingly limited.

2.128. The CAA argued that if a particular airline secures capacity through offering a higher price for it, it must be offering a higher net value product. However, we see a number of reasons why this general proposition frequently does not hold true in the case of the BAA airports.

2.129. First, the airline market is characterized by a number of aspects which reduce competition, including:

(a) bilateral treaties, which may limit the number of operators on individual routes, for example only four airlines are currently permitted to operate between Heathrow and the USA, which is likely to reduce competition on these routes and responsiveness to changes in charges;

(b) complex international regulatory systems, including EC slot allocation rules which require 50 per cent of slots returned to the pool to be awarded to new entrants potentially reducing the value of slots in alternative uses;

(c) varying degrees of state ownership of airlines, which are likely to affect the extent to which they respond to competitive or financial pressures;

(d) differing financial strengths of airlines, again affecting the response to competitive and financial pressure such as airport charges;

(e) different strategies pursued by different airlines (for example, a desire to continue to operate at an airport for future strategic gain or prestige) limiting responsiveness to higher charges; and

(f) possible other barriers to entry on particular routes, for example shortage of capacity at overseas airports; interlining and code-sharing arrangements; or commission override payments and frequent flyer points, as mentioned in previous reports.

2.130. Second, it was also suggested to us that the piecemeal release of spare slots by some airlines reduced the competitive opportunities for others, and the extent to which those slots would be more efficiently used by other airlines.

2.131. Third, such benefits are also likely to be very limited, given the very high level of excess demand currently prevailing particularly at Heathrow; the low price elasticity of demand; and the limited impact that would result from the dual till. We noted above the CAA's estimate that the premium on operating services from Heathrow rather than Gatwick could be £20 per passenger on short-haul routes and up to £110 per passenger on some services. In comparison, as shown in Table 2.6, the dual-till approach would increase prices by less than £2 per passenger above the single-till level (on the basis of including existing surface access within the commercial till). The argument was put to us that changes in the structure of landing charges in the 1980s had significantly reduced use of runways by smaller aircraft: but the movement from a weight-related to a flat rate landing charge resulted in substantial increases in charges on smaller aircraft, compared with the much more limited increases that would result from the dual till.

2.132. BAA and the CAA argued that although the above may be reasons why it could not be assumed that any slots released would be used by whichever airline valued them most, nonetheless, there should be some improvement in efficient utilization as a result. But they also appeared to accept that the effect on demand of the higher charges that would result from the dual till would be limited, hence that any effect on economic efficiency at Heathrow would be very limited in relation to the distortions caused by other factors, such as the slot allocation system. Nonetheless, BAA argued that even a limited improvement in allocation of scarce runway resources would be of value. BA, however, argued very limited improvements would be insufficient to justify the higher costs to airlines or fares.

2.133. We cannot rule out some improvement in efficient utilization of capacity. It will generally be true in any situation that higher charges are likely to give a greater incentive to improve efficient use of resources. But in the circumstances of the airline industry set out in paragraphs 2.129 to 2.131, any potential benefits of the dual-till approach are likely to be limited and speculative.

2.134. In principle the effect may be more significant in peak periods at Gatwick, fares being lower and airport charges higher as a percentage of fares. Any benefit would, however, be very dependent on adopting the CAA's concept of efficiency. The charter carriers, primarily at Gatwick, and LFCs, primarily at Stansted, being more price sensitive, were particularly concerned that they would be adversely affected by higher charges resulting from the dual till. In our view, such airlines have brought significant benefits through lower fares not only to their own passengers but also to passengers on traditional scheduled airlines. However, being more price sensitive and having lower fares and with airport charges a higher percentage of fares, they would be particularly adversely affected by higher charges. Charter airlines also operate larger aircraft at higher load factors and so in terms of passengers per slot are using runways relatively efficiently. Therefore, unless there is a switch towards a charging structure based primarily on movements (ie a switch away from passenger charges, which may beyond a point be difficult to justify since increased passenger capacity accounts for the bulk of investment costs), the effects could be perverse.

2.135. We would therefore be concerned that the impact of the dual till could be on airlines at Gatwick and, possibly, Stansted, who are more efficient in terms of physical use of capacity, who operate in a highly competitive sector of the market, reducing their ability to withstand higher charges, and who (particularly in the case of LFCs) have put significant competitive pressure on other sectors of the market which would be reduced if their operations had to be scaled back. The value of slots at Gatwick is also significantly lower than Heathrow, further limiting the potential benefits of any reallocation of slots.

2.136. A number of other concerns were raised with us about the effect on particular operators and particular services and environmental aspects which we now consider.

2.137. There was particular concern that higher airport charges resulting from the dual till could adversely affect airlines operating services from Heathrow to regional airports in the UK (for example, Leeds Bradford, Teesside and Belfast City airports)—adversely affecting not only those services but also the respective regional economies. It is uncertain how serious the risk to services would be if charges rose for any reason. They are operated by UK airlines which already use their slots in the most profitable way that is open to them. For there to be a risk to these services, any rise in airport charges would have to be so large that these airlines gave up slots and, as discussed above, we do not think that a move to the dual till would represent such a large change. Rather any risk to regional services may be more likely to arise from possible regulatory changes, for example to Bermuda 2, which provided the relevant airlines with new opportunities to operate more profitable services. But whether any withdrawal of such services that may result from higher charges is acceptable or not depends on the reason for the higher charges. If it reflected an increase in costs or the overall pressure of demand to use Heathrow, this may be acceptable, although if the Government saw some wider economic benefit from such services, it may need to consider whether they should be directly financed. If, however, it was the result mainly of a windfall gain to BAA it would not be acceptable, and we believe this would be the case if the dual till were adopted. This also applies to a similar concern expressed about the effect on airmail.

2.138. We also, however, see further possible disbenefits of higher airport charges resulting from the dual till to hub airlines based at the London airports, which compete for transfer traffic with airlines based outside the UK. Such effects may again be acceptable if higher charges reflect higher costs or changes in demand: but not otherwise.

2.139. On the other hand, environmental groups were concerned, as also at the time of our last report, that the single till artificially increased demand. It was regarded as one of a number of distortions, as they saw it, favouring the airline industry, including preferential taxation of fuel. Protecting the environment is not among the duties of the CAA, and in our view would need to be more directly addressed by Government as part of environment policies and, if necessary, tax policies rather than airport charges.

2.140. We regard increases in airport charges as a result of application of the dual till, therefore, as unlikely significantly to improve the efficient allocation of scarce runway capacity or thereby to benefit the reasonable interest of users or the economic and efficient operation of the airports in this respect. Such an objective would, in our view, be far more effectively addressed through reconsideration of EC rules on allocation of slots. Article 8 of the Council Regulation 95/93/EEC on slot allocation, gives support to grandfather rights and preference to new entrants in allocating any additional slots or slots returned to the pool. Subject to some qualifications, the article permits the free exchange of slots between carriers and the transfer of slots between routes and between types of service. The European Commission claims that while exchange of slots is permitted, transfers between airlines are not. There is some uncertainty in this area notwithstanding a 1999 decision of the High Court which ruled that an exchange of slots between KLM-UK and BA was an 'exchange' within the meaning of the article even though money had changed hands and KLM did not intend to use the slots it had acquired under the deal. The Government has suggested limiting the period of grandfather rights, allowing trading, or auctioning of any newly created slots. These matters are being considered by the EC, but the EC is also, however, considering action to prevent slot trading. BAA said the latter possibility would result in airport charges being the only means available to improve slot allocation: to do so, however, they would have to be very much higher than under the single or dual till.

2.141. While therefore the dual till could improve the efficient utilization of capacity, the benefits are unlikely to be more than marginal, even at Heathrow, by some degree the most congested of the airports and with the highest excess demand. Any such benefits are quite insufficient without other benefits to justify the dual-till approach. Indeed in Q4, with which this review is concerned, the application of the dual till is effectively confined to Gatwick and Stansted, rather than Heathrow, although any consideration of more efficient utilization of resources suggest it is at Heathrow rather than the other airports where it would be applied. There are, therefore, no such benefits at Heathrow in Q4 under the CAA proposals. Applying the dual till, and higher airport charges, at Gatwick, where there is spare capacity in off-peak periods, or Stansted where there is currently limited pressure on runway capacity, could therefore reduce the efficient utilization of resources in Q4. Hence, even in the longer term, any benefits at Heathrow might be offset by reduction in efficient utilization of resources at Gatwick or Stansted, if charges rose even further above incremental cost at either of those two airports.

Implications for commercial activities

2.142. The CAA's third rationale for the dual till was that it would eliminate de facto regulation of commercial activities at the airports. However, the difference between the dual-till and single-till approach only arises because of the greater profitability of commercial activities. Table 2.7 shows the estimated rate of return of the three airports for the last five years on the basis of the CAA proposed dual till (including surface access in the commercial till, much reducing returns at Heathrow).

TABLE 2.7 **Return on average capital employed of commercial activities under the CAA proposed dual till**

					per cent
	1996/97	*1997/98*	*1998/99*	*1999/00*	*2000/01*
HAL—incl surface access	22.3	15.6	15.2	14.4	14.5
HAL—excl surface access	N/A	N/A	N/A	N/A	30.2*
GAL	37.2	37.3	42.3	28.2	25.3
STAL	24.3	20.5	25.9	23.4	20.9

Source: CC study.

*From analysis in Table 2.5, based on a method of calculation somewhat different to those of the other figures in this table.
Note: N/A = Not available.

The rate of return on commercial activities at Heathrow excluding surface access in 2000/01 was some 30 per cent (see Table 2.5. The other figures in Table 2.7 are not exactly consistent with the estimates in Table 2.5 given the assumptions that have had to be made in deriving both sets of figures and the different sources of data that have to be used). The downward trend in return on commercial activities reflects the loss of intra-EC duty- and tax-free sales in 1999, and, in the case of Heathrow, the addition to assets and costs when the Heathrow Express came into service.

2.143. Under the CAA's projections, there are excess rates of return (taking a reasonable rate of return as 7.5 per cent, discussed further below) on commercial activities, with surface access included in the commercial till, of up to almost 30 per cent for individual airports: see Table 2.8.

TABLE 2.8 **Returns on assets over selected periods under CAA projections**

% rates of return

	Average Q4	2007/08	Average Q5	2012/13
Heathrow				
Single till: total airport	6.8	6.8	6.8	6.8
RRCB adjusted				
Aeronautical	6.8	6.8	6.8	6.8
Commercial till (incl surface access)	11.4	10.7	12.5	13.5
Total	8.3	7.8	8.2	8.4
CAA proposal				
Aeronautical	4.7	4.5	7.5	8.4
Commercial till (incl surface access)	11.4	10.6	12.5	13.5
Total	6.8	6.1	8.8	9.6
Gatwick				
Single till: total airport	7.2	7.2	7.2	7.2
RRCB adjusted				
Aeronautical	7.2	7.2	7.2	7.2
Commercial till (incl surface access)	23.8	24.4	25.5	27.6
Total	12.4	12.3	12.2	12.4
CAA proposal				
Aeronautical	4.3	6.1	7.4	7.7
Commercial till (incl surface access)	23.8	24.4	25.5	27.6
Total	10.4	11.5	12.3	12.7
Stansted				
Single till: total airport	7.2	7.2	7.2	7.2
RRCB adjusted				
Aeronautical	7.2	7.2	7.2	7.2
Commercial till (incl surface access)	31.2	34.1	34.5	35.3
Total	11.9	12.4	12.5	12.6
CAA proposal				
Aeronautical	3.8	7.2	11.8	15.3
Commercial till (incl surface access)	31.2	34.1	34.5	35.2
Total	9.1	12.4	16.0	19.1

Source: CC based on CAA projections.

Notes:
1. The RRCB and the CAA proposal cases still exclude existing surface access from aeronautical till.
2. The figures for Stansted assume that Stansted prices up to the maximum allowed: the CAA believe this unlikely to occur in practice.
3. The CAA proposals are based on longer-term projections than the period set out in this table, in which projected returns on aeronautical activities reflect the cost of capital.

2.144. A number of airlines argued that commercial activities are as monopolistic as aeronautical. In contrast, the CAA argued that these profits reflect significant 'locational scarcity rents' as opposed to 'monopoly rents'. While in theory, these two concepts can be regarded as distinct, in this context locational rents arise in our view only because of BAA's locational advantage, arising from its monopoly over aeronautical activities: a situation quite unlike the examples of a high street or Oxford Street quoted to us. Against that, BAA also argued that the requirement on concessionaires not to price above high-street levels itself showed there was no monopoly profit. However, there can be no presumption that there are no monopoly profits just because prices are the same as in different location: sales per square metre in BAA outlets may well be much higher than in many of those other locations. The very fact that BAA finds it necessary to constrain the prices in its retail outlets shows the market power they would have if it did not adopt this approach.

45

2.145. BAA also argued that to regard its commercial profits as equivalent to monopoly rents was an extreme position: that each activity should be looked at on its merits, and those activities which were clearly being provided in competition with off airport operators, should fall outside the regulatory domain. It quoted long-term car parking and landside retailing as examples where its only advantage was location, and consumers had clear alternatives (BAA acknowledged short-term car parking should be in the aeronautical till). In our view, BAA has, nonetheless, substantial monopoly power in those locations; even in the case of long-term car parking where there are off-airport operators, its share ranges from about 60 per cent at Heathrow and Gatwick to 97 per cent at Stansted (where competitive developments are generally not being allowed), and it is the nearest and easiest to find at each, putting it in a strong market position at each airport. Moreover, without the aeronautical investment and the presence of passengers at the airport, those facilities would be worth very little. To the extent it earns profits above the cost of capital from these activities, we believe it right these should be offset within the single till against airport charges rather than be regarded as purely for the benefit of BAA's shareholders.

2.146. If a dual-till approach were to be adopted there would also be a risk of increased prices where the airport enjoys market power—since, unlike at present, it would fully retain the benefits. This further increases the risk of requiring greater regulatory intervention (or threat thereof) to reduce the excess profits of the commercial activities and the windfall benefits to BAA shareholders as a result of moving from the single-till approach used at privatization. The CAA argued that if there are excess commercial profits, the single till does nothing to eliminate them: this should be directly addressed through, for example, the Competition Act 1998 (CA 98). The single till does, however, in our view channel them to airlines and to some extent to passengers (see our discussion of fares in paragraph 2.177 et seq). It is true that all passengers gain via the single till, whereas only those spending at airports would gain under any alternative approaches designed to reduce the prices of commercial activities, but this more focussed effect is in our view a small benefit to be set against the much more costly form of regulation that would be required.

2.147. Hence, if a dual-till approach were to be adopted, we believe there is a risk of requiring greater regulatory intervention or threat thereof to reduce the profits of commercial activities that would be implied by that approach; it is more desirable that any such excess commercial profits should be included in the single till which ensures that the rents accrue to the airport users who are the source of that rent. To date, users (airlines and passengers), and to some extent regulators may have been less concerned about the extent of those profits (which arise mainly from duty- and tax-free shops and short-term car parks), since they are used to offset airport charges, to the benefit of the airlines and/or passengers, hence the incentive to regulate these activities by other means has been negligible.

2.148. We are therefore not persuaded that the distinction between monopoly and locational rents is useful in this context, and in any event do not see it as supporting any case for disregarding excess profits made by BAA in its commercial activities. In so far as airport charges affect fares, the current relatively high profits of commercial activities are applied to the benefit of passengers; the dual-till approach would be likely to require increased regulation of such activities and increased regulatory costs with broadly the same outcome: we note below the need for detailed involvement of the CAA in apportioning costs, of existing and new assets, between the aeronautical and commercial activities and the scope for continuous disputes between BAA and users to which the dual till would give rise. We do not therefore see significant benefits from the deregulation of commercial facilities; the dual till could in practice increase rather than minimize the burden of restrictions in the regulatory system.

- *Effect on commercial investment and the balance between commercial and aeronautical activities*

2.149. One of the benefits of deregulating commercial activities put to us was that at present the incentive to develop commercial activities is reduced because commercial profits are taken into account in setting airport charges (in effect 'taxed') at the five-yearly review, ie shareholders get the benefit for a maximum of five years. The CAA suggested that as a consequence there was a 'different type of investment' at BAA airports than at Continental airports—with more 'short-term' investment by BAA. It acknowledged, however, that the effect of the dual till on investment in commercial facilities could lead to either more or less investment.

2.150. We acknowledge that the single till reduces long-term returns on commercial investments. However, we are not as yet aware of any desirable commercial developments that have not been undertaken as a result of the single till. We have noted, moreover, that even if the current approach, by effectively capping commercial and aeronautical investment to the cost of capital at each review, reduces returns on commercial investments, returns on aeronautical investments are also restricted to that figure and can take no account of wider economic benefits of additional capacity (as evidenced by the premium fares from Heathrow to which we referred above), which are likely significantly to exceed return to BAA, irrespective of the single or dual till. The dual till, however, by increasing return on commercial relative to aeronautical investment, would lead to a significant shift away from aeronautical investment, offsetting any benefits of deregulation.

2.151. We also acknowledge the argument that the single till may appear to provide a return on commercial investment, through its inclusion in the RAB, irrespective of its merits. The amount of commercial, in particular retail investment, is, however, relatively small. Table 2.5, for example, suggests commercial activities (excluding surface access but including property) account for only 16 per cent of the RCV of the three airports, but 57 per cent of the operating profit. BAA also estimated that retail activities are expected to account for only 8 to 10 per cent of T5 floor-space or even less net of the circulation and seating that would be required without the retail facilities; we have also seen CAA figures suggesting non-aeronautical use of terminals accounts for only 3 per cent of net assets. Retail profits however currently account for about 40 per cent of BAA's operating profit and may be even more profitable in T5. We have seen no evidence that BAA has been undertaking commercial investment which does not generate a reasonable commercial return or that it has persisted with facilities of no value commercially or to its users; on the contrary it has the considerable incentive of retaining additional profits from maximizing the value of its facilities within each quinquennium. Even were it to undertake unnecessary investment, this could be disallowed from the RAB in future reviews.

2.152. We do not therefore see any material benefits to users from any effect of the dual till on incentives to commercial investment.

2.153. Indeed underlying some of the points raised below in the context of the public interest, is the implication that BAA has to date even under the single till put excessive emphasis on commercial as opposed to aeronautical activities. For example, BAA required that it be compensated for loss of commercial income if that resulted from development of facilities for airlines and diversion of passengers via retail activities. BAA said this was the result of the single till, an argument we have taken into account in considering those complaints; but the incentives to impose such requirements would be even greater under the dual till.

2.154. Several airlines argued that the tendency to develop commercial activities at the expense of aeronautical activities would be greatly magnified under the dual till because of the much higher return on commercial activities that it would generate. A number of points tend to support this.

2.155. First, we noted evidence of the International Air Transport Association (IATA) that ratings of passengers perception of shopping facilities at Heathrow is significantly higher than the average of airports compared, while ratings tend to be significantly lower than average on other aspects of the airport (except those relating to range of services). This might suggest there has been too much development of commercial activities at the expense of developments that would improve passenger perception of aeronautical facilities. BAA disputed that ratings for non-retail elements of service quality had been significantly lower than average. The complaint, it said, only cited Heathrow, and Gatwick's performance was better. It did, however, acknowledge that there are two areas where this complaint could be justified, notably ease of way-findings/signposting and 'connections'. The first of these is addressed in the context of service quality (see below); the second is a joint responsibility between BAA and the airlines and BAA believes great strides have been made to improve performance. On comfort of passengers waiting at gate areas, Gatwick is above average and Heathrow slightly below average.

2.156. Some airlines suggested that in the USA where airlines tend to own terminals, and hence can choose the balance between commercial and aeronautical facilities, there are fewer shopping facilities, indicating that BAA's provision of them was excessive. BAA suggested this merely reflected poor performance in developing such facilities.

2.157. It was also suggested to us that retail space does now amount to a very significant proportion of floor area used by passengers (for example, at Heathrow T1) at the expense of space that could be used to improve other facilities for passengers; also that the layout of retail outlets requires passengers to walk through them (for example, in Terminal 3 (T3)). On that example, BAA argued that the T3 World Duty Free Shop (WDF) could be bypassed by fast track customers and regulars, effectively acknowledging that others have to walk through the WDF shop, albeit with 'no material increase in walking distances'. It also said there was very little negative customer feedback. We did, however, note very low ratings from BAA's Quality of Service Monitor (QSM) survey of passengers on seating in T3: although this is being improved by the current development, the provision of seating prior to and during the redevelopment appears to have been regarded as secondary to the quality of commercial facilities. Airlines also complained about way-finding often being obscured by commercial advertising; we noted that BAA acknowledged there was scope to improve way-finding.

2.158. Some airlines argue they have already been adversely affected by 'massive' commercial development, at the expense of seating, toilets etc, distracting of passengers and leading to delays. Others thought this unfair. Some said the situation had been tolerated only because of the benefits to them via the single-till approach.

2.159. In our view, even under the single till, BAA is likely to prefer commercial developments to aeronautical developments. This is because it is able to retain the benefits of greater than expected commercial revenues for the remaining period of a quinquennium Ultimately, however, under the single till, airlines and passengers subsequently share in these benefits: hence, we do not believe that the public interest has been adversely affected to date. However, as we have noted above given the relative profitability of the commercial and aeronautical tills, this problem would be exacerbated under the dual till. Currently, for example, the same rate of return (of about 7.5 per cent) is, in effect, permitted on both commercial and aeronautical tills; under the dual till that return would be allowed on aeronautical investment, but there could be a much greater return, currently some 30 per cent or more, on commercial activities. BAA argued that, even if the amount of commercial investment and its proportion of total investment were increased, aeronautical investment would be maintained rather than reduced: but since there are likely to be constraints not only of funding but also of space, we believe there would be detriment to aeronautical facilities.

2.160. We accept that BAA is not likely to put at risk aeronautical investments that increase capacity, and which generate commercial as well as aeronautical revenues. The dual-till approach is, however, likely to lead to too much investment in commercial activities to the detriment of aeronautical facilities that affect quality of service—for example, more shops, less seating, or greater difficulty in getting to the gate. BAA believes that any such effects would be adequately measured by quality of service criteria (see below) with penalty payments if standards were not met: or a code of conduct to ensure problems do not occur. It believed such a code of conduct would alleviate airline concerns on space utilization under a dual till and 'enable the business to focus on core operational performance and passenger service'. BAA would commit itself to collection and distribution of data on space utilization in common user terminal areas; maintain aeronautical space levels to meet quality standards; and consult on development proposals in common user terminal areas. Local approaches could supplement quality of service measurements at the airport level to alleviate specific airline concerns and provide additional information on other areas as required. For example, an airport would share its 'late-to-gate' surveys with airlines and handling agents. BAA acknowledged that some improvement in its space data would be necessary.

2.161. In our view, however, the dual till would risk unduly benefiting commercial activities, at the expense of non-capacity-enhancing aeronautical activities, which may not attract sufficient funds or attention. The safeguards put forward by BAA are unlikely in our view to reassure the airlines, given the uncertainties inherent in measuring such quality factors. The dual till is likely to involve intense and protracted argument as to the development of commercial and aeronautical facilities, because, unlike the single till, there will be a systemic conflict of interest between BAA and its airline customers. We do not therefore see the dual till approach as having any benefit to users in its effect on commercial activities; any benefits in encouraging investment in commercial activities are not in our view material and there could be disbenefits; nor do we see it as having any material benefits in minimizing restrictions in the regulatory system.

Disadvantages of the dual till

2.162. There is therefore no evidence that the single till has led to any general under-investment in aeronautical assets at the three airports, nor any expectation that it will do so over the next five years, or that the dual till is likely to lead to better aeronautical investment in the future. The dual till could improve the efficient utilization of capacity, but the benefits are unlikely to be more than marginal. Nor do we see any benefits from deregulation of commercial activities. We therefore see minimal benefits from the dual till. We have noted that the dual till could unduly benefit commercial activities, at the expense of aeronautical; we now consider the other problems the dual till might have.

The separability of the businesses concerned

2.163. The dual till requires a separation of costs and assets between commercial and aeronautical activities. We have noted in Table 2.1 that some separation of profitability between airport charges and other activities is already undertaken in BAA's accounts as required by the Airports Act (see paragraph 4.24). However, while there is no doubt that such separation can be done and may be appropriate for some purposes, it is necessary to consider whether it is sensible in regulatory and economic terms to regard the activities as separable in the context of the proposed dual till such that no account should be taken of the apparent profits of commercial operations in setting airport charges.

2.164. Among airlines' views, BA argued that commercial revenues were a by-product and an inseparable part of the aeronautical business—totally dependent on the regulated business. It argued that where demand complementarities between goods or services existed, single-till type arrangements often operated. In contrast, BAA in its submission to us described commercial activities as 'purely incremental', with the incremental costs readily identified. We noted, however, that in its statutory accounts for the individual airports, BAA has for many years stated that in the opinion of the directors it would be misleading to apportion operating costs and net assets to individual segments of the business, hence in its statutory accounts it dis-aggregates only revenue between airport and other traffic charges, retail property, and other operational facilities.

2.165. Much of the debate about whether costs and assets can be meaningfully separated between aeronautical and other activities has been concerned with two criteria, namely whether commercial activities can be regarded as 'essential' to an airport operation, and/or whether commercial and aeronautical activities can be regarded as 'joint' products. On the first of these, it would not in our view be valid to regard many commercial activities as an 'essential' part of an airport operation, but it is almost inconceivable that a major airport would not provide a certain level of catering and retail activity to meet passengers' needs while waiting to board aircraft, nor the means of accessing the airport or parking cars at the airport. On the second, aeronautical and many commercial operations cannot properly be regarded as 'joint products' because there is no fixed relationship between the two: commercial revenues are not auto-matically generated by aeronautical facilities, but require the appropriate facilities to be provided and promoted by the airport.

2.166. Such strict criteria are not, however, in our view relevant. Demand for use of com-mercial facilities can be regarded as to a large extent dependent on the usage of aeronautical facilities. Although the range and quality of commercial outlets is attributable to BAA's initiative in developing the business, and helps to maximize the revenue from commercial activities, there would be no commercial income to the regulated company without aeronautical facilities, and to a considerable extent expansion of commercial revenues depends upon expansion of aeronautical facilities. There are also unlikely to be any aeronautical investments that generate increased capacity and throughput that do not also generate increased commercial revenues. Hence, it is to be expected in undertaking capital investment that airports would take into account both commercial and aeronautical revenues in deciding whether, for example, to invest in a new terminal. It would be economically inefficient for an airport operator not to undertake an aeronautical investment because landing charges to airlines failed to cover aeronautical costs while ignoring the substantial profits from commercial activities that would more than cover any losses on the aeronautical sales. More limited investments too, such as air bridges, both provide aeronautical services and generate commercial revenues through advertising; the recent expansions of the international departure lounges (IDLs) at Heathrow and Gatwick have also improved aeronautical facilities while taking every opportunity to increase and promote commercial facilities (to the point, as noted above, of routing passengers through the retail outlets and location of seating areas in the middle of retail outlets).

2.167. Although the circumstances of individual airports vary considerably, in a hypo-thetical fully competitive market, it would generally be expected that an airport that lost airline customers would lose commercial revenue. Accordingly, it would be forced to set its airport charges so that its profit from both aeronautical and commercial activities reflected its cost of capital and no more. (Some airlines argued that this practice does indeed occur where airports are in competition—for example, Gulf State airports in competing for stop-over traffic.) Thus in any such competitive situation, only overall profitability would be of relevance, and the benefits from the commercial activities would also be shared with airlines and airline users. Clearly this is not a direct analogy where there is congestion, but nonetheless provides a useful indication that in principle under competitive conditions, aeronautical and commercial activities would naturally be regarded as interdependent.

2.168. Commercial activities can therefore be regarded as incremental only in a relatively limited sense: rather, airports are in most respects a unified business in which investment to expand aeronautical facilities generates additional aeronautical and commercial revenue. To the extent that commercial revenues can be regarded as generated to a large extent by aeronautical facilities and investment, it would be valid to expect them to contribute to aeronautical costs, rather than as generating profits in their own right for the use of the airport operator without any such contribution to aeronautical costs.

2.169. Also from the perception of many passengers, retail activities are an inherent part of airport services. The close relationship between the two activities is also shown when there is any downturn of traffic: commercial as well as aeronautical revenues are affected, the two being intrinsically linked. The practice of BAA and its concessionaires in adapting the products offered at retail outlets to the passenger profile of particular terminals (or even at particular times of day) also shows the close linkage between the two activities.

2.170. Given therefore the close relationship between commercial revenues at the three BAA London airports and the aeronautical facilities, in particular that commercial revenues accruing to the regulated company cannot be generated without aeronautical facilities, we believe it is difficult sensibly to separate commercial and aeronautical facilities and we think that they should be regarded as one business: they can not realistically be regarded as separate businesses, and it makes no practical sense to try to do so.

2.171. The profitable development of commercial activities also depends on the activities of the airlines, which are among the users of the airports. The objectives of the CAA imposed by the Airports Act include furthering the reasonable interests of users of airports and promoting the profitable use of airports. Mr Justice Lightman said in *R v Director General of Telecommunications ex parte Cellcom and others* in 1998 in relation to the equivalent provision in the telecommunications legislation (see Chapter 3 for a fuller quote): 'In my view it is plain that the various duties in section 3(2) may pull in different directions and may conflict ... The Director is not paralysed because such conflict arises: rather he is given the choice how that conflict is to be resolved and to decide priorities ...'. The successful development of commercial revenues requires airlines to deliver passengers to or from the airport. It can therefore be attributed to a large extent to the activities of the airlines and we therefore consider the benefits of commercial activities should be shared with airlines and airline users.

2.172. BAA argued that, under the single-till approach, it did not share in the benefits from commercial activities beyond the rate of return it was allowed for new investment, and the gains or losses from better or worse than expected performance between quinquennial reviews. However, we see no reason why the long-term benchmark for profit from its commercial investments should be higher than the cost of capital, while in the shorter term BAA has the opportunity within the period of the quinquennial review to retain the benefits of better than expected performance.

2.173. Airlines also argued that the distinction between aeronautical and non-aeronautical assets, and appropriate accounting treatment would be a source of regular and ongoing disagreement and friction, associated, for example, with new investment, as well as allocation of costs of existing assets, and of operating costs. In a situation where aeronautical and commercial activities cannot sensibly be regarded as separate businesses and, as apparent from Table 2.5, aeronautical activities (excluding surface access) which would be fully charged to airlines represent 55 per cent of the assets and 70 per cent of operating expenditure (opex), but non-aeronautical activities would receive almost 75 per cent of the operating profit, we accept this.

Effects of the dual till on profitability and fares

2.174. As we discuss below, there may be valid reasons why BAA charges should increase from current levels, in particular from the need to invest in new capacity at high incremental cost: the CAA's suggestion of a formula of RPI+6 in Q4 at Heathrow consistent with the single till reflects an assumption of such cost increases. The effect of the dual till at HAL over the longer term, however, would be to increase airport charges beyond that which may be necessary to reflect increases in costs net of commercial revenues. This is also the case in the shorter term at Gatwick and Stansted if they charge up to the cap.

2.175. As noted, the CAA objective in the review has been to approach regulated charges from the standpoint of economic efficiency, rather than equity between the BAA shareholders and airport users. As shown in Table 2.9 the dual-till approach would result in a significant increase in rates of return and revenues compared with the single till in both Q4 and Q5; the CAA proposals, by not implementing the dual till at Heathrow in Q4, would reduce the increase in profitability in Q4, but with a greater increase in Q5.

TABLE 2.9 **BAA projected rate of return under single and dual till**

	BAA Q4 %	BAA Q5 %
Single till: total airport	6.9	6.9
RRCB adjusted		
Aeronautical	6.9	6.9
Commercial till (incl surface access)	15.1	16.7
Total	9.4	9.3
CAA proposal		
Aeronautical	4.4	8.0
Commercial till (incl surface access)	15.1	16.7
Total	7.6	10.2

Source: CC based on CAA projections.

These projections include existing surface access in the commercial till. If airport charges were set to give, for example, a 7.5 per cent rate of return on the aeronautical till, including surface access, BAA's overall rate of return would be about 2 per cent higher.

2.176. We have noted above that the CAA's projections suggest that BAA would gain a net present value (NPV) of additional revenues of between £3.2 billion and £3.7 billion by adoption of the dual-till approach. The CAA described this estimate as 'simply a model output' and BAA also thought it too high—but neither BAA nor the CAA put forward what they would regard as a more accurate figure. We find this surprising given the magnitude of the transfer of resources that is implied.

● *Effect on fares*

2.177. Whether there is an effect on fares is an important aspect of the dual till. The CAA argued that there would be no effect on fares, merely a transfer of rent between BAA and airlines, which it regarded as not relevant to its duties under the Airports Act. We have not accepted that the effect on airlines is irrelevant to the CAA's duties, but if there were an effect on fares, this would be directly relevant to its duties even on the CAA's interpretation of them.

2.178. The CAA argued that at congested airports, such as Heathrow, where there was excess demand from airlines for access to the airport, the resulting scarcity rents accrue to incumbent airlines and fares would not rise as a result of the higher charges generated by the dual till. Thus, the increase in the profits of BAA over the longer term would not be at the expense of passengers, but would merely involve a transfer of scarcity rents between airport and airlines. The CAA subsequently acknowledged that some fares, on routes where capacity was withdrawn, would increase, while others on routes where capacity was added would decrease, but it believed average fares would not significantly increase and greater efficiency would result from the process. The argument is as follows:

(a) in normal circumstances, where there are no airport capacity constraints, airlines sell seats for as much as they can get given their previous decisions on route capacity (weekly number of flights, size of aircraft);

(b) decisions on route capacity are taken in the light of expected profitability; and

(c) in general a long-run increase in airport charges per passenger may result in lower airline route capacity (for example, cancelling a flight will be relatively more attractive than previously) and hence an increase in prices. Route capacity decisions are lumpy so small changes in airport charges in most cases would not have any effect, but, by the same logic, there are a few cases where they would have a big impact as they would tip the balance towards lower route capacity.

However, at congested airports the above argument does not apply as the airlines are already constrained to lower route capacity than they would wish and prices therefore will be set so as to constrain demand to the level which can be met by the airport capacity. Increases in airport charges would affect the level of airline costs—but not the level of fares which are above, and unaffected by the level of costs.

2.179. The last step would apply only at congested airports. It is clear to us that at an uncongested airport, such as Gatwick in off-peak periods or Stansted, an increase in charges will represent an increase in marginal costs, and therefore almost certainly cause fares to rise. There would be a particular impact on low-fare airlines—the LFCs and charter carriers—where the increase in charges would represent a higher percentage of fares. But even at congested airports, we believe this argument is incorrect.

2.180. The argument that there are significant rents to airlines at Heathrow sits oddly with the lack of profitability of Heathrow airlines. Almost all are currently making little or no profit. The CAA argued that some of these rents were absorbed in airlines' high cost structures, but we find it difficult to regard all Heathrow airlines as operating inefficiently. We are therefore doubtful whether such rents do accrue to airlines on the scale assumed by the CAA. More plausibly, competition between airlines is likely to result in some of these potential rents being passed on to passengers. However, even if rents did in part currently accrue to airlines, as profits or subsumed in high costs, there is no reason in our view to disregard the issue of to whom the rents accrue. If, for example, the rents currently took the form of high costs to the airlines, there would seem little justification for adding to those costs through higher charges as a result of the dual till.

2.181. Airlines strongly disputed the existence of such rents that would allow them to absorb any increase in charges. BA argued that higher yields at Heathrow reflect the superior network it operates there, rather than any intrinsic value of Heathrow, but that any such benefits were also offset by higher costs, including congestion costs, of operating at Heathrow. The impact of higher charges, given current average profitability per passenger, would be such that fares would have to increase, although it also acknowledged the possibility that it would have to withdraw from some routes. Another scheduled carrier also said the increased charges envisaged were of such scale as to result in significant losses—fares would have to be raised.

2.182. A number of airlines also argued that fares are to an extent constrained by competition between airlines on any particular route both from the same airport and from other airports, and, for some passengers, from other routes. Since the increase in airport charges would be common to all airlines, airlines would not only need, but also be able to increase fares to reflect that. Airlines suggested to us that at least some of the increases in other costs—insurance, fuel or air passenger duty—were similarly passed on in fares for that reason. We also noted the view of the DfT that the argument that there would be no effect on fares could be regarded as an 'extreme case' since scarcity rents are not necessarily captured by airlines in their entirety with some going to passengers.

2.183. In order to consider the argument that fares would be unaffected, we asked BAA a number of questions about effective capacity constraints particularly at Heathrow. The general picture which emerged was that:

(a) the main effective constraint at Heathrow is the runway;

(b) through time, various incremental improvements to the runway will produce a limited increase in capacity, and capacity will also be increased by additional T5 stands;

(c) this, together with the use of larger planes and/or higher load factors would allow ever increasing passenger numbers; and

(d) this would put ever-increasing strain on terminal facilities at peak periods, which T5 will eliminate; without T5, peak terminal capacity would in time become the effective constraint. More passengers can, however, be handled at lower standards of service: the number of passengers at Heathrow at existing terminals of 64 million in 2000/01 already exceeded the level of 60 million BAA assumes can be handled with adequate quality of service and is intended to increase to over 70 million before T5 opens, then reducing to 60 million.

There is also spare terminal capacity off-peak but this cannot to any great extent be seen as substitutable for peak terminal capacity. Given, however, the scope for more passengers in peak periods, albeit at reduced standards of service, as well as off-peak periods none of the airlines from whom we heard appeared to regard terminal capacity as a constraint on the number of passengers they could carry.

2.184. The effective airport constraint is therefore the number of ATMs. Given the planes deployed there is a theoretical maximum number of passengers, determined by the average number of seats per aircraft. However, as shown in the analysis by National Economic Research Associates (NERA) at Appendix 2.2, although there is little spare runway capacity, there is spare seat capacity on the services operated; hence the theoretical maximum number of passengers is only infrequently reached.[1] The BAA evidence we have noted above is that while more passengers at peak times would degrade services, there is no rigid terminal constraint on passengers.

2.185. Airlines therefore have the ability if they so wished to vary fares upwards or downwards, attracting fewer or more passengers accordingly. No doubt many factors come into the pricing equation, but it is implausible in theory and contrary to the evidence to believe that the marginal costs and marginal revenues per passenger are not among them.

2.186. It follows that any change in the per passenger landing charges (currently about two-thirds of the total landing charge) would, by affecting marginal cost per passenger, affect fares. As noted in Chapter 12, airlines we approached confirmed the NERA analysis, that in setting airfares they did take account of marginal cost; hence an increase in airport charges would be expected to increase marginal costs, and lead to an increase in fares. (In some cases, taxes including per passenger airport charges were separately identified on air tickets, and if per passenger charges increased, fares would increase automatically.) We noted that the theoretical arguments used by the CAA, in contrast, did not draw on any evidence as to how airlines actually set fares or sought to respond to the inconsistency between that evidence and the CAA's theoretical points.

2.187. We doubt whether precisely the same argument would apply to increase in per aircraft landing charges. Theoretically, an increase in the per aircraft landing charge (about one-

---

[1] Where this is a serious problem, airlines can use larger planes—see next section.

third of the total) may be thought unlikely to have such an effect, since it would merely raise the fixed costs of each aircraft landing, but not affect the marginal cost per passenger. A significant shift towards per aircraft landing charges would, however, seem unlikely given the high costs of new investment in terminal facilities, particularly at Heathrow.

2.188. We considered, however, whether an increase in landing charges could in other ways have an effect on fares. Airlines argued fares would increase irrespective of whether the increase in airport charges was brought about through increasing passenger charges or fixed-rate landing charges. First, they could change the size of plane, hence considerations of marginal cost per passenger would still arise. Second, if the marginal cost of a flight were to increase, they would need to recover the additional costs by adjusting fares, which they would be able to do since all airlines would be affected.

2.189. Whether this would necessarily be the case is less obvious. But, in a context of oligopolistic competition which results from the limited number of operators on most routes, such an increase in fares may in our view be expected. In practice, on most if not all routes, with limited numbers of competitors on the route, the decision as to what fares to charge will be heavily dependent on how one airline anticipates others will respond to price change. Thus, if the marginal cost per flight of only one airline, having optimised its route, flight and fare decisions in the light of all relevant considerations, increased, it would not be optimal (ie profitable) to raise fares to cover the extra cost because, if it were, it would have been optimal to raise fares before the increase in costs. Whatever the costs of a flight, the fares are already set to maximize profits taking account of the impact of fares on demand and any costs that vary per passenger. But in this situation the impact of any potential fares increase on demand will assume that no other airline raises its fares, because no other airline faces the same increase in costs.

2.190. If, however, all airlines experience an increase in per aircraft landing charges, each may well expect its competitors to follow any fare increase, particularly in the knowledge that the profitability of all airlines is under great pressure, and that they all need to recover any such cost increase. The loss of demand will thus typically be much smaller and may be minimal. This will affect the expected marginal revenue impact associated with an increase in fares, and the new optimum level of fares will almost certainly then be higher than before. Similarly, an increase in the per passenger charge could also affect fares by affecting all suppliers equally and creating the expectation that competitors will also be raising fares. This is all the more likely to be the case with per passenger charges since they are indicated as a separate charge on tickets.

2.191. We believe this is consistent with generally accepted developments in game theory that suggest that in an oligopoly there may be multiple possible equilibria for pricing decisions, and the effect of an event common to all suppliers may be to shift them on to an alternative equilibrium where higher prices prevail. Indeed, for suppliers to keep their prices unchanged on the assumption competitors would also not increase their prices in such a situation may itself require a rather unrealistic assumption that others are operating on the basis that only one equilibrium is possible.

2.192. There are, therefore, quite strong reasons to expect that a rise in either type of landing charge will lead to a rise in fares. We considered whether there could be an offsetting reduction in fares if, as the CAA suggested, there were a change in the usage of slots as a result of higher charges. However, it is only where demand for a route is sufficiently weak that the new optimum level of fares after the increase in marginal cost is loss-making, whereas previously it was profitable, leading to release of the slot that even the possibility of any offsetting effects came into play.

2.193. As we noted above, there are a number of reasons why even this effect may be limited. Some newly loss-making flights may be essential if aircraft are to be in the right place for other, profitable, flights. Some slots may be held, even though loss-making, because releasing them brings the threat of bigger losses if a competitor enters or expands its number of flights as a result. Some shorter-term losses may be accepted because of the prospect of profitability later, provided the slot is held; or because of the prospect of being able to realize some or all of the capital value of the slot at a future date, even though this would not currently be permitted. Some state-owned airlines will not respond to such losses.

2.194. Therefore, the situation envisaged by the CAA, namely release of slots to a more valuable use, is likely to be a very limited offset to the factors leading to fare increases. Moreover, even some of these cases, if they occur, will still raise fares. Suppose, for example, competition on a route has generated very low profits, so that the rise in the landing charge drives an airline into losses on the route and it withdraws. If the slot is taken up by its competitor it may now be in a position to raise fares with little or no loss of demand, because its competitor has been eliminated. In addition, 50 per cent of slots released will go to new entrants who may not, as it turns out, be more efficient at providing value for money to passengers, so that fares are not effectively lower.

● *Conclusions*

2.195. The CAA, therefore, focus on two mechanisms for arguing that an increase in landing charges will not affect fares. The first is that fares at a congested airport are set so as to ration demand to capacity, in which case changes in marginal cost will not affect fares. We do not, however, accept this in relation to per passenger charges because there is not an effective constraint on passenger numbers and fares are clearly not set on this basis. Nor do we accept this in relation to per landing charges where anticipated marginal revenue depends on expectations as to whether price changes will be followed or not, and this in turn depends on the reasons for a change in such cost. Given these factors, the very strong probability is that fares will rise generally across many, if not most, routes.

2.196. The second mechanism is that some slots will become available as a result of increased landing charges which, when taken up by another airline which can profitably use the slot, leads to a gain to passengers, either in the form of lower fares or, equivalently, better value for money, as seen by the fact that the new use of the slot is sustainable whereas the old use was not. However, this will, first, only ever, in principle, apply to that limited number of slots at Heathrow which were on the margin of profitability. Second, even a substantial number of these may not be offered up. And third, not all of those offered up will result in lower fares or better value. It therefore seems inherently unlikely that any residual effect applying to a very limited number of slots would or could offset the factors generating fare increases. Certainly we were supplied with no evidence or analysis that would justify our accepting this.

2.197. We therefore believe that average fares on services to and from even Heathrow, where excess demand is greatest, would be affected by the higher airport charges that would result from adoption of the dual-till approach. Where an increase in charges is required as a result of cost increases or the need for investment, it may be justified: but it would not be justified when it arises from application of the dual till, with little or no offsetting benefits. We cannot be precise as to the extent to which fares would increase, or the profits of airlines would be reduced but we believe on both theoretical and empirical grounds that the effect on fares is likely to be significant. Moreover, in Q4 the effect of the CAA's proposals is to implement the dual till at Gatwick and Stansted rather than Heathrow. Fares on services to and from Gatwick and Stansted would almost certainly increase if the dual till were to lead to charges being set above the single-till levels. The CAA's theoretical arguments that there would be no effect on fares at a congested airport would therefore not apply in Q4, when the dual till is only applied to the two less congested airports. The effects of the dual till on passengers is clearly relevant to considering the reasonable interests of users as required under the Airports Act.

2.198. As we noted in paragraph 2.64, the CAA estimated that an increase in charges of RPI+6 at Heathrow would be necessary under the single till due to the costs of T5, which may also be expected to have an effect on fares. The dual till does, however, further increase charges, at Gatwick and Stansted (in so far as these could be recovered) in Q4, and at all three airports in Q5 and thereafter (including recovery in Q5 and thereafter of the effect of not applying the dual till at Heathrow in Q4). In our view, the resulting difference between the price trajectories of the single till and the dual till—an NPV of between £3.2 billion and £3.7 billion—noted in paragraph 2.67 is significant, a proportion of which is likely to be passed on to passenger particularly in Q4 at Gatwick and, possibly, Stansted, and in the longer term also at Heathrow, when the dual till is applied there.

2.199. However, even if there was no effect on fares, and the effect of the dual till was merely to transfer rents from the airlines to the airports, we do not believe we can be indifferent to such a transfer of resources to a regulated utility. We regard it as undesirable on grounds of regulatory consistency to introduce such a major change in regulatory approach, unless there are significant benefits from doing so. Adoption of a dual till would significantly increase the value of BAA, which is as undesirable as significantly reducing a utility's value as a result of regulatory change unless there are clear and strong reasons to do so. Although BAA drew our attention to other utilities which had received windfall gains—for example, NGC when selling Energis, or the property gains of Transco and Railtrack—none represented as substantial a shift from the basis on which the utility was privatized. Moreover, these were less instances of regulatory windfalls than of exploitation of the existing assets; even so, in some of these cases, gains were foreseen and implicit mechanisms put in place to clawback the profits. The implication for users of changing the regulatory approach has therefore to be considered.

2.200. Hence, even if the effect of the dual till was merely to transfer rents from airlines to the airport, with no effect on fares, we believe that would be undesirable from a regulatory perspective and contrary to the reasonable interests of users without there being sufficient compensating benefits to investment or efficient utilization of resources. The CAA acknowledged that any such transfer of rents was sizeable relative to the market value of some airlines. Regulatory stability is, in our view, of value not just to the regulated utility but also to its users—in this case the airlines—and their shareholders. The airline industry is itself a higher risk, more competitive industry than that of the airports, as evidenced by its significant losses following 11 September, and the consequences to airlines of any transfer of rents is likely to exceed those of any benefits to BAA. We would have expected airlines to have planned on the basis that the single-till policy would be maintained, and they should also not be put in a worse position than that established by the regulatory settlement at privatization of BAA, unless there are strong reasons for doing so. However, for the reasons given above we believe that adverse effects of the dual till on users would go beyond airlines to passengers, with some increase in fares at congested airports, as well as uncongested airports. Hence, we believe that a move from the single till to the dual till would in the longer term mean a substantial transfer of income to airports from airlines and/or their passengers. This would be contrary to the reasonable interests of users, but also potentially undermine regulatory credibility and create regulatory uncertainty.

2.201. We considered whether the effect of any adoption of the dual till on charges and fares could be ameliorated if an alternative approach was adopted to valuing the RRCB rather than, as the CAA proposed, merely to value it by apportioning costs. In most regulatory cases, the CC has accepted that investors should be remunerated for what they invested at privatization plus subsequent investment. Where there was a difference between initial market value (IMV) and asset values, a privatization discount has been applied (for example, water and gas). In the case of BAA the IMV and book asset values (as a whole) broadly corresponded, so a privatization discount was not an issue. If the commercial and aeronautical businesses were now to be split, then arguably it would be necessary to split the value of the businesses rather than merely the assets, by reference to the IMV of shareholders' investment in BAA. Given that the commercial side is potentially more profitable than the aeronautical side, then more of the IMV should be allocated to the commercial side and less to the aeronautical side (thereby offsetting the effect of the dual till on aeronautical charges). An alternative to reopening the IMV at privatization would be to allocate assets between the commercial and aeronautical till, not with reference to cost but to profits. However, the effect of either approach would be broadly to replicate the pattern of charges of the single till. Hence, there would be little point in departing from the current single-till approach.

2.202. The CAA suggested that any windfall gains (which would accrue mainly in Q5 or thereafter) could be more directly addressed by the Treasury, the Airport Passenger Duty (APD) (although this is a tax on airlines, not the airport) being a possible analogy. We have, however, no grounds for believing that any particular level of excess profit would result in Parliament imposing a windfall tax. In any event, although a windfall tax may offset significant gains to BAA shareholders, it would do nothing to reduce the detriment to users—airlines and/or passengers—of higher charges. Potentially, moreover, we have noted that the scale of the windfall (up to £3.7 billion) is sizeable relative to the existing value of BAA (some £6 billion): any tax commensurate with that would be proportionately greater than previous windfall taxes imposed on any individual utility. It would be extremely difficult to structure such a tax other than as an annual tax on profit, removing most if not all of the improvement to incentives which the CAA argued would result from the dual till. Possible alternatives would be to allow a one-off windfall tax or annual windfall tax, but both could jeopardize BAA's ability to finance investment.

2.203. As argued by some airlines, moreover, the single till, by constraining BAA's overall level of profits, has been successful in creating the pressure for efficiency with which BAA has utilized its existing assets, as partly reflected in the relatively low charges at the London area airports. The looser form of regulation implied by the dual till is likely to act as a weaker incentive to improve efficiency of BAA; hence, while the dual till may promote the profitable operation of the BAA airports, to an unreasonable extent in our view, we believe it would be less successful than the single till in promoting the economic and efficient operation of the airports.

Practical difficulties in allocating costs

2.204. We also considered the practical difficulty in allocating particular activities to one or other of the two tills, about which different parties held different views. We have noted the CAA's allocation of activities between the two tills in paragraph 2.59. BAA, although agreeing with the dual till in principle, and stressing it was not seeking a more favourable outcome in terms of the level of airport charges, disagreed with the split proposed by the CAA. It argued that all surface access, including existing Heathrow Express assets but also short-term car parking, should be included in the aeronautical till (which, from Table 2.5, could increase the value of aeronautical assets by as much as £1.4 billion above the £2.9 billion under the CAA's proposals). It also argued that the value of aeronautical assets should be increased by a further £600 million by reallocation between the two tills of current liabilities and recovery of revenue advancement and under-investment.

2.205. The CAA had considered various possibilities for allocating activities between the tills but the only basic principle it put forward was the 'monopolistic bottleneck approach'—ie to be included within an aeronautical till a facility would have to be both essential and significantly monopolizable; users had a choice of whether or not to use retail, catering and other commercial activities and they should be excluded from the aeronautical till. Hence, we have noted above that if the CAA's proposals were to be followed, BAA's aeronautical activities would exclude not only retail facilities, but also surface access (unless required as a planning condition), car parks, and some airline facilities such as CIP facilities and non-terminal offices. Interpretation of both criteria—of being essential and monopolizable—is, however, in our view to a significant extent arbitrary.

2.206. A key particular difficulty, vital to the resulting level of airport charges, arises over the treatment of surface access. The CAA in proposals prior to the reference allocated all surface access to commercial activities. On the CAA's approach, surface access facilities including Heathrow Express were neither essential nor significantly monopolizable, since there is a choice of whether or not to use the facility: hence they should not be included within an aeronautical till. (The same also applied to car parking and other surface access costs.) The CAA believed that surface access was capable of generating its own revenue stream and that there was no reason why it could not cover its cost. Unprofitable but environmentally desirable projects should, in its view, be dealt with separately, by the Strategic Rail Authority. In its final proposals, the CAA did include the extension of the Heathrow Express and Piccadilly Line to T5 in the aeronautical till, since this is a requirement of the planning provision for T5.

2.207. BAA believed it would be inconsistent with previous regulatory practice to do other than to allocate all surface access activities to aeronautical costs. It also suggested it was illogical to include the extension of the Heathrow Express to T5, but not the existing facilities: a distinction we also found difficult to accept, given the extension serves no purpose without the existing facility. Consistent with this, BAA also suggested short-term car parks be included in the aeronautical till, while the CAA allocated these to the commercial till.

2.208. Some airlines while being against the dual till nevertheless commented that surface access projects should be funded like any other surface transport and if the dual till were introduced, it should at most be confined to aeronautical activities within the airport boundaries. Government policy (for example, in the Transport White Paper) has, however, been that the aviation industry should bear some of the costs of improving surface access to airports. Airlines also argued that surface access was related to commercial as well as aeronautical activities (for example, being necessary for staff and deliveries etc to retail activities) raising the problem of how to allocate surface access under a dual-till regime. But more important in our view is that the more general consideration raised in paragraph 2.168 would also apply to surface access: namely that without surface access which enables passengers to reach the airport, less commercial revenues would be generated, commercial and aeronautical facilities being essentially one unified business.

2.209. How to treat surface access is in our view a good example (and quantitatively a very significant one) of the problems, controversial nature and essential arbitrariness of distinguishing aeronautical and commercial tills. Clearly, BAA has a monopoly in the gateways to the airport: but the question arises as to how much beyond the gateways one should go in including surface access in the aeronautical till. It might, for example, be argued that strictly speaking neither car parking nor the Heathrow Express facility could be regarded as essential. Car parking adjacent to terminals is monopolizable but not car parking in general; similarly, Heathrow Express is monopolizable but not train access. On this basis, neither would be included in the aeronautical till. Yet it would be extraordinary to regard car parking as anything other than a critically important facility for airports, and congestion would be considerably worse without the Heathrow Express.

2.210. The alternative approach would be to consider the totality of surface access. Here the argument is more clear cut, since each mode is a substitute for the others, but an airport can clearly not function without any form of surface access, and the facilities as a whole are clearly monopolizable: ie it would be logical to include all surface access in the aeronautical till. But this undoubtedly then includes facilities supplied by BAA at the airports which to some extent are supplied by other operators in competition, for example, off-airport parking, underground access to Heathrow, and coaches. Presumably the same applies to catering at the airport and, indeed to retail services. To include all surface access (a significant part of which, though very valuable in reducing congestion, is loss-making) in the aeronautical till, but exclude all catering, retail and other commercial activities (which makes very substantial profits) would seem largely arbitrary, yet very disadvantageous to airlines and their passengers. To do so could add between five and ten percentage points to the value of X under any dual till at

Heathrow, whereas the losses on existing surface access could readily be financed by BAA's substantial commercial profits, as in effect they are under the single till.

2.211. If, however, surface access is included in the commercial till, as proposed by the CAA, this would give little incentive to invest in or maintain loss-making public transport investment, even those that may be necessary, by reducing congestion, to allow reasonable access to and from the airport. But more fundamentally, passengers who use surface access generate both aeronautical and commercial revenues, surface access is of value to both aeronautical and commercial activities, and the debate merely emphasizes the arbitrary basis of any distinction.

2.212. As indicated above, the arbitrary nature of any allocation of costs applies, in our view, to other activities. The CAA have employed a number of consultants to advise on how a wide range of other particular activities are classified, and their costs allocated (for example, within terminal buildings, by space occupied). Broadly, these studies have confirmed that BAA's existing profit centre reporting system can be adopted for this purpose, although the process could not be finalized until a final view on the application of any dual-till approach was agreed. BA, however, said that the CAA had found it is impossible to separate the tills 'in any fair and sustainable way' and that use of space occupied as a basis of cost allocation was artificial. Allocation of costs and revenues of the T3 South Wing was put forward as one example: there was concern that the bulk of the costs but few of the revenues would be allocated to aeronautical, and conversely several million pounds of income but only a small share of cost would be allocated to commercial. Similarly in the case of the extension to the T1 baggage hall, BA argued that the additional costs of stronger load-bearing structures to support commercial developments above it would be allocated to the aeronautical till. As a further example, BA said that T5 costs were increased by devoting a whole floor to retail developments, with further costs of escalators etc, and inconvenience to passengers of having to change levels, in order to ensure they passed the retail areas.

2.213. Some airlines suggested an alternative approach would be to consider how a terminal would be constructed without such facilities, and believed this would show that commercial, particularly retail activities, would bear a larger share of the costs. However, a study by BAA suggested the results would be little different if that was done. We have noted, however, that some two-thirds of operating costs would be treated as aeronautical, but about three-quarters of operating profit would be generated by commercial revenues (including car parking) that are not possible unless those costs are incurred. These are in our view examples of the more general problem referred to above, that commercial revenues are highly dependent on aeronautical investment. However, to allocate assets with reference to profitability, which would appear to be a reasonable way of addressing this issue, would merely replicate the single-till outcome.

2.214. The existence of significant common costs also suggest that aeronautical activities cannot be regarded as separate from commercial activities. For example, the allocation methods used by BAA and the CAA increase the space allocated to aeronautical activities by 15 per cent above that currently used to allow for the current saving in aeronautical space from passengers using commercial facilities (ie when shopping, eating etc). Such common costs, however, could be allocated to either till.

2.215. BAA also argued that recovery of revenue advancement in Q3 should be allocated to the commercial as well as to the aeronautical asset base and by not doing so the CAA had further reduced aeronautical RRCB by £410 million. It also objected to the CAA's assumption that all current liabilities should be deducted from aeronautical assets, rather than some allocated to commercial assets, understating the value of the aeronautical RRCB by £180 million (although neither the CAA nor ourselves regard current liabilities as relevant to the RAB). This again in our view merely shows the arbitrary nature of any allocation between the two tills.

2.216. It is therefore in our view difficult, in practice, to allocate both investments and operating costs between aeronautical and commercial activities; such practical difficulties are avoided under the single till. To the extent that some of the judgements that have to be made are arbitrary, future disputes about cost allocation could harm relations between the airport and its users. We acknowledge that BAA already allocates cost, on an incremental cost basis, meeting its regulatory requirement to provide figures on profitability of different parts of its business, and of certain services to airlines (such as check-in desks) excluded from airport charges. The fact that this has been done for the purpose of allocating costs, however, does not mean it could reasonably be applied to a quite different purpose, namely as a basis for setting airport charges which airlines will have to pay over the next five years.

2.217. There are therefore considerable practical difficulties in allocating costs and assets between the two tills. This is not necessarily a determinative argument against adoption of a dual-till approach. If there were strong reasons to do so, then no doubt some allocation, although essentially arbitrary and perhaps contested, could be made in order to implement the regime. But the practical difficulties nonetheless constitute a further objection to the use of the dual till.

Summary of difficulties with the dual-till approach

2.218. We have noted that, overall, there are standard arguments for pricing equal to LRIC which, in the case of a rising LRIC do not give rise to losses; and the dual till will, ceteris paribus give prices higher, and hence nearer to LRIC than the single till. But, in the actual circumstances of Heathrow, a switch to the dual till would in our view make very little difference if any to the actual demand for slots, space and investment experienced by Heathrow, and very little difference if any to the investment that will be carried out. Moreover, the single till applied so as to cover the average value of LRIC over the investment programme preserves the benefits to users while avoiding the costs and allowing BAA to meet its cost of capital.

2.219. We have also noted that aeronautical and commercial activities represent one business, and aeronautical facilities generate both aeronautical and commercial revenues: hence, it is not sensible to split the two businesses. A move from the single till to the dual till would in the longer term also mean a substantial transfer of income to airports from airlines and/or their passengers. It would have significant adverse consequences on the reasonable interests of users as a result of higher charges than necessary and higher fares, contrary in our view to the basic rationale for regulation of a monopoly supplier and potentially undermining regulatory credibility and creating regulatory uncertainty. Users would therefore be faced with a substantial loss of benefits via higher charges and fares, for little discernible gain in terms of investment, indeed, they may find that aeronautical investment suffers. In this respect, the reasonable interest of users is better served by the single till than the dual till.

Possible variations on a dual-till approach

2.220. During the inquiry, BAA suggested that the dual till could apply only to new investment. BAA saw this retaining the potential benefits of the dual-till approach as an incentive to investment, while avoiding some of the substantial windfall gains inherent in the CAA's approach. Nonetheless, new investment accounts for a substantial share of BAA's asset base; the problems identified above would still apply, if to a slightly lesser extent, and in our view with no net benefit. It would still require what, in our view, is a largely arbitrary allocation of assets between new investment in commercial and aeronautical resources. Indeed it may also require an arbitrary allocation between existing and new assets and give rise to perverse incentives, for example to refurbish existing facilities in order to count it as new investment and increase the proportion of commercial profits attributable to such new investment. It would still over time increase BAA revenue substantially, if not as significantly as under the CAA proposals, but fail in our view to generate significant benefits in resource allocation or to new investment.

Conclusions on single/dual till

2.221. Because the issue of single or dual till understandably preoccupied us and many of the parties to the inquiry in its internal stages, on 11 July 2002 we issued a statement of our, then, thinking on the issue (see Appendix 2.3). We said we had found the arguments and current evidence for moving to a dual till at any of the three BAA London airports not persuasive. None of the evidence we subsequently received led us to change that view: we therefore believe it appropriate to retain the single-till approach in setting airport charges for Q4.

2.222. Our main reasons are as follows:

(a) There is no evidence that the single till has led to any general under-investment in aeronautical assets at the three BAA London airports in the past, nor any expectation that it will do so over the next five years (see paragraph 2.122).

(b) It is not clear that the dual till, as opposed to the single till, would be likely to lead to significantly better aeronautical investment in the future and in some respects is likely to be worse (see paragraph 2.122).

(c) The dual till could improve the efficient utilization of capacity, but the benefits are unlikely to be more than marginal even at Heathrow, where they would not occur until Q5 (see paragraph 2.141).

(d) Nor do we see significant benefits from any deregulation of commercial activities. We are not persuaded that the distinction between locational and monopoly rents is useful in this context. In so far as airport charges affect fares, the current relatively high profits from commercial activities are applied to the benefit of passengers; the dual-till approach is likely to require increased regulation of such activities (see paragraph 2.148).

(e) The dual till could also risk unduly benefiting commercial activities, at the expense of non-capacity-enhancing aeronautical activities, which may not attract sufficient space, funds or attention (see paragraph 2.161).

(f) It is difficult sensibly to separate commercial and aeronautical facilities. Commercial revenues at the three BAA London airports cannot be generated without aeronautical facilities: they should therefore be regarded as one business (see paragraph 2.170).

(g) Since the successful development of commercial revenues requires airlines to deliver passengers to or from the airport, the benefits of commercial activities should be shared with airlines and airline users (see paragraph 2.171).

(h) We believe that average fares would be affected at both congested and uncongested airports if airport charges were to be higher at the three BAA London airports as a result of a switch to a dual-till regime, and we do not think that effect can be justified where it arises from application of dual-till regulation with little or no offsetting benefits (see paragraph 2.197).

(i) A move from the single till to the dual till would in the longer term mean a substantial transfer of income to airports from airlines and/or their passengers and be to their

detriment, potentially undermining regulatory credibility and creating regulatory uncertainty (see paragraph 2.200*).

2.223. We also note:

(a) No useful inferences can be drawn at this time from overseas airports which use the dual till in whole or in part, as their circumstances are different from those of the three BAA London airports (see paragraph 2.74).

(b) Nor are we persuaded that the dual-till approach would act as an effective incentive on BAA to maintain or improve performance by providing 'something to lose' (through reversion to a single-till approach) at future regulatory reviews should it fail to do so (see paragraph 2.121).

(c) The CAA proposal of raising the price cap above single-till levels at Gatwick and Stansted in Q4 but not at Heathrow would be contrary to efficient resource allocation in Q4 (see paragraph 2.141).

(d) It is difficult, in practice, to allocate both investments and operating costs between aeronautical and commercial activities. To the extent that some of the judgements that have to be made are arbitrary, future disputes about cost allocation could harm relations between the airport and its users (see paragraph 2.216).

2.224. We noted in paragraph 2.31 that the CAA regarded its approach as best promoting its statutory objectives under the Airports Act. There are clearly no grounds for considering the single-till approach to be inconsistent with the statutory duties on the CAA, given the consistent and successful regulation of the BAA on the single-till basis since privatization. However:

(a) Given the increase in the profitability of the BAA airports that would result from the dual till, at the expense of higher charges to airlines and higher fares to their passengers, we believe the reasonable interests of users, to which section 39(2)(a) of the Airports Act refers, are in this respect better served by the single till than by the dual till (see paragraph 2.200); nor do we see the dual till as more than marginally promoting the reasonable interests of users in respect of the more efficient use of airport capacity, (relevant also to the duties under section 39 (2)(b) of the Airports Act) (see paragraphs 2.140 and 2.141) ; nor do we see the dual till promoting the reasonable interests of users in its effect on commercial activities (see paragraph 2.161).

(b) Also as regards section 39(2)(b) of the Airports Act, the dual till would be less successful in promoting the economic and efficient operation of the airports in terms of the efficient utilization by BAA of existing assets (see paragraph 2.203).

(c) As regards section 39(2)(c) of the Airports Act, it is not clear that the dual till provides a necessary and acceptable means of encouraging investment in aeronautical facilities (see paragraph 2.122) and in some respects is likely to be worse than the single till in encouraging such investment by unduly favouring commercial investment if there are financial or other constraints; nor do we see any material benefits in encouraging investment in commercial facilities beyond that resulting from the current level of incentives (see paragraph 2.152).

(d) The dual till would not have any material benefits in minimizing restrictions in the regulatory system (section 39(2)(d) of the Airports Act) (see paragraph 2.148).

In conclusion, we do not therefore share the view of the CAA that the dual till is best calculated to meet the objectives of the Airports Act as listed above. In the light of all the considerations we have set out above, it would in our view be unreasonable and inappropriate to allow prices to be determined by the application of dual till.

2.225. We have noted above that under the CAA's proposals the dual-till approach would affect price controls in Q4 only at Gatwick and Stansted; its effect on Heathrow would not be until Q5. Even if the dual till were adopted in Q4, neither the CAA nor the CC could bind itself in the approach to be adopted in subsequent quinquennia; and conversely, whereas we have concluded that the dual till should not be adopted in Q4, it would be for our successors to decide on whether it should be adopted subsequently. Our current view, however, is that on the basis of the factors we considered in this review, it would require a very significant change in circumstances to change the balance of the arguments in future reviews.

Incremental cost/value-based incentives at Heathrow

2.226. There are a number of other elements to the CAA's approach, particularly at Heathrow, which we now consider.

2.227. The CAA proposed a price cap in relation to existing assets based on throughput up to the pre-T5 level of capacity. This was initially taken by the CAA as 70 mppa, but BAA objected that the base level of traffic at 70 mppa was excessive: the T5 Inspector had assumed a base level of traffic of 60 mppa. Throughput in 2000 was about 63 mppa, and BAA had variously said that Heathrow could handle 68 or even 71 mppa but at reduced quality. The intention, however, is to reduce the capacity of existing assets during their refurbishment when T5 opens. The CAA subsequently took 60 mppa as the base level of throughput.

2.228. There would then be a price increase when T5 opened (probably not until the subsequent quinquennium). The size of that increase is based on the incremental cost of T5 (taken by the CAA for this purpose at £18 per passenger on the dual till, £15 on the single till), which is substantially above the average cost of about £5 per passenger with the existing capacity. As we have noted above, to apply that incremental cost to all Heathrow passengers (which would be a theoretically more rigorous incremental cost approach) would generate substantial 'intra marginal rents' on the existing asset base and rates of return on the airport as a whole considerably above the cost of capital. Hence, the CAA approach is to apply the incremental cost only to the number of passengers over 60 mppa and to adjust the price cap on the base level of passengers to secure the appropriate overall NPV of revenues, thus producing a price cap that averages the cost of existing assets and of T5. Although T5 is unlikely to open in Q4 there would be, in so far as the Airports Act permits this, a PPC to adopt the proposed profile of such charges for at least 20 years subject only to the build up of traffic over 60 mppa, and any additional incremental costs of further increases in capacity. (There is also provision for further incentive payments for additional peak ATM capacity, stand capacity, and the opening of the airside road tunnel, which we discuss below.)

2.229. This incremental cost approach involves a number of issues. There are alternative ways of measuring such costs: for example, with reference to a discrete investment project such as T5, as the CAA propose; to the investment programme as a whole; or to small variances around the investment programme. To base price on short-run marginal cost, which could in turn be based on opportunity costs to users or value of slots, has sometimes been proposed— but the CAA argued convincingly against this, ie to allow very high prices at times of congestion could be regarded as an appropriate way of rationing available capacity, but would reduce the incentive to avoid congestion and hence discourage investment. If an incremental cost approach were to be applied, it would in our view be reasonable to base it on the costs of T5. In its consultation document, the CAA also raised the issue of whether incremental prices should be based on peak throughput rather than annual throughput. This would produce a higher incremental charge, but only applied during peak periods. The CAA acknowledged, however, the difficulties of defining the peak (or, conversely, an off-peak period where a significantly lower charge would be appropriate), and we also see little scope at Heathrow for applying an incremental cost approach only in peak periods.

2.230. There are inevitable uncertainties in identifying the incremental cost of any such project. The CAA initially showed alternative methodologies for deriving incremental cost, with an overall range from £17 to £30.5 per passenger and a 'central' range of £17 to £24: BAA put forward a £33.50 figure. BA and BATA said that the basis of the £18 figure was unclear, and not supported by facts. bmi british midland (bmi) argued that the scale of costs proposed indicated the design of T5 was not economic for users and the details of T5 should be reviewed in depth with airlines.

2.231. Airlines also suggested that the trigger for the incremental cost charges should be based on capacity coming on-stream rather than throughput: to prevent 'cramming in' of passengers above capacity. BA put forward a detailed specification of the T5 facilities to be fully functioning on 'Phase 1/Day 1' as a condition of the additional charges. We return to this suggestion below. More generally, some airlines objected to any additional financial incentivization, believing it unnecessary.

2.232. BAA, however, also argued that the incremental cost approach could increase risk and the cost of capital. The effect on revenue of unexpected variations in passenger growth would be enhanced: at present, a greater or lesser than expected number of passengers affects revenue by the average revenue per passenger—for example, the current £5; under the incremental cost approach it would affect revenues by £18 per passenger (on the dual till, £15 on the single till). BAA estimated that this greater risk could increase the cost of capital by about 1.5 per cent.

2.233. The incremental cost approach relates to other aspects of the CAA's proposals, in particular the dual till and the PPC. It would be possible to apply the incremental cost approach under the single till, but the CAA argued that the high-powered incentives of PPC were better under the dual-till than under the single-till approach. The CAA's £18 per passenger is on a dual-till basis: the figure would be about £15 under the single till.

2.234. However, the incremental cost approach requires substantial increases in charges when T5 opens. If, as is envisaged, this is in Q5, it is not possible for the CAA or ourselves to give any commitment as part of the current review: this is a general problem with the PPC approach we discuss below. Under the approach the MMC had previously adopted (and which we also discuss further below), we have allowed for a return on AICC: hence there would already be provision for that element of the incremental costs of T5 accounted for by the return on AICC in Q4 and there would already be some adjustment in Q4 towards the higher charges necessary to earn a return in Q5. Allowing for AICC therefore makes the return on T5 less dependent on a future 'step increase'—ie a one-off, large increase—in prices, thereby also reducing risk of investment.

2.235. Even allowing for AICC, there would still be an incremental cost on opening of T5, but reflecting only depreciation and operating cost—lower than the £18 or £15 figure. That could either be taken as a step increase in charges on opening of T5, or a 'smoothed' increase in charges over Q5 that could generate the same revenue over the period as a whole (a dual-till approach could also be applied in either of those ways). Either way, the full cost of the project is recovered over the timescale of the project, but there would be less uncertainty about BAA's ability to continue in Q5 a more gradual increase in charges that would have started in Q4, than to rely on the prospect of a larger step increase in charges when T5 opens. A further option we discuss below is to profile returns at Heathrow, after allowing for AICC, between Q4 and Q5, to generate more funds during Q4; to reduce further the price increases at Heathrow necessary in Q5; and hence the risk they may not be achieved. Some uncertainty as to prices in subsequent quinquennium would still be unavoidable, but would also be much reduced by continuing with the consistent approach to regulation, of allowing a return on assets on a single-till basis equivalent to cost of capital, adopted since BAA was privatized.

2.236. On balance, therefore, we see disadvantages with the incremental cost approach and believe it should not be adopted. The return on T5 would entirely depend on there being a significant increase in charges when T5 comes on-stream at the beginning of Q5, to which, however, neither the CAA nor ourselves can give any commitment as part of this review. 'Smoothing' of charges through allowance for AICC of T5 in Q4, and the possibility of additional explicit smoothing of returns between Q4 and Q5, are more credible than the assumption of a step increase in charges as part of any PPC approach in Q5. Such an alternative approach would also reduce the risk of increasing the cost of capital, and thus increasing airport charges, which could result from the incremental cost approach. We do, however, see value in adopting a series of 'triggers' relating charges to progress particularly of the T5 investment as well as to the operating costs and depreciation on opening of T5 given the uncertainties relating to its timing. We return to this below.

Price path commitment

2.237. As already noted, the CAA have proposed that the long-run incremental cost approach should be part of a PPC for future quinquennia that would ensure a return on the current expected investment in T5. This would comprise:

(a) The pricing components, for existing levels of throughput/assets and for T5 through put/assets, being set, for 20 years (although the CAA also said 'by implication, longer'): but average charges would change in line with the mix of existing passengers, T5 incremental passengers, and the incremental costs of any further major investments and passengers attributed to them.

(b) This commitment would apply irrespective of the actual costs of operating or enhancing existing assets or T5.

2.238. There would be a similar PPC at Gatwick—but, with no major capacity investments currently planned at Gatwick, there is no equivalent of the £18 per passenger incremental price. The CAA envisages that future major capacity increments at Heathrow and Gatwick would be rewarded through incremental pricing incentives similar to that for T5.

2.239. BAA (while agreeing in principle with the PPC approach) expressed concern that under the current legislation there can be no commitment as to the appropriate level of prices in future reviews: it therefore attached very little significance to it. BA and IATA also regarded the proposed PPC as inconsistent with the principle that neither we nor the CAA could bind our successors, and ultra vires. The CAA suggested that, if a revised Airports Act were to be introduced in the next five years, it could allow a ten-year price cap—but this is not a proposal we can take into account.

2.240. BA and BATA, among others, also expressed concern that the proposed prices already take insufficient account of scope for efficiency improvements. In consequence, they believed the proposed prices were excessive and enhanced BAA's monopoly power. They also argued that such a framework would be unsustainable given the uncertainty and volatility in the industry. BA said that the focus of setting prices in Q4 should be on Q4 alone.

2.241. It is in our view questionable whether it is desirable or realistic to expect a commitment to future prices, based on current estimated costs of existing operations or estimated costs of T5. BAA would retain the benefits of any reduction in costs. This would be a strong incentive to cut the capital costs of T5, but irrespective of whether any associated reduction in the quality of aeronautical assets was justified or not. Similar considerations would apply to

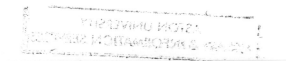

operating costs. But costs greater than expected would fall entirely on BAA, which could be regarded as significantly increasing project risks and cost of capital. This would clearly constitute a significant change in regulatory approach.

2.242. We note that other regulators have insisted benefits of efficiency savings on operating costs or investment projects be passed on to users in the longer term, while tight price controls are also seen as providing pressure to ensure operating efficiency. The CAA argued that airports were different in this respect in that, even if there were efficiency savings, there is no reason on resource allocation grounds for these to be shared with users, demand being inelastic and prices too low anyway given excess demand and increasing marginal costs. However, we do not accept this should be the overriding criterion for regulating airports.

2.243. We see a further disadvantage in that the PPC (in combination with other aspects of the CAA proposals) could distort investment. By fixing prices for existing assets and major projects to expand capacity, no return would be allowed on additional investment that may prove desirable to improve quality of service other than small and relatively uncertain amounts through the Q factor. Such distortion could also occur if the price cap fixed a level of incremental cost insufficient to justify some investments (as could well be the case at Gatwick).

2.244. Use of such fixed prices would also significantly increase the risks of investment in T5. Returns would be depressed for many years if costs proved greater than expected, but with scope for persistently higher returns if costs proved less than expected. Risks could also prove asymmetric, depending on the approach of future regulators. A regulator might, for example, be relaxed about higher than expected profits, regarding them as one possible outcome of the new regime; but if profitability was too low to allow significant aeronautical investment required by airlines, regard it is as necessary to increase prices. Nor would any future regulator be likely to let BAA face the risk of bankruptcy. However, the opposite possibility—that the regulator may feel the need to clawback excess returns but not, once investment in a major project such as T5 became a sunk cost, assist BAA if it was in difficulty—cannot fully be discounted. Neither possibility is attractive, but both have been avoided in the standard type of regime based on quinquennial reviews.

2.245. We are also concerned that such an approach could imply prices unrelated to costs in future quinquennia, possibly inconsistent with international agreements which stipulate that airport charges should be based on costs (see the summary of the relevant provision of Bermuda 2 in Chapter 3). The CAA argued that there was no such inconsistency. First, there may be amendment of such international obligations, in particular Bermuda 2, although in our view prospects for such an amendment may be uncertain. Second, such prices could, in the CAA's view, be regarded as related to 'forward looking costs'. Third, such an approach is not that different to the current setting of prices on the basis of projected cost over a five-year period. However, in our view there is a material difference between the current regulatory approach and the PPC in that the current system does allow five-yearly correction for excess or inadequate profits rather than attempting to set prices on the basis of 20-year projections that would be subject to even greater uncertainty.

2.246. In our view, therefore, it is neither possible nor desirable to adopt a PPC beyond Q4. There are, however, possible alternatives to the PPC to provide incentives to invest efficiently—namely to include AICC in the asset base and provide an element of smoothing of returns between quinquennia, thereby reducing reliance on future larger increases in prices, in which BAA could have no confidence; and, while acknowledging we cannot bind our successors nor the CAA, continue to adopt consistent principles in regulating revenues.

Correction for under-investment in Q3

2.247. As noted above, in recommending a formula of RPI–3 for the current quinquennium for the three BAA London airports, the MMC assumed the early commencement of

construction of T5, and allowed a return on T5 AICC. It also assumed a relatively high return in Q3 (8.5 per cent) with a suggestion of a relatively low return in Q4 (6.7 per cent) as a way of 'smoothing' the price profile for BAA with a return equal to cost of capital over Q3 and Q4 together. (Charges were, however, expected to increase in Q4, with RPI+2 suggested for that period.) For the same reason, the CAA subsequently adopted an RPI–3 rather than RPI–8 formula (we refer to this as an 'advancement of revenue for smoothing purposes').

2.248. We have noted that, as a result of delays in the planning inquiry, T5 construction did not commence in the original period of Q3 (although preparatory expenditure of £300 million was incurred in the period up to 2001/02).[1] As shown in Table 2.10, the effects on the volume of BAA expenditure has been partially offset by increased expenditure on non-T5 projects.

TABLE 2.10 **Comparison of MMC4 forecasts and actual spend**

£ million (2001/02 prices)

	MMC4 (1997/98– 2001/02)	Actual (1997/98– 2001/02)	Difference
T5 and related*	1,370.3	343.0	−1,027.3
Heathrow Express	122.1	169.4	47.3
Total	1,492.5	512.5	−980.0
Other Heathrow	850.6	1,050.8	200.2
Gatwick	355.6	442.6	87.0
Stansted	135.3	321.3	186.0
Total South-East	2,834.0	2,327.2	−506.8
Excluding T5 and related sub-total	1,341.6	1,814.7	473.1

Source: BAA.

*T5 related projects include extensions to Heathrow Express and Piccadilly Line; Visual Control Room; and Airside Road Tunnel.

Note: This table shows a higher level of actual capex and smaller difference from projected than Table 10.2, as Table 10.2 shows net capex after deducting proceeds of disposals.

2.249. Expenditure in the original period of Q3 up to 2001/02 on T5 and T5-related projects was about £1 billion less than assumed when the current formula was set. However, there has been almost £50 million greater expenditure on Heathrow Express and £200 million additional expenditure on other projects at Heathrow, £87 million at Gatwick and £186 million at Stansted. BAA believed that some £200 million expenditure at Heathrow and £65 million at Gatwick could be regarded as mitigating the effect of the delay in T5, as could all of the increased expenditure at Stansted since it regarded optimizing the use of existing capacity at Gatwick and Stansted and additional investment at those two airports as ways of meeting unfulfilled demand at Heathrow. (Some £20 million at Gatwick probably could not be attributed to the failure to build T5.) However, it believes another £100 million fixed expenditure on minor projects has occurred to replace worn out assets and deal with congestion conditions. It believes this is conservative as it has excluded some additional expenditure on CIP lounges and flight report centre. Changes in project scope are included within the additional £100 million element.

2.250. The CAA has recommended, first, that all of the smoothing adjustment implicit in its decision to adopt a price cap of RPI–3 rather than RPI–8 be removed from the RRCB.

---

[1] A further £310 million is expected to be spent this year.

Except for the timing of that recovery, this is not in dispute. The CAA estimated the value of revenue advancement at £300 million, including 2002/03. However, the MMC did not make definitive recommendations for 2002/03 nor was it covered by the CAA's 1996 statement about revenue advancement (ie the difference between RPI–8 and RPI–3). The price cap was extended for one year at RPI–3 in order that our inquiry could be delayed to take account of the T5 decision (and the possibility of changes to the Airports Act, in the event not implemented) at a time when BAA's position was already quite different to that which the MMC and the CAA had expected in 1996, in particular because of the delay to T5. So the original projections (in which MMC had suggested an indicative RPI+2) seem of no relevance. The revenue advancement would be increased from £300 million to about £350 million if 2002/03 were excluded (see Table 10.1).

2.251. Second, the CAA recommended recovery of 50 per cent of the gains in present value terms that BAA has earned (in addition to the smoothing) through the lower than expected capital investment. In its initial submission to us in February 2002, it referred to applying only a 50 per cent adjustment as being 'to ensure there is no danger of regulatory appropriation of legitimate efficiency gains that should accrue to the airports (to maintain incentives)'; in later evidence to ourselves, it described this as a judgement, to avoid full cost-plus treatment of investment. Airlines have suggested full recovery of under-investment. As we discuss further below, some airlines, including BA and bmi, also refer to informal undertakings given by BAA to request a mid-term review if there was significant delay to T5. There was, however, an asymmetry in arrangements for any mid-term review, in that it could only be sought by BAA, and BAA had subsequently not agreed to such a review. The airlines felt this undermined any similar provision for the future. Some airlines, including BA, have argued that the full amount should be refunded in Q4—not by lower charges stretching into the indefinite future. bmi appeared to suggest refund in the last year of Q3.

2.252. BAA objected to any implication of automatic recovery of underspend, since, among other things, it believed that such an approach would be a disincentive to efficient investment and its rate of return had been broadly as projected; hence, there were no windfall gains—factors it believed were recognized in the CAA's 50:50 approach. BAA argued that clawback of underspend should only be considered if underspend has been to some degree engineered by the company or it has made a windfall gain. It believed total returns, however, were very close to forecast because of high operating cost and depreciation due to the need to manage terminal congestion: high depreciation was partially caused by the purchase of shorter-life assets. Reduction of RAB would be arbitrary and mere punishment with no regulatory precedent and a very poor incentive for future capital projects.

2.253. We have therefore to consider whether and to what extent under-investment in Q3 resulting from delay in T5 should be recovered. We have noted BAA's argument that its rate of return has been broadly as forecast when its current maximum level of charges was set, so there may be a case for no recovery: the benefits to BAA of under-investment would have been off-set by other disadvantageous factors. However, BAA's arguments depend in part on its estimate of its asset base on a different basis to that which we used in our last report: as noted in paragraph 2.29, on a comparable basis, its return has exceeded that projected when the current formula was set, although it is only the variation in capex and its consequences which are relevant to our consideration of clawback.

2.254. Some Heathrow airlines argued that the increase in investment at Gatwick or Stansted was of no benefit to them and no other projects at Heathrow had been undertaken to compensate for the delay in T5. We have received no criticism that there has been excessive spend on non-T5 projects at Heathrow: hence, they should in our view be allowed for, even if they were not included in the original investment schedule. They will, indeed, help to maintain service quality despite number of passengers at Heathrow exceeding projections at Q3 by about 3 per cent (see Table 10.2) and the continued growth forecast at Heathrow despite the delay to T5. Such alternative investments, however, have also been on assets that have come into use earlier than was expected for T5, increasing depreciation. We believe it is valid to take that additional depreciation into account (but we do not include depreciation of investment properties).

2.255. We have noted BAA's argument that account should be taken of additional investment at Stansted and Gatwick, on the basis that this was to meet the growth in system demand, including that which could not be accommodated at Heathrow, rather than merely demand at those two airports. However, as shown in paragraph 10.12, due to the significantly higher than expected growth in passenger numbers at Stansted, airport charges at Stansted were £36 million greater than projected (and other revenue £40 million greater than expected): significantly greater than the £24 million of additional depreciation and return on RCV associated with additional capex at Stansted. The additional capex at Stansted was therefore more than financed by the additional growth at Stansted; passenger growth at Heathrow was also greater than expected, despite any diversion of passenger numbers from Heathrow to Stansted. The same applies at Gatwick, where in any case the costs associated with additional investment were negligible (see paragraph 10.7). Since additional capex at Stansted could be associated with additional growth in demand, we do not think the costs of additional capex at Stansted should be set against the effects of the underspend associated with delay to T5.

2.256. As to the amount of underspend therefore to be allowed for, the CAA estimated the effect of capital underspend on revenue was some £200 million to the end of 2002/03. We estimate that the effect at Heathrow alone at the end of 2001/02, consistent with our approach to revenue advancement above, would be £150 million. Allowing for additional depreciation, however, reduces the effect of capital underspend to £64 million (see Table 10.2). BAA argued the effect should be still smaller if (as well as allowing for additional expenditure at other airports) the following allowances were made (indeed there would be net overspend):

(a) Under-recovery of airport charges. However, we have allowed for this in the calculation of revenue advancement above.

(b) Centralized capital costs treated in individual airport accounts as operating costs for tax reasons—a factor the CAA did not take into account. We acknowledge it has been BAA's practice to capitalize such costs. Much of these were associated with T5, and therefore should be allowed for and we have done so in calculating the amount of underspend above. However, we found it unsatisfactory that it was far from clear how such costs had been treated in the projections for Q3 and we believe BAA should be more transparent in the information it provides to the CAA on such costs.

(c) The greater effect of loss of duty-free revenues than predicted at the time of our last report. However, we see no reason only to adjust for factors unfavourable to BAA: passenger growth was significantly better, to BAA's benefit, and it also benefited from an unexpected pensions holiday in this period.

(d) The CAA's allowance of £100 million for what BAA interpreted as capex efficiency. We noted above this was judgmental: but acknowledge it is undesirable to apply a 100 per cent clawback which could disincentivize efficiency improvements and give an incentive to maintain investment, even if there was no value from doing so: we believe it is appropriate to make some allowance for efficiency of the capex programme. We saw no evidence that any of the lower level of expenditure on T5 could be attributed to capital expenditure efficiency as opposed merely to delay in the planning process. But BAA has, for example, handled more passengers than projected despite a lower overall investment programme; its projects have generally been completed on time and within target; and the Stansted investment in particular offers significant increase in throughput for reasonable cost. A 5 per cent efficiency saving on its actual capex at Heathrow would reduce the £64 million to £46 million.

2.257. It is also necessary to consider whether any recovery of under-investment should be allocated to airports other than Heathrow. The MMC's projections at the time of the previous review were of returns above the cost of capital at Heathrow, but broadly similar to the cost of capital at Gatwick. Subsequently, the net underspend was only at Heathrow, and there has been higher investment at the other airports. It is therefore in our view appropriate for the adjustments for revenue advancement and underspend also to be confined to Heathrow.

2.258. Finally, it is necessary to consider whether any such recovery of under-investment (and also the revenue advancement) should be spread into the indefinite future (through adjustment to the RAB) or confined to Q4. In paragraph 181 of CAP 664 announcing its decision on charges for Q3, the CAA stated that 'the underlying philosophy is that any supernormal profit in Q3 [resulting from revenue advancement] will be paid back in Q4'. BAA, however, drew our attention to the subsequent qualification that the CAA cannot bind itself to act or not act in any particular way in a future review and, in order to meet its statutory objectives in subsequent reviews, 'it could be some time before the advancement could be unwound'. The CAA itself, in incorporating revenue advancement and recovery of under-investment in the RAB, has changed its approach. We accept that we also have the flexibility to make recovery over a longer period, but, to be consistent with the clear logic of what the MMC recommended six years ago, believe it desirable in principle for both elements of recovery to be made in Q4.

2.259. BAA also argued that, if a dual till were to be adopted, recovery should be applied not just to aeronautical charges but should also be allocated to commercial activities. The CAA argued that the under-recovery affected what was paid for in airport charges, hence, under a dual-till approach only airport charges should be adjusted. Given our view on dual till, however, it is not necessary for us to consider this point, but since the effect of revenue advancement and the assumed level of investment was fully reflected in airport charges, we would also see no reason why the recovery should not be fully recovered against airport charges.

2.260. In our view, therefore, there should in principle be recovery in Q4 of revenue advancement and correction for under-investment in Q3. We acknowledge that treatment of past under-investment may be regarded as a guide to the future, and therefore have an effect on incentives, and that a principle of full recovery of under-investment could result in BAA investing in projects even where it becomes apparent they are not necessary. But if there is no recovery of under-investment, users effectively pay twice. The circumstances we are considering—of delay to expected expenditure on one major project for which a specific adjustment to charges was made—are, however, exceptional. There is therefore no presumption that lower expenditure due to capital efficiency would ever be treated analogously and more general issues of incentives or inferences from the approach we have put forward do not arise.

Assets in the course of construction

2.261. We have discussed in previous reports whether a return should be allowed on AICC, ie in advance of output being generated (in effect, prefunding of investment, although BAA have argued that it should not be regarded as prefunding), or only when the assets come into use. One way of applying an incremental cost approach would be to allow income only when T5 increases passenger throughput with no allowance for AICC. The CAA accept AICC should be retained for all non-T5 investment—but when adopting a single-till approach for Q4, in fact continued to allow for AICC also for T5. As noted above, the MMC previously allowed for AICC.

2.262. Most airlines objected strongly to the allowance for AICC, particularly given the allowance for T5 assets in the course of construction during the current quinquennium that, due to planning delays, have not been constructed at all: prices should not increase, they argued, until they receive the benefits of investments, particularly given the congestion costs imposed on them until that occurs. BA, however, was not opposed to AICC, but only if there were separate airport tills, refund of previous prefunding, retention of the single till, and a clear definition of 'Phase 1/Day 1' opening facilities (which we referred to above) which were necessary to provide a balanced overall settlement. Virgin argued against prefunding since it should be for the airport to bear the risk.

2.263.   BAA argued that to increase charges only when a project was on-stream, rather than during the period of excess demand before that occurs, is inappropriate and cannot be relied upon to happen (it quoted experience in Hong Kong, where airlines prevented increases in charges when a new airport opened). It believed it could not finance T5 on that basis, or could not do so without increasing its financing costs. Airlines argued BAA should have no difficulty in funding a project such as T5, and for BAA to do so was less costly than for it, in effect, to pass the funding requirement on to airlines, via AICC.

2.264.   In our view, some addition to revenue while assets are being constructed remains necessary to secure funding for a major project and/or reduce the costs of funding. Allowance for AICC is also desirable to avoid undue volatility in prices: a factor in previous MMC reports, airlines previously telling us they disliked volatility. Allowance for AICC would also, in our view, reflect what would be expected in more competitive markets, with prices some- what higher when pressure on existing demand is greatest, and lower when new capacity comes on-stream. Given, however, the problems that occurred in Q3 with an allowance from AICC on T5 that were not constructed, we see value in a system of 'triggers' relating charges to progress of projects, which we discuss below.

Air transport movement/stand/airside road tunnel incentives

2.265.   The CAA also proposed an ATM incentive for Heathrow: a premium of £300 for each addition to air transport movement capacity at Heathrow in the peak period above current average peak throughput, in order to encourage BAA to make more use of the runways, for example by operating them in mixed mode. It proposed a further incentive related to the airside road tunnel (ART) and additional T5 stands. BAA and BA agreed with the CAA's suggestion. Some others disagreed with any such incentives: and with there being no guarantee of delivery. BATA 'reluctantly supported' the proposed peak ATM incentive but regarded it as made necessary by deliberate restriction of Heathrow runway capacity. Some airlines challenged whether any incentive in addition to the increase in revenue from airport charges or commercial revenues generated by additional ATMs and stand capacity is necessary.

2.266.   In our view, a mechanism is desirable to ensure the delivery of projects on which a return is allowed in the asset base, to avert the risk of extra revenue being provided to the airport for no purpose. We believe, however, this would be more comprehensively provided for by means of 'triggers' relating airport charges to progress of investment in T5 rather than the specific more limited incentives related to stands and the ART put forward by the CAA. We return to this below.

2.267.   As to the ATM incentive, planning permission for T5 is subject to the condition that the number of ATMs at Heathrow on the opening of T5 should be subject to a limit of 480,000; the incentive proposed by the CAA is therefore related only to peak movements. In our view, BAA has previously been successful in increasing the capacity of its existing runways, and already has sufficient incentives to increase the number of peak movements, when demand is obviously greatest, through the additional airport charges and commercial revenues that would be generated. We therefore see no need for any further peak ATM incentives.

The general approach—other issues

Revenue yield

2.268. As noted elsewhere, the current formula is based on revenue from airport charges per passenger. An alternative approach is that of the 'tariff basket' (see Chapter 5), based on weighted average change in each element of the charging formula (ie each item of landing, passenger and parking charges as listed in Table 1 of Appendix 2.5). The CAA (which rejected the MMC's recommendation of a tariff basket in the first Manchester Airport report in 1987) initially proposed to adopt a tariff basket approach for Heathrow and Gatwick in Q4: all but one of the airlines regarded it as too complex ('unconvincing, unproven and at times impenetrable' as one group of airlines put it) and preferred 'the devil they know'. The CAA subsequently did not pursue the tariff basket. Given the lack of support for the tariff basket and its greater complexity (for example, in predicting the level of revenue that would result from it) we agree the revenue yield approach should be retained.

Volume term

2.269. Over the longer term, growth in passenger throughput at the BAA airports (and in UK airports as a whole) has averaged between 5 and 6 per cent a year, but subject to un-predictable variations around that long-term trend. Further uncertainty is introduced by capacity constraints, which may limit the extent to which individual airports can accommodate such long-term growth but which in practice are often overcome: hence, at the last inquiry we assumed growth at the BAA London airports, particularly Heathrow, significantly below 6 per cent, but prior to 11 September growth of the three airports as a whole had been sustained at only a little below the former 6 per cent level. The events of 11 September have introduced a further and more significant uncertainty.

2.270. The expectation of BAA and others is that growth will ultimately revert towards its longer-term trend, but with uncertainty as to the period taken to recover. The greater the traffic growth within existing capacity levels above that assumed in setting X, the greater the profits to BAA, given that marginal costs in the short term are low (although we have noted that in Q3 the effects of higher than expected passenger growth were largely offset by other factors). Previous reports have considered whether there should be a volume term which would increase charges in the event of low growth, and reduce charges in the event of higher growth than expected: thus limiting 'windfall' gains and losses to the airport. (An extreme form of volume term, used in some utilities, would be a revenue rather than price cap.) There have also been suggestions for an asymmetric volume term. If traffic grows less than expected, it may be relatively easy to cut investment expenditure, but if traffic grows more than expected, it may be difficult to increase investment to an equivalent extent due to planning constraints. Hence, the concern of some airlines (for example, BA) about the downward bias in BAA's previous traffic forecasts and suggestions that the term should apply only to volume above projected levels—effectively a ceiling but no floor to revenue.

2.271. Such a volume term has, however, previously been rejected and we continue to see a number of disadvantages to it. Prices would decrease if volumes increased (or vice versa): which would be appropriate only if costs do not vary with volume. Although in the short term there may be little scope to adjust costs or capex to unpredicted variations in demand—hence the effect on profitability—this does not apply in the longer term, over which long-run marginal costs are significant and (for Heathrow) increasing, as shown by the high incremental cost of T5. When volumes increase, additional capital or operating costs may soon be incurred: to reduce prices would, therefore, be inappropriate and act as a disincentive to further investment. Similarly, if volumes fell, prices would increase despite spare capacity. The CAA said that it disliked a volume factor due to the perverse movement of prices that would result, and that it was better to give incentive for additional volume and to complete capacity-enhancing investment during a five-year period rather than reducing prices when demand exceeded forecasts. A further practical difficulty of a volume term suggested in previous reports is the lag before a volume term could be applied: it is only at the end of a particular year (after charges for the subsequent year have been set) that the actual volume is apparent: hence any volume term could only be applied with a two-year delay, by which time it may be inappropriate since traffic growth may have recovered to trend. (This would, however, mitigate the price signals effect noted above.) Airlines would also face higher prices when their own volumes and profits are likely to be under pressure and vice versa, thus increasing the riskiness of their income profile (this could be mitigated, or aggravated, by the time lags involved).

2.272. BA was previously the strongest advocate of a volume term. However, during the current inquiry, BA said that it agreed it was important to preserve the airports' incentives to accommodate growth. At the same time, it was crucial to ensure that, if passenger growth was higher than expected, then the airport spent the additional revenue on projects that increased capacity, relieved congestion and maintained service quality. BA therefore regarded the use of a volume term as a fallback solution if there were inadequate incentives in the regulatory settlement, by providing lower charges if an airport was more congested. Its preferred solution was to see the introduction of financial mechanisms, such as a delay term in the price cap, the imposition of service standards with compensation arrangements, and improvements in the capex consultation arrangements (as discussed below).

2.273. For the reasons we have set out above, a volume term should not be included in airport charges for Q4. In the event of any catastrophic event leading to a significant and sustained fall in volume, there is a possibility of an interim review.

The S factor

2.274. The current formula allows the pass-through of 95 per cent of the costs of any additional security requirement introduced during the quinquennium under review. The CAA has proposed, with support from the airlines, that that cost pass-through approach for additional security costs should be abandoned. However, this alternative approach would require security costs to be predicted more accurately. The CAA suggested that the uncertainties of abandoning the S factor would only be of importance if there was a tight price cap, which they were proposing to avoid; but even then there was provision for interim determination if there was a problem. Airlines believed the S term does not encourage BAA to be as stringent and cost conscious as possible; costs relating to additional security requirements were also difficult to distinguish from costs of other projects being undertaken at the same time, for example refurbishment of terminals. Nor were airlines in a position to discuss the efficiency of the process (one suggested there may be scope to tender such services). Some argued that security at airports was now sufficient; if there were to be new requirements, there was no more reason for BAA to be able to pass on such extra costs than for airlines to do so, which in the short term they were unable to do. IATA argued security costs should be borne by the state, and pointed to changes in arrangements in the USA, and the assistance given more generally to civil aviation in the USA after 11 September. We have, however, seen no evidence to suggest any such change in arrangements is likely in Q4, and have to make definitive recommendations on the basis of present policy.

2.275. BAA argued that security costs following the events of the 11 September were highly uncertain and that if there was to be any abandonment of the cost pass-through mechanism, it would be necessary to include a possible allowance in the price cap calculations for the costs of any additional security requirements, which would itself be subject to considerable uncertainty. The DfT also expressed concern about abandoning the S term.

2.276. The uncertainties as to future security requirements, after 11 September, could not in our view be adequately encompassed by an allowance for additional and currently unknown security requirements in the base formula. Hence, we see retention of the current security term as the better way of incorporating such uncertainty and avoiding any undesirable incentive for BAA to cut corners in its security provision. (Use of an S term would also be appropriate where additional security requirements could prove temporary.) Suggestions were put to us that operation of the S term could otherwise be improved. KLM and bmi suggested reduction of the cost pass-through to 75 per cent and more involvement by Transec (the DfT's security arm) or the CAA in agreeing efficient costs of implementation. The current formula gives BAA a modest incentive to be as stringent and cost conscious as possible: given the critical importance of security at airports, we are not persuaded there is any reason to modify the current S factor at present.

The Q factor

2.277. To avoid giving BAA an incentive to increase throughput at the expense of lower service quality (for example, overcrowding), the CAA recommended that up to 3 per cent of airport charges at Heathrow and Gatwick should be subject to meeting particular standards of service. The CAA said that the limitation of the Q factor to 3 per cent was because of uncertainty as to whether the initial specification of Q would be adequate, and because of the danger in an untried system that perverse incentives could result. Over the five years 1996/97 to 2000/01, the 3 per cent limit would have amounted to a maximum of some £60 million at Heathrow and Gatwick, 18 per cent of their operating profit from airport charges, 3 per cent of their total operating profit.

2.278. The standards of service would include measures of quality of service to airlines (the Q_A term); to passengers (the Q_P term, based on BAA's QSM surveys of passenger opinion); and congestion or delays (the Q_D term). The components of the Q factor proposed by the CAA are shown in Table 2.11; Table 2.11 also shows the elements of service proposed by BAA for inclusion in the Q term, together with those BA believed should be subject to service standards, although not through use of any Q term.

TABLE 2.11 **Proposed components of Q term**

	CAA	BAA	BA
Q_A			
Stand availability	✔	✔	✔
Jetty availability	✔	✔	✔
Pier service	✔	✘	✔
FEGP	✔	✘	✔
People movers	✔	✔	✔
Transit system	✔	✔	✔
Security queues	✔	✔	✔
Arrivals reclaim	✔	✔	✔
Runways	✘	✔	✔
Taxiways	✘	✔	✔
Departure baggage	✘	✘	✔
Q_P			
Departure lounge seat Availability	✔	✔	✘
Cleanliness	✔	✔	✘
Way-finding	✔	✔	✘
Flight information	✔	✔	✘
Delay	✔	✘	✔

Source: CC from information provided by CAA, BAA and BA.

2.279. Under the CAA proposals the Q_A term could effect charges by up to 1.5 per cent; the Q_P term by up to 0.5 per cent; and the Q_D term by 1 per cent. These maximum penalties could, however, be triggered if BAA failed to reach the minimum standard for only a majority of the individual measures. Moreover, the Q_A term would be asymmetric (ie a penalty for under-performance but no reward for over-performance).

2.280. BAA said that detailed service monitoring linked to the price formula was not necessary for BAA and might be counter productive: however, it said it had considered the issues involved and developed the Q factor concept in a way that might achieve the benefits whilst minimizing the disadvantages. But, it argued, the CAA should not adopt such a proposal unless or until it was satisfied that formal service quality regulation of this type would not cause distortions. It also, however, suggested possible alternative approaches, including additional transparency of service quality performance data, but without any effect on airport charges; and a minimum service quality protection system, where penalties would be incurred only if performance fell below prescribed minimum levels.

2.281. BAA argued the maximum effect on charges should be no more than 1 to 2 per cent which it believed would be consistent with the approach to other utilities. It suggested equal weighting of the 11 elements it proposed, with a maximum impact of 1.5 per cent of regulated airport charges which would be reached for very poor performance across the entire range of performance indicators. Par values should be based on existing target levels where they exist, but may need to change to take account of changing traffic levels or circumstances over five years. It also argued against an asymmetrical approach to the Q factor: but even with a symmetrical approach marginal improvements in service quality were increasingly difficult and costly as performance levels get closer to 100 per cent, introducing a degree of asymmetry.

2.282. BAA also queried the inclusion in those standards of service of a delay term. It believed that delays were difficult to measure and largely outside its control given the various causes not attributable to poor performance on the part of BAA. It believed it inappropriate to base any delay term on information gleaned from the subjective and simplified attribution of delays by airline or handling agent staff. BAA also provided figures showing that some 35 per cent of BA aircraft push back more than ten minutes after scheduled time of departure, but the time between a pushback request and actual time of pushback was very much smaller: 92 per cent of flights have no such delay and only 2.7 per cent have delays of more than 3 to 4 minutes. Even delay in granting a pushback request was not necessarily BAA's fault: it could result from variability in pushback request times and hence bunching. Delay would also be caused by peaking of the demand on the system imposed by the airlines that would not forgo their grandfather rights. At times, more flights were scheduled than could be handled. Similarly, delays in the stack resulted from a range of factors. However, it did not object to a delay term in principle as long as the measure reasonably reflected BAA's and National Air Traffic Service Limited's (NATS) performance, accurate data could be collected, and there was sufficient understanding and experience of the measure to allow appropriate targets to be set: it believed the CAA's proposals failed to pass these tests, but if a measurement system could be developed that would do so, then BAA would be willing for a delay term to be incorporated by mutual consent into a Q factor midway through the next quinquennium.

2.283. BAA also argued that fixed electrical ground power (FEGP) should be excluded since FEGP was outside regulated airport charges and charged for separately. It believed pier service should also be excluded because BAA did not carry out the day-to-day stand allocation which was an important determinant of pier service. The scale of infrastructure was the primary driver of pier service levels, but the way the stands were allocated led to significant variations around these levels. There were also practical difficulties in predicting appropriate target values given that the level of performance depends critically on the nature of demand and provision of pier service stands. It also argued that departures baggage system performance should be excluded since increasingly bespoke financially incentivized agreements would be developed for individual baggage systems. On the other hand, it proposed inclusion of runway and taxiway availability. Initially runway and taxiway availability would be measured, to inform decisions on appropriate targets by late 2003, and which may also have to be included part-way into the quinquennium by 'mutual consent'.

2.284. Several airlines (including BA) said that the proposal was 'much too weak'. They argued that the 3 per cent figure for the overall effects of the Q term should be increased to as much as 10 per cent. There also needed to be a clearer and more immediate link between performance and reward—under the Q term it could take up to two years for performance to be reflected in charges. Most airlines also 'strongly opposed' any 'averaging' in service standards, or rewards for overachievement as opposed to penalties for underachievement against target, as they believed these could lead to improvements in service standards where easily achieved, at the expense of others. Rather, they argued they needed all aspects of performance to function properly, since failure of any one element could cause serious detriments. Some of the measures could also reflect factors unrelated to performance—for example, quality of service may improve if passenger numbers declined; if there was averaging, the impact of such factors could obscure inadequate service against other standards.

2.285. BA said that service standards currently tended to be presentational rather than effective. Rather than a Q term in the airport charges condition, BA and other airlines believed that there were aspects of current service performance which were against the public interest, the formal remedies for which should be included in the conditions to levy airport charges. (We discuss this approach further below.)

2.286. On the measures to be included, many airlines argued strongly in favour of a delay term. Some airlines claimed that a system is feasible building on what they already do in attributing delays to airports, airlines and other factors: they also claimed that NATS (in the control tower) and Eurocontrol/Central Flow Management Unit (CFMU) already have such data; some suggested that airport delays account for well over 20 per cent of delays at Heathrow and have a very high cost to the airlines.

2.287. BA and a number of airlines objected to passenger perception being incorporated in any Q term, and queried whether the results of BAA's QSM are sufficiently robust for this purpose. Some airlines (Virgin, IATA, BA) argued that 'soft' targets—levels of service which are only normally to be expected—should not be incorporated in any Q term (or equivalent service standards), particularly if there was to be any 'averaging' of performance: resources would be diverted into those aspects of service most easily achieved. BA argued that passenger perception was also more difficult to measure than those aspects of performance relevant to airlines; whereas the CAA included some measures based on BAA's QSM—a passenger survey—BA believed this was biased and should form no part of any measure of service standards.

2.288. Particular criticisms of the QSM made by BA (see paragraph 12.112) were that the study was conducted by BAA themselves; that the QSM neither fully represented nor adequately captured the interviewee's opinions (which consequently implied bias); that it should ensure representative samples from each segment; that it was suspended during times of operational disruption; and that use of a five-point scale meant that many people may feel reluctant to choose either extreme, and prefer a neutral response (the so-called error of central tendency). Hence, BA argued, bias was inherent in the results. The QSM surveys were also designed for internal monitoring and decision-making, and hence were not appropriate for use as a tool to measure quality for presentation in a public forum. Some airlines supported the CAA's recommendation of an external audit: BAA had no objection to any such audit.

2.289. It was also argued that existing data from monitoring of service level agreements (SLAs)—which we discuss below—was not adequate for incorporation in any Q factor: for example, it excluded planned maintenance and there was inadequate measurement (for example, of time taken to pass through central security queues). There were also criticisms of incomplete or no standards on pier availability.

2.290. BA also suggested targets of 100 per cent serviceability, compared with current targets of 95 to 98 per cent serviceability.

2.291. BAA suggested any expected levels of payments under the Q term (or other standards of service compensation arrangements)—or risk of making such payments—should be reflected in the level of airport charges, in particular if the Q term was asymmetric. A number of airlines were concerned with this approach arguing, for example, that in effect this took away any penalty from failing to meet the standards.

2.292. Commenting on some of the above points, BAA said it recognized the concerns about a scheme whereby service quality performance did not affect airport charges until between 13 and 24 months later; however, it said that operational managers would be focused on performance from the very start of the scheme as they would be very well aware it would have a financial impact, albeit deferred. An alternative was for monthly airport charges invoices to be adjusted using monthly service quality performance results: but such an approach would be very complex and administratively burdensome. As to averaging, it said it was important to have a basket of measures in any Q factor to reflect the range of BAA's outputs: having set the maximum impact of a Q factor it would be inappropriate for performance of individual elements to give rise to penalties representing a large proportion of the maximum impact. It added there was a clear rationale for a symmetrical structure. Use of a basket of measures, together with the capping of individual elements and symmetry of bonuses and penalties necessarily meant that the overall balance of bonuses and discounts would reflect average performance across the standards. It had sought to reduce the impact of averaging by retaining monthly rather than annual targets for many parts of the Q factor. It was disappointed at criticisms of its approach and believed it had taken a very constructive stance to developing a ground-breaking, practical and effective mechanism, which put at risk over 5 per cent of its post-tax profits. It certainly would not put airlines in a worse position: if they truly believed this was the case, it would withdraw its Q proposal.

2.293. BAA regarded BA's proposal of targets of 100 per cent in some areas as unreasonable, and creating a very poor management incentive. The current infrastructure, for example, made a pier service target of 100 per cent unachievable, and an extremely large level of investment would be required to achieve it. Elsewhere, BA had proposed retaining existing percentage targets but changing the measurement definition to include planned maintenance: such a change in definition, which BAA agreed to do, would also require targets to be reduced. There would also be significant resource implications from adoption of a 6-minute generic standard, compared with the existing service level agreement (SLA) target of 10 minutes for security queuing of the SLA. BA had also argued for inclusion of baggage systems and FEGP. As noted above, BAA argued that these should be excluded as they were not covered by core airport charges, and use of a single serviceability target for baggage handling would be inconsistent with the range of measures which the joint working group of BAA and BA concluded was necessary to judge the effectiveness of a particular baggage system. Were baggage system performance to be incorporated in a Q factor, then BAA would be forced to remove the financial incentives from the existing Heathrow baggage system SLAs to avoid double jeopardy.

2.294. We have noted the argument of some airlines that it would be better to deal with performance standards as public interest questions with the possibility of there being an airport charging condition, subject to rebates in the event of poor performance. We return to the question of possible service standards in the context of public interest issues below.

Default price cap

2.295. The CAA proposed that there should be explicit provision for airport charges payable at Heathrow and Gatwick under individual contracts between individual airlines and the airports for different levels of service and specific facilities to be outside of the normal regulated price cap. (At Stansted the CAA said that there was no need for a formally implemented default price cap, because the price cap was not expected to be 'binding'—ie it would be more than the market would bear—but there would also need to be a mechanism for excluding costs associated with direct contracts from the RAB.) This could involve particular airlines entering into contracts under which, in return for higher than standard airport charges (for example, landing fees) they would either:

(a) receive marginal improvements in facilities and quality of service above a minimum standard; or

(b) be entitled at no extra charge to services for which non-airport charges are normally made.

2.296. The issue of a 'default price cap' in relation to service quality interrelates with the Q term above, and public interest issues on standards of service discussed below. The CAA's preference was for a broad-based Q term—but with scope also for contractual agreements where performance was easily reviewed and responsibilities clear (for example, pier/jetty services).

2.297. The CAA proposed that if under an individually negotiated agreement an airline agreed to pay higher airport charges than standard, the extra should be disregarded in calculating the maximum charge per passenger.

2.298. Originally the CAA believed that where individually negotiated contracts involved the payment of airport charges, these should be subject to a price cap separate from the cap applying to the payment of standard published charges. It initially proposed that the cap for charges payable under such agreements should be set at 'a deliberately non-binding level'. Subsequently, it considered that such special arrangements should merely be treated in the same way as non-published discounts at Manchester: ie when comparing out-turn yields with the price cap, it should be assumed the full published charges were levied. The proposals would be of relevance only in cases where the extra charges were themselves 'airport charges' as defined in the Airport Act. The CAA told us that, according to its legal advice, a payment for the supply of specified service elements under individual deals would not normally count as airport charges. Accordingly, it seems to us that the proposals were unlikely in any event to be of much practical importance.

2.299. In an opinion of 30 July 1987, Mark Littman QC expressed the view that the then MMC were under an obligation to fix maximum charges and it could not use its powers under section 40(5) to impose limits on one category of airport charges while leaving the remainder at large. The CAA appear to accept this. However, Mr Littman also said that he did not think the MMC could comply with its obligations by fixing an arbitrary maximum rate well above that which any airport operator is likely to want to charge, but that section 45 obliged the MMC to give its bona fide conclusion on the maximum amounts. Thus, if Mr Littman is correct, the CC cannot fix a charge at 'a deliberately non-binding level' but nor can any such charges not be capped at all and the question of how the charges should be capped would need to be addressed.

2.300. It would therefore be legally necessary to cap any top-up charges which are airport charges, but this is clearly impractical: it would require provision now for future arrangements, the scope of which are totally unpredictable. We therefore conclude that there should be no default price cap. We discuss any discounts for lower than any generic standard of service in the next section. Some airlines expressed concern that direct contracting may enable discriminatory or anti-competitive practices and that contracts should be limited to requests for service above an agreed generic standard with no possibility for contracting downwards. There is also the question of whether such arrangements are consistent with Articles 103 to 107 of the Air Navigation Order 2000. However, in the light of our conclusion we do not need to consider these questions.

Discounts

2.301. At Manchester, the price cap is required by the formula to be calculated as if users pay published charges: otherwise, a discount to one user can be offset by a premium to the rest. There is no such requirement for the BAA airports. For Stansted, the airport director has discretion to abate or waive charges to encourage traffic development. This discretion is used at Stansted in relation to a small number of new routes, to aircraft parking and to general aviation. The airport's quoted yields are net of these discounts which in 2001/02 amounted to £2 million. For the majority of new routes at the airport, however, the incentives given are treated as marketing expenditure, which in 2001 amounted to approximately £15 million a year. This marketing expenditure is disregarded by BAA and the CAA in calculating the price cap, ie in effect treating the expenditure as a cost rather than a revenue offset (in practice following the same procedure used in Manchester).

2.302. The CAA suggested that the Manchester approach formally be used for the BAA airports—which would affect the first of these types of discount—to which BAA agreed. We accept the formula should be revised to require that for yield calculation purposes the full published charge is used, in order that unpublished discounts to one carrier cannot merely be financed by raising charges to other operators. This principle should also apply to discounts agreed for service lower than any generic standard set, ie they should be disregarded for purposes of the price cap, and users should be assumed to pay the full published charge, in order that such discounts cannot merely be financed by higher charges to other users. (This would not, however, apply to the current remote stand rebate, as the rebates are published in the Condition of Use. They are also an aspect of the charging structure; as only the net charge counts towards the price cap, lower charges to users of remote stands can be offset by higher charges to users with pier service.)

2.303. Airlines argued against any non-cost-based discounts which are discriminatory/ distort competition or non-transparent, but this raises issues wider than the airport charges formula. Neither BAA nor the CAA wanted full transparency of discounts, BAA also suggested that the carriers themselves would not wish such information to be published, since they would reveal the strategy of the airlines on each route. Discount arrangements at Stansted could in our view be regarded as one of the few examples of competitive pressures on airport charges at any of the three airports; competition between airlines at Stansted has been to the significant benefit of users; and BAA's prices have, despite discounts, been sufficient to cover marginal cost and increase Stansted's profitability towards the point where it can earn a rate of return equivalent to cost of capital. However, these considerations do not affect our conclusions on the treatment of discounts in the charge cap formula.

Non-passenger flights

2.304. The revenue per passenger approach implies that extra revenue from non-passenger flights be offset by reduced revenue from passenger flights. In 2000, Manchester was allowed by the CAA to remove revenues from non-passenger flights from the cap (subject to a condition that charges should be no more than passenger flights): the CAA suggested that this be extended to BAA. BAA agreed with the CAA suggestion, but questioned whether it was desirable to signal an implied regulatory incentive to non-passenger flights at Heathrow and Gatwick or indeed Stansted which was likely to be congested in the short to medium term. However, as the CAA had suggested, the slot mechanism would prevent any encouragement to such flights, hence this was 'only a technical adjustment'. It felt the respecification of the pricing formula would also have no practical incentive effect: it would only allow theoretically slightly higher charges for passenger aircraft if each airport was close to the maximum allowable yield. It believed competition with other airports with cargo facilities would deter increases in charges at airports where there was capacity, and that non-discrimination provisions would ensure that charges for cargo aircraft at airports with limited capacity could not be increased to deter cargo aircraft. The effect on yield was less than 1 per cent at Heathrow/Gatwick but 7 per cent at Stansted. Some airlines supported the proposal.

2.305. We agree with this suggestion of the CAA; otherwise, the current formula acts as a disincentive to non-passenger flights, since the revenue from these flights counts against permitted revenue, and other charges have to be reduced. Some LFCs have queried whether the impact of different treatment of cargo flights at Stansted is allowed for in projections. We have done so.

2.306. We accordingly conclude that aircraft charges relating to non-passenger flights should not be included in the normal cap, but should be subject to a separate condition that they must not exceed the charges relating to equivalent passenger flights.

Regulation at Stansted

2.307. The CAA suggested a separate price cap at Stansted, based on Stansted costs under the dual-till approach. However, although it dismissed arguments that Stansted was in a significantly more competitive position than Heathrow or Gatwick, or subject to greater countervailing power of airlines, it suggested its approach to setting prices should be 'light-handed' and that charges could not in practice be raised to the level of the price cap given the price elasticity of demand at Stansted and BAA's development objectives. (Hence, it also did not propose a Q factor or default price cap at Stansted, with which BAA agreed.) It also suggested possible long-term contracts with low-cost airlines at Stansted.

2.308. Airlines were unconvinced, some of the LFCs arguing that:

(a) the CAA's approach would rely on the goodwill of BAA in that circumstances could change as Stansted begins to fill up which would allow BAA to charge up to the level of the cap;

(b) there should be more not less protection given their dependence on the airport providing a low-cost, 'no-frills' approach;

(c) competition from other airports was constrained, for example by restricted stand capacity of Luton; and

(d) relatively tight regulation would itself act as an incentive to reduce cost at Stansted.

2.309. We accept the argument of airlines that circumstances at Stansted could change. In our view, there is a prospect within Q4 or Q5 that increasing demand at Stansted could allow charges to be raised to the level of the price cap proposed by the CAA, given that capacity at other airports to provide competition to Stansted is limited. We accept, given that the large majority of traffic at Stansted is from LFCs, that there should be effective protection to ensure Stansted does not earn an unreasonable rate of return and to continue to provide an incentive to reduce costs at Stansted.

2.310. We estimate that Stansted's current revenue per passenger (gross of all discounts and marketing support and excluding cargo flights) is about £4.20 (2000/01 prices), while its estimated net yield is over £1 lower (see Table 10.7). Our modelling assumes its net yield increases gradually towards Gatwick's projected yield: but remains slightly below Gatwick's yield in Q5, which is sufficient for Stansted to earn a return equivalent to its cost of capital in 2008. Stansted's estimated average cost (excluding any future projects such as new runways) over the ten years of Q4 and Q5 is about £3.90 excluding projected marketing costs and £4.60 including BAA's projected marketing costs. We believe the cap should however be set at such a level that those Stansted users not in a position to negotiate discounts should not be required to pay charges significantly above the level of Gatwick. We therefore propose a price cap of £4.20 on the basis of its current gross yield.

2.311. In practice we expect it to charge somewhat less than this: as well as the risk that higher charges could cause it to lose business given the nature of its traffic, we were told that some contracts with airlines fix prices for the next two or three years, and in our modelling we have assumed that its yield net of marketing costs rises from its present level of £2.99 to £4.20 only by the middle of Q5.

Transfer baggage infrastructure charge

2.312. During the course of the inquiry, the Heathrow AOC proposed the inclusion within airport charges of transfer baggage infrastructure funding at Heathrow, some 43p per passenger (excluding under-recovery, see paragraph 8.14). The proposal excluded, however, the bulk of the costs of the T1 to T4 baggage tunnel, developed by BA and BAA, and initially intended to be funded only by BA. Users other than BA argued the costs of the tunnel should not be included in airport charges, this project having been undertaken at considerable cost without their involvement, and being used primarily by BA: BA regarded it as a facility valuable to the airport as a whole. BAA proposed that exclusion of the tunnel would be reviewed when BA moved from T4, which is likely to be at the beginning of Q5. We believe the proposal to include costs of transfer baggage facilities, excluding the T1–T4 tunnel in Q4, is reasonable: the appropriate treatment of the baggage tunnel should be considered in the next quinquennial review.

Conclusion on general approach

2.313. We have therefore concluded:

(a) The RPI–X form of control should be maintained (see paragraph 2.39).

(b) The three airports should still be regulated with reference to the system rate of return (see paragraph 2.57).

(c) The single-till approach should be retained for Q4 (see paragraph 2.221).

(d) The incremental cost approach proposed by the CAA should not be adopted (see paragraph 2.236).

(e) There should be no PPC for quinquennia beyond Q4 (see paragraph 2.246).

(f) Recovery of revenue advancement in Q3 and correction for under-investment in T5 should in principle be in Q4 rather than over the longer term (see paragraph 2.260).

(g) There should be allowance for a return on AICC (see paragraph 2.264), but with a series of triggers relating charges to progress of T5 (see paragraph 2.266) which we discuss further below.

(h) The revenue yield approach should be retained (see paragraph 2.268).

(i) There should be no volume term (see paragraph 2.273).

(j) The current S factor should be retained (see paragraph 2.276).

(k) There should be no default price cap (see paragraph 2.300).

(l) The formula should apply to charges as if users pay the full published price, ie before unpublished discounts (see paragraph 2.302).

(m) Revenues for non-passenger flights should be removed from the normal cap. Aircraft charges relating to non-passenger flights should be subject to a separate condition that they must not exceed the charges relating to equivalent passenger flights (see paragraph 2.306).

(n) Maximum charges at Stansted should be based on its current gross yield (see paragraph 2.311).

(o) Transfer baggage infrastructure charges (excluding the T1 to T4 tunnel) should be included in airport charges in Q4 (see paragraph 2.312).

We return to the CAA's proposed Q factor below.

The level of X within the general approach adopted

2.314. As noted above, the CAA proposed an increase in charges at Heathrow, of RPI+6 in Q4. This was consistent with the single-till rather than dual-till approach (though with recovery of the difference in Q5); but was also regarded by the CAA as the maximum increase in charges that was reasonable in Q4. It proposed only slightly lower increases at Gatwick and slightly higher at Stansted (assumed not to be fully recovered), consistent with the dual till at those two airports rather than the single-till approach. The CAA recommendations implied, however, a 33 per cent increase in charges at Heathrow when T5 opens. BAA proposed a formula of RPI+7 at Heathrow, RPI+3 at Gatwick and RPI+1 at Stansted (in practice, BAA assumed prices at Stansted would increase by a similar extent to those at Gatwick, as current marketing allowances were reduced). Many airlines criticized the CAA's RPI+6 proposal for Q4 as 'perpetuating prefinancing of T5'. BA believed increases in charges were not necessary: it proposed formulae of RPI-4.4 at Heathrow and RPI-6 at Gatwick, largely due to its preferred treatment of prefunding and a lower cost of capital.

2.315. As well as the issues relating to the general approach to the setting of charges discussed above, a number of more specific issues are relevant in considering the appropriate value of 'X'.

Passenger forecasts

2.316. We referred above to the uncertainty of passenger forecasts. BAA initially responded to 11 September by suggesting the uncertainties were such that the price controls should be lifted at least for two years by dedesignating the airports (ie removing the current requirement for regulation). BAA's latest forecasts in its 2002 CIP, compared with those of the CAA, are summarized in Table 2.12. The CAA forecasts exceed those of BAA, particularly at Stansted.

TABLE 2.12 **Traffic forecasts**

	2000/01	2001/02	2002/03	2003/04	2004/05	2005/06	2006/07	2007/08
Traffic forecasts at Heathrow (mppa)								
BAA2002 CIP			63.3	67.1	69.0	69.9	70.3	70.7
CAA 2002	64.3	60.4	62.1	67.9	68.8	69.5	70.0	71.3
Traffic forecasts at Gatwick (mppa)								
BAA 2002 CIP			28.4	31.2	33.8	36.0	38.6	39.7
CAA 2002	32.1	30.5	28.8	31.8	34.4	36.3	38.2	39.8
Traffic forecasts at Stansted (mppa)								
BAA 2002 CIP			15.5	16.4	17.1	18.0	19.3	20.5
CAA 2002	12.3	14.1	16.0	17.5	19.3	20.3	21.1	22.3
Total								
BAA 2002 CIP			107.1	114.7	119.9	123.9	128.2	130.9
CAA 2002	108.7	105.0	106.9	116.3	122.5	126.1	129.3	133.4
CC*				115.8	122.1	126.2	130.0	132.7

Source: CC study.

*BAA forecasts for Heathrow and Gatwick, CAA for Stansted—see paragraph 2.318.

2.317. BAA's main arguments in support of its latest forecast compared with that of the CAA were the evidence of worldwide sluggish and in some cases non-existent recovery from 11 September in terms of air travel demands; the faltering nature of economic recovery; and airline strategies of cutting capacity which it said had never been seen before. It believed that the CAA failed to take into account the persistent decline in average loads at Heathrow since February 2001; and that the CAA's short-term forecast for Gatwick looked unrealistic. It believed that traffic growth at Stansted would decelerate as the low-cost market matured and new route opportunities diminished: such growth had declined from over 30 per cent to close to single figures in the space of three years, for which there were parallels with the charter growth in the early 1960s and 1970s. It also noted the much lower forecast for Heathrow growth in the recent SERAS report.

2.318. We have noted that all forecasts at the time of the previous report proved too low, and that current forecasts even of the CAA are for growth rates significantly below historic trends of between 5 and 6 per cent a year reflecting capacity constraints. Although BAA has previously been able partially to overcome capacity constraints at Heathrow and Gatwick and handle more traffic than it expected, we accept that the opportunity to do so is now more limited. We have accepted BAA's view of capacity constraints at these two airports, and adopted the resulting BAA figures for Heathrow and Gatwick. Capacity constraints are un-likely, however, to limit growth at Stansted, which has been granted planning permission to increase terminal capacity to 25 mppa and which remains in a position to absorb some of the longer-term growth in demand which is unlikely to be accommodated at Heathrow or Gatwick. We have therefore adopted the CAA figures for Stansted (although in practice, it may be, as in Q3, that some of the Stansted growth we are assuming can be handled at the other airports). We acknowledge, however, the interdependence between the volume forecast for Stansted and future level of landing charges: hence we have assumed above that Stansted can only gradually increase charges, net of marketing expenditure, to the level of Gatwick by the beginning of Q5. BAA argued that the higher passenger growth at Stansted would require additional investment, for which we have allowed.

2.319. The resulting figures for total passengers handled at the three airports is shown in Table 2.12. The figures we have used—3 per cent a year growth from 2000/01 to 2007/08— being based on capacity constraints are significantly below the historic growth in demand of between 5 and 6 per cent a year. In our view the assumptions we have used adequately allow for the current uncertainties in recovery of air travel demand after 11 September 2001, and as much liable to upward as to downward error.

Cost of capital

2.320. Our previous report adopted a cost of capital of between 6.4 and 8.3 per cent for BAA (a mid-point of 7.4 per cent, although projections of returns on the RCV averaged 7.6 per cent over ten years).

2.321. The CAA (in its PPC approach) distinguish between an estimated 7 per cent cost of capital on existing assets at Heathrow, 8.5 per cent on T5 (assuming prices were set on incremental cost above a base level of traffic of 60 mppa, an approach we have rejected above), and 7.5 per cent at Gatwick and Stansted. For an RAB approach the CAA adopted 7 per cent at Heathrow, 7.5 per cent at Gatwick and Stansted.

2.322. BAA argued that its cost of capital is currently somewhat higher than the CAA propose, but also that it may be expected to increase as it undertakes the very substantial and risky investment in T5. In response to the CAA consultation document it said 'the cost of capital for the aeronautical till should be set at least 8 per cent for the airports taken together. The use of the 8 per cent dual till should provide sufficient headroom to allow BAA to proceed with investment with confidence'. However, it said that the figure would be higher if other aspects of the CAA proposals are adopted, for example individual airport regulation; PPC; 3 per cent Q factor; and no S term. BAA subsequently submitted to us a paper by Oxera suggesting a pre-tax cost of capital of 7.4 to 11.2 per cent (a mid-point of 9.3 per cent), and 7.69 to 11.6 per cent (a mid-point of 9.65 per cent) with T5 on an RAB basis—higher (a mid-point of 11.21 per cent) on an LRIC basis.

2.323. BA argued that the cost of capital for BAA is within the range of 5.6 to 7.7 per cent, a mid-point of 6.65 per cent.

2.324. The range of figures proposed for the cost of capital depends to a large extent on different assumptions as to the key components of the capital asset pricing model (CAPM) as summarized in Table 2.13.

TABLE 2.13 **Comparison of proposed WACCs for BAA**

	1996 MMC report		CAA—single and dual tills*		BAA		BA
	Low	High	LHR	LGW & STN	Low	High	LHR & LGW
Real risk free rate	3.5	3.8	3.0	3.0	2.75	3.25	2.75
Equity risk premium	4.0	5.0	4.0	4.0	4.0	6.0	3.5
Equity beta (number)	0.7	0.9	0.7	0.8	0.86	0.96	0.75
Cost of equity (post-tax)	6.3	8.3	5.8	6.2	6.19	9.01	5.38
Taxation adjustment	16.25	16.25	30.0	30.0	30.0	30.0	30.0
Cost of equity (pre-tax)†	7.52	9.91	8.29	8.86	8.84	12.87	7.68
Gearing	30.0	30.0	25.0	25.0	30.0	20.0	25.0
Debt premium	0.3	0.8	0.9	0.9	1.2	1.4	0.5
Cost of debt	3.8	4.6	3.9	3.9	3.95	4.65	3.25
Pre-tax WACC:							
Calculated figure	6.40	8.32	7.19	7.62	7.38	11.23	6.57
Mid point used	7.36				9.31		
Figure used by CAA			7.0	7.5			

Source: CC study.

*8.5 per cent for T5 if an incremental cost approach to pricing were adopted.
†The high figure quoted by BAA was 12.91, but actually grossed up to a pre-tax rate of 12.87 per cent, using the tax rate indicated of 30 per cent.

2.325. We discuss our view on the main elements of the CAPM in detail in Chapter 4. On the basis of that discussion, we regard a realistic range for cost of capital in Q4 as follows.

TABLE 2.14 **CC estimate of BAA cost of capital**

	%
Real risk-free rate	2.5–2.75
Equity risk premium	2.5–4.5
Equity beta (number)	0.8–1.0
Cost of equity (post tax)	4.5–7.25
Taxation adjustment	30.0
Cost of equity (pre-tax)	6.43–10.36
Gearing	25.0–25.0
Debt premium	0.9–1.2
Cost of debt	3.4–3.95
Pre-tax WACC	5.67–8.76
Mid-point	7.21

Source: CC study.

2.326. The mid-point of that range is 7.2 per cent, lower than in our previous report, reflecting subsequent reduction in the risk-free rate, and more recent research suggesting the equity risk premium (ERP) is lower than was previously believed to be the case. We believe, however, that, given the uncertainty of any estimates of the cost of capital or of the individual component of the CAPM, we should be cautious in adjusting estimates of the cost of capital to reflect recent developments, and adopt a degree of smoothing of the resulting variations to avoid undue fluctuation. A figure of 7.5 per cent, somewhat above the mid-point of the range would be appropriate on that basis in the light particularly of the downward movement in the ERP.

2.327. We also, however, believe in the current circumstances of BAA, a further increase in the cost of capital would be appropriate. First, we believe that the scale of the T5 project and consequential increase in borrowings and gearing will increase BAA's risks: it represents a considerable investment, with very long-term returns, subject not only to construction risks, but also risks of uncertain demand. Although passenger demand to use Heathrow should be strong, growth in the number of passengers per ATM is necessary if the additional capacity of T5 is to be fully utilized, but passengers per ATM have recently declined, adding to project risks. An increase in the cost of capital would also allow for the foreclosure of the options for BAA to postpone or cancel the project in the light of more data on air travel demand following 11 September, and for the effect of higher gearing and cost of new equity in the event of any major shocks. A further element of risk is introduced by the triggers associated with the development of T5 we mention below that could result in reduction in airport charges if trigger points are not met, despite considerable expenditure having been incurred. We have therefore adopted a figure for cost of capital of 7.75 per cent. Although this is to some extent based on the risks associated with T5, we believe these risks impact on the cost of capital to BAA as a whole and hence apply to each of the three airports. In particular an unexpected large fall in demand is more likely to impact on Gatwick than T5, because any spare capacity at T5 is likely to result in the transfer of flights from Gatwick. (The net result of the factors lowering the cost of capital and those company specific elements is that the annual rate of return is roughly the same as that used in our last report.)

Regulatory asset base and depreciation

2.328. In the last report, the MMC adopted an RAB slightly different to that reported in the BAA report and accounts as a way of removing some of the discontinuities and subjectivity of any company's accounts.

86

2.329. BAA claimed that the CAA adopted a method of valuation of the RAB inconsistent with the previous report and the CAA comments when setting the current charges. Its comments included treatment of depreciation (use by the CAA of actual depreciation charge in the accounts rather than that projected for the airports when the value of X was set), and value of asset disposals (use by the CAA of market rather than book values).

2.330. As we discuss further in Chapter 10, the advantage of using actual depreciation is that it treats capex and depreciation in a consistent manner—RAB is rolled forward for actual capex and actual depreciation—avoiding the CAA method's implicit over- or under-depreciation of assets in the RAB leading to effects after the expiry of the asset's life. We have also noted above, however, the difference in depreciation profile of the additional non-T5 projects carried out in Q3 instead of T5. Given that depreciation can be affected by the particular investment undertaken, there would seem a strong case to take actual depreciation costs into account.

2.331. As also noted in paragraph 10.19, the advantage of using projected depreciation, on the other hand, is that it reduces the company's incentive to exaggerate depreciation before price controls are set (though, in practice BAA has, up to now, tended to understate rather than overstate depreciation). It also removes the need, when rolling forward the RAB, for the actual depreciation charge to be adjusted for any accounting changes since the previous review—but it should be open to the regulator to adjust for such charges if it is thought appropriate to do so.

2.332. More generally, it is possible to identify various incentives affecting the regulated company arising from the depreciation regime. Use of projected depreciation reduces the disincentive to carry out additional non-revenue-earning capex over and above that included in the projection, since the company would not recover return and depreciation on it. Use of projected depreciation may also give more incentive to inefficiently substitute higher cost short-life capex for long-life capex. However, use of actual depreciation gives a stronger incentive to achieve capex efficiencies, but also a stronger incentive to delay capex or even not carry it out at all.

2.333. There are, therefore, arguments for and against either approach, and over the longer term there would be little difference from adopting one or the other. But it is important that the treatment of depreciation in rolling forward assets is consistent with the assumptions made when the price cap is set. In our previous report there was no suggestion that actual depreciation would not be used, and given the desirability of regulatory consistency, we believe there are insufficient reasons to change this approach. But at the least, if the CAA believes an alternative approach should be adopted five years hence in relation to Q4, it would need to consult widely, and if necessary incorporate the results into the annual calculation of RCV.

2.334. On accounting for disposals, the alternatives are to roll forward the RAB subtracting either the net book value (NBV) or the proceeds of disposals. In the 1996 report, the MMC rolled forward from 1991 for the proceeds of disposals and this was also the basis of the MMC's projections for 1996/97 to 2002/03. This suggests the roll forward from March 1995 to March 2003 should also be on the basis of disposal proceeds. BAA's objections to using disposal proceeds related to what happens when an asset with positive NBV is written off with no proceeds from the disposal. The asset would stop being depreciated and BAA would not recover the remaining NBV via the depreciation allowance in required revenue; the RAB would however be higher (by an amount equal to the remaining NBV of the disposed asset) than it otherwise would have been and hence return on the RAB (in £ million) would be higher in perpetuity. However, BAA would have to wait into the indefinite future to fully recover the NBV of the disposed-of asset which it would prefer to recover immediately. The CAA argued (see paragraph 16.12 of submission) that the BAA proposed treatment gives an incentive to 'cherry pick' assets for disposal: the company would gain every time it disposed of an asset for more than NBV.

2.335. In our projections, the treatment of disposals makes almost no difference to the value of X. This suggests that BAA's point is of little practical significance, at least over the next ten years, and that RAB should be rolled forward for disposal proceeds as proposed by the CAA rather than NBV, consistent with our past practice and with practice in other regulated sectors.

2.336. We consider BAA's approach to the RCV in paragraphs 10.23 and 10.24. We note that BAA based its projections of the RCV on the NBV of fixed assets plus working capital (its projected 31 March 2003 working capital was slightly negative, as trade creditors was projected to exceed trade debtors plus stocks). But the NBV of fixed assets in March 1995 (£3,667 million) was different from the RCV in the MMC report, namely £3,390 million. The MMC report was clear on the methodology used (see paragraph 2.153) and the consequent value of the RAB at 31 March 1995 was clearly shown in Table 10.6 and Appendix 10.3 of the 1996 report. This has also been used by the CAA in its calculations. BAA thinking appears to assume that the RAB should be equal to the value of the assets in its accounts. This was not the approach taken by the MMC in 1996: the MMC took what it regarded as the implicit 1991 regulatory value of the business and rolled it forward for net new investment up to March 1995 (noting also that this was somewhat greater than the value implied by rolling forward the market capitalization at the end of the first day's trading after privatization). There seems no reason to now adopt a different figure: to do so would give rise to considerable regulatory uncertainty. With regard to working capital, our view is that the RCV established by the MMC reflected working capital at that time and that there is no evidence of significant change since then in working capital relevant to the business (stocks and net trade debtors). With regard to the future, BAA said that, in order for the RCV roll forward to be clear and unambiguous, it would be preferable for change in working capital to be excluded. We agree, and have excluded changes in working capital from the RCV roll forward.

Investment

2.337. The RCV currently amounts to some £6 billion for the three BAA airports; capex over Q4 is currently projected to amount to £5 billion at 2002 prices (over 80 per cent of which is at Heathrow, in particular T5 the costs of which are almost £3 billion) leading to a significant increase in RAB. Expenditure of £2.4 billion is forecast for Q5. The size of the investment programme over Q3 and Q4 together has increased by about 20 per cent primarily due to increases in the cost of T5, although passenger numbers have increased by about 10 per cent.

2.338. We discuss capex in Chapter 9. The CAA commended BAA for following best practice through its framework agreements and new forms of contract with contractors, often referred to as partnering. These arrangements, rather than being fixed costs, share rewards of any cost reduction with the contractors, and provide no profit margin on any costs greater than expected: they do therefore expose BAA to greater risk of increased costs. BAA believes this approach is appropriate given the advantages of such a form of contracting, namely to produce greater cooperation with contractors, whose experience of working on airport projects would enable them to do so again at lower costs by introducing innovative methodologies, and believes this will help to avoid some of the significant cost increases that have occurred on other large projects. The approach has worked well on relatively small projects (such as the Stansted terminal extension), but BAA acknowledged that it has yet to be fully tested on a major project such as T5. Our own consultants, however, (see Chapter 9) were concerned that almost exclusive reliance on framework agreements rather than competitive tendering could increase the risk of cost overruns but, in our view, it is an approach which has worked well to date, one which is being adopted elsewhere in the construction industry, and seems sensible given the nature of the airport business.

2.339. BAA cannot, however, assume that any increases in the cost of T5 will be passed on in the next review. It therefore has in our view every incentive to make its approach work effectively.

2.340. Some airlines were also concerned about T5 costs. BA, for example, believed a £2.7 billion cost may be reasonable, but the £3.1 billion quoted now was not. It also criticized contingencies of 20 per cent, and the costs of the baggage tunnel which were to be reimbursed by BA or a third party when fully operational, rather than financed out of airport charges. bmi (which would not be accommodated in T5) referred to the design of T5—which it estimated accounts for the majority of the projected increase in its charges from BAA—as 'not economic for airlines'. It said that it had not been consulted on T5, and that T5 details have not, aside from connectivity, yet been discussed with most airlines but should be reviewed before commitments were made. Costings were based on specifications only agreed between BA and BAA—and had risen substantially. BAA accepted the suggestion by our consultants of a peer group review to review the costs of T5; we welcome this. It is important that any cost review be carried out by a company independent of any contractors involved in the project.

2.341. Our consultants were also critical that the benchmarking studies carried out on T5 costs were not adequate, although this partly reflects the unique scale and characteristics of the projects involved. BAA believed its benchmarking of T5 was the best that comparator data would allow. Our consultants were also concerned that BAA appeared to make allowances for contingencies at several levels, which in aggregate could lead to double counting and be excessive. BAA believed that its contingencies were prudent given project risks (for example, delay, externally imposed changes in requirements, supplier performance, wages and other costs, direct action, fraud/theft).

2.342. More generally, many airlines said they had insufficient information to comment adequately on BAA's capex programme: an issue to which we return below. However, there was as much concern about the scale of expenditure being too little, as concerns about project costs being too great. Views on specific projects varied. BA wished for greater expenditure on connectivity (in particular for a TTS between T5 and the CTA, presented in the CIP as a possible 'additional investment') and less on redeveloping the CTA. Others objected to any further expenditure on connectivity (depending also on the cost to be allowed for in airport charges) but argued that the CTA should be brought up to T5 standards before T5 opens to prevent competitive disadvantage (without which, some suggested, differential fees should apply). Similarly, some questioned BAA's intention to develop Gatwick to 40 mppa—but others supported this.

2.343. Even if there is scope for lower costs on some projects, there is in our view likely to be demand for any cost savings to be spent on additional projects. It would not, therefore, be appropriate for us to base charges on a lower level of expenditure. Expenditure on T5 in Q4, and possibly total expenditure, would, however, be less if there were any slippage in the project.

2.344. Hence, uncertainty as to the timing of that expenditure should in our view be recognized in the 'triggers' relating airport charges to progress of the project to which we referred in paragraph 2.266. Once agreed, they would give BAA a strong incentive to complete T5 quickly. BAA suggested that for a project to be suitable as triggers for charging increases, its scope would need to be financially significant; the scope would need to have been already established together with some confidence over programme timing; the projects would need to be supported by the airline community as a whole and providing aeronautical outputs; and the airport concerned would need to be one where charging was based around the maximum cap rather than the market (ie not Stansted).

2.345. BAA initially believed only T5 fulfilled these criteria, and proposed four triggers:

(a) completion of diversion of twin rivers 2004/05;

(b) early release stands (ERS) completion, same year;

(c) visual control room (VCR) handed over to NATS 2005/06; and

(d) core terminal building weather proof 2006/07.

The opening of T5, which appears to be an obvious trigger, is more likely to be in Q5: hence its current omission from the list. Failure to meet any trigger would reduce the value of X by 2 (per trigger): when the trigger was met, charges would return to the original trajectory (ie if a one-year delay, X would be 2 above the value set for the following year to get back on trend).

2.346.   BA made a number of further suggestions to us:

(a) BAA should commit ERS to T5 when T5 opens. BAA argued that although those stands would be primarily used for T5, it was desirable to maintain flexibility in their use, an argument we accept.

(b) Commitment of NATS to use VCR. BAA argued this was unnecessary: the VCR had to be used when T5 opened, NATS would wish to occupy it earlier than that, and NATS would also be charged rent, which would provide an incentive to make the best use of it. We accept BAA's arguments.

(c) Satellite 1 also weather proof. BAA argued that if there were unexpected shocks—financial, regulatory or traffic—this was the one aspect of Phase 1 of T5 it may wish to delay. However, its development on schedule is of importance to airlines, while the savings to BAA from delay could be substantial: we believe this should represent a further trigger.

(d) No twin river trigger. BAA said that if airlines did not want this trigger, it would drop it; however, it was the earliest of the triggers, important to the completion of the project, and we see no reason to drop it.

(e) Availability of T5 baggage system for testing by end of 2006/07; passenger TTS available for testing by end 2006/07. BAA regarded these dates as earlier than necessary, but also that there would be little point to a trigger in 2007/08 since this could be taken into account in the next review. In our view, it is likely to be necessary for these facilities to be available for testing in 2007/08, but agree it is more appropriate to regard availability for testing in that year, for introduction the subsequent year, as a matter to be taken into account by our successors in the next review.

(f) A minimum of 41 operational stands to be operational on day one of T5 opening, for which they would need to be built and commissioned by the end of 2007. BAA argued that this was more a Q5 issue and for the next review. We accept this is more a matter for Q5, to be taken into account in the next review.

(g) Acquisition of residual T5 site 2006/07. BAA argued that such a requirement would weaken its negotiating position for acquisition of that site, which we accept.

(h) Gatwick Pier 6 in operation 2004/05. BAA itself subsequently proposed the opening of Pier 6 as a trigger (but with an effect on X of 1 rather than 2 for other triggers), but in 2005/06, BAA believing it was not feasible for it to open earlier. We regard 2005/06 as an adequate date for this purpose.

2.347.   We acknowledge that the effect of the T5 triggers, about 2 per cent of charges for each trigger not met (1 per cent for Pier 6 at Gatwick), could prove significantly less than the cost savings of protracted delay to T5 as a whole. A higher value could, however, significantly increase BAA's risks: only a small delay in meeting a trigger could affect charges by up to a year, even if there was little reduction in value of expenditure. On the other hand, we also believe that to reduce charges for a whole year if a trigger is not met could be unreasonable, imposing more penalty on BAA than the effects of any shorter delay would justify. We therefore propose the triggers should apply on a monthly basis and, in order to do so, retro-spectively, ie the charges set for a particular year should take into account whether or not the above triggers have been met in the previous year, the number of months or part of any month for which they were not met, and the appropriate adjustment to be applied. We also accept there is sufficient uncertainty in projects other than T5 and Gatwick Pier 6 to enable such an approach to be more widely adopted. We therefore recommend the adoption of BAA's proposals, but modified to include T5 Satellite 1 and Gatwick Pier 6 as noted above and the monthly rather than annual triggers we have proposed. It would be for the CAA, maybe in conjunction with independent consultants, to finalize the specification of these triggers and confirm whether or not they are met.

Operating expenditure

2.348.   We discuss opex in Chapter 7. We note that the CAA did not undertake an in-depth review of operating efficiencies, believing BAA's projections did not look unreasonable, and that it did not see value in attempting to disallow forward projections of operating cost, particularly where prices were, and would continue to be, well below market-clearing levels and LRIC. We do not share this view, but believe it important that prices to users should reflect an efficient level of cost. We acknowledge, however, the difficulty in assessing what a reasonable level of costs would be, particularly in benchmarking performance against other airports, given the wide range of factors that affect cost.

2.349.   We did, however, see a number of grounds for concern as to BAA's approach to productivity. BAA was unable to give us data, whether on earnings, overtime working, or absence, which was broken down as between manual workers and non-manual workers. Since the major published data on these matters distinguishes between elements of the workforce in this way it seems evident that BAA does not seek to benchmark its own performance against these published sources. Our concern is that this may be indicative of an attitude within BAA that it does not need to undertake such benchmarking.

2.350.   The average basic pay of BAA employees (ie excluding shift pay and overtime) is about 20 per cent higher than the average of all employees in the areas in which they operate. We also noted that BAA is projecting increases in salaries per employee at some 1.5 per cent a year. BAA told us that it had previously restrained pay growth, for example by offering lower rates to new employees, but it was now experiencing difficulty in recruiting the right quality of staff for functions such as security, and there was no scope for below-average increases. We have no objection to such an assumption of real pay increases as long as it is financed by real productivity increases.

2.351.   We also noted that the productivity trends targeted by BAA appear considerably less challenging than previous performance at the airports—see Table 2.15—and appear primarily to result from increase in passengers rather than improved methods of delivery per se. As shown in Table 2.15, growth in passengers per employee at Heathrow between 1995/96 to 2000/01 at 4.8 per cent was above passenger growth of 3.2 per cent; for Q4 it is projected to be below passenger growth (1.3 per cent compared with 1.9 per cent). At Gatwick, growth in passengers per employee in the five years to 2000/01 was below passenger growth: over the seven years to 2007/08 it is projected to be about the same as passenger growth. At Stansted, growth in passenger per employee was about three-quarters of passenger growth in the five years to 2000/01; it is projected to be one-half of passenger growth after over the seven years from 2000/01.

TABLE 2.15 **Trends in productivity and passengers**

	1995/96	2000/01	Percentage change pa 1995/6– 2000/01	2007/08	Percentage change pa* 2002/03– 2007/08
Passengers					
HAL	54.8	64.3	3.2	70.7	1.9
GAL	23.0	32.1	6.9	39.7	4.3
STAL	4.1	12.3	24.6	20.5	10.8
Total	81.9	108.7	5.8	130.9	3.8
Passengers/man-year					
HAL	13.9	17.6	4.8	18.8	1.3
GAL	13.5	16.9	4.6	20.8	4.2
STAL	7.0	16.3	18.4	21.1	5.3
Total	13.1	17.2	5.6	19.7	2.8

Source: CC study.

*Given the exceptional downturn in traffic in 2001/02, it is not appropriate to base our analysis on 2001/02 figures: we have therefore assumed passengers per man-year are the same in 2002/03 as in 2000/01. The results of our analysis would be the same (all figures being changed by broadly the same proportion) if we based the annual percentage change on the seven years from 2000/01.

2.352. BAA argued that traffic growth was a main determinant of increase in passengers per employee—hence, with the expected slowdown of growth, there would be less scope for increase in passengers per employee. Scope for productivity improvements was limited by the requirements for security and safety imposed on BAA, but BAA believed that projected productivity improvements were nonetheless significant and further improvements could not be made without putting standards of service at risk, particularly at Heathrow where more staff were necessary to handle the congestion that would arise as passenger numbers grow before the opening of T5. As we note in paragraph 7.116, we also analysed BAA's recent and forecast levels of passenger growth and productivity in terms of passengers per man-year applying varying elasticities to the data: the calculation showed that future productivity increases predicted by BAA at Heathrow and Stansted are significantly less than those achieved in Q3 regardless of what elasticities are used. At Gatwick productivity increases are projected to be marginally better, once the figures are adjusted for the effect of passenger growth. We acknowledge these results reflect a range of factors: elasticities may well vary over time, in particular the recent very high growth in passengers per man-year at Stansted reflect the under-utilization of capacity at the beginning of Q3 and the subsequent ability to increase passengers with very little increase in manpower. This may no longer apply. We also acknowledge pressure on capacity and the need to maintain quality of service at Heathrow, and the need to increase staffing at the end of Q4 for the eventual opening of T5. Our view of the scope for productivity improvement also, however, depends on other aspects of BAA's approach to manpower planning.

2.353. In our report in 1992 we were critical of, among other things, the extent to which the delegation to departmental level of manpower management issues within BAA had resulted in a marked absence of standardized approaches either to productivity improvement or to the examination of absolute productivity levels. We expressed concern that there was no use made of work measurement or other techniques for evaluating performance, nor any regular basis for reviewing productivity indices. During the current inquiry, BAA said that such developments were delayed by the need to concentrate IT resources on Y2K issues, but they were about to be introduced, and were allowed for in the productivity projections.

2.354. During the current reference BAA also told us that it had come to the end of being able to make 'easy' productivity gains, and yet it indicated that it was not in favour of developing techniques for measuring the efficiency of different groups of employees on the basis that it had done well enough in the past without them. We believe that these two statements are not reconcilable. We are doubtful about the productivity assumptions which BAA has put into its manpower model. Moreover, although we were reassured in previous inquiries that no restrictive labour practices existed, BAA is only now making increased use of its informal right to move staff between terminals, and there is not a lot of resistance to this. BAA said that it was only circumspect about moving staff between terminals for purely pragmatic reasons (for example, the time wasted in doing so).

2.355. We hope that any future review of BAA's manpower costs and efficiency will be informed by detailed information about the productivity of the main groups of employees, based on suitable yardsticks, and that these same yardsticks can be related to estimates of future workloads in a way which allows BAA to demonstrate to the CC that its manpower projections are justified.

2.356. We also noted that absence in BAA is running at high levels, which, to an extent, BAA accepted and believed reflected the high stress levels particularly on security staff: it hoped to reduce such absence. However, the company was unable to supply us with dis-aggregated data, as indicated above, but eventually argued that some 80 per cent of its employees were in functions—security, engineering, terminal operations and airfield oper-ations—which consisted almost wholly of manual workers, and that therefore its whole workforce should be compared with the data for manuals in the Confederation of British Industry (CBI) absence survey. We do not believe it appropriate to compare BAA figures, comprising both manual and non-manual staff, with figures for manual workers alone elsewhere.

2.357. BAA also argued that its absence levels should be compared with those in the transport and communications sector, and said that on this basis BAA's performance was satisfactory. The CBI report noted that within the private sector the transport and com-munication sector had the highest absence rate, and that looking back over recent years, the transport and communications sector had been one of the worst performing sectors. We do not think that that record should leave room for complacency within BAA, which describes itself as a world-class company. We think that such a company would be distinctly concerned to reduce substantially the levels of absence which it is experiencing. If BAA reduced overtime to a realistic benchmark figure of ten days a year (a weighted average reduction of 2.9 days for each employee), the saving would be just over 1 per cent of the total wage bill.

2.358. We noted in paragraph 7.77 that almost 10 per cent of all hours worked in BAA were overtime hours—a workforce of 5,774 employees was working 573 man-years of over-time. Since this would attract payments of at least time-and-a-half of basic rates of pay, it is the equivalent of BAA employing a further 810 staff. We noted that overtime working at this level is built into manpower plans at the airports, and that the absolute level of overtime working had remained broadly constant over the past five years. We believe and BAA has confirmed that there is scope for reducing overtime through better rostering arrangements. We believe that future reduction of costs may be achieved by the adoption of greater control of overtime.

2.359. We also noted BAA had a central contingency cost, to allow for the probability that managers would not be able to meet the stringent targets set for them. We do not accept this is reasonable if targets are to be both challenging and achievable.

2.360. We do therefore see some grounds for concern as to whether BAA's financial projections are based on sufficiently demanding productivity targets and cost constraints. We have therefore considered the implications in our financial projections, first, for a 1 per cent saving in labour costs for improved absence. As to productivity, the statistical evidence of reduction in productivity improvements to which we referred in paragraph 2.352 is in our view reinforced by the evidence of scope to improve BAA's manpower planning. We have, however, acknowledged that, as well as the effects of slower growth in numbers of passengers, there are other factors which may lead to slower growth in productivity in Q4 than in Q3, hence do not believe it appropriate to assume the full scope for improved productivity that the figures based on the elasticity analysis in Appendix 7.6 would suggest. We have, however, examined the sensitivity of financial projections to an assumption of 1.5 per cent a year additional productivity improvement at Heathrow and Stansted plus 1 per cent savings in staff cost from lower absences, but, in our recommendations acknowledge the uncertainty of this judgement.

Pension costs

2.361. We have also noted that during Q3, BAA was able to take a pension holiday due to general increases in share prices; before that, the cost of pensions was about 14 per cent of pensionable pay, and had been assumed to remain at that level in Q3. The evidence we saw in the current inquiry showed that a surplus on past service had increased significantly, from 118 per cent of liabilities in 1992 to 142 per cent in September 1995 (the valuation for 1995 being available in 1996) and 150 per cent of liabilities in 1996. This was due in part to out-performance compared with share prices generally and most other schemes. (From 1992 to 1996, for example, the average annual benchmark return had increased by some 15 per cent, return to the fund by 18 per cent, ie an outperformance of 3 per cent a year in that period.) A pension holiday was declared from 1 April 1997, the start of Q3, with a view to eliminate the surplus by 2014.

2.362. The extent of the surplus subsequently varied between 126 and 142 per cent of liabilities until 2001, despite increases in benefits and liabilities in that period (BAA told us the increase in benefits had been a factor reducing wage settlements in Q3). BAA also said that the superior level of benefits compared with other schemes partly explained the differences between the 22 per cent assumed contribution requirement were there no surplus, and the average 15 per cent contribution of other schemes. BAA had told us that the recent surpluses reflected out-performance in the late 1990s—but this was not consistent with the data supplied: performance of the scheme was slightly below the average of other schemes in Q3 (an annual increase of 7.9 per cent compared with medium average performance of 8.1 per cent). With recent movements in share prices, however, the estimated value of the surplus was very low by the end of our inquiry—an asset value of 103 per cent of liabilities in 2002 estimated on a spot basis (although the full valuation would be on a three-year moving average basis). Between 1997/98 and 2000/01, BAA included a charge in the airport accounts for pensions of about 3 per cent of salary cost but this rose to 18 per cent in 2001/02 although no actual contributions to the main scheme were made.

2.363. BAA's forecasts (prepared before the recent preliminary valuation) included a pension cost to each airport of 9 per cent—the amount it judged necessary on the basis of the previous valuation of the surplus, but which it said could well increase given recent falls in share prices. However, there was a further centralized cost projected of 13 per cent, giving 22 per cent of pensionable pay overall, the amount it believed would be required if there were no surplus. On the basis of its 2002 estimates of the value of its remaining surplus, a contribution of 19.3 per cent would be needed. It acknowledged this would be a high level of contributions, but said this reflected the benefits given, and the characteristics of its employee base. As noted in Chapter 14, it argued that to reduce projected pension costs for the amount of the surplus would be expropriating the gains of it outperforming other schemes, and lead it to change the basis of its pensions policy.

2.364. We noted, however, that the funding level of the scheme was at its highest—150 per cent—at the time of the previous review (although the formal valuation was not carried out until the autumn of 1996). Despite the surplus (which on the basis of information supplied to us we believe was evident to BAA during that review) BAA, ourselves and the CAA assumed contributions would continue—it is a matter of serious concern to us that this situation should have arisen. The current projection of a required contribution of 19 per cent partly results from that pension holiday, without which a contribution of only about 15.4 per cent would be needed. Hence, charges in Q3 allowed for payments that were not paid; to have higher charges than would otherwise be necessary in Q4 because of contributions allowed for in charges but not made in Q3, would represent in effect a double charging of airlines for that element of pension cost. If that element of pension costs is excluded, then the appropriate level to be included in the financial projections is 15.4 per cent, which we have taken into account in our modelling below.

Commercial revenues

2.365. The study of BAA's commercial revenues by our consultants is at Appendix 8.1. They broadly supported BAA's approach to its commercial activities, although some of their comments would merit consideration by BAA to improve its performance further (although others we do not necessarily accept). BAA assumes a decline in some of the main commercial revenues per passenger, consistent with past trend (over and above the effect of loss of intra-EC duty- and tax-free sales). In Q4, commercial revenues proved worse than expected: we have seen no evidence to suggest we should adopt a different assumption to that of BAA.

2.366. We did, however, note that, since our last report, the operation of tax- and duty-free sales at the three airports has been operated by WDFE, a subsidiary of BAA, rather than by independent concessionaires. BAA told us this was necessary given the declining number of independent operators able to carry out this business, particularly with the end of intra-EC tax- and duty-free sales. It would be surprising, however, if there were no other serious bidders for what appears to be a substantial and profitable operation. The current concessions have been given for about ten years. BAA told us that it had not, and did not, intend to tender the operation of tax- and duty-free sales, but did monitor the terms in comparison with those previously obtained from independent concessionaires. There is also a code of conduct to ensure arms-length relations between BAA and WDFE. We noted, however, the increasing profits of WDFE at the London airports—some £18 million of profits in 2001/02 (after allocation of central costs), a return on capital employed of over 50 per cent, and a significant increase over the last four years from some £7 million in 1999. There has been some change in terms between BAA and WDFE, but this is also not unusual in arrangements between BAA and independent concessionaires.

2.367. To have such a concession operated by a subsidiary of BAA and in the absence of competitive tendering, gives rise to a number of concerns. First, transfer prices could be established such as to redistribute the profit from such services from BAA to WDFE. But second, it is not possible to judge in the absence of competitive tendering whether the current level of profits of WDFE is more or less than an independent concessionaire could have expected to earn, nor whether concession payments by WDFE to BAA are more or less than would otherwise have been the case. Over a concession of such length independent concession-aires may also have been expected to retain at least some of the benefits of any better than expected performance. WDFE return on capital is now high, but we accept, as BAA argued, that book value of capital may not necessarily be the most appropriate measure of capital for such a retail business. BAA argued that return on turnover is comparable with other retail businesses: but since WDFE does not own its retail outlets, this may also, in our view, not be a valid comparator. Comparisons with previous margins of concessionaires may also be inappropriate, given the effect on margins of loss of intra-EC taxes and duty-free sales; but comparison with other concessions, or similar concessions in other airports is also difficult given the different circumstances of other such operations. The adequacy of transfer prices can therefore only be judged by competitive tendering. A further concern is the absence of competition between outlets selling duty-free products.

2.368. We considered, therefore, and raised with BAA, whether an element of profit of WDFE should be included in the single till. However, there is insufficient evidence currently to justify doing so, and we also accept that to extend the scope of the single till to include the operation of the concessions, rather than merely BAA's rental income from them, would itself be undesirable. We believe, however, it is important that BAA takes measures to improve transparency of these arrangements to the CAA—including the profitability of WDFE operations at the airport, its relative performance and any further changes in terms during Q4—to ensure BAA receives no less favourable terms from WDFE than if the concession had been tendered. But we would also expect the concessions when renewed to be subject to competitive tendering, some of which would be before the next review. (BAA itself indeed offered an undertaking on competitive tendering.) To ensure the process of competitive tendering is adequate, it should in our view be conducted in such a way as to attract competition from a number of bidders, for a shorter period than the current ten years, and with independent monitoring and auditing of the tendering process. If there has not been satisfactory progress by the time of the next review, it may prove necessary for our successors to reconsider the treatment of WDFE, either its inclusion in the single till, or whether its operation and ownership by BAA give rise to public interest issues. The CAA should also be alert to any extension of BAA's ownership of other concessionaires, to ensure that the considerations noted above are addressed.

Other financial variables

2.369. Consideration is also necessary of other financial variables. BAA's medium- to long-term regulatory forecasts of June 2002, based on RPI+2 in Q4 (as indicated in our last report as a possible price control for Q4) and RPI thereafter, project return on capital value in Q4 declining from 6.9 to 5.1 per cent (below the 6.7 per cent (after smoothing) put forward in the last report). It also projected interest cover of [✂] by the end of Q4, but below [✂] by 2008/09 and for the rest of Q4, compared with covenant requirements of 2; and gearing (debt: equity) of [✂] per cent by 2007/08 rising to over [✂] per cent by the end of Q5. The decline in interest cover was regarded as more serious by putting its covenants and investment grade credit rating at risk. Such projections take no account of a possible share issue; we acknowledge, however, that such an option should be held in reserve for expenditure on any new runway, or should there be any further major disruption to the civil aviation industry.

Financial modelling

2.370. Our financial modelling of the relationship between airport charges and the rate of return for the airport is based on the general approach and the assumptions of the key inputs set out above.

2.371. We referred above to the CAA's own financial projections, based on its preferred price path, initially of RPI+6 at Heathrow, slightly higher at Stansted and slightly lower increases at Gatwick, but with the claim that BAA could not fully recover the permitted charges at Stansted. Its pricing proposals then implied an extremely large rise in prices, of 30 per cent, at Heathrow when T5 opens, partly due to the dual-till approach adopted by the CAA for Q5 and thereafter, but also including recovery of the difference between the single-till and dual-till approach in Q4.

2.372. We have noted airlines' understandable arguments that repayment for capex underspend and revenue advancement in Q3 should be in Q4 rather than incorporated in the asset base and spread into the future. In paragraph 2.260 we accepted the principle that revenue advancement and underinvestment in Q3 should be recovered in Q4, as our approach does.

2.373. It is also, however, necessary to consider whether we should recommend a maximum level of airport charges on the basis only of Q4, or of a longer period, for example Q4 plus Q5, or the CAA's approach of equity return to the cost of capital over 25 years. BAA supported continuing with a ten-year rather than five-year analysis. It said it was strongly against significant oscillations in inter-quinquennial charges levels, and believed a strong price signal was needed in particular for T5 so current users started to pay earlier in Q4 for the costs of a terminal expansion which the airline community has been requesting. It also believed that was necessary for the financing of T5: we noted above its reference to the Hong Kong experience where, it claimed, it was not possible once the new airport opened to bring about the increases in charges necessary to recover the cost of the investment.

2.374. In our view, to attempt to recover a rate of return equivalent to the cost of capital in each quinquennium could imply significant variation in charges between quinquennia at Heathrow, where the impact of T5 on charges is considerable; return on new investment would depend on future large step increases in prices which BAA cannot have full confidence would occur, increasing the risk to BAA and tending to deter investment. The CAA's approach, on the other hand, based on NPV of future revenues over a 20-year period, makes charges in any one quinquennium largely a matter of choice and increases uncertainty as to the view taken in future quinquennial reviews. We believe it is appropriate therefore to allow a rate of return equivalent to the cost of capital over Q4 and Q5 together at Heathrow, by smoothing or advancing revenues between quinquennia and we make our recommendations for Q4 on that basis; it will of course be for our successors to decide on the appropriate approach for Q5. But the full recovery for airlines in Q4 of revenue advancement and such adjustment for under-investment in Q3 as we believe appropriate for Heathrow should give some comfort in the CC's approach to regulatory consistency. At Gatwick, there is no equivalent major investment, and no need to smooth changes between quinquennia; we therefore base our recommendation for Gatwick on the charges appropriate to earn the cost of capital in Q4 and Q5 separately.

2.375. Profiling of return within quinquennia may also be necessary if particular values of X would result in inadequate values of other financial ratios in any year. This is not the case in either quinquennium on the basis of our projections below, but could be necessary in Q5 if, at the time of the next review, BAA's financial ratios in any one year prove worse than expected.

2.376. Our projections have therefore been based on a constant value of X for HAL throughout Q4 and Q5, a value of X for Gatwick that varies between the two quinquennia, and a price cap for Stansted based on current charges gross of marketing costs, such that the three airports together achieve a 7.75 per cent rate of return (equivalent to cost of capital) over ten years: in practice, however, they also each achieve that rate of return. (Since revenue advancement from Q4 to Q3 was intended to provide return higher than cost of capital in Q3, and below cost of capital in Q4 it is the returns after crediting BAA with recovery of revenue advancement and under-investment in Q3, which are equated to the cost of capital. BAA returns in Q4 before credit of these amounts are between 1 and 1.5 per cent less than the figures quoted below.) These projections also assume:

(a) BAA's assumption on operating costs, except we have not allowed the central contingency cost and assumed only 19.3 per cent pension contribution, and marketing support has been excluded from Stansted operating cost but treated as an airport charges discount (therefore with no effect on the estimated rates of return);

(b) BAA's assumption on capex (including BAA's assessment of additional capex at Stansted for the higher passenger forecast we have used) (we have not allowed for any expenditure on a new runway since this is subject to future government decision and would need to be remunerated separately);

(c) passenger forecasts as shown in Table 2.12;

(d) initial RAB of £6,013 million, after allowing for centrally capitalized costs, with £46 million clawback for under-investment in Q3, and £348 million for revenue advancement, both annuitized over Q4 and all allocated to Heathrow. The value of

clawback is based on offsetting additional capex only at Heathrow against underspend on T5;

(e) cargo flights excluded from the cap (but the revenue separately included in the projections); Heathrow transfer infrastructure covered by the transfer system charge (TSC) is included, as are additional security costs in 2002/03 on the assumption of no S claim in this year; and

(f) Stansted yield converges towards that of Gatwick.

2.377. We acknowledged above, however, the uncertainty as to two aspects of opex: the allowance for savings from higher productivity and lower absence levels than assumed by BAA; and pension contributions. With no allowance for these factors, a formula of RPI+6.8 would be appropriate at Heathrow and RPI+0.22 at Gatwick. With an allowance for 1.5 per cent a year additional productivity savings at HAL and STAL, 1 per cent reduction in manpower costs at all three airports for lower absences, and an assumed pension contribution rate of 15.4 per cent—which still allows for a level of benefits above the average of such schemes, itself a factor in encouraging additional productivity—these formulae would be reduced to RPI+6.22 at Heathrow and RPI–0.17 at Gatwick. Given the uncertainty of those adjustments, we have chosen assumptions which incorporate two-thirds of the productivity and pension adjustments and give RPI+6.50 at Heathrow and RPI+0 at Gatwick. The price cap at Stansted would not necessarily be affected, being based on £4.20 throughout, the current level of charges gross of marketing costs (but, as noted above, with an assumption that the net yield at Stansted is lower, but increasing towards £4.20 in Q5).

2.378. Projections consistent with that preferred approach are shown in Table 2.16.

TABLE 2.16 **Financial projections**

	2002/ 03	2003/ 04*	2004/ 05	2005/ 06	2006/ 07	2007/ 08	Average Q4	2012/ 13	Average Q5
Heathrow									
X (in RPI+X)			6.50	6.50	6.50	6.50	6.50	6.50	6.50
Revenue yield (£)	5.78	6.12	6.50	6.92	7.36	7.82		10.64	
Adjusted return on RAB (%)†‡		10.44	9.39	8.48	8.03	7.63	9.16	7.62	6.28
Gatwick									
X (in RPI+X)			0.00	0.00	0.00	0.00	0.00	1.80	1.80
Revenue yield (£)	4.08	4.08	4.08	4.08	4.08	4.08		4.45	
Return on RAB (%)		6.26	7.23	7.95	8.36	7.68	7.75	7.81	7.75
Stansted									
X (in RPI+X)§			0.00	0.00	0.00	0.00	0.00	0.00	0.00
Revenue yield (£)¶	2.99	3.15	3.32	3.50	3.69	3.89		4.40	
Return on RAB (%)		5.58	6.64	6.44	6.84	7.38	6.78	9.66	8.94
Total BAA									
Adjusted return on RAB (%)‡		9.04	8.69	8.17	7.95	7.61	8.65	7.86	6.76
Debt/equity (%)				Figures omitted.					
HCA interest cover				See note on page iv.					

Source: CC study.

*Heathrow and Gatwick revenue yield in 2003/04 was set so that the cost of capital was earned exactly over the ten-year period (see paragraph 10.39). The implied 2003/04 X for Heathrow is 5.9 and for Gatwick is –0.1.

†Revenue less capex less depreciation as per cent of opening and closing RCV. Reflects significant drop in 2008/09 when T5 opens, then increase.

‡Revenue reflects credit for recovery of revenue advancement and clawback of capex underspend in Q3: see paragraph 2.376.

§Current price cap £5.28: but £4.20 assumed unchanged until 2008/09, then same as Gatwick.

¶Revenue yield.

2.379. Formulae of RPI+6.50 at Heathrow over ten years and RPI+0 at Gatwick over Q4 and RPI+1.80 in Q5 result in a rate of return in Q4 of the three airports together above the cost of capital (8.65 per cent), and in Q5 below the cost of capital (6.76 per cent), but equivalent to the cost of capital over the ten years as a whole. As noted in paragraph 2.310, we have based STAL's cap on its current yield gross of marketing expenditure of £4.20 with the expectation it will converge towards those of GAL, but, for the purposes of the projections, STAL is assumed to remain below the cap throughout Q4. On this basis, all airports earn almost exactly their cost of capital over Q4 and Q5 together. If STAL was able to recover up to the level of its cap sooner, return on the three airports would be slightly above BAA's cost of capital, but we do not believe an adjustment for this is necessary, nor would it be should STAL's charges and BAA's return prove lower than assumed.

2.380. As to other financial variables, in the base case interest cover remains above [✂] throughout Q4, but falls to [✂] in 2008/09, then increasing for the remainder of Q5.

2.381. We noted in Chapter 12 BA's arguments that increases in charges were not necessary for growth in capex; and indeed that there should be decline in charges in Q4. On the first of these arguments, BA compared investment and passenger numbers over the ten years from our previous report and the ten years from now; on that basis increase in investment was less than the increase in passengers between the two reports. Investment, however, is only one factor relevant to determining the maximum level of charges. It is also necessary to allow, for example, for the increased depreciation on recent investments compared with T5, and the lower than expected commercial revenues BAA has earned since our last report. BA's suggestion of a decline in charges in Q4 is also based on full recovery of £200 million under-investment (a figure we believe too high) and revenue advancement in Q4; a rate of return in Q4 based on a lower cost of capital than we believe appropriate (before such recovery) and for Heathrow and Gatwick regulated separately; and no smoothing between Q4 and Q5. It would subsequently require a very substantial increase in charges in Q5, in which BAA could not have full confidence, and therefore put at risk BAA's ability to finance its investment and the longer-term interests of users. Our approach provides full refund of the revenue advancement and underinvestment in Q4, but in smoothing revenues between Q4 and Q5 ensures BAA's ability to finance T5 is not put at risk.

2.382. We also believe we have made full allowance for the points raised by BAA in paragraph 2.123. In principle, we have continued to apply the system approach, although it makes negligible difference in Q4; the cost of capital adequately reflects risk; we have allowed for AICC; we believe the effect of smoothing returns at Heathrow between quinquennia also provides a significant margin in Q4 in the event of major disruption (for which there is also the scope for interim review—any such disruption would also be taken into account in the next review in considering return in Q5); and our proposed clawback of capital underspend takes into account a range of factors relevant to the particular circumstances in which it occurred, including allowance for depreciation on alternative investments.

2.383. The need for price increases is primarily at Heathrow, reflecting the incremental cost of T5. In our view an increase in airport charges of RPI+6.5 at Heathrow, of RPI+0 at Gatwick and a constant cap of £4.20 at Stansted is therefore necessary to meet the statutory objectives set out in paragraph 2.4. This provides a return equivalent to the 7.75 per cent cost of capital for the three airports together, and each airport separately, over Q4 and Q5 combined. It produces an overall return above the cost of capital in Q4, below the cost of capital in Q5. But, as we have noted, to do otherwise would require a significant increase in charges at the beginning of Q5, discourage BAA's investment programme and fail to promote the reasonable interests of users given the value of increased capacity at Heathrow. (For example, a lower increase in airport charges at Heathrow in Q4, RPI+0.42 would give a return equivalent to cost of capital in Q4, but require a one-off increase in charges of RPI+83 at the beginning of Q5 when T5 comes on-stream, or increases of over 20 per cent a year in real terms throughout Q5.) We believe our recommendations are therefore consistent with the statutory duties of the CAA.

2.384. We acknowledge the price increases we have put forward represent a significant reversal of the decline in airport charges of the last three quinquennia. Since privatization, however, charges have been subject to RPI–1 in Q1 for the three airports as a whole; an average of RPI–4.5 in Q2 (for each airport); and RPI–3 in Q3 (at Heathrow and Gatwick combined), but RPI+1 at Stansted—a cumulative decline for Heathrow and Gatwick of almost one-third (excluding the S factor and D factor). However, in our previous report we recognized the likelihood of price increases being required in Q4 in our suggestion of RPI+2 for that period: the extension of the former RPI–3 price control for a year lowered the level of charges in 2002/03 to 5 per cent below that previously implied, which itself would have required a higher increase in charges than RPI+2 for the rest of Q4. We regard such an increase in charges as now unavoidable, reflecting the increasing marginal cost of development at Heathrow and poorer commercial returns than previously expected. Even at RPI+6.5, the charge cap will not have increased to its level at Heathrow at privatization until the first year of Q5 (£8.32 at 2000/01 prices): that at Gatwick will remain well below the level of privatization.

2.385. We have also noted in Table 5.7 that, in 2002, charges at Heathrow ranked 35 out of 50 international airports and slightly more than 25 per cent below major European airports such as Amsterdam, Paris and Frankfurt; only by the end of Q4, would its charges equal those of those three other airports, if they are maintained at current levels. Gatwick, currently ranked 49 of the 50 airports compared, will remain far below the average of these 50 airports.

2.386. In summary we have therefore concluded on the value of X:

(a) For Heathrow, from a base yield of £6.12 (in 2000/01 prices) in 2003/4, airport charges per passenger should increase by no more than RPI+6.5 for Q4. (For all airports, there would be a similar increase in charges on a comparable basis between 2002/03 and 2003/04—see note to Table 2.16 and Table 10.9.)

(b) For Gatwick, from a base yield of £4.08 (in 2000/01 prices) in 2003/4, airport charges per passenger should increase by no more than RPI+0 for Q4;

(c) For Stansted, airport charges per passenger gross of marketing expenditure should be capped at £4.20 in 2000/01 prices throughout Q4 (although we expect actual yields only gradually to increase towards that level).

(d) The formula at Heathrow should be subject to the following triggers;

    (i)   completion of diversion of twin rivers in 2004/05;

    (ii) completion of early release stands in the same year;

    (iii) the handing over of the visual control room to NATS in 2005/06;

    (iv) the core terminal building weather proof in 2006/07; and

    (v) Satellite 1 weather proof in 2006/07.

One-sixth of a percentage point should be taken off X for each month or part of the month any trigger has not been met in the previous year; when the trigger is subsequently met, the maximum level of airport charges should revert in the following financial year to the levels previously envisaged.

(e) That at Gatwick should be subject to the opening of Pier 6 at Gatwick in 2005/06 with the value of X reduced by one-twelfth of a percentage point if that trigger is not met for any month or part of a month in the previous year.

The formula should remain subject to a correction factor—but with no correction factor to be applied in the first two years as it would be inappropriate for BAA to be compensated for the intentional under-recovery against the 2001/02 and 2002/03 price caps.

Public interest issues

2.387. During the course of the inquiry a wide range of public interest issues were raised with us, some of which were also potentially relevant to airport charges.

Investment and consultation

2.388. We have noted above that there is no statutory requirement on BAA to invest. A number of issues were raised with us about BAA's record of investment relating both to specific investments and to its general procedures, including its planning standards, general planning processes and the consultation procedures it adopts. The details of the complaints and BAA's comments on them are included in Chapters 12 and 14.

Runways

2.389. On specific aspects of investment, we have noted above the objections of the airlines to BAA's appearing to rule out a new runway at Heathrow during the course of the T5 planning inquiry. BAA, however, argued that much of the local opposition to T5 was based on the fear of the third runway; it believed it was apparent the Inspector understood this fear and found it difficult to find a way to recommend the approval of any development without trying to close the door to such a runway. We accept that BAA's concern was primarily to ensure planning approval of T5. The Government's subsequent announcement that the option of an additional runway at Heathrow is nevertheless still under consideration suggests that BAA's statement made no difference. We do not therefore believe that BAA's conduct in this respect gives rise to public interest concerns.

2.390. Airlines were also critical that BAA had not consulted on the issuing of its statement to the T5 inquiry: BAA believed it could not have consulted airlines publicly on such a statement since that would have invited massive criticism, indeed it had to be able to say its stance had not been driven by airline views. It said that it was in no doubt that BA did not wish it to make this statement, but it felt that it was the price which had to be paid to secure the T5 consent. We acknowledge that consultation would have been very difficult in the circumstances of the T5 inquiry and would have served no useful purpose.

2.391. Airtours also complained about the lack of runway development at Gatwick, which it said increased delays and added significantly to its costs. BAA said that the level of delays at Gatwick had declined; there had been improvements in the capacity of its single runway; and any suggestion of another runway was subject to the role of Government in approving construction of any new runway. We have noted above that the agreement with local authorities not to build a new runway at Gatwick until 2019 predates privatization of the BAA, and also that the Government has now ruled out the option of any further runway development at Gatwick at least before 2019. We do not therefore think that BAA's conduct gives rise to public interest concerns.

T5 and effect on charges in Q3

2.392. As we have also noted above, the main investment planned for Q4 was construction of T5. None of the airlines believed that BAA could be blamed for delays resulting from the planning inquiry into T5 (although some did believe BAA should have sought planning permission earlier). They were, however, highly critical of BAA's failure to seek an interim review of charges or not to have more significantly reduced its charges in response to the delay in constructing T5.

2.393. We have noted in paragraph 2.24 the statement of the CAA in its decision on airport charges in Q3 that there should be a mid-term review in the event that T5 did not go ahead or, for reasons connected to planning permission, T5 was proceeded with on a significantly different scale. However, in an appendix to CAP 664, the circumstances under which BAA would seek a mid-term review were confined to planning permission being refused for T5 or being granted subject to conditions which would significantly reduce the scale of T5; or if BAA voluntarily reduced significantly the scale of T5 in order to secure planning permission; or if planning permission were granted subject to conditions which rendered BAA unwilling to proceed with the project on the basis of the price formula that was set. The possibility of prolonged delay before planning permission was granted was not envisaged by the CAA or, indeed, us in our last report. BAA also argued that the first airline request made for it to seek interim review was not until autumn 1999: too late, it argued, for revised charges to be introduced during the current quinquennium given the time that an interim review would require. We have also noted above BAA's arguments that its return on capital value was broadly similar to that which was assumed when the current charges formula was set, despite the reduction in investment from that originally envisaged (although we have noted that on a basis of calculation consistent with that in our previous report, that would not have been the case). One reason for this, it said, was that it had set charges in the last three years of the quinquennium such that it expected to under-recover charges by 3 per cent a year because of the delay in starting T5.

2.394. We noted above that BAA did set charges in order to under-recover against the maximum allowable by 3 per cent in each of the last three years. However, although it did under-recover charges by that amount in 2000/01, for 2001/02, the actual yield was very close to that permitted because of the 'concentration' of revenue in that year (ie yield per passenger being greater than expected), resulting particularly from the effects of 11 September and the reduction in number of passengers per movement. Its under-recovery in 2002/03 was calculated on the basis of a maximum level of charges that would have permitted it to recover the under-recovery which it deliberately brought about in 2000/2001: allowing for that, it more or less fully recovered charges in 2002/03. Hence, it can only be regarded as having under-recovered charges by 3 per cent in only one year of Q3: a very small amount compared with the financial advantage to it of delay in T5.

2.395. We have noted that requests for BAA to increase charges by less than the permitted amounts, or even reduce charges, to allow for delays to T5, were made in early 1999; in April 1999, one airline stated the current formula was no longer appropriate and should be adjusted to exclude the T5 element. An inquiry at that time could have been completed in time to affect charges the following year. However, we are not aware of a formal request for a mid-term review until November 1999: letters from one airline at that time also mentioned other factors such as increased passenger numbers, and lower duty-free income that, it argued, would need to be taken into account. Given this, it seems likely that the terms of reference would themselves have taken some time to agree. A wide ranging review, however, taking into account a range of factors, including growth in passengers, lower duty-free revenues, and the alternative investments being undertaken by BAA and their effect on depreciation, would not have been possible in time to affect charges for 2000/01. We also accept that BAA was under no obligation to agree to such a review, and that its own assessment of its profitability suggested it was not making excess profits despite the delay to T5. The CAA (which in May 1999 announced the one-year delay to the current review) also told us it did not regard an interim review as desirable. Given these factors, in our view, BAA's failure to seek an interim review could not be regarded as conduct operating against the public interest.

2.396. We asked ourselves whether under competitive conditions failure to undertake a major investment would have been expected to lead to a reduction in price. However, BAA regarded its profitability as little above its cost of capital (although our own calculations subsequently showed otherwise), hence reluctance to reduce charges significantly is not surprising. It did, however, reduce charges to some extent. We also noted that revenue advancement was due to be unwound in the next quinquennium anyway (with a cost of capital applied to compensate airlines for the time lag before that occurred); and the scale of under-investment, as evident from our discussion above, is significantly below some of the figures quoted. Hence we do not regard BAA's failure to reduce charges more significantly than it did as against the public interest.

Other projects

2.397. There was criticism also of a number of aspects of BAA's investment performance in Q3. First, we received criticisms of delays in improvements to transfer baggage facilities in T1 (due in part to the need to move the incumbent occupier of the space required). BAA acknowledged that there had been disruption for bmi, as a result of which BAA had made a concession on the rent of the bmi hangar, and subsequent financial concessions. During our inquiry, we were told that a further financial settlement had been agreed.

2.398. Second, there were complaints about BAA's failure to date to provide jetty service at the Metro stands adjacent to T4 at Heathrow, where pier service, at 85 per cent and declining, is significantly below BAA's planning standard of 90 to 95 per cent pier service. BAA attributed this to uncertainty about future airline demands, particularly given the uncertainty following 11 September (although BA argued that delay had also occurred before this). The decision to delay the project, BAA said, was taken at a time when Heathrow's traffic had fallen by 20 per cent, and followed BA's announcement of massive staff and service cuts and demand for emergency relief. BAA believed that temporarily pausing non-essential projects was a sensible step at that time. BA was also then undertaking its major 'size and shape' review, including among other options restructuring of its Heathrow short-haul market which could have weakened the case for providing jetty service to the Metro stands. When BA decided to transfer services from Gatwick to Heathrow, the scheme was reinstated in the draft CIP but still subject to consultation. If users attached high priority to this scheme, BAA said it would be sympathetic to bringing it forward. BAA did acknowledge that with the benefit of hindsight it was possible it could have progressed more speedily with the extension of Victor Pier to the Metro stands, but it was confident that at each stage of the process it had taken the appropriate decisions.

2.399. Third, there were similar criticisms of BAA's failure to develop Pier 6 at Gatwick which would have increased pier service at the North Terminal from the current level of about 79 per cent, significantly below its planning standard. BAA said that Gatwick Pier 6 was also originally conceived by BA and agreed with BAA as part of the former BA strategy to develop Gatwick as a second major hub. BAA was subsequently concerned that the cost of Pier 6 alone could exceed the benefits accruing to airlines. It therefore asked BA repeatedly for assistance in identifying and quantifying the benefits, but no such information was forthcoming. Stage one of the work, the reconfiguration of stands, had been completed, but after 11 September Gatwick traffic collapsed and BA abandoned its second hub strategy. Other supporters of the project were US airlines who also intended to shift services to Heathrow if an 'open skies' agreement was achieved. BA's release of slots at Gatwick was also uncertain, and BAA felt that the airline most likely to pick up any unused slots was easyJet which had a lower priority for jetty service than BA. Hence, BAA decided to pause the project. Completion of Pier 6 was nonetheless subsequently included in the CIP since other airlines supported it (we noted, for example, the Charter Group—Air 2000, Airtours International, Britannia Airways, JMC Airlines and Monarch Airlines—believed the project was important, since there were fewer delays in boarding when airbridges were used) and it would be restarted as and when the prospects justified it.

2.400. Fourth, there were also significant criticisms of delays in completion and reductions in scope of the Iceberg project at T1 at Heathrow, a project which would have allowed BA to transfer some long-haul services from T4 to T1. (Other aspects of this project are also referred to below.) BA said that the completion date had been delayed from April 2001 to at least 2003; BAA said that it always had reservations about the achievability of April 2001, and BA's own board of directors had not approved the project until October 2000 because of its complexity. BA also believed that performance on the project was symptomatic of consistently poor overall management of capital projects; BAA, however, said that the project was massively complex, and BA staff had been appointed to the management board and to that degree shared accountability for the project. Reductions in scope of the project had occurred after 11 September: in particular, the baggage systems had been reduced and the Europier extension cancelled, impacting on baggage handling capacity and performance and pier service. BAA said that the baggage system had subsequently been reinstated; it was also open to reinstating the extension of Europier, if airlines could establish this represented a project which gave appropriate benefits.

2.401. There were also criticisms of the lack of consultation on the creation of an additional security screening area (referred to as 'Little America') in T3 dedicated to US departures and arrivals following the events of 11 September. However, it was evident in the BAA comments on that scheme that the history of this project involved consultation not only between BAA and airlines but also with the DfT and the US Government concerning the requirements, as a result of which the project was not implemented as proposed.

2.402. A main cause of delays to the Metro Stand, Pier 6 and Iceberg projects was the uncertainty associated with 11 September. Airlines, however, criticized the reductions in expenditure after 11 September, particularly in the absence of what they regarded as adequate consultation, or any compensating reduction in airport charges. As to criticism of the lack of consultation on these cutbacks, BAA said that it had written to all airlines inviting their views, and had discussions with a number of airlines and their representative bodies. As to it not making any compensating reduction in airport charges, BAA said that the effect of the reduction in capex on airport charges (through the depreciation and return on the expenditure) would have been very small (about 1p per passenger).

2.403. However, there was also criticism in the context of three of the above projects of BAA's failure to give any apparent weight to its planning standards, particularly that for 90 to 95 per cent pier service. BAA said that the purpose of its planning standards, more recently redesignated as 'planning objectives', had been to help its managers in assessing the capacity of existing facilities and in identifying the appropriate size of new facilities: it had never been its understanding that such standards or the planning objectives were an immediate and blanket obligation and there was no regulatory obligation around them. Their role was not to create an operational performance-monitoring tool, for which SLAs had been developed. Operational performance in many of the areas covered by the planning objectives including pier service, was a shared responsibility, performance depending on the allocation by handling agents of particular flights to pier served stands (although BAA did acknowledge that the main case of current low level of pier service was the absence of sufficient pier-served stands). There were also practical difficulties associated with assessing whether planning standards/objectives were more generally being met.

2.404. Some of the airlines regarded the above cases as examples of systematic under-investment, and that BAA had generally failed to increase investment in line with greater than expected growth in number of passengers. BAA, on the other hand, denied there was any such systemic under-investment.

2.405. BA was also critical of what it described as BAA seeking to eliminate investment risk or offset it to the airlines, as shown by its reluctance to invest in the T4 baggage structure, and seeking to negotiate rescue contributions when the Iceberg project fell short of BAA's target rate of return. It said that BAA often broke projects down into component parts and requested a contribution to some of them. BAA said that it was currently expecting to make at most a small rate of return on the Iceberg project. However, much of the original intention of Iceberg as proposed by BA was not to increase capacity but to improve the quality of BA's product and allow it to reorganize its flights to optimize its transfer operations, ie for BA's competitive advantage. The project was now divided into two parts: bespoke elements to be separately remunerated under a bilateral agreement, and common elements to be remunerated by airport charges. The rescue contribution was directed only at CIP lounges, without which contribution those lounges were forecast not to make an adequate return: BA's need for additional CIP space arose only because of its wish to reorganize services between terminals to its own advantage. Hence, it would be unreasonable for BA to expect those lounges to be remunerated only through airport charges paid by all airlines.

Assessment

2.406. We believe the complaints raised with us have to be seen against a level of investment performance we regard as broadly satisfactory (aside from the delays attributable to the T5 inquiry). We have noted above that, although investment in T5 was much below expected levels in Q3, investment in other projects was above that which had been expected when the current charging formula was set. In our view, except for the delays in T5 that have been largely outside its control, BAA cannot be regarded as having systemically under-invested during Q3.

2.407. On the individual examples put to us, we believe delays can primarily be attributed to the particular difficulties identified in proceeding more quickly, and/or to uncertainty as to the benefits of the projects. The T1 transfer baggage facilities, for example, were initially delayed by the need to move the incumbent occupier. We have noted the delays to projects following the events of 11 September and criticisms of them. We do not find that BAA's reaction to the events of 11 September were against the public interest, given the considerable uncertainty to which those events gave rise.[1] This is supported by the reaction of some airlines to those events and their request for, for example, substantial reduction in airport charges.

2.408. Particularly in the case of Gatwick, there was uncertainty as to who the main users of Pier 6 were going to be, and whether pier service would be of value to them. Indeed, doubts about the value of pier service underlie some of the delays on BAA's part: this would apply less at Heathrow, where indeed BAA acknowledged work could have started sooner.

2.409. All but one of the projects have either eventually gone ahead (T1 baggage transfer and Iceberg), or BAA has said it is now prepared to undertake them, if airlines want it to do so (pier service to Metro stands and Pier 6). In the other case (Little America), where there were objections to the project proceeding, it did not (for various reasons) go ahead. No doubt some of the delays have caused inconvenience to airlines, but are not sufficient in our view to be regarded as against the public interest.

---

[1]This also applies to a further Gatwick project raised with us—the South Terminal Arrivals Extension Project—which BAA told us was suspended due to the uncertainty over the timing and extent of recovery in passenger numbers at Gatwick; but with the signs of recovery of traffic there, this project may now be started earlier than proposed in the CIP.

2.410. However, underlying the complaints to us is a view of inadequate consultation between BAA and other airlines: a feeling among airlines that BAA does not appear to listen to points raised; and by BAA that the airlines are not prepared to provide the feedback necessary for consultation to serve a purpose. As we discuss below, the consultation process in Q3 has been further hindered by the uncertainties as to the outcome of the T5 inquiry, and the delay that it has involved, to which are added the uncertainties of the outcome of SERAS. Given those difficulties, and the intention of BAA to improve not only its consultation process but also procedure for handling complaints, we do not currently think an adverse finding either on BAA's conduct as regards investment or consultation would be justified.

2.411. As to planning standards, there was no criticism that new investments failed to have regard to them, and we do not believe they can be rigidly applied to existing facilities without considering the costs and benefits in each case. It may nonetheless be appropriate more systematically to report performance against these standards, together with other indicators of quality of service, as part of the improved consultation process on capex to which we refer below, particularly in the context of the redevelopment of the CTA and the need to ensure airlines operating in the CTA do not suffer competitive disadvantage compared with those in T5. The particular cases are, however, indicative of weaknesses both in consultation processes (and in approach to quality of service) to which we return below.

2.412. On the terms on which BAA is willing to invest, BAA's basic approach is that investment in facilities dedicated to particular airlines and to their competitive advantage, such as CIP lounges, should not be reflected in charges to users generally. But investment to achieve a general standard should be financed out of airport charges and should not be subject to any additional charges. We do not therefore think that this approach gives rise to public interest concerns. The current difficulties relate to a large extent to the absence of generic standards (albeit ones which cannot be regarded as rigid guidelines).

2.413. We also saw criticism of BAA not allowing third parties to invest. BAA said that this was incorrect in factual and in policy terms, and there were numerous examples of such investment such as maintenance hangars, cargo sheds and transfer baggage facilities; furthermore, it was unaware of any cases where airlines had required investment and the company had been unprepared to undertake this. However, it would seek to build in accordance with its planning guidelines and in a manner which complied with its sustainability objectives. We saw no evidence that BAA's policy in this respect could be regarded as against the public interest.

Current investment programme and consultation

2.414. As we have noted above, most airlines from whom we heard were critical of the absence of sufficient information in the CIP to enable them to judge its adequacy: particularly on projects that might develop the CTA to a standard equivalent to that of T5. Several airlines criticized lack of quantitative information on development options: one, for example, said that it needed a greater understanding of each project and its costs and benefits including the high-level business case, an indication of the likely impact on airport charges for each project (including the method of cost recovery to be applied), along with definition of alternatives for comparison and consideration. More generally, several criticized lack of a master plan or development strategy, as a result of which users had not been given the opportunity to consider and comment on BAA's approach and long-term vision for the development of Heathrow. Users, it was argued, were deprived of the necessary future context when assessing individual projects; development was piecemeal and could therefore be wasteful if inconsistent with longer-term projects. This could make comprehensive development more costly and disruptive. On the other hand, some correspondence we saw said that for some airlines there was too much information contained in the CIP.

2.415. Airlines therefore believed that BAA's investment and consultation processes operated against the public interest and put various alternative approaches to us. Virgin, for example, referred to investment plans being determined by airport users in conjunction with airports and with continual involvement of the regulator. bmi considered that charges be subject to delivery of the investment programme. BA told us that there should be a mechanism that would require consultation on a development/capex plan for the South-East generally and for each airport concerned; this should be subject to specification by the CAA of the information to be provided and include participation by the CAA in settling disputes about deferment or cancellation of capex. As part of this process, BA said that the airport-by-airport capital programme needed to be agreed at regulatory reviews, with agreed changes incorporated in subsequent annual capex reviews, which would in time be an input to the process of setting charges.

2.416. We noted in paragraph 2.342 the range of views among airlines on the schemes incorporated in the CIP, reflecting their different interests, particularly at Heathrow between BA, envisaged as the main occupier of T5, and those airlines likely to remain in the CTA. We have noted BA's criticism of the absence of specific plans to develop 'connectivity', to provide a TTS for passengers between the CTA and T5. BA believed that without such connectivity it would not be possible for BAA to meet its planning standards for minimum connection times; airlines remaining in the central terminal area believed such connectivity was not desirable (depending in one case on the costs that would be passed on in airport charges). We have also noted above criticisms by bmi of the costs of T5, but also the concern of a number of airlines remaining in the CTA that the facilities available to them should be comparable to those to be provided in T5. There were also criticisms of inadequate consultation on decisions as to which airlines would occupy T5. BAA said the decision that BA would be the prime occupier resulted from analysis of the most cost-effective use of T5 and minimization of inter-terminal transfer requirements, about which airlines had been fully informed.

2.417. BAA said that it had made great efforts to improve consultation arrangements on its investment programme with very positive feedback from recipients. It believed that it was used as an example of best practice by airlines around the world. More generally, it referred to over 80 examples of consultation at Heathrow in one-quarter of this year, and a structure of consultation up to the level of Chief Executive Officer.

2.418. BAA felt, however, that master plans would prove inflexible in the face of changing airline demands (had it, for example, invested on the basis of any inflexible master plan at Gatwick five or six years ago, there would have been substantial investment in satellite facilities as part of BA's strategy of developing Gatwick as a second hub, a strategy that was then abandoned). But to produce a fully specified single plan would require an assumption as to whether, when and where a third runway was to be built, on which the Government had made no final decision. BAA had therefore to operate a broad development strategy which could accommodate evolving conditions rather than work to a fixed master plan.

2.419. Nonetheless, BAA had agreed with the CAA the contents of enhanced information disclosure and consultation documents, which would allow users to understand the principle business drivers, forecast demand and capacity and implications for quality of service, options for the development of the airport around the central plan, resourcing implications, cost estimates of individual projects, and expected outputs. The document would be produced on an annual basis, and provide users with an account of how the plan had changed and why. BAA intended that the plan would act as a basis for consultation only and would not represent a mandatory programme. It should, however, form the basis of an effective consultation process: BAA also noted that the CAA had said that failure by BAA to produce sufficient information, evidence that it had not consulted with all major users, or demonstration that it had consistently ignored reasonable requests of users in the consultation process without good reason and contrary to the interests of airport users generally could jeopardize the sustainability of the regulatory framework. Airlines themselves, however, would also need to cooperate in the provision of such information. We noted also that the CAA, in proposing additional information requirements and improved consultation procedures, believed they should not be statutory requirements.

2.420. For its part, BAA said that while it did not view legally binding agreements as appropriate for airport investment, it was sympathetic to airlines' views that charges should in some way be linked to delivery. This required either airports undertaking to provide a given level of throughput at a certain level of service standards (with the incentive provided by its Q factor proposals); or charges being either linked to the provision of certain predefined outputs or contingent on major project milestones throughout Q4 as we have discussed above. As noted in paragraph 2.347 we see merit in this approach. It also proposed an improved complaints procedure including written responses, meetings and appeal to senior levels within BAA (see paragraph 14.178).

2.421. On criticisms of inadequate planning for connectivity with T5, BAA said a number of factors argued against early construction of a TTS. It would increase dislocation in the CTA while congestion was already increasing before the opening of T5; it could not be undertaken until Satellite 2 of T5 was completed, and land acquired from Thames Water plc (TW); its location depended on whether or not there would be a new runway at Heathrow, and on which airlines would operate from which terminal after T5 opened; and it would be very costly, for relatively few transfer passengers.

2.422. We understand why airlines have been concerned about lack of a coherent vision of Heathrow's long-term development objectives being shared with them but in our view this can to a large extent be attributed to the uncertainties as to T5 and any new runway development. Only with the recent approval of T5, and the outcome of the SERAS process as to whether a further runway is to be located at Heathrow, will consultation on the long-term development vision for Heathrow be possible and we expect this then to occur. The agreement of the CAA and BAA to improve the process on consultation of the CIP in future years will be an important part of this process of consultation. BAA's intention to introduce a formal complaints procedure should also assist this, and resolve many of the capex, quality of service and other issues which arise between regulatory reviews, and which form the basis for such a large volume of complaints at each review. We believe these are the most useful ways forward, but ones in which the CAA should also be involved: a matter to which we return below.

2.423. However, although effective consultation is important, given the disparate views and interest of airlines it is unrealistic to believe BAA should have sought 'agreement' on the CIP. Consultation with all airlines on T5 also remains important (although we acknowledge the poor participation of some airlines in the present consultation processes) because all airlines in effect will pay the cost of T5, and the standard applied to T5 would then be applied to other parts of the airport. However, as we have noted above, BAA told us it accepted a suggestion of a peer-group review of T5 costs with involvement of the airlines.

2.424. In our view given the constraints and uncertainties of the last five to six years, BAA could not have done significantly more in its consultation processes and there is insufficient basis for us to establish conduct against the public interest; but as these uncertainties become resolved, we would expect to see significant improvements in those processes in Q4.

Stansted

2.425. There was also some criticism of 'gold plating' facilities at Stansted. However, the existing facilities at Stansted reflect the investment decisions taken in the mid-1980s, when it was assumed that there would be more significant constraints on the development of Heathrow. Recent developments at Stansted have had to be in keeping with the high quality of the original designs, but nonetheless have been of lower cost facilities, reflecting the requirement of the

LFCs at Stansted (for example lower standards of jetty service). We also noted in paragraph 2.54 that investment has, if anything, been undertaken 'just too late', rather than at all prematurely. Hence, we find it difficult to see any evidence of excessive investment at Stansted.

Quality of service

2.426. We have noted that many airlines regarded aspects of quality of service provided by BAA in Q3 to be against the public interest. In addition, we referred in paragraph 2.277 et seq to the CAA's proposals for inclusion of a Q term in the airport charges formula. We therefore now consider, first BAA's performance in terms of quality of service in Q3; second, issues concerning standards which were raised with us during the inquiry; and third, the implications for the approach to service standards in future.

Performance

2.427. As apparent in Chapter 6, BAA's performance in relation to the standards agreed or set by BAA have generally been satisfactory, but there has been poor performance in certain areas. There has been a slight deterioration in BAA's overall performance as measured by its QSM scores over Q3, particularly at Stansted where it was, however, largely to be expected given the very high scores there at the beginning of Q3, when it was relatively under-utilized. QSM scores are, however, not far above 3.5 out of 5—which BAA regard as the threshold of reasonableness—for departure lounge crowding and indeed are below that in certain terminals. (We also noted BAA's response to low ratings of landside seating in T3 was to remove some seats to encourage passengers to go airside: where, however, ratings were as low. Ratings should, however, much improve when the current expansion of the T3 IDL is completed.) BAA's targets under SLAs for stands, jetties and security queues have generally been met, but targets have been achieved only about 75 per cent of the time for people movers, which include passenger conveyors, escalators and lifts (of which the target for passenger conveyors has been achieved only 55 per cent of the time).

2.428. Airlines have criticized individual aspects of quality of service, as well as those aspects of SLAs where BAA has sometimes failed to reach its targets (as noted in Chapter 12, they also did not accept that the results of BAA's QSM surveys were valid).

2.429. We have noted above criticisms that BAA has failed to create an adequate number of jetty-served stands to meet its planning standards, particularly at T4 and Gatwick North Terminal. This is partly acknowledged by BAA, although BAA also argued that to some extent the achievement of pier service levels was determined by operating practices of airlines and their handling agents. However, extension of the Victor Pier into the Metro stands would significantly increase pier service in T4. There were also complaints that some airbridges at T4 had been unserviceable for up to three weeks in December 2001 and January 2002, for which the standard remote stand rebate gave inadequate compensation for the cost to airlines (including extra staffing and the costs of passenger dissatisfaction); and about the closure of Victor Pier for structural repair. BAA said that this resulted from unforeseen and serious faults with airbridges which required the acquisition of spares that were not normally stock items; but except for those two months its targets had been reached, as they had over the year as a whole.

2.430. There were also complaints about various aspects of security staffing and quality of facilities (including leaking roofs and air conditioning not adequately functioning, and time taken to repair operational systems such as PA systems at T1). As noted in Chapter 14 some of these points were accepted by BAA, with remedial action currently being taken. There was also criticism of short notice closure of stands for insurance inspections, about which BAA told us it was now undertaking a more carefully planned approach; but also of the closure of a large number of airbridge-served stands for painting as part of an advertising agreement: BAA told us that this did not involve only external repainting but also internal refurbishment sought by airlines, and that the programme was carried out within the allowances made for stand closures for maintenance for scheduling purposes. There were also criticisms of way-finding, the relatively poor quality of which was apparent also from IATA surveys of Heathrow performance compared with that of other international airports, and to an extent accepted by BAA.

Service level agreements

2.431. As well as citing such specific instances, airlines were critical of three aspects of BAA's approach to service standards, first its approach to SLAs. In the last report, the MMC expressed its view that the absence of quality standards was a deficiency inherent in the then regulatory regime. We also noted that the progress of introducing SLAs had been disappointing, although it was unclear whether this could be regarded as solely the responsibility of BAA. We believed, however, that adoption of formally agreed standards was necessary to ensure both that no deterioration of service would occur in future and that recent improvements up to the date of that report would be maintained. We welcomed the joint initiative then being undertaken between BAA and BA and the associated trial of SLAs, and believed this represented the best way forward, by agreement between BAA and airlines, and that SLAs should be made generally applicable after experience of those trials. Given that many of the key processes to which standards should apply were shared between BAA and airlines, the proposed trial was necessary to show that the responsibility for failure to meet standards could be properly and consistently identified. If the trials showed compensation could be feasible, we believed it would be desirable for SLAs to include provision for compensation, but that, where appropriate, compensation should be on a reciprocal basis if any party by failing to meet service standards imposed significant costs upon the others.

2.432. We have noted in Chapter 6 that SLAs have been developed for most facilities in most BAA terminals, but mainly only as a system of measurement against targets, without involving compensation should performance fall short of target. (Such SLAs are referred to as 'best endeavours' SLAs.) Only the bilateral SLAs between BAA and BA, concerning departure baggage facilities and T1–T4 transfer baggage, require compensation in the event of failure, or bonuses in the event of performance above standard.

2.433. A number of airlines said that existing SLAs 'lacked teeth'; they excluded capital intensive activities; there was a lack of compensation in SLAs, other than relating to jetties, where it had been insufficient to make BAA adhere to standards, and SLAs failed to cover all the key aspects of service provisions, or any at all at Gatwick, or to meet the standards set.

2.434. BA, for example, said it was disappointed in the rate of progress of SLAs, both in implementation and in improvement resulting from them. Existing SLAs covering jetty availability and security queuing had little credibility with the front line operational teams, because of their design, measurement and exclusions. It argued that many SLAs were flawed, for example not taking into account maintenance time and long-term outages, and using manual measurements for security queuing, which may miss peak flows, and that service credit payments should take the form of penalty payments to have sufficient bite to persuade BAA to meet the standards. The incentivized bilateral SLAs referred to above, BA said, had proved more successful in extracting improved levels of service and facilities—but BAA was insistent compensation in them should be reciprocal. Because of BAA's insistence on bonus payments, only less effective, best endeavours SLAs had been introduced for services provided to all airlines: most airlines were unwilling to enter into arrangements whereby they might end up paying more to BAA for a level of service they did not want. Service standards should cover all services—they currently fail to include runway and taxiway availability, navigation services and terminal 'fabric' (for example, cleanliness and condition). QSM scores were not a satisfactory alternative. SLAs therefore fell short of their goal: being focused, clear, simple, easily measured, well reported and used as the springboard for action to correct poor performance. Moreover, SLAs were only bilateral—there were no generic standards.

2.435. Specifically on security, BA said there was a target under the relevant SLA that no passenger should queue for more than 10 minutes, but no compensation for failure to meet it. (We noted however that the current target only requires that passengers should queue for less than ten minutes on 95 per cent of occasions when the queue is checked.) The target was too low, and poorly monitored by BAA itself, which had never failed to meet it. At Heathrow carriers had to resort to funding separate Fast Track search facilities to meet expectations of premium passengers and relieve congestion in the standard facility: they were effectively being charged twice, and with no apparent account taken of advertising revenue received by BAA in the Fast Track area—the basis of charges was insufficiently transparent to confirm this.

2.436. In response, BAA said that BA was involved in the creation of SLAs and had had ample opportunities in the last few years, as had other airlines to raise any concerns. It had not made BAA aware of any more extensive concerns about SLAs; nor had other airlines. BAA believed its approach to compensation under SLAs was consistent with the suggestion of our previous report, namely that this was possible with bilateral agreements but significantly more difficult for any multilateral agreements. Even if no system of payments were involved, monitoring of performance provided sufficient incentivization including incorporation of SLA performance into management incentive schemes. Other than BA, airlines had shown no particular interest in extending the scope even of penalty-only SLAs to new areas. Nor had BA consistently argued in favour of financial incentives. BAA's proposed Q factor would provide clear financial incentives and circumvented the difficulty of creating a payment mechanism separate to airport charges. Contrary to the complaint above, SLAs had been in place at Gatwick for several years (albeit only on a best endeavours basis).

2.437. BAA said that there was nothing intrinsically wrong with current performance measures, but it had committed in principle to move to a CCTV-based monitoring system for security queues. BAA agreed that its measures excluded planned maintenance from the amount of time assets were regarded as being unavailable. Subsequently, BAA suggested reducing the number of current exclusions for planned maintenance from the various measures, with the targets adjusted by 1 per cent where appropriate. On jetty availability, it had proved very difficult to adjust the measurements to include data on timing of dockings integrated with data on serviceability of equipment and the trial ended in agreement to continue to use the existing jetty service availability measure.

2.438. On security, BAA said that Fast Track was a marketing product which airlines at Heathrow chose to ask BAA to provide as a specific facility to support their product differentiation requirements. BAA said that it responded positively to this request. Agreement was reached on how it would be funded. Advertising was visible from both the fast track and the standard track and would have been located there whether or not a separate channel existed. Income from this source was not therefore included in fast track charging calculations.

Lack of generic service standards

2.439. Airlines were concerned about lack of generic standards, BA, for example, believing that failure to adopt and publicize the basic level of service/generic service standards covered by charges, or negotiate SLAs to cover all key aspects of services covered by charges was against the public interest. It believed that in the specific cases referred to above, service quality had been compromised by the behaviour of BAA, reflecting its incentives under the current framework to limit the quality of services covered by regulated charges and sacrifice service quality in pursuit of commercial activities; this should be remedied by linking part of the future price control formula to achievement of satisfactory planning standards, and giving greater regulatory force to obligations on BAA to maintain service quality through the licence.

2.440. BAA told us that it had undertaken an initial piece of work which it had thought would clarify the service quality level that airlines might expect to achieve in each of the areas covered by airport charges: the results of the exercise were shared with BA. However, the exercise highlighted how difficult it was to quantify the expected level of service in many of the areas not at present covered by SLAs and that BAA's performance in a number of areas was covered by safety regulation. It therefore did not believe it was possible to develop a statement quantifying the level of service which all users could expect for each area covered by airport charges. Partly as a result of the difficulties inherent in that approach, BAA and the airlines had developed SLAs, and BAA had more recently developed the Q-factor concept.

2.441. Moreover, BAA did not believe the absence of service levels could be a public interest issue of itself: if all services were being carried out to appropriate levels then the fact there were no service targets was of no concern. Rather any public interest issue would have to be related to a service failure and proper thought needed to be given as to how that failing might be remedied or prevented.

Conditions of use

2.442. There were complaints about 'one-sided Conditions of Use' with unreasonable disclaimers. Namely the condition that:

> Neither BAA, nor the airport company, nor their respective servants or agents shall be liable for loss of damage to the aircraft, its parts or accessories or any property contained in the aircraft, occurring while the aircraft is on the airport or is in the course of landing or taking-off at the airport, arising or resulting directly or indirectly from any act, omission, neglect or default on the part of BAA, the airport company or their servants or agents unless done with intent to cause damage or recklessly and with knowledge that damage would probably result. In any event neither BAA nor the airport company nor their respective servants or agents shall be under any liability whatever for any indirect loss and/or expense (including loss of profit) suffered by an operator.

Airlines argued that BAA should be liable for negligence, not just deliberate damage etc: the failure of main power supply was one instance in which airlines were unable to seek damages for negligence (of BAA's contractors).

2.443. As regards the first sentence, BAA said that the identical sentence was examined by the High Court in the case of *Monarch Airlines versus London Luton Airport* (1998 *1 Lloyds Reports* p 403). It was held that the exclusion clause satisfied the test of reasonableness under the Unfair Contract Terms Act 1972, it being generally accepted in the market including the insurance market and that it had a clear meaning and that the insurance arrangements of the parties were then made on the basis of the contract. As regards the second sentence, BAA asserted it was standard practice in commercial contracts to exclude economic loss arising as a result of negligence and breach of contract. Both parties would make their insurance arrangements on the basis of this condition. Under the law of negligence, it was not possible to recover for economic loss unless physical damage had been caused by the defendant's negligence. Accordingly the airlines would not have been able to claim in the example referred to. We noted, however, that *Monarch* was only a preliminary ruling, made on the basis of assumed facts. In general, we believe it more appropriate for airlines to bear insurance costs for damage as part of their overall insurance cover, but it is still open for them to seek a ruling from the courts if they consider that BAA's exclusion of liability is unreasonable in the circumstances of any particular case.

Assessment

2.444. We have noted that BAA has met the majority of its SLAs over Q3 and performance from its QSM surveys are generally satisfactory. However, there were instances of poor standards of service against some of these targets and against some QSM measures, as well as particular complaints raised by airlines as to poor performance and poor standard of facilities. Some of these were acknowledged by BAA and it intends to rectify them. In total, they are in our view, indicative of the variable service despite largely fixed charges; this is exacerbated by the absence of specified standards for what can be expected in return for those charges. We have noted that in our previous report we believed that the development of SLAs was appropriate with associated financial compensation. In only two areas of activity, however, have SLAs been developed with financial compensation. Furthermore, it is a weakness of the SLAs with incentives that they require bilateral agreements between BAA and individual airlines, and payments are made only to individual airlines with whom there are such bilateral agreements. The limitations in the Conditions of Use are also evidence of unequal bargaining power.

2.445. We do not believe the average level of service in Q3 has been poor. But we have noted: a variability of quality of service provided; that although standards were agreed, they were not comprehensive; that variability in standards has been reflected in equivalent variations in charges in only a few areas; and that users have not known what quality of service they were entitled to expect.

2.446. We believe that, in determining whether BAA has pursued a course of conduct that has operated or may be expected to operate against the public interest, we are entitled to compare its conduct in conducting its business with the conduct we would expect of a reasonable and efficient operator in a fully competitive market. BAA itself said in response to a question about wayleaves, 'Regulation should be about mimicking competition where possible'. We considered whether the factors we discussed in paragraph 2.445 would be expected to apply in the analogy of a competitive market.

2.447. There are various ways in which suppliers of services respond to full competition. They can, for example, build up a reputation for providing high-quality service and charge high prices. When it is clear that a supplier with a strong reputation for quality is determined to defend its reputation, this will often provide a sufficient guarantee to customers of a high quality service. It is understood that losing its reputation will have serious consequences for the supplier. There is then a strong incentive for consistent quality standards to be maintained and it is likely, in the unlikely event of a lapse, the supplier will go to considerable lengths to avoid any adverse effect on its customers. Others may offer lower standards but will be forced to accept lower prices for them. Suppliers offering a poor quality service but trying to charge high prices will rapidly lose customers to those offering better value for money.

2.448. The general outcome is that prices will tend to vary according to the level of service that is actually provided whatever the specific circumstances.

2.449. Suppliers, particularly those lacking the strongest reputation for service quality, may choose to strengthen their reputation for quality by entering into binding commitments to provide specified standards; they may even bind themselves to fixed discounts whenever the standards are not reached. In particular, some providers of high-value services to commercial customers may find it necessary to enter into binding contractual obligations to meet specified performance standards. Such contracts may set out an agreed scale of discounts or rebates that are to apply when the standards are not met, so that the customers, in effect, pay only for the service they actually receive. This kind of provision is commonly found in commercial contracts where the loss for breach would not be large, would vary substantially from case to case and would be expensive to determine in legal proceedings.

2.450. These considerations apply to airports. For example, poor or unreliable facilities may disrupt flight schedules at great cost to airlines. Equipment such as escalators failing to work could result in the airlines having dissatisfied customers, a dissatisfied customer may have the option of using a different airport and hence probably a different airline in future, but it would be difficult to prove actual loss for the airline in any particular case.

2.451. As regards Heathrow and Gatwick, we are in no doubt that in a fully competitive market airport charges would vary according to the level of service provided. During the last quinquennium, this occurred only to a minimal extent. There was a remote stand rebate in the Conditions of Use but, as we have noted, this does not necessarily relate to service failure as such and is more an aspect of pricing structure, rebates to some users being offset by higher charges to others. There has also been a jetty rebate (not in the Conditions of Use and for which airlines have had to apply). BAA agreed SLAs with various airlines, but only a few of these provided for compensation and were expressed not to be legally binding. We are satisfied that BAA could have conducted itself so as to make prices paid reflect levels of service to a far greater extent. It could have, for example, published service levels and undertaken to pay rebates whenever those standards were not met according to a published scale, the rebates reflecting that there was a difference between the value of a service provided in accordance with published standards and the service actually provided. We find that in failing to conduct themselves so as to make prices paid sufficiently reflect the level of service provided, HAL and GAL have pursued a course of conduct which may be expected to operate against the public interest.

2.452. We recognize that the failure to provide pier service to an airline on a particular occasion is reflected in a rebate. However, as the rebates are taken into account in calculating the charges subject to the cap, poor service is not reflected in a reduction of total charges levied. In the case of at least some airlines (the bigger users in particular) the existence of rebates might not put them in a better position than if the rebates did not exist, however poor the level of service. If, for example, a number of piers were out of service for a substantial period of time, rebates would be payable to a number of airlines and some of those who had received rebates could end up paying more charges than if the piers had been in service throughout the year. We also recognize that rebates have been paid on occasions when jetties were not serviceable, but only on application and not as a published commitment. Having regard to these matters, we include pier and jetty service in the finding we make in paragraph 2.451.

2.453. Our adverse finding does not include outbound and transfer baggage to the extent to which it is already covered by SLAs that involve payments, and which are commonly regarded as having been highly successful in improving performance. Our adverse finding does, however, include outbound baggage services where no SLA involving payment currently exists, for example where the service is provided to an airline that is not party to an SLA that provides for rebates.

2.454. In making this finding we are not in any way suggesting that BAA has been in breach of an obligation, legal or otherwise. We also recognize the significant efforts BAA has made to do as the MMC suggested in its last report and that BAA alone was not responsible: one reason financial adjustments have not been used more widely was indeed the suggestion in our last report that they should be symmetrical, and the refusal of many airlines to proceed on that basis. Nevertheless, we think BAA could have done more to provide for compensation which was a key part of the MMC suggestion. Furthermore, although its development of the Q factor was to its credit, BAA's proposals would also have resulted in a symmetrical approach within the Q factor based on current targets that are generally achieved, with the likely prospect of additional payments by airlines to BAA without significant improvements in service. The question for us is whether BAA has conducted itself in a manner that operated or may be expected to operate against the public interest; not whether it should be blamed for doing so. Its actual conduct did not provide sufficient degree of variation of charges in relation to variations in service.

2.455. The adverse effect of this conduct is that prices do not reflect the quality of service provided to the extent that would occur in a competitive market and in consequence that there is an absence of the financial incentive to provide the combination of price and quality of service which would obtain in a competitive market.

2.456. As regards Stansted, BAA put it to us that it did face competition and that, accordingly, prices did have to reflect quality. As we are not able to say on the evidence before us that this would happen to a greater extent in a fully competitive market, we accept this argument and make no adverse finding.

2.457. We have therefore found that HAL and GAL have pursued a course of conduct in relation to Heathrow and Gatwick that may be expected to operate against the public interest. As stated in paragraph 2.447, there are many ways in which players in a competitive market typically respond to competition. In devising a remedy we have sought a condition that, in broad terms, would make BAA operate in one of these ways. In choosing the most appropriate condition we are looking for the approach that: would put BAA under the kind of pressures to maintain standards that it would meet under full competition; would be readily implementable and practicable; and would produce a result that was fair as between BAA and the airlines and that was fair between airlines.

2.458. We identified two alternative ways of remedying the adverse effects we have identified. Our preferred remedy is to set standards with rebates when they are not met. The CAA had proposed that there should be a Q factor in the charge cap formula and BAA agreed with this approach, and we considered whether a Q factor could be a satisfactory remedy to the adverse effects we have identified. However, we see the following advantages or potential advantages in a condition that would require BAA to make rebates in accordance with a specified scale whenever specified standards are not met:

(a) Unlike a Q factor, the condition would not have to be finalized before the start of Q4. We note below that there are currently no standards or measures relating to runway and taxiway availability or delays.

(b) Unlike a Q factor, the specified standards and specified scale could be varied in the light of experience during the course of Q4 without the consent of BAA. The condition could be expressed in terms of standards and rebate scales 'as from time to time specified by the CAA'.

(c) Without a radical change in the nature of the charge cap formula a Q factor would result in a long time lag between a failure to meet a standard and recovery by the airlines. At best it would result in the money being recovered over the course of the whole of the following year.

(d) As a Q factor would operate by reducing future airport charges, it could not benefit an airline that had ceased to use the BAA airports soon after a period during which standards were not met.

(e) Without a radical change in the nature of the charge cap formula a Q factor could not enable rebates to be on a terminal-by-terminal basis.

2.459. A problem with the Q factor as proposed by the CAA is that good performance in one dimension offsets poor performance in another: hence it fails to address our central concern of lower prices in the event of poor service.

2.460. One potential advantage of a Q factor is that it could be so formulated that the airlines would pay extra if specified standards were exceeded, ie it could be symmetrical. But, if the targets were to be set below current or expected performances, this could itself require an overall increase in payments from airlines to BAA, without any improvement in quality of service, and thereby reduce the incentive on BAA to improve performance which falls short of standard.

2.461. We conclude that a condition requiring BAA to pay rebates according to a specified scale whenever specified standards are not met would be a better approach than a Q factor. Our preference would have been rebates to specific airlines affected by performance below the standard set, but we accept there would be practical difficulties identifying and compensating those airlines, of the many at BAA's airports, that were affected. Nonetheless, rebates should be as specific to an individual airline affected as possible, for which we propose rebates on a terminal-by-terminal basis. Compared with an overall adjustment of charges, this has the advantage that it recognizes that quality does vary by terminal, and will assist in compensating for any lack of a 'level playing field' between airlines in different terminals, including between airlines in the CTA and those in T5 when it opens. Allocation to airlines within terminals would seem most appropriately related to their share of passengers.

2.462. By 'rebates' we mean neither a system of penalties to be imposed on HAL and GAL, nor arrangements for compensation against which users can make claims when standards are not met. What we have in mind is a mechanism that will seek to align the charges that airlines pay to the quality of service that HAL and GAL deliver. This means that where service delivery meets the specified standards, then the full charge is payable, but if the delivery of a particular service falls short of the specified standards, then the airport will be required to pay a rebate of some or all of the charge related to that service.

2.463. Accordingly, we recommend that the CAA implement a system of quality-based rebates at Heathrow and Gatwick. This scheme should build on the work undertaken for the Q-term proposals that the CAA has already developed in consultation with BAA and the airlines but be implemented by the specified standards and rebates systems we have proposed. Where we have not specified to the contrary, the details of the scheme should be as proposed in the CAA's proposals set out in Annex A to our consultation paper of 5 July 2002. As the CAA's proposals are not yet complete, we recommend that it should vary the details of the scheme within the guidelines set out in paragraphs 2.464 to 2.481 and Appendix 2.4. Any such variations should take account of BAA's detailed proposals set out in Appendix 6.2 where they are compatible with our guidelines, should only be made after consultation with BAA and the airlines and should, so far as practicable, take account of their views.

2.464. Rebates should be paid after the end of each year, on the basis of performance in that year and should be distributed among the airlines on the basis of passenger share. The scheme should initially have a maximum impact on BAA, in terms either of rebates or adjustments to the price cap, equivalent to 2 per cent of the airport charges otherwise permitted by the price cap (referred to below as 'charges revenue') in each of the first two years, and 3 per cent subsequently after some experience is gained. (Such payments, unlike the current remote stand rebate, would not count against the limit on the maximum level of airport charges—ie the total of the airport charges levied should be calculated without taking such payments into account, so that BAA would not be able to recover the amount from the airlines by raising airport charges.) It should consist of a component based on objective measures of services provided to airlines (derived from those put forward as part of the CAA's Q_A term), a component based on passengers' perception of services in other areas that affect the service provided to them, and a component based on delays caused by airfield congestion attributable to the airport operator. At the outset, it is difficult to assess the appropriate weightings between these three elements, so we suggest adopting the figures proposed by the CAA, subject to the results of the consultation to be carried out by the CAA on this point. We recommend that in the first two years the airline standards should have a maximum impact of 1.5 per cent of charges revenue and the passenger standards should have a maximum impact of 0.5 per cent of charges revenue. The airline standards should be increased to 2.5 per cent after two years' experience of operating the scheme; but when the delay factor is introduced, it should have a maximum impact of 1 per cent of charges revenue and airline standards 1.5 per cent (if the delay factor is introduced prior to two years, the weights of each element should be adjusted accordingly). This gives a relatively large weighting to airline standards compared with passenger standards, but we believe this is reasonable given that the airline standards are

116

themselves of importance to passengers. It may well be appropriate over time for the weightings to be changed in the light of evidence received.

2.465. Some airlines argued that the overall limit on the impact on airport charges should be more than the 3 per cent proposed by the CAA; BAA regarded that amount as too high, pointing to other utilities where the effect of performance standards was between 1 and 2 per cent of total revenues. We see some arguments for the airlines' view. However, since this is a new, untried approach, we believe the initial limit should be no more than 2 per cent, to be increased to 3 per cent after two years by increasing the maximum impact of the airline standard to 2.5 per cent of charges revenue. We do not, however, rule out the possibility of this being increased in future. These figures should apply whatever dimensions may initially or subsequently be introduced. In particular, we consider that, for the practical reasons set out in paragraphs 6.127 to 6.137 and Appendix 2.4, the delay factor probably cannot be introduced for about two years; hence our proposal that, when the CAA, after consulting the airlines and BAA, has devised a workable delay factor it should be introduced with a maximum impact of 1 per cent, the airline standards being correspondingly reduced.

2.466. We do not consider that BAA should be able to use good performance in one element of service to cancel out the effect on rebates of bad performance in another, otherwise BAA may focus on areas where performance can be most easily improved, and the incentive to improve areas of poor performance would be much reduced. This implies that the individual elements of airline and passenger standards should be assessed separately. For each individual element of service, we recommend that BAA should be permitted to use good performance in one month to offset bad performance in another during the same year. This approach should, however, be limited to mitigating any rebates, or reductions in charges, due from BAA to the airlines and should not of course result in net payments from airlines to BAA over the year concerned.

2.467. It is in principle desirable that differences in service quality between terminals should, at least to some extent, be reflected in differences in the overall charges to the airlines based in each terminal. BAA objected to such an approach arguing that it could encourage airlines to request differentiation of airport charges by terminal; that charges would still fail to reflect services to individual airlines; and it would be costly to administer. The CAA agreed with us that it was reasonable. We see no reason why such a limited measure should lead to any wider demand for separate terminal charges; we believe that a terminal approach would better, although not fully, reflect experience of individual airlines, and that administration costs should not be excessive given data is already recorded by terminal. We therefore recommend that the CAA should ensure that some elements of the scheme be assessed and implemented at terminal level where this is practicable.

2.468. We recommend that the airline standards should initially include rebates related to the serviceability of stands, jetties, FEGP, people movers, transit systems and baggage reclaim carousels and to the time passengers spend in security queues.[1] We consider that additional work is needed to develop appropriate rebates related to the serviceability of runways and taxiways. Nonetheless, we recommend that these should be incorporated into airline standards when the CAA has determined the details, after discussion with BAA and the airlines. Similarly, we consider that additional work is needed on pier service levels. The existing remote stand rebate results in differences in charges to different airlines but does not affect the overall level of charges: it therefore fails to provide any incentive for BAA to meet the target level of pier service. BAA were concerned that the level of pier service partly reflected the allocation of stands by airlines and/or ground handlers. We believe this should be taken into

---

[1] In relation to a possible Q-factor approach, BAA argued that in principle a discount off airport charges may be inappropriate for failure to meet standards for facilities subject to separate charges: but BAA were prepared to include FEGP given its importance to airlines. However, as we are not recommending a Q-factor approach, this is not relevant.

account by the CAA in setting the appropriate standards; alternatively, BAA might have to take over responsibility for allocating stands itself, which may not be desirable. We therefore recommend that pier service be incorporated in the standards when the CAA has determined details, and is confident a workable rebate scheme exists. In the interim the total potential airline standard rebate or charge reduction of 1.5 or 2.5 per cent (see paragraph 2.465) should be divided between the elements included in this component of the rebate system at any particular time.

2.469.   Our adverse finding does not include outbound and transfer baggage to the extent to which it is already covered by SLAs involving payments, and which are commonly regarded as having been highly successful in improving performance. Such SLAs are, however, limited to particular airlines, although BAA's intention is to extend them to other terminals. However, we recognize that BAA has offered to extend these SLAs to airlines other than BA, which have been slow to respond. The existing baggage SLAs are more complex in approach than the measures we are putting forward for other activities, and the standards to a considerable extent reflect performance not only of BAA but also of other parties involved in the baggage process. Hence, outbound and transfer baggage systems would, in our view, be better covered by extending the existing SLAs to cover other airlines, but this cannot be done without the co-operation of those airlines. Whilst there would be scope for BAA to make voluntary payments (cf jetties) when they were at fault in the absence of agreement, we are not convinced that a satisfactory scheme could be imposed by a condition.

2.470.   We recommend that performance targets should in principle be set at the level incorporated in existing SLAs. We do, however, consider that planned maintenance should normally be included within the performance measures, subject to detailed consideration by the CAA of the possible exceptions discussed in Appendix 2.4. This implies that a small downward adjustment in each affected target would be necessary. We further recommend that the CAA review the lists of other events excluded from the present SLA measures. Such exclusions should be reduced to the minimum consistent with avoiding undesirable operational incentives that may affect the efficient management of each airport. Performance targets should be appropriately adjusted to take account of the likely effect of removing any such exclusions.

2.471.   We have noted the suggestion of BA that there should be 100 per cent standards to be met at all times. We have, however, doubts about the broader implications of such an approach at Heathrow and Gatwick, being very congested. In certain cases, a 100 per cent target would not be achievable; but secondly, to the extent that actual performance was expected to be below 100 per cent, the base level of airport charges (before offsetting service discounts) would need to be increased to allow for the 'normal' level of payments or the costs that would be incurred to avoid such payments. If, consequently, BAA exceeded the expected performance, then BAA would benefit: ie a 100 per cent standard could have the effect of introducing a symmetrical rather than asymmetrical basis of payment, and raising charges to airlines, contrary to the wishes of the airlines. Under the approach we have set out above, any bonuses to BAA would only offset any payments due to the airlines, and there would never be an actual payment to BAA for achieving performance above the current SLA targets.

2.472.   We consider that, within each element of service, the maximum rebate or charge reduction should normally be payable when the relevant performance target has been missed in six months of the year concerned. We set out further guidelines for the treatment of the elements of the airline standards, including their relative weighting, in Appendix 2.4.

2.473.   Although we have recommended inclusion of pier service in airline standards, we consider that the existing remote stand rebate should be retained since it remains important to reflect in the pricing structure the additional costs imposed on airlines who have to use remote stands.

2.474.   We recommend that the passenger standards should include rebates related to passenger perception of departure lounge seat availability, cleanliness, way-finding and flight information. (We acknowledge that this excludes one major area of concern to passengers—check-in queues: but this is an aspect of performance that depends not only on BAA in providing adequate facilities, but also airlines and handling agents in determining the number of desks to use.) Performance should be measured using the results of BAA's QSM surveys. However, it is necessary to ensure that this process is independent and protected from undue influence from BAA's management. We consider that the condition should require BAA to set up a regular independent audit both of the methodology and of its application to ensure that it is in accord with best market research practice, and that the methodology is adequately implemented to make sure that samples accurately reflect the overall mix of passengers at all times of operation. The auditor should be appointed by the CAA (in consultation with the airlines) and report to the CAA.

2.475. We recommend that performance targets for the relevant QSM measures should normally be set at a level determined by the relevant performance of each airport or terminal in a base year of the 12 months ending in August 2001. In any cases where the base year performance is below 3.5, the CAA should consider progressively increasing the level of the target over the next quinquennium until at least this level is reached; it is, however, important that targets remain reasonable and achievable. We set out further guidelines for the treatment of passenger standards in Appendix 2.4.

2.476. We recommend that delay rebates should be introduced when the CAA, after consulting the airlines and BAA, has devised a satisfactory basis for measuring the airfield congestion delays that are attributable to each airport. We believe that, at the moment, neither adequately robust measures of delay nor sufficiently uncontentious methods of attributing their cause are available. We discuss the issues involved in Appendix 2.4. (The CAA may also wish to consider whether any other developments that may require passenger compensation for delays have implications for delay rebates.)

2.477. We recommend that the CAA, from time to time, consider the appropriateness of the standards, and if it has any reason to consider them too easy or too demanding, to amend them after consulting BAA and the airlines. Although the CAA wished to avoid changes to the standards between quinquennial reviews, we believe flexibility is desirable given this is a new and untried approach for BAA, but it would be necessary to ensure that any revisions to standards should be considered from the perspective of both BAA and users. On the basis of the standards we have proposed, however, the targets generally being at or near the level of current performance, there should not be a significant financial impact on BAA unless it allows service to deteriorate significantly: we therefore see no need to increase projected operating costs or cost of capital as a result of introducing standards and rebates for failure to meet them.

2.478. We do not believe it appropriate to include planning standards in this approach, since we accept they cannot rigidly be applied to existing buildings, and could require substantial increases in investment, which may take years to implement and may not always be feasible at reasonable cost within heavily congested sites. A possible exception would be pier service; but the CAA may well take the view that the standard set should be lower than the current planning standard given the level of investment needed at T4 and Gatwick to meet the standards.

2.479. The introduction of generic standards would have the further advantage that those airlines wishing to pay for a quality of service above that of the generic standard would have a firmer basis for doing so: the generic standards would provide a base line above which any higher standards could be specified. Introduction of generic standards would also in our view be more appropriate than amending the current Conditions of Use. We do not share the concern of airlines that those Conditions of Use could themselves prevent development of service standards. The Conditions of Use would not override any conditions imposed by the CAA as a result of our findings. In any event, airlines can always negotiate an SLA that overrode these terms in the Conditions of Use.

2.480. Our adverse finding does not include Stansted, hence the above recommendations do not refer to Stansted. But as Stansted becomes more fully utilized, the CAA should consider the case for introducing appropriate standards at Stansted, although it could not do so within Q4 without the agreement of BAA.

2.481. As is clear from the above, the detailed operation of this approach is for the CAA to consider. If significant administrative problems emerge, it may wish to consider the alternative of the Q factor, but we would expect this to be less successful for the reasons we have set out.

2.482. We conclude that the adverse effect could be remedied by the CAA imposing a condition in relation to Heathrow Airport and a condition in relation to Gatwick Airport along the following lines:

(a) The condition would require HAL or GAL (as the case may be) to pay specified rebates to the airlines whenever their quality of service fails to meet specified performance standards. By 'specified' we mean as specified from time to time by the CAA. The condition would contain exceptions.

(b) The condition would require HAL or GAL (as the case may be) to arrange for regular independent audits of the QSM methodology and of its application to ensure that it is in accord with best market research practice, and that the methodology is adequately implemented to make sure that samples accurately reflect the overall mix of passengers at all times of operation. The auditor should be appointed by the CAA (in consultation with the airlines) and report to the CAA.

We recommend that the CAA impose such a condition. In specifying the scales of rebates and the standards, we recommend that it act in accordance with the principles set out above and in Appendix 2.4.

Airport charging issues

2.483. We considered whether three aspects of airport charges gave rise to public interest concerns: the absence of peak passenger charges; the basis for aircraft parking charges; and the level of charges at Stansted.

2.484. In its recommendations, the CAA said that it would endorse moves that airports made to increase the level of peak pricing. However, it did not propose itself to impose peak pricing on the airports. We thought it appropriate ourselves to consider whether the absence of peak passenger charges in the period up to the date of the reference could be regarded as against the public interest.

2.485. There are peak- and off-peak charges for both runway and parking elements at HAL and GAL, and STAL has a seasonal peak- and off-peak component to its runway charge. Peak international passenger charges at Heathrow are, however, precluded, until T5 opens, by the results of the US:UK arbitration in 1992.

2.486. BAA said that introduction of peak passenger charges only at Stansted and Gatwick would pose several problems. Given the ban on peak passenger charges at Heathrow there would be increased risk of legal challenge to any extension of this principal to Gatwick and Stansted; having a peak passenger charge at Gatwick and Stansted but not Heathrow would lead to perverse pricing differentials, with higher peak pricing at either of those airports than at Heathrow, although pressure on Stansted and Gatwick was less than at Heathrow at such times; and peak passenger charges were very unpopular with airlines who usually claimed they have little choice but to operate at peak times in order to secure the necessary number of rotations a day. The increase in prices in peak hours would be far more significant than pricing increases suggested by the dual-till approach at Gatwick in Q4.

2.487. We received no complaints about the absence of peak charging, and given the current constraint on use of peak international passenger charges at Heathrow, we see no grounds to regard the absence of peak passenger charges at any of the airports as against the public interest, although we recognize it may be an issue worth pursuing.

2.488. Within airport charges, BA and BATA also criticized airport parking charges which include taxiing times which vary within the airport and discriminate, they alleged, against users of T4. BAA said that use of average taxiing times was necessary because of poor data. It was not apparent that T4 airlines would be systematically disbenefited, T3 airlines having longer taxi times when departing towards the West on R27L. T4 was also well placed for BA's maintenance area which would reduce fuel burn. Hence, it would be necessary to establish the impact of such factors in order to determine whether use of average taxi times discriminated against T4.

2.489. We believe this issue is best resolved through the use of best endeavours by BAA and all Heathrow airlines. Any disadvantages from this element of the pricing structure to T4 airlines may well, in the case of BA, be offset by the advantages of concentrating much of its operations in T4. BAA may also have to address this issue when BA moves to T5 and it becomes necessary to attract other airlines into T4. We do not see it as giving rise to public interest issues in itself.

2.490. Concern was also expressed by Luton that BAA should not establish a minimum level of charge at Stansted which is cross-subsidized by other BAA airports, allowing it to compete unfairly; that the existing formula has kept BAA charges artificially low and had the effect of making other airports' own cost-based charges look high; and that BAA was also using its ability to cross-subsidize its charges, enabling it to incentivize traffic to move to its airports, at the expense of other airports. There was also concern about BAA's application to expand Stansted to 25 mppa, and that any development of Stansted would potentially adversely affect capacity and development opportunities at London.

2.491. Hence, Luton argued that BAA should not in the future be able to cross-subsidize operations at Stansted from the monopoly rents gained at Heathrow and Gatwick. (Luton also argued in favour of application of the dual till at Stansted.)

2.492. BAA commented that predatory pricing had been investigated several times by the CAA, the MMC and DGIV in the European Commission and no evidence ever found. The fact that Stansted's tariffs and average revenue yield have both increased since these investigations was in itself substantial evidence that predatory pricing is unlikely. Moreover, BAA made a policy decision never to charge below variable costs. Stansted airport as a whole now met its full operating costs and was forecast to be making real pre-tax returns of 7.5 per cent, ie approximately its cost of capital, by around 2010.

2.493. In our view, Luton would have cause for concern, only if there was evidence of anti-competitive behaviour. Stansted's charges have to a large extent been market-determined, and we expect that will continue to be the case. We have noted, moreover, in Chapter 4 the increasing profitability of STAL over Q3, indicating that charges were above marginal cost in that period. As to whether there has been undue investment, to the detriment of Luton, the early losses of Stansted, as we have noted above, reflect unexpected developments after its construction, in particular, removal of the runway limit at Heathrow, which allowed growth in traffic at Heathrow rather than Stansted. We have also noted in Table 2.16 above that STAL's rate of return could increase to over 7 per cent by the end of Q4, and to above its cost of capital in Q5 even if its charges remained below Gatwick's level and despite the expansion to 25 mppa intended, suggesting its charges are now sufficient to cover the marginal cost of that development. We would find it difficult therefore to regard its charges as too low or that it had engaged in anti-competitive behaviour in pricing, or investment.

Non-regulated charges

2.494. As noted in Chapter 8, BAA currently charges separately for a number of facilities necessary for airlines to operate at the airports, and the charges for which are not regarded as airport charges, although the activities are included in the scope of 'relevant activities' in the Airports Act. (Relevant activities means the provision at the airport of any service or facilities for the purpose of landing, parking or taking-off of aircraft, servicing of aircraft or handling of passengers or their baggage on the airport; section 41 of the Airports Act allows complaints to the CAA about various specified courses of conduct in relation to such relevant activities.) Some of those charges are also 'specified activities' for which, under conditions imposed by the CAA following the 1991 reference, information has to be published on the revenues costs and profits. There is, however, no requirement that either separately or in aggregate those activities should do no more than cover their costs although in practice they do not do so in aggregate on the basis of BAA's current cost allocation system (but with very significant variation in the profitability of individual activities—see Chapter 8).

2.495. In setting the level of airport charges for a particular quinquennium, the MMC took into account projected revenues from non-regulated charges, as with other commercial revenues. It is open to BAA to increase charges for such facilities during a quinquennium by more than we may assume: but to do so could lead to complaint to the CAA under section 41 of the Airports Act relating to relevant activities; or there could be clawback of any unpredicted additional profitability at the next quinquennial review. We discuss the implication of this further in paragraph 2.507.

2.496. Detailed complaints and BAA's response to them are again included in Chapters 12, 13 and 14. Only the main points are included in this chapter.

2.497. A number of issues were raised with us concerning ground handling:

(a) There were complaints about the effect of loss of traffic and relocation of airlines between terminals at Gatwick resulting in loss of economies of scale. BAA, however, regarded this as an issue relating more to the general environment and market conditions of baggage handling, rather than conduct by BAA, with which we agree.

(b) There were suggestions that GAL had failed to police the business plans of new handling agents allowing them to buy market share by offering below-cost handling, putting at risk the viability of existing handlers. BAA believed that it would not be open to it, or desirable, to police the business plans and operations of ground handlers in such a way, with which we also agree.

(c) There were objections to the intended appointment a fourth handler at Gatwick which would lead to further loss of business, further reducing handling charges and profit-ability. The appointment of a fourth ground handler would be outside our terms of reference (as it does not relate to conduct prior to 28 February 2002) but BAA said that the CAA had previously rejected GAL's proposals to limit the number of handlers to three. Concerns about the appointment of a fourth handler, however, were not shared by at least one of the airlines, who believed BAA should have been quicker to have appointed a fourth ground handler at Gatwick and was critical of the criteria on which that handler was chosen (also outside the period with which we are concerned), but that process is now nearing completion. We do not believe BAA has operated against the public interest in this issue in the period we have to consider.

(d) There were also criticisms of BAA insisting on an airport-by-airport relationship, but it was unclear to us that that is necessarily undesirable.

(e) There were criticisms of BAA stipulating service standards as part of ground handling licences with penalties for non-compliance, but where achievement was often

determined by the requirements of the airline on the ground handler. We have no public interest concerns in BAA attempting to impose service standards in their licences. Their obligations under the licences would be a matter for ground handlers to take into account when negotiating contracts with the airlines. In practice, as noted above, BAA can do very little to enforce such conditions on ground handlers, other than by suspending licences, which it is very reluctant to do given the disruption that would be caused.

(f) Ground handlers were also concerned that in the event of failure of an airline, the handling agent remained responsible for meeting the BAA overhead. BAA said that occupation of accommodation such as desks is often on one-month notice periods, but the terms of occupancy are subject to individual negotiation and agreement and it was important for the handling agent to advise the airport management team on its particular requirements. We also regard this as a matter to be taken into account in the initial terms agreed between the handlers and the airlines.

(g) We were also told that there had been delays in signing of licences which BAA acknowledged, but it attributed these to the fact that handlers were already operating at Gatwick and there was no pressing need to conclude documentation.

2.498. We find it difficult therefore to regard any of the above matters as giving rise to public interest concerns about conduct on the part of BAA.

2.499. There was also concern about check-in desks and other rentals. As noted in Chapter 8, check-in desk rentals at Gatwick do not cover the costs of the desks and associated baggage facilities. However, concerns were expressed about the structure of charges, in particular charging per row, hence with higher charges for relatively unutilized rows, and, it was alleged, making it more difficult for new entrants to compete. BAA acknowledged its present charging structure did result in higher charges for desks on less utilized rows, but it had sometimes adjusted charges to reduce the resulting disparities or given rebates. Its proposed hourly charging structure would, however, overcome this problem, and variation in charges per desk would relate only to quality of facilities. Again we found it difficult to regard this as raising public interest concerns.

2.500. There was also concern that since the level of fees was determined by dividing the full costs of operating check-in desk and departure baggage facilities by timed desk usage, with any over- or undercharging carried forward, GAL would have an incentive to under-forecast usage so the level of charges per time period was set higher, hence the risk associated with under-recovery was lower; this would also enable GAL to earn interest on any over-recovery before crediting the amount to airlines in subsequent periods. BAA acknowledged that a number of assumptions were made in calculating hourly charges and for this reason had made provision that revised hourly charges could be introduced on one month's notice in the circumstances of significant over-recovery or under-recovery. However, it had at the request of some airlines deferred the introduction of hourly charging until winter 2002.

2.501. There were also complaints about increases in rental income at Gatwick of some 48 per cent since the time of our previous report, and of increases for particular accommodation, which airlines felt would be less if guidelines used at Heathrow for calculating formulae for rent increases were also applied to Gatwick. The increase in total rent income since our previous report primarily reflects the volume of accommodation rather than increases in rents of individual properties and rents themselves seem reasonable. As noted in Appendix 8.1, we have not found evidence of rents at Gatwick significantly out of line with appropriate comparators, and BAA's calculations showed that rent increases would be higher rather than lower if the Heathrow formula had been applied. There was also criticism of some very high rents at Heathrow, for example £64 per square foot for CIP lounges, but given the demand for CIP accommodation, we find it difficult to regard this as against the public interest. As noted in the appendix from our commercial consultants, we find BAA's approach to rents and property management broadly satisfactory and not indicative of any conduct against the public interest.

2.502. In addition to the rents charged, however, we received a number of complaints about requirements to compensate BAA for lost retail income. One example arose from a proposal by one airline to share a CIP lounge with another airline, where a requirement was imposed by BAA that passengers walk through retail outlets between the lounge and the pier, and that a lift which passengers would otherwise have used be disabled to make sure that they did so; there was also a requirement to compensate BAA for lost car parking when BA wished to establish fly-through check-in facilities. BAA said that the first of these cases was simply an opening negotiating position. On the other hand, it also argued that compensation for lost retail income was reasonable in the context of the single till.

2.503. It is in our view not against the public interest for BAA to seek compensation when providing privileged services to a particular airline, since otherwise such services would under the single till be at the expense of other airlines, as long as it is not excessive.

2.504. A number of other complaints were received (and reproduced at much greater length in Chapter 12) about particular non-airport charges, namely:

(a) Waste disposal charges, for which BAA had changed the services and facilities offered and previously included in airport charges; but also introduced new charges, and increased charges for terminal waste disposal of 50 per cent at Heathrow. BAA attributed these developments to the need to improve handling of waste, following previous abuse of bins provided (see paragraph 14.263) and, in the case of Gatwick, a prohibition notice for transportation of waste by GAL's waste contractor in an unacceptable manner. The 50 per cent increase in terminal waste charges was necessary to cover the costs of the waste contract.

(b) Charges for staff car parking, where there was concern about the very large allocated costs of, for example, constabulary, and the structure of charges which did not vary with time parked and acted as a disincentive for part-time staff. BAA argued that staff car parking costs at Heathrow had significantly under-recovered and compared favourably with other local car parks. It also argued that costs were determined by peak use rather than time parked—in its view, a flat rate charge was less inappropriate than a time-related charge.

(c) FEGP, where there were complaints about frequent outages which caused considerable disruption and cost (hence its inclusion in the service specification proposed by airlines to which we referred above), but also charging on the basis of periods of 15 minutes even when an aircraft was not connected to the system. BAA said that moving to a timed-base system would be expensive and increase overall costs.

(d) Water and sewerage fees which were regarded as excessive compared with prices from other suppliers. BAA argued that water and sewerage charges were cost based, including the capital costs of its utility infrastructure, and under-recovered. Similar considerations apply to electricity.

(e) Cable wayleave charges, which BAA had significantly increased. BAA said that recent increases in cable wayleave charges reflected in part the need to improve on current excessive cable installations by airport occupants/tenants, and complaints were unreasonable.

(f) Substantial fuel fees paid to BAA, both at Gatwick and Stansted. BAA acknowledged that Gatwick charges were not directly derived from actual costs but had been

established by reference to annual increases and RPI for several years. In a single-till environment, if the fuel levy did not exist, its income shortfall would have to be met by an increase in airport charges which would not necessarily be desirable. (There would, of course, be no automatic reduction in airport charges if levies were increased within a quinquennium: a general concern which we discuss below.) Similarly at Stansted, it believed current charges did not recover capex. It also argued that fuel fees were relatively cheap compared with other airports.

2.505. In the context of the single till, excess charges to airlines for such relevant activities are offset by other charges. This would to an extent also apply under the dual till to activities included within the aeronautical till; but the dual till would make the basis of allocation of costs between commercial and aeronautical tills more important (the less the costs allocated to non-aeronautical activities under the dual till, the greater the profit that can be retained by BAA; under the single till, any such effect is merely offset by lower airport charges). Specified activities are also subject to the requirement on BAA to provide information on costs, revenues and profits; a summary of the profits of specified activities in 2000/01 is at Table 8.3 which shows overall costs (including indirect costs) are very close to income.

2.506. Indirect costs account for almost 30 per cent of total costs allocated to specified activities; and airlines said there was insufficient transparency of the basis on which indirect costs were allocated. BAA argued that its profit centre reporting (PCR) cost allocation system was introduced to deal with the conditions, and ensured costs were allocated on a consistent basis for activities, which prevented double counting of cost to more than one activity. BAA offered to give users further explanations of its PCR system, including a full cost breakdown if requested. The specified activity statements are currently audited but primarily to ensure BAA's methodology is consistently applied, rather than that the methodology is valid. Consistent application of the methodology is probably as important to users as its basis, and we see insufficient grounds to find lack of transparency has operated against the public interest. However, we noted in Chapter 8 that BAA's system of PCR has recently been considered by the CAA's consultants, in the context of the CAA's proposed dual till. They commented that BAA's approach to cost allocation was in the main sensible, but did note that insufficient methodology documentation and inconsistent overhead cost definitions/reporting meant that it had been difficult for them to gain a full understanding of how BAA had carried out the allocations. Avia Solutions noted five areas (police, property, corporate charge, terminal facilities and management, and public relations) where BAA's methodology was debatable. They noted proposed changes to the PCR and commented that BAA had accepted the need for many of the changes and had formed a working group to review and implement short-term improvements to the system. Even if the dual till is not adopted, there is value in this process being continued and the CAA being involved in it.

2.507. Underlying the specific complaints, above, however, is the justifiable concern of airlines about BAA's ability to increase existing non-regulated charges between quinquennial reviews, to introduce new charges including new charges for activities which users may currently assume are covered by airport charges, or to reduce the scope of the services and facilities provided, as with waste services. The main safeguards against any such conduct between quinquennial reviews are first the scope to complain under section 41 of the Airports Act. A number of airlines said that they were reluctant to use this provision given the anticipated length of such inquiries, the cost, the risk of worsening working relationships with BAA, and the uncertain outcome: we noted that there had been no complaints to the CAA concerning BAA airports in Q4, and only one concerning another airport. We understand these concerns, but it is clearly not acceptable that section 41 is effectively not usable: if, for example, it is clearly not possible to handle section 41 complaints in significantly less than six months, the legislation is clearly not working as intended. There would therefore be a benefit if the CAA made the application of section 41 procedures more workable for airlines. The second safeguard is the scope for clawback at the time of the next quinquennial review, by when, however, the circumstances of any increase in charges may be unclear. The complaints also, therefore, raise the question of whether the definition of 'airport charges' in the Airports Act should be amended so as to widen the classes of charges that fall within the definition. BAA also itself offered an undertaking that average income per passenger from the main categories of unregulated charges should be linked to RPI; such a linkage would also be applied to some of the more minor specified services for which there were no market benchmarks (and for which BAA believed it should no longer have to publish information on profitability). Finally, the improved complaints procedure BAA intends to introduce may be of benefit in this respect.

2.508. We considered whether a more formal approach would be desirable, namely to include in the condition imposing the charge cap a list of services covered by the cap for which no extra charges are made, and a list of services for which charges are made (not being airport charges) and the amounts of the charges assumed in Q4 when we determine the charge cap. (BAA's list of services covered by these categories is in Appendix 2.5.) The charge cap formula would have a factor comprising any extra money raised through new or increased charges for these items during the quinquennium (a U factor): the U factor would be negative so that any new or increased charge would result in a corresponding reduction in the maximum level of airport charges. The CAA would be able to give its consent to a new charge (or increase in an existing one) not being deducted from the cap if it is satisfied that there are grounds (for example, unavoidable increases in costs) for doing so.

2.509. Given that the U factor could be more complex to administer, we recommend that the CAA adopt the suggestion of BAA of an undertaking to limit the increase in revenues per passenger from such charges to RPI; should this not prove successful, it would open to the CAA to implement the U factor for Q5 (or, in the event of specific complaints from users about any unreasonable increase in charges in Q4, to investigate under section 41 of the Airports Act). We would, however, see it as important that BAA continue to provide to the CAA and airlines and others as appropriate the information required under the present transparency arrangements.

2.510. We referred in paragraph 2.312 to the proposed inclusion of transfer infrastructure baggage in the activities regarded as covered by airport charges. BA also suggested that airport navigation services, provided by NATS and charged for separately, should be included within the scope of airport charges. This is subject to a separate consultation exercise by the CAA, the results of which, and decision by the Secretary of State, will not be known until after we have reported. There are advantages and disadvantages of this approach; BAA argued that such a move was too complex to be incorporated in charges in Q4. If a decision was taken before airport charges for Q4 are set, it would be open to the CAA to adjust the pricing formula to include such services; alternatively this could be done by mutual consent between the CAA and BAA during Q4.

Other specific complaints

2.511. A number of other specific complaints summarized in more detail in Chapter 13, with BAA's response in Chapter 14, were raised with us.

2.512. One tour operator referred to the charges levied by contractors to airlines for handling handicapped passengers, which were passed on to the passengers; it said that prices should be the same to everyone. BAA said that it shared the correspondent's concern about any instances where passengers with reduced mobility are directly charged for the extra costs incurred: it did not believe this was an acceptable practice. This was made clear in the European airports voluntary commitment on passenger service. However, a very small number of airlines persisted in directly charging passengers with reduced mobility. This led to the suggestion that airports should organize the assistant services to these passengers. BAA told us it did trial taking on more direct responsibility for provision of services to reduced mobility passengers at Gatwick, but it was not supported by one of the main airlines, and costs would therefore have been prohibitive.

2.513. Although BAA understood the concerns expressed and stood ready to deal with the problem, it did not believe a centrally organized service was necessarily the appropriate solution. In these circumstances, this is a matter for airlines to resolve. (We also note that legal proceedings have recently been instituted against an airline and BAA concerning arrangements for disabled passengers at Stansted.)

2.514. We received a number of complaints about charges levied on car hire operators. These included:

(a) the percentage basis of the concession fee;

(b) the application of a concession fee percentage to revenues including those derived from fuel sold, albeit at more limited margins, resulting in higher fuel prices to users, and vehicle licence and registration fee;

(c) whether the level of the concession fee was fair;

(d) BAA's cap on car hire charges to off-airport levels;

(e) service at Stansted for turnaround being unsatisfactory;

(f) the requirement for investment by the operator;

(g) rent for property being set at levels higher than in neighbouring areas;

(h) BAA's requirement that it be able to reacquire sites at nominal value, including the benefits of any investment by the concessionaire on those sites, if an operator withdraw from the market; and

(i) more generally, the strong negotiation position of BAA with respect to its ability to control rents and impose charges that could not be challenged by using comparables or appeal, rents within airport land being artificially higher than the potential market rent elsewhere: it was suggested BAA should be covered by the same regulation on comparables and approaches that apply elsewhere.

2.515. BAA responded that all car hire contracts were tendered on the open market or sometimes negotiated individually. This process ensured that market forces determined the value of the on-airport site for rental locations. The only additional costs imposed were for backup areas, concession fee and utility charges. BAA believed tendering on the basis of price was the most suitable way of rationing the scarce resource of land, and if charges to the operators were lower, there would merely be additional profits generated by them, and, under the single till, higher airport charges to users. It also pointed out that the requirement to price at national rates only applied to 'walk-up' prices, a relatively small part of the market. If an operator went bankrupt, it was necessary for BAA rapidly to recover the site; the value of any asset it acquired when it did so would be offset by the liabilities to BAA; but BAA sometimes did allow assets to be recovered.

2.516. These appear to be sound reasons for BAA wishing to apply such conditions. Given, in our view, that the car hire companies can reflect such conditions, being well known and fully transparent, in their tenders, we do not see grounds for an adverse finding.

2.517. We also received complaints about discouragement of international business or air taxi traffic, in particular that Stansted had a very poor reputation for handling of and attitude to general aviation (GA) aircraft. BAA said that Stansted had arguably the best dedicated GA facilities of any major south-east airport. It did not actively market the airport to GA, preferring to rely on the fixed base operators to do so, but it did ensure that both operators could develop their facilities in line with growing demand. In most cases GA operators were required to apply to Airport Coordination Ltd (ACL) for runway slots, for which regular commercial services took precedence. If Stansted became busier, particularly at certain times of day, it was likely that GA taxi operators would find it more difficult than previously to gain runway access at peak times. However, at other times they had full and open access to the airport.

2.518. Given the pressure of demand from scheduled services to use the BAA airports, particularly for passenger services, the EC regulation that determines the way that ACL operates allocates runway slots, and the greater range of other airports available for business or air taxi traffic, we do not regard BAA's conduct as against the public interest in this respect.

2.519. We also received criticisms of recent changes in arrangements for taxi services at Gatwick. Until February 2001, two Private Hire contractors provided the South and North terminals of Gatwick Airport with Private Hire Services. These contracts expired in 2001 and were the subject of a rigorous tendering process by BAA. BAA accepted tenders from two independent contractors, one to provide the service at Gatwick South Terminal and another to provide the service at Gatwick North Terminal. The contractor providing the South Terminal service was subsequently appointed at the North Terminal due, we were told, to pressure from the incumbent owner-drivers. BAA said that it had become apparent that to have two taxi operators at each terminal did not work in the best interest of the customer. Competition had been effectively abandoned in order to allocate work evenly between the drivers and ensure drivers were retained at Gatwick. Service had declined. Hence, contracts were subsequently awarded on the basis of one operator per terminal. However, due to the uneven and seasonal split of passenger numbers between the terminal and the very different profile/mix, this led to a similar situation and the drivers working solely from the North Terminal were disadvantaged in their earning capabilities. It became apparent that one operator with one pool of drivers serving both terminals was the best option providing flexibility and better service to the customer, including the prequoting of fares prior to boarding the taxi which most customers preferred. Complaints had significantly reduced and there was investment in new vehicles and a computerized booking facility.

2.520. In our view, the current arrangements are not ideal; but users appear to have benefited and it would still be open to other operators to compete for the contract when renewed. We do not therefore regard current arrangements as raising public interest concerns.

2.521. There were also complaints about the granting of exclusive concessions to operate VAT refunds at Heathrow and Gatwick, including recent extensions without tender of the current exclusive concession, which increased costs and reduced quality of service offered. BAA believed that the current method of providing the VAT cash refund service did not operate against the public interest, as there was no increase in cost to customers; quality of service had improved; having one VAT cash refund point was a simpler solution for a customer and the most efficient and cost-effective solution; and operation of the service through an independent operator meant all those refund operators who wished to offer their customers the option of receiving their VAT refund in cash were able to do so on a level playing field. Hence, BAA believed that the provision of the service by a sole operator was essential to derive and develop the substantial customer service benefits arising from a close working relationship that had been developed with HM Customs. Given these benefits from the current arrangements, we do not believe BAA's conduct can be regarded as against the public interest in this respect.

2.522. A company set up at Stansted to carry out airside driver training and fire evacuation training said it was undercut by a £10 per person BAA charge for fire and evacuation training, which resulted from unfair cross-subsidy by BAA. BAA said that the training of BAA staff was previously undertaken by various trained facilitators on a departmental basis. In order to improve efficiency, enhance consistency and effectively increase the number of fire training sessions available to staff it was concluded that all such training should be led by BAA fire service personnel. Given the courses being run for BAA staff, the offer was made to third parties to book their staff on these two-hour courses at £10 a head if spare places existed. This had the effect of ensuring that frequent courses accommodating around 40 people were available on predetermined dates throughout the year. As a result, the marginal costs of providing third party training were very low and there could be, therefore, no question of cross-subsidy. The course was not obligatory for non-BAA staff: indeed BAA also offered a 'train the trainer' course to enable other organizations to undertake the regular annual training themselves in future. The primary objective therefore had been to improve BAA processes and take the opportunity of contributing positively to fire safety at Stansted.

2.523. We are sympathetic to the complaints raised. BAA's approach to charging implies charges are set below fully attributable cost, with the risk of adversely affecting competition. However, any adverse consequences are likely to be offset by the benefits to users of having frequent courses available at low cost. On balance we find it difficult therefore to find its conduct against the public interest. We do, however, invite BAA to ensure that, given it does not appear to be including any cost of its own facilities in its charges, it make them available on the same, free terms to any new entrants seeking to provide such services; this is not, however, likely to be enough to ensure new entrants could operate profitably.

Heathrow taxis

The complaints

2.524. A taxi driver complained that Heathrow Airport Licensed Taxis Limited (HALT) unfairly used its bargaining position by refusing to produce a written commercial agreement setting out the terms and conditions under which self-employed taxi drivers are granted access to the airport's taxi ranks. Last October it informed drivers the written terms and conditions were about to be drawn up but nothing more on the matter had been heard. One of the unwritten rules for Heathrow taxi drivers enforced by HAL was that they have to make a payment of 49p to a taxi drivers friendly society known as HALT each time they use the taxi system. The airport bylaws were totally silent on this, but HAL insisted it could rely on them to prevent a taxi driver from working at Heathrow should he or she refuse to make payments to HALT. HALT was employed as a contractor by HAL to supply taxi support services and one of HALT's main duties was to provide taxi information desks in the passenger terminals and to take bookings from taxi passengers travelling from Heathrow to London and vice versa. However, although HALT registered as a friendly society in 1992, it had not elected an Executive Committee since 1994. Second, its 'Executives' were members of the Transport & General Workers' Union (T&G) and yet in the London taxi trade as a whole, less than 2 per cent of drivers are union members. Without doubt the T&G's taxi branch acquired through its control of HALT an unacceptably high degree of control over Heathrow taxi drivers which it certainly could not acquire through the ballot box. According to the taxi driver, BAA also claimed to have lost basic information on the contract entered into with HALT in 1993, the terms of which require all Heathrow taxi drivers to pay subscriptions to HALT irrespective of their membership status. It had subsequently failed to exercise due diligence to reorganize and replace lost paperwork covering transactions involving millions of pounds of taxi drivers' money.

2.525. It was argued that HAL's rule on compulsory payments to HALT represented a violation of statutory right to freedom of association. Conditions should be imposed on HAL as a means to remedy the adverse effects of their funding rules for the dysfunctional HALT friendly society that HAL must agree to publish the terms and conditions of the commercial agreement by which HAL and taxi drivers are bound in the Heathrow taxi system, including terms covering compulsory payments to trade organizations, and must agree to publish the terms and conditions of the commercial agreement concluded by HAL and HALT in 1993, including the identity of parties represented during negotiations.

2.526. In 2000, another taxi driver, acting as a litigant in person, issued county court proceedings against HAL. He claimed £348 being the total sums paid by him under the HALT levy during 1999. He alleged that HALT did not hold quorate annual general meetings for 1997, 1998 or 1999; that the taxi drivers who controlled HALT's funds were not elected to office; that it was a condition of the agreement between him and HAL that HALT was managed in accordance with its rules; and that HAL had collected £348 in breach of that condition. He abandoned the action after a defence had been filed. He told us that the court decided that the case was too complex to be handled as a small claim and he discontinued the action rather than face the costs risks through not having copies of the contract documents to refer to at a full trial.

Heathrow Airport Licensed Taxis Limited

2.527. HALT is a society registered under the Industrial and Provident Societies Act 1965 and is not a friendly society. It was registered on 14 September 1992. Membership is open to any licensed cab driver who is a member of a 'Cab Trade Organisation recognised by the Department for Transport, the Metropolitan Police and the London Taxi Board'. However, the executive committee can accept applications from any other licensed cab driver wishing to use the facilities of the society. Shares are not transferable and carry no right to a dividend. However, the profits can be applied in paying a bonus to members. As at 31 January 2002, there were 3,100 members. In the year ending 31 January 2002, the turnover was £443,097 and the accumulated profit was £42,405. The accounts do not record any bonuses being paid in the accounting years 1996/1997 to 2001/2002. We have not seen any earlier accounts. Further details are set out in Appendix 2.6.

Operation of taxis at Heathrow

2.528. BAA told us that it imposes an obligatory taxi control system at Heathrow. It told us that it is designed to regulate the number of taxis waiting on the ranks at each of the four terminals by use of a holding area away from the terminals known as the Taxi Feeder Park. The system automatically directs each taxi leaving the Taxi Feeder Park to the next available place on the rank at one of the four terminals, thereby keeping each of the terminals supplied with the appropriate number of taxis for hire. Save for an exception that applies when a taxi driver has returned after completing a local journey, a taxi cannot gain access to the ranks at any of the terminals to ply for hire without first going through the Taxi Feeder Park.

2.529. The Heathrow Airport—London Bylaws 1996 prevent a taxi plying for hire at the airport other than at an authorized taxi rank. They also prevent a taxi entering an authorized taxi rank without first passing through the Taxi Feeder Park unless authorized by a constable, traffic warden or airport official.

2.530. From the time a taxi driver enters the Taxi Feeder Park to the time he leaves the terminal rank, he has to display a device known as Cabtag on his windscreen. This requirement and the manner in which the control system operates is now set out in the Taxi Feeder Park and Terminal Ranks Cabtag System Terms and Conditions of Use (Cabtag Terms and Conditions of Use) which became effective from 1 August 2002. The control system is largely automatic. A Cabtag is an electronic device on which the system depends. HALT have nothing to do with the operation of the Cabtag system.

2.531. BAA told us that the Cabtag Terms and Conditions of Use are displayed in the Taxi Feeder Park. It is stated in that document that the Bylaws are also displayed there, but the taxi driver who made the complaint told us that they are not and never have been displayed there.

2.532. BAA believes that there are between 3,500 and 4,000 regular taxi drivers at Heathrow, although it has issued 7,500 Cabtags.

2.533. BAA told us that HALT provides support services to all taxi drivers at Heathrow. These principally comprise the operation of the taxi information desks at each of the terminals. The desks are manned by retired taxi drivers who assist the public with any inquiries regarding the provision of taxi services at the airport.

2.534. BAA told us that it is not under any contractual obligation to the taxi drivers to provide the support services. BAA regards HALT as licensees at a reduced rent who are not any contractual obligation to BAA to provide the HALT services. There is in existence a written licence agreement between BAA and HALT. All of the original documentation went missing in the Heathrow tunnel collapse.

2.535. So far as BAA is aware, there is no contractual relationship between a driver using the Taxi Feeder Park and HALT.

2.536. Fares within the Metropolitan and City Police Districts are restricted to the amount shown on the meters and there is no supplement for journeys starting at Heathrow. Fares for other journeys are fixed by agreement. Thus the levy could affect the availability of taxis for journeys to destinations in and outside the Metropolitan and City Police District. It could also affect the fares for journeys outside these Districts.

Charges to taxi drivers

2.537. BAA told us that taxi drivers are obliged to pay a charge upon each visit to the Taxi Feeder Park. They are required to pay £1.75 plus £0.31 VAT. They are also required to pay a sum of £0.49 (called the 'HALT levy') making a total of £2.55. BAA told us that the £1.75 is intended to cover the operational costs of running the control system. A notice of these charges is normally displayed on the Taxi Feeder Park. The notice of the charges currently in force has been taken down and BAA has not been able to provide us with a copy. There is, however, currently a notice of the charges coming into force on 1 November 2002 but BAA failed to provide us with a copy. The Cabtag Terms and Conditions of Use state that taxi drivers need to purchase credits. However, they do not state the amount of the charges or the existence of the HALT levy.

2.538. BAA told us that the taxi driver has to pay the levy whether he or she is or is not a member of HALT. The levy is reviewed annually following a consultation exercise with the Heathrow taxi trade representatives HALT, the London Taxi Drivers Club, the Licensed Taxi Drivers Association and the T&G. All minutes are published and placed on the taxi notice board within the Taxi Feeder Park for any comments by the drivers.

2.539. BAA believes that it receives the levy as collection agent and not as principal. It charges HALT a 2 per cent collection fee.

2.540. BAA said that, according to its calculations, it made an under-recovery of 48 per cent. The under-recovery relates to the overall cost of running the taxi operation including the Cabtag costs and traffic wardens. It is not clear whether the rent reduction has been taken into account in this calculation.

Origins of establishment of Heathrow Airport Licensed Taxis Limited and the compulsory levy

2.541. BAA told us that HALT has received funding from the Heathrow taxi drivers since the early 1990s and was in response to an original request from the taxi trade. It said that it was agreed that HALT would be set up as a 'registered Friendly Society'. BAA became involved in collection of the levy when the former bucket collection created concern as to coercion and misuse of funds. It became involved with the consent of the trade representative bodies.

The issues and BAA's comments

2.542. As we see it, the complaint gave rise to two potential public interest questions that, in our view, needed further consideration:

(a) Has BAA acted against the public interest by imposing the HALT levy on all taxi drivers without first ascertaining, by tender or otherwise, such questions as whether all aspects of the service are necessary; whether it could be obtained at a lower price from a commercial provider; or whether a better service could be obtained for the same price?

(b) Is the levy sufficiently transparent as to the purpose for which it is made?

2.543. As to *(a)*, BAA told us that all trade organizations agreed that the desks are of benefit to the trade as a whole. If the majority view were to change or circumstances were to alter, then BAA would review the HALT funding but at present it has no evidence of this. BAA also said that it was highly questionable whether a commercial provider could operate the support services profitably without a huge increase in the charge to taxi drivers. It also said that if it were minded to invite tenders for the provision of the services, the majority of taxi drivers would be likely to try to stop it.

2.544. As to *(b)*, BAA said that drivers using the Taxi Feeder Park for the first time will have the charge explained to them by its agents, currently traffic wardens. It agreed that the Cabtag Terms and Conditions of Use could be altered to include details of the services provided by BAA and the charge could be better published. It said that there may be a lack of transparency about the HALT levy but believed this was for HALT's members to question and not BAA.

Assessment

2.545. In our view, taxi drivers are not users as defined in the Airports Act but the services they provide at Heathrow are operational activities. The question of the levy relates, in our view, to the granting of a right by virtue of which operational activities are carried out, that is to say, the right to use the taxi ranks. Accordingly, we are required by section 43(5) to have regard to the reasonable interests of the taxi drivers.

2.546. In the time available to us, we found this to be a complex and non-transparent issue. We accordingly make such findings as we feel able to make on the basis of the evidence available to us.

2.547. In our view, since the services have not been tendered, it is more likely than not that costs are higher than necessary. However, our conclusion does not depend on this view.

2.548. We find that HAL has pursued a course of conduct during the relevant period which operates and may be expected to operate against the public interest in that it imposed the HALT levy on all taxi drivers without first ascertaining, by tender or otherwise, such questions as whether all aspects of the service are necessary; whether they could be obtained at a lower price from a commercial provider; or whether a better service could be obtained from a commercial provider for the same price.

2.549. The adverse effects of this conduct are:

(a) that a levy has been imposed on taxi drivers without any basis for the regulatory authorities to determine whether the services provided by HALT are of benefit to taxi drivers (whether or not members of HALT) or represent value for money to them, and to passengers, and whether the methods used are currently cost-effective; and

(b) that taxi drivers (whether or not members of HALT) do not have the protection against excess charges that would be afforded if the services were provided under normal commercial arrangements or if BAA had taken the steps set out in paragraph 2.548.

2.550. Having found that BAA has pursued a course of conduct that is expected to operate against the public interest, we now need to consider remedies.

2.551. We recommend that the CAA should invite BAA to produce evidence within six months that satisfies the CAA that the HALT service is of benefit to the taxi drivers who use Heathrow (whether or not members of HALT) and their passengers; that the benefits outweigh the costs of providing the service; and if so that the service could not be provided in a more efficient and cost-effective manner. The CAA should then in due course decide whether to give a direction under the condition we are recommending below. However, if the CAA is at any time minded to give a direction under the condition, it should consult HALT before coming to a final decision.

2.552. If BAA produce evidence that satisfies the CAA that the HALT service is of benefit to the taxi drivers and their passengers, the CAA should from time to time, say every five years, invite BAA to provide evidence that that is still the case.

2.553. The condition we are recommending would enable the CAA to give a direction preventing BAA collecting the HALT levy on a compulsory basis while the direction remained in force. The power would arise if at any time it appeared to the CAA that it was not in the public interest that the HALT levy should continue on a compulsory basis. We envisage the CAA imposing the condition at the same time as it invites BAA to produce the evidence. We believe that the condition would give all concerned the necessary incentive to demonstrate that the levy represented value for money, etc. So long as they were able to do so, taxi drivers would be protected. If they fail, the levy would cease. Either way, the adverse effects would be remedied. We accordingly find that the adverse effects could be remedied by the imposition of such a condition.

2.554. BAA told us that it is willing to invite tenders for the HALT services and that this would probably be preceded by a consultation exercise with the whole trade. This is one of the ways that could satisfy the CAA that the HALT services provide value for money and are of benefit to taxi drivers. Further action might, however, be needed to show that the services are of benefit to the public.

2.555. As BAA was not able to provide us with a copy of the contents of the notice in use during the relevant period and we have no grounds for believing that taxi drivers were not fully aware of the levy during the relevant period, we make no adverse public interest finding on whether the purpose of the levy was sufficiently transparent. We nevertheless hope that BAA will make the arrangements more transparent by including full details of the charges in the Cabtag Terms and Conditions of Use. BAA has told us that it is willing to do this. We also hope that the Cabtag Terms and Conditions of Use along with the bylaws will be made available on BAA's web site. We would also like to see it stated that payment of the levy does not give rise to any contractual relationship between the taxi driver and HALT (if that is HALT's intention) and the fact the HAL is not under any obligation to the taxi drivers to ensure that the support services are provided (so long as that is BAA's intention).

Old public interest condition

2.556. The CAA also said that it would value advice on lifting old public interest conditions. In particular, BAA had argued that it had proved impossible to attract a second travel agent to the Gatwick concourse as required following our last report. Hence it wished to remove the requirement to do so. It would seek tenders for the remaining outlet to be run as a travel shop when its contract expired—but would not necessarily do so in future.

2.557. The existing agent, however, attributed the difficulties of having two agents in part to the way the contract was awarded—based on turnover rather than fixed rent—and by providing for a shop rather than desk. The first point was acknowledged by BAA but with a guaranteed minimum being based on the concessionaries sales forecast. BAA had not considered the rental of desks alone for these contracts: when the two travel shops were open the concessionaire requirements were for space for four to six staff who could both deal face to face and answer phone calls. However, methods of booking holidays had dramatically changed. A change to rental of a desk would not offer any financial advantage to a travel shop operator—the current minimum guarantee payment of the existing agent was less than the amount they would pay using the rate applied to airline or handling agent ticket sales desks, even if the existing frontage was reduced by 25 per cent and not have any office behind the desk. BAA would consider a change in the form of space requirement, subject to availability of desk space.

2.558. Section 51(6) of the Airports Act gives the CAA power to modify the condition whether or not we make an adverse finding in this report. We see no evidence that BAA has been pursuing a course of conduct against the public interest as regards these matters. In the absence of such a finding, the question of whether the condition should be modified is outside our terms of reference.

Summary of public interest conclusions and recommendations

2.559. During the inquiry we received a substantial number of complaints on a wide range of public interest issues. It is clearly unsatisfactory that the airlines in particular have to use five-yearly reviews as to the main means to pursue such complaints; the proposed improvements in consultation on the CIP, and BAA's proposals to improve its handling of complaints may make it less necessary for such issues to be raised with us, but we were also concerned that the need to raise such issues with ourselves resulted from a perception by airlines of a lack of involvement by the CAA in the relationship between airlines and users between quinquennial reviews. We therefore share the concerns of airlines about any policy of the CAA of standing back from such issues, and suggest not only, as we have mentioned above, it examines whether the operation of procedures under section 41 of the Airports Act can be pursued, but also whether it does not have more scope to be involved aside from its formal role under section 41.

2.560. On two of the issues raised with us, we have concluded that:

(a) in failing to conduct themselves so as to make prices paid sufficiently reflect the level of service provided, HAL and GAL have pursued a course of conduct which may be expected to operate against the public interest (see paragraphs 2.451 to 2.453). The adverse effect of this conduct is that prices do not reflect the quality of service provided to the extent that would occur in a competitive market and in consequence that there is an absence of the financial incentive to provide the combination of price and quality of service that would obtain in a competitive market; and

(b) HAL has pursued a course of conduct which operates and may be expected to operate against the public interest in that it imposes a levy—the HALT levy—on all taxi drivers without first ascertaining, by tender or otherwise, such questions as whether all aspects of the service are in the interests of taxi drivers; whether they could be obtained at a lower price from a commercial provider; or whether a better service could be obtained from a commercial provider for the same price (see paragraph 2.548). The adverse effects of this conduct are that a levy has been imposed on taxi drivers without any basis for the regulatory authorities to determine whether the services provided by HALT are of benefit to taxi drivers (whether or not members of HALT) or represent value for money to them, and to passengers and whether the methods used are currently cost-effective; and that taxi drivers (whether or not members of HALT) do not have the protection against excess charges that would be afforded if the services were provided under normal commercial arrangements or if BAA had taken the steps previously referred to in this paragraph.

2.561. In paragraph 2.18 we referred to the arguments of some airlines for further consideration of separate ownership of the three airports: none of the adverse effects we have identified in the current review would justify our recommending such a remedy. To remedy the adverse effects identified above, we have recommended:

(a) That a condition be imposed in relation to Heathrow Airport and a condition in relation to Gatwick Airport that HAL or GAL (as the case may be) pay specified rebates to the airlines whenever their quality of service fails to meet specified performance standards. By 'specified' we mean as specified from time to time by the CAA. In specifying the scales of rebates and the standards, we recommend the CAA acts in accordance with the principles set out in paragraphs 2.461 to 2.481 and Appendix 2.4.

(b) The conditions would require that HAL or GAL (as the case may be) arrange for regular independent audits of the QSM methodology and of its application to ensure that it is in accord with best market research practice, and that the methodology is adequately implemented to make sure that samples accurately reflect the overall mix of passengers at all times of operation. The auditor should be appointed by the CAA (in consultation with the airlines) and report to the CAA.

(c) That a condition should be imposed that would enable the CAA to give a direction preventing BAA collecting the HALT levy on a compulsory basis while the direction remained in force. The power would arise if at any time it appeared to the CAA that it was not in the public interest that the HALT levy should continue on a compulsory basis. For that purpose, we recommend that the CAA should invite BAA to produce evidence within six months that satisfies the CAA that the HALT service is of benefit to the taxi drivers who use Heathrow (whether or not members of HALT) and their passengers; that the benefits outweigh the costs of providing the service; and that the service could not be provided in a more efficient and cost-effective manner. The CAA should then in due course decide whether to give a direction under the condition. However, if the CAA is at anytime minded to give a direction under the condition, it should consult HALT before coming to a final decision. If BAA produce evidence that satisfies the CAA that the HALT service is of benefit to the taxi drivers and their passengers, the CAA should from time to time, say every five years, invite BAA to provide evidence that that is still the case.

Part II

Background and evidence

3 Background

Contents

Introduction

3.1. This chapter gives background information on BAA; the history and development of demand at the airports; the system of regulation; and the regulatory history.

BAA history and organization

3.2. The British Airports Authority was established by the Airports Authority Act 1965, and assumed ownership and responsibility for the three London airports, Heathrow, Gatwick, Stansted, as well as Prestwick airport in Scotland, in April 1966. (Later, Edinburgh, Aberdeen, Glasgow and Southampton Airports were added. Prestwick was subsequently sold.) The Government announced its intention to privatize the British Airports Authority in the Airports Policy White Paper (Cmnd 9542) and the Authority was dissolved, and its property, rights and liabilities transferred to BAA, under the Airports Act 1986. BAA had been formed on 13 December 1985. We refer to Heathrow, Stansted and Gatwick airports as the BAA London airports.

3.3. Separate companies were established to operate the airports, namely HAL, GAL, STAL and Scottish Airports Ltd. We refer to HAL, GAL and STAL as the 'airport companies'. The holding company of each of the three airport companies is LAL, which is in turn a subsidiary of BAA. On 16 July 1987, 500 million shares in BAA were offered for sale and the company was listed on the International Stock Exchange, London, on 28 July 1987, becoming the world's first listed airport operator. Since then the company's shares have been listed on both the Canadian and Australian Stock Exchanges.

3.4. BAA currently has approximately 400,000 shareholders, over 95 per cent of whom are private individuals, who together hold just over 15 per cent of the share capital. The two most substantial shareholders are FMR Corporation and Fidelity International Ltd, which together have interests of approximately 4.17 per cent in the company's share capital. After privatization, the Government retained a residual 2.9 per cent stake in BAA, but it sold this stake in 1996 for approximately £145 million. The Secretary of State, however, still retains a Special Share in BAA (referred to as a 'golden share'). Under BAA's articles, certain matters are deemed to be a variation of the rights attached to the Special Share and would therefore require the consent in writing of the Secretary of State. Such matters include a provision preventing any individual from owning more than 15 per cent of the shares of BAA, and another restricting the disposal outside BAA of any airport designated for price regulation (currently BAA's London airports: Heathrow, Gatwick and Stansted). The issue of golden shares is currently being reviewed by the European Commission which has argued that these types of shares—which give national governments a casting vote over takeovers and major decisions in firms in which they no longer hold a majority stake—are contrary to EC rules on the free movement of capital, and therefore should not be allowed. In 2000, the European Commission filed a case against the UK Government over its failure to relinquish its golden share in BAA. This case is still pending before the European court.

BAA other business activities

3.5. After privatization BAA evolved into an international airports and retail operator. Management pursued a strategy to expand away from regulated activities as much as possible, by developing new streams of unregulated income. Areas that were expanded into included hotel development, cargo handling, duty-free retailing, property development and, more recently, rail operations.

BAA Lynton

3.6. BAA acquired Lynton plc (Lynton), a property company, in 1988 to develop its airport land holdings. Lynton was subsequently relaunched in April 1997 as BAA Lynton, the specialist airport property developer, focusing on property development and investment at and around airports, including locations which have or will have transport links to airports. In 2002 BAA Lynton signed an agreement with Radisson SAS to open a 500-bed, four-star hotel at Stansted, to open in 2003.

BAA McArthurGlen

3.7. In March 1995, BAA opened Cheshire Oaks, an outlet centre for designer and brand label surplus stock, in a joint venture with McArthurGlen. BAA McArthurGlen has now expanded with 12 centres operating in six countries, comprising over 1,000 shops. BAA and McArthurGlen dissolved the joint venture, however, with effect from 30 August 2002, as BAA furthered its strategy of exiting from non-core airport interests.

World Duty Free

3.8. In July 1997, BAA acquired the US company Duty Free International (DFI). In May 1998 DFI was renamed World Duty Free Americas and merged with the UK-based operation, WDFE, to create a new integrated duty free global holding company called WDF. World Duty Free Americas, however, was considered to be under-performing, and BAA subsequently sold it in October 2001, returning its focus to core UK airports business. BAA's UK operations now include 58 stores across BAA's seven UK airports. As well as the WDF stores, BAA also operates a range of stand-alone specialist stores including World of Whiskies, The Cigar House, The Wine Collection, and the Beauty Studio.

3.9. In February 1998, BAA's in-flight retail division, Inflight Duty Free Shop Inc (IDFS), was awarded a five-year contract by bmi to operate its in-flight tax- and duty-free sales business; the first time a major in-flight contract from a British airline had been awarded to third party specialists. However, IDFS was subsequently sold due to poor performance.

3.10. In March 1999, BAA signed a major contract with Eurotunnel to operate retail facilities in its Folkestone and Calais/Coquelles terminals. However, BAA rescinded the contract in June 2000 and initiated a High Court action against Eurotunnel for damages for misrepresentation and breach of warranty. This action was settled to BAA's satisfaction.

Heathrow Express

3.11. BAA launched the £500 million Heathrow Express in 1998, providing a direct link between central London and Heathrow. In 2001/02 over 4.8 million passengers used the service (around 11 per cent of Heathrow non-transfer passengers).

International management and consultancy

3.12. BAA has continued its involvement in international consultancy and the management of airport facilities. Outside the UK, the group now has management contracts or stakes in 12 airports including Pittsburgh, Indianapolis, and Boston Logan in the USA, six in Australia, including Melbourne and Perth, Naples in Italy and two in Oman.

BAA London airports

The airport businesses

3.13. Within the airport framework BAA is directly responsible for the provision and maintenance of airport infrastructure, such as runways, terminals and equipment; and the provision of essential services, including passenger and staff search, perimeter security, and fire-fighting. The airports contract out cleaning, catering, retailing, car parks management, electricity distribution and a large proportion of maintenance. BAA also allocates resources, both between airlines (for example, check-in desks) and between commercial concessionaires (such as car hire franchises).

3.14. Some services are not undertaken by the airport companies or any contractors on their behalf, but are carried out by licensees acting on their own behalf. These services include Air Traffic Control (ATC) (provided by NATS) and baggage and passenger handling (provided by the airlines themselves or handling agents employed by the airlines).

History and development

Heathrow

3.15. Heathrow was designated as London's main airport in 1944 and commercial services began in 1946. It has grown consistently and is now the world's fourth largest airport, and the world's busiest international airport, handling 64.3 million passengers in 2000/01. It is also the oldest of the world aviation hubs.

3.16. Heathrow has two runways and four terminals. Terminal 2 (T2) opened in 1955, T1 opened in 1968, and T3 opened in 1970. By 1977 demand for Heathrow had developed to such an extent that the Government implemented traffic distribution rules to redirect certain categories of traffic to Gatwick whilst a fourth terminal was being planned for Heathrow. T4 eventually opened in 1986. These terminals have all subsequently been extensively remodelled and extended. On 17 February 1993, an application for planning permission for a fifth terminal was submitted. It was approved in outline (subject to conditions) on 20 November 2001, following the longest planning inquiry in history. T5 is now planned to open in spring 2008 (ie after the end of Q4).

3.17. Heathrow is the closest of the BAA airports to central London, and is connected by road, and rail links: including both the London Underground and the BAA Heathrow Express.

Gatwick

3.18. Gatwick was developed as a second airport for the South-East following a public inquiry in 1954. The terminal building was opened in 1958. The restrictions on the categories of traffic allowed to use Heathrow from 1977 assisted traffic growth at Gatwick, leading to the construction of a second 'North' terminal, which opened in 1988. These traffic distribution rules were relaxed in 1991, resulting in a significant transfer of scheduled services from Gatwick to Heathrow.

3.19. Gatwick has only a single runway, but it is one of the busiest in the world with 48 movements per hour scheduled throughout most of the day. In 1979, the British Airports Authority (forerunner of BAA) signed an agreement with West Sussex County Council not to build a second runway during the next 40 years.

3.20. Gatwick is 24 miles from Central London, and has rail connections to central London and the rest of south-east England, and links to the national motorway system.

Stansted

3.21. The Government identified the development of Stansted as the third London airport in December 1979, to accommodate the overspill from Heathrow and Gatwick. The growth in air travel demand during the 1980s resulted in BAA being requested to bring forward the proposals for Stansted's development. The plans were approved in 1985 and a new terminal opened in 1991.

3.22. Demand for Stansted in the beginning did not meet expected forecasts, due in part to the Gulf War and the removal of the traffic distribution rules referred to above. However, it has grown strongly in the last five years, and has become one of the fastest-growing airports in Europe, largely due to the unprecedented growth of the low-fares airlines.

3.23. Stansted currently has one runway and one terminal. It has a rail link to Central London and is connected to the national motorway network.

3.24. In September 2002 permission was granted to develop the airport to serve another 10 mppa, beyond its then existing consent of about 15 million. BAA has indicated that it expects work to start on a further terminal extension in 2004, and the airport is expected to handle about 25 mppa, by around 2010.

Capacity and demand at the BAA London airports

3.25. Heathrow, Gatwick and Stansted are the main airports serving London and the South-East of England. Table 3.1 shows that BAA's three London airports currently account for 92.8 per cent of the passengers and 88 per cent of the ATMs of the 'London area airports' as classified by the CAA.

TABLE 3.1 **Number of passengers and ATMs at London airports, 2001**

	ATMs		Passengers	
	'000	%	m	%
Heathrow	457.6	47.1	60.4	53.3
Gatwick	245.2	25.2	31.1	27.4
Stansted	152.5	15.7	13.7	12.1
Luton	59.7	6.2	6.5	5.8
London City	54.9	5.7	1.6	1.4
Southend	1.4	0.1	0.0	0.0
Total all London area airports	971.3	100.0	113.3	100.0

Source: BAA—Initial Position Paper to the CC, February 2002.

3.26. The main elements of airport capacity are reviewed twice a year (summer and winter season) as part of the schedule coordination process. Heathrow and Gatwick declare a set of scheduling limits (hourly aircraft movements on the runways, passenger flows in the terminals and at Heathrow, the number of aircraft parking stands), which cannot be exceeded by the schedule coordinator. The scheduling process at the London airports is coordinated by an independent company, Airport Coordination Limited (ACL). ACL aims to match demand to fly with available capacity.

3.27. Airport capacity in the wider sense is usually expressed in terms of mppa and is a function of the individual capacities of the airport's runways, terminal buildings, aprons and ground access.

3.28. At Heathrow and Gatwick, runway capacity is primarily assessed by NATS in consultation with airlines and BAA. NATS defines capacity as the number of movements that can be handled on the runway over a period of time, such that the average delay to individual movements is 10 minutes. Runway capacity in practice may vary from hour to hour, depending on factors such as the proportions of aircraft of different sizes and weather conditions. The actual hourly movement rate may also vary considerably from these figures due to the random bunching of actual operations.

TABLE 3.2 **Airport capacity, 2001/02**

Airport	Current utilization (mppa)	Likely future capacity limits (mppa approx)
Heathrow	60.4	90.0
Gatwick	30.5	40.0
Stansted	14.1	25.0

Source: BAA Annual Report 2001/02 and airport announcements.

3.29. Terminal capacity is based on hourly flows of passengers, and is measured by BAA as the flow of passengers which each facility (for example, check-in and security search) can handle whilst just meeting BAA's service standards. The overall capacity of the arrivals or departures process in the terminal is dependent on the lowest capacity for any individual facility.

3.30. The effective constraint at Heathrow is the runway. Current capacity is about 79 movements per hour (averaged on a 17.5-hour day) or about 500,000 on an annual basis, about 92.5 per cent of which is utilized (100 per cent for most of the day).

3.31. Through time, various incremental improvements to the runway are expected to increase its capacity to about 82 movements per hour, which will then require increased stand capacity, to which the

T5 stands will contribute. This together with the use of larger planes and/or higher load factors would allow increasing passenger numbers. There is some spare terminal capacity off-peak but this cannot to any great extent be seen as substitutable for peak terminal capacity. T5 will eliminate the increased strain on terminal facilities at peak periods. Without T5, peak terminal capacity would in time become the effective constraint.

3.32. Similarly at Gatwick, the annual passenger-carrying capacity of the runway will grow as a result of some minor increases in the number of movements which can be scheduled in a day (currently at about 46 movements an hour, averaged over a 17.5-hour day, to increase to around 49 by the end of Q4), higher utilization of that capacity, and growth in the average number of passengers per aircraft.

Heathrow

3.33. Heathrow is the busiest international airport in the world, with 60.4 mppa in 2001, and it is London's primary scheduled service hub. Heathrow is also one of the most congested airports in the world, with demand far exceeding capacity. Current runway capacity is completely full through most of the day with planned capacity reflecting a 10-minute average delay. Supply is rationed using a system of slot allocation, regulated under EC law, which includes grandfather rights.[1]

3.34. The level of demand for Heathrow has developed for a number of reasons. It is the closest full-service airport to central London, and is situated on the side of London from which the highest level of demand originates. Heathrow is also the primary business airport for the South-East. The busiest routes are to New York, Paris, Amsterdam and Dublin.

TABLE 3.3 **BAA London airports: purpose of travel, 2001**

	per cent	
	Leisure	Business
Heathrow	62.5	37.5
Gatwick	81.0	19.0
Stansted	79.8	20.2

Source: BAA—Initial Position Paper to the CC, February 2002.

3.35. Heathrow is overwhelmingly used for scheduled flights, with virtually no charter traffic or non-passenger/freight-only flights. None of the main low-fares carriers currently operate out of Heathrow.

3.36. BA is the most dominant single user of the airport, with approximately 38 per cent of the runway slots and 40 per cent of passenger traffic.

3.37. As the long-established base of the major international scheduled airlines, Heathrow has a wide range of frequent interconnecting services, to some 152 destinations, and a high proportion of transfer passengers. In 2001 an estimated 30.4 per cent of passengers were transferring from one aircraft to another.

TABLE 3.4 **BAA London airports: proportion of passengers transferring, 2001**

	% transfers
Heathrow	30.4
Gatwick	20.4
Stansted	6.3

Source: BAA—Initial Position Paper to the CC, February 2002.

[1]Airlines that hold a slot in one summer or winter season have the right to the same slot in the following season, provided they have used it for at least 80 per cent of the time. These rights of airlines are known as 'grandfather rights' and are set out in the EC slot regulation.

Gatwick

3.38. Gatwick, with 31.1 mppa, is Europe's sixth largest airport and the UK's largest holiday charter airport; a point reinforced by the Heathrow ban on charters from 1977 to 1991.

TABLE 3.5 **Proportion of charter passengers at BAA London airports, 2001**

	Charter passengers '000	Total passengers '000	%
Heathrow	120	60,432	0.2
Gatwick	11,203	31,098	36.0
Stansted	1,174	13,650	8.6

Source: BAA—Initial Position Paper to the CC, February 2002.

3.39. It is also a secondary scheduled service hub. Scheduled services built up originally as a result of the traffic distribution rules. When these were largely withdrawn in 1991 Gatwick lost some 19 international airlines to Heathrow. However, Gatwick still benefits from the continued exclusion of certain US airlines and routes from Heathrow under the Bermuda 2 agreement (see paragraph 3.74).

TABLE 3.6 **Proportion of long-haul passengers BAA London airports, 2001**

	Long-haul passengers '000	% of total	Total passengers '000	% by airport
Heathrow	25,309	66.7	60,432	41.9
Gatwick	12,215	32.2	31,098	39.3
Stansted	397	1.1	13,650	2.9
BAA London total	37,921	100.0	105,180	

Source: BAA—Initial Position Paper to the CC, February 2002.

3.40. Like Heathrow, Gatwick is also described as congested, with the two terminals under considerable pressure at peak periods, particularly in relation to pier service and stand availability. There is currently some terminal capacity available off-peak.

3.41. Following 11 September 2001, Gatwick suffered a significant reduction in passenger numbers, with both passenger numbers and air traffic movements falling by 16 per cent compared with the previous year (December 2001 data). BA, the airport's biggest airline, was already restructuring its Gatwick operation following an announcement in December 2000 of a rationalization of its short-haul network and the transfer of a number of long-haul services to Heathrow. This restructuring—which would have cut Gatwick capacity by 40 per cent by summer 2003 (relative to summer 1999)—was accelerated and intensified following 11 September and the announcement of BA's Future Size and Shape strategy on 13 February 2002. Latest estimates suggest that BA will effect a 60 per cent reduction in its capacity in terms of available seat kilometres at Gatwick over the four years 1999 to 2003. However, the impact on passenger numbers will be less significant with the BA seat count, which will actually determine the number of passengers within the airport, likely to be down by 40 per cent and the number of aircraft movements down by 30 per cent. Therefore, the impact on airport revenues will be less marked than the 60 per cent network reduction suggests. Also, the network reductions at Gatwick occur because services are being moved to Heathrow where the revenue lost at Gatwick from reduced flight movements will be offset by BAA from the resultant increase in movements and passengers at Heathrow. Meanwhile, however, other airlines are moving in to take up the capacity BA is leaving at Gatwick. easyJet has recently begun new services from the airport.

Stansted

3.42. Stansted is Europe's fastest-growing airport. In the five years to 1991 Stansted was the subject of a £400 million investment programme to develop it as the third London airport. The new facilities opened in inauspicious circumstances, during the Gulf War, and just as the air traffic distribution rules were being relaxed. While starting off slowly, the advent of the LFC market has caused a recent boom at Stansted, with current levels peaking above 13 mppa and growing rapidly. Demand and capacity profiles currently demonstrate that Stansted is the least congested of the BAA London airports, with runway utilization only reaching capacity during three daily peak periods (early morning, late morning and late afternoon), reflecting the operational needs of the low fares airlines that make up the majority of the airport's traffic.

TABLE 3.7 **Proportion of passengers on low-fares airlines BAA London airports, 2001**

	Passengers on low-fares airlines '000	Total passengers '000	%
Heathrow	27	60,432	0.0
Gatwick	685	31,098	2.2
Stansted	11,045	13,650	80.9

Source: BAA—Initial Position Paper to the CC, February 2002.

Government policy framework

3.43. The Government has stated that it intends to publish an air transport White Paper, in early 2003, which will provide a policy framework for the long-term future of both aviation and airports in the UK. Prefacing this, the DfT has released a consultation document on the future of air transport in the UK, which seeks to determine how much additional airport capacity will be needed over the next 30 years, and where it should be sited. This builds on earlier work undertaken in both the 1993 RUCATSE (Runway Capacity to Serve the South East) and the 1999 SERAS programmes of studies.

3.44. For the South-East, the consultation document outlined a range of potential options, which included consideration as to the importance of a world-class global hub airport in the South-East. With the practical limitations at Heathrow, the question is raised as to whether to maintain Heathrow as the premier airport; or to develop an alternative airport into a major hub; or whether the UK needs two hubs. The consultation document identified three options. One option outlined is to build on Heathrow; this could mean an additional shorter runway to complement the runways already there. A second option is to build at Stansted; to develop it as either a hub itself, or to complement Heathrow. A third option is to build a completely new airport, at Cliffe in north Kent. The consultation document also sets out the potential combinations of airport development options.

3.45. The consultation document also looked at where any other new capacity should be located. The Government has stated that it does not propose to overturn the legal agreement that rules out construction of a new runway at Gatwick before 2019. While not putting forward any option for a new runway at Gatwick, the document does, however, note that there is some capacity that can still be developed at Gatwick, and states that this has already been agreed locally.

3.46. As described in Chapter 2, any decision regarding the preferred development option is not likely to be taken until some time after our inquiry is completed. Therefore we have not sought to make a specific allowance for the cost of any new runway in our recommendations. Should work start on a new runway at any of the BAA airports during Q4, however, it would be open to BAA under the Airports Act to seek an interim review if higher charges were necessary in Q4 to finance it.

The system of regulation

The legislation

3.47. The Airports Act provides in Part IV for the economic regulation of airports. The Airports Act prohibits the levying of airport charges at an airport 'subject to economic regulation' (as defined in the

Airports Act) unless permission by the CAA is in force in relation to the airport. Permission is given by the CAA. Four airports subject to economic regulation have been designated by order of the Secretary of State under Part IV.[1] They are Heathrow, Stansted, Gatwick and Manchester. We shall describe the legislation as it applies to designated airports.

3.48. When the permissions were granted in 1986, a condition limiting the amount of airport charges was imposed for five years from 1 April 1987. In the case of Manchester, the permission was granted in February 1988 and a condition limiting the amount of airport charges was imposed for five years from 1 April 1988. Section 40(4) of the Airports Act requires the CAA, each time the condition is due to expire, to extend it for a further five years with or without modification. The CAA can, however, at any time while the condition is in force, extend the period for up to 12 months. In the case of the BAA airports, the charge cap imposed for Q3 was due to expire on 31 March 2002, but the CAA extended the period until 31 March 2003.

3.49. Before the CAA extends a condition imposing a charge cap on airport charges for the following quinquennium it must, unless the Secretary of State otherwise directs, make a reference to the CC under section 43 of the Airport Act. We shall refer to such a reference as a 'quinquennial reference'. The reference has to cover two aspects:

(a) *airport charges:* the maximum amounts that may be levied by the airport by way of such charges for five years; and

(b) *public interest:* whether between the date of the previous reference and the date of the reference, the airport has pursued a course of conduct which has operated or might be expected to operate against the public interest.

The questions in the reference and the procedures following a CC report are discussed later (see paragraphs 3.61 to 3.68).

Definitions of key terms

Airport charges

3.50. Section 36 of the Airports Act defines airport charges as:

(a) charges levied on operators of aircraft in connection with the landing, parking or taking off of aircraft (including charges that are to any extent determined by reference to the number of passengers on board the aircraft, excluding charges payable by virtue of section 73 of the Transport Act 2000 (charges for services);[2] and

(b) charges levied on aircraft passengers in connection with their arrival at or departure from the airport by air.

3.51. The nature of the charges levied that fall within the definition of airport charges vary from airport to airport. At the BAA London airports, all the charges regarded as airport charges are set out in the Conditions of Use and have three components: charges on landing, charges on departing passengers and aircraft parking charges. The landing charges are differentiated by time (with higher charges at peak times), aircraft size (with larger aircraft paying more off-peak) and noise characteristics (with aircraft in higher noise categories paying more). Passenger charges are regarded as being levied on airlines,[3] are levied per departing passenger, and are less for domestic passengers than international passengers. Aircraft parking charges are higher at peak times and include a weight-related element.

---

[1] The CAA (Economic Designation of Airports) Regulations 1986 (SI 1986/1544).
[2] These relate to charges for air traffic services—see paragraph 3.93.
[3] The Conditions of Use describe these charges as being 'collected by airlines/agents'. This would, at any rate, at first sight suggest that this was a charge on passengers with the airlines collecting the charges as agents for one party or the other. However, the airlines regarded the charge as a charge on airlines and not a charge on passengers.

Operational activities

3.52. Section 30(4) of the Airports Act defines operational activities, in relation to an airport, as meaning any activities:

(a) which are carried on wholly or mainly for the benefit of users of the airport; or

(b) the revenues from which are wholly or mainly attributable to payments by users.

3.53. Section 82 of the Airports Act defines user in relation to an airport as meaning:

(a) a person for whom any service or facilities falling within the definition of relevant activities in section 36(1) are provided at the airport; or

(b) a person using any of the air transport services operating at the airport.

3.54. Section 36(1) defines relevant activities in relation to an airport as meaning the provision at the airport of facilities for the purposes of:

(a) the landing, parking or taking-off of aircraft;

(b) the servicing of aircraft (including the supply of fuel); and

(c) the handling of passengers or their baggage or of cargo at all stages while on airport premises (including the transfer of passengers, their baggage or cargo to and from aircraft).

The section goes on to declare that *(c)* does not include the provision of facilities for car parking, for the refreshment of passengers or for the supply of consumer goods.

3.55. Section 82 defines air transport services as meaning services for the carriage by air of passengers or cargo.

3.56. It follows that an operator of a cafe for air travellers at an airport is engaged in operational activities, but is not a user of the airport. The same applies to a company supplying fuelling facilities for the aircraft.

3.57. Further instances of operational activities are activities carried out for passengers at airports, such as retailing and catering; and activities carried out for airlines, such as rents of check-in desks and offices and licences for services such as baggage handling.

The roles of the CAA and the CC with regard to airport charges

3.58. The task of the CAA under section 40(4) of the Airports Act is (in effect) to impose conditions on the operators of designated airports to regulate the maximum amount they may levy in airport charges over a five-year period, or quinquennium (see paragraph 3.48).

3.59. The airport charges conditions:

(a) may provide:

   (i)   for an overall limit that may be levied by the airport operator by way of all airport charges at the airport; or

   (ii)   for limits to apply to particular categories of charges; or

   (iii) for a combination of any such limits;

(b) may operate to restrict increases in any such charges or to require reductions in them whether by reference to any formula or otherwise; and

(c) may provide for different limits to apply in relation to different periods of time falling within the period of five years for which the conditions are in force.

Where a group of airports is concerned, the maximum level of charges may apply to each airport separately or to the airports together as a group. Once set for the five-year period, an airport charging condition cannot be modified by the CAA except with the agreement of the airport operator.

3.60. Before imposing conditions, the CAA must make a reference to the CC, unless the Secretary of State directs otherwise. In making the reference to the CC, the CAA may specify its own view as to the appropriate maximum level of charges. The reference has to require the CC to investigate and report on the maximum airport charges that the airport operator may levy during the five-year period specified in the reference. The CC's conclusions have to take the form of recommendations as to what the maximum amounts should be. Following receipt of the CC report, the CAA has to extend by five years the conditions attached to the permission to levy charges for each airport with such modifications as it thinks appropriate. In setting the maximum level of charges, the CAA must have regard to the CC's recommendations.

The roles of the CAA and the CC with regard to public interest issues

3.61. Every quinquennial reference to the CC has to require the CC to investigate and report on whether between the date of the previous reference and the date of the reference, the airport operator has pursued a course of conduct which has operated or might be expected to operate against the public interest, in relation to (a) any airport charges levied at the airport; (b) any operational activities which it has carried out in relation to the airport; or (c) the granting of a right to carry out operational activities at the airport. In cases where an associated company of the airport operator carries on operational activities or is entitled to grant a right to carry out operational activities, the reference has to require the CC also to report on whether the associated company has pursued such a course of conduct in relation to (a) any operational activities which it has carried out in relation to the airport; or (b) the granting of a right to carry out operational activities at the airport. The CAA may specify in the reference its opinion about courses of conduct considered contrary to the public interest; the CC can also find other conduct to be contrary to the public interest.

3.62. If the CC finds effects adverse to the public interest, it must report on whether the adverse effects could be remedied by means of conditions and if so what conditions should be imposed. If the CC concludes that the adverse effects could be remedied in this way and makes recommendations as to how it should be done, the CAA has to impose such conditions as it considers appropriate for the purpose of remedying the adverse effects specified in the report.

3.63. Section 41 of the Airports Act enables the CAA to impose conditions, other than as a consequence of a conclusion following a quinquennial reference. It can do so only to remedy adverse effects resulting from a course of conduct in relation to relevant activities. (The meaning of 'relevant activities' is explained in paragraph 3.54.) If following investigations the CAA is minded to impose a condition under section 41, it has to notify the airport operator of the course of conduct concerned and the condition it intends to impose. If the operator objects, the CAA either has to abandon its proposal or make a reference to the CC. The CAA cannot impose a condition unless the CC concludes that the airport operator has pursued the course of conduct referred to in the CAA's notification and that it operates against the public interest. Otherwise the process after the CC report is similar to the process after a quinquennial report.

3.64. The Airports Act specifies that the CAA must perform its functions relating to the economic regulation of airports, in the manner which it considers best calculated:

(a) to further the reasonable interest of users of airports within the UK;

(b) to promote the efficient, economic and profitable operation of such airports;

(c) to encourage investment in new facilities at airports in time to satisfy anticipated demands by the users of such airports; and

(d) to impose the minimum restrictions that are consistent with the performance by the CAA of these functions.

149

3.65. The CAA is also required to take into account such of the international obligations of the UK as may be notified to it by the Secretary of State. These are currently:

(a) the obligations under Article 15 of the 1944 Chicago Convention, which provides a framework of non-discrimination and states that airports should be made available on uniform conditions, including charges, to aircraft of different nations; and

(b) the obligations under provisions relating to airline charges contained in the 1977 Bermuda 2 agreement between the UK and the USA and a 1994 Exchange of Notes modifying this agreement. This states that, in relation to user charges, regard should be had to such factors as efficiency, economy, environmental impact and safety of operation; and, as revised in 1994, additionally stated that user charges should not exceed by more than a reasonable margin, over a reasonable period of time, the full cost of providing the service to users. Such full cost might include a reasonable return on assets, after depreciation.

3.66. We are explicitly required to have regard to the above objectives in considering the public interest. In considering any matter relating to the granting of a right by virtue of which any operational activities may be carried on, we are also required to have regard to those objectives and to an additional objective, namely the furtherance of the reasonable interests of persons granted such rights. The Airports Act does not explicitly require the CC to have regard to those objectives in recommending the maximum level of airport charges. However, such a recommendation is a recommendation as to how the CAA should perform its functions and, accordingly, we need to have regard to the CAA's duty to act in the manner which it considers best calculated to achieve its objectives, and to its duty to take account of notified international obligations. The CAA disagreed, arguing we were only required to recommend what the maximum amounts should be in the five years in question. We disagree with its view, but in any event our conclusions would be the same irrespective of this point.

3.67. The Airports Act does not provide any guidance of the interpretation of these objectives and does not set out how trade-offs, if any, between the objectives should be judged. However, the CAA has stated that it believes that trade-offs between the objectives should be judged against the criterion that where there are potential inequality in benefits between airport users and airports from different regulatory options, the aim should be to choose the policy that is expected to maximize net gains to users and airports combined. We note that in *R v Director General of Telecommunications, ex parte Cellcom Ltd and others* (*The Independent*, 3 December 1998; *The Times*, 7 December 1998), Mr Justice Lightman said:

> 25. Section 3(2) requires the Director to exercise his functions in the manner which he considers best calculated (a) to promote the interests of consumers, purchasers and other users and (b) to maintain and promote effective competition between persons engaged in commercial activities connected with telecommunications. The question has been raised as to the relationship of these duties with each other and of the duties inter se in respect of consumers and other purchasers (and in particular ISPs). In my view it is plain that the various duties imposed by s.3(2) may pull in different directions and may conflict; there may be a conflict between the duties in s.3(2)(a) and s.3(2)(b); there may be a conflict between the interest of the consumers, purchasers and other users specified in s.3(2)(a), and what may promote competition eg between network operators may have a negative effect on competition between service providers. The Director is not paralysed because such a conflict arises: rather he is given the choice how that conflict is to be resolved and to decide priorities, and so long he bears in mind the entirety of his duties, has a predisposition to fulfil all the duties so far as this practicable and with those duties in mind makes a decision which promotes one or other of the objectives specified (and is rational) his decision stands and is not open to challenge.

3.68. Although there are obviously environmental issues regarding airport expansion, these are primarily addressed under the Town and Country Planning legislation, not by the CAA under the Airports Act.

Regulatory history

3.69. As mentioned above, since privatization BAA's London airports have been subject to regulation on a quinquennium or five-year basis. During this review, the CC is concerned with recommending the appropriate maximum level of charges for Q4.

3.70. At the time of privatization in 1987, the Government decided that BAA's London airports would best be regulated by an incentive-based system centred on an RPI–X price control formula. During Q1 charges imposed by LAL were subject to a cap of RPI–1. In 1991 the CC and the CAA undertook the first examination of BAA's prices. The CAA decided that there should continue to be separate caps for Heathrow and Gatwick and the system as a whole with the following formulae: RPI–8 (1992/93), RPI–8 (1993/94), RPI–4 (1994/95), RPI–1 (1995/96) and RPI–1 (1996/97).

3.71. The CAA last referred BAA's London airports to the MMC in December 1995 and in October 1996 set a price cap for the period from 1 April 1997 to 31 March 2002. Manchester was referred a year later, in December 1996, and a price cap was set for the five years from 1 April 1998 to 31 March 2003. The CAA's decision regarding the BAA London airports for Q3 was broadly that a formula of RPI–3 should be set for Heathrow and Gatwick combined for each of the five years, with a formula of RPI+1 for Stansted.

3.72. In May 1999, the CAA extended the price cap for BAA's London airports by one year to 31 March 2003 to allow it to take into account the Government's final decision on BAA's planning application for a fifth terminal at Heathrow on the working assumption that this could be published in late 2001. The result of this is that the reviews of the BAA London airports and Manchester took place at the same time. The CAA had previously assumed that these reviews would be conducted under new regulatory arrangements, under which the CAA would carry out the reviews of the price caps with the CC acting in an appellate role. However, the changes to the regulatory procedures were not in place by the time of the reviews. The CAA was content to conduct the BAA and Manchester reviews in parallel so as to help achieve consistency of regulatory approach and to allow common issues to be addressed jointly. Consequently, the new price caps will be set for each of the four designated airports for the five years from 1 April 2003 to 31 March 2008.

Review of regulation

3.73. In its 1998 White Paper on utility regulation, the Government announced its intention that the CAA should become the prime airport regulator with the CC in an appellate role. The CAA supports this intention. The CC agrees that the challenges of airport regulation in the future are likely to demand a more flexible and accountable regulatory framework. However, this change, designed to bring airport regulation more into line with the standard utility regulation model, will require primary legislation or the use of the Regulatory Reform Act, which, as discussed above, has not yet been brought forward. The CC is therefore working on the basis that the statutory framework for the current reviews is unchanged.

International obligations

3.74. The UK Government is subject to a number of international obligations in relation to airport charges. Article 15 of the Chicago Convention (reproduced at Appendix 3.1) provides a basic framework of non-discrimination, stipulating that no airline should be penalized with regard to access or level of charges compared with a national carrier.

3.75. The 1977 US/UK Air Service Agreement, known as Bermuda 2, provides more detail about the structure of charges. In 1994, agreement was reached in a dispute between the USA and UK, which centred on Article 10 of Bermuda 2 and the related 1983 Memorandum of Understanding. This agreement, formalized in an Exchange of Notes between the two Governments, provided for compensation of nearly $30 million in settlement of a dispute over Heathrow charges. It was agreed that peak passenger charges at Heathrow would be phased out (and not reintroduced until at least 2003) while the relative levels of landing, passenger and parking charges would be maintained (with no weight-related element introduced into landing charges). Finally, Bermuda 2 was amended, to eliminate passenger charges from the definition of user charges. Extracts from the Exchange of Notes are contained in Appendix 3.1 and its effect on the level of airport charges is described in paragraph 3.65*(b)*.

The record of the negotiations shows that the UK Government did not require the adoption of a single-till, and the USA did not dispute this. The 1994 Exchange of Notes cancelled the 1983 Memorandum of Understanding, which had been the basis of the US Government's claims for a single till at UK airports.

The International Civil Aviation Organization guidelines

3.76. The ICAO was created in 1944 to promote the safe and orderly development of air traffic services in the world. It is a specialized agency of the United Nations. Its governing body is a Council, with headquarters in Montreal. It sets international standards and regulations necessary for the safety, security, efficiency and regularity of air transport and serves as the medium for cooperation in all fields of civil aviation among contracting states, numbering over 180.

3.77. Within an overall policy that the operations at each airport should be considered on a case-by-case basis, the ICAO issues statements from time to time on charges at airports. Some of these are of relevance in the debate on the single- and dual-till approaches to airport charges. The ICAO's 1997 guidelines on the appropriate cost basis for charges as set out in its Statement by the Council to Contracting States on Charges for Airports and Airport Navigation Systems reads, in particular: 'In determining the cost basis for airport charges the following principles should be applied: (i) The cost to be shared is the full cost of providing the airport and its essential ancillary services, ... but allowing for all revenues, aeronautical or non-aeronautical, accruing from the operation of the airport to its operators.' (See Appendix 3.1.)

3.78. Commenting on these guidelines, the 1996 and 1997 MMC reports on, respectively, BAA (see paragraph 8.14) and Manchester (see paragraph 8.16) stated that: 'Although only guidelines, several parties referred to this [ICAO] statement as morally binding on the UK Government as a signatory to those guidelines, failure to observe which could lead to adverse consequences for UK airlines operating at overseas airports.'

3.79. In June 2000, however, at an ICAO conference held to discuss charging principles, there was considerable support for more flexibility in the interpretation and application of the single till in view of different airports' differing circumstances. The report of this conference records the following, among other things:

> The Conference held a comprehensive and extensive discussion on the concept of the single till. Many delegates supported continued endorsement of the single till concept as it reflects the special role of airports in promoting and developing air transport, serves the purpose of reducing the cost base for charges, motivates airports to develop revenues from non-aeronautical activities, and provides for capital investment ... On the other hand there was considerable support for more flexibility in the interpretation and application of the single till in view of the varying situations among airports, the need to adjust to the changing airport environment, including autonomous organizational and financial structures, and investment requirements ... . The conference therefore agreed that ICAO conduct a study as a matter of high priority ...

(See Appendix 3.1 for the relevant conference report excerpt.)

3.80. The result of this study was a change in wording in the ICAO 1997 guidelines quoted above. This was adopted on 8 December 2000, and the current guidelines, in subparagraph 22, now state: 'The cost to be shared is the full cost of providing the airport and its essential ancillary services, ... but allowing for all aeronautical revenues *plus contributions* from non-aeronautical revenues' (emphasis added)—see Appendix 3.1.

3.81. The reference to 'contributions from non-aeronautical revenues' implies a greater degree of flexibility for the future as to what the actual level of a contribution should be. With those guidelines established, the ICAO Secretariat on 6 April 2001 issued guidance and an interpretation of the remarks on the single till, relevant sections include (see Appendix 3.1):

> ... Reaching a common understanding on the contribution of non-aeronautical revenues to defray the cost base for charges is an acknowledgement of the partnership between airports and users.

... Given the different local circumstances and fast changing conditions, with respect to airport ownership and management, as well as regulatory regimes, there are likely to be a range of different appropriate treatments of non-aeronautical income by airports.

... it may be appropriate for airports to retain non-aeronautical revenues rather than use such revenues to defray charges. However, there is no requirement for airports to do so and, in appropriate circumstances, there may be solid grounds for charges to be lower...

Other regulation

3.82. In addition to the economic regulation provided for under the Airports Act, airports are subject to a number of other regulatory measures which prescribe their behaviour.

3.83. The Air Navigation Order 2000 broadly requires aerodromes to be licensed by the CAA if aircraft over certain weights (and certain other aircraft) are to land there or take-off from there. The CAA can grant a licence subject to the condition that the airport shall, at all times when it is available for the take-off or landing of aircraft, be so available to all persons on equal terms and conditions. Such a licence is known as a 'licence for public use'. BAA's airports are each subject to a licence for public use.

3.84. A licence may be granted subject to such conditions as the CAA think fit. The aerodrome licences impose requirements on the operator as to the safe operation of the airport, including rescue and fire-fighting, provision of safety equipment and night use.

3.85. The Secretary of State has powers under section 31 of the Airports Act to direct traffic between airports serving the same area through traffic distribution rules. Such rules are currently only applied to peak-time operations by general and business aviation and all-cargo operators at Heathrow and Gatwick.

3.86. Under sections 12, 13, 13A, 14 and 15 of the Aviation Security Act 1982, the Secretary of State may issue directions to an airport operator in respect of security. Such directions may relate, for example, to baggage search or to the segregation of arriving from departing passengers.

3.87. The allocation of aircraft movements (slots) at the busy airports in the UK is carried out by ACL in accordance with the terms of EC Council Regulation 95/93, supplemented by IATA Scheduling Procedures Guide. This Regulation was incorporated into UK national legislation by means of Airports Slot Allocation Regulations 1993 (SI 1993/1067).

3.88. Section 32 of the Airports Act enables the Secretary of State to make an order imposing a limit on the number of ATMs during any specified period at under-used airports. Stansted is subject to such a limit.[1]

3.89. The Secretary of State has made an order designating the BAA's airports under section 80 of the Civil Aviation Act.[2] This gives the Secretary of State power under section 78 to control airborne aircraft noise and to make a scheme requiring an airport operator to make grants under section 79 towards the cost of soundproofing buildings.

3.90. The Secretary of State has imposed a requirement under section 78 that aircraft taking off from Heathrow, Gatwick and Stansted shall follow specified routes (noise preferential routes) in order to avoid, so far as possible, the overflying of the largest concentrations of population; and imposed a system of night quotas limiting aircraft movements at night.

3.91. Various schemes (now complete) were made under section 79 of the Civil Aviation Act under which HAL and GAL had to bear the cost of insulating dwellings close to the ends of the main runways against noise. A comparable scheme was also carried out by STAL on a voluntary basis, but with Government approval.

---

[1]The Stansted Airport Aircraft Movement Limit Order 1987 (SI 1987/874 as amended).
[2]The Civil Aviation (Designation of Aerodromes) Order 1981 (SI 1981/651).

3.92. Section 73 of the Transport Act 2000 (the 2000 Act) gives the CAA certain powers in relation to 'chargeable air services'. It can specify such things as the amount, the operators and owners of aircraft who are to pay the charges and the persons (including companies) to whom they are to be paid.

3.93. 'Chargeable air services' are defined in section 77 of the 2000 Act and covers air traffic services. However, air traffic services provided by or on behalf of the owner or manager of an airport are not chargeable air services unless the airport has been designated under the section by an order made by the Secretary of State. The Secretary of State has made an order designating (among others) the BAA airports[1] but not Manchester.

3.94. At Manchester, air traffic services are provided by NATS under contract with the airport operator. The operator pays NATS under the terms of the contract and the cost could be taken into account in assessing the charge cap. In this way the operator would recover the cost through airport charges. These charges are regulated under the Airports Act. As Manchester has not been designated, these charges are not subject to section 73 of the 2000 Act.

3.95. At the BAA airports, as a consequence of the designation and section 73 of the 2000 Act, the airlines pay NATS directly for air traffic services. Accordingly, the cost of providing the services is not borne by the airport companies.

3.96. The DfT has asked the CAA to review the way in which airport air traffic services are charged and to advise on whether direct charging of airlines should be extended to all airports or should be discontinued. In July 2002, the CAA published a consultation paper on this, mentioning the linkages with the reviews of Manchester and the BAA airports under the Airports Act. Were the designation order to be revoked during Q4, arrangements would have to be made for the airport companies to pay NATS under contract and for the airport charges to be raised accordingly. When the Secretary of State makes an order under section 77 of the 2000 Act, he has power under section 103(2) to include incidental, consequential or transitional provisions. This power could possibly be used to make the necessary changes, but it would be for the DfT to decide whether that were possible and appropriate.

---

[1] The Aerodromes (Designation) (Chargeable Air Services) Order 2001 (SI 2001 No 354).

4   Financial performance and cost of capital

Contents

Introduction

4.1. The purpose of this chapter is to review the financial performance of BAA, of the three companies operating airports in the London area which are owned by LAL (a subsidiary of BAA), and of Heathrow Express Operating Company Ltd (HEOC) which operates the rail link to Heathrow airport. In addition in this chapter we also consider the cost of capital of the designated airport companies.

The BAA group

4.2. BAA was privatized in 1987. At that time it was the holding company for a business owning and operating airports in the South-East of England and in Scotland. BAA later diversified in a number of ways. Lynton, a property investment and development company, was acquired in 1988 in order to provide BAA with property expertise to develop more fully the property potential of its airport sites; in 1998/99 the business of Lynton was transferred to BAA where it operates as BAA Lynton. Another property diversification involved the construction of hotels by BAA Hotels Ltd, but the programme was subsequently scaled down and the hotels that had been developed, and were operated by third parties on lease, were sold to the individual airport operating companies concerned in 1994/95. The hotel assets were subsequently transferred to BAA Lynton and in 1999/2000 sold to a partnership in which BAA retains a 10.2 per cent holding. WDFE was established by BAA in November 1996 to take over and run airport and tax-free shops. The duty-free activity was extended in August 1997 with the purchase of Duty Free International Inc (renamed World Duty Free Americas Inc (WDFA)) for £429 million, but the company was disposed of in October 2001 for £4 million in order that BAA could concentrate on its core duty-free business in the UK. BAA has now also closed or disposed of its duty-free activities in China, Italy, Mauritius and South Africa. A joint venture with McArthurGlen, BAA McArthurGlen, was established in 1995 and it became Europe's largest developer and operator of designer outlet centres. In September 2002 BAA announced that the joint venture with McArthurGlen had been terminated, with BAA retaining three centres and minority interests in a further two centres.

4.3. BAA has expanded its airport activities overseas and now has interests in six airports in Australia, three airports in the USA, one in Italy and two in Oman. BAA also offers retail and operational consultancy services to airports throughout the world.

4.4. The Heathrow Express rail connection between London Paddington and the airport was opened in June 1998. The fixed asset investment in the project is held by HAL and the service is managed by HEOC which is a wholly-owned subsidiary of BAA. Ticket revenue for Heathrow Express is collected by HEOC and passed to HAL. Costs incurred by HEOC on behalf of HAL are charged to HAL together with a management fee of 10 per cent. In the two most recent years HEOC has reported pre-tax profits of around £4 million a year.

4.5. BAA currently owns three airports in the London area, Heathrow, Gatwick and Stansted, and the operating company of each airport is a subsidiary of LAL. As a sub holding company LAL does not itself publish consolidated accounts; however, BAA prepares a pro forma aggregation of the regulatory accounts (see paragraph 4.14) of the three London airport companies, together with the accounts of HEOC, which it submits to the CAA. In 2001/02 the three London airports accounted for 59 per cent of BAA's turnover, 85 per cent of operating profit and 78 per cent of net operating assets. In addition, Heathrow Express accounted for a further 3 per cent of turnover, 1 per cent of operating profit and 9 per cent of net operating assets. The role of BAA is to provide corporate and financial management for its operating subsidiaries.

BAA results in the third quinquennium

4.6. BAA prepares its accounts on the historical cost accounting (HCA) convention, as modified by the revaluation of investment properties. Fully completed properties, let to and operated by third parties and held for long-term retention, including those at airport locations, are accounted for as investment properties and valued at the balance sheet date at open market value. All investment properties are revalued annually and by external valuers at least once every five years. No depreciation is provided in respect of freehold or long leasehold investment properties. This is a departure from the Companies Act 1985 requirement for all properties to be depreciated, but is permitted under statement of standard accounting practice 19 (accounting for investment properties); the properties are held not for consumption but for investment and the directors consider that to depreciate them would not give a true and fair view. Operating assets such as terminal complexes, airfield assets, plant and group occupied properties are stated at cost less accumulated depreciation. AICC are stated at cost less provision for impairment. Where appropriate, cost includes interest, own labour and associated overheads.

4.7. The results of the BAA group to date in Q3, together with those for 1996/97 the last year of Q2, are shown in Table 4.1. The duration of Q3 was extended by the CAA for one year so as to run to 31 March 2003; financial results for 2002/03 the final year of Q3 will not be available until mid-2003. Fuller profit and loss accounts and balance sheets are shown in Appendices 4.1 and 4.2; the results for 2000/01 and 2001/02 include the effect of applying Financial Reporting Standard (FRS) 17 (retirement benefits) and accordingly are not fully comparable with earlier years.

TABLE 4.1 **BAA: financial performance***

	(Q2) 1996/97	1997/98	1998/99	1999/00	2000/01	£ million 2001/02
Revenue	1,373	1,679	1,959	2,121	2,226	1,987
Operating profit	491	521	576	402	560	550
Enterprise value†	4,614	5,570	6,078	6,033	6,399	6,458
Mean enterprise value	4,414	5,092	5,824	6,056	6,216	6,428
						per cent
Return of profit on:						
Revenue	35.8	31.0	29.4	19.0	25.2	27.7
Mean enterprise value	11.1	10.2	9.9	6.6	9.0	8.5

Source: BAA.

*During 2001/02 BAA applied three new accounting standards—FRS 17 (retirement benefits), 18 (accounting policies) and 19 (deferred tax). The results for 2000/01 in the above table have been restated to take account of the changes resulting from the application of the new standards.
†Shareholders' funds plus net debt.

4.8. There were a number of developments in the period which had a significant effect on the results of BAA:

(a) Revenue in 1997/98 included £337 million resulting from the establishment of the duty-free activity as a separate business. Of this, £113 million related to WDFE (much of which in earlier years had formed part of the turnover of the airport companies) and £224 million related to the WDFA acquisition. The turnover of the duty-free activity increased to £738 million in 2000/01 before falling to £480 million in 2001/02 following the disposal of WDFA. Operating profit from the duty-free activity in Europe and the Americas ranged from a loss of £153 million (including a goodwill write-down of £147 million) in 1999/2000 to a profit of £14 million in 2001/02. There was a further loss on the sale of WDFA in 2001/02 of £190 million.

(b) The loss of duty- and tax-free sales to passengers travelling within the EC came into effect on 1 July 1999 and resulted in a loss of income for BAA.

(c) Heathrow Express generated income of £28 million in 1998/99, the first year of operation, and this increased to £63 million in 2000/01 before falling slightly to £58 million in 2001/02. There was a loss of £2 million on the activity in 1998/99 and operating profits in other years with a peak of £10 million in 2001/02.

(d) Along with other companies in the air transport industry, BAA was materially affected by the events of 11 September.

Overall the operating margin fell from 35.8 per cent in 1996/97 to 19.0 per cent in 1999/2000 before recovering to 27.7 per cent in 2001/02. The return on mean enterprise value has fallen from 11.1 per cent in 1996/97 to 8.6 per cent in 2001/02, with a low point of 6.6 per cent in 1999/2000.

Capital expenditure and funding

4.9. Despite the postponement of the T5 project BAA incurred substantial capex in Q3, mainly on airport assets and further capex is expected to take place in 2002/03. The net cash outflows on capex of the BAA group since the 1997 review by the MMC (including 1996/97, the last year of Q2) are shown in Table 4.2 and a summary of its sources and use of funds in Table 4.3. Table 4.3 also shows some of BAA's main financial ratios.

TABLE 4.2 **BAA: capital expenditure and financial investment, cash outflows**

£ million

	1996/97	1997/98	1998/99	1999/00	2000/01	2001/02
Heathrow	313	390	257	178	233	364
Gatwick	61	68	68	72	107	82
Stansted	14	21	43	44	100	84
Total London airports	388	478	368	294	440	530
Other airports and sundry	51	45	105	132	87	98
Total operational capex	439	523	473	426	527	628
Non-airport investment property and other assets	6	43	18	22	9	1
Change in long-term investments	15	41	−37	−3	25	55
	460	607	454	445	561	684
Less proceeds from asset disposals	−48	−51	−46	−337	−141	−49
Total BAA group	412	556	408	108	420	635

Source: BAA.

TABLE 4.3 **BAA: cash flows and financial ratios**

£ million

	1996/97	1997/98	1998/99	1999/00	2000/01	2001/02
Net cash inflow from operations	586	683	774	798	879	858
Interest (net) and dividends paid	−188	−240	−239	−268	−295	−260
Tax paid	−107	−144	−145	−112	−125	−135
Net operating cash flow	291	299	390	418	459	463
Capital expenditure (Table 4.2)	−412	−556	−408	−108	−420	−635
Acquisition and disposals	0	−404	0	0	−11	−23
Net cash inflow/outflow before financing	−121	−661	−18	310	28	−195
Financing						
Issue of share capital	13	21	19	12	18	21
Repayment of share capital	0	0	0	0	−141	0
Net increase/repayment of borrowings	258	405	132	−71	3	731
Management of liquid resources	−121	223	−131	−183	102	−578
Increase/decrease in cash and cash equivalents	29	−12	2	68	10	−21
Financial indicators						
Share capital and reserves	3,461	3,739	4,234	4,517	4,826	4,807
Year-end borrowing less cash	1,153	1,831	1,844	1,516	1,573	1,651
Profit before interest	494	532	614	495	585	369
Net interest including capitalized interest*	138	121	144	146	135	131
Post-tax profit†	296	277	401	262	393	167
Dividends	130	144	159	175	187	194
Financial ratios						
Capital expenditure as % of net operating cash flow	142	186	105	26	92	137
Gearing: D/D+E (%)	25.0	32.9	30.3	25.1	24.6	25.6
Interest cover (times)	3.6	4.4	4.3	3.4	4.3	2.8
Dividend cover (times)	2.3	1.9	2.5	1.5	2.1	0.9
Dividend growth (%)	12.1	10.8	10.4	10.1	6.9	3.7

Source: BAA.

*The basis for capitalizing interest in the group was changed (see paragraph 4.15(b)). The interest figure of £138 million for 1996/97 includes a charge for £40 million of interest capitalized in earlier years which was written off in 1996/97.

†In addition to the tax charge on the profits of the year, BAA paid windfall tax of £102 million in 1997/98.

BAA's share price in Q3

4.10. Shares in BAA were offered for sale in the July 1987 privatization at 245p and at the close of business on the first dealing day, 28 July 1987, were quoted at 291p, valuing the equity at £1.225 billon and £1.455 million respectively. At the time of the previous report by the MMC, the share price (at 29 March 1996, the last dealing day of the 1995/96 accounting year and after taking account of one-for-one capitalization in July 1994) was 535p (at which price the BAA equity was valued at £5.537 billion. Figure 4.1 shows the movement of BAA's share price from April 1996 to September 2002 together with the movement relative to the rebased *Financial Times* (FT) SE-All Share Index. In 2000/01, under a share buy-back programme, BAA purchased and cancelled 26.9 million shares at a total cost of £141 million. The BAA share price at end-September 2002 was 529p at which price the BAA equity was valued at £5.511 billion. On that date the gross dividend yield was 3.5 per cent and the historical price earnings ratio was 16.4. The book net asset value per share at 31 March 2002 was £4.51. As in previous years, the operational assets were valued by external valuers. This revaluation, which is not incorporated in the balance sheet, would have increased the net asset value per share to £9.36 at 31 March 2002.

Comparison with other companies

4.11. BAA is by far the largest airport operator in the UK, so it is difficult to identify suitable private sector companies for comparisons of financial performance. TBI plc (TBI) has substantial airport interests both in the UK and overseas, but it is a much smaller company with a market capitalization less than one-tenth that of BAA and its three airports in the UK (Belfast, Cardiff and Luton) are not subject to price regulation. In 2001/02 TBI's operating profit as a percentage of mean enterprise value was 4.8 per cent, compared with the equivalent figure for BAA of 8.6 per cent. It should be noted that such comparisons made on a modified HCA basis tend to be affected by differences of accounting practice on asset revaluations.

Financial performance of LAL

4.12. The statutory accounts of the three airport companies are now prepared on substantially the same accounting bases as those used in the BAA group. Prior to 1996/97 the accounts of the airport companies included operational assets at depreciated replacement cost, whereas BAA included the assets at depreciated historical cost.

4.13. In addition to statutory accounts, the three airport companies have since 1996/97 prepared regulatory accounts, the purpose of which is broadly to report their results in line with the accounting basis used by the CAA in setting airport charges in Q3. The regulatory accounts for the airport companies are audited. The main accounting differences between the statutory and regulatory accounts relate to asset values and were discussed between BAA and the CAA following the 1996 report by the MMC; they are:

(a) The gross value of the fixed assets recorded in the regulatory accounts represents the replacement value at which they were included in the statutory accounts at 31 March 1995 adjusted to reflect changes in the RPI since that date, with additions and disposals since 31 March 1995 being adjusted to reflect changes in RPI since the dates of acquisition and disposal respectively. The depreciation charge and accumulated depreciation is also adjusted to reflect the gross values of fixed assets as set out above.

(b) Investment properties, excluding land, have been depreciated in the regulatory accounts as from 1 April 1995 using the BAA group depreciation policy applicable to comparable operational assets.

(c) No interest on loans to finance capital investment has been capitalized in the regulatory accounts with effect from 1 April 1995. Interest capitalized in the statutory accounts for years up to and including 1994/95 is included in the asset value.

FIGURE 4.1

**BAA share price from end-April 1996 to September 2002
(BAA performance against FTAS)**

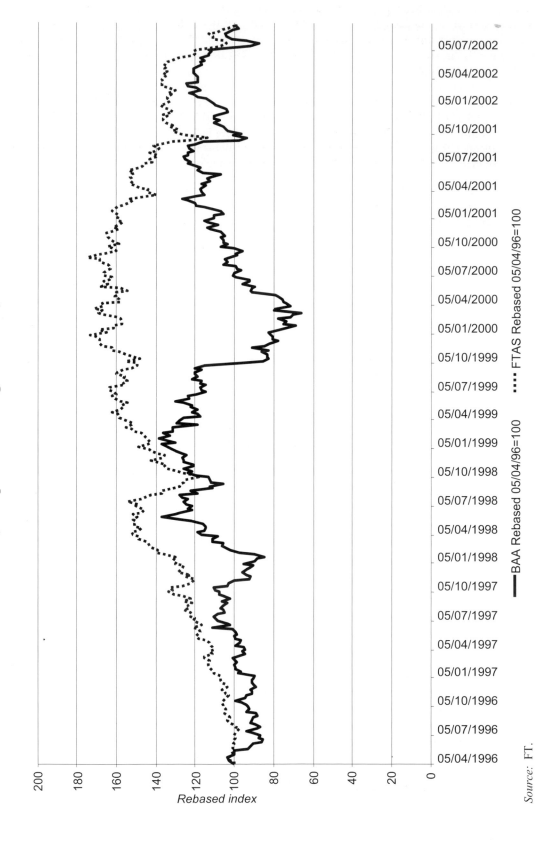

Rebased index

······ FTAS Rebased 05/04/96=100

——BAA Rebased 05/04/96=100

Source: FT.

4.14. Statutory accounts are prepared for LAL, the holding company for the three London airports, but not on a consolidated basis, as consolidated accounts are prepared by BAA, the ultimate holding company. A pro forma aggregation is, however, prepared of the regulatory accounts of the three London airports together with the accounts of HEOC. The pro forma aggregation, which is not audited, includes a number of further adjustments to the accounts of the underlying companies and a notional capital structure which is intended to represent the London airports as if they were a stand-alone group. Table 4.4, which compares the financial results of the airport companies with the projections made by the MMC in its 1996 inquiry, shows details of revenue, operating profit and capital value. The further adjustments which affect these items are:

(a) The airport companies owned a number of hotels in the early part of Q3 (see paragraph 4.2) which have now been transferred from the airport companies to BAA and subsequently disposed of. The results of the hotels activity was not regarded by the CAA as part of the activities of the airports when setting airport charges and accordingly the revenue, operating profits and fixed assets involved have been excluded from the aggregation.

(b) Although the staff at the airports are employed by BAA, the costs are charged to the airport companies and appear in their accounts. Some of these costs, as well as those for staff working centrally on behalf of the airports, are capitalized. Since 1995/96 further costs relating to T5 and Heathrow Express (written off as operating costs in the accounts of airport companies) have been capitalized in the accounts of BAA group and will be written off over periods of between 10 and 25 years. The additional capitalization of central costs at BAA group level is included in the aggregation, with an effect on both operating profit and fixed assets. At 31 March 2002 the cumulative sum involved (after depreciation) was £50.8 million. The value of the assets involved is, however, not adjusted to reflect movements in the RPI.

(c) When the RCV of the London airports was determined at the beginning of Q3 there was a difference of £29 million between the RCV and the capital employed of the airport companies in their regulatory accounts. This sum, adjusted for movements in the RPI, is included in the aggregation.

Changes in accounting policies and presentation

4.15. During Q3 a number of changes in accounting policy took place in the airport companies, including:

(a) From 1996/97 operational assets in the statutory accounts have been accounted for on a historical cost basis, having previously been accounted for on a depreciated replacement cost basis.

(b) Up to 31 March 1997, capitalization of interest was based on all costs incurred from commencement of a project until it was complete and income producing. This policy was refined in 1997/98 so that interest is capitalized now only on costs incurred once planning permission has been obtained and a firm decision to proceed with the project has been taken. BAA told us that the result of this change was to write off in the restated 1996/97 accounts interest of £20.2 million which had been capitalized in earlier years and to reduce the interest capitalized in that year by £11.5 million. Further, from 31 March 2000, in accordance with FRS 15 (tangible fixed assets), capitalization of interest now ceases once a project has been completed, without the need for it to have become income producing as well.

(c) The adoption of FRS 15 has resulted in runway surfaces from 1999/2000 being treated as a separate class of asset and depreciated over the expected useful lives of 10 to 15 years. BAA told us that the effect of the change on the accounts for the year to 31 March 2000 was insignificant.

(d) From 1 April 2000, the depreciation life of runways aprons and taxiways has been reduced to 50 years from 100 years. The effect on the results for the year to 31 March 2001 was to increase the depreciation charge by £1.1 million.

(e) For compliance with FRS 12 (provisions, contingent liabilities and assets) the policy of deferring income relating to aircraft charges invoiced over and above the permitted yield was changed in 1999/2000 and all remaining provisions against amounts invoiced above the permitted yield were released in that year. BAA told us that effect of releasing the provisions in the year was an increase in profit at Heathrow of £0.7 million and of £4.4 million at Gatwick; as these amounts were not considered material no prior year adjustment was made.

(f) Changes have taken place in the amounts of own costs capitalized in the accounts of the airport companies with a reduction resulting from a refinement of the overhead absorption rate calculation. Prior to 1998/99 the basis of capitalization of staff costs was cost plus an overhead rate of between 30 and 65 per cent; the basis now used is salary plus other direct employee costs.

Treatment of AICC

4.16. As already noted (see paragraph 4.15*(b)*), interest on AICC is capitalized in the statutory accounts of BAA group companies. The 1996 MMC report recommended that, in setting prices for airport charges, capitalized interest should be excluded from the regulatory asset values. However, provision was made for a return on AICC by the inclusion of such assets in the RCV. A number of airlines made known to us their view that users which paid airport charges while assets were being constructed might not be the eventual users of the assets when they were brought into use; and that the allowance of the rate of return on AICC involved prefunding, a concept to which many airlines were opposed. We considered an alternative approach involving the capitalization of expenditure on new investment at the cost of capital (as opposed to the capitalization only of interest actually incurred) and not allowing for such investment in the regulatory capital value until the assets became operational. Such an approach would produce a much lower RCV initially and a considerably higher RCV thereafter, with implications of significantly lower airport charges in the short term and a significant increase in charges subsequently, but with no advantage over time to either shareholders or users as a whole.

Results in the third quinquennium

4.17. The aggregated financial results for LAL in Q3 (including those for 1996/97, the last year of Q2) are shown in Table 4.4 in out-turn prices. These results are compared with the forecasting model outputs in 1996 on which the MMC recommendations for the levels of X in Q3 were based. Details of the aggregation of the results of the companies and the adjustments made are shown in Appendix 4.3, and a summary of the regulatory accounts of the three airport companies are shown in Appendices 4.7 to 4.9 respectively. The statutory accounting results of the three airport companies are shown in Appendices 4.4 to 4.6 (see paragraph 4.18). When extending Q3 by one year with the inclusion of 2002/03, the CAA continued the price control for HAL and GAL at RPI–3 per cent and the one at STAL at RPI+1. The MMC's projections in 1996 assumed an X of +2 per cent for 2002/03 and the remaining years of what was then intended to be Q4.

162

£ million (out-turn prices)

	1996/97	1997/98	1998/99	1999/00	2000/01	2001/02
Forecast from 1996 model						
Movement in RPI (1995/96=100)	1.024	1.058	1.091	1.108	1.142	1.159
Passenger numbers	85.4	88.7	91.3	93.3	94.8	96.3
Revenue	1,137	1,223	1,321	1,374	1,425	1,456
Operating profit	400	423	452	459	468	486
Mean regulatory capital value	3,960	4,405	4,880	5,335	5,922	6,453
Capex	403	445	482	574	595	607
Return of profit:						
On revenue (%)	35.2	34.6	34.2	33.4	32.8	33.4
On mean RCV (%)	10.1	9.6	9.3	8.6	7.9	7.5
Actual						
Passenger numbers	85.6	90.9	98.0	102.6	108.7	104.9
Revenue	1,156	1,178	1,251	1,247	1,337	1,363
Operating profit†	409	393	445	427	461	419
Value of fixed assets‡	4,298	4,776	5,006	5,242	5,594	5,928
Mean fixed asset value	N/A*	4,537	4,892	5,124	5,418	5,761
Capex (Table 4.2)	388	478	368	294	440	530
Return of profit:						
On revenue (%)	35.4	33.3	35.6	34.2	34.6	30.7
On mean fixed asset value (%)	N/A*	8.7	9.1	8.3	8.5	7.3

Source: BAA and CC.

---

*N/A = not applicable.

†A charge of £92 million was made by BAA to HAL and GAL in 1997/98 for the effect of the windfall tax, which was treated as an operating cost in the accounts of the airport companies. This amount has been added back to operating profit for 1997/98 in the table above.

‡The RCV is not calculated on an ongoing basis. As a proxy, the value of fixed assets, which are updated each year by reference to movements in the RPI, has been used as an approximation in calculating actual returns on the value of investment made.

Financial performance of HAL, GAL and STAL

4.18. The financial results in the statutory accounts of each airport in 1996/97 and in Q3 to date are shown in Table 4.5 for HAL, Table 4.6 for GAL and Table 4.7 for STAL. Additional financial information is shown in Appendices 4.4 to 4.6 for the respective operating companies. The results in Tables 4.5 to 4.7 are prepared on the same accounting basis as that used in the BAA group, the results of which are in Table 4.1. This basis differs from the basis used for the aggregated regulatory accounts of LAL shown in Table 4.4.

TABLE 4.5 **HAL: summary of financial results for Q3 to date**

£ million (out-turn prices)

	1996/97	1997/98	1998/99	1999/00	2000/01	2001/02
Revenue	793.8	786.0	810.0	834.2	893.6	903.7
Operating profit	337.3	240.0	323.0	324.5	349.2	324.5
Enterprise value	2,402.2	2,761.5	3,033.9	3,141.4	3,085.5	3,322.4
Mean enterprise value	2,166.3	2,581.9	2,897.7	3,087.7	3,113.5	3,204.0
Return of profit:						
On revenue (%)	42.5	30.5	39.9	38.9	39.1	35.9
On mean enterprise value (%)	15.6	9.3	11.1	10.5	11.2	10.1

Source: BAA.

TABLE 4.6 **GAL: summary of financial results for Q3 to date**

£ million (out-turn prices)

	1996/97	1997/98	1998/99	1999/00	2000/01	2001/02
Revenue	305.6	331.4	359.8	317.5	325.3	321.7
Operating profit	101.0	88.2	127.8	112.1	119.5	100.9
Enterprise value	856.8	867.4	871.7	1,014.8	1,032.6	1,056.9
Mean enterprise value	841.6	862.1	869.6	943.3	1,023.7	1,044.8
Return of profit:						
On revenue (%)	33.0	26.6	35.5	35.3	36.7	31.4
On mean enterprise value (%)	12.0	10.2	14.7	11.9	11.7	9.7

Source: BAA.

TABLE 4.7 **STAL: summary of financial results for Q3 to date**

£ million (out-turn prices)

	1996/97	1997/98	1998/99	1999/00	2000/01	2001/02
Revenue	67.2	62.1	82.0	95.5	118.4	137.9
Operating profit	-	4.1	17.4	21.1	28.1	36.3
Enterprise value	586.7	601.2	656.6	726.9	794.6	949.7
Mean enterprise value	579.8	594.0	628.9	691.8	760.8	872.2
Return of profit:						
On revenue (%)	-	6.6	21.2	22.1	23.7	26.3
On mean enterprise value (%)	-	0.7	2.8	3.1	3.7	4.2

Source: BAA.

4.19. As noted in paragraph 4.8, BAA established a separate unit in 1997/98 to operate the duty-free facilities at its airports. WDFE was formed in November 1996 and progressively took over the duty-free franchises at the airports as the management agreements for them expired. The process was completed in the course of Q3. WDFE also operated in Q3 at BAA airports outside London and at Eurotunnel terminals. Under the management agreements with third parties which applied prior to the transfers, the duty-free sales and cost of sales of a concession appeared in the accounts of the airport company and the management fee was treated as a cost. This meant that the whole of the profit on the activity accrued to the airport, subject only to payment of the management fee. After the transfer to WDFE, a separate company, this arrangement was replaced by payment by WDFE to the airport company of a concession fee for the facility. These concessions fees were linked to the volume of sales in the same way as in agreements with third party retailers.

4.20. BAA told us that the reason it took the duty-free activity within the BAA group was that, following the loss of the EC duty- and tax-free allowance, there were insufficient stable and well-capitalized companies to maintain a competitive market for effective tendering. This would have impacted on operational and financial performance at the airports. It said that in negotiating the amounts payable by WDFE it had sought to apply terms no less favourable than those which applied under the previous management contracts. The contracts with WDFE ran for a period of up to nine years (depending on the start date and investment) compared with a period of some five to seven years for pre-WDFE duty-free contracts. There was a code of conduct in operation to ensure an arm's length relationship between WDFE and the airport companies.

4.21. The effect of the transfers on the revenue and operating costs of the airport companies was substantial, but operating profit was affected only to the extent that WDFE itself made an operating profit on the transferred concession different from the previous management charge. BAA told us that the returns to WDFE from its business had been above those initially projected. By 2001/02 operating profit of WDFE was £22 million (having increased from £10 million in 1998/99) on sales of £342 million and net assets of £41 million, of which operating profit of some £18 million was attributable to the London airports on sales of £317 million.

4.22. BAA told us that the margin on sales of WDFE at the airports in 2001/02 was 5.9 per cent and the margin in previous years had been similar or less. It said that bearing in mind that WDFE took volume, price and capital expenditure risk, this sort of margin did not seem excessive compared with other industries where profits were driven by margins on sales rather than by rates of returns on assets. BAA provided us with an analysis of operating margins (operating profit divided by sales) for UK retailers over the period 1992 to 2002 which showed an average return on sales of 7.3 per cent.

4.23. BAA made group management charges in 1997/98 to HAL (£69.3 million) and GAL (£22.7 million) in respect of the windfall tax levied on the group. This was charged as an operating cost in the accounts of the companies and so reduced operating profit and the returns in that year.

Analysis of revenues and profits of HAL, GAL and STAL

4.24. Under the Airports Act the CAA must impose conditions on each designated airport requiring it to disclose certain information in its accounts. The conditions in force in effect require the airport operator to include in its audited accounts a statement of revenues and profits broken down between airport charges (aircraft landing and parking fees and charges levied on aircraft passengers), other operational activities (income from tax-free and duty-free concessions, other shops, car parks and rental of other airport property) and non-operational activities. Table 4.8 summarizes the results for Q3 to date, together with those for 1996/97 the last year of Q3.

4.25. The conditions imposed by the CAA under the Airports Act also require the statement of revenues and operating profits to be supported by a description of the broad principles of cost allocation used in the statement. Appendix 4.10 reproduces BAA's current description of the broad principles used. BAA has made detailed assumptions to create a system of cost allocation which reflects the principles shown in Appendix 4.10, and this is used for preparation of PCRs which form part of BAA's management information; this approach is consistently applied by all airports. The allocation of costs requires a degree of judgement and, though BAA's system has been developed in accordance with widely accepted accounting methods and in consultation with the CAA, it is possible that other accountants would make different judgements and thus arrive at analyses different from those shown in Table 4.8.

4.26. The statutory accounts of each airport company, drawn up in accordance with the provisions of the Companies Act 1985, include in a note to the accounts a segmental analysis of revenue between airport and other traffic charges, retail income, property and operational facilities, rail and other activities. The note does not include a segmental analysis of either profit or assets along similar lines as: 'In the opinion of the directors it would be misleading to apportion operating costs and net assets to individual segments.'

4.27. Under a condition imposed under section 46(2) of the Airports Act, BAA also provides cost information to users showing the revenue costs and financial result of various specified activities such as check-in desks, staff car parks, staff ID cards, airside licences, FEGP, bus and coach operators and utility services (heating water and electricity). BAA's system of cost allocation is used for these statements which are accompanied by a more detailed description of the principles of cost allocation in use and by a report from the auditors of each company. In their report the auditors confirm that these PCRs present fairly the information set forth therein on the basis of the broad principles of cost allocation set out.

4.28. Considerable work has been carried out in the past two years by both BAA and the CAA on the system of cost allocation, against the background of the possible introduction by the CAA of an RRCB (dual-till) system for setting airport charges, and there have been a number of studies by consultants. BAA and the CAA told us that the studies were broadly supportive of the existing cost allocation and PCR systems, though some refinement would be required for a dual-till environment, in particular the allocation of facilities between the aeronautical and commercial tills.

4.29. As an indication of the way that the results shown in Table 4.8 could be affected by the CAA's proposed distinction between an aeronautical and a commercial till, we have calculated a comparison of the returns on average capital employed for the two tills for the years 1996/97 to 2000/01. This is shown in Table 4.9.

TABLE 4.8 **Analysis of revenue and profit for HAL, GAL and STAL by type of activity**

	1996/97		1997/98		1998/99		1999/00		2000/01		2001/02	
	Revenue	Operating profit	Revenue	Operating profit	Revenue	Operating profit	Revenue	Operating profit	Revenue	Operating profit	Revenue	Operating profit
HAL												
Airport charges	267	49	276	28	298	70	309	84	337	116	338	94
Other operational activities	515	283	497	207	494	244	505	228	525	214	534	210
	782	332	773	235	792	314	814	312	862	330	872	304
Non-operational activities	12	5	13	5	18	9	20	12	32	19	32	21
Total	794	337	786	240	810	323	834	324	894	349	904	325
GAL												
Airport charges	91	-11	100	-17	110	-	125	6	130	3	130	-5
Other operational activities	212	111	227	103	245	125	189	104	190	113	187	103
	303	100	327	86	355	125	314	110	320	116	317	98
Non-operational activities	3	1	4	2	5	3	3	2	5	3	5	3
Total	306	101	331	88	360	128	317	112	325	119	322	101
STAL												
Airport charges	18	-22	20	-21	28	-16	39	-13	54	-12	63	-13
Other operational activities	48	21	41	25	53	33	55	33	62	39	73	48
	66	-1	61	4	81	17	94	20	116	27	136	35
Non-operational activities	1	1	1	-	1	-	1	1	2	1	2	1
Total	67	-	62	4	82	17	95	21	118	28	138	36
Total for three airports												
Airport charges	376	16	396	-10	436	54	473	77	521	107	531	76
Other operational activities	775	415	765	335	792	402	749	365	777	366	794	361
	1,151	431	1,161	325	1,228	456	1,222	442	1,298	473	1,325	437
Non-operational activities	16	7	18	7	24	12	24	15	39	23	39	25
Total	1,167	438	1,179	332	1,252	468	1,246	457	1,337	496	1,364	462

Source: BAA.

166

TABLE 4.9 **BAA: illustrative returns on capital employed of aeronautical and commercial tills under the CAA's RRCB proposal**

per cent

	1996/97	1997/98	1998/99	1999/00	2000/01
Aeronautical till					
HAL	8.4	2.6	6.7	6.2	6.7
GAL	−3.4	−6.4	−2.2	1.9	2.5
STAL	−5.5	−3.8	−2.5	−1.7	−0.8
Commercial till					
HAL	22.3	15.6	15.2	14.4	14.5
GAL	37.2	37.3	42.3	28.2	25.3
STAL	24.3	20.5	25.9	23.4	20.9

Source: CC from BAA and CAA data.

The returns shown in Table 4.9 were derived by applying to the results in the airport accounts the apportionments between the tills proposed by the CAA in its submission to us. The data provided by the CAA showed a split of assets at 31 March 2001 and the projected splits of opex and non-regulated revenue over the course of Q4. Figures were not available on a year-by-year basis for Q3 and earlier years. Use of these apportionments therefore provides an illustrative indication only of the relative profitability of the two tills, as the splits will have varied from year to year. In particular the asset split at 31 March 2001 included the substantial investment in Heathrow Express in the commercial till, though the extent of this investment was considerably less in earlier years. As in Table 4.8, figures from the statutory accounts have been used and these tend to show higher returns on capital employed than the regulatory accounts due to the higher asset values and depreciation in the regulatory accounts.

Future investment

4.30. The ability of the south-eastern airports to maintain and develop their businesses is dependent on various factors such as the growth in airport traffic, the level of regulatory control applied to airport charges and their success in controlling costs. A further major factor will be the level of new investment in fixed assets, including in future quinquennia the investment in T5. Despite the postponement of T5 due to the delay in the grant of planning permission, investment since the MMC's 1996 report has been considerable (see Table 4.2). Additional details comparing new investment with that forecast in 1996 is given in Chapter 9. BAA is projecting (at constant 2002 prices) capex for 2002/03 of £675 million, for Q4 of £5 billion and for Q5 of a further £2.4 billion.

Cost of capital

4.31. The cost of capital was an important input used in 1996 by the MMC in making recommendations on the airport charging formula to apply to BAA in Q3. It has also figured prominently in the pricing formula proposals of other regulators. In the light of the evidence submitted by the CAA, BAA and some third parties, the relevant literature on these matters and the position taken by the MMC and the CC in previous inquiries involving regulated industries, we have made estimates of the range of rates of return to apply to BAA. For this purpose we have primarily used the framework of the CAPM which was used by both BAA and the CAA in their submissions to us. All calculations of cost of capital in this section of our report are made in real terms.

The CAA's submission

4.32. The CAA proposed different costs of capital figures for the three airports, reflecting the variation with respect to investment and the levels of risk faced at the airports. The proposed costs of capital for each airport were the same under both a single-till and dual-till approach and these are shown in Table 4.10. In the case of Heathrow the CAA proposed different cost of capital figures for existing and new assets, reflecting different levels of risk and the cost of financing large projects.

TABLE 4.10 **BAA: CAA proposals for BAA's cost of capital on both a single- and dual-till basis**

				per cent*
	Heathrow	Gatwick	Stansted	Heathrow (new assets under PPC)
1. Risk-free rate	3.00	3.00	3.00	3.00
2. Equity risk premium	4.00	4.00	4.00	4.00
3. Equity beta	0.70	0.80	0.80	1.30
4. Cost of equity (post-tax) Line 1+(line 2 x line 3)	5.80	6.20	6.20	8.20
5. Taxation adjustment	30.00	30.00	30.00	30.00
6. Cost of equity (pre-tax) Line 4 ÷ (100 – line 5)	8.29	8.86	8.86	11.71
7. Gearing	25.00	25.00	25.00	45.00
8. Debt premium	0.90	0.90	0.90	1.60
9. Cost of debt Line 1 + line 8	3.90	3.90	3.90	4.60
10. Pre-tax WACC Line 6 x (1 – line 7) + Line 9 x line 7	7.19	7.62	7.62	8.51
11. Rounded pre-tax WACC proposed by the CAA	7.00	7.50	7.50	8.50

Source: CAA.

*Excluding line 3, which is a number.

4.33. The CAA told us that under its PPC proposals, output-based pricing would apply to new assets at Heathrow, such as T5, which resulted in increased outputs. Most of the risks involved in building projects such as T5, for instance the risk of cost overruns, could be seen as diversifiable risk. Under the PPC, BAA faced a higher level of risk as the large planned new investments relied on passenger volume for their success and it was therefore appropriate to increase BAA's equity beta under the PPC to 1.3 for new assets. For existing assets, which were of much lower risk, an equity beta of 0.7 remained appropriate. In addition the CAA assumed a higher debt premium for new assets of 1.6 per cent and a gearing level of 45 per cent. Together these factors increased the CAA's proposed real pre-tax WACC to 8.5 per cent for new assets at Heathrow.

4.34. The approach used by us (see paragraph 4.64) has been to arrive at a single cost of capital for both existing and new assets, but in doing so we have applied a higher equity beta than that used by the CAA for existing assets at all three airports; the beta of 0.70 used by the CAA for Heathrow is similar to the most recent reported historical beta for BAA of 0.71. The higher range for beta used by us in Table 4.13 of 0.8 to 1.0 in part recognizes the special factors applying to large new capital projects such as T5.

BAA's submission

4.35. BAA provided two submissions to us on the cost of capital. In the first submission BAA took as its starting point the existing regulatory structure prior to the changes proposed by the CAA to the price-setting process and the construction of T5. In the second submission BAA described the impact of T5 on its cost of capital. Table 4.11 shows BAA's proposals for a base cost of capital of 9.3 per cent, prior to any changes to the price-setting process and the construction of T5.

168

TABLE 4.11 **BAA: the company's proposals for the base cost of capital**

		per cent*	
	Low	Mid-point	High
1. Risk-free rate	2.75		3.25
2. Equity risk premium	4.00		6.00
3. Equity beta	0.86		0.96
4. Cost of equity (post-tax)			
Line 1+(line 2 x line 3)	6.19		9.01
5. Taxation adjustment	30.00		30.00
6. Pre-tax cost of equity			
Line 4 ÷ (100 − line 5)†	8.84		12.87
7. Gearing	30.00		20.00
8. Debt premium	1.20		1.40
9. Cost of debt			
Line 1 + line 8	3.95		4.65
10. Pre-tax WACC			
Line 6 x (1 − line 7) + line 9 x line 7	7.38		11.23
11. Proposed mid-point for pre-tax WACC		9.31	

Source: BAA.

*Excluding line 3, which is a number.
†The BAA submission showed a figure of 12.91 for the high level of pre-tax cost of equity.

4.36. In its second submission BAA proposed figures for the cost of capital taking account of T5 under two bases—first under the conventional process linked to a return on the RCV (9.65 per cent) and second under an LRIC approach as proposed by the CAA with its PPC (11.21 per cent). The details of both BAA's proposals for the cost of capital with T5 are shown in Table 4.12.

TABLE 4.12 **BAA: the company's proposals for cost of capital with inclusion of the effect of T5**

				per cent*		
	Under RCV system			Under LRIC		
	Low	Mid-point	High	Low	Mid-point	High
1. Risk-free rate	2.75		3.25	2.75		3.25
2. Equity risk premium	4.00		6.00	4.00		6.00
3. Equity beta	1.03		1.31	1.37		1.69
4. Cost of equity (post-tax)						
Line 1+(line 2 x line 3)	6.87		11.11	8.23		13.39
5. Taxation adjustment	30.00		30.00	30.00		30.00
6. Pre-tax cost of equity						
Line 4 ÷ (100 − line 5)	9.81		15.87	11.76		19.13
7. Gearing	(✂)		(✂)			(✂)
8. Debt premium	1.75		1.95	1.75		1.95
9. Cost of debt						
Line 1 + line 8	4.50		5.20	4.50		5.20
10. Pre-tax WACC						
Line 6 x (1 − line 7) + Line 9 x line 7	7.69		11.60	8.85		13.56
11. Proposed mid-point for pre-tax WACC		9.65			11.21	

Source. BAA.

*Excluding line 3, which is a number.

4.37. BAA told us that the distinctive nature of the T5 project meant that several aspects of the determination of its cost of capital were different from the standard regulatory model. Failure to give adequate recognition to this in Q4 would undermine an infrastructure project that was of fundamental importance to the British economy and might threaten the viability of BAA itself. BAA referred to the financial failure of a number of recent projects as indicative of the risks inherent in large infrastructure projects.

4.38. BAA made a number of points about the exceptional nature of its investment in T5:

(a) In the decade from 2002/03 to 2010/11, investment in T5 was expected to total £3.7 billion, nearly half of BAA's total capex over the same period of £8 billion. At its peak in 2005/06, T5 investment would be 63 per cent of BAA's total capex in the year. The T5 investment was of a similar magnitude to other major transport infrastructure projects such as the Channel Tunnel (£8.9 billion), the Channel Tunnel Rail Link (£4.2 billion) and the West Coast Route Modernisation (£5.8 billion).

(b) Not only was the T5 investment large, but it was a fixed expenditure and would raise BAA's operational gearing appreciably. BAA defined operational gearing as the ratio of capex to the total of capex and opex for the regulated airports group. On this basis operational gearing rose from the 2001/02 level of 46 per cent to [✄] per cent in 2005/06 before falling to [✄] per cent in 2010/11.

(c) The investment in T5 was irreversible. Once expenditure had begun, BAA was committed and abandonment of the project was not a viable option. BAA was foregoing an option to defer starting the project to a later date. The loss of this option was not reflected in the standard CAPM measure of the cost of capital.

(d) Although the base case financial projections did not necessitate new equity issues, cost overruns or unanticipated revenue shortfalls on existing assets could force the company into them. BAA said it considered that the cost of raising new equity to fund T5 would be substantially in excess of the cost of internal and debt finance.

(e) The regulatory treatment for T5 proposed by the CAA was a radical departure from the methods employed in the past. The traditional approach involved determining allowed revenues from an RCV, a cost of capital and allowed operating costs. Instead the CAA's proposal for a PPC involved an LRIC approach that set charges on the basis of the long-run marginal costs of building T5 and a per passenger price for each passenger in excess of a benchmark level. This procedure substantially increased the risk to BAA in relation to one based on the traditional use of an RCV, as marginal revenues were substantially in excess of average revenues above the benchmark level. This implied that under the CAA's proposed PPC mechanism, there would be a much higher sensitivity of BAA's revenues to out-turn volumes.

These risk factors and the additional levels of finance required identified by BAA for the T5 project resulted in the higher equity betas, gearing and debt premia shown in Table 4.12 as compared with the base case without T5 shown in Table 4.11.

BA's submission

4.39. In its submission to us BA said that adequate but not excessive returns should be permitted. The interests of users required that BAA's charges were as low as possible, commensurate with BAA achieving a fair return on its investment. This return should reflect risk and be set at a level that did not compromise quality. BA proposed lower levels for both equity and debt finance and a central estimate cost of capital for both Heathrow and Gatwick of 6.6 per cent, well below the level proposed by BAA and the CAA. BA said that it did not believe it was appropriate to use different cost of capital estimates for the three London airports, or to distinguish between new outputs and existing outputs in the treatment of Heathrow capex. BA said that the CAA's proposals for a higher cost of capital to be applied to T5 were intrinsically linked with its proposals for a long-term price cap which BA rejected and that BA did not believe a robust methodology existed to ensure that the appropriate differential was applied. BA proposed lower levels than either BAA or the CAA for most elements of the CAPM and a gearing level of 25 per cent. BA suggested a debt premium of 0.5 per cent which, together with a risk-free rate of 2.75 per cent, gave a cost of debt of 3.25 per cent, well below the base cases of the CAA (3.9 per cent) and BAA (3.95 to 4.65 per cent). It said that BAA, with investment grade ratings of A1 (Moody's) and AA- (Standard & Poor's), should be able to attract lending well below 50 basis points. According to BA, BAA's 7.875 bonds due 2007 were trading at the equivalent of London inter bank offered rate (LIBOR) plus 25 basis points on 12 August 2002, the longer-dated issue of 11.75 bonds due 2016 at LIBOR plus 55 basis points and even the recent 30-year bonds due 2031 were trading at LIBOR plus 80 basis points. BAA was also able to access very attractive banking facilities from the European Investment Bank and the Japan Bank for International Co-operation. BA assumed the same gearing level used by the CAA of 25 per cent for BAA, which it said might not be optimal. It was concerned that there were no incentives in place to seek a lower cost of capital through an improved funding structure (ie an increased level of gearing).

CC illustrative range for the cost of capital

4.40. Inputs to the CAPM are continually changing, not only as a result of movements in financial markets, but also as a result of continuing work by financial and academic analysts on new data and on the reinterpretation of existing data. In addition, there can be considerable uncertainty over the appropriate level for some inputs and a degree of judgement is therefore required. This can result in changes over time to the WACC of an individual company and, in the case of airport companies, from one quinquennial review to another. In view of these uncertainties, the approach we have adopted has been to identify what we consider to be reasonable ranges for each input to the CAPM on an illustrative basis, and from the resulting high and low WACCs to take a mid-point as our base case for BAA.

4.41. We have then considered the special additional features which are expected to apply to BAA in Q4, principally as a result of its commitment to the construction of T5, and made what we consider to be an appropriate adjustment to BAA's WACC. It has been put to us that the changes to the CAPM inputs referred to above, as a result of activity in the markets, could lead to undue volatility in our assessment of BAA's WACC; and that the resulting uncertainty would have a detrimental effect on investment decisions by BAA. Accordingly we have also considered whether to apply a degree of smoothing for changes in some elements of the CAPM so that long-term trends in inputs are recognized over time, but without excessive fluctuations in the short term.

4.42. An illustrative range of rates of return for BAA in real terms is shown in Table 4.13. The rates of pre-tax WACC range from 5.67 to 8.76 per cent with a mean of 7.21 per cent. The bases for the ranges of input values in Table 4.13 are described below.

TABLE 4.13 **BAA: CC illustrative calculation of BAA's cost of capital**

	Low	Mid-point	High
		per cent*	
1. Risk-free rate	2.50		2.75
2. Equity risk premium	2.50		4.50
3. Equity beta	0.80		1.00
4. Cost of equity (post-tax) Line 1+(line 2 x line 3)	4.50		7.25
5. Taxation adjustment	30.00		30.00
6. Pre-tax cost of equity Line 4 ÷ (100 – line 5)	6.43		10.36
7. Gearing	25.00		25.0
8. Debt premium	0.90		1.20
9. Cost of debt Line 1 + line 8	3.40		3.95
10. Pre-tax WACC Line 6 x (1 – line 7) + Line 9 x line 7	5.67		8.76
11. Proposed mid-point for pre-tax WACC		7.21	

Source: CC.

*Excluding line 3, which is a number.

Risk-free rate

4.43. Unlike other inputs to the CAPM, the current risk-free rate can be observed directly from trading in liquid markets. The UK Government has issued index-linked securities (index-linked gilts) which are generally considered to have negligible default risk and inflation risk (inflation measured by the RPI, though lagged eight months). The redemption yield on these gilts provides an estimate of the real risk-free rate for different maturities. The Bank of England makes regular estimates of such rates over the whole yield curve which are, in addition, adjusted to a zero coupon basis which helps to deal with tax and other complications.

4.44. Figure 4.2 shows index-linked yields from January 1985 to June 2002. Since 1997 yields for all maturities have fallen from over 3.5 per cent to under 2.5 per cent. At June 2002 the respective yields on short term (5 years), medium term (10 years) and long term (20 years) were 2.28 per cent, 2.32 per cent and 2.16 per cent. It will be seen from Figure 4.2 that these yields are well below most previous levels.

FIGURE 4.2

Real redemption yields on index-linked gilts 1985 to 2002*

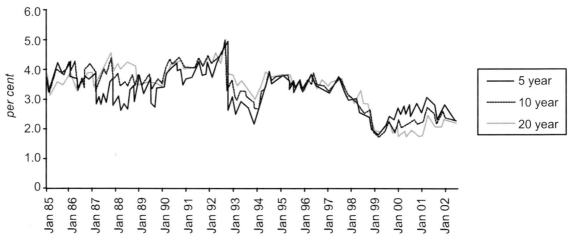

Source: Bank of England.
*Estimated by the Bank of England from a smoothed zero coupon yield curve.

4.45. Figure 4.3 shows real yield curves (at six-monthly intervals) over the most recent three years and again shows how yields in general have declined. We are concerned primarily with the costs of debt and equity over the next five years, during which the price control will operate. However, the financial modelling for setting the level of the price control takes place over a ten-year period, while decisions on equity investments are typically made in an even longer time scale. The yield curve also provides information on expected future yields: for example, the expected yield on a ten-year index-linked gilt security in three years' time can be worked out from the current yields on a 13-year gilt and a three-year one.

4.46. Two main arguments were put to us suggesting that the risk-free rate should be set at a higher level than the current yields on index-linked gilts: first, that historic yields may be more important than current yields as a predictor of future yields, since yields may revert towards the mean; and second, that current yields had been affected by special factors such as the increased demand for gilts as a result of the minimum funding requirement (MFR) for pension funds. We consider each of these in turn.

FIGURE 4.3

Real yield, December 1999 to June 2002 (spot rates)

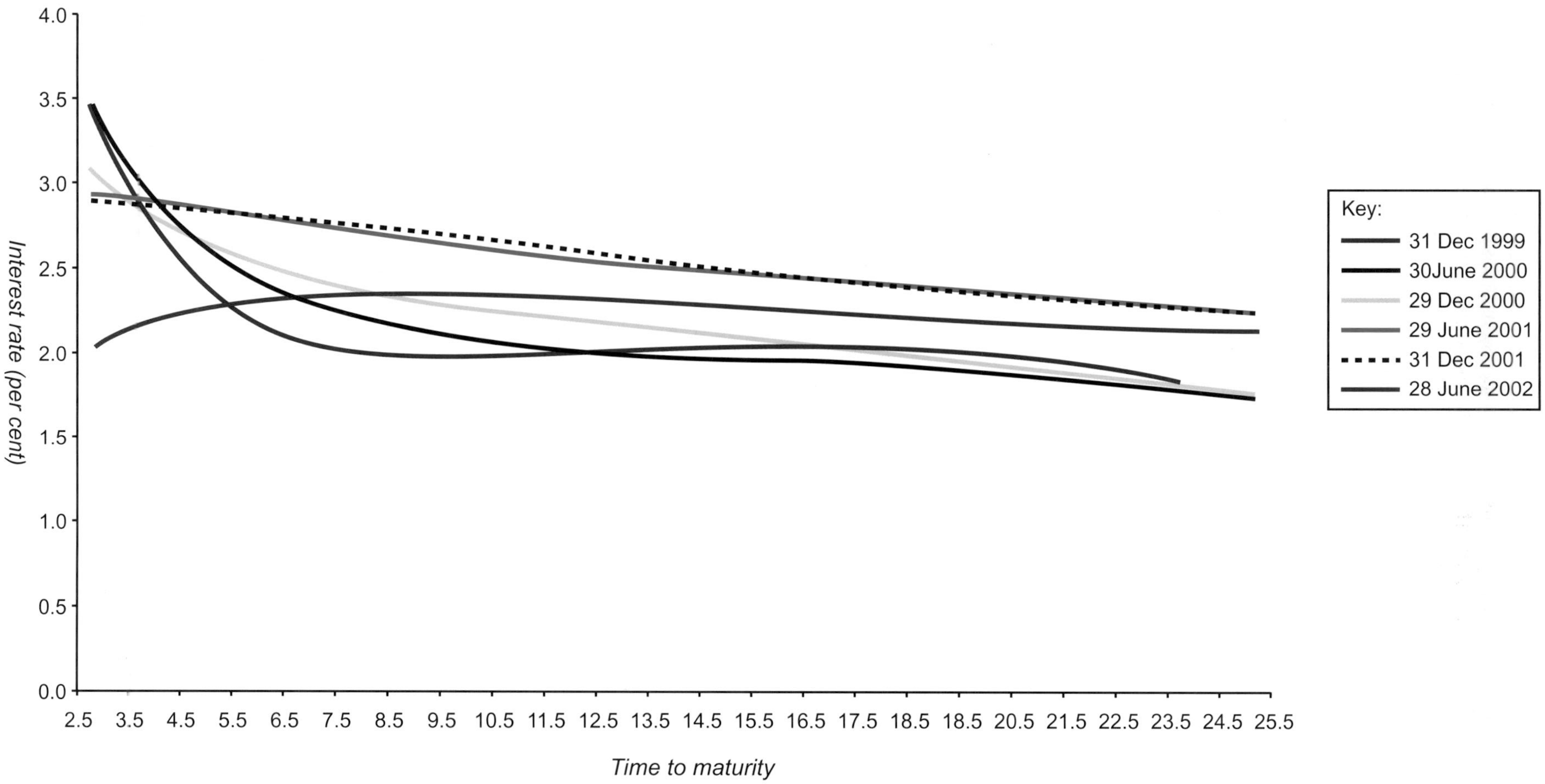

Key:
31 Dec 1999
30 June 2000
29 Dec 2000
29 June 2001
31 Dec 2001
28 June 2002

Interest rate (per cent)

Time to maturity

Source: Bank of England.

4.47. We received no formal evidence of mean reversion in index-linked gilts (or any other bond) yields. Conventional gilt yields over the past 15 to 20 years have been relatively high when compared with longer periods of up to a century.[1] Consequently, even if there is long-run mean reversion, it is unclear that the rate to which yields revert is the yield over the period since 1982 for which index-linked gilts have been available. We accept, however, that markets can be volatile and that it would be unwise to place too much reliance on just the most recent figure if it is substantially different from previous figures. In the most recent reports on Cellnet and Vodafone[2] and on two water companies[3] the MMC/CC based its ranges for the risk-free rate on both recent and longer-term evidence. In the Cellnet/Vodafone inquiry in 1998 a range of 3.5 to 3.8 per cent was used, but this was at an early stage in the decline in real index-linked yields. The Mid Kent Water/Sutton and East Surrey inquiries took place in 2000 when the CC had to take account of more recent evidence of the failure of yields to recover to their earlier levels: in recognition of this a risk-free rate of 3.0 per cent (the mid-point of a range between 2.75 and 3.25 per cent) was used by the CC in those inquiries. This level for the risk-free rate was above the then current rates for index-linked gilts of around 2 per cent, but took account of the downward trend in index-linked rates.

4.48. There appears to be widespread recognition that gilt yields have been affected by special factors, including an increased demand from pension funds as a result of the introduction of the MFR requirements in 1997, just before the decline in gilt yields started. The strong demand has placed upward pressure on prices of both conventional and index-linked government securities. Relatively low UK Government borrowing in recent years could be another factor contributing to the upward pressure on gilts prices (and hence lower yields); this position could change in the next few years if increased government borrowing became necessary to finance expenditure commitments. Between 1998 and 2000, the spread between yields on corporate bonds and on conventional gilts widened, supporting the contention that specific institutional factors had affected gilt yields. More recently corporate bond spreads have declined. Index-linked government securities in other countries are currently yielding somewhat higher amounts of the order of 3 per cent and a little above.[4] Caution is needed in interpreting these figures as some foreign markets are less mature than that in the UK and may in consequence be less liquid. In addition, the arrangements for index liking and tax treatment may differ from those in the UK, as may the construction of the inflation index to which the securities are indexed.

4.49. In the light of all these considerations, we have used in Table 4.13 a range for the risk-free rate from 2.5 to 2.75 per cent. This is below the range of 2.75 to 3.25 used by the MMC in the water inquiries and reflects recognition of a continuation of the downward trend in the underlying rate, although above the current spot rates which have recovered slightly to around 2.2 per cent from their level in 2000 of around 2 per cent.

Equity risk premium

4.50. ERP represents the additional return that investors require to compensate them for the additional risk associated with investing in equities, rather than in risk-free assets. It is not directly measurable from market data because the future cash flow from equities, unlike that on bonds, is uncertain. There are two main methods in use to estimate the ERP; historical averages of realized equity returns over the risk-free rate; and surveys and other evidence of investors' current expectations on the ERP. Both methods attempt to proxy investors' expectations over the next few years. In its evidence BAA cited evidence from academic and practitioner studies giving ERPs ranging from 1 to 8.5 per cent and suggested that the evidence pointed to an ERP in the range 4 to 6 per cent.

4.51. If it is assumed that the ERP is constant over time and that, on average, investors' expectations are realized, then current and future ERPs can be estimated from a historical average of the difference between past equity returns and risk-free rates. Since equity returns tend to be volatile from year to year, it is common practice in the finance literature to consider returns over an extended period.

---

[1]The compound real rate of return on conventional gilts was 8.2 per cent over 1980 to 2000 and 8.9 per cent over 1990 to 2000, compared with only 1.3 per cent over the whole of the twentieth century. (Elroy Dimson, Paul Marsh and Mike Staunton, *Triumph of the Optimists: 101 years of global investing.*)

[2]*Cellnet and Vodafone: reports on the references under section 12 of the Telecommunications Act on the charges made by Cellnet and Vodafone for terminating calls from fixed-line networks,* The Stationery Office, December 1998.

[3]*Mid Kent Water plc: a report on the references under sections 12 and 14 of the Water Industry Act,* The Stationery Office, ugust 2000. *Sutton and East Surrey Water plc: a report on the references under sections 12 and 14 of the Water Industry Act,* The Stationery Office, August 2000.

[4]*FT* from Merrill Lynch *Global Bond Issues,* October 2002.

4.52. Table 4.14 shows the UK ERP relative to gilts and Treasury bills over various periods in the twentieth century. The figure derived for the ERP is sensitive to the holding period assumed.

TABLE 4.14 **UK mean ERPs over various periods**

per cent

Period	Relative to gilts	Relative to Treasury bills
1900–2000	4.4	4.8
1900–1949	2.1	2.4
1950–2000	6.8	7.1
1960–2000	4.6	5.3
1970–2000	3.5	5.6
1980–2000	3.6	7.3
1990–2000	0.4	4.8

Source: ABN AMRO/LBS indexes.

The equity return relative to gilts over the century was 4.4 per cent, with an annual return of 2.1 per cent from 1900 to 1949 and one of 6.8 per cent from 1950 to 2000. With the downturn in the stock market towards the end of the 1990s, the annual return relative to gilts was only 0.4 per cent from 1990 to 2000 and in 2000 there was a negative return of 11.6 per cent.

4.53. Calculation of the mean historical premium over a period depends on whether the premium is computed relative to gilts or to Treasury bills and on whether geometric or arithmetic means are used. The choice of statistical method is important since there is a difference of about 1.9 per cent between the geometric and arithmetic means of total returns on equities during the twentieth century, based on one-year holding periods.

4.54. The figures in Table 4.14 are geometric means. The equivalent arithmetic ERPs relative to gilts and Treasury bills over the period 1900 to 2000 were 5.6 and 6.5 per cent respectively, compared with the geometric ERPs of 4.4 and 4.8 per cent in Table 4.14. The figures given in the table are lower than historical figures that have previously been cited because the ABN AMRO/LBS study discovered survivorship bias[1] in previous estimates of total equity returns for the first half of the century and because earlier figures sometimes ignored the 1900 to 1919 period. The ABN AMRO/LBS study also showed that the UK average historical equity premium was slightly below the average for 11 other countries.

4.55. In a more recent paper extending and updating the ABN AMRO/LBS study, Dimson, Marsh and Staunton[2] arrived at an expected geometric risk premium of 2.3 per cent for the UK, 4.0 per cent for the USA and 2.9 per cent for the world equity market; the arithmetic premiums were 3.6 per cent, 5.3 per cent and 3.9 per cent. The Dimson, Marsh and Staunton results for the USA were similar to those obtained recently by Fama and French.[3] Based on dividend yields and growth estimates Fama and French computed the US equity premium from 1872 to 1999. They found a premium of 3.8 per cent before 1949 and one of 3.4 per cent for the subsequent period, below the 4.0 per cent for the USA shown in the Dimson, Marsh and Staunton study.

4.56. BAA drew our attention to a survey published by Welch in 1999[4] of more than 100 leading financial economists, mainly in the USA, which suggested a consensus forecast of the long-term (ie 30 years) ERP of about 6 per cent. The forecast for shorter horizons of five to ten years was between 5.3 and 5.7 per cent based on arithmetic means. In a revision to the survey[5] in the following year a higher estimate of the long-term equity premium of 7 per cent was reported.

---

[1]Previous indices had overstated returns as they had been calculated for companies that were subsequently incorporated into a larger company index and had excluded companies that had not survived.

[2]E Dimson, P Marsh and P Staunton, 'Global evidence on the equity risk premium', unpublished 2002 paper.

[3]E F Fama and K R French, *The equity premium*, Journal of Finance, April 2002.

[4]I Welch, *Views of financial economist on the equity premium and other issues*, Anderson Graduate School of Management UCLA, May 1998.

[5]I Welch, *Views of financial economists on the equity risk premium and professional controversies*, Anderson Graduate School of Management UCLA, June 1999.

4.57. The future expected returns on equities can also be estimated from the dividend growth model (DGM) using an estimate for the future growth in dividends. On the basis of the April 2002 yield on the FT All Share index of 2.69 per cent and an assumption of future GDP growth of 2.25 per cent (taken as an approximation for the future growth in company dividends), the expected future return on equities is 5 to 5.3 per cent if GDP growth of 2.5 per cent is assumed. Taken with the current yields on index-linked gilts at the time of around 2.3 per cent, the implied expected ERP is 2.7 to 3.0 per cent.

4.58. We turn now to the second method of estimating the ERP mentioned in paragraph 4.50, the use of survey and other evidence of investors' current views. In 1997 a report on strategic asset management by Mercury Asset Management stated that many estimates of the expected annualized real return fell between 5 and 7 per cent, implying an ERP of 2 to 4 per cent on the basis of a then risk-free rate of around 3 per cent. In his final determination in 1999 the Director General of Water Services referred to a 1998 survey by Price Waterhouse which found a range for the ERP of 2.7 to 4.5 per cent; recent research published by equity analysts at a broad range of investment banks showing a range of 2 to 4 per cent; and a January 1999 survey by NERA which suggested an average premium of 3 to 4 per cent. In the draft proposals for the electricity transmission price control Ofgem referred to a 1998 report on electricity companies by Merrill Lynch which indicated that some fund managers had started to use estimates for the ERP as low as 2 to 3 per cent and to a report on cost of capital by SBC Warburg which used 3.5 per cent as an estimate of the ERP.

4.59. A report in 2000 by a group of actuaries[1] assumed future real returns on UK equities of 4.5 per cent, implying an ERP of only 2 per cent if taken with a risk-free rate of 2.5 per cent. Such figures are in line with the estimates for future returns used in valuing pension funds and disclosed by companies in their annual accounts. In the most recent accounts of BAA the actuaries valuing the pension fund adopted an expected nominal return on equities of 7 per cent, equivalent after adjusting for expected inflation to an expected real return of 4 to 4.5 per cent. BAA commented that actuarial valuations of pension funds would be likely to take a prudent view of future liabilities and to incorporate relatively low estimates of future returns.

4.60. Survey and other evidence may be subject to biases which are difficult to quantify and assess. Fund managers could have an incentive to quote lower figures to make their achievements look better. On the other hand, if they knew the use to be made of their evidence, they might have the incentive to bias their figures.

4.61. In the light of the submissions to us on the level of the ERP and the considerations above, we have used a range from 2.5 to 4.5 per cent for the ERP in Table 4.13. This is primarily based on ex ante data and the more recent analyses of ex post data. We note the importance of recognizing changes in views on the ERP as they develop, but at the same time we consider that it would be inappropriate to introduce undue volatility. For this reason, a degree of smoothing of changes over time seems appropriate. The range in Table 4.13 excludes the more extreme results, with the lower figure based on the recent evidence from Dimson, Marsh and Staunton and at the upper figure derived from evidence of historical returns in the UK market over the long term. The mid-point of the range at 3.5 per cent is below the 4 per cent used by the CC for the ERP in its reports on the water companies, and below the mid-point (4.25 per cent) of the range of 3.5 to 5.0 per cent used in its earlier MMC reports on Cellnet and Vodafone. In its report on the water companies the CC noted that its best estimate of 4 per cent for the ERP was somewhat below the historical average but above current estimates of market expectations. Although the continuing downward trend reflects recent evidence, there remains considerable uncertainty over the appropriate level for the ERP and we return to the matter in paragraph 4.69.

Equity beta

4.62. As with the ERP, the beta of a company is not directly observable from market data. However, statistical estimates of equity betas are made on an ex post basis by regression analysis (total returns from holding a particular share or portfolio of shares are regressed against total returns from the market portfolio). The most recent equity beta (July to September 2002) for BAA published by the LBS risk measurement service was 0.71, down from 0.74 for the previous quarter. The LBS risk measurement

---

[1]P M Meredith, N P Horsfall, J M Harrison, K Kneller, J M Knight, and R F Murphy, *Pensions and low inflation,* The Staple Inn Actuarial Society, 2000.

service uses data over a period of 60 months. The most recent published beta for the only other UK airport company, TBI (see paragraph 4.11), was 0.94, but as noted, TBI has no regulated airports and is considerably smaller than BAA.

4.63. In its submission BAA proposed an equity beta of 0.86 to 0.96, before taking account of the impact in Q4 of T5. BAA pointed out that its current level for beta was below historical levels and that since 11 September 2001 there seemed to have been an increase in BAA's beta as investors better appreciated the company's exposure to passenger volume risk. In addition the changes proposed by the CAA to the S term and the introduction of a Q factor would represent an increased exposure to non-diversifiable risk. When account was taken of T5, BAA proposed higher equity betas—1.03 to 1.31 with continuation of an RCV-based price control and 1.37 to 1.99 under an LRIC-based system. In support of the higher equity betas, BAA pointed to increases in both the financial gearing and operational gearing of its regulated airports (see paragraph 4.38). Mainly as a result of T5, financial gearing was expected to rise in Q4 from between [✂] per cent, while operational gearing (measured by BAA as the ratio of capex to capex plus opex) would rise from 46 per cent in 2001/02 to a peak of [✂] per cent by 2005/06. The CAA used an equity beta for existing assets of 0.7 at Heathrow and one of 0.8 at Gatwick and Stansted. Under its PPC, the CAA proposed an equity beta of 1.3 for new assets at Heathrow such as T5, accompanied by an increase in gearing to 45 per cent.

4.64. In Table 4.13 we have used an equity beta of 0.8 to 1.0, significantly above the recent published levels, which we consider adequately recognizes any impact from recent events on BAA's business and the substantial CIP envisaged for Q4. We return in paragraph 4.70 to the overall impact of T5. In view of the integrated nature of BAA's activities and the centralized financing arrangements in place, we have not sought to disaggregate the beta between the individual London airports and the other businesses of BAA. As noted in paragraph 4.34 that the range for beta is consistent with the level adopted by the CAA with its distinction between new and existing assets.

Taxation adjustment

4.65. The financial modelling underlying the recommendations for the price control takes place in pre-tax terms, so it is necessary to convert post-tax estimates of the cost of capital to a pre-tax basis. The conversion can be made either using the standard rate of corporate taxation (currently 30 per cent) or by using estimates of the tax that will actually be paid by BAA. There are a number of reasons why actual tax payments can differ from the effect of applying the standard rate of tax within the CAPM. They include the effect of capital allowances, other timing differences, delay in the payment of tax and the receipt of relief for tax on interest at a nominal rather than a real rate. Any projections of BAA's future tax profile involve a considerable degree of uncertainty. BAA is making substantial investment in assets which will receive capital allowances and tend to lower the actual tax rate. The capital allowances applying to a substantial element of the new investment are at relatively low levels and the difference between actual and standard rates of tax is thought unlikely to be significant over the long term. We have therefore used the standard tax rate in Table 4.13 and we note that the use of the standard rate of taxation is likely to be, on balance, to the advantage of BAA. This treatment is consistent with that proposed by both the CAA and BAA.

Cost of debt

4.66. There are a number of ways that regulated companies can borrow, including the issue of index-linked bonds, conventional bonds convertible debt and borrowing from banks. The three designated airport companies do not usually borrow on their own account and are financed by a mixture of equity and intra-group debt, with most of the borrowing being undertaken by BAA. At 31 March 2002 the book net debt of the BAA group was £1.7 billion and its gearing (D/D+E) was 25.6 per cent (book values) and 21.9 per cent (using market values), as shown in Table 4.15.

TABLE 4.15 **BAA: group net borrowing at 31 March 2002**

	£ million	
	Book value	Market value
Secured		
Due after one year	30	30
Unsecured		
Due within one year	57	57
Bank loans due after one year	350	350
7.875% £200 million bonds due 2007	199	215
11.75% £300 million bonds due 2016	308	454
8.5% £250 million bonds due 2021	247	314
6.375% £200 million bonds due 2028	197	208
5.75% £900 million bonds due 2031	891	869
4.875% £314 million convertible bonds due 2004	311	332
	2,590	2,829
Offsetting cash and short-term investments		
Cash	−99	−99
Short-term investments	−840	−840
	1,651	1,890
Shareholders' funds	4,807	
Equity market capitalization (31 March 2002)		6,758
Gearing (D/D+E) (%):	25.6	21.9

Source: FT and BAA.

In addition, there were undrawn committed borrowing facilities at 31 March 2002 of £384 million. On 4 April 2002, BAA issued £424 million 2.94 per cent convertible bonds due 2008.

4.67. In order to estimate the cost of debt we need to make an assumption about the level of interest rates over the medium term. The premium for corporate borrowing compared with government bonds varies with the maturity of the debt, with spreads widening on longer maturities. At April 2002 the corporate spread for a typical company with an AA-- rating in the transportation sector ranged between 69 basis points (one year) up to 165 basis points (30 years). BAA told us that in mid-October 2002 the spread on its bond due in 2031 had increased to 1.3 per cent over the reference gilt and that the bonds had been issued at a 1.6 per cent premium. For the illustrative calculation in Table 4.13 we have assumed that the total debt would be spread over a range of maturities and have added a premium of between 0.9 and 1.2 per cent to the same risk-free rate as we have used for the calculation of the cost of equity. The resulting range for the cost of debt of 3.4 to 3.95 per cent compares with 3.95 to 4.65 per cent proposed by BAA and 3.9 per cent proposed by the CAA.

4.68. Although according to BA (see paragraph 4.39) the prices in the markets of BAA's debt recently represented a margin of 50 to 80 basis points over LIBOR, we have arrived at the cost of debt by using our estimate of the risk-free rate rather than LIBOR. The margin between LIBOR and the risk-free rate is variable, but an excess of around 40 basis points is normal and this has informed the range used by us of 80 to 120 basis points.

Movement in the equity risk premium

4.69. In paragraph 4.61 we indicated the basis of our choice of a range of 2.5 to 4.5 per cent for the level of the ERP. This range is below that used in the two previous regulatory reports of the MMC/CC, reflecting further analysis of historical data and modification of the expectations of investors in present market conditions. The exact extent to which the appropriate level for the ERP has been moving downwards in recent years is uncertain and, if market conditions altered, an increase might occur. In view of this uncertainty we would wish to be cautious over implementing in full the decline represented by our range of 2.5 to 4.5 per cent. We consider that a degree of smoothing of the downward trend in the ERP would be appropriate, an approach which would also help to prevent volatility in the short term. We consider that the most appropriate way of recognizing this factor is not by modifying our judgement of the range for the ERP, but by an increase of 0.25 per cent in the overall level of the WACC for BAA.

Impact of T5

4.70. Both BAA and the CAA recognized in their proposals for BAA's cost of capital the exceptional circumstances represented by the construction of T5, work on which is now under way. Because of changes in the specification, the project is likely to have a proportionately greater impact on BAA's financial position than did the proposals extant at the time of our 1996 review. In recognition of T5 the CAA proposed a WACC of 8.5 per cent for investment in new assets at Heathrow where output-based pricing was to apply, some 1.5 per cent above its proposal for existing investment at the airport. BAA's proposed mid-point for its WACC excluding T5 was 9.31 per cent. When account was taken of T5 the figure rose to 9.65 per cent with if the existing the existing RCV-based approach continued, and to 11.21 per cent if LRIC pricing as proposed by the CAA was applied.

4.71. In our view there are four special factors linked to T5 which could affect BAA's cost of capital of which account needs to be taken:

(a) Our proposals for the price control include a trigger mechanism under which the level of permitted airport charges will increase only when the specified construction landmarks have been met. Were delays in construction to occur, some of which might be outwith the control of BAA, the company would suffer a significant financial penalty. This represents a definite increase in the risks faced by BAA.

(b) In a competitive market companies will tend to delay capital projects and only embark on them at the latest possible moment, as the option to discontinue a project has a value to the company. It is arguable that, in keeping with its responsibilities as a regulated company, BAA is undertaking construction of T5 earlier than might otherwise have been the case and in doing so is giving up its option on timing; something for which it should be compensated.

(c) The increase in borrowing to fund the construction of T5 is expected to increase BAA's gearing from [✂] per cent to more than [✂] per cent by the end of Q4. The increase in gearing will have an effect both through an increase in the debt premium through the perceived greater risk of default, and an increase in the equity beta reflecting the greater risks to equity shareholders. In particular, any major adverse change in the financial circumstances of BAA could lead to the requirement for a rights issue by the company. At present the possibility of a rights issue is implicitly being regarded as a contingency against either another major event such as 11 September or the need to raise funds should the SERAS study lead to construction of one or more new runways at BAA's London airports. A rights issue would represent a definite cost to the BAA, including the possible cost of an adverse change in market sentiment, and the fact that T5 increases BAA's exposure to one in Q4 needs to be recognized.

(d) In the course of the construction of T5 the scope for BAA to outperform the price control set for Q4 is limited, but there is real scope for the expectations incorporated in the price control not to be met and for BAA thereby to be financially disadvantaged.

4.72. Although these factors arise because BAA is undertaking the T5 project, there are also potential implications for Gatwick and Stansted. For instance, if demand for air travel were to decline severely in response to an event similar to 11 September, the airport most likely to be adversely affected is Gatwick, with traffic moving from there to fill any capacity becoming available at Heathrow. Similarly, if financial problems occurred on the construction of T5, these would apply more generally to BAA and affect the rates at which the group could raise capital for investment at other airports. In our view the factors in paragraph 4.71 can best be recognized by way of a further T5-related uplift to the WACC of some 0.25 per cent. Addition of this to the allowance of 0.25 per cent for smoothing of the movement in the ERP would increase BAA's WAC from the mid-point of 7.21 per cent shown in Table 4.13 to some 7.75 per cent. We consider that a WACC of 7.75 per cent should be sufficient to enable BAA to raise the finance needed for T5, to compensate the company for the loss of its real option on the T5 project and to recognize the increased risk to the company as a whole.

Lending covenants and financial ratios

4.73. Details of BAA's existing debt are given in paragraph 4.66. All BAA's loan, bond and guarantee documentation contains legally binding covenants on the group for the duration of the borrowing intended to ensure the continued soundness of the lender's asset. The covenants fall into three categories:

(a) *Provision of information:* Generally this takes the form of forwarding audited accounts and interim statements to the banks, institutional lenders and bond trustees involved within a set time period—typically 150 days after the financial year end.

(b) *Financial covenant:* These consist of negative pledges on security, maximum levels of gearing and minimum levels of interest cover. A negative pledge is an undertaking not to grant security over a borrower's assets to third parties; its purpose being to ensure that no other creditor of the company is put in a better position than the lender. Such a clause will prohibit the creation or continuation of any encumbrance over any asset of the company, subject to a de minimis level or a specific carve out clause. BAA told us that most of its debt documents contained covenants on gearing expressed as a percentage of consolidated net worth, usually 90 per cent. At 30 June 2002 the gearing under this definition was 45 per cent. Only the sterling long bonds due 2016, 2021 and 2028 contained an interest cover covenant; in this case that profit before interest and tax should would exceed interest payable by at least two times over a rolling three years. BAA's position was that this was a measure of lender protection that should not be ceded lightly and should only be extended to investors with the longest term exposure. BAA said that interest cover on the basis laid down was 3.8 times in the year to 31 March 2002 and 3.1 and 4.6 in the two previous years.

(c) *Other covenants:* Other covenants include restrictions on the sale of assets and revenue streams, clauses preventing a material change in the scope of the business of BAA, required levels of credit rating, pari passu clauses (which ensure that all unsecured and unsubordinated creditors have equal ranking), obligations to keep assets of the company insured and (in the case of the Heathrow Express project) undertakings on compliance with environmental legislation and EC tendering procedures.

Breach of a covenant typically gives the lender the right to demand repayment and/or to cancel its obligation to make further advances. A material adverse change in the financial condition of the group is generally deemed an event of default. BAA said that material adverse change clauses were subjective, and that its policy was not to include such clauses in bond documentation.

5 Airport charges and their regulation

Introduction

5.1. This chapter discusses regulation of airport charges; the level and structure of airport charges at BAA's London airports and comparisons with other UK and foreign airport charges. This chapter is limited to airport charges, as defined in the Airports Act: that is charges for landing, parking or taking-off of aircraft and charges levied on airlines in connection with passengers' arrival at or departure from the airport. Charges for other activities carried on by or at BAA's London airports are considered in Chapter 8.

Approach to regulation

5.2. There are a number of different approaches to regulating a continuing monopoly, which were set out in the 1996 MMC report. There was no support in the evidence submitted to us for moving away from an RPI–X formula as the main control on BAA's prices.

5.3. At the two previous reviews, the RPI–X formula was set broadly at a level that enabled the regulated business as a whole (comprising HAL, GAL and STAL) to earn the cost of capital[1] on the value of its capital. To this end, the MMC and the CAA considered projections of capital and operating expenditure for the whole business and of revenue from sources other than airport charges. The proposed level of airport charges was determined by the difference between total revenue required for the business to earn the cost of capital and projected revenue from sources other than airport charges.

5.4. This overall approach is similar to that taken to the regulation of water companies and of electricity and gas transmission and distribution businesses, in that all the revenue and costs of the regulated business are taken into account. However, the percentage of BAA's revenue accounted for by airport charges is much lower than the percentage of the other regulated businesses' revenue accounted for by their regulated charges and the boundary between the regulated business and the remainder of BAA has been less closely defined than in some other cases, where the regulated business is strictly 'ring-fenced'. In airports and also the other regulated businesses the RPI–X formulae, and hence the overall level of prices, have been reviewed every five years. Regulators and the CC have, however, maintained consistency between reviews in their approach to the capital value of the regulated businesses.

5.5. As a result of prices being reviewed every five years, cost savings and/or increases in unregulated revenue (compared with the previous projections) that have been achieved by the regulated business over the previous five years are retained by the company but the future effects of such savings are passed on to customers. Unexpected cost changes will also be passed on at the next review. Five-year reviews are designed to provide incentives to companies to control costs but assurance to customers that benefits will be passed on within five years. However, incentives to achieve cost savings may weaken towards the end of each five-year period, since the companies only keep the savings for a short period.

CAA proposals

5.6. The CAA proposed a number of important changes to this approach. The CAA suggested that:

(a) Costs and revenue of each airport should be considered separately, so that there would be three regulated businesses (Heathrow, Gatwick and Stansted) rather than one and any shortfall against the cost of capital at Stansted would no longer be added to required revenue at the other two airports.

(b) Costs and revenue at each airport should be divided into two tills, aeronautical and non-aeronautical, with the RPI–X formula set on the basis of the aeronautical till only (the 'dual-till' approach—see Chapter 8).

(c) T5, and future major capacity-enhancing projects at Heathrow and Gatwick, should be remunerated directly on the basis of their incremental cost. To give effect to this, the CAA proposed to make a 20-year commitment, which it described as a PPC to: the base formula at Heathrow and Gatwick; to terms remunerating the outputs of T5 (initially completion of the ART and new stands,

---

[1] In 1991, the MMC referred to a reasonable rate of return rather than the cost of capital.

subsequently, after T5 opened, excess of passenger numbers over 60 million up to a ceiling of 90 million); and to a term remunerating additional peak runway movements at Heathrow. The CAA's proposed PPC is set out in Appendix 5.1.

(d) At Heathrow and Gatwick, a service quality term (Q term) should be added to the formula: this would reduce the airport's revenue if quality fell below specified levels (see Chapter 6) and increase it if quality was above these levels.

(e) At Heathrow and Gatwick, the price cap should be regarded as a 'default price cap' covering the default standard of service and a higher non-binding cap considered for any voluntarily entered-into contracts that provided a higher standard of service for facilities covered by airport charges (during the course of the inquiry the CAA revised its views on how a default price cap would work and no longer saw a need for a separate non-binding cap).

The CAA's proposals, and the reasoning behind them, are set out in more detail in Chapter 11 and in its submission, which is available on the CAA web site.

The price cap formulae during the third quinquennium

5.7. During Q3, the main elements of the airport charging formula for the three London airports have been as follows:[1]

(a) Airport charges per passenger should not increase by more than RPI–3 at Heathrow and Gatwick combined for each of the five years, with a formula of RPI+1 for Stansted.

(b) Within the overall formula for Heathrow and Gatwick the differential between charges at the two airports should increase by at least 1 per cent in each year.

(c) The airports should continue to be allowed to recover 95 per cent of additional security costs in the year after they were first incurred (referred to as the S factor).

(d) The maximum level of airport charges for Heathrow and Gatwick combined and for Stansted should increase by 70p per passenger partly in the year when the concession on intra-EC sales of duty-free and tax-free goods was withdrawn and partly in the following year (referred to as the D factor).

(e) The formulae also contain a correction factor should the actual yield differ from that expected when charges are set.

The formulae were subsequently extended for one year to enable this inquiry to take into account the T5 decision.[2] The following paragraphs consider the main elements of the above.

Type of formula

5.8. Regulation by reference to airport charges per passenger—*(a)* above—is sometimes referred to as a revenue yield approach. An alternative approach is that of the tariff basket, based on the weighted average change in each element of the charging formula (ie each landing, passenger and parking charge) where the weights are volumes or revenue for the most recent full year for which data is available at the time tariffs are set. A form of tariff basket is used in the formulae for BT and for the water companies and an illustration of the difference between the revenue yield and tariff basket was shown in Appendix 5.2 of the 1996 MMC report. The CAA (which rejected the MMC's recommendation of a tariff basket in the first Manchester Airport report) initially proposed to adopt a tariff basket approach for Heathrow and Gatwick in Q4: all but one of the airlines regarded it as too complex and the CAA subsequently did not pursue the tariff basket. The tariff basket approach is more comprehensive since it applies to all elements of output, not just total number of passengers, and may therefore be theoretically preferable. Use of the tariff basket may also

---

[1] CAP 664, Economic Regulation of BAA London Airports 1998–2002.
[2] The extension of the conditions was notified in a letter from the CAA to BAA on 18 May 1999.

remove undesirable incentive effects of the revenue yield formula,[1] but there is no evidence that these have been a problem in practice.

5.9. As apparent in *(b)* above, there is some variation in the formulae applied to the three airports. However, as noted in paragraph 5.3, in assessing the appropriate level of airport charges, regard was had to generating a reasonable rate of return across the three London area airports as a whole, rather than at each airport separately—this is sometimes described as a system approach as opposed to the individual airport approach recommended at this review by the CAA.

Adjustments for additional costs

5.10. As regards *(c)* above, BAA is currently permitted to pass on 95 per cent of additional security costs imposed by the DfT with a one-year delay. In Q1, BAA was allowed to pass on 75 per cent of security costs with a two-year delay (the two-year delay avoided the need for corrections due to out-turn figures for the previous year not being available when charges are set). The 1991 MMC report recommended that 85 per cent of security costs be passed on in Q2, but the CAA decided on 95 per cent with a one-year delay. At this review, the CAA proposed that no pass through of security costs should be included in the formula.

5.11. The formulae in Q3 also contained an allowance—*(d)* above—for increase in charges when the concession on intra-EC sales of duty- and tax-free goods was withdrawn—the D factor. The concession having been withdrawn in 1999, and the maximum level of charges increased, the D factor is now in effect subsumed in the current level of charges.

Other factors affecting the formulae

5.12. The formulae also contain a correction factor—*(e)* above—one reason for which is that, in contrast to the tariff basket approach, which can be set at the start of a year, the actual revenue per passenger is only known at the end of a year and may differ from that expected when charges are set.

5.13. The increase in airport charge revenue per passenger may fall short of the average increase in actual airport charges if, for example, the number of passengers per aircraft increases (because landing charges revenue per passenger is lower) or if patterns in aircraft parking change. This is referred to as 'dilution'. If the opposite occurs, and the increase in airport charge revenue per passenger is greater than the average increase in charges, it is referred to as 'concentration'. The exact yield, however, will not be known until after the end of the charging year, when charges have already been set for the next year. Hence, a correction factor is applied two years after any such under-recovery or over-recovery with a rate of interest applied to compensate for the time lag involved.

5.14. In the CAA's decision, it also said that there should be a mid-term review in the event that T5 did not go ahead or, for reasons connected to planning permission, proceeded on a significantly different scale (paragraph 187(c), CAP 664, summarizing the CAA's decision). In Appendix 1 of the decision it was stated that BAA would cooperate in a mid-term review in the circumstances of planning permission being refused for T5, or granted subject to conditions which would significantly reduce the scale of T5, or BAA voluntarily reducing significantly the scale of T5 to secure planning permission which was subsequently granted, or if it was granted subject to conditions which rendered BAA unwilling to proceed with the project. As discussed elsewhere in this report (see paragraph 14.126), although there was an unexpectedly lengthy delay before planning permission was given for T5, and construction failed to commence in the original five-year period of Q3, there was no interim review.

---

[1]The revenue yield approach may give the regulated company the incentive to price some services (those where price is more responsive to demand) below marginal cost (Appendix 5.1 of the 1996 MMC report showed this for a hypothetical example of two airports, one congested and one uncongested). However, the incentive to under-price Stansted would only occur if there was a single revenue yield formula covering all three airports and can be removed by setting a separate price cap for Stansted, as was done in 1996. In relation to the existing revenue yield formulae, there is no evidence that they have encouraged excessively low off-peak pricing—rather, concern has been expressed that there is insufficient differentiation between peak and off-peak prices. Tariff basket formulae also have some incentive drawbacks, in particular (since the tariff basket weights are based on historical data), there is an incentive to increase the prices of services where volume is growing more rapidly: this would tend to give BAA the incentive to increase passenger charges and reduce landing charges.

Charges in Q3

5.15. Table 5.1 shows the trend in airport charges revenue per passenger at BAA's London airports. For the third quinquennium, revenue yield at HAL has increased by 18 per cent, and GAL has seen an increase of 15 per cent. Stansted has seen the greatest rise by 24 per cent. These figures are all in nominal prices.

TABLE 5.1 **Airport charges revenue at BAA's London airports**

£ per passenger, out-turn prices

	1996/97	1997/98	1998/99	1999/00	2000/01	2001/02
HAL	4.76	4.82	4.89	4.89	5.23	5.62
GAL	3.70	3.77	3.89	3.86	4.06	4.26
STAL	3.64	3.55	3.75	3.91	4.36	4.39

Source: BAA.

5.16. A breakdown of the components of the charging conditions and comparison with the allowed level of charges is shown in Table 5.2. Revenue yield has increased principally because of the D factor (compensation for loss of revenue from duty-free sales).

TABLE 5.2 **Application of price formulae to derive maximum allowable yields, Q3 (1997/98 to 2001/02) and 2002/03**

£

	1996/97	1997/98	1998/99	1999/2000	2000/01	2001/02	20002/03
Heathrow and Gatwick combined maximum yields							
Base yield	N/A	4.443	4.403	4.439	4.713	5.065	5.079
Estimate of +S (security factor)		0.000	0.010	0.007	0.004	0.000	0.043
+S correction		0.000	0.000	−0.004	0.000	−0.001	0.000
Total		4.443	4.413	4.442	4.717	5.064	5.122
Application of RPI−3		−0.040	0.026	0.009	−0.090	0.015	−0.067
RPI=		*2.1*	*3.6*	*3.2*	*1.1*	*3.3*	*1.7*
R (special one-off correction factor)		0.000	0.056	0.000	0.000	0.000	0.000
D (duty-free factor)		0.000	0.000	0.262	0.438	0.000	0.000
K (standard correction factor)		0.000	0.000	−0.099	−0.075	0.074	0.165
Maximum yields allowable	4.490	4.403	4.495	4.614	4.990	5.153	5.220
Actual yield		4.485	4.559	4.549	4.841	5.145	5.140*
Over/under-recovery		0.082	0.064	−0.065	−0.149	−0.008	−0.08
Over/under-recovery (£m)		7.0	5.8	−6.0	−14.4	−0.7	−7.3
Stansted maximum allowable yields							
Base yield	N/A	3.494	3.602	3.768	4.188	4.714	4.917
Estimate of +S (security factor)		0.000	0.000	0.000	0.000	0.000	0.000
+S correction		0.000	0.000	0.000	0.000	0.000	0.000
Total		3.494	3.602	3.768	4.188	4.714	4.917
Application of RPI+1		0.108	0.166	0.158	0.088	0.203	0.133
RPI=		*2.1*	*3.6*	*3.2*	*1.1*	*3.3*	*1.7*
D (duty-free factor)		0.000	0.000	0.262	0.438	0.000	0.000
K (standard correction factor)		0.000	0.000	0.055	0.019	0.373	0.415
Maximum yields allowable		3.602	3.768	4.243	4.733	5.290	5.465
Actual yield		3.554	3.750	3.910	4.359	4.394	4.590*
Over/under-recovery		−0.048	−0.018	−0.333	−0.374	−0.896	−0.875
Over/under-recovery (£m)		−0.3	−0.1	−3.3	−4.6	−12.6	−13.6

Source: BAA.

*Estimate.
Note: N/A = Not available.

5.17. BAA told us that it voluntarily set airport charges 3 per cent below the expected allowable level for Heathrow and Gatwick over the last three years in recognition of the lower capex. However, we noted that the expected under-recovery in 2001/02 was offset by unexpected concentration (see paragraph 5.13) in that year with the result that out-turn revenue per passenger was only very slightly below the maximum allowable (see Table 5.2). We were told that this occurred in 2001/02 as a result of a reduction in passengers per ATM following the events of 11 September. Moreover, any under-recovery in 2002/03 will arise only after applying the correction factor for the deliberate under-recovery in 2000/01, (indeed Table 5.2 shows an expected under-recovery in 2002/03 of only about half of the correction factor in that year).[1] Effectively, therefore, there has been under-recovery in only one of the three years (2000/01).

5.18. The price cap for Stansted was not expected by the MMC and the CAA in 1996 to be binding and this has proved to be the case: BAA under-recovered against the maximum allowable yield at Stansted in every year (see Table 5.2). The cumulative effect of these under-recoveries is that the maximum allowable yield at Stansted has increased to above the level at Heathrow and Gatwick.

5.19. As noted in paragraph 5.13, the actual percentage change in tariffs may differ from the change in revenue yield due to dilution or concentration. Table 5.3 shows BAA's estimate of dilution or concentration over the last five years.

TABLE 5.3 **Dilution/concentration at south-east airports, Q3**

Year	Heathrow	Gatwick	Stansted
1997/98	−0.2	−1.8	5.7
1998/99	0.1	−2.4	−1.0
1999/00	0.3	−0.1	−2.2
2000/01	0.8	1.8	−2.2
2001/02	−3.5	−2.1	1.2

Source: BAA.

Note: Negative figures represent concentration.

Discounts

5.20. BAA told us that, at Stansted, the airport director had discretion to abate or waive charges to encourage traffic development. This discretion is used at Stansted in relation to a small number of new routes, to aircraft parking and to general aviation. The airport's quoted yields are net of these discounts which in 2001/02 amounted to £2 million. We were told there were no similar discounts at Heathrow and Gatwick. At Manchester, the price cap is required by the formula to be calculated as if users pay published charges:[2] in contrast, at the BAA airports discounts to one user can in principle be offset by a premium to the rest. In practice, this has not been a problem since unpublished discounts are not given at Heathrow and Gatwick and the Stansted cap has not been binding. Nevertheless, the CAA suggested that the Manchester approach be used in future for the BAA airports as well.

5.21. Other forms of incentive are also offered to assist carriers to develop the majority of new routes at the airport. These are treated as marketing expenditure and in 2001 amounted to approximately £15.5 million. This is accounted for as a cost rather than a revenue offset and hence does not reduce revenue yield.

Non-passenger flights

5.22. The revenue per passenger approach implies that extra revenue from non-passenger flights be offset by reduced revenue from passenger flights. In March 2000, Manchester was allowed by the CAA to remove revenues from non-passenger flights from the cap (subject to a condition that charges should be no

---

[1]Similarly, the over-recovery for 1997/98 and 1998/99 and under-recovery in 1999/2000 were absorbed into maximum allowable yields for later years (see Table 5.2).
[2]The calculation takes into account any published discounts.

more than passenger flights).[1] The CAA suggested that this be extended to BAA. The effect would be to reduce yield by less than 1 per cent at Heathrow/Gatwick but 7 per cent at Stansted.

Structure of charges

5.23. Airport charges are currently structured into:

(a) Landing charges, with a distinction (except for large aircraft at Stansted) between off-peak and peak charges. Landing charges are generally flat rate, but with a small degree of differentiation between weight bands, mainly in off-peak periods. There is also some differentiation according to noise classification of aircraft.

(b) Charges on terminal departing passengers, those for international passengers being above those for domestic passengers.

(c) Aircraft parking charges, based on maximum authorized weight of the aircraft. At Heathrow and Gatwick, a higher rate is applied in peak periods. At Heathrow and Gatwick parking charges accrue immediately after landing subject to a taxi time allowance of eight minutes. At Stansted, parking charges accrue after five minutes.

Air traffic services at the three airports are provided by NATS and charged for separately, being statutorily excluded from the regulatory formula. At Manchester, by contrast, the cost of air traffic services are currently recovered through landing charges which are included in the formula. At the Secretary of State's request, the CAA is currently reviewing the regulatory treatment of air traffic services (it issued a consultation paper in August 2002).

5.24. BAA currently pays a rebate of £3 per departing passengers to airlines which have to coach their passengers to remote stands. From 2001/02, this has been applied separately at the rate of £1.50 per arriving or departing passenger on remote stands. The scale of such rebates was almost £5 million at Heathrow and almost £6 million at Gatwick in 2001/02. Payments of the rebate are offset against airport charges—hence other charges can be increased to compensate, and it has a neutral effect on BAA's revenue and profits. We noted in our previous report that BAA argued that this was appropriate as the use of remote stands was a normal feature of airport operations, and the rebate was a means of distributing charges among airlines according to the level of benefit they receive (the lower the level of pier service, the lower the net charges paid).

5.25. The breakdown of published charges between landing fees, passenger charges and parking charges is shown in Table 5.4 for representative aircraft, and for charges as a whole in Table 5.5.

---

[1] This amendment to the Manchester condition (CAP 679) was made in CAA Official Record Series 6 Part 2, No 123.

TABLE 5.4 **Comparison of airport charges for typical aircraft, 2002/03**

| | Boeing 747-400 | | Boeing 757-200 | | Boeing 737-400 | | DC 9-30 | |
	Peak	Off-peak	Peak	Off-peak	Peak	Off-peak	Peak	Off-peak
Heathrow charges (£)								
Landing fee	465.0	335.0	418.5	301.5	418.5	301.5	930.0	390.0
Parking charge	918.7	306.2	110.7	36.9	86.5	28.8	77.8	25.9
Total landing and parking charge	1,383.7	641.2	529.2	338.4	505.0	330.3	1,007.8	415.9
Charge per departing passenger	7.7	7.7	7.7	7.7	7.7	7.7	7.7	7.7
Total passenger charges paid	2,262.6	2,262.6	1,127.5	1,127.5	851.4	851.4	621.3	621.3
Total paid per visit	3,646.4	2,903.9	1,656.7	1,465.9	1,356.4	1,181.7	1,629.0	1,037.2
Total paid per passenger	6.2	4.9	5.6	5.0	6.1	5.3	10.1	6.4
Gatwick charges (£)								
Landing fee	345.0	115.0	310.5	103.5	310.5	103.5	690.0	170.0
Parking charge	751.5	250.5	93.4	31.1	73.9	24.6	66.9	22.3
Total landing and parking charge	1,096.5	365.5	403.9	134.6	384.4	128.1	756.9	252.3
Charge per departing passenger	6.5	6.5	6.5	6.5	6.5	65	65	6.5
Total passenger charges paid	1,908.6	1,908.6	951.1	951.1	718.2	718.2	524.1	524.1
Total paid per visit	3,005.1	2,274.1	1,254.9	1,085.7	1,102.6	846.3	1,281.0	716.4
Total paid per passenger	5.1	3.8	4.6	3.7	5.0	3.8	7.9	4.4
Stansted charges (£)								
Landing fee	335.0	335.0	175.5	85.5	175.5	85.5	240.0	170.0
Parking charge	641.4	641.4	62.5	62.5	43.8	43.8	37.0	37.0
Total landing and parking charge	976.0	976.4	238.0	148.0	219.3	129.3	277.0	207.0
Charge per departing passenger	6.4	6.4	6.4	6.4	6.4	6.4	6.4	6.4
Total passenger charges paid	1,888.0	1,888.0	940.8	940.8	710.4	710.4	518.4	518.4
Total paid per visit	2,864.4	2,864.4	1,178.8	1,088.8	929.7	839.7	795.4	725.4
Total paid per passenger	4.8	4.8	4.0	3.7	4.2	3.8	4.9	4.5
Assumptions								
Noise category	Chapter 3		Chapter 3 (-)		Chapter 3 (-)		Chapter 2*	
Maximum authorized weight in tonnes	395	395	104	104	68	68	55	55
Seat capacity	393	393	196	196	148	148	108	108
Load factor	0.75	0.75	0.75	0.75	0.75	0.75	0.75	0.75
Passengers carried	295	295	147	147	111	111	81	81
Parking time (hours)	3	3	1	1	1	1	1	1
Flight	International		International		International		International	

Source: CC analysis of data provided by BAA.

---

*For comparative purposes only: Chapter 2 aircraft are not now permitted.

TABLE 5.5 **Percentage of airport charges revenue accounted for by different charges, 2001/02**

	Heathrow	Gatwick	Stansted
Landing fees	22.7	15.6	17.4
Parking charges	13.9	14.9	18.1
Passenger charges	63.4	69.5	64.5
Total	100.0	100.0	100.0

Source: BAA.

5.26. Following the results in 1992 of the arbitration between the US and UK Governments on user charges at Heathrow, and a subsequent Exchange of Notes between the US and UK Governments, BAA was required to phase out the differential between peak and off-peak international passenger charges at Heathrow by 1 April 1998. The Exchange of Notes also contained commitments by the UK Government regarding the structure of Heathrow tariffs including:

(a) no reintroduction of a peak international passenger charge before 1 April 2003 or, if later, the opening of T5;

(b) no change in the level of parking charges relative to the charges generally before 2003; and

(c) no weight-related peak landing charges before 2003.

5.27. The impact of these commitments was to increase charges paid for off-peak operations: off-peak average charges per passenger in Table 5.4 have risen in comparison with the equivalent table in our previous report.

Comparison of airport charges at BAA London airports with charges at other airports

5.28. Table 5.6 shows the level of traffic and revenue from airport charges at some UK airports. The comparison in Table 5.6 reflects prices actually paid (after discounts) but does not reflect marketing support to airlines, since this is treated as a cost rather than a deduction from revenue (see paragraph 5.20). The comparison does not reflect charges other than airport charges and is affected by the nature of traffic, in particular the importance of cargo flights and general aviation and also the average size of passenger flights (average revenue per passenger tends to be higher the smaller the aircraft handled as aircraft landing charges have to be spread over fewer passengers).

TABLE 5.6 **Traffic and revenue from airport charges at larger UK airports 2000/01**

	Terminal passengers '000	Cargo and mail '000 tonnes	Aircraft movement		Revenue from airport charges*	
			ATMs '000	Other '000	Total £m	Per passenger £
BAA London airports						
Heathrow	64,328	1,385	459.5	6.7	336.5	5.23
Gatwick	32,134	336	256.9	3.0	130.4	4.06
Stansted	12,378	187	147.5	19.2	53.9	4.36
Other BAA airports						
Glasgow	6,978	10	92.1	12.2	43.4	6.22
Edinburgh	5,618	48	89.9	11.1	34.0	6.05
Aberdeen	2,423	6	82.4	17.1	16.1	6.64
Other						
Manchester	18,630	123	194.2	N/A	129.2	6.93
Birmingham	7,619	12	111.1	15.6	59.3	7.79
Luton	6,331	35	61.1	24.4	23.3	3.68
Newcastle	3,287	4	43.1	39.1	27.2	8.29
Belfast International	3,156	47	56.4	40.3	23.6	7.49
East Midlands	2,229	194	47.2	29.5	21.8	9.79
Bristol	2,172	N/A	38.5	24.1	17.5	8.04

Source: CRI 2000/2001.

---

*Charges for airport air traffic services are included in airport charges at non-BAA airports. Luton—1999/2000 data amended for prior year adjustments.
Note: N/A = Not available.

5.29. Table 5.7 shows a comparison of airport charges at 50 international airports. This is based on total airport charges for 2002 and 2001 and averages eight aircraft types, which vary in weight and capacity for international routes. Such comparisons are affected by the following factors:

(a) only aeronautical charges, including ATC charges, are considered;

(b) it excludes government taxes, although for the USA a proportion of Federal funding has been included;

(c) the chosen eight aircraft may not represent the traffic at all airports;

(d) the comparison is based on published prices, so does not consider any discounts available or marketing support paid to airlines; and

(e) it should also be noted that the comparison is affected by fluctuations in exchange rates.

TABLE 5.7 **Airport charges index (ranking of 50 airports worldwide)**

	Airport	2002	2001
1.	Osaka	100	100
2.	Tokyo	86	85
3.	New Jersey-EWR	84	65
4.	New York-JFK	78	58
5.	Athens	66	68
6.	Moscow	66	64
7.	Sao Paulo	56	76
8.	Vienna	50	48
9.	Washington	50	35
10.	Budapest	47	45
11.	Chicago	47	38
12.	Paris-CDG	46	40
13.	Dallas/Fort Worth	45	20
14.	Amsterdam	45	39
15.	Frankfurt	45	40
16.	Berlin	42	36
17.	Vancouver	42	37
18.	Sydney	41	34
19.	Zurich	41	37
20.	Miami	41	24
21.	Lisbon	40	38
22.	Munich	40	37
23.	Brussels	40	31
24.	Seoul	39	34
25.	San Francisco	38	29
26.	Toronto	38	31
27.	Jeddah	37	36
28.	Stockholm	37	30
29.	Dusseldorf	36	34
30.	Milan-MXP	36	26
31.	Mexico City	34	48
32.	Oslo	34	29
33.	Copenhagen	34	31
34.	Bangkok	34	31
35.	Heathrow	33	32
36.	Orlando	32	20
37.	Taipei	31	30
38.	Singapore	31	25
39.	Helsinki	30	28
40.	Hong Kong	30	26
41.	Honolulu	28	18
42.	Madrid	28	25
43.	Bombay	28	28
44.	Rome	27	23
45.	Johannesburg	25	23
46.	Kuala Lumpur	25	22
47.	Dublin	24	26
48.	Los Angeles	23	12
49.	Gatwick	23	23
50.	Dubai	7	6

Source: TRL.

Note: Based on an average of peak and off-peak charges for eight aircraft types (international arrivals and departures). ATC charges are included for all airports.

6 Quality of service

Contents

Introduction

6.1. In this chapter we consider the CAA's proposals for a Q term in the price cap formula and the quality of service currently provided by BAA both to airlines and to passengers. We examine BAA's approach to quality management, its performance, as shown by BAA's own performance indicators, the SLAs at the BAA London airports, and the views of BAA's customers. The chapter does not cover the quality of service provided by BAA as a landlord, which is considered in Chapter 8.

6.2. We received critical representations about the quality of service provided to airlines (see Chapter 12). In particular, the Heathrow AOC told us that Heathrow suffered from being heavily congested owing to a lack of investment. This had resulted in inadequate service quality, despite some improvements in areas covered by SLAs. Some airlines were concerned about the absence both of defined specifications for the service being provided and of any relationship between prices and performance standards. They felt that, without these, BAA had an incentive to improve its profits by increasing throughput at the expense of lower standards. These airlines felt that the CAA's Q-term proposals would not sufficiently reduce this incentive. BA accordingly proposed an alternative system of quality incentives, which we describe in paragraph 6.38.

6.3. BAA told us that its mission was to become the most successful airport group in the world. This meant always focusing on customers' needs and safety; achieving continuous improvements in the profitability, costs and quality of processes and services; enabling staff to give their best; and growing with the support and trust of neighbours. BAA added that its success depended on satisfying airlines, passengers and other customers. To achieve its mission it would ensure that the services it provided were excellent and good value for money. It therefore worked with suppliers and business partners to measure and improve processes and services and create value added for all concerned. Examples of measurement systems included the monitoring of performance against SLAs (see paragraph 6.47) and the QSM surveys (see paragraph 6.138).

6.4. BAA told us that it aimed to approach customer service by leading the world in market research; making continuous efforts to maintain a culture of customer service; ensuring that staff delivered a high quality of customer service; investing in capacity, quality and new products; having a high degree of transparency in products and prices; building partnerships with suppliers and good relationships with major airlines; and making a strong commitment to safety, security and sustainable environmental performance.

6.5. BAA added that customer service was a key aspect of its objectives, goals, strategies and measures (see Chapter 7). Customer service would be developed further through the ongoing core process review (CPR), which aimed to maximize the throughput of BAA's airports whilst continuing to improve service quality and maintain profitability.

Proposed quality of service incentive schemes

The CAA's Q-term proposals

6.6. The CAA recommended to us that service quality should be directly reflected in charges through a quality term (the Q term) in the charges formula at Heathrow and Gatwick. It did not recommend this approach at Stansted, as it did not expect the airport to price up to the cap it had proposed with the result that any Q term would be ineffective. The CAA also believed that, as the operating environment there was less capacity constrained, there were fewer pressures on quality at Stansted.

6.7. The CAA recommended that a quality term in the price cap at Heathrow and Gatwick should include three distinct elements:

(a) QA: a component based on objective measures which have a direct bearing on service performance for airlines;

(b) QP: a component based on passenger perceptions of quality in other areas which have a significant influence on service quality; and *(c)* QD: an airfield congestion component based on aspects of service for which the airport has responsibility, such as queuing arising from the airport declaring capacity close to the physical capability of the runways, taxiways and ATC services.

6.8. Mathematically, the CAA's proposed price cap would take the following simplified form:

Maximum charge = Basic formula – QA – QP – QD.

We discuss the CAA's proposals in more depth in Appendix 6.1.

6.9. The CAA told us that choosing the scale of the potential impact of the quality term was a matter of judgement. It proposed that the maximum effect should be 3 per cent of annual revenue from charges. It recommended that, of this 3 per cent, QA should amount to a maximum of 1.5 per cent, QP 0.5 per cent and QD 1 per cent. Although the CAA considered that the 1 per cent limit on QD was far from commensurate with impact of delays on users, it had proposed this figure because of the untried nature of the measurement systems. It felt that the division of the remaining 2 per cent between QA and QP reflected the greater relative importance of airline operational factors compared with passenger perceptions.

6.10. The CAA proposed a penalty-only approach to the QA component. It told us that this recognized the strongly-held view of airlines that airports should not be rewarded for outperformance. The CAA also considered that this approach would indicate the level of service to be provided in return for airport charges and would thus provide a contractual baseline for negotiating different levels of service. The QA component is discussed further in paragraph 6.12.

6.11. With respect to QP and QD, the CAA proposed a scheme that allowed bonuses for outperformance as well as penalties (which is referred to as being 'symmetrical'). The QP and QD components are discussed further in paragraphs 6.16 and 6.20 respectively.

QA

6.12. The detailed calculation of the QA component of the CAA's Q term is set out in Appendix 6.1. Broadly, the approach starts by allocating potential penalty points to a range of elements of the service provided to airlines. The performance on these service elements would be assessed on the basis of performance relative to par values, mainly set at or near the current SLA parameters. They would be stand serviceability, jetty serviceability, the percentage of passengers receiving pier service, FEGP serviceability, people mover serviceability, transit system serviceability, the length of security queues and arrivals reclaim serviceability.

6.13. Either 1 or 0.5 penalty points, depending on the element, would be incurred each time BAA failed to meet a standard in any month. The CAA told us that the points attached to each element broadly reflected the views of airlines. It had, however, increased the weighting for people movers in response to comments by BAA.

6.14. At Heathrow, a total of 66 points[1] would be at risk over the year, that is each point would be equivalent to about 0.023 per cent of airport charge revenue. The total number of points incurred at each airport over the year across all the QA service elements would determine the associated adjustment to airport charges in the next year.

6.15. Weightings could be set in many ways. The CAA suggested two approaches: either that the maximum penalty should be paid only if the theoretical maximum number of points is incurred or that the maximum penalty should be paid if half the maximum number of points is incurred. The CAA favoured the second alternative. Appendix 6.1 sets out an example of how penalty points would be calculated.

---

[1] At Gatwick, there would be 72 points after allowing further points for the transit systems.

QP

6.16. Under the CAA Q-term proposals, all services to passengers assessed on the basis of QSM scores would be addressed through QP. This would cover departure lounge seat availability, cleanliness, way-finding and flight information. As the same quality incentive scheme could be applied to all the elements, they are discussed jointly. In most cases, the QSM results for average passenger perceptions throughout each airport would be used.

6.17. BAA agreed with the elements that the CAA had included in its proposed QP component. Airlines were concerned that, if the QP component were to be based on the QSM scores, BAA would have a vested interest in its results. The CAA told us that the QSM should therefore be subject to external audit to eliminate any biases in the samples. In particular it should be checked to make sure that the sample interviewed had no inherent biases: non-English speakers and regular business passengers should be fully represented and the survey should not be discontinued in periods of operational dislocation.

6.18. Under the CAA approach the average QSM scores for each of the four elements would be summed at the end of each year and divided by four. QP would then be calculated using a formula involving this amount, an equivalent par value determined from BAA's performance in a base year, a base level of performance and a value coefficient. The base level of performance would either be 1 (the theoretical minimum QSM score) or a higher threshold score (assumed to be 2 in the CAA's worked example). The value coefficient would be calculated such that the maximum penalty was 0.5 per cent of airport charges. This method would allow for bonus payments when the targets were exceeded on average. The detailed calculation of QP is set out in Appendix 6.1.

6.19. Although many airlines were opposed to the inclusion of passenger perception measures in the price cap formula, the CAA believed that these should be included in the Q term to address important areas of quality that were not amenable to objective measures. It told us that passenger representative bodies had supported these measures.

QD

6.20. The CAA felt that there was a case for developing measures for airfield congestion delays and a mechanism that would reflect the airport's delay performance in its future price caps. It therefore proposed the QD component to provide an incentive to reduce those airfield congestion delays that were within each airport's control. Details of the CAA's proposals for the QD component are set out in Appendix 6.1. The CAA felt that potential actions by an airport that could cause delays included: declaring capacity close to the physical capability of the runways, taxiways and associated ATC services; and delays in the performance of ATC ground control and approach services.

6.21. Some causes of delays, for example the non-serviceability of stands and jetties, are included in the QA component. Within the QD component, the CAA intended to capture the airport's performance in other areas, such as the aerodrome navigation service (ANS) and queuing and stacking arising from the airport declaring a high level of capacity. At BAA's London airports, NATS provides ANS under contract to the airport, although it makes a direct charge to users for the service. As each airport can choose the service provider and negotiates the terms of the contract, it has overall accountability to users for the service provided.

6.22. To provide an incentive to the airport not to declare an excessive level of capacity, the CAA proposed that the airfield delay component should include the following two elements:

(a) on departure: the time from the aircraft doors closing, with the aircraft having received an air traffic flow management[1] (ATFM) slot, to take-off, less an allowance for taxiing time; and

(b) on arrival: the time spent by the aircraft in the arrival stack plus any ATFM delay attributed to the airport by Eurocontrol.

---

[1]The method of controlling and attributing delays at a European level by the central flow management unit of Eurocontrol. It is based on restrictions to traffic flow requested by ATC service providers.

6.23. The average values of these elements over the year would be added and a par value would be subtracted from this total. The payment would be calculated by multiplying the result by a value co-efficient equal to 1.19 times the annual number of ATMs divided by the annual number of passengers. This calculation is designed to be consistent with a related formula in a NATS en-route charge condition. At Heathrow it would result in a penalty or bonus of 0.85p per passenger per minute of delay. The overall payment would be subject to a limit of 1 per cent of airport charges.

BAA's views on the Q term

6.24. BAA told us that it broadly accepted the CAA's approach to the Q term; it had been instrumental in creating the concept and had taken the lead in developing the methodology. BAA proposed to us a penalty and bonus regime with a financial impact limited to a specified percentage of airport charges income. BAA added that it was prepared to give an undertaking that, if the CC gave the CAA firm guidance on the implementation of a Q-term scheme, it would accept the CAA's rulings on details of the scheme, where these were consistent with the guidance.

6.25. BAA differed with the CAA on a number of important points, which we discuss below and in Appendix 6.1. In brief, BAA considered that the 3 per cent of airport charges ceiling for the Q term was too high compared with similar schemes in other industries; it felt that all the components should include the possibility of bonuses as well as penalties; and it opposed the QD element. Given the inadequate measurement system and historical data in some areas, BAA felt that the maximum impact of the Q term should be limited to 1.5 per cent for the next quinquennium. BAA considered that, for an element to be included in the Q term, it should:

(a) be important to passengers and/or airlines;

(b) affect a high proportion of passengers and/or airlines;

(c) be capable of being influenced by BAA to a substantial extent; and

(d) be relatively easy to monitor.

6.26. Although BAA had questioned the need for segmenting the Q term into three components, it agreed with the CAA that the QA component should include elements related to the serviceability of stands, jetties, people movers and baggage reclaim facilities and to the queuing time at departure security. BAA felt, however, that FEGP should be excluded as payments for this service fell outside core airport charges; it was nevertheless prepared to consider introducing a service quality incentive into FEGP charges (see paragraph 6.117). BAA also thought that pier service should be excluded. It considered that, although pier service levels depended mainly on the amount of pier infrastructure, it had limited operational control over performance at terminals where it did not carry out day-to-day stand allocation (see paragraph 6.83).

6.27. BAA proposed that additional elements linked to runway serviceability and taxiway service-ability measures should be included in the QA component of the CAA's Q term, as an alternative to the QD component. Both runway and taxiway serviceability would be measured in terms of annual hours of unplanned closure. Taxiway serviceability measures would only apply to taxiways adjacent to a runway. The CAA felt that QD, the airfield delay component, was a better way of addressing issues concerned with the serviceability of airfield facilities.

6.28. BAA told us that it had wide-ranging concerns about the QD component. It considered that most of the variation in punctuality was caused by factors outside the control of BAA and NATS. These included the weather, the performance of other parties including pilots, and the stochastic arrival and departure of flights. Given the importance of these factors, BAA told us that none of the available measures adequately reflected its airfield performance (or that of NATS as BAA's contractor). The data for on-stand and off-stand times was poor. Even for the existing measures, BAA did not think that there were accurate ways of collecting the necessary data or of attributing blame among the various parties that might have been responsible for any delay. It also felt that more experience of any proposed measures would be needed before appropriate targets could be set.

6.29. The CAA did not accept BAA's arguments on QD. It agreed that many factors were outside BAA's control but felt that BAA had to take a position on these factors when assessing its level of capacity. BAA should be accountable for such judgements.

6.30. BAA produced further detailed comments on the CAA proposals that are summarized in Appendices 6.1 and 6.2.

Views of airlines on the Q term

6.31. The views of the airlines on the CAA's proposals are set out in Chapter 12. In brief, many airlines considered that any failure by BAA to achieve a fixed performance standard should result in agreed rebates or compensation payments. They felt that realistic rebates or compensation payments were necessary if the standards were to be taken seriously; they would also help to redress the imbalance of power caused by BAA's position as a monopoly supplier.

6.32. Airlines were strongly opposed to any symmetrical approach to incentives as they felt that BAA should not be rewarded for providing a standard of service above the level they required. The airlines considered that this was contrary to normal commercial practice and would reduce the incentive effect of the rebates or compensation payments by allowing them to be offset by unrequested over-performance in other areas, which had no value for the customer. They felt that customer service consisted of getting all aspects right—getting only some right did not achieve the required result.

6.33. The airlines also felt that any incentive scheme should focus entirely on those elements identified in BA's alternative proposals and on the CAA's QD component. Those that expressed a view supported the alternative incentive proposals put forward by BA (see paragraph 6.38).

6.34. Airlines have argued for the inclusion of measures of runway and taxiway serviceability. A joint BAA/airline working group had been discussing this as part of a broader discussion of service quality in the run-up to the regulatory review; it had, however, failed to achieve a useful agreement and had ceased work.

6.35. BA broadly supported the CAA's proposals for a QD component but put forward an alternative way of measuring departure delays. We consider BA's and BAA's views on measuring and attributing delays in Appendix 6.3. BA considered that adequate measures were already in place to measure delays and attribute responsibility for them. It would, therefore, be possible to introduce a QD component at the beginning of the quinquennium. BA considered that the CAA's proposed limit on the QD component of 1 per cent of airport charges was too low.

Summary of differences between positions of the CAA, BAA and BA

6.36. Table 6.1 summarizes the elements of service covered by the various proposals. It shows the components of the Q term proposed by the CAA, together with the elements of service proposed by BAA for inclusion in the Q term and those BA believed should be subject to service standards (through its own scheme of generic service standards rather than the Q term). We discuss BAA's performance on the individual elements of service to airlines in paragraphs 6.61 to 6.116, on the individual elements of service to passengers in paragraphs 6.140 to 6.155 and on delays in paragraphs 6.120 to 6.137.

TABLE 6.1 **Views of parties on proposed components of Q term**

	CAA	BAA	BA
QA			
Stand serviceability	✔	✔	✔
Jetty serviceability	✔	✔	✔
Pier service	✔	✘	✔
FEGP	✔	✘	✔
People movers	✔	✔	✔
Transit system	✔	✔	✔
Security queues	✔	✔	✔
Arrivals reclaim	✔	✔	✔
Runways	✘	✔	✔
Taxiways	✘	✔	✔
Departure baggage	✘	✘	✔
QP			
Departure lounge seat availability	✔	✔	✘
Cleanliness	✔	✔	✘
Way-finding	✔	✔	✘
Flight information	✔	✔	✘
QD			
Delay	✔	✘	✔

Source: CAA, BAA and BA.

6.37. A major difference between the BAA and CAA proposals concerns the level of performance necessary to incur the maximum penalty for each element. Under the BAA proposals, the maximum penalty could only be incurred if there was very poor performance across the entire range of service elements. By contrast under the CAA proposals, very bad performance for any element within one of the three components could incur a high proportion of the maximum penalty for that component.

BA's alternative generic standards scheme

6.38. BA told us that the attractiveness of the CAA's Q-term proposals had been weakened by a number of decisions taken by the CAA. First, the Q term had been limited to a level that might be ignored by BAA. Second, any resulting price cap adjustments would take place only after a long delay that would weaken the incentive effect. Third, the proposed measures involved the averaging of performance across a range of different elements of performance. Despite an airport performing poorly on a factor critical to airlines any resulting penalty could be diluted, or its incentive effect offset by over-performance in other, possibly less important areas (see paragraph 6.32). Fourth, BA regarded the CAA's proposals as a form of tokenism that would create the illusion of progress whilst leaving airlines in a worse position.

6.39. Given these views, BA chose to put forward an alternative package of quality of service incentives to replace the CAA's QA and QP components. We describe them in detail in Appendix 6.4. In outline they consist of the following short-, medium- and long-term elements.

Short term

6.40. BA proposed a system of short-term quality incentives modelled on the existing remote stand rebate (which BA, however, considered to be set at an inadequate level). Under the remote stand rebate, all airlines receive a rebate of £1.50 for each passenger that has to arrive or depart on an aircraft that does not obtain pier service. Under BA's proposal, generic service standards would be set out in BAA's permission to levy charges (usually referred to as its licence). Airlines would be entitled to expect that BAA would always meet these service standards; any failure to do so would give the affected airline the right to receive a rebate, or compensation for services denied or costs incurred, because the airport did not achieve the generic standard. The rebate or compensation payments received would be set at a realistic level and open ended, depending only on the number of service failures experienced.

6.41. The generic service standards proposed by BA cover the availability of serviceable runways, taxiways, stands, airbridges, pier service, people movers, baggage systems and FEGP. A standard for waiting time at security queues is also included.

6.42. The generic service standards would also provide a baseline, above which airlines could contract with the airport for any additional services on the basis of bilateral negotiations.

Medium term

6.43. BA's proposal for medium-term incentives was based on BAA's planning standards (see paragraph 6.159). The intention was to provide an incentive to build adequate terminal capacity. BA proposed that an audit process should be developed to assess whether the existing terminals complied with the planning standards. Where the standards were not met, possible remedies could include annual price adjustments, reopening the price cap or representations to the CAA under section 41 of the Airports Act.

Long term

6.44. The third element in BA's alternative proposals was designed to encourage the timely development of airport infrastructure. To achieve this, BA proposed that future major projects should only be remunerated on a 'pay-for-what-you-get' basis. Any future increases in an airport's price cap needed to finance capital projects would be implemented only when the CIP was delivered as planned. If BAA failed to deliver major agreed projects, it would be penalized by adjustments to its price cap until the projects in question were delivered—including adjustments in the following quinquennia.

Default price cap

6.45. The CAA favoured a system that would encourage greater direct contracting between airlines and airports about the quality of service to be provided. Under this approach, the regulated price cap would act as a default price cap (see Chapter 5). As the basic quality of service to be expected would be defined by the par values incorporated in the Q term, the default price cap would provide a firm basis for negotiating higher or lower levels of service. Airlines would then be able to negotiate with an airport to pay more or less for any changes in service relative to this base level. BAA told us that it did not have strong views for or against the CAA's default price cap proposal.

BAA's current quality of service

Services to airlines

6.46. Many aspects of the quality of service BAA provides to airlines are measured through parameters set out in SLAs agreed between BAA and the AOCs and these would form the basis of the QA component of the CAA's proposed Q term (see Appendix 6.1).

Service level agreements

6.47. In the MMC's last inquiry into BAA's London Airports, the MMC welcomed a joint initiative by BAA and BA to develop SLAs on a trial basis.[1] It recommended that SLAs should be made available to all airlines after the trials. The MMC also proposed that, if the trial showed compensation to be feasible, SLAs should include provision for compensation, and that, where appropriate, compensation should be on a reciprocal basis if any party (for example, BAA, the airlines or their handling agents) imposed significant costs upon the others by failing to meet service standards.

---

[1]See paragraphs 2.40 and 2.41 of MMC4.

6.48. There is a strong interaction between different processes: for example, check-in delays caused by inadequate airline staffing can disrupt the security search process. Consequently, BAA and the airlines had originally felt that any SLAs should be set by consultation between the airports and users at local AOC level.

- *Best endeavours SLAs*

6.49. The first SLAs did not involve penalties or bonuses and are commonly referred to as best endeavours SLAs. Performance measurement trials were begun in 1996 in the following areas: the management of capital projects, baggage belts, queuing standards, stand serviceability, people mover serviceability, jetty serviceability and transfer standards. BAA and BA subsequently proposed that SLAs should be introduced in the following areas: aircraft stands, passenger jetties, people movers, security queuing, investment projects, transfer connections and departure baggage systems. SLAs covering the first four of these areas were introduced in 1997. The SLAs were initially piloted at three trial locations (T1 and T4 at Heathrow and the North Terminal at Gatwick) and, by the end of 1998, the four pilot SLAs had been extended to cover the relevant parts of all terminals at Heathrow and Gatwick. By June 1999, similar SLAs were also in force at Stansted. BAA said that the target levels adopted reflected the high expectations of users, rather than standards based on analysing the cost-effective level of service.

6.50. BAA describes these SLAs as 'performance target agreements'. These are non-legally-binding agreements between an airport company and the AOC setting out the level of service to be provided by the airport to the airlines, for example the target level of stand serviceability. As no financial compensation payments are involved for any failure to meet the standards, these agreements are also referred to as best endeavours SLAs. Appendix 6.5 outlines the features of a typical SLA.

6.51. During 1998, BAA replaced the proposed investment projects SLA by a commitment to apply its Continuous Improvement of the Projects Process (CIPP) policy which is discussed in Chapter 9.

6.52. Trials for an SLA for connecting passengers were held in 1997 an 1998 at the North Terminal at Gatwick but the SLA was not taken any further, owing to difficulties in monitoring the airport and airline responsibilities covered by the SLA.

6.53. The early discussions on SLAs mainly involved BAA and BA, reflecting the strong interest from BA and a significantly lower level of interest from other airlines. Discussions were extended to other airlines during 1998 and local SLA discussion forums were established at each airport early in 1999. These forums included representatives of the airport management team and of the relevant AOC.

6.54. The Heathrow AOC told us that the SLAs had generally worked satisfactorily, partly by highlighting deficiencies in the areas they covered.

- *Baggage system SLAs*

6.55. Separately, BAA had progressed the development of baggage system SLAs with penalties and bonuses. This proved significantly more challenging. BAA told us that it was committed to working with all the parties involved to improve baggage performance. It had therefore worked hard, with BA, to identify appropriate measures and a financial structure. After BAA's detailed work on baggage SLAs, and particularly baggage transfers, it proposed that the resulting SLAs should be described as 'facility agreements'. These were to be similar to the other SLAs but would set out the roles and responsibilities of each party involved in operating a facility and would include compensation payments. The development of these SLAs included a calibration period, which allowed existing performance levels to be properly understood, before financial incentives were implemented. Unlike the other SLAs these were to be bilateral agreements, initially between BAA and BA. Appendix 6.5 outlines an example of a baggage system SLA.

- *Further developments*

6.56. During 1999, BA reviewed the way that the best endeavours SLAs were operating and recommended a number of improvements in the way that performance was reported. Discussions also took place about the development of further SLAs. BA told us that the baggage SLAs, which incorporated financial incentives, had proved significantly more successful than the SLAs without such incentives. They had enabled BA to obtain improved service and facilities from BAA. BA felt that SLAs without incentives 'lacked teeth' as poor performance in the areas they covered could actually increase BAA's revenue. BA added that SLAs should cover all services that were part of the passenger experience of the airports. It was concerned that a number of areas were currently excluded, particularly planned maintenance (see paragraph 6.167). Others included runway and taxiway serviceability, ATC services and the maintenance of the fabric of the terminals. BA's views on SLAs and related incentives are set out in Chapter 12.

Equipment serviceability

6.57. BAA records data on the 'availability' of critical equipment, such as stands, jetties, escalators, passenger conveyors, lifts and baggage conveyors. We discuss each of these in turn in paragraphs 6.61 to 6.104. Availability is defined in terms of the proportion of time for which the equipment is ready for use, rather than the proportion of occasions that it is available when an airline requires it. We refer to this measure as 'serviceability' to avoid confusion with the availability of the equipment to a particular airline when needed. These measures, which are used in the existing SLAs, either use measures of downtime produced automatically by BAA's Maximo fault-reporting system (see Chapter 7) or involve manual examination of records. Performance is calculated separately for each terminal and statistics are circulated to the relevant AOCs each month.

6.58. The serviceability targets in the current SLAs all exclude notified planned maintenance (see paragraph 6.167): equipment is not classed as being unserviceable when it is undergoing notified planned maintenance. Airlines favoured the inclusion of planned maintenance in any future measures, as the current system gave BAA an incentive to declare high levels of planned maintenance. BAA reviewed this and expressed its willingness to adapt the definitions to include planned maintenance; it suggested that most of the targets would need to be lowered if planned maintenance were to be included. It considered that the following downtime could be counted against serviceability targets: annual insurance inspections; special insurance inspections; standard cleaning; deep cleaning; vandalism, misuse and operator error (with an exception set out below); operational activations, such as emergency stops; engineering faults; basic maintenance; and extra maintenance.

6.59. BAA added that there were several situations where downtime should not be counted against a serviceability target. These events were:

(a) a fault being logged by BAA's fault reporting system but the equipment being found to be working when examined by BAA or its contractor;

(b) vandalism, misuse and operator errors at goods lifts, which were prone to a high degree of damage through incorrect use;

(c) major damage of jetties and FEGP equipment by non-BAA users;

(d) equipment being taken out of service during a major investment project in the vicinity, after consultation with users;

(e) equipment being taken out of service for replacement or major refurbishment work, when this had been done in agreement with the appropriate consultation group (such as a terminal's AOC) and the period was specified in advance; and

(f) risk-assessed deep cleaning of equipment, where this is needed to reduce the danger of fire.

If other planned maintenance were to be included, but these circumstances were excluded, BAA considered that the associated QA targets for jetties, people movers and arrivals baggage systems should be 1 per cent below the current SLA targets. It was opposed to including planned maintenance in the assessment of stand serviceability (see paragraph 6.167).

6.60. Serviceability is often measured over the key operational hours, rather than over a 24-hour day. It may be easier to achieve a target if performance is not measured over the full 24 hours—particularly if planned maintenance were to be included in the calculations. On the other hand, if performance in peak hours is critical, it may be appropriate for incentive systems to operate over a more limited period that encourages repairs and maintenance to be carried out at other times. BAA told us that the current periods had been chosen by the airlines.

Stand serviceability

6.61. BAA told us that aircraft parking stand capacity is provided to meet forecast maximum stand demand. The SLAs for stands use serviceability targets that apply to all stands, including remote stands. At Heathrow, a 99 per cent target has been set; at Gatwick and Stansted the corresponding targets are set at 98 per cent.

6.62. At Gatwick the target excludes stand closures caused by the unserviceability of stand entry guidance equipment, fire hydrants, floodlights, spillages and obstructions by equipment.

6.63. At Heathrow and Stansted performance is assessed over a period of 24 hours. At Gatwick performance is assessed over the key operational hours of 04.00 to 13.30 and 17.30 to 20.30.

6.64. At Heathrow, the stand allocation unit records stand outages daily and checks them against planned maintenance schedules before calculating the percentage serviceability. At Gatwick and Stansted, the airfield operations section records stand outages daily and checks the reasons for closure before calculating the percentage serviceability.

6.65. The performance achieved in the 12 months ending March 2002 is set out in Table 6.2.

TABLE 6.2 **Stand serviceability: performance over 12 months to March 2002**

Terminal	Target %	Months target met	Average score %	Lowest score %
Heathrow T1	99	12	100	100
Heathrow T2	99	12	100	100
Heathrow T3	99	12	100	100
Heathrow T4	99	12	100	100
Gatwick NT	98	12	100	100
Gatwick ST	98	12	100	100
Stansted	98	12	100	100

Source: BAA.

6.66. BA considered that the exclusion of planned maintenance and long-term outages from the equipment serviceability SLAs was a serious flaw. In response, BAA told us that planned maintenance resulted mainly from development works, scheduled cleaning and jetty maintenance. The development works included modifying stands to accommodate different types of aircraft. BAA added that major planned maintenance projects at Heathrow and Gatwick were carefully programmed to minimize operational disruption; wherever possible, information on these projects was communicated to airlines twice a year as part of each airport's capacity declaration discussions. BAA considered that planned maintenance should continue to be excluded from any incentive scheme for stand serviceability. The need to reconstruct stands was highly unpredictable and had to be carried out promptly to maintain airport safety and capacity. Any serviceability targets that included planned maintenance would therefore need to be set at low levels. Unplanned outage was largely the result of fuel spillage.

6.67. Under the CAA's QA proposals, one penalty point would be incurred for each monthly failure to achieve the stand serviceability target. The CAA has yet to determine the level of its proposed targets. BAA proposed that the targets should be set at 99 per cent (excluding planned maintenance) at both Heathrow and Gatwick. BAA also proposed a penalty and bonus regime with a financial impact limited to a specified percentage of airport charges income.

Jetty serviceability

6.68. A jetty rebate, currently standing at £15.36 per instance, is payable on application to BAA, when the jetty is not available on a jetty-served stand. The SLAs for jetties incorporate a 98 per cent serviceability target at all three airports. The target excludes planned maintenance.

6.69. At Heathrow performance is monitored over a period of 18 hours agreed with the AOCs for each terminal. Performance at Gatwick is monitored between the hours of 04.00 to 23.00 (South Terminal) or 04.00 to 11.00 and 16.00 to 21.00 (North Terminal). At Stansted, jetty serviceability is monitored between 05.00 and 23.59. The method of monitoring jetty serviceability was the subject of discussion between BAA and the airlines. It had been suggested that it might be more appropriate to monitor the proportion of unsuccessful 'dockings', ie the number of times a handling agent wished to use a jetty but was unable to do so because it was unserviceable. Data was collected in a trial of this form of monitoring. The conclusion was, however, that the alternative approach to performance measurement did not provide better information.

6.70. In additional to being circulated to the AOC for each airport, at Gatwick the statistics are also discussed at airbridge liaison meetings with handling agents.

6.71. The performance achieved in the 12 months ending March 2002 is set out in Table 6.3.

TABLE 6.3 **Jetty serviceability: performance over 12 months to March 2002**

Terminal	Target %	Months target met	Average score %	Lowest score %
Heathrow T1	98	12	98.8	98
Heathrow T2	98	12	99.4	98
Heathrow T3	98	12	98.9	98
Heathrow T4	98	10	97.8	95
Gatwick NT	98	12	99.8	98
Gatwick ST	98	12	100	100
Stansted	98	11	99.4	97

Source: BAA.

6.72. BA told us that the SLA for jetty serviceability had little credibility with front-line operational teams because of its design, measurement and exclusions.

6.73. Under the CAA's QA proposals, one penalty point would be incurred for each monthly failure to achieve the jetty serviceability target. The CAA has proposed a target of 98 per cent serviceability, excluding planned maintenance. BAA proposed a target of 97 per cent, including planned maintenance.

Pier service

6.74. Passengers express a strong preference for pier service over being coached to a remote stand. In BAA's QSM surveys, passengers receiving pier service typically rate it above 4[1] while coached passengers rate that method of disembarkation in the range from 2.5 to 3.5. Nevertheless, BAA told us that its research indicated that passengers thought pier service was less important than many other factors in determining the quality of their airport experience. It would not be economic for airports to provide sufficient pier capacity to permit pier and jetty service to be provided in all circumstances, particularly at peak times.

6.75. There is no SLA for pier service. Airlines are, however, compensated through the remote stand rebate, which is provided for in BAA's Conditions of Use, every time they do not receive pier service. The payment was initially intended to recognize that passengers were receiving a less attractive service.

[1]On a scale where 5 is 'excellent', 4 is 'good', 3 is 'average', 2 is 'poor' and 1 is 'extremely poor'.

After airlines complained that the rebate did not cover the cost of hiring coaches, BAA increased it to £3 per departing passenger (or £1.50 for each passenger). Although this represents a substantial proportion of the airport charge per departing passenger, airlines claimed that the rebate still did not fully cover their consequential costs or marketing effects on them. The way that the payments are treated in the price cap results in a redistribution of cash between airlines, rather than a net cost to BAA.

6.76. The provision of off-pier coaching services has historically been the responsibility of airlines. BAA told us that, at Heathrow, it had, at the airlines' request, sought to help them arrange coaching operations. It had set up a contract for the airlines in T3, with the exception of Virgin and BA, which retained their own arrangements. BAA told us that, at the request of the AOC, it was currently investigating an opportunity to establish a common approach across all terminals, whilst protecting airlines' legal right to arrange their own coaching operations. The Heathrow AOC said that, although some improvements had resulted, more improvements were needed to meet increased demand.

6.77. BAA measures the level of pier service in terms of the percentage of passengers who board aircraft from pier-served stands. It includes both those who use a jetty and those who have to walk from the pier across the apron to board their aircraft. This may be necessary where an aircraft is incompatible with the jetty, where a jetty could not be docked successfully or where a multiple aircraft ramp service (MARS) stand is being used by two small aircraft and the jetty can only be used by the aircraft on the left-hand side of the stand. BAA has a planning objective that '90 to 95 per cent' of the passengers in each terminal should receive pier service over a year.

6.78. Pier service statistics are shown in Table 6.4. At Heathrow there have been significant declines at T1 and T4. There have also been smaller declines at T2 and at the South Terminal at Gatwick.

TABLE 6.4 **Passengers receiving pier service**

					per cent
Terminal	*1996/97*	*1997/98*	*1998/99*	*1999/00*	*2000/01*
Heathrow T1 domestic	92.6	96.1	93.8	92.6	90.3
Heathrow T1 international	83.3	93.9	83.2	82.4	81.5
Heathrow T2	99.5	99.2	99.5	99.0	96.8
Heathrow T3	96.1	96.2	95.0	94.9	96.9
Heathrow T4	94.5	90.4	89.4	88.9	87.4
Gatwick NT	80.7	78.9	75.8	76.8	79.3
Gatwick ST	98.9	98.8	97.7	96.5	96.1
Stansted	99.9	99.9	99.7	99.7	99.6
Including forward coaching facility*	N/A	N/A	0.3	2.5	2.8

Source: BAA.

*See paragraph 6.82.
Note: N/A = not applicable.

6.79. BAA told us that the higher than expected traffic growth had made it difficult to respond quickly with the necessary pier infrastructure. Furthermore, it had reacted positively to airline requests for moves between terminals and between airports, some of which had had detrimental effect on pier service levels.

6.80. Issues concerning investment projects to improve pier service levels at T4 and the North Terminal at Gatwick are considered in Chapter 9. BAA said that one consideration that led to the delay in extending pier service to the Metro stands at Heathrow was that they offered the only possibility of handling the Airbus A380 at T4. Allowing for two A380 stands affected the design of the scheme. BAA added that BA's decision to move some long-haul services from Gatwick to Heathrow had itself reduced the level of pier service at Heathrow.

6.81. BAA told us that the pier service statistics for Gatwick understated the level of pier service in recent years. There were a number of North Terminal flights that, although they departed from a pier-served stand, were held on a remote stand awaiting a runway slot. Since BAA's database recorded the last stand occupied by an aircraft, these flights were not counted as receiving pier service; taking account of this, true pier service levels would have been 1 to 2 per cent higher. BAA added that, whilst three additional stands at the North Terminal had received pier service at the end of 1999, this change was not reflected in the data until the beginning of 2001; the effect on monitored pier service levels would, however, have been less than 1 per cent. The level of pier service at Gatwick from 2002 onwards[1] had been affected by the decision to delay the Pier 6 project. This was a deliberate decision in the light of the uncertain position of airlines after 11 September 2001.

6.82. At Stansted the statistics record the percentage of passengers arriving or departing on aircraft parked on pier-served stands. BAA told us that, as in some cases passengers have been coached to or from aircraft parked on pier-served stands, the statistics slightly overestimated the level of pier service. The Stansted pier-service data also includes passengers who arrived or departed on aircraft parked adjacent to the forward coaching facility. (Passengers are coached to this building, which effectively operates as a remote satellite.)

6.83. BAA opposed the inclusion of pier service in QA. Although it controlled the level of pier infrastructure, BAA often could not ensure that pier-served stands were allocated efficiently. The precise level of pier service was affected by the way in which stands were allocated. At T1 and T4 at Heathrow and at both terminals at Gatwick, the airlines or their handling agents allocated the stands. Tactical decisions taken by handling agents could, therefore, affect the overall level of pier service.

6.84. Under the CAA's QA proposals, one penalty point would be incurred for each monthly failure to achieve the pier service target. The CAA has yet to determine the level of the target.

People mover serviceability

6.85. Under this heading, BAA includes passenger lifts, goods lifts, escalators and passenger conveyors. There are SLAs with serviceability targets for all types of people movers. At Heathrow and Gatwick, targets of 99 per cent have been set for all people movers; at Stansted, targets of 98 per cent have been set. At Heathrow, data on the performance of the CTA subway passenger conveyors and the lifts in the multi-storey car parks are included in the overall performance reports but not in the average performance for each terminal.

6.86. At Heathrow serviceability is measured over a period from 05.00 to 23.00 each day at T1 and T3. At T2 serviceability is measured over a period from 04.30 to 23.30 and at T4 from 04.00 to 23.00. At Gatwick, serviceability is assessed over a period from 04.00 to 22.00 at the North Terminal and 04.00 to 11.00 and 16.00 to 21.00 at the South Terminal. At Stansted serviceability is monitored over a period from 00.00 to 23.59 each day.

6.87. The performance achieved in the 12 months ending March 2002 is set out in Tables 6.5 to 6.8.

TABLE 6.5 **Escalator serviceability: performance over 12 months to March 2002**

Terminal	Target %	Months target met	Average score %	Lowest score %
Heathrow T1	99	8	98.6	97
Heathrow T2	99	11	99.7	98
Heathrow T3	99	10	99.3	98
Heathrow T4	99	11	99.8	98
Gatwick NT	99	12	99.7	99
Gatwick ST	99	10	99.3	98
Stansted	98	12	100	100

Source: BAA.

---

[1]The original earliest completion date for the Pier 6 project.

TABLE 6.6 **Passenger lift serviceability: performance over 12 months to March 2002**

Terminal	Target %	Months target met	Average score %	Lowest score %
Heathrow T1	99	9	99.0	98
Heathrow T2	99	7	98.4	94
Heathrow T3	99	7	99.8	97
Heathrow T4	99	6	97.8	93
CTA subways, car parks and bus station	99	4	97.2	91
Gatwick NT	99	12	99.9	99
Gatwick ST	99	11	99.4	98
Stansted	98	12	99.3	98

Source: BAA.

TABLE 6.7 **Goods lift serviceability: performance over 12 months to March 2002**

Terminal	Target %	Months target met	Average score %	Lowest score %
Heathrow T1	99	9	99.3	98
Heathrow T2	99	12	99.9	99
Heathrow T3	99	12	99.5	99
Heathrow T4	99	10	99.4	98
Gatwick NT	99	12	99.9	99
Gatwick ST	99	10	99.3	94
Stansted	98	11	99.3	97

Source: BAA.

TABLE 6.8 **Passenger conveyor serviceability: performance over 12 months to March 2002**

Terminal	Target %	Months target met	Average score %	Lowest score %
Heathrow T1	99	5	98.4	96
Heathrow T2	99	11	99.6	97
Heathrow T3	99	2	95.5	90
Heathrow T4	99	6	98.7	97
CTA subways	99	3	98.1	97
Gatwick NT	99	12	99.8	99
Gatwick ST	99	7	98.7	98

Source: BAA.

6.88. The Heathrow AOC told us that there had been some improvement in the serviceability of the passenger conveyors in the CTA subways. It felt that further improvements could be made by extending the automatic electronic reporting of equipment faults to expedite repairs.

6.89. Under the CAA's QA proposals, half a penalty point would be incurred for each monthly failure to achieve the people mover serviceability target. (In practice the points BAA risked incurring might need to be divided up between the different types of people movers.) The CAA and BAA have both proposed targets of 98 per cent serviceability, including planned maintenance.

● *Fault repair times*

6.90. Until the end of 1999, BAA included information on the mean time taken to repair faults in its SLA reports for people movers. Early in 2000 it proposed that that the mean time to repair targets should be dropped. BAA told us that, after discussion in SLA forums, airline representatives at each airport had agreed this change. BAA had felt that the targets provided inappropriate incentives to its maintenance engineers: the percentage serviceability targets were better incentives to carry out rapid and effective repairs. It added that this move was part of an internal exercise to change its approach from one based on simply fixing problems that occurred to one of improving performance by adopting maintenance planning and scheduling based on how critical a fault would be (see paragraph 6.167).

Transit systems

6.91. At Gatwick, SLAs with serviceability targets have been established for the passenger transit systems. The target for the inter-terminal transit system is set at 97 per cent (excluding planned maintenance) for the serviceability of both cars. There are two targets for the Pier 3 transit system: 99 per cent for the serviceability of at least one car and 97 per cent for the serviceability of both cars. At Stansted, a 97 per cent serviceability target has been set for the transit system.

6.92. The performance achieved in the 12 months ending March 2002 is set out in Table 6.9.

TABLE 6.9 **Tracked transit serviceability: performance over 12 months to March 2002**

Terminal	Target %	Months target met	Average score %	Lowest score %
Gatwick inter-terminal	97	10	97.8	92
Gatwick Pier 3 (2 cars)	97	9	97.8	92
Gatwick Pier 3 (1 car)	99	12	99.9	99
Stansted	97	12	99.6	97

Source: BAA.

6.93. BAA told us that HM Railway Inspectorate (HMRI) required planned maintenance equivalent to 8,500 man-hours to be carried out on the Gatwick transit systems each year. It added that the current SLA measurement period, which is the same as for people movers, would cause a conflict with these maintenance requirements if planned maintenance were to be included in the measures. BAA therefore considered that measurement periods should be revised to take account of the present operational profile. This would permit planned maintenance to be carried out in quieter hours without affecting BAA's performance assessment. HMRI commented that it would not specify a required number of hours of planned maintenance. Health and safety law required maintenance regimes for equipment that were suitable and appropriate for the use to which it was put. The duty holder (BAA) would have to decide the exact amount of time and effort required in the particular circumstances.

6.94. Under the CAA's QA proposals, half a penalty point would be incurred for each monthly failure to achieve the tracked transit serviceability target. The CAA has proposed a target of 98 per cent serviceability. BAA proposed targets for both Gatwick transit systems of 99 per cent serviceability of one car and 97 per cent serviceability of two cars. BAA also proposed a penalty and bonus regime with a financial impact limited to a specified percentage of airport charges income.

Baggage handling

6.95. Baggage handling services are either provided by the airlines themselves, or by handling agents on their behalf, using fixed equipment provided by BAA.

● *Departures baggage systems*

6.96. At Heathrow, bilateral SLAs between BAA and BA have been established for the departure baggage systems at T1 and T4 and for the baggage tunnel between these two terminals. These SLAs include legally enforceable financial incentives and focus on end-to-end baggage system times and the service provided at system input and output points, as well as equipment serviceability (see paragraph 6.57). The SLAs also take account of the effect that operators have on baggage delivery, for example by failing to clear baggage chutes properly. The operational responsibilities and financial incentives in the SLA are therefore reciprocal, that is the bonuses and penalties take account of BA's performance as well as BAA's performance. BA told us that, while accepting that such arrangements might be acceptable in private bilateral agreements, airlines would be completely opposed to such symmetry in generic standards. BAA told us that it was working with BA to integrate these SLAs into a single end-to-end system for T1 and T4.

6.97. Although other airlines and handling agents are not yet included, BAA told us that they had been offered similar SLAs, with or without reciprocal financial incentives. BAA added that it was working with airlines and handling agents to implement new SLAs for the departures baggage systems in T2 and T3 at Heathrow and the North Terminal at Gatwick.

6.98. The SLAs at T2 and T3 were being calibrated, although airlines only showed limited interest in the financial dimensions. At the North Terminal, after investigating how it might provide departures baggage system SLAs, BAA concluded that it could not offer any at this stage. It did not believe that it had sufficient control over key aspects of the system's operation; BAA told us that it was therefore reviewing the management of baggage at Gatwick and developing a five-year strategy. BAA also told us that it was working to develop further end-to-end route SLAs for inter-terminal baggage flows at Heathrow. These were now in place for transfers between T1 and T4 and for the activities of the independent transfer operators.

6.99. The CAA told us that departures baggage systems were not included in its proposals for QA because:

(a) outbound baggage was not paid for through airport charges;

(b) users had varying requirements;

(c) there was scope for particular requirements to be addressed by differentiated payments, at least for substantial users; and

(d) there was scope for bilateral SLAs with incentives, as demonstrated by the arrangements between BAA and BA.

BAA told us that it shared the CAA's views on excluding outward and transfer baggage systems from a Q term.

● *Incoming baggage systems*

6.100. Airlines and their handling agents are responsible for delivering incoming baggage to BAA's baggage systems in each terminal. BAA told us that the licences it issued to ground handlers (and self-handling airlines) included a set of minimum service standards that had been agreed with the airlines. The licences also included provision for a performance review process, through which service quality could be discussed and action plans agreed. After exhausting the performance review process, BAA could in extreme cases threaten to serve notice on the handling agent.

6.101 In the ground-handling licences, BAA has set the performance standards shown in Table 6.10 for the delivery times of incoming baggage to the reclaim carousels. Times are measured relative to the arrival of aircraft on stand. The standards set vary slightly by airport, when compared with a similar minimum percentage of flights standard. Different standards apply to narrow-bodied and wide-bodied aircraft, reflecting the different lengths of time taken to unload them. This tends to result in longer delivery times for long-haul aircraft at a given airport. Performance against the standards is monitored and reported monthly.

TABLE 6.10 **Ground handling licence standards for maximum baggage delivery times**

Maximum delivery times

	Time for first bag mins	Minimum percentage of flights	Time for last bag mins	Minimum percentage of flights	Time for first bag mins	Minimum percentage of flights	Time for last bag mins	Minimum percentage of flights
	Narrow-bodied aircraft				*Wide-bodied aircraft*			
Heathrow	15	95	25	90	20	95	35	90
	All aircraft							
Gatwick	N/A	N/A	35	85	N/A	N/A	N/A	N/A
			45	98				
			60	100				
	All aircraft							
Stansted	30	90	45	95	N/A	N/A	N/A	N/A
			60	100				

Source: BAA.

Note: N/A = not applicable.

6.102. Following an SLA trial for the reliability of the arrivals baggage reclaim carousels at T4, similar SLAs have been introduced to cover parts of the operation at Gatwick. Subject to discussions with airlines, BAA intends to introduce arrivals baggage reclaim SLAs with serviceability targets throughout Heathrow and possibly at Stansted.

6.103. The target for the serviceability of arrivals baggage reclaim carousels at Gatwick is 99 per cent. It excludes planned maintenance and is measured over the core operational hours of 04.00 to 11.00 and 16.00 to 21.00 (North Terminal) and 04.00 to 22.00 (South Terminal). Performance is assessed using downtime data from the Maximo fault reporting system.

6.104. Under the CAA's QA proposals, half a penalty point would be incurred for each monthly failure to achieve the arrivals baggage reclaim serviceability target. The CAA proposed a target of 99 per cent serviceability, excluding planned maintenance. BAA proposed a target of 98 per cent, including planned maintenance. BAA also proposed a penalty and bonus regime with a financial impact limited to a specified percentage of airport charges income.

● *Transfer baggage*

6.105. The Heathrow AOC told us that, after a near collapse of transfer baggage arrangements in 1997, there had been significant improvements. It considered that further upgrading was, however, required: the facility used by T2 airlines was totally inadequate; and three separate facilities were in use at T3, one of which needed replacing. The AOC felt that the whole transfer baggage system should be reviewed to ensure efficient connections between all five terminals.

6.106. BAA commented that, at the time of the last review, it had become clear that it needed to work closely with the airlines to ensure that transfer baggage was delivered more quickly and reliably. Airlines were traditionally responsible for the handling of baggage and contracts had typically been organized by the AOC. Even so, BAA told us that it took the lead in developing a strategy for action with the guidance of the AOC. This involved: understanding the baggage transfer process; getting the best from existing facilities; process development; infrastructure investment and development; and IT development.

6.107. BAA established teams to manage the facilities and processes at eight locations in all the terminals, and to measure performance in handling baggage. These teams were responsible for ensuring that all the relevant parties worked together to deliver over 30,000 connecting bags each day. New baggage facilities costing over £140 million had been introduced together with new IT systems.

6.108. BAA believed that this had resulted in a significant improvement in performance. It cited comments from airlines, which had said that Heathrow's approach to connections now ranked above its European competitors and had praised the collective focus on problem resolution, rather than apportioning blame.

6.109. We consider future connections between the terminals after the completion of T5, in Chapter 9.

Security queues

6.110. The SLAs for security queues incorporate the target that queue lengths should be less than ten minutes on at least 95 per cent of the occasions when they are checked. At Heathrow, BAA is committed to checking the queue length at least every 30 minutes during the agreed period. At Gatwick and Stansted, BAA is committed to checking the queue length at least every 15 minutes during the agreed period. The SLAs do not apply when:

(a) operations are severely disrupted by weather or an evacuation;

(b) planned passenger throughput exceeds declared capacity; or

(c) airlines are sending passengers with hold bags to the gate.

6.111. The monitoring periods selected by the AOCs are shown in Table 6.11.

TABLE 6.11 **Security queue monitoring hours**

Terminal	Monitoring hours
Heathrow T1 international	06.30 to 11.00 and 13.30 to 19.30
Heathrow T1 domestic	07.30 to 10.00 and 16.00 to 21.00
Heathrow T2	06.30 to 10.00 and 15.00 to 20.00
Heathrow T3	08.30 to 12.30 and 16.30 to 20.30
Heathrow T4	09.00 to 11.00 and 19.00 to 21.00
Gatwick North Terminal	05.00 to 10.45 and 17.00 to 19.30
Gatwick South Terminal	05.00 to 14.00 and 18.00 to 22.00
Stansted	06.00 to 18.00

Source: BAA.

6.112. At Heathrow and Gatwick, BAA's supervisory staff monitor how the length of security queues compares with the standards. To collect the data, the last passenger in the queue is identified and the time taken to reach the head of the queue is measured. At Stansted the queues are monitored using CCTV and performance against the targets is assessed by reviewing the CCTV videotapes. As this arrangement is preferred by the airlines, BAA has agreed in principle to move towards CCTV monitoring at Heathrow and Gatwick.

6.113. The performance achieved in the 12 months ended March 2002 is set out in Table 6.12. Performance each month is calculated by dividing the number of occasions when the SLA standard was achieved by the total number of observations. At T1, the performance of the international and domestic queues is measured separately.

TABLE 6.12 **Security queuing: performance over 12 months to March 2002**

Terminal	Target %	Months target met	Average score %	Lowest score %
Heathrow T1 international	95	12	99.0	97
Heathrow T1 domestic	95	12	99.2	97
Heathrow T2	95	12	99.8	98
Heathrow T3*	95	9	96.6*	92*
Heathrow T4	95	12	98.8	95
Gatwick NT	95	12	98.8	97
Gatwick ST	95	12	98.3	95
Stansted	94	11	95.6	92

Source: BAA.

*T3 failed to record a figure in one month.

6.114. BA told us that the SLA for security queues had little credibility with front-line operational teams because of small sample sizes, exclusions and the use of manual measurement.

6.115. BAA told us that changing security requirements following the events of 11 September 2001 had had major implications for departing passenger security screening. It had been required to increase staffing which was a slow process, given the need for security vetting and training. BAA therefore considered that it should be able to apply to the CAA for a temporary suspension of the security queuing element of the Q term in the event of further significant changes in security requirements that necessitated substantial increases in staffing.

6.116. Under the CAA's QA proposals, one penalty point would be incurred for each monthly failure to achieve the security queuing target. The CAA has proposed a target of 95 per cent achievement of the ten-minute queuing time standard. BAA proposed a penalty and bonus regime with a financial impact limited to a specified percentage of airport charges income.

Fixed electrical ground power

6.117. FEGP is financed through a separate charge rather than airport charges.[1] BAA told us that the charge at Heathrow was based on the time an aircraft was parked on its stand. When FEGP was not available, the charge was not payable. At Gatwick and Stansted, the charge was based on the time each aircraft was connected to the FEGP system. When aircraft did not use the system, no charge was payable.

6.118. At Gatwick (but not at Heathrow or Stansted), an SLA has been developed for the serviceability of FEGP systems. The target of 99 per cent serviceability applies to all stands where FEGP is available and is measured over the same core operational hours as stand serviceability. Performance is measured using downtime data from the Maximo fault reporting system. Monthly results are reported to the AOC. At Heathrow BAA has reported to airlines on the availability of FEGP for some time, against a target of 98 per cent, and has had discussions with BA about the introduction of a formal SLA for FEGP.

6.119. Under the CAA's QA proposals, half a penalty point would be incurred for each monthly failure to achieve the FEGP serviceability target. The CAA has yet to determine the level of the target. BAA questioned whether it would be lawful or appropriate for FEGP to be included in a Q term as it was financed through a separate charge rather than airport charges. Nonetheless, subject to the legal position being clarified, BAA told us that it would not oppose an FEGP serviceability measure being included in a Q term. Alternatively, it was prepared to include a service quality incentive in the FEGP charging arrangements.

[1]It can be argued that the charge at Heathrow falls within the definition of an 'airport charge'. When we put this point to BAA and the CAA, neither accepted that it was the case.

Airfield operations

6.120. The airport company is only one of many parties that can affect air transport punctuality. Many of the most crucial aspects of airport operations are not directly the responsibility of BAA. For example, whether or not aircraft landings and take-offs occur on time is largely determined by ATC performance, the greatest part of which is dependent on en-route ATC. Airport ATC services are provided by NATS under contract to BAA. Keeping to the published schedules requires close coordination between the airlines, ground handling agents, NATS and BAA, any one of which could cause a delay. Road traffic delays in the approaches to Heathrow can also delay departures. Generally, the proportion of delays attributable to airports is low. Passengers and airlines nonetheless incur significant time costs caused by activities for which the airport has some responsibility.

6.121. The CAA told us that concentrating on punctuality alone might underestimate the impact of airfield congestion. A large part of the additional aircraft holding times had been absorbed into scheduled times and thus did not feature in reported delays. In some cases, quite long additions to scheduled times had been made to protect punctuality.

6.122. There are at present no serviceability measures or SLAs for runways or taxiways. BAA has proposed that runway and taxiway serviceability measures should be included in QA; airlines also support this addition, if BA's alternative approach to incentives were not to be adopted. BAA proposed that the taxiway element of QA should only cover those taxiways immediately adjacent to runways. As there is at present no data on taxiway serviceability, this element of QA would require a data collection exercise before the effect of any proposed targets could be assessed. We set out BAA's comments on this proposal further in Appendix 6.2.

- *Capacity declarations*

6.123. In planning runway capacity, BAA aims for a ten-minute average delay. Each airport declares hourly capacities twice a year after consultation with NATS and the airlines. Given random variations in the actual rates of aircraft arriving and departing, some delays are inevitable unless the airport declares a low level of capacity. In principle, therefore, the airport could cause airlines and passengers to experience delays if it were to declare a level of capacity that was too close to the maximum capability of runways, taxiways and the ANS.

6.124. Although airlines are the main beneficiaries of additional capacity, airports have a strong incentive to maximize throughput between price reviews by declaring high capacities; any increased queuing that results has no direct impact on their financial performance. BAA told us that its capacity declarations were made on the basis of queuing time criteria agreed with the airlines. Its estimates of runway capacity were developed in close consultation with NATS, which collected survey data as the basis for simulating airfield operations. Runway and taxiway capacity were then assessed using simulation modelling that took account of the effect of changes to the taxiway layout.

6.125. The results from the NATS simulation models can be used to examine the trade-off between the level of declared capacity and the resulting forecast delays. They are discussed with airlines at each airport as part of a twice-yearly consultation process on airport scheduling capacities. The key delay assumptions used in the NATS modelling work are that the average forecast delay should not exceed ten minutes and that peak delays should not exceed 20 minutes for arriving aircraft and 25 minutes for departing aircraft.

6.126. Given the effect of the differing layouts of its airports, BAA does not use planning objectives in determining the provision of runway, taxiway and apron facilities. It does, however, apply safety standards and general guidance notes on the capacity of airfield facilities; this guidance is currently under review.

- *Problems with delay data*

6.127. In practice present measures of the times required for the CAA's calculations are controversial, as are the possible methods of attributing fault. Various measures suggested by the CAA

211

are considered in Appendix 6.1. Many of these are subject to objections from BAA; BAA's comments and proposals from BA are set out in Appendix 6.3.

6.128. BAA told us that there was a wealth of performance statistics, each measuring different facets of this complex issue. Many were flawed either because it was difficult to capture accurate data or because they were misused. Ultimately, NATS intends to introduce a system that may automatically record the times at which key stages of arrival and departure take place. This is, however, likely to take several years.

6.129. We are aware of two sources of information on causes of delays. The first is the records of the reasons for delays made by the dispatchers employed by airlines and their ground handlers. These are likely to be subjective and possibly over-simplified where there are multiple causes. Moreover, the dispatcher may not be in a position to know the real reason for the delay. The second source of delay attribution data is Eurocontrol's Central Office for Delay Analysis (CODA). BAA told us that CODA attempts to ascribe delays to the most constricting cause.

6.130. After considering the available data, the CAA concluded that there was no prospect of satisfactory measurement systems being in place to support the QD component by April 2003. It felt, however, that improvements could be achieved during the next quinquennium, in particular through the new data collection systems that NATS was developing.

6.131. In the short term, the CAA felt that BAA should be required to commission NATS to extend its ad hoc sample surveys of airfield activity (see paragraph 6.124) to cover a representative sample of weather and operating conditions. This would provide unbiased estimates of the par values for the parameters required for the QD component, which could be used until the new NATS systems were available. Performance could then be measured against them until the automated systems became available. BAA told us that it did not believe the CAA's sampling proposal to be an appropriate way forward in view of the likelihood of sampling errors, resulting from weather or other extraneous factors.

- *Delay performance*

6.132. CODA published data[1] on planned delays for 2001 covering flights to and from 48 airports. Overall, it attributed 25 per cent of delays to 'airports', although this category also covered some causes outside the control of the airport managing bodies. The detailed data showed an average departure delay of 4.0 minutes at Heathrow, 5.3 minutes at Gatwick and 4.4 minutes at Stansted, but did not provide any analysis of the causes at individual airports. For comparison, the longest average departure delay at any of the airports reported on was 7.1 minutes and the shortest was 2.5 minutes. CODA's analysis of arrivals showed an average delay of 4.0 minutes at Heathrow, 4.1 minutes at Gatwick and 4.3 minutes at Stansted. The longest average arrival delay at any of the airports was 8.1 minutes and the shortest was 2.2 minutes. CODA's monthly data for 2002 shows significant increases in delays to flights to and from the London airports. This may, however, be partly caused by problems associated with the movement of the NATS en-route ATC centre to Swanwick.

6.133. Data published by the Association of European Airlines (AEA)[2] showed that 23.9 per cent of departures at Heathrow were delayed by more than 15 minutes in 2001. It attributed 42 per cent of these delayed flights to the airport and ATC. AEA reported that 19.3 per cent of departures at Gatwick were delayed by more than 15 minutes, 34 per cent of which were attributed to the airport and ATC. For comparison, AEA's data showed an overall average of 24.2 per cent of departures being delayed for all European operations.

6.134. AEA data for arrivals showed that 26.8 per cent of arrivals at Heathrow were delayed by over 15 minutes, as were 20.8 per cent of arrivals at Gatwick. AEA did not attribute causes to arrival delays or publish any data for Stansted. AEA's general comments said that most delays were infrastructure-related and in particular could be traced to ATC. It added that Europe's fragmented airspace was unable to cope satisfactorily with normal levels of traffic. Airlines told us that they were concerned that increasing congestion might result in more delays, particularly at Heathrow before the opening of T5.

[1]*Delays to Air Transport in Europe, Annual 2001*, CODA, European Organisation for the Safety of Air Navigation.
[2]*European Airline Delays in 2001*, Association of European Airlines, 11 February 2002.

6.135. AEA told us that, as its data only covered about one-quarter of the total movements in the area reported on by CODA, they were normally different from the CODA data; on close examination, however, they showed the same trends. BAA commented that the two sets of data measured different things. CODA's departure data measured 'planned' delays, that is the difference between pilots' requested departure times and the time windows granted by CODA. AEA's data estimated the difference between the scheduled departure time and AEA's assessment of the actual departure time. BAA added that, where AEA attributed delays to 'airports' this included ATC and a number of reasons outside the airport operators' control.

6.136. BAA has kept its own analysis of punctuality since 1995. Its arrival statistic depends on estimating the time of each aircraft's arrival on stand by adding an allowance of five minutes for taxiing time to the landing time. This arrival time is compared with the scheduled arrival-on-stand time. BAA's departure statistic depends on its airfield staff estimating each aircraft's time of departure from the stand. This departure time is compared with scheduled departure-from-stand times. Figure 6.1 shows an analysis of the sum of BAA's arrival and departure delay statistics for Heathrow from May 1995 to March 2002.

FIGURE 6.1

Sum of median arrival and departure delays at Heathrow

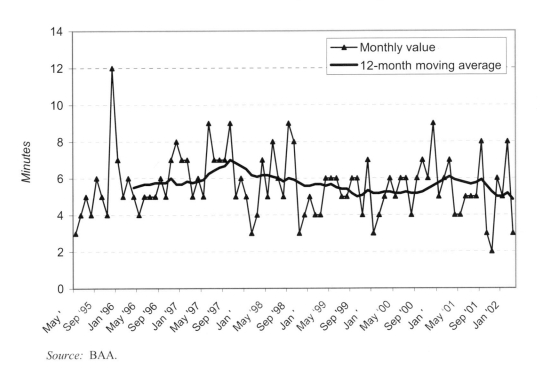

Source: BAA.

6.137. Figure 6.2 shows an analysis of the sum of BAA's arrival and departure delay statistics for Gatwick from May 1995 to March 2002. In both cases, these analyses show considerable fluctuations in the median monthly delay but no evidence of any upward trend. BAA did, however, acknowledge that its statistics were an imperfect measure of delay and did not capture the reasons for delays.

Services to passengers

6.138. BAA measures the quality of service it provides to passengers through its QSM passenger surveys. QSM started in 1990/91 and measures passengers' perceptions of the service they receive in departures, arrivals and retail areas. To prepare the QSM results, about 50,000 passengers are interviewed throughout each year. Interviewers employed by BAA ask them a number of standard questions. BAA employs 185 interviewers and each interview takes five to ten minutes. For each activity, passengers assess the service received on a five-point scale from 'extremely poor' (1) through 'average' (3) to 'excellent' (5). BAA told us that it gave particular consideration to any areas with QSM scores below 3.5 (see paragraph 6.158). Although it represented a score halfway between 'good' and 'average', BAA regarded this score as being the 'threshold of reasonableness'.

FIGURE 6.2

Sum of median arrival and departure delays at Gatwick

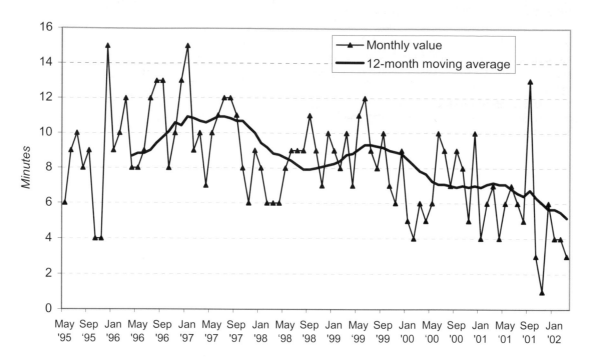

Source: BAA.

6.139. Some airlines questioned whether the passenger samples used in the QSM surveys adequately represented all types of passenger and all times of operation. BAA commented that it would be happy for the QSM to be audited to ensure that it was fit for purpose. It added that as QP was based on comparing future performance with past experience, it was important to maintain a consistent survey methodology. We discuss the methodology BAA uses in its QSM surveys in more detail in Appendix 6.6.

Passenger perception of performance

6.140. Figure 6.3 shows the trends in the QSM scores for passengers' overall satisfaction by airport. In each case, the score is an average of scores for arrivals and departures. Over the six years since the last MMC inquiry, there has been some deterioration in passengers' perception of the airports, particularly at Stansted (although in this case the fall was from a very high initial level of satisfaction). To put these scores in context, they remain close to 4, which is equivalent to 'good'; a score of 3 would be equivalent to 'average'. The decline in passenger perception contrasts with the generally satisfactory performance reported by the MMC in its last report. Then nearly all areas had either shown some improvement over the previous five years or were unchanged. As found by the MMC, Stansted still achieves the highest level of customer satisfaction and Gatwick still scores slightly better than Heathrow.

● *Heathrow*

6.141. Figure 6.4 shows the QSM scores for overall passenger satisfaction with each terminal. The scores are close to 4, which corresponds to 'good'. T4 achieves consistently higher scores than the other terminals. Passengers have in the past assessed T1 and T2 as being less satisfactory than T3 and T4. In recent years, however, passengers' perception of T3 has declined significantly and it has reached a similar QSM score to those of T1 and T2.

FIGURE 6.3

Overall QSM scores: annual average for each airport

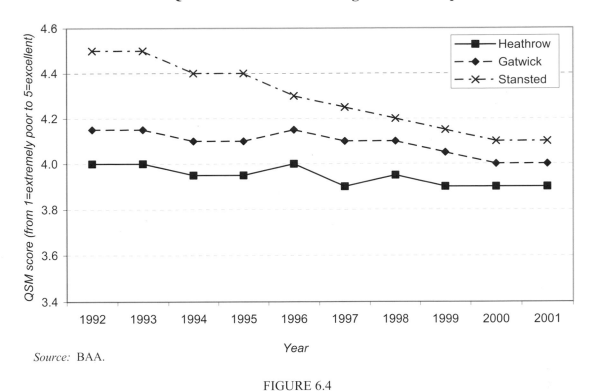

Source: BAA.

FIGURE 6.4

Overall QSM scores: annual average for each terminal at Heathrow

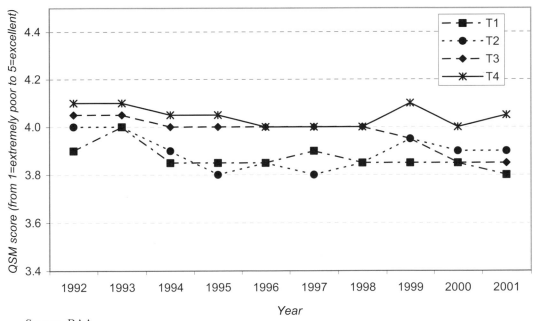

Source: BAA.
Note: In each case, the score is an average of arrivals and departures

6.142. BAA told us that Heathrow's existing terminals and aprons were already operating above their rated capacities and there was heavy airline pressure to accommodate both growth and transfers from Gatwick. The airlines' priority was for BAA to accommodate as much growth as possible whilst preventing service quality from slipping too far. With floor space effectively fixed, short-term growth would inevitably lead to some increase in crowding and congestion.

6.143. The Heathrow AOC told us that BAA had been too focused on its QSM data, rather than its core activities and input from airlines. Passengers were unable to comment on infrastructure and systems outside the public view: these were vital to airlines.

6.144. Figure 6.5 shows the trends in BAA's performance at Heathrow on the QSM elements proposed by the CAA for inclusion in the QP component of the Q term (see paragraph 6.16).[1] The detailed QSM scores for other elements of service are discussed in Appendix 6.6.

FIGURE 6.5

Heathrow QSM scores for possible Q-term elements

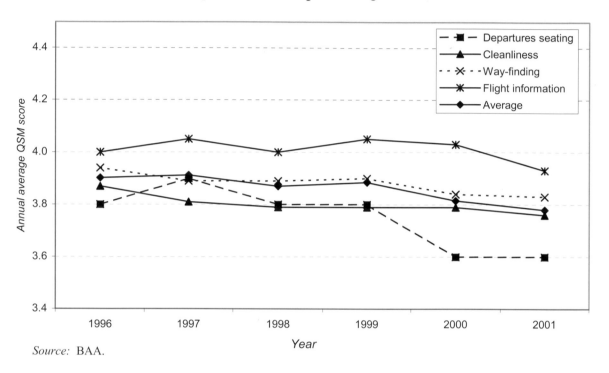

Source: BAA.

● *Gatwick*

6.145. Figure 6.6 shows the QSM scores for overall passenger satisfaction with each terminal. Both terminals currently achieve scores close to 4, which corresponds to 'good'. Their QSM scores are higher than those of T1 to T3 at Heathrow. There was, however, a significant slippage in passengers' perception of them between 1995 and 2000, followed by some improvement in 2001.

---

[1]For Heathrow and Gatwick, Figures 6.5 and 6.7 are based on data supplied by BAA in which each of the QSM scores for the subcomponents making up each element of service was weighted, according to the number of passengers using the particular service, in calculating a combined QSM score for each element. 'Departures seating' in the figures covers airside seating only. The data for 2001 are affected by the events of 11 September: interviewing ceased from 11 September until November 2001.

FIGURE 6.6

Overall QSM scores: annual average for each terminal at Gatwick

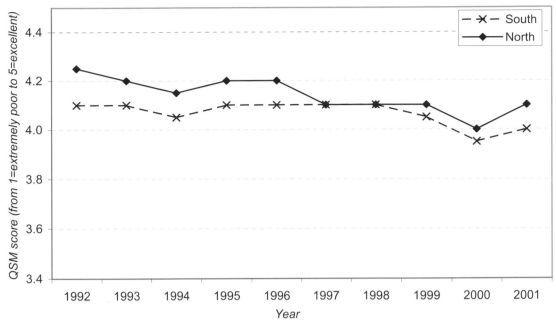

Source: BAA.
Note: In each case, the score is an average of arrivals and departures.

6.146. Figure 6.7 shows the trends in BAA's performance on the QSM elements at Gatwick proposed for inclusion in the Q term. The detailed QSM scores for other elements of service are discussed in Appendix 6.6.

FIGURE 6.7

Gatwick QSM scores for possible Q-term elements

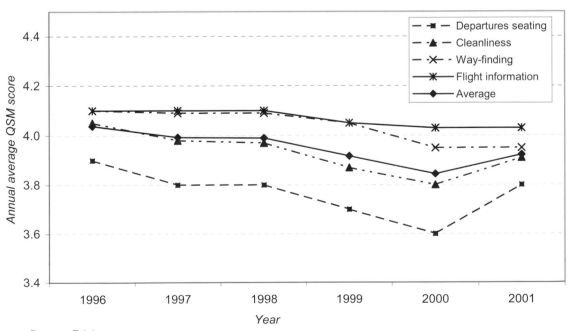

Source: BAA.

• *Stansted*

6.147. Figure 6.3 shows the QSM scores for overall passenger satisfaction with the terminal at Stansted. As we noted in paragraph 6.140, passengers' perception of the airport has declined significantly but it still achieves a higher overall QSM score than any terminal at Heathrow or the South Terminal at Gatwick.

6.148. Figure 6.8 shows the trends in BAA's performance on the QSM elements at Stansted that the CAA proposes for inclusion in the Q term at Heathrow and Gatwick.[1] The detailed QSM scores for other elements of service are discussed in Appendix 6.6.

FIGURE 6.8

Stansted QSM scores for possible Q-term elements

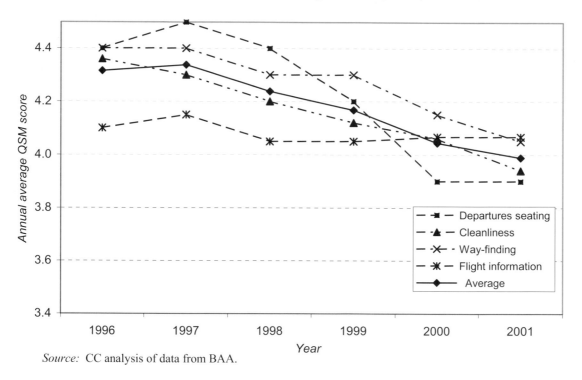

Source: CC analysis of data from BAA.

• *Departure lounge seat availability*

6.149. Figures 6.5 and 6.7 show that passengers' perception of seat availability in the departure lounges at both Heathrow and Gatwick had fallen to 3.6 in 2000 and was barely above what BAA regards as the 'threshold of reasonableness' (3.5). Gatwick, however, achieved a significant improvement on this measure in 2001. Although Figure 6.8 shows that passenger satisfaction has fallen at Stansted, it remains significantly higher than at Heathrow and Gatwick.

• *Cleanliness*

6.150. The CAA's proposed Q-term cleanliness measure is an average of QSM results for the cleanliness of the arrivals concourse, arrivals toilets, departures toilets, departures check-in, and the departures lounge. Cleanliness scores have fallen but at 3.8 (Heathrow) and 3.9 (Gatwick and Stansted) are still above BAA's 'threshold of reasonableness'.

---

[1]As BAA did not supply weighted data for Stansted, we have weighted the QSM scores for each subcomponent equally in calculating a combined QSM score for each element of service.

● *Way-finding*

6.151. The CAA's proposed Q-term measure was an average of QSM scores for arrivals and within-terminal departures (ie excluding inter-terminal transfers). BAA told us that it had initially proposed that inter-terminal transfers should be excluded, as these only involved a small proportion of passengers; it had subsequently suggested their inclusion and would accept either approach.[1] The CAA commented that it agreed with the proposed revision to the measure to include inter-terminal transfers; this was an area of service where way-finding was particularly important. Figures 6.5, 6.7 and 6.8 show that the QSM scores have fallen but are still at acceptable levels.

6.152. Several airlines told us that they were concerned that functional airport signs were insufficiently prominent relative to advertising displays and felt that this could delay passengers' arrival in gaterooms.

6.153. Since the last MMC report, BAA has introduced signs indicating the expected travel time to each gate. It told us that it had adopted a facility guideline for way-finding and had appointed information and way-finding planning consultants to assist with way-finding projects, refurbishment projects and major developments, including T5.

6.154. Information desks in each terminal are provided both by BAA and by the airlines. BAA provides numerous telephone help points and a total of nine BAA-staffed information desks in the seven terminals, normally including a desk in each of the arrivals areas. It also has an information desk in each departure lounge and mobile information assistants.

● *Flight information*

6.155. The score that the CAA proposed should be used in its Q term is an average of QSM scores for ease of finding, ease of reading and ease of understanding the information screens. The flight information QSM scores shown in Figures 6.5, 6.7 and 6.8 correspond to passengers on average rating the service 'good' and are higher than the scores for the other elements. There was, however, some slippage in 2001 at Heathrow.

Performance monitoring

6.156. BAA produces monthly reports on its performance against the SLA targets. It told us that these reports were sent to the secretary of the relevant AOC and shared with each business unit's airlines at their monthly AOC meetings. Discussions then focus on the areas for which targets have not been achieved. The management at each airport arranges meetings about twice a year with AOC representatives to discuss matters relating to SLAs.

6.157. A quarterly report with a commentary highlighting any trends and exceptional performance is sent to the CAA. Summary results are also published in BAA's annual report.

6.158. BAA expects its managers to use the QSM results to benchmark their own area against other operations and airports with the aim of identifying areas of weakness, highlighting areas for action and monitoring the effectiveness of programmes. Quality of service measures, including the relevant QSM scores, are incorporated into senior and middle management incentive schemes and, where appropriate, into concessionaires' and contractors' bonus schemes. BAA told us that particular consideration is given to any areas with QSM scores below 3.5. BAA's managers at all levels monitor their own performance using monthly results.

Planning guidelines

6.159. When it plans new developments, BAA safeguards service standards by applying planning objectives and planning guidance for the facilities required; these include such factors as the space

---

[1] They are included in the data shown in Figures 6.5, 6.7 and 6.8.

allowed per passenger and planned queuing times. BAA told us that the purpose of its planning objectives and related guidance were to help its managers to assess the capacity of existing facilities in relation to the hourly passenger throughput and to identify the appropriate size of future facilities. Space standards could, however, be varied where a case could be made. BAA added that it did not consider the planning objectives to be a contract with, or an immediate obligation to, airlines. Planning standards were never intended for use in operational monitoring. BAA's planning process is considered in Chapter 9.

6.160. At the time of the last MMC inquiry, BAA's planning standards covered matters such as waiting times, space per standing passenger, space per seated passenger and the amount of seating to be provided. They were intended to provide guidance to BAA staff and architects planning new developments.

6.161. The nature of BAA's planning standards and guidance are reviewed from time to time, in conjunction with the airlines, in the light of changing operational practices and the QSM results for existing terminals. A review that took place in 1998 led to BAA's 'Planning Standards, Targets and Guidelines' consultation proposal, issued in November 1999. This said that BAA's planning standards had become disconnected from the way that BAA and its customers ran their businesses. It suggested a number of alternative approaches and recommended a way forward based on replacing its space and time-based planning standards by targets intended to achieve specified levels of passenger satisfaction, ie an extension of the QSM approach.

6.162. This led to a great deal of disagreement and debate. BAA considered the responses to its first consultation before producing significantly revised proposals in June 2000. In these it referred to space and time-based planning objectives, which it intended to retain subject to:

(a) reviewing them in the light of research into passenger expectations and industry needs;

(b) recognizing the need for them to be subject to local circumstances and 'real world checks and balances'; and

(c) initiating joint studies with airlines to understand how planning could deliver good airfield performance and support the drive for punctuality.

The proposed checks and balances included: taking account of the different needs of different airlines; recognizing that strict adherence to standards could result in inappropriate capacity limitations; ensuring that the overall benefits of projects needed to outweigh their overall costs; considering different approaches where required by technical change or process improvements; and recognizing that BAA, the airlines and others were jointly responsible for service performance.

6.163. This approach was formally adopted in February 2001, subject to adding an additional constraint, namely recognizing that Government policy objectives, and the need to obtain planning permission, may affect the eventual development solution. The resulting planning objectives are set out in Appendix 6.7. BAA also discussed certain aspects, including airfield planning, with BA and IATA but concluded that it was not appropriate to create additional planning objectives at that time. A range of internal intranet-based facilities guidelines is now available to provide design guidance tools for various airport facilities. These have replaced the previous suite of 'planning standards', 'planning guidelines, and 'planning calculations' documents.

6.164. BAA told us that at Heathrow and Gatwick it designed new projects in accordance with its planning objectives. Lack of space often meant that they could not easily be achieved; BAA therefore had to consider whether the extra cost would be sensible in each case. BAA said that the actual level of crowding that occurred after a project was completed depended on the throughput that airlines wanted to achieve. Airlines often pressed for higher throughputs than projects were designed to accommodate. Achieving some planning objectives, such as check-in queuing times, was dependent on the airlines and their handling agents. BAA added that, apart from the decision to delay the Pier 6 project (see paragraph 6.81), it always attempted to plan facilities at Gatwick using its planning objectives.

6.165. At Stansted, BAA was pragmatic about the planning objectives, given that the low-fares airlines there were more interested in keeping costs down than in customer service.

6.166. BA has proposed an incentive based on the achievement of planning guidelines in existing terminals (see paragraph 6.43). Planning guidelines are an aid to designing new projects. Given rising expectations, it is unlikely that many buildings built before the standards were devised will satisfy them. A penalty scheme based on planning standards could, therefore, result in regular penalty payments at all terminals that have not been substantially rebuilt in the last few years.

Planned maintenance

6.167. BAA told us that it established its approach to maintaining each type of equipment by analysing the impact of its failure. It said that the first step was to understand how critical each asset was. BAA measured this in terms of safety, service to customers, environmental impact, and the cost to BAA and its business partners. In the light of these assessments, BAA adopted one of five maintenance strategies. It dealt with all but low impact events through one of three preventative strategies; the one chosen for each type of equipment was dependent on its failure characteristics. The three preventative strategies were:

(a) condition-based maintenance: monitoring wear and intervening before failure occurred;

(b) cycle-based maintenance: monitoring time run or cycles completed and making a planned replacement before the historically predicted failure point; and

(c) calendar-based maintenance: replacing components before the historically predicted failure time, according to a schedule.

6.168. The fourth strategy was a 'planned failure strategy'. Under this, it was accepted that a failure might occur but mitigation and reinstatement plans were preplanned, ready to be activated within an appropriate time scale. BAA told us that the planned failure strategy was reserved for equipment whose failure had a very low impact on operations and which did not need to be returned to use immediately.

6.169. The final strategy was a 'reactive strategy'. This involved responding to unplanned failures within reaction times established through the assessment of asset criticality. BAA said that the reactive strategy was only appropriate where a preventative approach had failed. BAA said that, even then, it first reviewed the use of the preventative strategy to reduce the potential for similar reactive faults.

Timing of planned maintenance

6.170. BAA told us that it identified when each type of equipment was needed and, if at all possible, avoided taking it out of service during these periods. Nevertheless, planned maintenance occasionally had to be carried out during the SLA measurement periods for three reasons:

(a) The work required for major repairs took too long to be completed during the night. In such cases, BAA said that it tended to programme the work for quieter parts of the year.

(b) It was not always cost-effective to carry out major maintenance work during the night.

(c) Maintenance carried out at night could be of lower quality than work carried out during the day.

Cargo and mail

6.171. Aviance told us that it had been constrained by inadequate cargo facilities at Gatwick; it had requested purpose-built facilities, which it had been unable to secure (see Chapter 13). We have received no other significant comments on facilities for cargo or mail operators or on the quality of service they receive.

Consultation

6.172. BAA produces six-monthly reports on the main ways that it has consulted airlines at Heathrow. In the May 2002 report, BAA outlined a large number of issues that had been discussed at regular meetings with the AOCs at each terminal and with individual airlines. These issues included capital projects, security, check-in allocation, stand allocation and other operational problems. BAA said that monthly key account meetings were held with airlines. The ATUC met quarterly and discussed issues such as ramp safety and the EC Ground Handling Directive. BAA added that monthly meetings were held with the ground handlers in each terminal to discuss issues associated with the ramp. Various ad hoc teams, forums and steering groups also met regularly to consider such matters as connections and transfer baggage. BAA told us that it adopted a similar approach to consultation at Gatwick and Stansted, although in these cases it did not produce formal reports.

International comparisons

6.173. BAA provided us with the results of international comparative surveys of airports carried out by IATA. These each compared passenger perception of 24 aspects of quality of service each year by interviewing some 90,000 passengers at 48 airports, including Heathrow and Gatwick but not Stansted. BAA commented that it was increasingly concerned about IATA's methodology (see paragraph 6.182).

6.174. The main analysis stressed by IATA is that of 'overall passenger satisfaction'. In 2001, Gatwick ranked 20th (out of 48 airports covered) on this measure and Heathrow came in 30th position. In 1995 the MMC found that, on the slightly different measure then stressed by IATA of 'overall passenger convenience', Gatwick ranked 12th (out of 43 airports covered) and Heathrow came in 26th position.

Comparison with the largest airports in the world

6.175. IATA has collected data for 'overall passenger satisfaction' since 1998. Table 6.13 shows the results since then for the airports handling more than 25 mppa that were included in all three surveys.

TABLE 6.13 IATA Global Airport Monitor: mean scores of largest airports

Airport		Overall satisfaction with airport, all passengers, 1998		Overall satisfaction with airport, all passengers, 1999		Overall satisfaction with airport, all passengers, January 2000 to April 2001	
		Score*	Rank†	Score‡	Rank†	Score§	Rank†
Amsterdam Schiphol	AMS	7.82	2	4.05	2	3.55	4
Atlanta Hartsfield	ATL	7.49	3	3.92	5	3.43	5
Bangkok	BKK	6.87	18	3.60	14	3.31	8
Dallas Fort Worth	DFW	7.46	4	3.85	8	3.17	11
Detroit Wayne County	DTW	6.09	22	3.23	22	2.73	22
Newark	EWR	7.05	14	3.63	13	2.93	18
Rome Fiumicino	FCO	6.73	19	3.54	18	3.18	10
Frankfurt Main	FRA	7.03	15	3.59	15	3.12	14
Hong Kong International	HKG	7.46	4	4.03	3	3.81	2
Houston	IAH	7.34	9	3.88	7	3.24	9
New York JFK	JFK	6.16	21	3.32	21	2.93	18
Los Angeles	LAX	6.71	20	3.39	20	2.90	20
London Gatwick	**LGW**	**7.39**	**7**	**3.79**	**9**	**3.37**	**7**
London Heathrow	**LHR**	**7.09**	**12**	**3.64**	**12**	**3.16**	**12**
Madrid Barajas	MAD	7.08	13	3.55	16	3.03	16
Miami	MIA	6.92	17	3.44	19	3.01	17
Minneapolis/St Paul	MSP	7.43	6	3.97	4	3.70	3
Chicago O'Hare	ORD	7.39	7	3.73	10	3.15	13
Seattle Tacoma	SEA	7.32	10	3.91	6	3.43	5
San Francisco	SFO	7.02	16	3.55	16	2.83	21
Singapore Changi	SIN	8.32	1	4.31	1	4.01	1
Toronto Lester Pearson	YYZ	7.31	11	3.67	11	3.05	15
Average		7.16		3.71		3.23	

Source: IATA.

*Scores from 10 to 0.
†Out of 22.
‡Scores are: 5 = excellent, 4 = good, 3 = fair, 2 = poor and 1 = very poor.
§Scores are: 5 = excellent, 4 = very good, 3 = good, 2 = fair and 1 = poor.

6.176. Owing to the number of changes in IATA's methodology, it is more meaningful to compare trends in the rankings than trends in the absolute scores. Figure 6.9 shows how the rank positions of the large airports have changed over the three periods. It is apparent that Heathrow and Gatwick have retained stable middle-ranking positions, despite dramatic movements in the rankings of some other airports.

6.177. In Appendix 6.8, we set out a comparative analysis of passengers' assessment of the 22 airports in the IATA 2001 survey that handled over 25 mppa. Our analysis of the responses on what IATA considered to be the eight key service elements to passengers shows that Heathrow and Gatwick featured in the top quartile of these airports (ie 6 out of 22) for the following factors:

(a) Heathrow

— Shopping facilities.

(b) Gatwick

— Overall leisure passenger satisfaction.

— Courtesy, helpfulness of airport staff.

— Shopping facilities.

— Ground transportation to/from airport.

— Parking facilities.

FIGURE 6.9

IATA airport monitor, rankings of large airports for overall passenger satisfaction

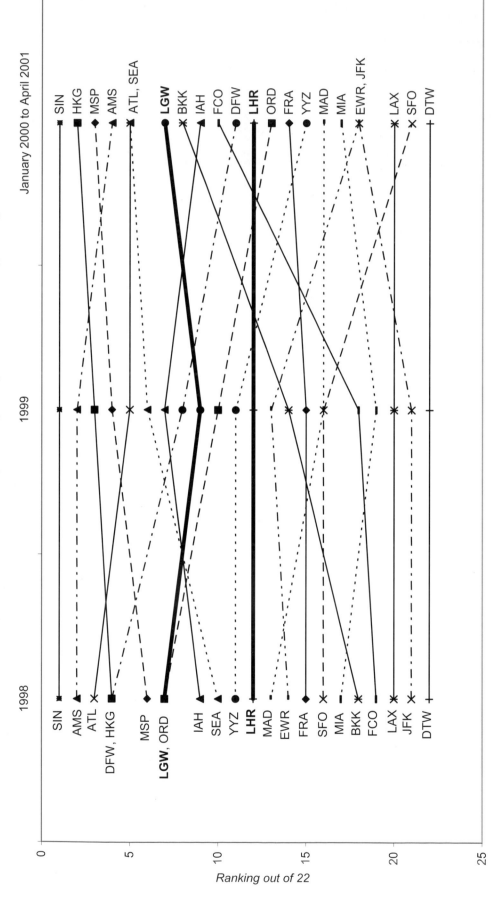

January 2000 to April 2001

Ranking out of 22

Source: CC analysis of IATA data.
Note: The airports corresponding to the codes are set out in Table 6.13.

6.178. Although Gatwick did not feature in the bottom quartile of assessments for any of these key service elements, Heathrow appeared in the bottom quartile for 'comfortable waiting/gate areas'.

6.179. The BAA airports had a middle-ranking performance in the second and third quartiles for the following factors:

(a)   Heathrow

— Ease of finding your way through the airport/signposting.

— Ease of making connections with other flights.

— Courtesy, helpfulness of airport staff.

— Restaurants/eating facilities.

— Ground transportation to/from airport.

— Parking facilities.

(b)   Gatwick

— Ease of finding your way through the airport/signposting.

— Ease of making connections with other flights.

— Restaurants/eating facilities.

— Comfortable waiting/gate areas.

Comparison with main European airports

6.180. Appendix 6.8 also shows a comparative analysis of passenger perception of the main European airports included in the IATA survey. The only factor for which Heathrow featured in the top quartile (ie 6 out of 26) of major European airports was business/executive lounges. Gatwick did not feature in the top quartile of major European airports for any service element.

IATA comments

6.181. In its 2001 report IATA commented that both BAA airports received high ratings for 'shopping facilities' and for 'ground transport to/from airport'. It added that Heathrow's main weakness, compared with the other large airports, was 'comfortable waiting/gate areas'. IATA commented that passengers' perception of Gatwick was favourable and it outperformed Heathrow in all service elements, other than 'shopping facilities'. It added that Gatwick was competitively strong, compared with other large airports, on 'courtesy and helpfulness of airport staff' and 'parking facilities'. Gatwick's main weakness was in 'ease of finding your way through the airport/signposting'.

6.182. BAA commented that IATA's airport monitor results were seriously flawed because of its questionable methodology. It said that, as the surveys were carried out in various ways at different airports and in different years, the results were inconsistent. As examples, BAA cited sample sizes that varied greatly, and were sometimes very small, and biased samples at some airports that excluded short-haul passengers. BAA told us that it was working with ACI to develop an alternative benchmarking survey based on its own QSM system.

7   Operating costs and efficiency

Contents

Introduction

The CAA's position

7.1. The CAA noted in its first submission to the CC that operating costs per passenger at Heathrow appeared to be higher in 2001/02 to 2002/03 than in the immediately preceding years. It went on to say of that airport:

> While the CAA has not undertaken an in depth review of operating efficiencies it does not believe that BAA's current operating cost projections look unreasonable. It is in the nature of price cap regulation that actual performance may well exceed ex ante projections, and the CAA does not see value in attempting to pre-judge the magnitudes of any out-performance or to 'disallow' BAA's forward projections of operating costs. This is particularly justified where prices are, and will continue to be, well below market clearing levels and long run incremental costs.

7.2. The CAA made similar comments as to the other two airports:

(a)   Gatwick

> The CAA's work on benchmarking has not raised any evidence that Gatwick's operating costs are likely to be excessive (although the benchmarking study is not itself robust enough to demonstrate that costs are indeed efficient). Combined with the high level inspection above, the evidence does not suggest a need for a detailed review of Gatwick's operating cost projections. As for Heathrow, attempting to disallow part of the projections to take into account possible out-performance by BAA is unlikely to yield economic benefits where charges remain below market clearing levels.

(b)   Stansted

> It is likely that an RCCB-based price cap would not be tightly binding on the airport, even if a tough line were taken on operating expenditure, capital expenditure and non-regulated revenue. For this reason, and because the CAA prefers to rely on the incentive properties of price cap regulation, the CAA has not undertaken a detailed review of BAA's projections of these variables. However, it notes that in the case of operating expenditure, projections are for operating expenditure per passenger to continue to fall, as would be expected.

7.3. In its conclusions, the CAA said of all three airports: 'In the CAA's view the scope for efficiencies should be achieved through price cap incentives, rather than through attempting to project efficiency gains up front.'

7.4. We nevertheless decided that a detailed review of BAA's costs was appropriate (see paragraph 2.348). In this chapter we consider whether costs in the last quinquennium were at a level compatible with efficient performance, and examine the company's cost projections for the next quinquennium.

BAA's position

7.5. BAA provided us with a great deal of information, both in writing and orally. As well as putting forward arguments on the various elements of what follows in this chapter, the company expressed great concern that there was a need to ensure that manpower costs should not be considered in isolation from quality of service. The company believed that this was particularly true when active consideration was being given to introducing a regime which would penalize the company for failing to meet prescribed quality of service targets.

Performance during Q3

Operating expenditure

7.6. BAA told us that at least half of the London airports' costs were largely uncontrollable. These costs were related to property management (for example, rates, maintenance), imposed as a result of safety and security requirements (for example, police costs, CAA Safety Regulation Group licences, insurance) or were recharged services provided by third parties (for example, utilities).

7.7. BAA said that, where it had a degree of control over non-staff costs, it used regular tendering whenever possible (for example, for utilities, cleaning, maintenance, other goods and services) and added that these processes had been extensively upgraded as part of the Enterprise Programme implementation (see paragraph 7.53). It added that it had carried out a number of change management initiatives targeted at various areas of the airports' business. These are referred to in more detail in paragraph 7.52 et seq.

7.8. BAA said that these developments had all depended on improvements to information technology (IT) systems. In common with many FTSE 100 companies it had had a moratorium on the introduction of new systems over the period 1997/98 to early 2000, because of the need to give priority in developing systems to urgent year 2000 compliance work. BAA said that its first priority was to ensure compliance of business-critical systems such as baggage, airfield lighting, the flight information display system and security.

7.9. Development of new back-office IT products was, therefore, limited to systems analysis and planning process re-engineering; implementation had to be delayed until after 1 January 2000. BAA added that the proposed change management and new systems could not all be introduced at the same time, due to the disruption that this would cause. Implementation had, therefore, been phased over a period from the beginning of 2000. Some aspects of the Enterprise Programme and the Engineering Review (for example, absence level reporting and detailed resource management within Maximo) had therefore only just been implemented. Further details of these initiatives are in paragraph 7.59 et seq.

7.10. Table 7.1 shows the actual cash operating costs of the BAA London airports during Q3 in out-turn prices.

TABLE 7.1 **BAA London airports actual regulatory operating costs**

£ million, out-turn

	1997/98*	1998/99	1999/00	2000/01	2001/02	Total
Staff	196.8	204.1	196.3	199.0	219.7	1,016.0
Police	34.4	36.1	36.5	36.7	38.3	182.0
Rent and rates	57.1	57.6	66.1	71.3	63.5	315.5
Utility costs	72.7	77.4	78.2	78.9	86.9	394.1
Retail costs	20.2	20.7	10.8	14.4	13.1	79.2
Maintenance and equipment	68.9	74.7	75.3	80.4	86.1	385.4
Heathrow Express	7.6	28.6	34.3	37.7	35.8	144.0
Other costs	56.8	73.1	111.2	133.8	148.9	523.8
Total opex before depreciation	514.6	572.3	608.7	652.2	692.3	3,040.0
Capitalized costs included in 'other costs'	13.4	11.5	13.7	8.6	19.6	66.7

Source: BAA.

*Excluding windfall tax.

7.11. Table 7.2 shows the cash operating costs forecast for the BAA London airports at the time of the last MMC report for Q3, converted into out-turn prices. Overall operating costs were £128 million higher than expected by the MMC, largely resulting from the need to handle higher than expected numbers of passengers.

TABLE 7.2 **BAA London airports regulatory operating costs projected in the 1996 MMC report***

£ million, out-turn

	1997/98	1998/99	1999/00	2000/01	2001/02	Total
Staff	192.5	200.3	202.8	208.2	210.3	1,014.0
Police	36.7	37.9	42.4	43.6	47.0	207.6
Rent and rates	62.5	66.4	68.6	71.6	73.4	342.5
Utility costs	77.9	83.6	86.2	89.8	92.0	429.5
Retail costs	17.7	18.0	18.6	19.4	19.9	93.6
Maintenance and equipment	60.4	62.0	63.9	79.1	68.2	333.5
Heathrow Express	5.5	24.7	22.6	23.5	24.1	100.4
Other costs	69.7	71.2	79.5	82.4	88.0	390.8
Total opex before depreciation	522.8	564.2	584.5	617.6	623.0	2,912.0

Source: BAA.

*Constant price forecasts adjusted using RPI.

7.12. The percentage variances between the actual operating costs and those forecast in the MMC report are shown in Table 7.3. Although the total costs were only 4.4 per cent above the level predicted in the MMC report, there were substantial variances in a number of cost items.

TABLE 7.3 **BAA London airports percentage variance in regulatory operating costs**

percentage variance

	1997/98	1998/99	1999/00	2000/01	2001/02	Total
Staff	2.3	1.9	−3.2	−4.4	4.5	0.2
Police	−6.4	−4.8	−14.0	−15.6	−18.5	−12.3
Rent and rates	−8.7	−13.2	−3.7	−0.5	−13.5	−7.9
Utility costs	−6.6	−7.5	−9.3	−12.1	−5.6	−8.2
Retail costs	14.0	14.6	−41.9	−25.8	−33.9	−15.4
Maintenance and equipment	14.2	20.5	17.9	1.7	26.2	15.6
Heathrow Express	38.2	15.7	52.0	60.3	48.8	43.5
Other costs	−18.4	2.5	40.0	62.3	69.1	34.0
Total opex before depreciation	−1.6	1.4	4.1	5.6	11.1	4.4

Source: BAA.

7.13. The largest cost variances were in 'other costs' and the cost of the Heathrow Express. This increase in other costs is largely a reflection of a number of structural changes that BAA has made to its organization. These include the transfer of certain retail, IT, project and procurement functions from the airport companies to the Corporate Office budget. The most significant effect of this was to move projected expenditure from various cost items to recharges from BAA Group, which are included in other costs.

7.14. Heathrow Express costs were above forecast because of higher than expected staffing, track access fees and maintenance costs. Maintenance and equipment costs were above forecast because of higher than expected expenditure on the T1 to T4 baggage tunnel at Heathrow.

7.15. The saving in police costs resulted from the renegotiation of BAA's agreement with the police, which allowed the airports, particularly Heathrow and Gatwick, to be covered by fewer officers. Utilities costs fell following general reductions in electricity prices, which were reflected in BAA's negotiations with suppliers, and cost saving measures. Trends in non-manpower costs are discussed at greater length in paragraph 7.121 et seq.

7.16. Table 7.4 shows the percentage variance in the operating costs analysed by airport. The costs of the Heathrow Express are included in Heathrow Airport's costs.

TABLE 7.4 **Variance in operating costs by airport**

percentage variance

	1997/98	1998/99	1999/00	2000/01	2001/02	Total
Heathrow*	5.1	8.4	8.4	10.4	12.1	9.0
Gatwick	−4.7	−6.3	−5.8	−8.0	−1.1	−5.2
Stansted	−6.1	3.7	16.1	34.2	43.4	19.5
Total opex before depreciation	−1.6	1.4	4.1	5.6	11.1	4.4

Source: BAA.

*Including Heathrow Express.

7.17. The higher than expected costs at Heathrow reflect larger numbers of passengers handled there as well as the increased costs of the Heathrow Express (see Table 7.3). Higher costs at Stansted were due to greater than forecast passenger numbers.

Costs per passenger

7.18. Table 7.5 shows the variances between the actual cash operating costs and those projected at the time of the last MMC report expressed as costs per passenger.

TABLE 7.5 **Variances expressed in terms of costs per passenger**

£ per passenger, out-turn prices

Variance	1997/98	1998/99	1999/00	2000/01	2001/02	Total
Staff	−0.01	−0.11	−0.26	−0.36	−0.09	−0.17
Police	−0.04	−0.05	−0.10	−0.12	−0.12	−0.09
Rent and rates	−0.08	−0.14	−0.09	−0.10	−0.16	−0.11
Utility costs	−0.08	−0.13	−0.16	−0.22	−0.13	−0.14
Retail costs	0.02	0.01	−0.09	−0.07	−0.08	−0.04
Maintenance and equipment	0.08	0.08	0.05	−0.09	0.11	0.04
Heathrow Express	0.02	0.02	0.09	0.10	0.09	0.07
Other costs	−0.16	−0.03	0.23	0.36	0.50	0.20
Total opex before depreciation	−0.24	−0.34	−0.33	−0.51	0.13	−0.25

Source: BAA.

7.19. Table 7.5 shows that the effect of the higher than expected numbers of passengers more than outweighed the increase in the airports' costs. The effect of BAA's internal reorganization (see paragraph 7.140) resulted in a transfer of costs from various headings to other costs.

Projected operating expenditure for Q4

7.20. BAA told us that exogenous events were driving some costs up. Most notable of these were additional security staffing, police and insurance costs following the events of 11 September 2001. BAA added that the slower projected growth in passenger numbers reduced the potential for efficiency savings. Table 7.6 shows the total projected cash operating costs for BAA's London airports in Q4 in real prices. We consider trends in individual cost items in detail in paragraph 7.121 et seq.

TABLE 7.6 **BAA's total projected operating costs at Heathrow, Gatwick and Stansted**

	2002/03	2003/04	2004/05	2005/06	2006/07	2007/08	£ million, September 2002 prices Total Q4*	% change 2002/03– 2007/08
Staff	218.3	227.9	229.9	235.9	243.2	248.1	1,184.9	13.6
Police	44.3	45.7	52.1	53.4	54.9	55.9	261.9	26.1
Rents	6.0	6.1	5.5	10.0	10.0	10.0	41.8	68.7
Rates	67.6	68.8	69.9	72.6	76.0	80.6	368.0	19.3
Utility costs	65.9	68.6	70.0	74.3	76.5	77.7	367.1	17.9
Maintenance and equipment								
Other costs				*Figures omitted. See note on page iv.*				
Total								

Source: BAA.

*2003/04 to 2007/08.

Heathrow

7.21. Table 7.7 shows BAA's projections of the cash operating costs at Heathrow in Q4 in real prices.

TABLE 7.7 **BAA's projected operating costs at Heathrow**

	2002/03	2003/04	2004/05	2005/06	2006/07	2007/08	£ million, September 2002 prices Total Q4*	% change 2002/03– 2007/08
Staff	130.7	135.9	136.9	139.0	141.1	143.2	696.0	9.5
Police	26.4	27.5	33.9	34.4	34.9	35.4	166.1	33.9
Rents	5.2	5.5	4.7	9.3	9.3	9.3	38.0	78.3
Rates	46.1	46.4	46.4	48.8	51.2	54.1	246.9	17.4
Utility costs	42.0	43.5	43.6	45.6	46.4	46.5	225.6	10.7
Maintenance and equipment								
Other costs				*Figures omitted. See note on page iv.*				
Total								

Source: BAA.

*2003/04 to 2007/08.

7.22. BAA told us that many of the projected cost increases at Heathrow were associated with the planned capital programme. Rates and maintenance costs were, for example, driven by forecast increases in the buildings and equipment in use.

7.23. Table 7.8 shows the same data expressed in terms of costs per passenger.

TABLE 7.8 **BAA's projected operating costs per passenger at Heathrow**

	2002/03	2003/04	2004/05	2005/06	2006/07	2007/08	% change 2002/03– 2007/08
Staff	2.07	2.03	1.98	1.99	2.01	2.03	−2.0
Police	0.42	0.41	0.49	0.49	0.50	0.50	19.8
Rents	0.08	0.08	0.07	0.13	0.13	0.13	59.5
Rates	0.73	0.69	0.67	0.70	0.73	0.77	5.0
Utility costs	0.66	0.65	0.63	0.65	0.66	0.66	−0.9
Maintenance and equipment							
Other costs			*Figures omitted. See note on page iv.*				
Total							

£ per passenger, September 2002 prices

Source: BAA.

7.24. BAA told us that the complexity of the Heathrow site was a significant factor in its higher projected unit costs compared with Gatwick and Stansted. This particularly affected costs associated with surface access and the inter-terminal baggage transfer process. The heavily congested CTA required continuous management by a ground operations team, costing about £1.4 million a year, to maintain traffic flows. Contracts for inter-terminal passenger and baggage connections, which cost around £5 million a year, had no equivalent at the other airports.

7.25. Some additional activities at Heathrow produced compensating extra income streams. These activities included the transfer baggage system, whose £20.6 million a year cost was recharged to airlines, and extra advertising management.

Gatwick

7.26. Table 7.9 shows BAA's projections of the cash operating costs at Gatwick in Q4 in real prices.

TABLE 7.9 **BAA's projected operating costs at Gatwick**

						£ million, September 2002 prices		% change 2002/03–
	2002/03	2003/04	2004/05	2005/06	2006/07	2007/08	Total Q4*	2007/08
Staff	60.0	63.1	63.5	66.4	69.8	71.1	333.7	18.4
Police	13.6	13.7	13.7	14.3	15.0	15.3	71.9	12.4
Rents	0.2	0.2	0.2	0.2	0.2	0.2	1.2	8.3
Rates	15.3	15.6	16.6	16.7	17.1	18.1	84.1	18.5
Utility costs	17.2	17.6	18.0	18.9	20.0	20.6	95.1	20.0
Maintenance and equipment								
Other costs				*Figures omitted. See note on page iv.*				
Total								

Source: BAA.

*2003/04 to 2007/08.

7.27. Table 7.10 shows the same data expressed in terms of costs per passenger.

TABLE 7.10 **BAA's projected operating costs per passenger at Gatwick**

					£ per passenger, September 2002 prices		% change 2002/03–
	2002/03	2003/04	2004/05	2005/06	2006/07	2007/08	2007/08
Staff	2.11	2.02	1.88	1.84	1.81	1.79	−15.3
Police	0.48	0.44	0.40	0.40	0.39	0.39	−19.6
Rents	0.01	0.01	0.01	0.01	0.01	0.01	−22.5
Rates	0.54	0.50	0.49	0.46	0.44	0.46	−15.3
Utility costs	0.61	0.56	0.53	0.53	0.52	0.52	−14.2
Maintenance and equipment							
Other costs			*Figures omitted. See note on page iv.*				
Total							

Source: BAA.

7.28. BAA told us that unit operating costs at Gatwick had fallen, mainly as a result of increased passenger numbers reducing the level of fixed costs per passenger. In future, the reduction in unit costs would taper off, as the growth in passenger numbers was expected to be slower. BAA expected that Gatwick would struggle to regain the 2001/02 number of passengers by 2003/04.

7.29. BAA added that fixed costs were expected to increase at Gatwick as a result of greater security, police and insurance costs. Process improvements, such as the new roster management system (RMS), would compensate for some of these increases.

Stansted

7.30. Table 7.11 shows BAA's projections of the cash operating costs at Stansted in Q4 in real prices.

TABLE 7.11 **BAA's projected operating costs at Stansted**

	2002/03	2003/04	2004/05	2005/06	2006/07	2007/08	Total Q4*	£ million, September 2002 prices % change 2002/03– 2007/08
Staff	27.6	28.9	29.5	30.6	32.3	33.8	155.2	22.4
Police	4.3	4.5	4.5	4.7	5.0	5.2	23.9	21.1
Rents	0.5	0.4	0.6	0.6	0.6	0.6	2.6	1.5
Rates	6.2	6.8	6.8	7.2	7.7	8.4	37.0	35.4
Utility costs	6.8	7.4	8.4	9.8	10.2	10.6	46.3	56.4
Maintenance and equipment								
Other costs				Figures omitted. See note on page iv.				
Total								

Source: BAA.

*2003/04 to 2007/08.

7.31. Table 7.12 shows the same data expressed in terms of costs per passenger.

TABLE 7.12 **BAA's projected operating costs per passenger at Stansted**

	2002/03	2003/04	2004/05	2005/06	2006/07	2007/08	£ per passenger, September 2002 prices % change 2002/03– 2007/08
Staff	1.79	1.77	1.72	1.70	1.67	1.65	−7.7
Police	0.28	0.28	0.27	0.26	0.26	0.25	−8.8
Rents	0.04	0.03	0.03	0.03	0.03	0.03	−23.5
Rates	0.40	0.42	0.40	0.40	0.40	0.41	2.1
Utility costs	0.44	0.45	0.49	0.54	0.53	0.52	17.9
Maintenance and equipment							
Other costs			Figures omitted. See note on page iv.				
Total							

Source: BAA.

7.32. BAA commented that Stansted's cost base was largely fixed. Many costs, such as rates, had remained steady or fallen in real terms. Unit costs had consequently fallen sharply in earlier years when Stansted's passenger numbers grew strongly. BAA added that, although utility costs had grown, this cost increase was balanced by a corresponding increase in income. In future, Stansted's high growth rate would slow, reducing the potential for reductions in unit costs. BAA said that it expected Stansted's unit costs to reduce steadily and eventually converge with those of Gatwick.

Manpower costs and efficiency

7.33. Manpower costs represent the largest single cost item in BAA's opex, and the most controllable. This part of the chapter concerns the manpower costs and efficiency of the workforce at each of the London airports. It covers the following ground:

(a) an overview of the cost of manpower as detailed in annual reports and other evidence supplied by BAA;

(b) manpower planning arrangements and efficiency;

(c) pay, overtime and shiftworking;

(d) absence and labour turnover;

(e) trade union membership;

(f) a comparison between out-turns and forecasts made at the last review; and

(g) BAA's projections for the next quinquennium.

7.34. We noted from BAA's annual reports that none of the three airport companies under review employed any staff: all staff were directly employed by BAA.

Overview

7.35. Details of the numbers of staff employed at each location are in Appendix 7.1. Data supplied to us by BAA for the three London airports show that total staff costs of their employees in 2001/02 amounted to £219.7 million, representing 33.5 per cent of all opex excluding depreciation and Heathrow Express, at an average cost per staff member employed of £38,049 a year. Details for each airport are in Table 7.13.

TABLE 7.13 **Operating costs (excluding depreciation and Heathrow Express), 2001/02**

	Heathrow	Gatwick	Stansted	Total
Total costs (£'000)	404,766	174,685	80,318	659,769
Staff costs (£'000)	131,055	62,585	26,044	219,684
Staff costs as % of total	32.4	35.8	32.4	33.3
Average staff cost (£pa)	39,178	36,371	36,794	38,049

Source: BAA.

7.36. Staff costs represented about 37 per cent of airports' direct costs (before depreciation and inter-company charges).

7.37. BAA told us that corporate costs represented a further addition to operating costs. Details are shown in Table 7.14.

TABLE 7.14 **Corporate staff numbers and costs**

	2002/03	2003/04	2004/05	2005/06	2006/07	2007/08
Staff numbers	762	776	775	775	775	775
Staff costs (£'000)	50,506	50,548	50,684	51,445	52,216	53,000

Source: BAA.

7.38. About one-third of BAA's engineering work was contracted out. Contracting out varied between airports, and covered areas such as heating and ventilating, and air conditioning. Airfield activities were kept in-house.

7.39. There has been little recent change in the level of outsourcing. BAA said that over the last five years outsourcing had accounted for 13.6 jobs lost at Heathrow (4 in motor transport and 9.6 occupational health roles), 39.6 at Gatwick (36 porters and mailroom staff, and 3.6 occupational health positions) and 1.8 occupational health staff at Stansted.

Productivity measures

7.40. During the 1996 inquiry, BAA provided us with a list of 'Standard Productivity Indicators' and the variables from which they were calculated. They were:

(a) *Passengers per man-year*

Total fixed wing terminal passengers in the period.

Average full-time equivalent employees during the period plus overtime worked during the period (converted as 2,080 overtime hours = 1 full-time employee).

(b) *Passengers per employee*

Total fixed wing terminal passengers in the period.

Average full-time equivalent employees in the period (permanent, temporary, contract and agency, casual staff including trainees and YTS.

(c) *Pay-related costs per passenger*

Pay-related costs excluding terminal payments and pension top-up in the period.

(d) *Total staff costs per passenger*

Total staff costs excluding terminal payments and pension top-up in the period.

Each man-year represents 2,080 hours of overtime working, the aggregated number of all overtime hours worked being divided by 52 to reduce the number to a weekly figure, and then by 40 to reduce it to the relevant number of man-years.

7.41. Figures for passengers per man-year and passengers per employee are shown in Table 7.15. The figures in the table relating to overtime represent the difference between the average number of staff employed and the number of man-years worked.

7.42. The data in Table 7.15 shows that the ratio of passengers per employee is reduced by over 9 per cent in each year when overtime working is taken into account.

7.43. Table 7.16 gives details over the past five years of pay-related costs per passenger. It shows that employee numbers tend to increase at a slower rate than numbers of passengers (indeed, at both Heathrow and Gatwick, staff numbers fell as passenger volumes increased, although at Gatwick, numbers had previously increased sharply) thereby reducing pay-related costs per passenger. The table also demonstrates how the downturn in passenger volumes following the events of 11 September 2001 led to a marked upturn in pay-related costs per passenger. BAA told us that the period immediately following 11 September 2001 was marked by increased security arrangements and an unpredictable airline response. A programme of staff redundancies would have been counter-productive and jeopardize public safety.

TABLE 7.15 **Passengers, employees and man-years**

	passengers/average staff numbers (FTE)				
	1997/98	1998/99	1999/00	2000/01	2001/02
Heathrow					
Passengers ('000)	58,134	61,009	62,270	64,310	60,363
FTE average staff*	3,703	3,614	3,409	3,317	3,345
Passengers/employee					
('000)	15.7	16.9	18.3	19.4	18.0
Man-years total	4,054	3,972	3,761	3,670	3,697
Passengers/man-years					
('000)	14.3	15.4	16.6	17.5	16.3
Man-years overtime	351.0	357.5	351.3	353.9	351.9
Gatwick					
Passengers ('000)	27,325	29,549	30,426	32,131	30,490
FTE average staff*	1,890	1,831	1,766	1,749	1,721
Passengers/employee					
('000)	14.5	16.1	17.2	18.4	17.7
Man-years total	2,059	1,993	1,916	1,901	1,859
Passengers/man-years					
('000)	13.3	14.8	15.9	16.9	16.4
Man-years overtime	168.4	161.3	149.6	151.7	138.5
Stansted					
Passengers ('000)	5,471	7,408	9,902	12,260	14,084
FTE average staff*	568	615	660	680	708
Passengers/employee					
('000)	9.6	12.0	15.0	18.0	19.9
Man-yrs total	633	681	728	751	790
Passengers/man-years					
('000s)	8.6	10.9	13.6	16.3	17.8
Man-yrs overtime	64.3	65.7	68.1	71.3	82.1
All					
Passengers ('000)	90,930	97,966	102,598	108,700	104,937
FTE average staff*	6,161	6,061	5,835	5,745	5,774
Passengers/employee					
('000)	14.8	16.2	17.6	18.9	18.2
Man-years total	6,745	6,645	6,404	6,322	6,346
Passengers/man-years					
('000)	13.5	14.7	16.0	17.2	16.5
Man-years overtime	583.8	584.5	569.0	576.9	572.6

Source: BAA.

*Using actual historical manning numbers.

TABLE 7.16 **Pay-related costs per passenger**

					£, 2002/03 prices	
	1996/97	1997/98	1998/99	1999/00	2000/01	2001/02
All	2.29	2.28	2.13	1.94	1.81	2.05
Heathrow	2.14	2.19	2.08	1.89	1.81	2.13
Gatwick	2.32	2.23	2.07	1.94	1.80	2.01
Stansted	3.79	3.46	2.81	2.23	1.87	1.80

Source: BAA.

7.44. Total staff costs per passenger are shown in Table 7.17. Staff costs include all pay-related costs together with sundry other costs relating to training, recruitment, relocation and so on.

TABLE 7.17 **Total staff costs per passenger**

£, 2002/03 prices

	1996/97	1997/98	1998/99	1999/00	2000/01	2001/02
All	2.42	2.42	2.25	2.04	1.89	2.13
Heathrow	2.28	2.31	2.20	1.98	1.88	2.21
Gatwick	2.44	2.37	2.19	2.05	1.88	2.09
Stansted	4.05	3.72	2.98	2.36	1.98	1.88

Source: BAA.

7.45. Table 7.16 shows that Stansted's total staff costs per passenger were greater than those of Gatwick and Heathrow up to 2000/01 but were falling more rapidly. This reflects the fact that the large numbers of staff in fixed posts, being mainly in overhead functions, were relatively unaffected by increasing passenger volumes, and that any such increases could be handled with little increase in staff overall. Figures for 2001/02 indicate a substantial change, with Stansted's staff costs per passenger continuing to fall, but those at Heathrow and Gatwick rising.

7.46. Asked to comment on the latter point, BAA said that Stansted's more favourable ratios in 2001/02 arose from the differing extents to which airports had been affected by the events and consequences of 11 September. Stansted's traffic continued to grow, albeit at a slower rate, Gatwick's slumped but was forecast to recover, and Heathrow's had fallen moderately but recovered. By 2007/08 staff costs per passenger at Gatwick and Stansted would be comparable, with Heathrow's productivity lower as it dealt with the introduction of T5.

Manpower planning arrangements

7.47. Each department at each airport prepares an annual plan covering its staff needs for the coming year, the biggest factor being traffic variability. Various elements contribute to the plans, such as BAA's system of tactical forecasting, which seeks to match security staff to passenger flows. Flight scheduling is broken down to identify daily forecast figures, initially on a monthly basis and then further refined to an hour-by-hour basis. Operational research techniques are used on a regular basis, particularly as to security staff, for which the operational research team looks at, for example, optimum flow levels, bag search times, and the number of bags per passenger. A combination of such techniques produces an annual output total, broken down into months. The figures are then converted into man-years, both permanent and seasonal. The ratios of such types of employees change according to seasonal variations.

7.48. A description of this process is at Appendix 7.2, along with information about how BAA arranges for manning levels to match workloads in the days leading up to the expected demand.

7.49. BAA said that manpower plans for years 2 and 3 of the business plan were not as refined as those for year 1, and were based mainly on growth factors. The plans take into account labour turnover and absence. BAA said that the business planning process was subject to challenge and review at both local and corporate levels. Manpower was always a particular focus of these reviews. In the current year, local business plans were the subject of formal discussion between the local boards and the Deputy Chief Executive, the Group Services Director (who has overall responsibility for HR) and other members of the Executive. BAA said that the reviews provided a good opportunity to discuss relative manpower efficiencies between airports, with passengers per man-year being a key indicator.

7.50. We noted that BA had announced on 13 February 2002, in its *Future Size and Shape* review, that it would be transferring routes from Gatwick to Heathrow to the extent that 'by summer 2003, [BA's] Gatwick capacity will have reduced by a total of 60 per cent since summer 1999'. We asked BAA what difference this would make to passenger volumes at the two airports; how it affected each airport's manpower plans; and, in relation to Gatwick, to what extent easyJet would fill the gap.

7.51. In reply, BAA told us that its passenger forecasts in March 2002 took these factors into account; but that the impact would not be known until changes in load factors of BA and easyJet services became apparent. BAA said that there were considerable doubts over the timing of forecast market recovery at Gatwick: BA's strategic intentions at the airport were still unknown, charter operators had consolidated at Gatwick but cut capacity there by 20 per cent for summer 2002, and easyJet was performing well but in the context of smaller aircraft.

Efficiency reviews

7.52. BAA undertakes regular reviews of its efficiency and effectiveness as part of its philosophy of continuous improvement. The principal programmes to have emerged from this in the last five years were:

(a) the Enterprise programme;

(b) the Organisation Effectiveness Model (OEM);

(c) the core process review;

(d) the RMS; and

(e) CIPP in relation to capital investment (see paragraph 9.16).

7.53. The Enterprise programme stemmed from proposals put to the board in April 1997 for a system which would replace various IT systems that were ageing, expensive to maintain, and had been purchased and personalized in a haphazard way, which led to inefficiencies. The proposal to the board commented that whilst these systems provided endless data, it was often to the exclusion of useful management information.

7.54. The proposed system was seen as an opportunity to bring radical change to processes, jobs, working methods and organizational structures through the re-engineering of processes across the airports group. The system is based on computerization of BAA's business support areas including finance, human resources, procurement and project accounting. The project was initially introduced at Gatwick and BAA's Corporate Office in August 2000, and in a planned six-month time span it was then introduced at Heathrow and BAA's Scottish airports. It has now been introduced at all BAA's UK airports. The project, when completed, will have cost some £60 million to £80 million.

7.55. BAA claimed that the OEM was, in effect, a template which would allow it to bring about effective change, and which would ensure that staff understood the company's corporate vision. It said that through systematic implementation of all elements of the model, change would be sustained and benefits achieved.

7.56. The CPR was initiated in 2001 with the aims of identifying core processes in arrivals, departures, connections, baggage and aircraft turnaround; and considering levels of service, responsibility for them, performance measurement and how prospective improvements could be achieved.

7.57. At the time of our inquiry, BAA was mid-way through implementation of the RMS, the primary objective of which was to replace the current forecasting and staff management systems with an integrated and uniform system for security and passenger services staff at all BAA south-east airports. Details are in Appendix 7.3.

7.58. The two-phase project will have cost about £6.75 million when completed. Approval to proceed with the second phase was given in June 2002. BAA told us that introduction of the RMS would lead to better rostering, which would reduce overtime working. BAA said that this was allowed for in its financial model.

Maximo

7.59. Maximo is a maintenance management system which, at the time of our 1996 report, was being trialled at Gatwick and at Heathrow's T3. It is capable of recording engineers' tasks and staff time, and BAA was exploring the use of data from Maximo for short- and medium-term manpower planning.

7.60. In a discussion during the current reference of performance yardsticks, BAA said that the Maximo system recorded engineers' job times, attendance, and unproductive time, among other things. BAA said that it had found it had not used the full functionality of the system. As such, there were no trend measures of engineers' productivity. Maximo was being used increasingly to record staff skills, allocate work to individuals, register faults and plan maintenance. The system was beginning to be used to look at the percentage of time which engineers spent 'on tools', and was going to be used to monitor the survival rate of particular repairs and maintenance. About half of all maintenance work was planned under the Maximo system, as distinct from being reactive.

7.61. BAA provided us with copies of the latest Maximo reports for each airport but acknowledged that the quality of data recording at this stage was such that the reports were of limited use as a means of determining efficiency. BAA said that the data was in a fairly detailed but crude format. BAA told us that there were issues around the recording of actual versus scheduled time to perform tasks, and that the processes were quite new, with mistakes being made in booked times. There were also industrial relations issues, where some staff were over-booking time because of grievances over the time scheduled for blocks of work. BAA said that issues of this kind were not untypical in a significant change management programme.

7.62. BAA intended using Maximo as part of a pay system for engineers in which there would be rewards for skills. Negotiations had progressed to a point where the trade unions were balloting their members about acceptance of BAA's proposals.

Tactical forecasting

7.63. BAA sought to match workforce to workload by short-term forecasting, RMS, and planned maintenance. It was less appropriate to apply these tools to the fire service, terminal operations, airfield operations and overhead functions, as these areas were less directly related to passenger numbers.

Flexibility

7.64. 76 per cent of BAA's workforce work shifts. Shift cover at the airports is predominantly provided by employees working a two-shift system, covering a 16-hour period when the bulk of passenger traffic might be expected. Some departments are rostered continuously over 24 hours. Double-day shift working in BAA attracts a basic pay enhancement of 17.4 per cent, whilst continuous shift working attracts an enhancement of 20.3 per cent.

7.65. Many of the operational hours at airports were 'unsocial', and BAA sought to spread these hours among rostered full-time staff rather than to recruit part-time workers. Table 7.18 shows the numbers of part-time staff employed at the airports. BAA said that the ability to attract part-time staff was a function of the hours and the labour market at a particular location. The company said that it may, thus, not be appropriate to recruit part-time staff in some areas, for example Heathrow.

TABLE 7.18 **Part-time staff**

	Heathrow	Gatwick	Stansted
Part-time staff	336	167	189
Proportion of work-force (%)	10.6	10.2	30.8

Source: BAA.

7.66. Data in *Labour Market Trends* (September 2002) showed that in the period April to June 2002 there was an average of 16.8 million full-time workers in employment, compared with 6.3 million part-time workers.

7.67. BAA told us that virtually all part-time staff at Gatwick worked in Terminals and Security, and worked a rotational shift pattern which included unsocial hours. At Stansted, 179 part-time staff worked in Terminals and Security, with ten on non-operational work. A number of staff worked split shifts, working four hours in the morning and four in the evening to meet peak requirements. Job-sharing and working from home in appropriate cases were also becoming features of BAA's employment practices.

7.68. BAA told us that it had a contractual right to move staff between terminals and that this right was increasingly being invoked. It said that there was little resistance to this, which made manpower planning easier. BAA said that it was 'only circumspect about moving staff between terminals for purely pragmatic reasons (for example, the time wasted in doing so)'.

7.69. BAA said that there was low unemployment around its airports, and it had introduced arrangements under which people looking for a second income, older people, and those from outside local catchment areas, could work fixed hours with the same working times each shift. These shifts do not attract premium payments. Some 4 per cent of Stansted's security staff were employed on these terms.

Pay

Basic rates of pay and hours of work

7.70. The contractual basic hours for full-time employees are 40 hours a week, inclusive of meal breaks. Hours of full-time shiftworkers also average 40 a week over the shift cycle.

7.71. In its 1996 review, the MMC demonstrated that certain BAA pay rates were higher than justified by comparison with like grades elsewhere. The report noted BAA's belief that its pay rates were competitive, but not excessive.

7.72. In evidence to us in the current inquiry, BAA said that, by 1997, it had been clear from internal indicators and external market comparators, that pay rates were substantially higher than the market for operative, clerical and junior administrative posts. It undertook a comprehensive review of pay structures and rates at the three airports, which aimed to achieve alignment with local market conditions.

7.73. It introduced separate, lower pay bands for new employees. Existing staff retained previously obtained pay arrangements. The difference between the mid-points of the old and new pay scales varied according to job by between 5 and 19 per cent. For security staff and other operatives the differences were about 13 per cent.

7.74. At the time of our inquiry, 37 per cent of BAA's employees at Heathrow were on the new rates of pay, with 32 per cent at Gatwick and 48 per cent at Stansted. With the inclusion of 1,174 firemen and managerial grades, who were on pay rates which were broadly market-related and to whom new entrant pay scales did not apply, and some 430 engineering technicians who were employed on 'old' pay scales which were not significantly different from the current market norm, the percentage of staff on market-related pay scales was 56.4 per cent. The remaining 2,950 staff were on old pay rates.

7.75. BAA expected that there would be 3 per cent wastage from employees on the old pay scales in 2002/03. On that basis the overall figure on market-related pay scales would increase to 60 per cent by 2003. The proportion was expected to increase further as new starters replaced staff leaving under normal wastage and on early retirement, although the rate of attrition was not expected to be substantial.

7.76. Pay matters are discussed in more detail at Appendix 7.4.

Overtime pay and controls

7.77. Overtime working in BAA averaged four hours per employee per week, equating to 572.7 man-years. This level of overtime working was 53.8 per cent above the national average for all employees as shown in the New Earnings Survey (NES), but the proportion of manual workers in BAA is substantially greater than that in the NES.

7.78. BAA's records do not distinguish between manual and non-manual workers, but the company told us that its engineering, security, terminal operations and airfield operations staff were all fulfilling manual functions. Together they constituted some 89 per cent of the workforce at Heathrow, 83 per cent at Gatwick and 77 per cent at Stansted, whereas in the NES the ratio of manual to non-manual workers was about 3:4. For further analysis, see Appendix 7.4.

7.79. Overtime pay in BAA equated to some 15 per cent of basic pay. BAA told us that 33 per cent of overtime worked at Heathrow was at the weekend rate of time-and-three-quarters. The corresponding figures for Gatwick and Stansted were 31 per cent and 29 per cent respectively. It said that over the years it had moved away from patterns of shift work which manned the airports continuously. BAA said that it had now had matched its shift rostering arrangements to passenger flows, but in consequence some extra overtime was necessary to cover the busiest periods when insufficient staff were rostered. The company believed that its degree of overtime working was not out of line, either with industry generally, or with other employers in the airport environment. Nevertheless, BAA felt that there was room to reduce overtime levels, and that would come from revised rostering arrangements which it was introducing. It had built the reductions, which were relatively small, into its financial model.

Pension costs

7.80. The accounts of the airport companies include charges from BAA for pension fund contributions. Between 1997/98 and 2000/01 the aggregate charges in the accounts of the three airport companies represented around 3 per cent of total salary costs, but in 2001/02 this rose to 18 per cent. In the projections made at the time of the 1996 MMC report, BAA had included provision, within operating costs, for contributions at 14 per cent of eligible pay (a lower percentage of total pay, as not all staff remuneration is pensionable). In practice a pension holiday has applied throughout Q3: the BAA group made no payments to its defined benefit fund in the period. We discussed with BAA how pension contributions should be treated in a regulatory environment, since payments made to a scheme could fluctuate considerably. In this case provision had been made in the determination of charges for Q3 at a funding rate of 14 per cent, whereas actual contributions had been at a much lower rate. Details of the pension fund performance and of the relevant fund valuations are included in Appendix 7.5.

7.81. BAA told us that the previous surplus was now substantially reduced, as a result of recent poor performance in stock markets and some increase in benefits. It therefore proposed a long-term funding rate of 22 per cent of eligible pay for Q4. We put to BAA an estimate of what the projected pension-funding rate for Q4 would have been if contributions had been made in Q3 at the rate allowed for when airport charges were set for the quinquennium, and taking account of the remaining estimated pension surplus. This showed a notional funding rate of 15.4 per cent for Q4.

Absence

7.82. BAA said that its historical absence data was patchy and unreliable, and that it had no consistent detailed reports prior to the introduction of the Enterprise system (see paragraph 7.53). BAA said that in the early stages the Enterprise system was not providing reliable absence data. It had found this a complex issue to resolve, but was now satisfied that it had complete and reliable absence data from April 2002.

7.83. It provided annualized data for 2002/03 based on absence in April and May 2002, multiplied by six. This showed that staff at Gatwick were absent on 11.9 days in the year, at Heathrow 11.7, and at Stansted 9.0. An examination of monthly absence statistics from April 1995 to June 2000 showed that, in order to annualize data for April and May, it was necessary to multiply data for those months by an average of 6.7. This produced annualized absence data of 13.1 days per year per employee at Heathrow, 13.3 days at Gatwick and 10.1 days at Stansted.

7.84. BAA said that its security staff, which constituted 40 per cent of the airports' workforce, were subject to working conditions which were more likely to induce illness than such conditions elsewhere. The company referred to the repetitive processes involved, the stress caused by having to undertake continual checking on a basis which did not allow mistakes to occur, the bending and lifting of luggage, the fact that the employees were standing throughout their shifts, and through repeated contact with the public were likely to be more vulnerable than most employees elsewhere to catching various ailments. BAA also claimed that many BAA jobs were active rather than sedentary so that staff feeling unwell could not perform their duties satisfactorily, whereas an office worker with some degree of impairment might still be able to perform satisfactorily.

7.85. BAA told us that it believed that there was scope to make some minor improvements to the level of absence, but doubted whether they might be achievable over the next five years.

7.86. In November 2001, BAA tabled proposals to its recognized trade unions to implement a common 'Attendance Improvement Programme' to replace the various such programmes which applied at different airports. Managers were to assess an employee's absence record after three periods of absence in a rolling 12-month period, or after ten days of absence, which is broadly at the level of the worst quartile recorded in the CBI's absence survey. At the time of our report, BAA and the employees' representatives had not reached agreement on the November 2001 proposals because of the protracted pay discussions this year. BAA said that this was a long-term process, and that no early gains could be anticipated.

7.87. BAA sought to provide further information from other sources as to sickness absence over the five years to March 2002, but it was unable to give anything other than aggregated figures for the relevant years. Details of the average number of days lost per employee are shown in Table 7.19. The table shows a continuing rise in the levels of absence at Heathrow and Gatwick, whilst the level at Stansted was slightly below that of 1997/98.

TABLE 7.19 **Sickness absence: average days lost per employee**

	1997/98	1998/99	1999/00	2000/01	2001/02
Heathrow	8.6	9.3	9.6	10.1	10.8
Gatwick	8.1	8.2	9.0	10.8	11.1
Stansted	9.5	8.8	9.1	9.4	9.2

Source: BAA.

7.88. In discussing attendance improvement, BAA was asked to comment on the absence of guidance to airport managers in the guidelines sent from Head Office about the completion of manpower plans, and about manpower plans which catered for absence of ten days per employee. BAA said that absence control was a matter for the airports; and that it was not unreasonable to plan for an average of ten days absence per employee, when the CBI's absence data suggested a benchmark of 9.5 days for comparable staff.

7.89. Comparative data is at Appendix 7.6.

Labour turnover

7.90. Labour turnover within BAA was substantially below the national average. Details of labour turnover are in Appendix 7.6. BAA said that it sought to preserve low turnover because of the high investment which the company needed to make to ensure a high-quality workforce operating in a good employee relations environment. Additionally, labour turnover caused greater costs in terms of equipping staff with, for example, uniforms and identity cards, and, in the case of security staff, with providing training under statutory requirements.

7.91. The company said that it had not, to date, found it necessary to implement significant compulsory redundancies. This was not a formal policy and BAA kept the matter under review. The financial model did not permit manpower numbers to fall by more than 4 per cent in any one year since that would require compulsory redundancies.

7.92. BAA said that it had used voluntary severance and early retirement packages on a number of occasions when reductions in full-time staff were appropriate in certain areas. The schemes were rarely offered to operational staff because of the potential security and service standard implications of reducing the levels of these staff.

Trade union membership and collective bargaining machinery

7.93. Some 66 per cent of BAA's employees pay trade union subscriptions by voluntary deduction from payroll under 'check-off' arrangements. Additionally, it is usual for some employees to pay subscriptions by direct debit or other arrangements and BAA has no records relating to that. There is an extensive framework of consultative bodies at each of the airports.

Forecasts versus out-turns

7.94. BAA estimated that it had underspent on allowed manpower costs by 0.2 per cent in the last quinquennium.

7.95. Table 7.20 shows how staff numbers and costs have moved over the past five years, along with the MMC's projections made at the time of the last reference.

TABLE 7.20 **Forecasts versus actuals, 2001/02 prices**

	1997/98	1998/99	1999/00	2000/01	2001/02
Staff—projected	6,151	6,103	5,997	5,868	5,744
Staff—actual	6,161	6,061	5,835	5,774	5,766
Staff costs—projected (£'000)	192,452	200,312	202,763	208,213	210,301
Staff costs—actual (£'000)	196,832	204,114	196,304	199,037	219,684

Source: BAA.

7.96. Within each airport the position was as in Tables 7.21 to 7.23.

TABLE 7.21 **Heathrow**

	1997/98	1998/99	1999/00	2000/01	2001/02
Staff—projected	3,642	3,579	3,482	3,376	3,246
Staff—actual	3,703	3,614	3,409	3,317	3,345
Staff costs—projected (£'000)	117,198	120,848	121,294	123,690	123,260
Staff costs—actual (£'000)	120,593	123,834	115,851	117,067	131,054

Source: BAA.

TABLE 7.22 **Gatwick**

	1997/98	1998/99	1999/00	2000/01	2001/02
Staff—projected	1,872	1,884	1,866	1,827	1,801
Staff—actual	1,890	1,831	1,766	1,749	1,721
Staff costs—projected (£'000)	56,594	59,725	60,918	62,714	64,022
Staff costs—actual (£'000)	58,006	59,855	58,499	58,554	62,585

Source: BAA.

TABLE 7.23 **Stansted**

	1997/98	1998/99	1999/00	2000/01	2001/02
Staff—projected	637	640	649	665	697
Staff—actual	569	615	660	680	708
Staff costs—projected (£'000)	18,661	19,739	20,550	21,809	23,020
Staff costs—actual (£'000)	18,232	20,426	21,955	22,3415	26,044

Source: BAA.

7.97. The manpower numbers and manpower cost projections above replaced significantly higher projections submitted by BAA earlier in the inquiry. Details of the respective manpower forecasts submitted in 1996 are as shown in Table 7.24.

TABLE 7.24 **Manpower forecasts**

	1997/98	1998/99	1999/00	2000/01	2001/02
Initial projections	6,386	6,324	6,211	6,072	5,936
Revised projections	6,085	6,032	5,924	5,794	5,667
Difference	301	292	287	278	269
%	−4.7	−4.6	−4.6	−4.6	−4.5

Source: BAA.

Forecasts for the next quinquennium

Staff numbers and costs

7.98. Table 7.25 gives details of actual and forecast movements in staff and staff costs as provided by BAA.[1]

TABLE 7.25 **Passengers, man-years and costs—actual and forecast (2002/03 prices)**

	Actual					Forecast					
	1997/ 98	1998/ 99	1999/ 00	2000/ 01	2001/ 02	2002/ 03	2003/ 04	2004/ 05	2005/ 06	2006/ 07	2007/ 08
Passengers (m)	90.9	98.0	102.6	108.7	104.9	107.1	114.7	119.9	123.9	128.2	130.9
Man-years	6,745	6,645	6,404	6,322	6,346	6,365	6,461	6,421	6,494	6,597	6,633
Staff costs (£m)	219.6	220.8	209.2	205.8	223.9	212.5	220.1	222.0	227.8	234.9	239.5
Pax/man-year ('000)	13.5	14.7	16.0	17.2	16.6	16.8	17.8	18.7	19.1	19.4	19.7

Source: BAA.

7.99. The forecasts in Table 7.25 derive from BAA's current business plan for 2002/03 to 2004/05, and from BAA's latest projections in its financial model. The cost figures derive from forecasts of man-years.[1]

7.100. The forecast data in Table 7.25 can be broken down to show details for the three airports separately. Table 7.26 gives details.

---

[1]At a late stage in the reference, BAA revised its forecast data relating to security staff. It had initially intended to treat its additional security staff under a +S factor arrangement, but later decided that it would be better to include them in its financial model as with other employees. The additional staff are included in the modelling in Chapter 8, but are excluded from this chapter. Details are in Appendix 7.1.

TABLE 7.26 **Man-year forecasts**

| | Actual | Forecast | | | | | |
	2001/02	2002/03	2003/04	2004/05	2005/06	2006/07	2007/08
Heathrow	3,697	3,715	3,780	3,751	3,751	3,751	3,751
Gatwick	1,859	1,792	1,809	1,786	1,840	1,906	1,912
Stansted	790	858	872	884	903	940	969
Total	6,346	6,365	6,461	6,421	6,494	6,597	6,633

Staff costs (£ million, 2002/03 prices)

| | Actual | Forecast | | | | | |
	2001/02	2002/03	2003/04	2004/5	2005/6	2006/07	2007/08
Heathrow	133.5	127.2	131.4	132.4	134.4	136.4	138.4
Gatwick	63.8	58.4	61.0	61.3	64.1	67.5	68.7
Stansted	26.5	26.9	27.7	28.3	29.3	31.0	32.4
Total	223.9	212.5	220.1	222.0	227.8	234.9	239.5

Passenger forecasts (million)

| | Actual | Forecast | | | | | |
	2001/02	2002/03	2003/04	2004/5	2005/6	2006/07	2007/08
Heathrow	60.4	63.3	67.1	69.0	69.9	70.3	70.7
Gatwick	30.5	28.4	31.2	33.8	36.0	38.6	39.7
Stansted	14.1	15.5	16.4	17.1	18.0	19.3	20.5
Total	104.9	107.1	114.7	119.9	123.9	128.2	130.9

Passengers per man-year ('000)

| | Actual | Forecast | | | | | |
	2001/02	2002/03	2003/04	2004/5	2005/6	2006/07	2007/08
Heathrow	16.3	17.0	17.7	18.4	18.6	18.7	18.8
Gatwick	16.4	15.8	17.2	18.9	19.6	20.3	20.8
Stansted	17.8	18.0	18.8	19.4	19.9	20.5	21.1
Total	16.5	16.8	17.8	18.7	19.1	19.4	19.7

Source: BAA.

Productivity

7.101. During the 1996 review BAA told us that it used the passenger per man-year measure to manage and monitor year-on-year improvements in productivity, rather than to determine the total staffing requirement for an airport in a mechanistic way. Nevertheless, this measure is used in BAA's long-term financial model to forecast staff numbers and their associated costs—and in its base case BAA asked the CC to accept that costs predicted in this way should be accommodated in the pricing model.

7.102. BAA said that over the business plan period a detailed bottom-up review of staffing levels was carried out. For long-term forecasts this level of detailed forecasting was not possible as the necessary information was not available in sufficient detail. Hence, the long-term forecasts were made at a summary level using the key drivers of productivity and wage inflation, as appropriate at each location.

7.103. BAA's business plan is prepared annually and incorporates assumptions as to wage costs and staff productivity over the following three years. Its forecasts therefore cover only two years of the quinquennium under review. Forecasts for the final three years are in the company's long-term financial model.

7.104. BAA said that it had incorporated real wage growth of 1.5 per cent a year into its financial model. BAA reasoned that average real earnings growth in the economy as a whole had been 2 per cent over the long term. The company said that it was reasonable to expect that BAA's average staff costs per employee should lie between its historical trend of 1 per cent and the expected continuation of the economy's growth rate of 2 per cent. The company's long-term financial model provided for real wage increases of 1.75 per cent from 2008/09.

7.105. We asked BAA to explain how its model took into account the savings accruing from more staff coming on to new starters' pay rates (see paragraph 7.70 et seq). BAA said that since it was only inflating wage costs by 1.5 per cent in Q4 rather than the 2 per cent seen in the economy as a whole, the wage reductions did not need to be reflected in the model. It estimated that the savings to accrue under this heading over the next five years would amount to some £0.875 million, equivalent to about 0.4 per cent of the pay bill. This assumed that 350 staff per year would join on market-related pay scales at a saving of £2,500 per employee, about 8 to 9 per cent of staff costs.

7.106. The staff cost data which appears in the Group Strategic Model is derived from a separate modelling of such costs analysed in two components—productivity in terms of passengers handled per man-year and average staff costs per man-year. The model therefore rests on judgements by BAA of the extent to which it might vary the ratio of passengers per man-year, and the extent to which average pay costs should rise in real terms. BAA said that these two elements together provide the staff costs per passenger ratio which is used to drive the long-term financial forecast of staff costs beyond the business plan period.

7.107. In comparing the business plan and long-term financial model BAA said that the latter used the last year of the business plan as a starting point. BAA went on to say that some care was taken to ensure that the long-term forecasts matched historical experience and were not inconsistent with the business plan.

7.108. Within each BAA department a comparison was made of long-term trends in the UK economy at large (both historic and forecast) with the detailed picture of productivity gains and average staff costs per employee in the recent past. A forecast was made for each of the two components which were then combined to show forecast staff costs per passenger. BAA said that this methodology was consistent with BAA's approach at the last MMC review in 1996.

Relationship between productivity and passenger numbers

7.109. Some 80 per cent of BAA's staff are employed in the functions shown in Table 7.27.

TABLE 7.27 **Staff by function and activity**

Function	Activity
Security	Searching of staff and passengers entering restricted zone, guarding access to and patrol of restricted zone. Issue of ID cards.
Engineering	Maintenance of terminal and other buildings, airside infrastructure and electronic systems (ie flight information).
Terminal operations	Ensuring free flow of passengers, reliability of passenger sensitive equipment (lifts, escalators, travelators, etc), liaison with airline and handling agents, monitoring service standards, dealing with critical incidents, maintaining health and safety standards, traveller assistance and trolley service.
Airfield operations	Management of runways, taxiways, apron areas. Equipment checks, stand allocation, liaison with the CAA and NATS.
Airport fire service	Attendance at aircraft incidents, fuel spillage and, when requested, incidents such as traveller collapses and road traffic incidents.

Source: BAA.

7.110. Security staff represent about 40 per cent of the workforce as a whole; about half of the security staff are in fixed posts, which involve the manning of gates, entrances and crossover points.

The 20 per cent of staff not included in the above table have an indirect association with increases in volumes. BAA said that, nevertheless, more passengers equated to more transactions, more retail activity, more property demand, more planning and therefore more staff.

7.111. BAA said that security staff in fixed posts had duties which entailed security checks for transfer passengers, for staff within terminals, for staff and vehicle entry points around airport perimeters, and for passengers in lieu of segregation. We were told that manning levels at staff control posts were determined by the number of staff passing through these security points, which in turn was strongly related to the number of passengers.

7.112. BAA said that it continued to measure labour productivity in terms of passengers per man-year. It noted that, historically, productivity growth tends to follow passenger growth, and pointed out that productivity was negative at Gatwick and Stansted in 1991, when passenger growth was negative, and highest at Heathrow and Gatwick in 1992/93 and 1998/99 when passenger growth was highest. We noted, in paragraph 7.107, that BAA took care to make sure that the long-term forecasts matched historical experience.

7.113. We suggested to BAA that this implied that the company did not seek to improve manpower productivity when passenger levels were static or declining. BAA rejected this suggestion, saying that the data was simply a reflection of the measure on a per-passenger basis. The company said that in response to the downturn in traffic in the early 1990s, for example, BAA had undertaken a major voluntary severance programme.

Comparison of projected productivity gains in Q4 and actual gains in Q3

7.114. We compared BAA's Q3 actual and Q4 projected levels of passenger growth and productivity (in terms of passengers per man-year). For details, see Appendix 7.7.

7.115. Passenger movements in 2001/02 and 2002/03 were affected by the events of 11 September 2001, and we therefore based our historic analysis on the five years to 2000/01, which we took to be a representative period; our analysis for the quinquennium was based on an assumption that the trend level of passengers per man-year in 2002/03 was at the same level as actually reached in 2000/01.

7.116. A simple comparison then suggests that the projections for the increase in passengers per man-year for Q4 are significantly below those actually achieved in Q3 at Heathrow and Stansted, and slightly below at Gatwick. However, as passenger numbers are forecast to grow more slowly in Q4 than they did in Q3, it is to be expected that productivity growth would be somewhat less. We corrected for this by considering a range of elasticities (the proportionate increase in staff numbers required for a given increase in passenger numbers). The results, in Tables 7.28 to 7.30, show that future productivity increases predicted by BAA at Heathrow and Stansted are significantly less than those achieved in the last quinquennium, regardless of what elasticities are used, within reason. At Gatwick productivity increases are projected to be marginally better once the figures are corrected for volume effect. The overall analysis is not significantly changed if the projected results for 2002/03 are used, rather than the 2000/01 figures.

TABLE 7.28 **Heathrow**

Assumed elasticity	Actual—five years to 2000/01	Forecast—five years to 2007/08	
	Productivity increase unrelated to volume changes	Productivity increase unrelated to volume changes	Difference % per year
0.2	2.5	−0.1	2.5
0.3	2.8	0.1	2.7
0.4	3.1	0.3	2.8
0.5	3.4	0.5	2.9
0.6	3.7	0.7	3.0
0.7	4.0	0.9	3.1
0.8	4.3	1.1	3.2

Source: CC analysis of BAA data.

TABLE 7.29 **Gatwick**

	Actual—five years to 2000/01	Forecast—five years to 2007/08	
Assumed elasticity	Productivity increase unrelated to volume changes	Productivity increase unrelated to volume changes	Difference % per year
0.2	−0.9	0.9	−1.9
0.3	0.0	1.4	−1.4
0.4	0.8	1.9	−1.1
0.5	1.6	2.3	−0.7
0.6	2.3	2.8	−0.5
0.7	2.9	3.1	−0.2
0.8	3.5	3.5	0.0

Source: CC analysis of BAA data.

TABLE 7.30 **Stansted**

	Actual—five years to 2000/01	Forecast—five years to 2007/08	
Assumed elasticity	Productivity increase unrelated to volume changes	Productivity increase unrelated to volume changes	Difference % per year
0.2	3.6	−3.9	7.5
0.3	7.8	−2.0	9.8
0.4	10.7	−0.4	11.2
0.5	12.8	0.9	12.0
0.6	14.4	1.2	13.2
0.7	15.7	1.8	13.9
0.8	16.8	2.3	14.5

Source: CC analysis of BAA data.

7.117. BAA believed that as passenger numbers increased towards the end of the quinquennium, congestion in the existing terminals at Heathrow would be such that staff numbers would need to be kept at a level which would provide acceptable service standards. At Stansted there had been some under-utilization as passenger levels grew to match the airport's fixed costs. That situation no longer applied. It told us that over the past ten years it had achieved all the easy productivity gains. The company said that there were many reasons why it believed that, in its particular circumstances, it would not in future be able to achieve the productivity improvements made in the past ten years, and that the position going forward was quite different from the earlier period. BAA also told us that as it had been able to achieve historical productivity gains without the need for productivity yardsticks in respect of particular groups of workers, there was no prima facie case for introducing such yardsticks. It believed that the increases in passengers per man-year which it was forecasting were quite aggressive, and perhaps beyond the company's ability to achieve.

7.118. As noted in paragraph 7.40, BAA indicated during the last reference that one of its main standard productivity indicators was pay-related staff costs per passenger. The measure did not feature in its business plan, although relevant data in the plan allowed the projections in Table 7.31 to be obtained.

TABLE 7.31 **Pay-related costs per passenger**

£

	2001/02	2002/03	2003/04	2004/05
Heathrow	1.95	1.90	1.91	1.91
Gatwick	1.87	1.96	1.90	1.81
Stansted	1.66	1.65	1.65	1.65
Total	1.89	1.88	1.87	1.85

Source: CC analysis of BAA data.

7.119. BAA told us that pay-related costs per employee, which enabled this calculation to be made, did not feature in the long-term financial model and that no forecast was available beyond 2004/05.

Non-manpower operating expenditure

7.120. We set out BAA's projections of the opex at Heathrow, Gatwick and Stansted in paragraphs 7.20 to 7.32. We now consider how the projections at each airport relate to historical trends in unit costs.

Total operating costs

7.121. Figure 7.1 shows the historical and projected trends in total operating costs per passenger at each airport. Stansted's high initial unit operating costs reflected the low level of utilization of the terminal at the time; costs have subsequently declined to a level similar to the other BAA airports. The increase in the unit costs projected for Heathrow in 2008/09 is associated with the opening of T5.

FIGURE 7.1

Total operating costs per passenger

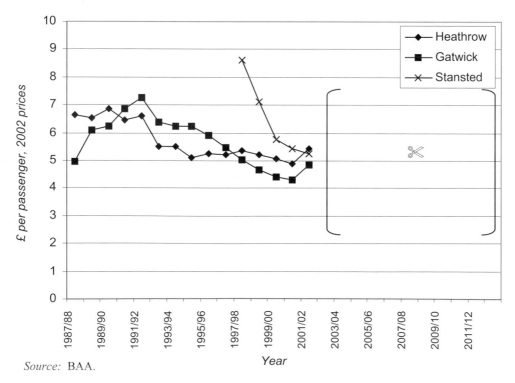

Source: BAA.

7.122. To understand the reasons for these cost trends in more detail we examine each major cost item separately in the following paragraphs.

Police

7.123. Figure 7.2 shows the historical and projected trends in police costs per passenger at each airport. Policing costs are negotiated between BAA and the police force concerned after taking account of any threats and the number of passengers. Unit costs at Heathrow and Gatwick are projected to increase as a result of increased security measures and a request from the local police force to increase the proportion of costs reimbursed by the airport.

FIGURE 7.2

Police costs per passenger

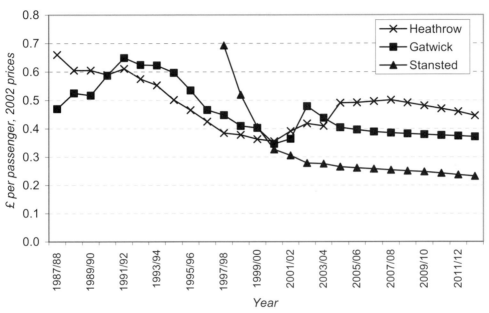

Source: BAA.

7.124. BAA told us that the primary reason for police costs being higher at Heathrow than at either Gatwick or Stansted was the perceived level of threat there, due to the type of flights, destinations and its profile as the major gateway into London. Police costs at Heathrow were forecast to increase significantly in 2004/05 because of heightened security requirements. In addition, Metropolitan Police wage rates were believed to be higher than those for the Sussex and Essex constabularies.

7.125. In the long term, BAA assumed that policing costs would increase in proportion to its own staff costs.

Rent

7.126. Figure 7.3 shows the historical and projected trends in rent per passenger at each airport. These costs normally cover the cost of renting accommodation for airport staff from non-BAA landlords. The cost of accommodation provided by other group companies is charged to inter-company accounts.

FIGURE 7.3

Rent per passenger

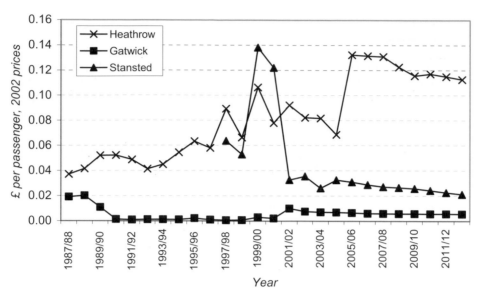

Source: BAA.

7.127. BAA said that the sums involved were very small, especially at Gatwick. BAA tended to view rent costs in absolute terms, as they were unrelated to passenger numbers. It believed that rent costs per passenger were not a meaningful measure. Similarly, comparisons by airport were not useful, as the costs were driven by land ownership and local costs specific to each location.

7.128. BAA told us that the higher costs at Heathrow were almost entirely related to rents paid for the Heathrow Point complex and BA's Cranford Lane car park. Heathrow Point provided accommodation for BAA support staff, releasing scarce space in the CTA to be rented to airlines. There would be a step increase in rents at Heathrow in 2005/06 under an agreement with TW to provide it with replacement accommodation. The associated amount (£4.3 million a year) was intended to cover the incremental costs that TW would incur as a result of moving its operations from the T5 site to Iver South.

7.129. The smaller rental costs at Gatwick and Stansted are related mainly to wayleaves needed for operational purposes. BAA told us that the increase at Gatwick in 2001/02 reflected a transfer of BAA properties (including Gatwick Gate sold for £5.4 million) from BAA Lynton to a developer, Airport Industrial Partnership (AIP), agreed by the CAA. (Previously GAL paid rent to Lynton, which was treated as an inter-company charge; it now pays rent to AIP, in which BAA has a 10 per cent shareholding, which is shown under this heading.) The peak in rent at Stansted relates to office accommodation that was temporarily transferred to a developer but is now part of BAA's portfolio.

Rates

7.130. Figure 7.4 shows the historical and projected trends in rates per passenger at each airport. Rates are determined by the size of the buildings occupied and have a five-year revaluation cycle that tends to result in sudden increases followed by reductions after appeal. The forecast growth at Heathrow is therefore linked to planned capital investment.

FIGURE 7.4

Rates per passenger

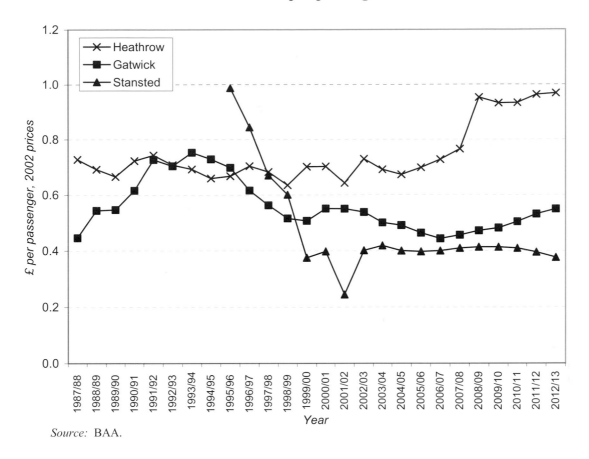

Source: BAA.

7.131. BAA said that rates at Heathrow were greater because of the high land values in the area relative to Gatwick and Stansted. Rates were also forecast to increase significantly there given the high level of capital investment. It added that the increase in projected rates per passenger at Heathrow also reflected the less intensive occupation of the terminals, following the opening of T5. At Gatwick rates fell during the 1990s as BAA released staff accommodation for other uses. Both there and at Stansted projected increases in rates are broadly in proportion to passenger numbers. BAA told us that Stansted had lower land values than Gatwick. The increase in rates per passenger there in 2002/03 is associated with the opening of the terminal extension and Satellite 3. Stansted's rates are projected to increase in 2004/05, when a rate rebate for under-occupation is expected to end.

Utility costs

7.132. Figure 7.5 shows the historical and projected trends in utility costs per passenger at each airport. Reductions in utility costs in the 1990s reflected one-off savings following changes in supplier and by price-cutting as a result of increased competition within the utility industries. In addition, BAA said that it now negotiated utility costs on a group-wide basis, rather than at individual airports, in order to maximize buying power.

FIGURE 7.5

Utility cost per passenger

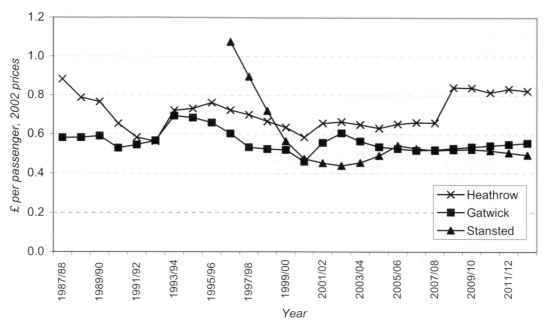

Source: BAA.

7.133. The increases in 2001/02 and 2002/03 are caused by the introduction of the climate change levy and, at Heathrow and Gatwick, falling passenger numbers following 11 September. Forecast increases owing to the opening of new buildings are broadly offset by reduced consumption to meet BAA's CO_2 emission targets. BAA told us that it was increasing its use of renewable energy, which was charged at premium rate. From 2005/06, BAA expected to source around 10 per cent of its electricity from renewable sources. This policy is part of BAA's approach to sustainability, which, it told us, was necessary to secure neighbourhood 'buy-in' to airport expansion. BAA argued that it was too early to consult the airlines on the cost implications of this policy. We would expect it to do so in a timely fashion.

7.134. BAA told us that the higher projected utility costs at Heathrow, relative to Gatwick and Stansted, reflected the nature and use of the site. The large site required greater utility consumption. There were also higher proportions of cargo and freight forwarding activities at Heathrow, relative to passenger numbers. BAA said that the projected increase at Heathrow followed the opening of T5, which would be an energy-intensive terminal with far more automated systems for baggage transfer and passenger movement than traditional terminals. T5 would be a large building but initially would only produce a small marginal increase in passengers. The increase in utility costs would largely be offset by higher revenue from tenants. BAA added that it intended to introduce technologies, such as electric vehicles and preconditioned air which, although being environmentally friendly, increased utility consumption.

Maintenance and equipment

7.135. Figure 7.6 shows the historical and projected trends in maintenance and equipment costs per passenger at each airport.

FIGURE 7.6

Maintenance and equipment costs per passenger

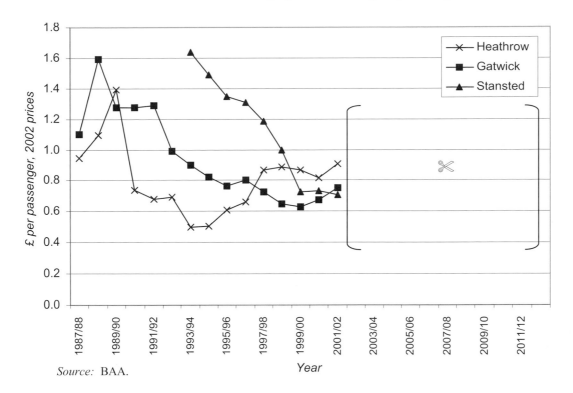

Source: BAA.

7.136. The increase in costs per passenger at Heathrow from 1995/96 to 2001/02 reflects the costs of the new T1 to T4 baggage transfer system, which are recharged to the airlines. BAA told us that, without these costs, Heathrow's unit maintenance costs would be similar to those of the other airports. There is a step increase associated with the opening of T5.

7.137. Costs per passenger at Gatwick fell during the 1990s, as passenger numbers rose faster than maintenance costs. Unit costs increased in 2000/01, when equipment in the South Terminal was refurbished. Increases in 2001/02 at Gatwick are caused by abortive project costs (primarily on earlier schemes for Pier 6), the fall in passenger numbers following 11 September and the increasing costs of maintaining ageing assets. At Stansted there is a step increase in 2005/06 caused by additional operating costs associated with the terminal extension.

Other costs

7.138. Figure 7.7 shows the historical and projected trends in other costs per passenger at each airport. Other costs include ground transport operations, general expenses, adjustments for the capitalization of revenue costs and inter-company costs.

FIGURE 7.7

Other costs per passenger

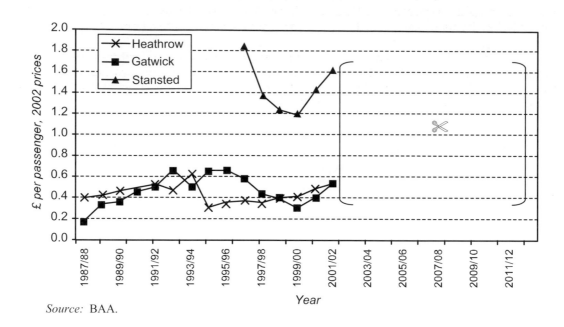

Source: BAA.

7.139. BAA told us that the increase in 2001/02 was driven by higher insurance premiums and the drop in passenger numbers following 11 September 2001. Table 7.32 shows a breakdown of other costs in 2001/02.

TABLE 7.32 **Breakdown of other costs for BAA south-east airports, 2001/02**

	£m
Property security costs	0.4
Property maintenance costs	0.2
General expenses	101.9
Inter-company costs	31.4
Corporate Office fees	76.1
Less	
Police costs recharged	−38.3
Capitalization of revenue	−14.4
Capitalization of inter-company costs	−5.2
Recharge of Heathrow Express costs	−3.3
Total other costs	148.9

SourcSource: BAA.

7.140. Capitalized revenue in 2002/03 is expected to amount to about £6.4 million at Heathrow, £0.7 million at Gatwick and £2.0 million at Stansted. In addition, BAA expects to capitalize further inter-company costs, associated with the T5 team based at Corporate Office, amounting to £9.3 million in 2002/03, and similar amounts in the following five years. Other costs at Heathrow fall in 2002/03 following the large credit from the capitalization of inter-company charges. There is an equal and opposite effect in centrally held costs. These effects disappear in 2008/09 when T5 opens.

7.141. Other costs per passenger at Gatwick are forecast to remain constant, except for the assumed effect of entry into the euro in 2005/06. At Stansted, marketing support and advertising costs designed to attract traffic to the airport were very high in the early 1990s. BAA plans to phase out this expenditure as the airport becomes busier.

Comparisons with other airports

7.142. The CAA told us that it had not 'got a lot of power out of' the benchmarking exercise undertaken for it by NERA. It said that a wide variety of factors required adjustments, and a need for much data mapping, particularly at Heathrow. It said that most of those attending its consultation meeting on benchmarking had forecast that the benchmarking exercise would prove fruitless.

7.143. We asked NERA whether the benchmarking data could provide a means of comparing BAA's performance with that of other major airports. NERA told us that the benchmarking exercise had not produced results which could be regarded as robust, and that it could not be relied upon as a satisfactory means of comparing expenditure with other airports.

8 Commercial and other activities

Contents

Introduction

8.1. Airport charges account for only part of the income of the airports. This chapter considers the other sources of the airports' income.

8.2. Under the Airports Act, airport charges are charges levied in connection with the landing, parking or taking-off of aircraft at the airport and charges levied on passengers in connection with passengers' arrival at or departure from the airport (see paragraphs 3.50 and 3.51). Appendix 3.2 of the 1996 MMC report (reproduced in Appendix 2.5, Table 1, of this report) set out the services that BAA regarded as covered by airport charges and Appendix 2.5, Table 2, of this report sets out the services that BAA currently regards as covered by airport charges. These are services for which no separate charges are levied. However, there is nothing in law to prevent BAA at any time introducing a specific charge for any of these services,[1] or withdrawing separate charges for other services.

8.3. The airports also levy charges that are not in connection with aircraft landing, parking and taking-off and passenger processing. Such charges are outside the definition of airport charges and, therefore, are not subject to the price cap, but projected revenue from such charges may be taken into account when the price cap is set. This means that BAA has an element of discretion as to whether a particular service, such as baggage transfer, is remunerated by a separate charge or through airport charges (if an aeronautical activity has no separate charge, airport charges will of course be higher than if it has a separate charge). It is, however, important that the airport subsequently charges its customers on the same basis that the regulator sets the price cap.

Airports' income and profit by activity

8.4. In addition to services that are separately charged for, the airports also derive significant amounts of income from property rents, car parking and from concessionaires operating businesses (principally retailing) at the airports. Table 8.1 summarizes the airports' income and HCA profits from all sources. There are a number of points to bear in mind in considering the figures in Table 8.1:

(a) It reflects an analysis according to one particular set of profit centres (defined by BAA) and results would be different with different profit centres. For example, the airport road infrastructure is not included as a profit centre and its costs are allocated across the existing profit centres. The CAA has said that airports should have the ability to impose road pricing for airports access, which would imply road infrastructure should be a separate profit centre (currently earning no revenue).

(b) Many costs have to be allocated across different profit centres and results are thus dependent on the allocation methods used. In the context of the CAA's proposed dual till (see paragraph 8.7), BAA's system of PCR has recently been considered by the CAA's consultants, Avia Solutions, who commented that BAA's approach to cost allocation was in the main sensible.[2] Avia Solutions said that they had not found an allocation methodology that was clearly inappropriate but did note that insufficient methodology documentation and inconsistent overhead cost definitions/reporting meant that it had been difficult for them to gain a full understanding of how BAA had carried out the allocations. Avia Solutions noted five areas (police, property, corporate charge, terminal facilities and management, and public relations) where BAA's methodology was debatable. Avia Solutions proposed changes to the PCR and commented that BAA had accepted the need for many of the changes and had formed a working group to review and implement short-term improvements to the system (they noted also that, if a dual-till approach was implemented, BAA had indicated a willingness to work with the CAA to address many of the issues). BAA told us that it had reviewed and updated the PCR rules and definitions documents and produced an up-to-date set of PCR guidance notes. It had also made efforts to make PCR at different locations more consistent.

(c) Profit figures reflect HCA depreciation without adjustment for inflation and thus differ from those used in the financial projections (see Chapter 10).

---

[1] If BAA introduces a charge for a service in the list, the charge might or might not fall within the definition of airport charges (it depends on the circumstances).
[2] The report is available on the CAA's web site.

(d) Profit figures are before any allowance for cost of capital.

Consequently, the profit figures in Table 8.1 do not necessarily reflect the excess of revenue over avoidable cost for commercial activities, which may be either above or below the level shown in Table 8.1.

TABLE 8.1 **Summary of BAA London airports' income and HCA profits, 2000/01**

£ million

	Heathrow	Gatwick	Stansted	Total
Income				
Airport charges*	339.3	129.8	53.9	523.0
Other services and facilities				
Specified activities†	78.0	34.9	10.7	123.8
Transfer baggage	36.8	0.0	0.0	36.8
Other‡	8.3	4.5	4.6	17.3
Property income				
Terminal property	43.5	7.8	1.9	53.2
Cargo	9.5	3.3	2.0	14.8
Other property	37.5	16.1	5.0	58.6
Income from concessionaires				
Retail	166.2	86.5	17.5	270.2
Car rental	13.1	3.4	1.2	17.7
Car parks	58.5	32.1	19.9	110.5
Heathrow Express	62.8	0.0	0.0	62.8
Advertising income	27.4	5.5	1.6	34.5
Total§	880.9	323.9	118.4	1,323.2
HCA profits				
Airport charges	109.2	4.0	−11.6	101.6
Other services and facilities				
Specified activities†	−11.1	4.8	2.4	−2.6
Transfer baggage	−5.4	0.0	0.0	−5.4
Other‡	−2.9	−3.0	−0.5	−7.5
Property income				
Terminal property	30.3	4.2	1.6	36.1
Cargo	6.9	1.6	1.5	10.0
Other property	23.7	4.8	0.5	29.0
Income from concessionaires				
Retail	122.4	71.5	14.0	207.7
Car rental	12.2	2.8	1.1	16.1
Car parks	42.4	24.7	18.0	85.1
Heathrow Express	4.7	0.0	0.0	4.7
Advertising income	16.8	4.1	1.0	21.9
Total	349.2	119.5	28.0	496.7

Source: BAA's Profit Centre Reports.

*Heathrow's airport charges profit centre includes a small amount of other income (total airport charges were £336.5 million).

†See paragraph 8.10.

‡See paragraph 8.17.

§Total revenue shown in the report and accounts is slightly greater than total income in the PCR.

8.5. Some additional information is provided in Table 8.2, which is based on CAA work and divides airport activities into four categories:

(a) Aeronautical: these are considered by the CAA to be activities which are necessary for the operation of the airlines but cannot be 'economically duplicated', that is supplied off airport. In practice the CAA regards as aeronautical everything on the airfield necessary for arriving and

departing aircraft,[1] facilities within terminals piers and satellites necessary for processing passengers,[2] baggage handling facilities, refuelling facilities and airline offices inside terminals (but not CIP lounges).

(b) *Commercial*: for the purposes of Table 8.2, commercial includes retail concessions and property (other than airline offices inside terminals and buildings occupied by BAA, which are considered aeronautical), including cargo buildings.

(c) Roads, car parking, car rental, buses, coaches and taxis.

(d) Rail, the Heathrow Express train company, which is owned and operated by BAA, and associated infrastructure.

The CAA split revenue, costs and assets between aeronautical and non-aeronautical; the additional division of non-aeronautical into commercial, roads etc and rail is our own based on CAA data. Certain assets, particularly in terminals, are used for both aeronautical and commercial activities: the CAA adopted a pragmatic approach to splitting these assets but the underlying principle was that the aeronautical activity should include the assets and costs needed to allow airlines to operate (thus, if an aeronautical only terminal would be 90 per cent of the existing terminal area, 90 per cent of the non-specific costs would be allocated to the aeronautical activity).

8.6. Table 8.2 shows the large profits made by the airports' commercial activities and the substantial shortfall (after allowing for the cost of capital) attributable to the Heathrow Express. Roads, car parking etc shows a small surplus but it is likely that this reflects a substantial surplus on public car parks offset by losses on roads provision (which currently earns no revenue) and road public transport.[3] Under the single-till principle, airport charges are capped so that the airport business as a whole is projected to earn the cost of capital. Hence, if the financial projections made at the time the price cap is set are correct, the shortfall for the aeronautical activity would be expected to be equal to the combined surplus for the other activities. In 2000/01 the aeronautical shortfall was smaller than the combined surplus for the other activities, and the airports business as a whole earned more than the cost of capital: the main reasons for this were revenue advancement (see paragraph 10.3) and outperformance against the MMC's 1996 projections (see paragraph 10.10).

---

[1] Air traffic management services from the control tower, runways, runway lighting and drainage, taxiways, aprons, stands, space for equipment storage for ground handling services, essential space and roads for third party access such as fire stations, airside roads and associated utilities.
[2] Check-in, security, departure lounges, way-finding, transit systems, people movers, departure gates, arrivals lounges, immigration, transit lounges and customs.
[3] We are unable to separate these out.

TABLE 8.2 **Approximate allocation of airport profit across activities, 2000/01**

£ million

	Revenue	Operating expenditure	Depreciation*	Profit†	Cost of capital*‡	Surplus of profit over cost of capital§	Surplus per passenger
Heathrow							
Total	893.6	429.6	142.8	321.2	253.4	67.8	1.05
Aeronautical	478.0	288.6	69.4	119.9	123.2	−3.2	−0.05
Non-aeronautical	415.6	141.0	73.4	201.3	130.2	71.1	1.10
Commercial	261.4	67.8	23.8	169.8	42.2	127.6	1.98
Road etc¶	90.4	28.7	22.2	39.5	39.4	0.2	0.00
Rail	63.9	44.5	27.4	−8.1	48.7	−56.8	−0.88
Gatwick							
Total	325.5	165.9	54.0	105.6	86.5	19.1	0.59
Aeronautical	170.4	123.6	33.5	13.3	53.7	−40.4	−1.26
Non-aeronautical	155.1	42.3	20.5	92.3	32.8	59.5	1.85
Commercial	114.3	31.4	9.3	73.6	14.8	58.8	1.83
Road etc¶	40.8	10.9	11.2	18.7	18.0	0.7	0.02
Rail							
Stansted							
Total	118.4	72.3	22.1	24.0	52.7	−28.7	−2.34
Aeronautical	66.9	57.6	18.0	−8.7	43.0	−51.7	−4.22
Non-aeronautical	51.5	14.7	4.1	32.7	9.7	23.0	1.88
Commercial	29.8	12.8	2.4	14.6	5.7	8.9	0.73
Road etc¶	21.7	1.9	1.7	18.1	4.0	14.1	1.15
Rail							
All three airports							
Total	1,337.5	667.8	218.9	450.8	393.2	58.2	0.54
Aeronautical	715.3	469.9	120.9	124.5	220.2	−95.3	−0.88
Non-aeronautical	622.2	197.9	98.0	326.3	173.0	153.5	1.41
Commercial	405.4	112.0	35.4	258.1	62.8	195.4	1.80
Road etc¶	152.9	41.5	35.1	76.3	61.5	14.9	0.14
Rail	63.9	44.5	27.4	−8.1	48.7	−56.8	−0.52

Source: CC calculations based on regulated accounts and RRCB annexes to the CAA submission and November 2001 preliminary proposals.

---

*Depreciation and cost of capital are allocated to airports pro rata with net book value of fixed assets at 31 March 2001. Depreciation is taken from regulated accounts and thus differs from that shown in Tables 10.2, 10.3 and Appendix 10.2 in that it includes depreciation on investment property and excludes depreciation on centrally capitalized costs.

†Profit is equal to revenue less opex and depreciation.

‡Cost of capital is calculated at 7.5 per cent of RCV, broadly in line with required return in 1996 MMC report. RCV figures taken from Appendix 10.2.

§Surplus is equal to revenue less operating expenditure, depreciation and cost of capital. Surplus exceeds zero due to revenue advancement (see paragraph 10.3) and outperformance against MMC's 1996 assumptions, in particular lower RCV and hence lower required return (see paragraph 10.10).

¶Includes all car parking (short-term, long-term and staff), car rental, buses, coaches and taxis.

Dual till

8.7. BAA and the CAA proposed that, in future, only the aeronautical activity should be taken into account when setting the airport charges price cap: there would then be two tills—aeronautical (taken into account when setting price cap) and non-aeronautical (not taken into account when setting the price cap). Assuming that both revenue and cost of the activities can be separated, this may be expected to have the following effects.

(a) Airport charges would rise. The size of any effect would depend on the precise definition of the aeronautical activity:

(i) Under the CAA's proposal, the aeronautical till is as shown in Table 8.2 with all other activities outside the aeronautical till: based on the approximate 2000/01 data in Table 8.2 the effect would be to increase required net airport charges revenue by about £150 million, just under £1.50 per passenger or 29 per cent of airport charges. The effect is somewhat smaller at Heathrow than the other two airports because at Heathrow commercial profits of about £2 per passenger are reduced by rail losses of £0.88 per passenger.

(ii) Under BAA's proposal, the aeronautical till would include also surface access (roads etc, rail) except for long-term car parking and the Heathrow Express operating company: based on the approximate 2000/01 data in Table 8.2 the effect would be to increase required airport charges revenue by more than £195 million, £1.80 per passenger or 37 per cent of airport charges.[1]

Future effects would depend on future profitability of activities outside the aeronautical till (BAA's projections show falling retail revenue per passenger—see paragraphs 8.32 to 8.35).

(b) BAA would have the incentive to introduce new charges for activities outside the aeronautical till that are not currently charged for. As noted above, a possible example is road access.

(c) BAA would also be incentivized to increase existing charges and rents on activities outside the aeronautical till above the level that would prevail under the single till. Under the single till, BAA derives only a short-term benefit from increases in such charges (since extra revenue is taken into account the next time the price cap is set) but under the dual till BAA derives a permanent benefit and this gives it a stronger incentive to seek price rises. Of course BAA may only be expected to increase prices under the dual till if it is profitable to do so, ie if it has unexploited market power in the supply of the relevant product. Given that BAA itself has strong market power in the airports market (the reason for its designation under the Airports Act and hence our current inquiry)[2] this depends principally on the ease with which customers can substitute the BAA product with products provided by off-airport suppliers. The CAA only considered activities to be aeronautical if they were both necessary for the operation of airlines and non-duplicable. It is quite possible that an activity would not meet either one or both of these requirements (and thus be outside the CAA's aeronautical till) but that BAA nevertheless has market power in its supply, for example because off-airport suppliers exist but are an imperfect substitute for BAA's on-airport supply.

8.8. The remainder of this chapter considers the main activities not covered by airport charges, according to the classification shown in Table 8.1. We have considered the extent of market power held by the airports in each of these activities, that is the extent to which they are constrained in raising prices. The main potential constraints include competition for airlines and passengers from other airports (which, as noted above is limited in the case of the BAA London airports), competition from off-airport suppliers and the willingness of customers to substitute other products for that supplied by BAA or its concessionaires. In the context of this inquiry we have not, however, been able to make a full competition analysis of the market for each service that BAA supplies.

Services and facilities not remunerated by airport charges

8.9. This category includes provision of facilities to airlines and their handling agents and also to other companies operating on the airports including retail concessionaires and transport companies.

Specified activities

8.10. Following a recommendation in the 1991 MMC report, the CAA requires the airports to publish trading statements for certain activities, known as specified activities, including:

---

[1] The exclusion of commercial activities, as defined in Table 8.2, would increase required airport charges revenue by £196 million and in addition BAA's proposal would increase it by surplus of long-term car parking plus notional profits/losses of Heathrow Express operating company (currently the Heathrow Express operating company earns a profit of about 10 per cent of its operating expenses (see paragraph 4.4).
[2] Stansted's market position is weaker than that of the other two airports as it faces competition from Luton.

(a) Check-in desks (including outbound baggage systems but not hold baggage screening (HBS) which is remunerated through airport charges[1]), for which a rental per desk is charged. Some desks are subject to common user arrangements and are charged on a per hour basis.

(b) Other desk licences, which include other airline desks (for example, ticket desks) and desks for non-airline organizations.

(c) Staff car parking (parking for those working at the airports, most of whom are not employed directly by BAA), for which a monthly fee per pass is usually charged.

(d) Staff identity cards, for which airlines are charged per pass.

(e) FEGP, which is currently charged on an hourly basis, either based on metered time or aircraft parking time, and which aircraft on stand are required to use in preference to their engines or ground power units for environmental reasons.

(f) Aviation fuel supplied through hydrants, on which airports levy a charge according to fuel taken on at the airport; this is additional to the charges for fuel and for fuel infrastructure (which at Stansted, but not Heathrow and Gatwick, is owned by BAA).

(g) Airside licences, which cover the costs of managing vehicles accessing and operating airside including safety checks and security control (these are required, for example, by cleaning and catering companies).

(h) Heating and ventilation, which is mostly charged according to space occupied, although some heating is charged according to usage.

(i) Electricity, gas and water, which is charged according to usage.

(j) Coach operators (including express, charter, hotel and courtesy coaches) are charged according to costs incurred including the use of facilities such as the central bus station at Heathrow and the coach parks. Local bus operators are not charged, as part of BAA's commitment to public transport, and in addition BAA uses the receipts of a levy on car parks, including staff car parks to contribute to various public transport initiatives including support for free local buses at Heathrow and Gatwick.

8.11. BAA told us that most specified activities were charged on the basis of costs. The exceptions were desk licences other than check-in desks, which were based on commercial negotiations, and aviation fuel supplies where BAA's charges were based on costs plus a levy. Costs include allocated overheads (see paragraph 8.4(b)) and a capital charge (based on annuitizing the inflation-adjusted historical cost of each asset over its assumed life[2]) and thus differ from those shown in Table 8.1. Income, costs and profits of specified activities are summarized in Table 8.3. Prices for most of the specified activities do not cover their full costs while total income from aviation fuel far exceeds cost, reflecting income from the levies. Thus, income from the fuel levies tends to offset losses on the other specified activities and specified activities as a whole probably do not contribute to an airport charges cap below allocated cost.[3] However, there seems no logical connection between the two and alternative arrangements could include higher charges for loss-making specified activities (except where supported by valid policy objectives, such as support for public transport) and either lower fuel levies or lower airport charges. BAA told us that other airports also had fuel levies; that, despite the levies, fuel charges at its airports were no higher than at other European airports and hence that reducing or eliminating the levies could provide an incentive for short-haul airlines to take on more fuel at Heathrow when they had a realistic expectation that the need to refuel elsewhere could be avoided.

8.12. BAA argued that the operation of the transparency undertakings should be streamlined, especially as some of the specified activities were de minimis in terms of income generated.

---

[1] Inbound baggage is remunerated via airport charges and transfer baggage is considered below.

[2] In most cases a real pre-tax cost of capital of 8 per cent is used. For Heathrow check-in desks, BAA quotes a current 'risk free post tax discount rate' of 9.25 per cent.

[3] The methodology for setting the airport charges pricing formula includes inflation-adjusted depreciation and return on capital in projected costs (see Chapter 10) and thus differs from the methodology used in the specified activity statements.

TABLE 8.3 **Summary of specified activities, 2001/02**

£'000

	Income	Costs	Profit
Heathrow			
Check-in desks	34,059	43,098	−9,039
Other desk licences	2,420	438	1,982
Staff car parks	16,401	17,010	−609
Staff ID passes	1,616	1,686	−70
FEGP	3,719	4,256	−537
Aviation fuel*			
Airside licences	777	927	−150
Heating and ventilation	5,254	6,658	−1,404
Gas			
Electricity†	27,683	28,422	−739
Water (and sewerage)	3,735	4,163	−428
Coach‡	1,043	3,849	−2,806
Gatwick			
Check-in desks	9,212	10,868	−1,656
Other desk licences	591	598	−7
Staff car parks	3,398	3,520	−122
Staff ID passes	732	986	−254
FEGP	1,609	1,264	345
Aviation fuel	7,186	385	6,801
Airside licences	49	11	38
Heating and ventilation	7,102	7,193	−91
Gas	532	1,097	−565
Electricity†	11,240	11,480	−240
Water (and sewerage)	1,763	1,833	−70
Coach	229	245	−16
Stansted			
Check-in desks	1,954	2,845	−891
Other desk licences			
Staff car parks	726	478	248
Staff ID passes	219	280	−61
FEGP	209	461	−252
Aviation fuel	4,530	1,520	3,010
Airside licences			
Heating and ventilation§	20	4,372	−4,352
Gas	222	504	−282
Electricity†	5,447	5,328	119
Water (and sewerage)	626	999	−373
Coach	0		

Source: BAA trading statements (which are the basis for consultation on specified activity charges).

Note: The trading statements are based on PCR adjusted for: notional income from BAA's usage of the facilities; inclusion of capital charge (see paragraph 8.11) and exclusion of depreciation; electricity costs (see note below)

*Income from hydrant refuelling (£13.4 million) is included in property income. The majority of the £13.4 million is attributable to an inflation-linked fuel rent from a lease granted to the Heathrow Consortium, which is due to expire in 2005.

†Based on 1992/93 costs indexed by the RPI, as agreed by BAA and airlines following the sale of electricity assets to LEC.

‡Includes notional revenue from local bus use of central bus station.

§The trading statement indicates that, at present, only a nominal sum is recovered via charges although further sums are included in service charges, but that STAL's intention is to introduce in 2002/03 a methodology whereby costs can ultimately be recovered. STAL's own usage accounts for a significant level of consumption.

8.13. There appears to be little opportunity for customers to substitute off-airport suppliers or other products for the specified activities listed at *(a)*, *(b)* and *(d)* to *(g)* of paragraph 8.10 and both BAA and the CAA included them[1] in their definitions of the aeronautical till. With respect to the other activities listed in paragraph 8.10:

(a) BAA appears to have potential market power in staff car parking as many staff would incur additional costs and inconvenience getting to work by other means. Moreover, BAA can influence the price of many alternative means of access to the airports (including rail and bus),

[1]The CAA allocated off-site check-in (Paddington) to the non-aeronautical till.

although we note that in practice BAA tends currently to subsidize public transport[1] rather than exploit its power to raise prices. BAA allocated staff car parking to the aeronautical till but the CAA allocated it to the non-aeronautical till, in line with its treatment of all surface access (see paragraph 8.43).

(h)–(i) As regards utilities (heating, gas, electricity and water) the extent of BAA's market power depends on the extent of market power in the properties to which the utilities are supplied (see paragraph 8.23). BAA allocated revenue and costs from utilities between aeronautical and non-aeronautical tills approximately on the basis of usage. The CAA allocated revenue and costs from utilities on the airfield to the aeronautical till, those relating to utilities within terminal buildings were split between both tills.

(j) As regards facilities for coach operators, BAA appears to have very strong market power since the facilities are valuable but account for a small proportion of the price charged for the service offered by the coach operators[2] (implying there is a very weak threat of passengers substituting alternative transport modes). Furthermore, BAA itself can influence the prices of many alternative transport modes including car parking, taxis and Heathrow Express and in future may also be able to introduce charges for road access.[3] BAA included facilities for coach operators in the aeronautical till, although the CAA did not do so in line with its general treatment of surface access.

Transfer baggage

8.14. Around one-quarter of Heathrow passengers are transferring between flights and around 70 per cent of these transferring passengers require their baggage to be transferred between terminals. Following the MMC's 1996 report, most transfer baggage infrastructure is financed by a per passenger TSC.[4] The TSC is based on costs under a methodology agreed by BAA and the airlines, and there is a committee, Transfer Infrastructure Group at Heathrow (TIFGAH), which meets regularly to review costs, approve infrastructure investments and recommend future levels of TSC to the User Charges Forum. The TIFGAH steering group told us that in 2001/02 BAA had voluntarily deferred part of the TSC and that BAA's total under-recovery against costs stood at £2.8 million by the end of 2002/03. Some costs of transfer baggage, in particular the facilities at T4 and the tunnel between T1 and T4,[5] are paid for separately by airlines. BAA told us that the 2002/03 costs associated with the TSC were £26.7 million (excluding under-recovery) and the other transfer costs were about £18 million.

8.15. The TIFGAH steering group also told us that, since the introduction of the TSC and the associated improvements in infrastructure, transfer performance had improved but that agreeing the TSC each year had been a lengthy process with a significant amount of management time invested in reviewing all costs, a point also made by BAA. BAA and TIFGAH proposed that the costs covered by TSC be included in airport charges from 1 April 2003: this would mean there was no need for a TSC after that date (BA argued that its other transfer costs should also be included in airport charges but this was not supported by BAA or other airlines on the grounds that BA had freely entered into the contract for the T1/T4 tunnel). BAA also told us that its ultimate vision for the remuneration of direct and transfer baggage systems was for airlines to pay using mechanisms that incentivized the efficient use of those facilities. This would involve a per bag charge covering all transfer baggage infrastructure. BAA's view was that cost calibration and airline agreement were likely to prove difficult in the short term and this was therefore a longer-term aim for Q5, when the T1/T4 tunnel agreement would be likely to have expired.

8.16. BAA appears to have strong market power in the provision of transfer baggage facilities as transfer passengers are important to many airlines operating at Heathrow and the relevant services cannot be supplied off-airport. Both the CAA and BAA included transfer baggage systems in the aeronautical till.

---

[1]BAA told us of the following activities which encouraged staff working at the airport to use public transport: support for free buses in the Heathrow local area; reduced prices for public transport (the Airport Travelcard); one of the largest car-sharing schemes in the UK; concessionary rates for staff on the Heathrow Express.
[2]Relevant services include express coaches, hotels and off-airport car parking.
[3]As noted above, the CAA has indicated that it would support legislation allowing such charges.
[4]The MMC recommended a per bag charge.
[5]4 per cent of the costs associated with the tunnel are included in the TSC. This reflects usage by airlines other than BA, which pays the costs of the tunnel under a contract that dates from before the TSC system.

Other

8.17. This category includes a variety of services and facilities for which BAA currently levies separate charges (see Appendix 2.5, Tables 4 and 5), including self-service check-in, off-airport check-in (Paddington), the cost of installing common user check-in equipment at Gatwick and taxi charges (described below). BAA is also proposing certain new charges (see Appendix 2.5, Table 6). BAA proposed that total revenue per passenger from some of these services and facilities together with specified activities (and TSC if continued) would be subject to an RPI+/–X cap.

8.18. As Heathrow is within the metropolitan area, licensed London taxis are allowed to ply for hire there but are required to wait at a feeder park before being dispatched by a computer system to the various terminal ranks. BAA currently charges drivers £2.55 (increasing to £2.70 from 1 November) for using the feeder park, of which 49p is a levy paid to Heathrow Airport Licensed Taxis to fund taxi information desks and the remainder contributes to BAA's costs in running the operation.[1] Taxis frequently have to wait up to two hours in the feeder park but those picking up passengers with a local destination are entitled to return straight to the rank without going through the feeder park, providing they do so within one hour. At Gatwick and Stansted, taxi ranks are operated by concessionaires paying a rent to BAA.

8.19. There are a wide variety of services and facilities included in this category (see Appendix 2.5, Tables 4 and 5) but, for the most part, competition from off-airport suppliers is likely to be limited or non-existent while customers would find it difficult to substitute other products for the BAA service or facility. Indeed, were this not the case, there would be no reason for BAA to propose a cap covering revenue from these services and facilities.

BAA's projections

8.20. Figure 8.1 shows BAA's projections of future revenue per passenger from other services and facilities. Projected revenue per passenger at Heathrow (which includes revenue from the TSC)[2] declines in particular after 2007/08 due to assumed loss of rental income from the T1/T4 baggage tunnel and to lower check-in rentals at T5 (where BAA's projections envisage the departure baggage system will be sold to BA). Projected revenue per passenger at Gatwick and Stansted is assumed to remain approximately constant.

Property

8.21. BAA's property activities at the London airports are described and evaluated by Donaldsons in Appendix 8.1. In their report, Donaldsons indicate that they believed BAA was an efficient manager of its property assets and that growth in BAA's underlying rental income over the last five years had not been excessive.

8.22. Donaldsons' conclusions are based on BAA's policy and incentives under the single till and do not in themselves imply either that BAA has no market power in the supply of airport property or that it would not exploit that market power under a different regime (for example, dual till).

8.23. The extent of BAA's market power depends on the type of property:

(a) Terminal offices and ramp areas appear necessary for airlines and cannot be supplied off airport. Both BAA and the CAA allocated them to the aeronautical till.

---

[1]The facilities include traffic wardens to manage the forecourts, police to deal with ticket touts, the control system and the taxi park. BAA told us that it expected 2002/03 charges to fall short of cost by £392,000.

[2]Our own projections assume that Heathrow's transfer baggage is funded from airport charges: hence, no TSC income is included (see paragraph 10.33).

FIGURE 8.1

Revenue per passenger from services and facilities not remunerated by airport charges

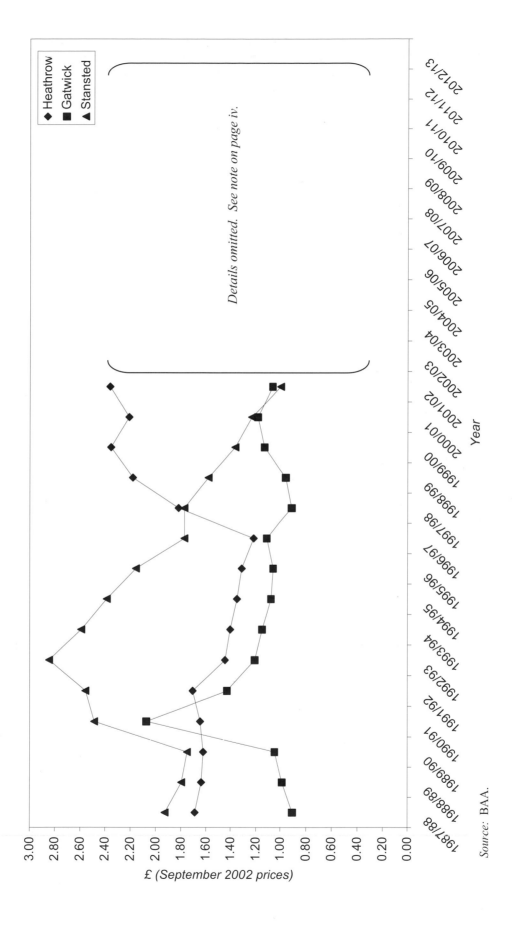

Details omitted. See note on page iv.

Source: BAA.

(b) CIP lounges are an important part of the product offered by some airlines, which would be impossible to provide off airport. Although existing rents are described by Donaldsons as very high, it seems probable that the value of CIP lounges to some airlines, as part of their offering to premium passengers, is such that some CIP rents could be increased further and thus that BAA does have market power in their provision. Despite this, both BAA and the CAA allocated CIP lounges to the non-aeronautical till.

(c) With regard to other offices (those not within the terminals), Donaldsons said they were not aware that tenants were deprived of the sort of choice or flexibility enjoyed in the wider market or that they lacked suitable alternatives. This suggests that BAA does not have market power in the supply of these offices. Both BAA and the CAA allocated them to the non-aeronautical till.[1]

(d) With regard to maintenance facilities, the CAA argued that airlines were able to choose between a number of airports when deciding where to carry out planned (but not unplanned) maintenance. We note, however, that UK scheduled airlines, which tend to have their main base at one of the London airports, may find it costly to shift major maintenance operations to other airports. Furthermore, the choice of maintenance base for major UK charter airlines may be limited to just two airports (Gatwick and Manchester). Consequently, BAA may have market power in the supply of planned as well as unplanned maintenance. In the event, the CAA allocated maintenance facilities to the aeronautical till on pragmatic grounds, as did BAA.

(e) With regard to cargo buildings, the CAA argued that they were not bottlenecks as most, if not all, cargo and freight commissioning could be done off airport if suitable space were available. However, BAA told us that the DfT security regulations required export checks to be carried out on-airport which would limit competition from off-airport suppliers to import traffic. BAA also suggested that suppliers of cargo facilities further from the airport tended to be attractive for a low-speed handling service and this suggests that off-airport competition may not tightly constrain the price of on-airport facilities required for a higher-speed handling service. Although BAA believed its market power to be very limited, it seems to us that off-airport sites are unlikely to be a close substitute for units at the airport and thus that BAA has market power in the supply of this type of accommodation. BAA and the CAA allocated cargo facilities to the non-aeronautical till.

BAA's projections

8.24. Figure 8.2 shows that property revenue per passenger at Heathrow is projected to remain broadly static until T5 opens when there is a step increase. At Gatwick and Stansted property revenue per passenger is forecast to decline: BAA told us that, at Gatwick, this reflects certain baggage facilities becoming fully paid under the terms of the relevant rental agreement, and, at Stansted, it reflected improved utilization of existing facilities. The higher level of property revenue at Heathrow reflects the greater demands of full service scheduled airlines, especially those with extensive long-haul operations (Gatwick's numbers also reflect low cargo revenue). Past trends reflect transfers (with the CAA's agreement) of property out of the regulated companies into BAA's unregulated property company (Lynton) and reclassification of some revenue.

Retail and car rental

8.25. Retailing is carried out at the airports by concessionaires: BAA chooses concessionaires through a process of bidding for turnover rents (subject to a minimum annual payment). Concessionaires are for the most part major retailing groups, such as Dixons, Boots and WHSmith. The duty-free concession is let on the basis of a percentage of profit and, at all three London airports, is held by WDFE, a subsidiary of BAA. BAA told us that WDFE was not required to tender for the duty-free concession in competition with other bidders (although it was required to tender for tax-free specialist shops) and that WDFE operated at arm's length from the airport companies. Although BAA's formal role is that of landlord, it exercises a degree of control over its concessionnaires' product lines more akin to a department store than a shopping centre landlord (see Appendix 8.1, paragraph 123).

---

[1] The CAA allocated offices occupied by BAA's own staff to the aeronautical till.

FIGURE 8.2

Property revenue per passenger

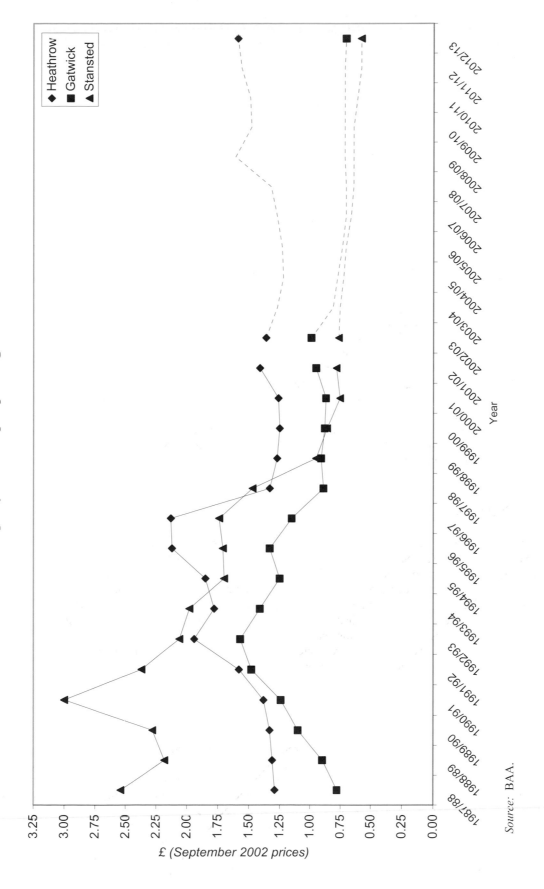

£ (September 2002 prices)

Year

Source: BAA.

271

8.26. BAA's retail activities at the London airports are described and evaluated by Donaldsons in Appendix 8.1. In their report, Donaldsons indicated that they believed BAA was an efficient manager of its retail assets but that there were a few areas offering scope for improvement, including opportunities for BAA to provide a better environment to passengers by embracing a stronger and more unified design concept within its public spaces. Donaldsons also stated that they believed growth in BAA's underlying concession income over the last five years had not been excessive. With regard to WDFE bidding successfully against third parties for tax-free concessions, Donaldsons believed there was a level playing field.

8.27. Table 8.1 shows that retail accounts for about 42 per cent of HCA profits and the percentage of profits would almost certainly be increased if allowance were made for cost of capital as retail accounts for a small percentage of the assets.[1] Table 8.4 shows that duty-free sales account for over one-third of retail revenue. Moreover, as duty-free has the highest revenue per square metre (apart from bureaux de change which occupy little space), it is likely to account for a higher proportion of profits than revenue (it was nearly two-thirds of retail HCA profits in 1999/2000—see Appendix 8.2). In 2001/02, BAA's duty-free concession fees were about 31 per cent of the shops' turnover and its concession fees from other airside shops were about 18 per cent of their turnover. BAA provided us with information on the profits and net assets of WDFE split between the three London airports and elsewhere (see Appendix 8.3): these suggested that in the years 1999/2000 to 2001/02 WDFE's profits at the three London airports were about £20 million per year, representing a return on capital of between 50 and 100 per cent.

TABLE 8.4 **Revenue from retail concessions, 2000/01**

				£ million
	Heathrow	Gatwick	Stansted	Total
Duty-free	59.1	32.6	4.6	96.3
Other airside	47.2	18.6	1.9	67.7
Landside	13.1	8.4	3.0	24.5
Catering	15.2	10.2	3.3	28.7
Bureaux de change	23.7	12.6	3.8	40.1
Other*	7.4	3.7	1.1	12.2
Total	165.7	86.0	17.8	269.5
				£ per square metre
Duty-free	5,885	6,786	3,435	5,950
Other airside	4,224	3,278	2,861	3,866
Landside	3,361	1,596	2,066	2,308
Catering	1,003	902	1,249	986
Bureaux de change	17,914	21,538	25,000	19,466

Source: BAA.

Note: Totals differ slightly from those shown in Table 8.1.
*Insurance, payphones, family entertainment, CTA petrol station, hotel bookings, VAT cash refunds and other concessions.

8.28. BAA requires its concessionaires to offer prices (or, in the case of bureaux de change, commissions) no higher than at their high-street locations. Airside shops (other than duty-free shops which are dealt with in the next paragraph) are required to sell to non-EC passengers at high street prices less VAT. Following the 1999 abolition of tax-free sales to EC passengers, BAA and its concessionaires have also pursued a policy of selling to EC passengers at the same price as to non-EC passengers even though VAT is payable on such sales (BAA told us it may wish to review this policy). BAA also told us that its shops and branded catering outlets were contractually obliged to supply information confirming their compliance on prices and BAA also carried out a biannual survey of 12 products per outlet. About 20 per cent of catering sales are from unbranded catering outlets and these are required to price at or below the price shown by a survey of 10 to 15 key lines in comparable high-street locations. Car rental operators were required to offer their national tariffs to customers who had not prebooked—BAA told us that such 'walk-up' tariffs were now relatively unimportant and also that car rental was a product area

---

[1]Non-aeronautical (mainly retail) use of terminals accounts for only about 3 per cent of total assets (2 per cent at Heathrow and Stansted and 5 per cent at Gatwick) according to the CAA's analysis of the net book value of assets over £1 million at 31 March 2001 (source: RRCB annex to CAA submission). On a similar basis, car rental accounts for about 3 per cent of profits and about 1 per cent of assets.

that was difficult to monitor as tariffs varied according to time of day, availability of cars and customer discounts from membership of airline loyalty schemes, motoring organizations etc.

8.29. BAA directly controls the price of duty-free goods that are sold only to non-EC passengers. BAA told us that, compared with the high-street price (including duty and VAT), its duty-free shops offered savings of 20 to 50 per cent on alcohol,[1] 50 per cent on cigarettes[2] and 25 to 50 per cent on cigars, more than 21 per cent off fragrances and the VAT rate (17.5 per cent) off the list price of skincare and cosmetics products (which are available to EC passengers as well as non-EC passengers). BAA compares the prices of alcohol, tobacco and fragrance products quarterly. Duty-free shops also sell some other goods, for which the pricing policy is similar to other airside shops.

8.30. BAA's role is essentially that of landlord but, as its concession fees are linked to concession-aires' turnover and/or profits, its retail revenue and profits depend on the prices charged by its concessionaires. Passengers at an airport often have time on their hands and may be, to some extent, a captive market: this may give retail businesses the opportunity to raise prices above those prevailing at off-airport locations (higher prices would discourage some purchases but may nevertheless be profitable). Additionally, BAA faces limited competition for duty-free purchases—this comes only from the airline and the airport at the other end of the passenger's route. As explained in the previous paragraphs, BAA limits the prices that concessionaires can charge and this would have the effect, at least in the first instance, of reducing its own revenue and profits (which are linked to the turnover of its concessionaires). BAA told us that it did this because it considered it vital to create and maintain the perception that airport retailing provided passengers with good value and quality. We note, however, that the need to control concessionaires' prices suggests that they have market power in retailing even though the profits would accrue to BAA;[3] that BAA, as a monopoly supplier of airports, may have limited incentives to continue to ensure low prices at its retail outlets; and that introduction of the dual till would give BAA a greater incentive to allow prices to be raised (under the single till extra profits would only be retained for up to five years; under the dual till they would be retained indefinitely). BAA did not accept this inference, stating that the aim of its current retail strategy and pricing, which would be unchanged under the dual till, was to maximize retail income by promoting the price advantages and value of airport shopping.

8.31. BAA and the CAA argued that consumers had a choice whether or not to use retail and catering services and they paid for the services directly. Hence, retail and catering services were not a bottleneck activity and should be outside the aeronautical till. The CAA also said that if excess prices were charged at the airports' shops and catering outlets the appropriate action would be for the Office of Fair Trading (OFT) to consider them directly, using the CA98.

BAA's projections

8.32. Figure 8.3 shows that BAA projects a decline in its duty- and tax-free revenue per international departing passenger (IDP). This reflects assumed lower purchases of alcohol and tobacco products due to increased health awareness, an assumed ban on tobacco sales phased in over 2005/06 to 2007/08 and an assumed increase in size of the EC in 2004/05 and 2008/09, although at Heathrow these factors are offset somewhat by the effect of increased retailing space when T5 opens. Donaldsons accepted that BAA's projections were reasonable, noting also that they expected continued erosion in general retail margins to translate into lower bids by retailers for concessions. Past trends reflect in particular the abolition of sales to EC passengers and also an underlying decline in sales per IDP over time, offset at particular points by the effects of increased retailing space. BAA told us that the Asian crisis of the late 1990s had also affected Heathrow revenue per IDP.

8.33. Figure 8.4 shows that BAA projects catering revenue per passenger to remain approximately constant at a level slightly lower than 2001/02. BAA told us that catering revenues had increased in 2001/02 due to increased dwell times after 11 September but that it had assumed that dwell times would return to previous levels.

---

[1] Duty and tax on 1 litre of spirits (40 per cent alcohol) costing £18.00 would be about 58 per cent of the price.
[2] Duty and tax on a packet of 20 cigarettes costing £4.00 would be about 69 per cent of the price.
[3] Any excess profits earned by concessionaires would be bid away on the next occasion that concessions were let.

FIGURE 8.3

Duty- and tax-free revenue per IDP

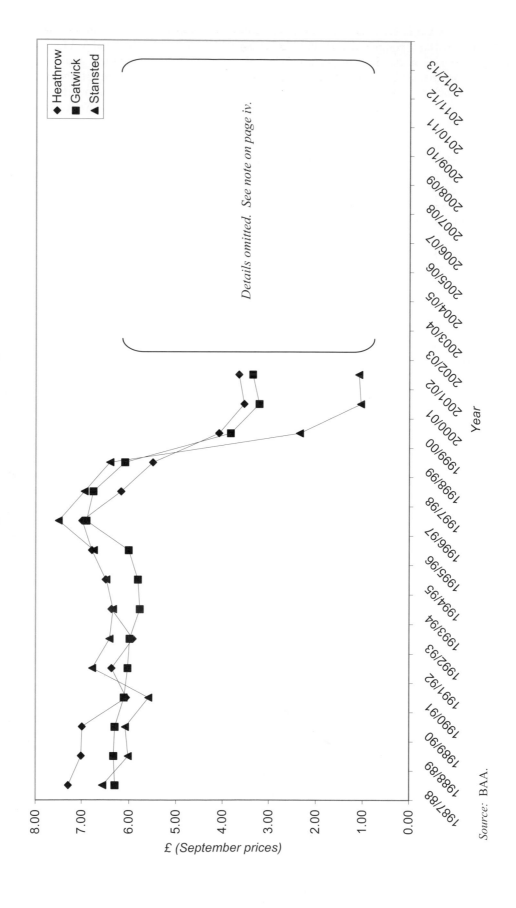

FIGURE 8.4

Catering revenue per passenger

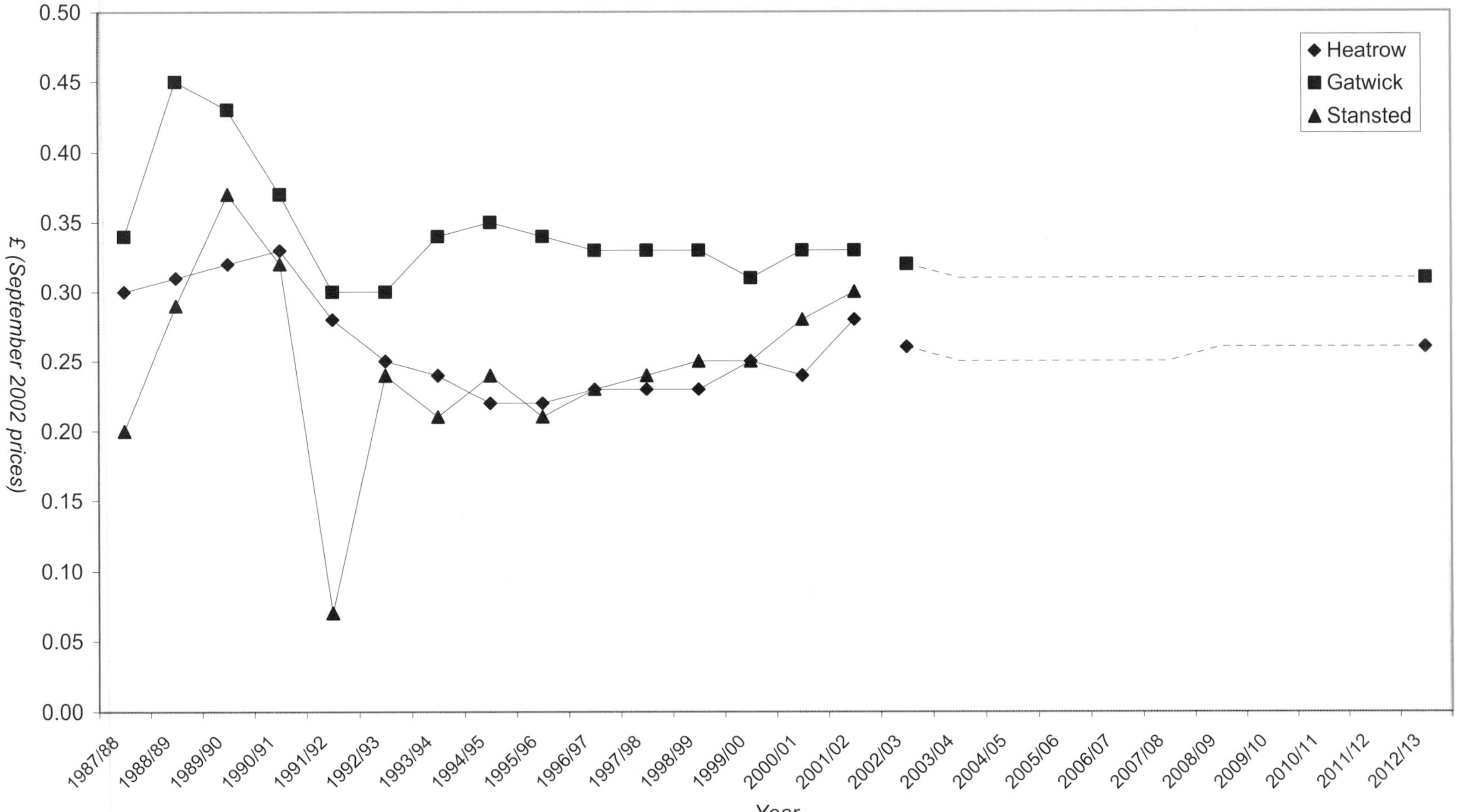

Source: BAA.

275

8.34. BAA assumes that its revenue from bureaux de change (Figure 8.5) will approximately halve due to the UK joining the euro in 2005/06. BAA also assumes bureaux de change revenues are affected by an adverse long-term trend due to increased ATM use by passengers.

8.35. Figure 8.6 shows BAA's projected revenue from other retailing activities (including car rental and advertising). BAA told us that it had assumed an adverse long-term trend due in particular to consolidation of the car rental sector, prebooking services on the Internet and continued decline in revenue from landside retail.

Car parking

8.36. BAA's public car parks[1] can be divided into two main categories: short-term car parks (within walking distance of the terminals) and long-term (which require a coach transfer[2]). Short-term car parks are used by family or friends meeting arriving passengers or seeing off departing passengers. They may also be used by passengers making short trips, who use their own car to get to/from the airport.[3] Long-term car parks are used by passengers making longer trips, who use their own car to get to/from the airport. Prices of long-term car parks are lower for similar periods: at Heathrow, one day's long-term car parking in 2001/02 cost £12.40 against £36.00 for one day's short-term car parking; at Gatwick the comparison for 2001/02 was £6.50 (£5.95 at off-peak times of year) for long-term against £16.80 for short-term; at Stansted, the figures were £6.00 for long-term against £13.00 for short-term parking. Prices per day/hour decline with the length of time parked and lower long-term prices may be obtained by prebooking either direct or through an intermediary.

8.37. BAA sets the prices of its short-term car parks which are operated under an open-book concession agreement. Long-term car parks are operated by concessionaires paying a 'turnover rent' with BAA setting maximum prices.

8.38. As illustrated in Appendix 8.4, BAA's short-term car park prices have increased substantially in real terms since the mid-1990s, and long-term prices have also increased materially, although it should be noted that long-term prices do vary between peak and off-peak times of the year and some customers may obtain discounts on the prebooked price. BAA indicated that there were a number of factors that influenced its pricing of car parks:

(a) Increasing car park prices gave effect to BAA's strategy of increasing the proportion of passengers arriving by public transport. This was in line with government policy and helped ease congestion around terminal buildings, which would otherwise occur due to planning and other constraints on the number of car parking spaces (similarly there was limited access capacity to Heathrow's CTA). A small part of the increase in prices was accounted for by an explicit Public Transport Levy, which funded public transport schemes such as the Heathrow Free Travel Zone and other improvements to bus services.

(b) On the other hand, excessive increases in short-term car park prices could aggravate congestion by encouraging those waiting to pick up passengers to drive round and round the airport to avoid parking charges.

(c) Price increases could attract significant critical press comment and the attention of the OFT under competition legislation (the OFT carried out some inquiries into BAA's pricing of car parks during 1999 and 2000).

8.39. Users of car parks in most cases potentially have alternative means of accessing the airports, including use of public transport, taxi and being dropped off/picked up by friends/relatives. Table 8.5 shows recent trends in use of different methods of transport.

---

[1] Staff car parking has been considered above under specified activities.
[2] At Heathrow, BAA offers business parking, involving a shorter coach journey, as well as standard long-term car parking.
[3] BAA told us that, at Heathrow, 87.5 per cent of short-term car park customers park for less than 2 hours.

FIGURE 8.5

Bureaux de change revenue per IDP

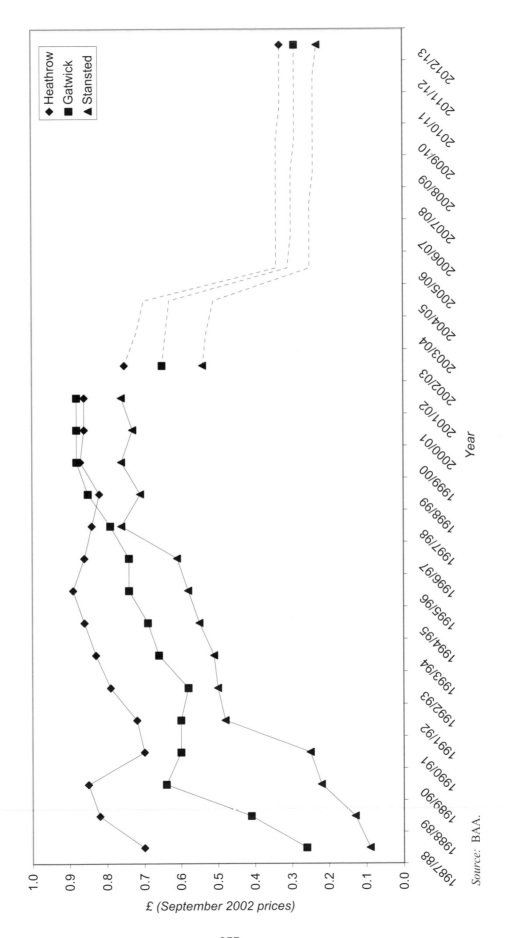

Source: BAA.

277

FIGURE 8.6

Other retail revenue per passenger

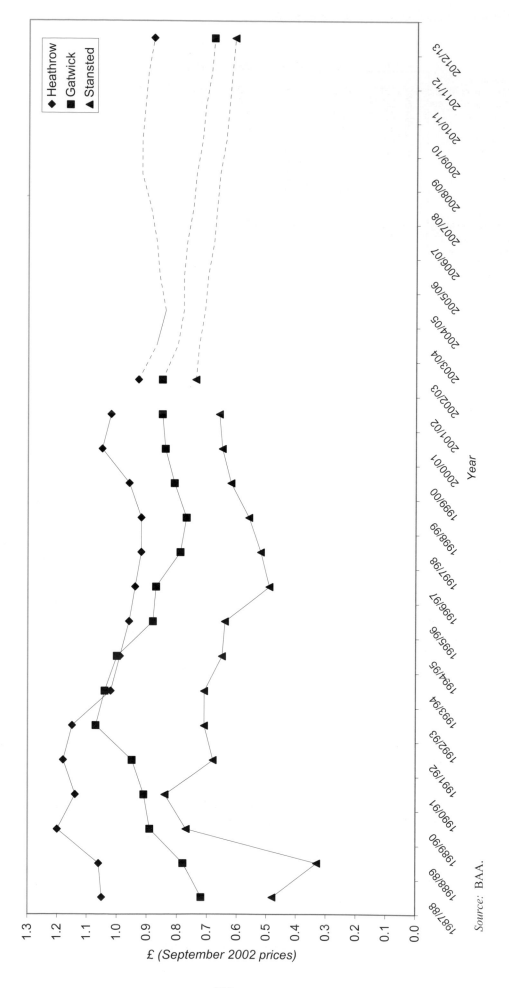

£ (September 2002 prices)

Year

Source: BAA.

278

TABLE 8.5 **Mode of access to BAA London airports**

					per cent
	1997	1998	1999	2000	2001
Heathrow					
Car—driven away*	25.0	16.8	16.5	17.2	18.8
Short-term car park*	3.7	9.9	9.0	7.6	7.3
Long-term car park	8.4	9.6	9.0	9.0	9.1
Hire car	4.4	4.0	3.7	3.6	3.2
Taxi/minicab	24.8	26.7	26.2	25.9	26.6
Bus/coach	16.3	15.0	13.9	13.9	13.0
Rail/tube	16.5	17.5	21.0	22.0	21.0
Other	0.9	0.5	0.7	0.8	1.0
Total	100.0	100.0	100.0	100.0	100.0
Gatwick					
Car—driven away*	24.2	19.1	20.2	20.2	21.2
Short-term car park*	4.5	8.8	6.8	5.8	5.5
Long-term car park	20.5	23.8	22.0	23.5	23.5
Hire car	2.6	2.7	2.7	2.7	2.0
Taxi/minicab	13.2	14.8	15.2	16.0	17.0
Bus/coach	14.3	10.3	10.9	10.0	9.4
Rail/tube	20.6	20.4	21.7	21.5	20.9
Other	0.1	0.1	0.5	0.3	0.5
Total	100.0	100.0	100.0	100.0	100.0
Stansted					
Car—driven away				16.2	18.8
Short-term car park†				11.3	8.2
Long-term car park†				25.3	25.0
Hire car				3.0	3.3
Taxi/minicab				10.1	10.6
Bus/coach				6.9	7.9
Rail/tube				27.1	26.2
Other				0.1	0.0
Total				100.0	100.0

Source: CAA airport surveys (analysed by BAA).

*The CAA told us that there was a tightening up of the definition of 'car—driven away' between 1997 and 1998: the 1997 survey probably included some who parked in the short-term car park in the category 'car—driven away'.

†Capacity problems with the short-term car parks, especially during the summer, caused short-stay passengers to use the long-term car parks. BAA said that this was due in part to the rapid growth of low fares airlines.

8.40. We asked BAA to estimate the effect of an increase in short-term car park prices on usage of the different access modes: this would have enabled us to assess the profitability of further price increases. BAA told us that, although it had a modal split model for Heathrow, results had been disappointing (for instance, in predicting Heathrow Express's share). The last major update of its model had been at the end of 1993 (based on CAA data for 1991) and BAA did not believe it sensible to attempt to utilize its current model to estimate the effect of increased car park prices. At a later stage in the inquiry BAA told us that, over time, its experience was that a 3 per cent year-on-year out-turn price increase (approximately 1 per cent real) for short-term car parks was associated with a 2 per cent increase in revenue per passenger (approximately 0 per cent real).[1] If the underlying trend (assuming constant prices) in demand per passenger is constant, this suggests a price elasticity of –1, implying that prices are now at a level where price increases do not generate increased revenue although BAA might benefit from any cost savings associated with servicing fewer customers than there would have been with lower prices.

8.41. BAA's long-term car parks face competition from off-airport suppliers, some of which have been authorized by the planning authorities and others which operate without authorization. BAA told us that there were around 11 off-airport car parks at Heathrow, 32 at Gatwick (including Gatwick hotels offering some long-term parking) and one at Stansted. As shown in Table 8.6, BAA's market share is about 60 per cent at Heathrow and Gatwick and 97 per cent at Stansted. Off-airport car parks typically offer lower prices than BAA and market their service either directly (for example, through Internet sites, travel agents and leaflets in ticket wallets) or through intermediaries.

---

[1]Figure 8.7, however, shows increasing car park revenue per passenger. Figure 8.7 does reflect contract fees and long-term car park revenue as well as short-term car park revenue.

TABLE 8.6 **Approximate market share in long-term car parks**

	Heathrow	Gatwick	Stansted
			per cent
BAA on airport car parks	55	48	97
BAA-owned off-airport car parks	0	12	-
Other car parks: authorized	4	31	-
Other car parks: unauthorized	42	9	3
Total	100	100	100

Source: Surveys commissioned by BAA for Heathrow (2001) and Gatwick (2002).

Note: Market share estimated from number of spaces.

8.42. While BAA faces competition from off-airport suppliers of long-term parking, the extent to which other suppliers can respond to increased demand (for instance, following a price increase at BAA car parks) may be limited by planning constraints on the number of spaces offered. BAA has a large market share and has been successful in implementing material price increases. These considerations suggest that BAA has market power in the supply of long-term as well as short-term car parking.

8.43. BAA accepted that it had a monopoly position in short-term car parks and allocated it to the aeronautical till. BAA considered that long-term car parking was a competitive market and hence long-term car parks should be outside the aeronautical till. The CAA considered that all surface access (including short-term car parks) should be outside the aeronautical till. Among the reasons for this were that airports did not necessarily fully control all modes of access to the airport and thus could not extract a full monopoly rent; that parking charges were paid by passengers who would not benefit from car parks being allocated to the aeronautical till since the profits would accrue to airlines who, at congested airports, would not pass it on to passengers in lower fares;[1] and that passengers were protected from excessive pricing by the competition legislation.

BAA's projections

8.44. Figure 8.7 shows that BAA projects total car park revenue per passenger to remain approximately constant. BAA told us that it expected any further increases in prices to be offset by declines in the percentage of passengers using the car parks. The projected level of revenue per passenger at Stansted remains much higher than at Heathrow or Gatwick due to a higher percentage of passengers leaving their car at the airport and BAA's higher share of long-term car parking.

Rail

8.45. BAA's existing rail activities comprise principally the rail infrastructure at Heathrow and the operation of the Heathrow Express train company. BAA told us that it had originally expected British Rail to operate the service but had been unable to stimulate any interest and had therefore decided to fund and operate it itself.

8.46. BAA invested heavily in the Heathrow Express and Table 8.2 suggests that operating profits fall far short of earning the cost of capital on the relevant assets. Given that Heathrow Express seeks to maximize profits, this suggests that, at present, competition from other transport modes, including London Underground, prevents BAA earning even an adequate return on its invested capital. Consequently, BAA does not have market power in the market for rail journeys to Heathrow. It is possible that this could change in future: for instance, if BAA is permitted to levy additional access charges on Heathrow road users, passenger volume and fares on the Heathrow Express would be expected to increase.

---

[1]The CAA accepted that Stansted was not a congested airport but argued that its cap was not likely to be binding.

FIGURE 8.7

Car park revenue per passenger

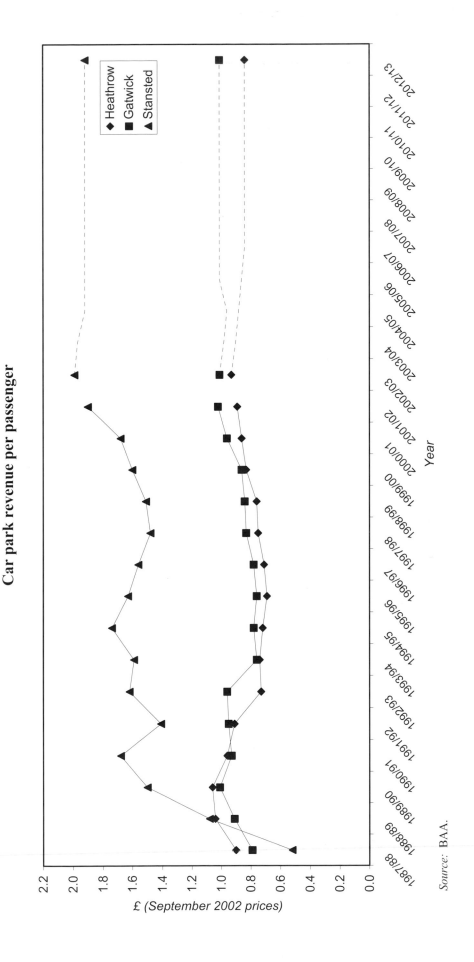

Source: BAA.

281

8.47. At present both the infrastructure and HEOC are included in the regulated till (the assets being included in RCV and revenue, opex and depreciation being included in the financial projections). BAA argued that under the dual till the Heathrow Express infrastructure should be included in the aeronautical till, along with road infrastructure and other public transport facilities, as this gave BAA the incentive to push forward with aeronautically beneficial schemes to improve airport access capacity, reduce travellers' delays and improve service quality. BAA also argued that another reason for including the Heathrow Express infrastructure in the aeronautical till was that the 1991 CAA decision on the price cap had been heavily conditional on BAA pursuing the Heathrow Express project. BAA suggested that HEOC should be outside the aeronautical till with an access fee paid for use of the infrastructure.

8.48. As noted above, the CAA proposed to exclude all surface access, including the Heathrow Express infrastructure, from the aeronautical till. An important aspect of the CAA's argument was that externality problems should be dealt with directly, for instance through road charging[1] and taxes on harmful emissions, rather than the airports subsidizing public transport projects. However, following the Government's decision that planning permission for T5 was conditional on completion of the extensions to the Heathrow Express and London Underground's Piccadilly Line, the CAA included these in its aeronautical till.

TABLE 8.7 **Projected net revenue from HEOC**

	£ per passenger, September 2002 prices
2002/03	0.44
2003/04	0.47
2004/05	0.46
2005/06	0.51
2006/07	0.52
2007/08	0.50
2008/09	0.46
2009/10	0.50
2010/11	0.52
2011/12	0.53
2012/13	0.54

Source: BAA.

Note: Net revenue per passenger is revenue less opex expressed as a proportion of all passengers at Heathrow. Net revenue from the Piccadilly Extension is included, although this is small (less than 5p per passenger).

8.49. Table 8.7 shows BAA's projections of net revenue from the Heathrow Express (the figures exclude depreciation and any return on capital). Net income increases up to 2006/07 due to a small assumed increase in Heathrow Express's modal share and increased prices; the trend after 2007/08 is affected by increased costs, in particular increased track access fees and operating costs of the T5 extension.

---

[1] The CAA also noted that new legislation introducing such charges could also provide for mechanisms to address concerns about monopoly abuse.

9 Capital investment

Contents

Introduction

9.1. This chapter considers BAA's capital investment performance. It first sets out BAA's actual investment in Q3 and its investment planning procedures. It then considers its projections of investment in Q4, paying particular attention to T5, which is by far the largest project. Finally, it sets out the airlines' views on BAA's investment performance.

Capital investment in the third quinquennium

9.2. Table 9.1 shows actual capital investment for 1997/98 to 2001/02 compared with the projections made at the time of the 1996 MMC report.

TABLE 9.1 **Comparison of MMC4 forecasts and actual spend in Q3**

£ million, 2001/02 prices

	MMC4 1997/98– 2001/02	Actual 1997/98– 2001/02	Difference
T5 and related*	1,370.3	343.0	−1,027.3
Heathrow Express	122.1	169.4	47.3
Total	1,492.5	512.5	−980.0
Other Heathrow	850.6	1,050.8	200.2
Gatwick	355.6	442.6	87.0
Stansted	135.3	321.3	186.0
Total South East	2,834.0	2,327.2	−506.8
Excluding T5 and related subtotal	1,341.6	1,814.7	473.1

Source: BAA.

*T5-related projects include extensions to Heathrow Express and Piccadilly Line; VCR; and ART.

9.3. It can be seen that, at 2001/02 prices, actual investment was £2.3 billion over the period, somewhat less than the forecast investment of £2.8 billion. The overall underspend against forecast of 18 per cent was more than accounted for by Heathrow where investment was 33 per cent below that previously forecast. Gatwick investment was 24 per cent above that previously forecast, whilst investment at Stansted was 138 per cent above that forecast.

9.4. The underspend at Heathrow of £780 million compared with the forecast capex at the MMC 1996 review was largely as a result of the length of the T5 planning inquiry. The MMC review in 1996 assumed that the public inquiry would conclude in 1997 and that construction of T5 would commence in 1998. The planning inquiry was actually completed in March 1999 and approval was granted in November 2001.

9.5. The underspend at T5 was partially offset by alternative investment at Heathrow and additional investment at Gatwick which BAA said would probably not have happened (at least in Q3) had T5 been built. Table 9.2 shows the projects at Heathrow and Gatwick which, according to BAA, were undertaken in lieu of the delay to T5. The total expenditure of £269.5 million (£204.9 million at Heathrow and £64.6 million at Gatwick) was thus not part of the forecast capital investment at the 1996 MMC review.

TABLE 9.2 **Major projects undertaken in lieu of the T5 delay**

£ million, 2001/02 prices

	1997/98	1998/99	1999/00	2000/01	2001/02	Total 1997/98– 2001/02
HAL						
Major projects						
T3 departure lounge extension	3.3	18.9	23.9	18.8	19.9	84.8
T1 departure baggage sortation	0.1	11.5	0.7	0.3	0.0	12.6
T1 arrivals concourse	0.6	6.9	1.0	0.0	0.0	8.5
T4 coaching station	1.3	9.5	3.2	0.1	0.0	14.0
Metro stands	0.0	0.0	2.3	4.4	0.6	7.3
T1 arrivals forecourt	0.9	2.1	0.0	0.0	0.0	3.0
MSCP1A ent & exit & link road	0.4	1.4	0.0	0.0	0.0	1.8
Additional baggage facility 1.5	0.0	0.0	1.4	0.6	0.0	2.0
Grass area 12 push and hold stands	0.0	0.0	2.4	1.0	0.0	3.4
Iceberg	0.0	0.0	0.0	6.5	0.0	6.5
T1 FC eastern extension (enabling)*	0.0	0.0	0.0	1.4	4.5	5.9
T1 FC eastern extension	0.0	0.0	0.0	0.0	28.9	28.9
T1 FC southern extension	0.0	0.0	0.0	0.0	26.3	26.3
HAL total	6.6	50.2	34.9	33.2	80.1	204.9
GAL						
Major projects						
New stands development (tower stands)	7.0	13.1	0.0	0.0	0.0	20.1
Runway 26L/08R resurfacing	0.0	0.0	2.7	13.4	0.0	16.1
Runway 26L RET	0.0	0.0	0.0	4.2	0.5	4.7
Concorde House extension	0.0	0.7	6.7	2.3	0.1	9.8
APV gates	0.8	0.0	0.0	0.0	0.0	0.8
NT airside coaching	0.0	0.0	0.0	1.9	0.0	1.9
NT temporary APV	0.7	1.0	0.0	0.0	0.0	1.7
Permanent APV, NT	0.0	1.3	8.0	0.2	0.0	9.5
GAL total	8.4	16.2	17.4	22.0	0.5	64.6
Total	15.0	66.4	52.3	55.3	80.6	269.5

Source: BAA.

*See paragraph 9.62.

9.6. According to BAA the £186 million additional spend at Stansted was to accommodate an unforeseen 60 per cent uplift in passenger numbers above that forecast and the requirement to provide appropriate passenger facilities. BAA said that much of this growth might not have occurred had T5 been open.

9.7. In addition to the impact of the delay of T5, BAA told us that the majority of projects for Heathrow and Gatwick in the 1996 MMC review were subsequently redefined for a variety of reasons, such as changing stakeholder requirements or planning issues. Overall, BAA believed that around £100 million additional actual expenditure had resulted from these factors at Heathrow and Gatwick. Changes in the nature of airline operations such as the growth in the low fares sector at Stansted had also led to a substantially revised capex requirement and profile.

9.8. In the latter half of 2001/02, following the events of 11 September and the subsequent reduction in passenger numbers, BAA undertook a review of current capital investment. In the light of this, a number of projects were postponed, with Gatwick being the most affected airport. Projects postponed at Gatwick airport included North Terminal Pier 6, North West zone stands and taxiways, long-term car parking expansion and the South Terminal Pier 2 reconfiguration. The only projects postponed at Heathrow were elements of the T1 future concepts project. The terminal arrivals extension project was put on hold at Stansted. These projects formed a relatively small part of the overall investment programme.

9.9. A number of major projects were completed during the 18 months to April 2002. At Heathrow these included the rehabilitation of the northern runway, the Victor cul de sac rehabilitation and the Heathrow transfer facilities sortation project. At Gatwick the completed major projects included the North and South Terminal IDL extensions, the South Terminal check-in 2001 project and the North Terminal Pier 4 extension. At Stansted the phased opening of the terminal extension was completed.

Investment planning

Project and investment evaluation

9.10. BAA told us that the key issues which underlay its investment decisions were:

(a) an accurate assessment of forecast demand/opportunity including key assumptions;

(b) the options considered, including those which might not require any, or required little, capex, ie 'do nothing' or 'do minimum';

(c) a proposed solution which is most appropriate to meet the business need and which maximizes shareholder value (or alternatively minimizes loss of shareholder value in the case, for example, of asset replacements);

(d) the appropriate balance between cost (capital and future operating costs), time (delivery programme) and quality of facility to be provided with the resulting impact on customer service, with supporting benchmarks against previous comparable projects where possible;

(e) a thorough and systematic assessment of risk (sensitivities should be performed to gauge the potential impact of cost and income fluctuations on the financial appraisal);

(f) the availability of appropriate funding or headroom within previously agreed capital budgets;

(g) the value that is added or subtracted from the group after taking into account all relevant cash flows and the payback period;

(h) the effect on the group's profit and loss accounts; and

(i) a clear understanding of how the business benefits and performance of the investment would be measured against predefined targets, using the Investment Performance Review process.

9.11. Discounted cash flow techniques are used by BAA to assess the incremental cash flows associated with investments. The NPV and the internal rate of return (IRR) of individual projects are calculated, and compared with the test discount rate or hurdle rate which has been set for that part of the business. These rates are based on BAA's estimate of the group's cost of capital which, at the time of our inquiry, was 9.5 per cent post-tax nominal.

9.12. Other risk premiums are added or subtracted according to the degree of protection or exposure to construction cost, price risk, volume risk and business experience. The basic hurdle rate is 12 per cent average (post-tax nominal) which can be increased by 3 per cent for business cases with a high risk on cost or a high dependency on traffic forecasts; and reduced by 3 per cent in low-risk areas.

9.13. All airport infrastructure projects are assessed against these hurdle rates. However, BAA told us that it was only part of the assessment criteria as there were a number of other factors which influenced BAA in its capital investment decision-making.

9.14. It appears from the above that value for money (VFM) is an important criterion in evaluating capital investment. This VFM assessment is, however, somewhat circular. Project appraisals assume a level of incremental revenue that depends on assumptions about future price controls. These price controls have themselves been assessed on the basis that BAA's future capital investment will earn a return equal to the cost of capital assessed by the CAA and the CC.

9.15. Some projects are non-remunerative as they either produce no return or the return is impossible to assess. Such projects are based on an assessment of the best VFM on an NPV basis. BAA told us that it would not formally take account of external benefits to airlines or other users in appraising a project. However, a key issue in evaluating investment was to demonstrate that schemes met the requirements of the users and others, such as statutory authorities, and then to examine alternative ways of meeting those requirements, often in consultation with users.

The project planning and development process

9.16. BAA has sophisticated guidelines and procedures for project planning and development. This is referred to as CIPP. It includes proprietary software for assessing the business case for projects. The guidelines and procedures are described in Appendix 9.1.

Master plans

9.17. Driven by the need for greater flexibility in order to meet rapid and unpredictable changes in the business environment, BAA had moved away from the concept of master plans for each airport in the 1970s and 1980s. During Q3, it reintroduced the concept and BAA told us that a long-term master plan for Heathrow was set out in the T5 planning application. BAA felt that the need to maintain a rigid plan through the long public inquiry process meant that it could not then publicly consider alternative development strategies for Heathrow. BAA also said that explicit master plans also exacerbate its difficulties in dealing with local planning authorities.

9.18. By 1998, BAA said that it was undertaking work to produce a range of strategic development options for the long-term development of Gatwick. Around 15 options were evaluated, in conjunction with BA and NATS. According to BAA, the developments were shaped according to the evolving needs of passengers, airlines and other business partners, and always with an eye to the future needs of the airport. Airlines were asked to respond to BAA Gatwick's Draft Development Strategy, before a preferred option was selected. BAA has still not chosen between the various options, partly it said at the request of BA, as it was awaiting more information regarding the Government's thinking about runway studies.

9.19. Concerns over the absence of master plans for Heathrow and Gatwick over a number of years have been voiced by the London Airports Consultative Committee (LACC) and some airlines. The views of these parties are detailed in paragraphs 12.126 to 12.141.

Planning standards

9.20. BAA applies its planning objectives and facilities guidelines when planning new developments to assist its managers in assessing the appropriate capacity and size of future facilities. These planning objectives are described in paragraphs 6.159 to 6.166.

South East and East of England Regional Air Services study

9.21. The Government and the aviation industry are faced with the problem of an increasing shortage of runway capacity in the South-East over the next 15 years and more. In 1999, the Government announced the SERAS study. The objectives of SERAS were to give a better understanding of the demand for, and constraints on, airports and air service development in the South-East and East of England over the next 30 years, and to consider options for sustainable development of airports and air services. The main consultation document was published in July 2002 and included a range of options including possible new runways at Heathrow and/or Stansted but not at Gatwick, where a second runway has been ruled out for the time being.

9.22. BAA has included an allowance for investment in additional runway capacity in the South-East, at an unspecified location, in its future capital programme. However, until a government decision is made, the site or scope of what is required is uncertain. BAA has made the assumption that costs would be incurred from 2005/06 and an allowance of £1.4 billion has been included for this project (though most of it falls in Q5).

The capital investment programme

9.23. BAA's internal procedures for developing and reviewing its CIP are orthodox. The Capital Projects Committee is responsible for reviewing the Group's annual proposals for investment in capital projects as part of the business planning cycle and recommending an annual capital budget to the

Management Committee. These proposals are prepared from submissions from each airport, prepared in accordance with set categories and guidelines, as shown in Table 9.3.

TABLE 9.3 **BAA London airports: project classifications and project examples, 2001/02**

Category	Classification of projects	Project example
1	Safety, security & environmental	Segregation of Pier 5, Heathrow
2	Capacity	T5, Heathrow
3	Service quality	Satellite 3, Stansted
4	Revenue generating	New aircraft hangar, Heathrow
5	Replacement/refurbishment of existing assets	Taxiway Y reconstruction, Gatwick
6	Process/productivity improvement	
7	Other	

Source: BAA.

9.24. Table 9.4 categorizes capital investment for BAA's London airports in terms of the 2001/02 spend. Table 9.5 gives the same figures as percentages of total spend at each airport.

TABLE 9.4 **BAA London airports: classification of capex, 2001/02**

					£ million, 2001/02 prices
Category	Classification of projects	HAL	GAL	STAL	Total
1	Safety, security & environmental	8.5	8.3	3.0	19.8
2	Capacity	244.8	17.9	49.3	312.0
3	Service quality	10.6	24.9	28.9	64.4
4	Revenue generating	53.3	14.0	1.0	68.4
5	Replacement/refurbishment of existing assets	42.9	13.2	3.7	59.8
6	Process/productivity improvement	0.0	0.0	0.0	0.0
7	Other, eg community projects, staff facilities	0.0	0.0	0.0	0.0
	Total	360.1	78.3	85.9	524.3

Source: BAA.

TABLE 9.5 **BAA London airports: percentage breakdown of capex, 2001/02**

					per cent
Category	Classification of projects	HAL	GAL	STAL	Total
1	Safety, security & environmental	2.4	10.6	3.5	3.8
2	Capacity	68.0	22.8	57.4	59.5
3	Service quality	3.0	31.8	33.6	12.3
4	Revenue generating	14.8	17.9	1.2	13.0
5	Replacement/refurbishment of existing assets	11.9	16.9	4.3	11.4
6	Process/productivity improvement	0.0	0.0	0.0	0.0
7	Other, eg community projects, staff facilities	0.0	0.0	0.0	0.0
	Total	100.0	100.0	100.0	100.0

Source: BAA.

9.25. Tables 9.4 and 9.5 classify each investment in one category alone. In practice, the majority of projects will have outputs covering several of these categories. For example, CIP lounges expenditure would cover categories 3 and 4, whilst a runway lighting system may include categories 1, 2 and 5.

Consultation

9.26. BAA's consultation processes are discussed under Quality of Service in Chapter 6. Important elements are consultation with airlines on the CIP and on individual projects.

BAA's partnership approach to capital investment

9.27. BAA told us that before the last review it had introduced a partnership approach to projects. This involved continuous improvement of its own processes, those of its suppliers and the way in which the client and supplier teams work together. BAA and the supplier(s) also share the risks and rewards of delivering the project, ie mutual objectives. BAA told us that the partnership approach has delivered greater efficiencies in its construction programme. It added that off-site manufacturing and standardization of construction products have led to more efficient on-site construction, reduced disruption to the busy airport environment and improved value. It said that standard solutions had been developed for a number of products including link bridges, toilets and car parks that had reduced costs by 20 per cent and on-site assembly by up to 75 per cent. BAA said that the £60 million terminal extension at Stansted had opened three months ahead of schedule and at a saving of around 8 per cent on the original 1991 budget forecasts. It claimed that, through collaborative design and re-engineering, the volume of soil disposed off-site for the M11 slip road project had been reduced by 70,000 cubic metres.

9.28. WT commented on BAA's procurement approach in their final report to the CC in September 2002. The comments are detailed in paragraphs 9.72 to 9.75.

Future capital investment

Investment strategy

9.29. BAA told us that its future CIP is a medium-term development strategy that aims to maximize utilization of existing runway capacity in the South-East, whilst ensuring high levels of safety and security and delivering a high level of service quality. It said that the key components of the strategy were:

(a) the completion of phase 1 of T5 as rapidly as possible;

(b) the implementation of early works to provide for the advanced release of stands prior to the opening of T5, in order to meet short-term demand, including the construction of the ART by 2005;

(c) the continuous build of phase 2 of T5 (subject to demand growth);

(d) the progressive redevelopment of the CTA at Heathrow to manage the anticipated high levels of traffic until T5 opens;

(e) the completion of works to the airfield Western Apron and piers to allow for the introduction of the A380 aircraft from spring 2006;

(f) the progressive build-out of Gatwick to ensure its passenger-handling capacity meets the full capacity of the existing runway. This is primarily focused on the expansion of the North Terminal, aprons and airside (the timing and specification of this part of the strategy is dependent on the mix of traffic that in turn depends on the resolution of 'open skies', the BA strategy, and the actions taken by other Gatwick airlines;

(g) the completion of the approved Stansted terminal by the construction of an eighth bay on the arrivals end of the building, and the progressive addition of further bays to take the terminal to 25 mppa and beyond subject to planning consent;

(h) the phased completion of the schemes at Heathrow and Gatwick to implement the segregation of arriving and departing passengers, in accordance with DfT requirements; and

(i) continued expenditure on the renewal of facilities and systems, to avoid degradation of assets and service quality.

9.30. BAA said that the aims of the strategy had evolved in consultation with stakeholders over the last five years but that two further options were available. The first was to reduce investment with the objective of holding down user charges. However, BAA had not detected support for this strategy. At Gatwick and Heathrow, it said, most pressure from airlines had been for the inclusion or acceleration of more projects.

The second option would be to spend more, and more quickly. BAA believed this to be unfeasible. In its view, the scale of current planned expenditure and its implications for charges, the difficulties of obtaining planning consents and the logistical difficulties of building on constrained and intensively utilized sites, particularly at Heathrow, formed an effective cap on the programme.

Overview of investment programme

9.31. Table 9.6 summarizes BAA's capex programme, at constant 2002 prices, distinguishing between investment in T5 and other investments at Heathrow, and the other two airports. T5 accounts for over 57 per cent of projected capex over Q4—some £2.9 billion out of a total of some £5.03 billion—and 17 per cent of expenditure in Q5.

TABLE 9.6 **BAA's capex programme at constant 2002 prices**

£ million, 2002 prices

	Q3	Q4					Q4	Q5	
	2002/03	*2003/04*	*2004/05*	*2005/06*	*2006/07*	*2007/08*	*2003/04– 2007/08*	*2008/09– 2012/13*	*Total cost*
HAL									
T5	275.1	560.6	621.4	678.7	512.2	522.3	2,895.3	414.2	3,584.6
Other specified projects	296.8	268.9	221.0	246.1	233.7	229.1	1,198.8	1,179.7	2,675.3
Other	61.8	46.9	44.1	67.1	70.6	71.9	300.5	284.5	646.7
Slippage	−38.5	−25.0	−25.0	−30.0	−40.0	−50.0	−170.0	−140.0	−348.5
Total	595.1	851.4	861.5	962.0	776.5	773.2	4,224.6	1,738.3	6,558.1
GAL									
Specified projects	17.0	58.6	72.5	88.5	115.8	128.4	463.8	375.9	856.7
Other	27.0	27.1	23.7	10.7	9.8	15.5	86.7	35.6	149.2
Slippage	−4.0	−8.0	−9.0	0.0	0.0	0.0	−17.0	0.0	−21.0
Total	40.0	77.7	87.2	99.2	125.6	143.9	533.5	411.5	985.0
STAL									
Specified projects	37.7	42.5	55.8	40.3	25.2	51.8	215.5	274.8	528.0
Other	7.3	6.2	9.1	18.4	3.7	33.2	70.6	15.6	93.5
Slippage	−5.0	−14.0	2.0	0.0	0.0	0.0	−12.0	0.0	−17.0
Total	40.0	34.7	66.9	58.7	28.9	85.0	274.2	290.4	604.6
All London airports	675.1	963.8	1,015.6	1,119.9	930.9	1,002.1	5,032.3	2,440.2	8,147.6

Source: BAA.

9.32. A breakdown of the CIP by airport and by individual project is shown in Appendix 9.3.

9.33. BAA suggested that the investment programme for each airport should be seen as having five elements being:

(a) a one-year budget, which is a specific and detailed estimate of capex built up from many individual projects that have already been costed in detail and agreed by the airlines through BAA's project approval process (see Appendix 9.1) and within consultation forums where appropriate;

(b) a business plan for the following two years that sets out the projects in considerable detail. These projects will be at varying stages of the project approval process and as such are subject to amendment but are unlikely to suffer significant shifts in the overall level of expenditure;

(c) major capacity and service quality projects that extend over several years such as T5, Gatwick North Terminal and the Stansted pre- and post-15 mppa developments. These projects have been subject to detailed specification and consultation to the extent that the business rationale has been developed and planning applications can be made. The main uncertainty with the projects is the timescale for planning permission. T5 was subject to a public inquiry and BAA hopes not to incur similar delays by seeking approval to the Stansted scheme without a public inquiry;

(d) broadly defined projects in the three- to ten-year period that are included in the plan in recognition of the likely need for investment in that area. These projects have not been designed or costed in

detail although BAA believes that the overall level of spending is likely to be in the order of the amount provisioned although subject to changes in industry conditions that lead to changes in intent or timing; and

(e) an allowance for continued spending on minor projects, including renewals, and an allowance for slippage of such expenditure.

9.34. Table 9.6 includes slippage provisions for each airport. These have been derived on a high level basis but are designed to reflect the possibility of time delays particularly given the difficulties in implementation at constrained sites operating in sensitive planning environments.

9.35. We next consider the major projects included in BAA's projections for the next five and ten years, and particularly T5; and the projections of expenditure on smaller projects.

Short-term plan

9.36. Within the overall investment strategy, the projects that have started or are planned to start at Heathrow over the next three years include: DfT passenger segregation projects; the start of onsite work at T5; the T1 'Future Concepts' project; T3 arrivals and departures improvements; construction of the ART, leading to additional aircraft stands on the western apron; phase 2 of the Pier 5 extension project; and various projects to accommodate the large new A380 aircraft.

9.37. At Gatwick, the short-term plan includes the extension of the South Terminal arrivals area, segregation work on Pier 2 and Pier 3 and the addition of aircraft stands.

9.38. At Stansted, the short-term plan includes an arrivals extension to the terminal, the completion of satellite 3 and the building of taxiway extensions.

9.39. These projects are discussed in more detail in Appendix 9.2.

Terminal 5

9.40. By far the most significant item of capex for BAA is T5. BAA forecast passenger numbers at its south-east airports were likely to reach around 153 mppa by 2012/13 and along with representatives of the airline industry argued that capacity in the South-East must be provided to meet this demand.

9.41. In February 1993, BAA applied for planning permission to develop a new fifth terminal at Heathrow. The development was the subject of a public inquiry that ended in March 1999. Government approval followed in November 2001 and phase 1 construction has commenced. BAA has obtained local planning consents for details including the diversion of the Duke of Northumberland and Longford rivers and substantive works on site have started.

9.42. The proposed site, formerly occupied by Perry Oaks sludge works, is on the western side of the airport between the two runways. T5 will be constructed in two phases, and once completed, will provide a new terminal complex at Heathrow with a total capacity of around 30 mppa bringing the total capacity of the airport to around 90 mppa.

Phasing of construction

9.43. Table 9.7 shows BAA's plans to phase the development of T5 capacity.

TABLE 9.7 **T5 development phasing**

Phase	Commencing	Opening year	Capacity mppa	Construction costs 2002 prices £m
1	2002	2008*	20–22	2,711†
2	2007	2011	10	422
Total			30–32	3,133

Source: BAA.

*Stands to be brought online from 2004.
†Includes all expenditure to date.

9.44. Phase 1 includes the clearance of the Perry Oaks site and construction of: a Core Terminal Building, one satellite building connected by automated TTS, associated roads, taxiways, stand infra-structure and ancillary facilities such as car parks, sub-stations, waste and sanitation facilities and security control posts. The Core Terminal Building will be built as a single box construction progressively fitted out to meet demand through phases 1 and 2. It will comprise 275,000 square metres of floor space over seven levels (four above and three below ground). The satellite building will occupy 81,000 square metres of floor space, also over seven levels. By comparison T4 occupies 100,000 square metres of floor space. A total of 42 stands will be provided in phase 1 (five more stands in 2009) providing capacity for 20 mppa. Phase 1 is scheduled to be operational for the summer season 2008, although BAA's objective is to bring aircraft stands online as soon as possible beginning in summer 2004.

9.45. Phase 2 will comprise a second satellite building, which is expected to provide additional capacity of around 10 mppa. The second satellite building will require an extension to the TTS system and deliver a further 12 aircraft stands (making 59 in total) and associated airside roads and taxiways. The need and timing of phase 2 together with the extension to phase 1 will be driven by the need to maintain pier service levels.

9.46. BAA has proposed that increases in airport charges should be related to project progress, giving it a strong incentive to complete T5 on schedule and ensuring that airlines only pay increased charges as and when there is demonstrable progress. The four 'triggers' proposed by BAA are:

(a) completion of diversion of twin rivers 2004/05;

(b) early release stands completion 2004/05;

(c) VCR handed over to NATS 2005/06; and

(d) core terminal building weatherproof 2006/07.

9.47. The CC asked BAA if it would consider an additional 2003/04 trigger for T5 and a Gatwick trigger. BAA replied that an additional T5 trigger has been looked at but that there is a need to retain flexibility in this area. BAA believed that the BA proposal for using Pier 6 as a charges trigger for Gatwick was a reasonable suggestion and should apply in financial year 2006/07. According to BAA, other projects over Q4 at Gatwick are much less certain in terms of their scope and timing and so their suitability as triggers is very limited.

Benchmarking and best practice

9.48. A benchmarking study was undertaken by BAA on the T5 project in early 2002. The main purpose of the exercise was to identify best practice and demonstrate that T5 project costs represented VFM when benchmarked against similar BAA projects as well as projects external to BAA.

9.49. The benchmarking task team comprised BAA's Single Commercial Team, EC Harris, Turner & Townsend and Parsons Brinckerhoff. Thirteen separate facilities were identified to be benchmarked and a series of internal and external projects were analysed at facility, system and component levels.

9.50. On the basis of the data analysed, the benchmarking exercise and associated report concluded that the majority of the current T5 costs for the facilities analysed were close to, if not less than, the benchmark mean for the sampled projects. Some facilities such as the surface and multi-storey car parks, the control tower and tunnelling indicated current T5 costs to be higher than the benchmark mean. The reasons for these adverse variances were outlined in the report, which also contained a proposal for the 'way forward' in terms of an ongoing benchmarking process.

9.51. WT, commenting on the T5 benchmarking, made recommendations in its final report to the CC in September 2002 (see paragraphs 9.74 and 9.75).

Risk assessment

9.52. PricewaterhouseCoopers (PwC) prepared a report for HAL in August 2001 in connection with HAL's consideration of project risks associated with the delivery of T5 at Heathrow. The analysis involved:

(a) aggregation of risk analysis performed by the BAA design and delivery teams on the individual project components and high-level assessment of project-wide risk. PwC applied this information to a project-wide, probability-based financial analysis to estimate the range of probable project costs; and

(b) contrast of the T5 project with performance of other major civil engineering projects in the airport and other industries, to produce a holistic analysis.

9.53. PwC found that the T5 project was complex and faced material risks throughout the key areas of commencement, scope change, construction, integration, significant disruption and commissioning. BAA's approach to risk mitigation and management was found to centre on design and procurement through partnership contracting, allowing much greater involvement and control over project development. PwC believed that this approach increased corporate exposure to project cost overruns and delays, subject to insurance protections that BAA puts in place.

9.54. PwC's assessment concluded that:

(a) the current level of contingency did not appear inappropriate, given the assumptions and a risk neutral perspective;

(b) though difficult to make a statistically-based assessment of the probability of a 'catastrophic event' occurring without further work, the impact on expected[1] costs of a single such event was not great but the impact on actual costs in the unlikely event it occurred would be significant;

(c) programme risks and major disruptions causing a hold-up to the programme once in full flow and running at maximum overhead cost, represented the largest source of risk; and

(d) the uncertainty surrounding the outcome of the planning inquiry and protestor and legal responses appeared to have a large impact on expected costs but that much of this uncertainty would be resolved as the results of the planning inquiry became known.

9.55. Based on this basic risk assessment, PwC concluded that the contingency of some £600 million established by BAA was of the right order of magnitude.

9.56. The review highlighted other areas that PwC believed would benefit from further analysis. These included:

(a) a more detailed risk assessment, focusing on areas of integration risk and catastrophic events;

(b) the appropriateness of BAA's attitude towards project risks;

(c) further consideration of the impact of cost overruns at the corporate level, in terms of cash flows and credit ratings; and

---

[1] Statistical measure calculated as the cost multiplied by its probability of occurrence.

(d) analysing T5 project contingency needs versus other corporate calls on funds to enable BAA better to manage risk exposure across the group.

9.57. WT's comments on BAA's assessment of risk are detailed in paragraph 9.70.

Occupancy of T5

9.58. In consultation with the industry BAA established three criteria for deciding the likely occupiers of T5. These were:

(a) the allocation should enable the best use of Heathrow's overall terminal and apron capacity;

(b) the number of passenger transfers able to take place without changing terminals to be maximized; and

(c) the number of airlines required to move between terminals to be minimized.

9.59. BAA employed consultants Economics Plus to build a computer model to test various options using these criteria. The tests demonstrated that the T5 occupancy best suited to the criteria was BA. BAA consulted individual carriers and groups of airlines to ensure that appropriate infrastructure will be in place for airlines remaining in the CTA when T5 opens. This resulted in a number of additional projects being included in the current CIP before T5 opens. The details of these projects and the inter-terminal connectivity projects are set out in Appendix 9.2.

9.60. BAA has not yet committed to a long-term allocation of airlines between the other terminals after the opening of T5. The opening of T5 is six years away and BAA believes airlines will be reluctant to commit plans to move or stay until nearer the time. Also, there may be a need by that time to accommodate more US carriers at the airport if an 'open skies agreement' is forged between the UK and the USA. BAA has said that it is continuing to discuss individual requirements with airlines. In about 2005, it will launch a full-scale consultation with the total airline community, on the distribution of airlines between the terminals.

Other major projects

9.61. Appendix 9.3 shows the phasing of expenditure on major projects by airport included in the BAA CIP. The following notes give an outline of the background to most of these projects and the reasons why they are required.

Heathrow

9.62. The purpose and general details of the highest expenditure major projects (more than £75 million) are detailed below. Other major projects are described in Appendix 9.2.

(a) The Pier 5 Extension Phase 2 and Segregation project provides pier service to an additional three aircraft stands and segregates the length of Pier 5 (total capex of £80 million).

(b) Pier 6 reconfiguration will provide a new segregated Pier 6 with ramp accommodation and service to three A380 stands. There is also potential for a new airside link to T2 to improve connectivity and enable stand usage by T2 airlines (total capex of £87 million).

(c) The Terminal 3 Departures Development is nearing completion, accommodating additional demand from T3 airlines and alliance groups until the opening of T5. A wide range of passenger facilities and an already operational new security search area are also provided (total capex of £108 million).

(d) The scope of the Terminal 3 Departures/Check-in/Arrivals Concourse Development project is yet to be determined in detail. The opportunity of expansion of the terminal landside facilities into the

area currently occupied by the T3 car park would enable expansion and improve the quality of the check-in area and the arrivals landside concourse (total capex of £205 million).

(e) T1 Eastern extension forms part of the Future Concepts Strategy for T1 which enables additional long-haul flights to operate from the terminal (total capex of £154 million). The chief elements of the project are:

(i) reconfiguration of four stands to create room for an extension of the building;

(ii) two-storey extension of the departures building; and

(iii) the additional space at apron level will enable reconfiguration of the baggage system.

(f) Terminal 1 Pier 3 Segregation and Future Development will provide segregation on the pier and includes a major refurbishment (total capex of £81 million).

(g) Multi-Storey Car Parks Structural Works and Upgrade refurbishes all of the existing short-stay multi-storey car parks within the CTA (total capex of £86 million).

(h) The CTA Long Term Development Strategy T1/T2/T3 Consolidation is a long-term development strategy for the airport devised by BAA and the LACC. Though in the early stages of development, it is likely that it will focus on the eastern apron and terminal complex and will provide additional integrated facilities for the forecast increase in long-haul passengers (total capex of £245 million).

(i) The CTA Landside Redevelopment Strategy project will deliver a reshaped road system; direct access to each of the terminals for public transport; elevated pedestrian access between the principal landside facilities and the terminals; new car parks; and provision for a hotel and additional office accommodation (total capex of £127 million).

(j) The Baggage Connections Post-T5 (System Solution) project has three phases and provides an automated integrated transfer baggage system linking all of the terminals post the opening of T5 (total capex of £297 million).

(k) The New Generation Large Aircraft (NGLA) Taxiways project upgrades the taxiway system to comply with new licensing requirements to enable the introduction of new aircraft types (total capex of £81 million).

(l) ART provides a road tunnel link from the CTA to the western apron and allows the use of the remote stands so improving capacity (total capex of £136 million).

Projects not included in the Core Programme

9.63. One of the additional investment proposals that BAA is considering is a TTS linking terminals at Heathrow. The project would be an extension of the T5 TTS with stations at T3, the flight communications centre and T4. The project is at the early stages of consideration but was presented to the LACC in February 2002. At this stage, BAA has assumed that investment in the project would start from 2005/06.

Gatwick

9.64. The purpose and general details of the highest expenditure major projects (more than £75 million) are detailed below. Other major projects are described in Appendix 9.2.

(a) The North Terminal Pier 6 project provides a new pier and additional pier-served stands and makes use of a revolutionary 'overbridge' to link them to Pier 4 (total capex of £85.4 million).

(b) The Midfield Pier (including TTS) project ensures an appropriate level of pier service to cater for future North Terminal traffic, with the provision of a baggage hall and a transit link for passengers from the North Terminal (total capex of £243.8 million).

(c) The North West (NW) Zone project has four phases and involves the construction of new stands within the NW zone, taxiway connections and necessary relocations (total capex of £133.5 million).

(d) Stands/Taxiways provides taxiway enhancements and additional remote stands (total capex of £64 million).

Stansted

9.65. The purpose and general details of the highest expenditure major projects (more than £50 million) are detailed below. Other major projects are described in Appendix 9.2.

(a) Phase 3 Other Projects represents development beyond Stansted's current planning permission, including further additions to the aprons, services, access and other facilities to meet expected growth in demand (total capex of £77.9 million).

(b) The Other Approved Terminal and Satellite Development project provides additional passenger circulation space, baggage reclaim capacity, pier-service and increased capacity/flexibility on the TTS network (total capex of £101.1 million).

(c) The Phase 3 Terminal Development project meets forecast passenger growth via an extension to the departures end of the terminal building. This allows for additional check-in facilities, baggage infrastructure and passenger circulation areas, together with support facilities and space for retail outlets (total capex of £57.2 million).

Our consultant's assessment of proposed projects

9.66. We asked WT to:

(a) examine BAA's past capital investment performance;

(b) examine the future plans of BAA's CIPs; and

(c) assess the efficiency and effectiveness with which BAA were likely to implement the programmes.

9.67. We asked WT to comment specifically on the proposed capex for the T5 project and to review a number of recently completed and future projects to be undertaken at the three airports. WT also reported on a number of issues surrounding BAA's procurement processes. BAA's response to the WT report is given in paragraphs 9.76 to 9.80.

Terminal 5

9.68. WT was asked to assess whether, under the stated assumptions, the capex programme reflected the likely capital costs that should be incurred by an efficient airport operator.

9.69. WT recommended that an independent review of the construction cost and risk provision for T5 be undertaken. They noted the trend of upwardly spiralling cost for T5. The cost of T5 in the CIP has increased from £1.8 billion in constant 1996/97 prices to £2.71 billion in April 2002. WT also noted that a number of the largest elements of phase 1 of the T5 project had challenging cost targets when benchmarked against similar facilities and that given the history of cost escalation to date, a further review would be beneficial.

9.70. WT noted that some £250 million of a corporate contingency provision of £420 million had been allocated as at July 2002. WT believed that the risk assessment should also be reviewed. Without further major investigation, WT was unable to discover the amount of contingency that had been built into the baseline figures within the Cost Plan.

Review of other past and future capital projects

9.71. WT reviewed one completed project and one future project from each of BAA's London airports to assess the efficiency and effectiveness of BAA's capital programmes. WT found that BAA had at times been too pessimistic in assessing contingency and risk and also that benchmarking needed to be more consistent and centrally controlled. WT also noted that BAA seemed very sensitive to criticisms of its procurement process which could lead to it discounting alternative methods or potential improvements.

BAA's procurement philosophy and processes

9.72. WT found that BAA is committed to a partnering[1] form of procurement, along the lines of that championed in the *Rethinking Construction* report prepared by the Construction Task Force in 1998. WT summarized the claimed key advantages gained from the collaborative nature of the partnering approach to procurement as:

(a) increased productivity, turnover and profits;

(b) continuous improvement and improved predictability of time and costs; and

(c) satisfied customers.

9.73. WT noted that the critics of the partnering approach voiced the following main disadvantages:

(a) the difficulty in realizing genuine collaborative working practices;

(b) the requirement for robust and accurate benchmarking in order to measure performance and assess VFM; and

(c) the partnering contractual arrangements may result in an increased exposure to risk.

9.74. WT found that the main potential problem resulting from the new approach to procurement related to benchmarking. Benchmarking is an important management tool for measuring continuous improvement and the effectiveness of the procurement process. From their investigation, WT concluded that although BAA's benchmarking in some areas and for some isolated components was good, benchmarking for whole projects was poor and for T5 was not of the highest quality, given the significant capex involved.

9.75. WT recommended that BAA improve its benchmarking by:

(a) taking a more rigorous approach when comparing whole project costs;

(b) ensuring that only genuinely comparable projects are compared and by being cautious when making use of international comparators and ensuring appropriate adjustments are made to the data;

(c) making use of project life-cycle costs as well as initial capital costs when benchmarking; and

(d) being cautious in the use of old data. Data for benchmarking may be invalidated over time due to changes such as technological advances and changes in construction techniques and/or in statutory requirements.

BAA's response to WT's report

9.76. BAA noted that the WT report had little content on the main area of interest that of WT's view on the reasonableness of BAA's capex estimates. BAA noted the WT proposal for an independent cost review

---

[1]As described in the 'Rethinking Construction' report, 'partnering' involves two or more organizations working together to improve performance through agreeing mutual objectives, devising a way for resolving any disputes and committing themselves to continuous improvement, measuring progress and sharing the gains'.

of T5 and agreed with the need for this, to provide comfort to the airline community and to the BAA board, prior to final approval of the scope and phasing of the project. BAA intends to appoint Franklyn and Andrews (F&A) in this role. We note that F&A are no longer fully 'independent' as they have now merged with Mott MacDonald, one of the design consultants for T5.

9.77. BAA has undertaken to provide a further consultation exercise on T5 costs in 2003. In the interim period, BAA will be concluding its current series of studies on finalizing scope and reviewing risk and internal peer reviews. As well as the appointment of F&A to carry out the independent review, an updated 2002/03 price base cost plan will be provided by BAA in January 2003.

9.78. BAA recognized that benchmarking is often constrained by the quality and quantity of comparable data available. Providing these limitations are understood and adjusted for, BAA does not believe that the T5 benchmarking project is invalidated. BAA therefore accepted that the earlier F&A benchmark exercise contained certain technical limitations and has adjusted certain comparisons within the benchmarking report to reflect these. BAA noted, however, that these changes made no significant difference to the overall findings of the F&A report. As part of the 2003 F&A exercise outlined in paragraph 9.76 above, the T5 benchmarking study will again be reviewed and latest estimates included.

9.79. BAA agreed that T5 costs had risen, chiefly due to changes in scope and price adjustments. In addition, BAA said that it had provided considerable information on T5's corporate contingency and that PwC had already reviewed these costs, concluding that they were reasonable.

9.80. BAA said that its partnership approach to procurement was the right one, rather than the traditional approach advocated by WT. BAA pointed to the government approach to procurement partnering highlighted in various reports commissioned by the Government such as *Rethinking Construction* chaired by Sir John Egan in 1998 which advocated the use of integrated supply teams and partnering within the teams. BAA also noted the 'Achieving Excellence' initiative launched by the Chief Secretary to the Treasury in 1999 which counted partnering, team working and integrated procurement as key action points.

Airlines' views on BAA's capital investment

9.81. More detailed views of third parties on BAA's investment programme are included in Chapters 12 and 13. Various parties responded to BAA's CIP, among them airlines such as BA, Virgin, bmi, Britannia, United and Lufthansa. The LACC and the AOC also commented. Overall, it was noted that the 2002 CIP document is significantly more detailed than previous CIP documents, but that there was still insufficient information on individual projects and their costs and the underlying assumptions behind each project justification. The main issues raised by these parties are summarized in the following paragraphs.

9.82. After review of the CIP, BA noted that the key capital investment issues for BA were that:

(a) BAA moves ahead with the T5 investment programme as soon as possible to achieve completion in 2011;

(b) the TTS and baggage link between T5 and the parts of CTA from which BA's services operate are fully operational on the opening day of T5 in 2008; and

(c) BAA seek to increase runway capacity at Heathrow in a sustainable way in the SERAS review process.

9.83. BA has also stated its concern over the need for master planning at Heathrow in part to form a more secure basis for effective consultation and to give greater clarity about the overall objectives, balance and size of the CIP. BA felt that there was a need to fundamentally review the eastern apron and maintenance area layout at Heathrow.

9.84. bmi said that it had not been involved in any of the consultations and planning of T5, despite the size of the capital investment involved. It noted that the size of the T5 capital programme suggested either that the project was hugely overcosted or overspecified. bmi also noted that the CTA development in the CIP was not scheduled to start until 2005 and would be completed after 2013. bmi believed this handed significant competitive advantage to BA operating out of T5. bmi wanted the CTA development brought forward to ensure that capacity and service quality for CTA carriers was protected and advanced. It believed that the consultation process could be improved by providing further specific information about each project, such as a business case, expected revenues and running costs of the projects and the sources of remuneration.

9.85. The LACC highlighted Heathrow connectivity between terminals as a main concern, in particular questioning the workability of a road-based option for connectivity and the arrangements for T5 opening with a hybrid baggage system. The LACC also stated that the CTA required an improvement in operational capacity and quality both before and after T5 opening.

9.86. The LACC also questioned why BAA's capital investment was not based on a long-term vision, for example 30 years like the government White Paper. The LACC asked for a clearer definition of specific project outputs and noted that, whilst T5 outputs were broadly known, the planning standards and intended levels of service were not clear. The LACC also noted the perception among many carriers that much of the 'investment' in the CIP related to maintenance of outdated structure and should be categorized as such.

9.87. Virgin Atlantic found that the CIP contained insufficiently detailed information on the justification for each project as well as the associated costs. It voiced concern that there were risks that the projects within the CIP would not be delivered on time or at all, to budget and to the agreed specifications. It asked for a clear separation of capacity-enhancing investment expenditure from expenditure that will improve quality of service for airlines.

9.88. Lufthansa voiced concern that the CIP was not supported by a long-term master plan, particularly for Heathrow. Lufthansa also believed that the consultation process with the airlines was insufficient, particularly with regard to the specification of facilities at Heathrow.

9.89. The Heathrow AOC commented that the CIP lacked any commentary on overall strategy and possible major future developments that had formed part of the airlines' Heathrow master plan proposals. It had concerns over the lack of options for passenger and baggage inter-terminal connections when T5 became operational and the lack of sufficient data for the AOC to form a view on the best connections method. In addition, the AOC believed that greater investment was necessary at T2 to improve facilities such as the arrivals hall, baggage-handling areas and off-pier coaching. It was the AOC's view that some of the individual project costs appeared expensive at Heathrow compared with similar projects at other airports and it was considering the use of consultants to provide an independent view on cost transparency and value for money.

9.90. The Gatwick AOC stated that the scale of development there seemed appropriate and that the key issues were the non-availability of Pier 6 until 2006, the delivery of the midfield pier only when Gatwick reached 40 mppa, and the seemingly excessive car-parking expenditure.

10 Financial projections

Contents

Introduction

10.1. In this chapter we set out our projections for Q4 and Q5 which underlie our assessment of the value of X. We start by considering some implications of the CAA's 1996 decision on the value of X for Q3 (which was largely based on the recommendations in the 1996 MMC report). We also compare BAA's performance in Q3 with the MMC's 1996 financial projections.

Value of X in Q3

10.2. The financial projections for Q3 and Q4, on which the MMC based its 1996 recommendations, and the CAA its decision, were affected by the costs associated with T5, which at that time was expected to receive planning permission early in Q3 and to commence operations in 2003/04. There are three aspects of this that are relevant to our current projections:

(a) The MMC recommended and the CAA decided to smooth prices by setting the price cap at a higher level (RPI–3) than would have been required for BAA to earn the cost of capital in Q3 alone (RPI–8). This is described as revenue advancement.

(b) The RPI–3 cap was continued for a sixth year (2002/03) in order to enable our current inquiry to take into account the Secretary of State's planning decision on T5.

(c) The unexpectedly long planning delay to the commencement of work on T5 (which was beyond the control of BAA, the CAA and the MMC) has given BAA an unexpected financial benefit since its capex has been lower than projected in 1996. As noted in paragraph 5.17, BAA deliberately under-recovered to a small extent against the (RPI–3) price cap.

We deal with each of these in turn.

Revenue Advancement

10.3. The CAA said in its 1996 decision document (CAP 664) that it accepted the need to smooth charges and that its underlying philosophy was that any super-normal profit in Q3 would be paid back in Q4.[1] The CAA stated that the yardstick for estimating the revenue advancement was a price cap (for Heathrow and Gatwick) of RPI–8, which was the price cap commensurate with BAA's cost of capital. Based on the difference between the notional maximum revenue per passenger (yield) under an RPI–8 price cap and BAA's actual revenue yield, we estimate the value of the revenue advancement at the start of Q4 (31 March 2003) was £348 million at 2000/01 prices[2] (see Table 8.1). As it is based on the actual revenue yield, our estimate is reduced by BAA's under-recovery against the RPI–3 cap.

---

[1]The CAA also noted that it could not bind its successors and that at the time of the next review other factors might well outweigh a highly prescriptive calculation setting advanced against future revenues; and hence that, it could be some time before the advancement could be unwound.

[2]To facilitate comparisons, all figures in this chapter are adjusted to 2000/01 prices using actual or projected movements in the RPI.

TABLE 10.1 **Calculation of revenue advancement at Heathrow and Gatwick**

	1997/98	1998/99	1999/00	2000/01	2001/02	31 March 2003
Passengers ('000)						
Heathrow	58,165	61,037	62,294	64,328	60,381	
Gatwick	27,331	29,556	30,432	32,135	30,494	
Total	85,496	90,593	92,726	96,463	90,875	
Out-turn revenue (£'000)						
Heathrow	280,360	298,229	304,312	336,537	338,073	
Gatwick	103,068	114,810	117,537	130,435	129,486	
Total	383,428	413,039	421,849	466,972	467,559	
Out-turn yield (revenue per passenger) (£)	4.485	4.559	4.549	4.841	5.145	
Calculation of notional maximum yield *(revenue per passenger) under RPI–8*						
Starting yield (£)*	4.443	4.181	4.003	4.080	4.239	
+ S factor (£)		0.010	0.007	0.004		
+ S factor correction (£)		−0.004		−0.001		
Total after S factor (£)	4.443	4.187	4.010	4.083	4.239	
RPI %†	2.1	3.6	3.2	1.1	3.3	
1+RPI–8	0.941	0.956	0.952	0.931	0.953	
R (special one-off correction factor)‡		0.056				
D (duty-free adjustment)				0.262	0.438	
Notional maximum yield (£)§	4.181	4.059	4.080	4.239	4.040	
Out-turn less notional maximum yield (£)	0.304	0.500	0.469	0.602	1.107	
Extra revenue (£'000)						
Out-turn prices¶	25,991	45,297	43,488	58,071	100,417	
2000/01 prices¤	28,038	47,387	44,787	58,071	98,939	
Compounded value at 31.3.03#	42,354	66,410	58,231	70,047	110,720	
Total compounded value at 31.3.03~						347,762
RPI index 2000/01=1.00	0.927	0.956	0.971	1.000	1.015	
Compounding factors (31/3/03 = 1.00)★	0.662	0.714	0.769	0.829	0.894	1.000

Source: CAA Performance report of BAA London Airports and Manchester Airport, August 1991, Table 6.1, and CC estimates based on BAA data for 2001/02.

---

*The starting yield for 1997/98 was specified by the CAA in its 1996 decision. The starting yield for later years is the notional maximum yield for the previous year excluding any correction factor.

†Annual percentage change in the RPI for September of the previous year.

‡This is a correction factor for under-recovery in 1996/97. The calculation of notional yield assumes no under- or over-recovery in 1997/98 to 1999/00, hence there is no correction factor for 1999/00 to 2001/02.

§Total after S factor multiplied by (1+RPI–8) plus (R+D).

¶Out-turn less notional maximum yield multiplied by total passengers.

¤Extra revenue at out-turn prices divided by RPI index.

#Extra revenue at 2000/01 prices divided by compounding factor (to allow for cost of capital on the extra revenue up to 31 March 2003).

~Total compounded value at 31 March 2002 was £322,797,000 (value at 31 March 2003 divided by (1 + cost of capital)).

★Assumes cost of capital of 7.79 per cent (consistent with accounting rate of return of 7.5 per cent assumed by the MMC in 1996).

10.4. The MMC's projections, which underlay the CAA's RPI–3 decision, showed returns above the cost of capital at Heathrow but returns broadly similar to the cost of capital at Gatwick. In these circumstances, we think it appropriate that the full amount of the revenue advancement should be set against expected future required revenue at Heathrow.

2002/03

10.5. The RPI–3 cap was extended for one year in order that our inquiry could be delayed to take into account the T5 planning decision. Our understanding is that, under the Airports Act, the CAA did not have discretion to vary the RPI–3 cap for the additional year and thus the RPI–3 cap for 2002/03 was not based on an assessment of BAA's projected performance. As it happens, however, BAA's current projections for 2002/03 suggest a return similar to the cost of capital. In these circumstances, we think it appropriate that 2002/03 should be treated as a one-off year. Consequently, any under-recovery against the cap should not be carried forward to Q4 and 2002/03 should also not affect the amount of revenue advancement in Q3 or the assessment of the financial benefit BAA received from the planning delay to T5.

Effects of delay to T5

10.6. In its 1996 decision, the CAA acknowledged that it could not bind its successors; it nevertheless indicated its hope that the next review would take into account, inter alia, BAA's performance in delivering its investment programme. As noted above, there has been a very long planning delay to T5, the most important aspect of BAA's Q3 investment programme. We have estimated the net effect of BAA's underspend on capex at Heathrow (the resulting benefit to BAA is additional to the revenue advancement mentioned in paragraph 10.3). The basis of our calculations is that the Q3 price cap reflected required return and depreciation on the 1996 projections of capex. Hence, the effect on BAA is the difference between:

(a) required return and depreciation on projected Heathrow Q3 capex; and

(b) required return and depreciation on actual Heathrow Q3 capex.[1]

This takes account of the costs of additional spending on non-T5 projects at Heathrow. Table 10.2 shows that the effect on return of lower than projected capex was offset to some extent by higher depreciation,[2] which occurred as actual expenditure started to be depreciated (by contrast there was no depreciation on T5 even in the projections as it was not projected to come into operation during Q3). On balance, Table 10.2 suggests the compounded value (at 31 March 2003) of return and depreciation on actual Heathrow capex was £64 million less than that of return and depreciation on projected capex.

---

[1] We refer to the depreciation charged in the regulatory accounts as 'actual depreciation'.
[2] The difference between actual and projected depreciation on Q3 capex is estimated from the difference between actual and projected depreciation on all assets (it is assumed that that projections of depreciation on existing assets are accurate).

TABLE 10.2 **Calculation of effects on BAA of Heathrow underspend on capex**

£ million

	1995/96	1996/97	1997/98	1998/99	1999/00	2000/01	2001/02
Actual Heathrow net capex:							
At out-turn prices	310.5	316.7	396.3	238.8	180.7	252.5	340.8
At 2000/01 prices	354.4	353.0	427.6	249.8	186.1	252.5	335.7
Projected Heathrow net capex:	0.0	0.0	0.0	0.0	0.0	0.0	0.0
At 1995/96 prices	324.2	316.5	328.5	363.2	441.8	423.7	448.1
At 2000/01 prices	370.1	361.3	375.0	414.7	504.4	483.7	511.5
Difference (actual less projected)	−15.7	−8.3	52.5	−164.9	−318.2	−231.2	−175.7
Impact on end-year RCV	−15.7	−24.0	28.5	−136.4	−454.6	−685.8	−861.6
Effect on return (at 7.5 per cent of average RCV)			0.2	−4.0	−22.2	−42.8	−58.0
Compounded value of return at 31.3.03*			0.3	−5.7	−28.8	−51.6	−64.9
Total for Q3							−150.8
Actual Heathrow depreciation:†							
At out-turn prices	46.2	58.9	64.7	93.4	115.3	128.6	148.7
At 2000/01 prices	52.1	64.7	68.5	97.2	116.7	127.6	145.5
Projected Heathrow depreciation:†							
At 1995/96 prices	51.8	53.5	66.2	79.7	91.6	90.8	89.1
At 2000/01 prices	59.2	61.1	75.5	90.9	104.5	103.7	101.7
Difference (actual less projected)	−7.1	3.6	−7.0	6.2	12.2	24.0	43.8
Impact on end-year RCV‡	7.1	3.4	10.4	4.2	−8.0	−31.9	−75.8
Effect on return (at 7.5 per cent of average RCV)‡			0.5	0.5	−0.1	−1.5	−4.0
Total depreciation effect§			−6.5	6.8	12.0	22.5	39.8
Compounded value of depreciation effect at 31.3.03*			−9.8	9.5	15.7	27.1	44.5
Total for Q3							87.0
Total effect for Q3 (return and depreciation)							−63.7
RPI 2000/01=1.00	0.876	0.897	0.927	0.956	0.971	1.000	1.015
Compounding factors (31.3.03 = 1.00)*			0.662	0.714	0.769	0.829	0.894

Source: CC calculations based on data in Appendix 10.2. Net capex and depreciation include centrally capitalized and HEOC expenditure.

---

*Compounding assumes cost of capital of 7.79 per cent (consistent with accounting rate of return of 7.5 per cent assumed by MMC in 1996).

†Depreciation on all Heathrow assets (see second footnote to paragraph 10.6) adjusted to exclude depreciation on investment property.

‡Higher depreciation reduces RCV and hence required return.

§Total depreciation effect is difference (actual depreciation less projected depreciation) plus effect on return.

10.7. BAA pointed out that its capex at Stansted and Gatwick[1] had also been greater than projected but we note that any additional costs were more than offset by additional revenue due to higher than expected passenger numbers.[2] Hence, we do not think costs of additional capex at the other airports should be set against the effects of the underspend associated with the delay to T5. BAA has also benefited from higher than expected passengers and revenue at Heathrow but the additional non-T5 capex at Heathrow was not necessarily related to the higher than expected passenger numbers.

10.8. The CAA estimated the effect of the underspend (before efficiency adjustment) at £201 million. The main reasons for the difference from our figure of £64 million (and their approximate quantitative impact—a positive figure is a reason why the CAA figure is larger than ours) are:

(a) The CAA included a projected underspend for 2002/03 but we excluded this in line with our general approach to 2002/03 (+£52 million).

(b) The CAA treated transfers to Lynton as negative capex but we did not do so as we understand the transfers were agreed by the CAA and that the lower RCV and required return resulting from these transfers is offset by lower income to the regulated company (+£29 million).

---

[1]At Gatwick, the overall costs (return and depreciation) were broadly in line with the projections (total capex for Q3 was higher than projected, but the timescale was later than projected).

[2]The price cap formula reflects projected return and depreciation per passenger. When the number of passengers exceeds that projected, the revenue yield formula used in Q3 allows BAA greater than projected revenue and profits (even if operating costs rise pro rata with passengers): this additional revenue is available to offset return and depreciation on higher than projected capex.

(c) The CAA excluded the effect on RCV of underspend against projections in 1995/96 and 1996/97 but we included this as it was an integral part of the MMC projections and, moreover, out-turn for 1997/98 to 2001/02 was affected by slippage and delays to 1995/96 and 1996/97 investment, in particular the Heathrow Express (–£27 million).

(d) The CAA capex figures excluded centrally capitalized costs but included major runway maintenance (see Appendix 10.2). Our capex figures were in line with our approach to RCV, which is set out in Appendix 10.2 (+£19 million).

(e) The CAA included the effects of capex at Gatwick and Stansted but, as explained above, we did not do so (–£22 million).

(f) The CAA excluded depreciation effects altogether, as they rolled forward RCV for net capex less projected depreciation (see paragraphs 10.19 and 10.20), but we included depreciation effects (+£87 million).

10.9. BAA argued that it had achieved efficiencies in its capex, implying that the size of the actual capex programme relative to projected was larger than suggested in Table 10.2 and the difference consequently smaller. We note that, if BAA had achieved 5 per cent efficiency savings on its actual Heathrow capex, this would reduce the estimated effect from £64 million to £46 million.

Performance in Q3

10.10. Table 10.3 compares BAA's Q3 performance with the MMC's 1996 projections, adjusted as far as possible onto a comparable basis. For the five years as a whole BAA outperformed the projections by about £240 million, representing a compounded value at 31 March 2003 of about £300 million. This reflects in particular:

(a) higher revenue, not fully offset by higher opex[1] and depreciation; and

(b) lower capital costs due to lower capex reducing RCV: lower than projected expenditure on T5 was not fully offset by greater expenditure elsewhere (the comparison is not affected by revenue advancement since it is in both actual and projected figures).

Our comparison also suggests that overall return on capital was on average 1.0 per cent higher than projected.

---

[1] We have excluded pensions costs from actual opex as BAA paid no pensions contribution. As discussed in Appendix 7.5, the projections included a pensions contribution of 14 per cent. We estimate that if BAA had made contributions at this level, it would have paid £102 million (2000/01 prices over Q3). Thus BAA's pensions holiday was a major reason for its outperformance.

TABLE 10.3 **Comparison of BAA's actual performance with MMC projections**

£ million

	1997/98	1998/99	1999/00	2000/01	2001/02	Total out-turn prices	Total 2000/01 prices
Actual performance							
Revenue	1,052.9	1,187.8	1,235.7	1,341.1	1,366.6	6,184.0	6,338.6
Opex	−514.6	−572.2	−608.7	−652.2	−692.3	−3,040.0	−3,115.0
Adjustment for pensions costs*	5.1	6.1	4.9	5.3	27.2	48.6	49.0
Depreciation†	−112.4	−142.5	−168.1	−194.7	−221.2	−839.0	−856.2
Adjusted operating profit	431.0	479.1	463.8	499.5	480.3	2,353.6	2,416.4
Cost of capital‡	−321.5	−349.7	−369.2	−392.6	−419.2	−1,852.2	−1,898.5
Surplus after cost of capital	109.5	129.4	94.5	106.8	61.1	501.4	517.9
RCV§	4,286.2	4,662.9	4,922.9	5,235.1	5,589.0		
Operating profit as % of RCV	10.1	10.3	9.4	9.5	8.6	9.6	
Projected performance							
Revenue	1,068.6	1,157.1	1,205.2	1,251.0	1,274.8	5,956.7	6,111.5
Adjustment for transfers¶	−11.5	−12.7	−13.7	−14.0	−14.4	−66.3	−68.0
Opex	−522.8	−564.2	−584.5	−617.6	−623.0	−2,912.0	−2,987.5
Depreciation	−122.7	−140.8	−161.6	−165.6	−166.6	−757.3	−775.9
Operating profit	411.6	439.4	445.5	453.8	470.8	2,221.0	2,280.1
Cost of capital‡	−320.5	−353.3	−386.0	−429.3	−468.5	−1,957.6	−2,003.8
Surplus after cost of capital	91.0	86.0	59.5	24.5	2.3	263.4	276.3
RCV§	4,407.4	4,881.2	5,337.7	5,924.1	6,450.7		
Adjusted RCV¶	4,273.9	4,711.3	5,146.2	5,723.9	6,246.7		
Operating profit as % of RCV	9.6	9.3	8.7	7.9	7.5	8.6	
Actual less projected performance (adjusted)							
Revenue	−4.2	43.4	44.1	104.1	106.2	293.7	295.1
Opex ¤	13.3	−1.9	−19.3	−29.3	−42.1	−79.4	−78.4
Depreciation¤	10.3	−1.8	−6.5	−29.1	−54.6	−81.7	−80.3
Cost of capital§¤	−0.9	3.6	16.7	36.7	49.3	105.5	105.3
Surplus after cost of capital	18.5	43.4	35.0	82.3	58.8	238.0	241.6
Return as % of adjusted RCV	0.4	1.0	0.8	1.6	1.0	1.0	

Source: CC estimates based on data provided by BAA and estimates of RCV in Appendix 10.2.

Note: In this table revenue is shown as positive and expenditure as negative.

*Adjustment to remove pensions costs from opex (BAA paid no pensions contributions from 1 April 1997).

†Depreciation on investment property is excluded (see Appendix 10.2) and the resulting figure adjusted to average year prices.

‡Cost of capital is calculated at 7.5 per cent of RCV.

§Average of start and end year RCV (see Appendix 10.2)

¶Revenue and RCV are adjusted for actual transfers from the regulated companies to Lynton.

¤Since costs are shown in the table as negative, a negative (positive) number in this row indicates that actual costs exceeded (were less than) projected.

10.11. Table 10.4 shows a breakdown of both actual and projected revenue (a breakdown of costs is shown in Chapter 7). Table 10.4 suggests the following main points:

(a) Revenue from airport charges was greater than projected due to higher passenger numbers (see paragraph 10.13). Other factors affecting airport charges include BAA's under-recovery against the formula in 2000/01 and its S factor claims (see Chapter 5).

(b) Other operational income was much greater than projected. BAA told us this was primarily due to new charges for transfer baggage (TSC), the revenue and costs of which were not included in the 1996 projections (as transfer of baggage was previously carried out by airlines). The TSC charge is agreed by the airline community through TIFGAH. Other operational income was also higher due to higher passengers.

(c) Duty- and tax-free revenue was significantly lower than projected, despite higher passenger numbers. This to some extent reflects that the BAA projections (which were adopted by the MMC) were over-ambitious and that the MMC and the CAA may have under-estimated the effect on revenue of the change in the legislation regarding duty-free sales to EC passengers. BAA told us that other reasons for lower than projected duty- and tax-free revenue included the effect of the late 1990s economic crisis in the Far East and increased health awareness affecting sales of alcoholic and tobacco products.

(d) Revenue from other retailing (bureaux de change, catering, car rental and landside shops) has also been lower than projected despite higher passenger numbers.

(e) Revenue from property has been higher than projected. As discussed in Appendix 8.1, this is attributable primarily to more space and facilities.

(f) Revenue from car parks has been higher than projected due to increased demand for parking spaces associated with higher passenger numbers and to real price increases (see paragraph 8.38).

(g) Revenue from utilities (electricity, gas, heating and water) was lower than projected. BAA said the reasons included cost savings passed on to customers.

(h) Revenue from Heathrow Express was lower than projected due principally to a delay in the start of services (lower than projected passenger numbers being largely offset by higher than projected prices).

(i) Other revenue (which includes advertising and car park passes) was higher than projected for a number of reasons, including the introduction of sponsorship (by HSBC) and improved terms from BAA's media sales agency (J C Decaux).

TABLE 10.4 **Comparison of actual with projected revenue**

£ million, 2000/01 prices

	Actual	Adjustments*	Actual adjusted	Projected	Adjustment†	Projected adjusted	Difference‡
Airport charges	2,414.3	−221.4	2,192.8	2,077.3		2,077.3	115.5
Other operating income	129.5		129.5	44.2		44.2	85.3
Duty/tax-free	953.0	176.1	1,129.2	1,351.3		1,351.3	−222.1
Other retail	660.9		660.9	701.4		701.4	−40.5
Car park	484.2		484.2	380.5		380.5	103.7
Property	961.0		961.0	892.9	−68.0	824.9	136.1
Utility	176.3		176.3	216.4		216.4	−40.0
HEX	202.7		202.7	244.1		244.1	−41.4
Other	356.6		356.6	203.4		203.4	153.1
Total revenue	6,338.6	−45.3	6,293.3	6,111.5	−68.0	6,043.5	249.8

Source: CC estimates based on data provided by BAA.

---

*Adjustment for D factor in the formula (£176 million is deducted from airport charges and added to duty/tax-free revenue) and for marketing support paid to airlines (£45 million). (Marketing support was netted off revenue in the projections.)

†Adjustment for transfers to Lynton.

‡Actual adjusted less projected adjusted.

10.12. At Stansted, airport charges revenue (net of marketing support) was about £36 million and total revenue £76 million more than projected, while Stansted's costs were about £24 million greater than projected, of which £20 million was accounted by depreciation and return on capital. Hence net out-performance at Stansted was about £52 million.

Passenger numbers

10.13. Table 10.5 shows that the actual number of passengers exceeded the MMC's 1996 projections (which were based on BAA's 1996 passenger projections with a small upwards adjustment for Stansted). BAA told us that the reasons for greater than projected total passenger numbers included:

(a) the unexpected growth of LFCs at Stansted;

(b) sustained economic growth over the period; and

(c) lower oil prices.

As a result of the events of 11 September 2001, the actual number of passengers at the three airports declined by 3.5 per cent in 2001/02 (Heathrow and Gatwick declined by 5.7 per cent but the LFCs at

Stansted continued to expand). However, the number of passengers at all three airports remained above the 1996 projections for that year. In the 1996 projections, Heathrow was assumed to be constrained to capacity of 60 million passengers before T5 opened. In fact, the passenger figures for 2000/01 show that capacity increased well above this level: the reasons for this included continued gradual increases in the number of hourly ATMs, increased use of slots at unpopular times and increased average number of passenger per ATM.

TABLE 10.5 **Comparison of actual with projected passenger numbers**

million

	1997/98	*1998/99*	*1999/00*	*2000/01*	*2001/02*	*Total*
Actual						
Heathrow	58.1	61.0	62.3	64.3	60.4	306.1
Gatwick	27.3	29.5	30.4	32.1	30.5	149.9
Stansted	5.5	7.4	9.9	12.3	14.1	49.1
Total	90.9	98.0	102.6	108.7	104.9	505.1
1996 MMC projections						
Heathrow	57.5	58.8	59.5	60.0	60.0	296.0
Gatwick	25.6	26.5	27.3	27.8	28.5	135.7
Stansted	5.6	6.0	6.5	7.0	7.8	32.9
Total	88.7	91.3	93.3	94.8	96.3	464.4
Actual less projected						
Heathrow	0.6	2.2	2.7	4.3	0.3	10.1
Gatwick	1.7	3.0	3.1	4.3	2.0	14.2
Stansted	−0.1	1.4	3.4	5.3	6.3	16.3
Total	2.1	6.5	9.1	13.7	8.4	39.8
Actual less projected as % of projected						
Heathrow	1	4	5	7	1	3
Gatwick	7	11	11	16	7	10
Stansted	−1	23	53	75	80	49
Total	3	7	10	15	9	9

Source: CC estimates based on BAA data for actual passengers.

10.14. As discussed in Appendix 10.1, over the past 35 years passenger numbers have tended to grow at just under 6 per cent per year both for the UK as a whole and for BAA London airports. Previous forecasts have tended to incorrectly predict a levelling off in the rate of growth (due, for instance, to consumers becoming to some extent satiated with travel). However, continued growth at previous rates at the London airports in the period up to summer 2001 was due to rapid expansion of the LCCs (which generated new journeys through offering very low prices as well as attracting passengers from existing airlines) and this may not necessarily be expected to continue through the next ten years. It is not axiomatic that growth in passenger numbers continues at previous rates and we consider that a reduction in the rate of growth is now likely. Furthermore, projections need to take into account the risk of lower passenger numbers due to further terrorist activity.

10.15. Table 10.6 shows BAA's and the CAA's passenger projections for Q4 and 2012/13 (the last year of Q5). The forecasts for Heathrow and Gatwick are similar and assume a resumption of growth following the downturn after 11 September 2001.[1] Given full or near full use of runways, the projections for Heathrow and Gatwick depend principally on trends in the number of passengers per ATM. At Stansted, where there still is spare off-peak runway capacity, the CAA has taken a somewhat more optimistic view of LFC growth, reflecting continued strong growth in Stansted passengers during 2002.[2] Even so, the CAA's implied compound rate of growth over the 12 years to 2012/13 is 3.1 per cent,[3] well below the past long-term growth rate. The DfT's projections are lower than those of BAA and the CAA,

---

[1]Recent BAA figures show August and September 2002 passengers at Heathrow were about 2 per cent down on the similar months in 2000, reflecting continuing recovery from the position in October 2001, when passengers were 20 per cent below October 2000, and in November 2001 (13.5 per cent below November 2000). At Gatwick, August and September 2002 passengers were about 4 per cent down on the similar months in 2000, compared with 13 per cent decline for October 2001 and 20 per cent decline for November 2001.

[2]BAA figures show that April to September 2002 passengers at Stansted were 12 per cent up on the comparable months of 2001 and 32 per cent up on the comparable months of 2000.

[3]Because of the drop in 2001/02 traffic the growth rate for the 11 years to 2012/13 is 3.8 per cent.

reflecting in particular a more pessimistic view of trends in passengers per ATM (which is important given runway constraints at Heathrow and Gatwick). The DfT told us it recognized that its profile of passengers per ATM was subject to some uncertainty and that the balance of risk was that this profile could be somewhat higher.

TABLE 10.6 **Projected passenger numbers for Q4 and 2012/13**

	2000/01 Actual	2001/02 Actual	2003/04 Projected	2004/05 Projected	2005/06 Projected	2006/07 Projected	2007/08 Projected	2012/13 Projected
Heathrow								
BAA	64.3	60.4	67.1	69.0	69.9	70.3	70.7	84.7
CAA	64.3	60.4	67.0	68.8	69.5	70.0	71.3	87.1
DfT*								76.9
Gatwick								
BAA	32.1	30.5	31.2	33.8	36.0	38.6	39.7	42.0
CAA	32.1	30.5	31.8	34.4	36.3	38.2	39.8	42.6
DfT*								36.6
Stansted								
BAA	12.3	14.1	16.4	17.1	18.0	19.3	20.5	26.3
CAA	12.3	14.1	17.5	19.3	20.3	21.1	22.3	27.9
DfT*								23.0
Total								
BAA	108.7	104.9	114.7	119.9	123.9	128.2	130.9	153.0
CAA	108.7	105.0	116.3	122.5	126.1	129.3	133.4	157.6
DfT*								136.6

Source: BAA, CAA and DfT.

*DfT forecasts for 2015.

10.16.   BA regarded the CAA's passenger projections as broadly plausible (see paragraph 12.118).

RCV

10.17.   The MMC's projections, which were the basis for both its recommendations and the CAA's subsequent decision on X, were based on an opening RCV (31 March 1995) of £3,390 million. We have rolled forward this RCV for capex less depreciation over the period 1995/96 to 2002/03 (figures for 2002/03 represent BAA's latest projections)—see Appendix 10.2. Our calculation of RCV is consistent with the MMC's roll forward of RCV from 31 March 1991 to 31 March 1995 and also with the MMC's 1996 projections.

10.18.   Prior to the MMC's 1996 report, BAA had not had an RCV similar to that of other regulated companies, the price caps for Q1 and Q2 being based on asset values from the accounts. The 1996 MMC report proposed a value for the RCV, which was accepted by the CAA. The CAA stated in its 1996 decision (CAP 664) that it was 'impressed by the MMC's analysis [of asset valuation], believes that its [the MMC's] approach gives a robust basis for this and future reviews and has adopted it in framing its initial proposals and the final decision'. Unfortunately the CAA did not institute a procedure for annually rolling forward the RCV. As a consequence, a number of disputed issues arose at this review, initially between BAA and the CAA, and subsequently between BAA and ourselves. These are discussed in the following paragraphs.

Depreciation used in roll forward of RCV

10.19.   The CAA argued that the RCV roll forward should be based on BAA's actual capex less the depreciation projected by the MMC. We note, however, that the CAA's proposed treatment involves some inconsistency between the resulting treatment of capex and of depreciation. If actual capex and depreciation differ from projected levels, then, under the CAA's proposed treatment, RCV will be different from what it would have been if the projections were correct. Additionally, as shown in Appendix 10.3, assets will be over- or under-depreciated over their book lives and there will be consequential effects on RCV after the assets are life-expired, with the result that the profile of prices may be distorted.

10.20. The CAA nevertheless argued that projected depreciation was what customers had paid for[1] and that its proposed treatment had a number of advantages:

(a) It avoided problems in dealing with any changes in accounting policies and asset book lives. In rolling forward RCV, actual depreciation would need to be adjusted for changes in accounting conventions in order to avoid unforeseen and potentially undesirable transfers from customers to shareholders[2] or vice versa. For example, the MMC's Q3 projections excluded depreciation on investment property whereas BAA's regulated accounts included depreciation on investment property after 31 March 1995 and thus it is necessary to adjust actual depreciation to exclude depreciation of investment property. We note that changes in accounting policies, in particular capitalization policy, may affect capex as well as depreciation and therefore it remains necessary for the regulator to consider accounting changes carefully even if RCV is rolled forward for projected rather than actual depreciation.

(b) It avoided arbitrary effects which might occur due to errors in the projections. The CAA noted, in particular, that price caps would be higher than necessary if projected depreciation was overstated, but that, if RCV was subsequently rolled forward for projected depreciation, this would be offset by lower price caps in future periods and that this would reduce any incentive to overstate depreciation in the projections. We note that there are many uncertainties about the projections and that it is possible for the regulator to carry out consistency checks, as with other aspects of the projections. Furthermore, if managers are concerned principally with the next five years rather than the longer term, they may still be tempted to overstate depreciation even under the CAA's proposal. There is, moreover, no evidence that BAA has in the past overstated projected depreciation.

(c) It reduced the disincentive to carry out additional non-revenue-earning capex over and above what was included in the projections used to set the price cap. This occurs because the company does not recover return and depreciation on any additional capex (unless passenger numbers are also higher or there are other effects[3]). If RCV is subsequently rolled forward for projected depreciation, RCV will be higher by the full amount of the additional capex. But, if RCV is rolled forward for actual depreciation, RCV will be higher by the additional capex less additional depreciation. Consequently, RCV and prices in subsequent periods will be slightly higher if RCV is rolled forward for projected depreciation and, if the company is aware of this, it should reduce the disincentive to carrying out additional capex.[4]

10.21. We note, however, that there may also be incentive drawbacks to rolling forward for projected depreciation including:

(a) weaker incentive to achieve capex efficiencies (due to the reverse of the above effect); and

(b) stronger incentive to substitute short-life assets for longer-life assets (since such substitution will result in actual depreciation being higher than projected, and RCV lower, if rolled forward for actual rather than projected depreciation).

10.22. There are a variety of possible approaches to rolling forward the RCV but it is important that the roll forward is consistent with the assumptions made at the time the price cap was set, as any inconsistency could undermine investment incentives. It is, however, possible to separate the issue of

---

[1]BAA's price cap is set on the basis of £ per passenger and hence the amount paid by passengers depends, among other things, on projected depreciation per passenger and the ratio of actual to projected passengers. During Q3 the number of passengers was greater than projected and therefore the amount implicitly paid by customers was greater than projected depreciation.
[2]Consider an asset of £100 million expected to be installed at the start of a five-year price cap period with a ten-year life. Depreciation will be £50 million in the first period and £50 million in the next period. If accounting conventions are changed so that reported depreciation is £70 million in the first period, the asset's RCV would be £30 million at the start of the next period. This would be anomalous if the price cap for the first period was set on the basis of £50 million depreciation: the company recovered only £50 million in the first period and thus needs to recover £50 million in the next period whatever the reported depreciation.
[3]Other effects could include improved quality of service if this is remunerated.
[4]The effect would be more marked for projects that would come into operation early in the period and on which depreciation would be charged for a number of years.

how depreciation is treated in the RCV roll forward to the start of Q4 from the issue of how the regulator intends to treat depreciation in future (the roll forward from the start to the end of Q4, Q5 etc):

(a) In relation to the roll forward to the start of Q4, there is no suggestion in the 1996 MMC report or the CAA's 1996 decision that RCV should be rolled forward in any way other than using actual depreciation. The benefits that the CAA expects from rolling forward using projected depreciation would only arise in future and do not require rolling forward using projected depreciation to the start of Q4. We have therefore rolled RCV forward to the start of Q4 using actual depreciation.

(b) In relation to the future, if investment incentives are to be maintained, it is important for the CAA to be clear in its forthcoming decision about the approach it assumes that the airports regulator will in future take to rolling forward through Q4. Although the CAA's proposed approach involves some inconsistency between the treatment of capex and depreciation with potential effects on the profile of prices, we accept that this is not an overriding problem. We nevertheless believe the advantages are smaller than suggested by the CAA and also that rolling forward using projected depreciation may be less suited to airports than other regulated sectors where uncertainties about both capex and volume are lower (and also in many cases where variances in volume have less impact on the price cap). We therefore believe that it would be acceptable for RCV to be rolled forward through Q4 either for projected depreciation (as proposed by the CAA) or for actual depreciation (as was preferred by BAA). It is important that the CAA makes clear the approach it intends to use and also puts in place a procedure for calculating the RCV numbers annually.

BAA's approach to the RCV

10.23.   BAA argued that the RCV should be based on the NBV of assets less net current liabilities in its notional consolidated regulatory accounts,[1] noting that the CAA had been fully involved in formulating the accounts and had not raised any objections or comments suggesting that they would not serve the purpose of regulation. The asset valuations in the regulatory accounts are adjusted annually by the RPI but nevertheless differ from the rolled forward RCV in the following material respects:

(a) Since 31 March 1995, investment property assets have been depreciated and hence the NBV of the assets has been reduced by depreciation on investment property. This is inconsistent with the 1996 projections (which excluded depreciation on investment property in line with previous accounting treatment) on which the Q3 price cap was based.[2] By contrast, the rolled forward RCV in Appendix 10.2 excludes depreciation on investment property up to 31 March 2002,[3] which is consistent with the 1996 projections and Q3 price cap. Similarly, the 1996 projections included projected expenditure on major periodic maintenance of runways but from 1999/2000 BAA has capitalized this expenditure in its accounts.[4] BAA's proposed RCV thus includes the NBV of major runway maintenance (about £15 million at Gatwick) even though this expenditure was included in the 1996 projections which were the basis of the Q3 price cap. By contrast, the rolled-forward RCV in Appendix 10.2 excludes Q3 expenditure on major runway maintenance.

(b) When BAA disposes of assets that are not fully depreciated, the NBV of assets is reduced by the remaining NBV of disposed-of assets. This is not consistent with the MMC's previous treatment of the RCV or with the 1996 projections, which assumed the RCV was reduced by the proceeds of the disposals. However, the roll forward of the RCV in Appendix 10.2 is consistent with the MMC projections as it takes account of the proceeds not the book value of disposals.

(c) BAA's calculation includes net current liabilities at the date in question. But the value of net current liabilities is affected by a number of factors that are not relevant to regulatory costs given the approach we have taken to the cost of capital. These factors may include loans from other

---

[1]At 1April 1995 this equalled the RCV of £3,390 million as a result of an addition of £29 million to the NBV of fixed assets in the notional consolidated regulatory accounts.
[2]This is disadvantageous to BAA shareholders since depreciation on investment property was not reflected in Q3 price caps and, under BAA's approach, will not be reflected in future price caps through the RCV.
[3]For the year 2002/03, investment property depreciation is included. This is in line with our treatment of 2002/03 as a one-off year that was not part of Q3 (see paragraph 10.5).
[4]This occurred as a result of BAA adopting FRS 15.

BAA subsidiaries, unpaid dividends and corporation tax.[1] Between 31 March 1995 and 31 March 2002 the value of net current liabilities in the notional consolidated regulatory accounts declined from £277 million (£328 million at March 2002 prices) to £113 million (in particular due to an increase in debtors and repayment during 1995/96 of £83 million owed by STAL to fellow BAA subsidiaries). This increases the value of BAA's proposed RCV by £215 million even though some of the movements are not relevant to regulatory costs.[2]

As it happens, these factors to some extent offset one another in the period between 31 March 1995 and 31 March 2002, with the result that BAA's proposed RCV is only about £50 million higher than the rolled-forward RCV in Appendix 10.2. However, the difference increases to a projected £157 million at 1 April 2003 as BAA's projections of RCV take account only of net trading liabilities (we note that, while this removes the problem (see *(c)* above) of RCV being affected by loans from other BAA subsidiaries and irrelevant tax and dividend liabilities, it introduces an inconsistency with the MMC's 1996 recommendations and the CAA's 1996 decision.[3]

10.24. We do not accept BAA's view that the RCV should necessarily be equal to the NBV of the assets shown in the accounts. This was not the approach taken by the MMC in 1996: the MMC took what it considered to be the implicit 1991 regulatory value of the business and rolled it forward for net new investment (noting that the resulting value was somewhat greater than the value implied by rolling forward the market capitalization immediately after privatization). We note also that, as BAA's approach to the RAB is not consistent with the MMC's 1996 report and the CAA's subsequent decision, its adoption might be expected to generate regulatory uncertainty and damage incentives.

Approach to calculating the value of X

10.25. We have adopted a similar approach to that adopted by the MMC in 1996 and also to that adopted for other regulated industries. We have considered projections for the next ten years (Q4 and Q5): this is similar to the approach of the 1996 MMC report.

10.26. The broad basis of our calculations is that BAA's required revenue from airport charges should equal its total costs including cost of capital on the RCV less all non-airport charge revenue. In order to estimate BAA's required revenue, projections are therefore required on:

(a) opex (see Chapter 7);

(b) depreciation;

(c) cost of capital (see Chapter 4);

(d) RCV at the start of Q4 (see Appendix 10.2);

(e) change in RCV: this is equal to projected net capex (see Chapter 9) less depreciation, adjusted for inflation; and

(f) revenue per passenger from non-airport charges (see Chapter 8) and projected number of passengers (see paragraphs 10.14 and 10.15 and Appendix 10.1).

Passenger projections also affect X directly as the formula specifies a cap on revenue per passenger, and impact on opex and capex as well. Within each quinquennium, higher passenger numbers tend to be

---

[1]Loans from other BAA subsidiaries and liabilities to pay dividends and corporation tax are a source of funds rather than a cost to the regulated business.

[2]We note also that it largely represents a reversal of movements in net current liabilities between 31 March 1991, when net current liabilities were £116 million (£154 million at March 2002 prices) and 31 March 1995, and that this increase in net current liabilities did not reduce the 31 March 1995 RCV under the MMC's 1996 approach.

[3]The notional consolidated regulatory accounts for 31 March 1995 equalled the MMC's RCV of £3,390 million on the basis of total net current liabilities, not net trading liabilities: if the notional consolidated regulatory accounts had taken account only of net trading liabilities it is likely that a deduction from, rather than a £29 million addition to, the NBV of fixed assets would have been required for consistency with the 1996 MMC report.

associated with a lower required price cap as the short-term impact on costs is less than pro rata. In the longer term, higher passenger numbers at Heathrow are likely to be associated with higher prices as extensive capex is required.[1]

Process

10.27. BAA published its passenger forecasts in April 2002 and provided us, at the end of June 2002, with its own projections of opex and capex, non-airport charges revenue and depreciation. BAA's projections were both for the full single till and for an aeronautical till.

10.28. The CAA developed its own view on passenger projections (included in its initial submission and revised during September 2002) but not on other aspects of the projections. However, as the CAA's definition of the aeronautical till was different from that of BAA (see Chapter 8) its projections for the aeronautical till were different from those of BAA. The CAA did not provide us with updated projections reflecting BAA's revised June 2002 projections.

10.29. The CAA developed its own financial model to use in setting X. We found it difficult to use the CAA's model to consider a full range of regulatory approaches (for example, system as well as individual airport approach). Additionally, the CAA did not update its model to include BAA's end-June projections rapidly enough to ensure that our modelling could be carried out within a timescale consistent with completing our inquiry by the end of October. We therefore decided to base our modelling on an adapted version of BAA's own financial model: we considered this preferable to developing another model running off the results of the CAA model.

10.30. We provided BAA and the CAA with illustrative projections, together with a full copy of our adapted version of BAA's financial model on 16 August 2002, 12 September 2002 and 21 October 2002.

CAA and BAA proposals for X

10.31. The CAA's proposed PPC involved price caps for Q4 of (RPI+6) at Heathrow and (RPI+5) at Gatwick (see Appendix 5.1) with a significant increase in the Heathrow price cap when T5 opened. Although the CAA favoured a dual-till approach, the actual price caps proposed by the CAA for Q4 are lower than the level implied by the dual till (RRCB). This remains the case for the full 20 years of the PPC: as noted in Appendix 5.1, the NPV of revenues from the CAA's proposed 20-year PPC is less than that implied by the RRCB, although in the CAA's modelling this is offset by a higher NPV of revenues after the end of the 20 years. For Stansted, the CAA proposed a Q4 cap of (RPI+6.7) although it did not expect the airport to price up to this cap. The reasoning behind the CAA's proposals is set out in Chapter 11 and in its submission to us (available on the CAA web site). These proposals were based on BAA's projections at the end of 2001.

10.32. BAA proposed price caps for Q4 of (RPI+7) for Heathrow, (RPI+3) for Gatwick and (RPI+1) for Stansted. BAA's proposals are further described in paragraph 14.116.

CC projections

10.33. We made projections of required revenue on two sets of assumptions. The basis of the first (described below as the base assumptions) was:

(a) BAA's projections of passengers at Heathrow and Gatwick and the CAA's projections of passengers at Stansted;

(b) BAA's projections of opex, adjusted as follows:

(i)   for the effects of higher passengers at Stansted;

---

[1]CAA estimates suggest the cost per incremental passenger of T5 is about £15 on a single-till basis, well above the level of the costs of existing capacity on either a single- or dual-till basis.

(ii)   to exclude BAA's £8 million contingency costs;

(iii) for the pensions contribution that BAA was expected, on the basis of the most recent actuarial valuation, to pay (19.3 per cent rather than the 22 per cent of pensionable pay, which was included in the projections); and

(iv)   to exclude expenditure on marketing support at Stansted (see paragraph 5.21). We excluded marketing expenditure as we wished to consider projections of the net price customers pay.

BAA submitted opex projections both including and excluding additional security costs following 11 September of £5.7 million in 2002/03 and £7.5 million in 2003/04 (at 2000/01 prices). We have used the numbers including additional security costs and thus our projections assume that BAA does not make an S factor claim for 2002/03 for these security costs (it would be appropriate to exclude these security costs if BAA does make an S factor claim).

(c) BAA's projections of capex (adjusted for the effects of higher passengers at Stansted), except that no expenditure on a new runway was included as this is subject to future government decisions and would need to be remunerated separately;

(d) BAA's projections of non-airport charges revenue, adjusted:

(i)   for the effects of higher passengers at Stansted;

(ii)   to exclude projected revenue from the Heathrow TSC which is in future to be included in airport charges (see paragraph 8.15); and

(iii) to include projected revenue from cargo flights (which occurs mainly at Stansted) as it is assumed to be excluded from airport charges: we have assumed revenue from cargo flights increases at the same rate as revenue from passenger flights;

(e) BAA's projections of depreciation, based on the straight-line approach[1] using BAA's accounting asset lives and with RPI adjustment of asset values;

(f) opening 31 March 2003 RCV of £6,013 million (2000/01 prices) as set out in Appendix 10.2;

(g) RCV is rolled forward for projected net capex less depreciation where net capex is capex less proceeds of disposals;[2]

(h) cost of capital of 7.75 per cent;

(i) Heathrow is credited with revenue of £94.4 million (2000/01 prices) per year during Q4, reflecting the annuitized effects over Q4 of the £348 million revenue advancement (£83.4 million a year) and the £46 million adjustment for net underspend on capex at Heathrow (£11.0 million a year);

(j) RPI out-turn for 2002/03 of 1.9 per cent and RPI of 2.5 per cent for 2003/04 to 2012/13; and

(k) a formula similar to that in Q3, but with no correction factor in 2003/04 and 2004/05 (as it would be inappropriate for BAA to be compensated for under-recovery against the 2001/02 and 2002/03 price caps).

10.34. We then considered projections with a lower level of opex (described as low assumptions), specifically:

---

[1]Depreciation on each asset equals RPI-adjusted cost of acquisition divided by assumed life. Depreciation starts when the asset comes into operation.
[2]BAA proposed an alternative approach where RCV is rolled forward for the NBV of disposals and loss/profit on disposals is treated as a cost. The CAA suggested that this would give a regulated company the incentive to cherry-pick assets for disposal on the basis of differences between book and market value, and we found BAA's alternative approach made little difference to the value of X.

(a) a lower pensions contribution (based on what the latest actuarial valuation suggests it would have had to pay if its Q3 contributions had been at the level assumed in the 1996 projections) of 15.4 per cent (see Appendix 7.5); and

(b) immediate savings in labour costs (compared with BAA's projections) of 1 per cent specifically due to better management of employees' absence and further savings of 1.5 per cent a year due to improved productivity.

We then considered a further set of projections with intermediate assumptions one-third up the range between the two sets of projections (nearer to the low assumptions).

10.35. For Heathrow and Gatwick we considered two profiles for X:[1]

(a) X is set so that the airport earns the cost of capital over Q4 with the same X for each year and similarly for Gatwick in Q5 (at Heathrow we assumed a one-off increase in the price cap at the start of Q5 followed by X of 0^2); and

(b) X is set so that the airport earns the cost of capital over Q4 and Q5 together with the same X for each year.

10.36. For Stansted we have assumed that average revenue from passenger flights (net of discounts and marketing support paid by BAA to airlines) increases gradually towards Gatwick's level by 2008/09. Where this results in Stansted earning above the cost of capital, Stansted's Q5 revenue yield is reduced below that of Gatwick so that Stansted just earns the cost of capital over Q4 and Q5 together. Where the assumption that Stansted has similar Q5 revenue yield to Gatwick results in Stansted earning below the cost of capital, X at Heathrow is altered so that the system as a whole earns the cost of capital.

10.37. We assume that, as in Q3, the CAA will set the 2003/04 revenue yield as a number rather than relating it to the maximum yield for 2002/03. We projected revenue yield for 2003/04 and X for 2004/05 to 2007/08 assuming a notional formula relating 2003/04 yield to projected actual 2002/03 yield.[3] Under our approach, therefore, the value of X depends on the projected revenue per passenger in 2002/03. Table 10.7 shows BAA's projected 2002/03 revenue per passenger[4] and the adjustments we have made for consistency with our projections for Q4 and Q5.

TABLE 10.7 **Projected 2002/03 revenue per passenger and adjustments**

£ per passenger, out-turn prices

	Heathrow	Gatwick	Stansted
Revenue yield (current formula basis)	5.57	4.24	4.59
Adjustment for cargo flights	−0.02	−0.02	−0.33
Adjustment for TSC*	0.43	-	-
Discounts†	-	-	0.09
Approximate yield from published tariffs	5.98	4.22	4.35
Discounts†	-	-	−0.09
Marketing support	-	-	−1.17
Yield net of discounts and marketing	5.98	4.22	3.09
Net yield adjusted to 2000/01 prices	5.78	4.08	2.99

Source: CC calculations (based on BAA data).

*Excluding under-recovery (see paragraph 8.14).
†Excluding cargo flights.

---

[1]This was achieved by using a spreadsheet iterative routine to solve the equation:
NPV (airport charges revenue) = NPV(opex + capex − non-airport charges revenue) + NPV(opening RCV) − NPV(closing RCV) where NPVs are evaluated using the cost of capital; opex, capex and revenue are assumed to accrue for discounting purposes in the middle of the year.
[2]Assuming the same Heathrow X for each year in Q5 tends to result in returns far exceeding the cost of capital by the end of Q5.
[3]The notional formula for 2003/04 is similar to the formulae for 2004/05 to 2007/08 except that we used projected RPI for 2003/04 of 2.5 per cent rather than the out-turn RPI for September 2002 of 1.7 per cent (this was to avoid any anomaly as a result of the difference between the two figures).
[4]Out-turn revenue yield will depend on dilution/concentration (see paragraph 5.13) during the year.

10.38. Table 10.8 shows a summary of the projections described above. Table 10.8 shows that targeting Heathrow's cost of capital in Q4 and Q5 separately would result in a relatively small increase in the price cap during Q4 (about 1 per cent) but would require an extremely large increase in the price cap (about 80 per cent) when T5 is projected to come into operation at the start of Q5.[1] Targeting the cost of capital over Q4 and Q5 together results in a value of Heathrow X of between 6.23 and 6.8 per cent.

TABLE 10.8 **Summary of financial projections**

per cent

Opex assumptions	Heathrow X*			Gatwick X†		Stansted net yield‡	
	Q4	2008/09	Rest of Q5	Q4	Q5	2003/04– 2008/09	Rest of Q5
Cost of capital targeted separately in Q4 and Q5							
Base	1.23	79.3	0.00	0.22	1.39	5.90	1.39
Low	0.12	83.9	0.00	−0.17	2.03	5.21	2.03
Intermediate	0.42	82.9	0.00	−0.04	1.82	5.54	1.82
Cost of capital targeted over Q4 and Q5 together							
Base	6.80	6.80	6.80	0.51	0.51	6.01	0.51
Low	6.22	6.22	6.22	0.38	0.38	5.59	0.38
Intermediate	6.39	6.39	6.39	0.42	0.42	5.86	0.42

Source: CC.

*Value of X in the formula (RPI+X). Under base opex assumptions, X is increased slightly to cover Stansted shortfall against cost of capital.
†Value of X in the formula (RPI+X).
‡Percentage change in revenue yield (net of discounts and marketing support). This is not a projected value of X as the formula relates to revenue yield before discounts and marketing support. With these net yields, Stansted covers its cost of capital (taking Q4 and Q5 together) under low and intermediate opex assumptions but not under the base assumptions.

10.39. We then considered a further set of projections with intermediate opex projections and Heathrow cost of capital targeted over Q4 and Q5 together (with a rounded cap of RPI+6.5[2]) and Gatwick cost of capital targeted in Q4 (with a rounded cap of RPI+0) and Q5 separately. The projected yield for 2003/04 at 2000/01 prices is £6.116 for Heathrow and £4.079 for Gatwick (at our projected out-turn prices, the projected yields are £6.484 for Heathrow and £4.324 for Gatwick). Table 10.9 shows further details for these projections. Net debt as a percentage of RCV (sometimes described as regulatory gearing) increases to [✂] per cent in 2007/08, the year before T5 is projected to open, and then declines. Interest cover declines to [✂] in 2008/09 and then increases.

---

[1] If the same X is assumed for each year of Q5, the required X is about 22, implying an overall increase in the price cap during Q5 in excess of 150 per cent.
[2] The opening 2003/04 yield was amended to ensure cost of capital was earned exactly.

TABLE 10.9 Projections assuming RPI+6.5 for Heathrow and RPI+0 for Gatwick (intermediate opex assumptions)

	2003/04	2004/05	2005/06	2006/07	2007/08	2008/09	2009/10	2010/11	2011/12	2012/13
Passenger numbers ('000)										
Heathrow	67,075	69,000	69,900	70,300	70,700	75,500	80,000	81,500	83,000	84,700
Gatwick	31,200	33,760	36,000	38,600	39,700	40,000	40,500	41,000	41,500	42,000
Stansted	17,500	19,300	20,300	21,100	22,300	23,600	24,700	25,800	26,800	27,900
Total	115,775	122,060	126,200	130,000	132,700	139,100	145,200	148,300	151,300	154,600
*Capex (£m, 2000/01 prices)**										
Heathrow	792.1	817.4	948.3	796.5	801.4	471.6	467.1	415.5	273.6	252.6
Gatwick	72.3	82.8	97.8	126.9	145.4	121.1	90.9	91.3	55.9	48.6
Stansted	32.2	68.2	68.0	78.5	81.4	86.3	59.9	62.7	87.7	58.5
Total	896.6	968.4	1,114.1	1,001.9	1,028.2	678.9	617.9	569.5	417.3	359.7
RCV at end-year† (£m, 2000/01 prices)										
Heathrow	*Figures omitted. See note on page iv.*									
Gatwick	1,186.1	1,209.4	1,250.6	1,317.3	1,397.2	1,450.1	1,466.5	1,482.9	1,464.8	1,440.4
Stansted	816.8	855.9	891.6	935.4	979.1	1,022.2	1,032.7	1,042.3	1,078.5	1,085.2
Total	*Figures omitted. See note on page iv.*									
Revenue yield (revenue per passenger)										
Heathrow‡	6.12	6.50	6.92	7.36	7.82	8.32	8.85	9.41	10.00	10.64
Gatwick§	4.08	4.08	4.08	4.08	4.08	4.15	4.22	4.30	4.37	4.45
Stansted¶	3.15	3.32	3.50	3.69	3.89	4.10	4.17	4.25	4.32	4.40
Summary financial projections for BAA regulated business (£m, 2000/01 prices)										
Airport charges	592.7	650.6	701.4	752.4	801.7	890.8	981.7	1,052.3	1,127.4	1,210.4
Other revenue	*Figures omitted. See note on page iv.*									
Opex¤	−241.9	−251.7	−254.0	−264.3	−283.8	−394.8	−423.5	−438.9	−463.3	−467.1
Depreciation	*Figures omitted. See note on page iv.*									
Unadjusted return										
Adjustments	94.4	94.4	94.4	94.4	94.4	0.0	0.0	0.0	0.0	0.0
Adjusted regulatory return	*Figures omitted. See note on page iv.*									
Adjusted return on RCV# (%)										
Heathrow	10.4	9.4	8.5	8.0	7.6	4.8	5.6	6.2	6.6	7.6
Gatwick	6.3	7.2	7.9	8.4	7.7	7.6	7.2	7.3	7.5	7.8
Stansted	5.6	6.6	6.4	6.8	7.4	7.9	7.9	8.4	9.2	9.7
Total	9.0	8.7	8.2	8.0	7.6	5.5	6.1	6.6	7.0	7.9
Unadjusted return on RCV~ (%)										
Heathrow	8.3	7.5	6.8	6.6	6.3	4.8	5.6	6.2	6.6	7.6
Total	7.6	7.3	7.0	6.9	6.6	5.5	6.1	6.6	7.0	7.9
Financial ratios for BAA regulated business★										
HCA debt/equity (end year, %)	*Figures omitted. See note on page iv.*									
Net debt/RCV (end year, %)										
HCA interest cover (times)										

Source: CC estimates.

*Capex after assumed real price increase of 1 per cent in 2002/03 and 2003/04 (costs are assumed to increase 1 per cent faster than RPI in these years but in line with RPI thereafter).

†Change in Heathrow RCV for 2008/09 reflects proceeds from sale of T5 departure baggage system. In other years, proceeds of disposals are assumed to be zero.

‡RPI+6.5 for 2004/05 to 2012/13. 2003/04 yield set to give 7.75 per cent cost of capital for Q4 and Q5 together (notional 2003/04 formula gives implied X of 5.9 per cent for 2003/04).

§RPI+0 for 2004/05 to 2007/08. 2003/04 yield set to give 7.75 per cent cost of capital for Q4 (notional 2003/04 formula gives implied X of −0.1 per cent for 2003/04). X for Q5 is 1.8 per cent.

¶Revenue yield net of discounts and marketing support. A price cap consistent with these projected revenue yields is discussed in Chapter 2.

¤Includes airport opex and central opex allocated to airports on basis of 2001/02 accounts. Central opex includes net charges from/to other parts of BAA plus a share of costs of the BAA board and BAA's senior management incentive scheme. It also includes additional pensions contributions of 16.1 per cent of pensionable costs.

#Revenue (adjusted to include credit for recovery of revenue advancement and adjustment for capex underspend) less opex less depreciation as percentage of average of opening and closing RCV.

~Excludes credit for recovery of revenue advancement and adjustment for capex underspend.

★Notional financial ratios for the regulated company based on the opening level of net debt and dividends in the notional consolidated regulatory accounts. BAA's other assumptions (which we have adopted in our projections) are that: dividends increase in real terms by 2 per cent in 2003/04, 2.7 per cent in 2004/05 and 5.4 per cent thereafter; that existing fixed rate debt is held until maturity and that new debt is taken on at a nominal interest rate of 6.5 per cent (equivalent to 3.9 per cent real interest rate at the assumed inflation rate of 2.5 per cent). BAA's fixed rate debt is allocated to the regulated company if BAA considers it was clearly taken on for the development of the London airports business (such debt includes EIB debt and the sterling bond and convertible bond issues in 2001 and 2002). Other debt is allocated to the regulated business pro rata with assets (about 86 per cent) unless it was clearly taken on for unregulated business development.

10.40. Table 10.10 shows, for the same set of projections, NPV of net revenue by airport: total net revenue over Q4 and Q5 together is zero as BAA is projected to earn the cost of capital, and no more, on its RCV. The NPV of net revenue at Heathrow in Q4 is positive reflecting our smoothing assumptions:

(a) at Heathrow our Q4 projections show a surplus of revenue over costs amounting to an NPV at 31 March 2003 of £300 million, which is assumed to reduce Heathrow's price cap in Q5 (compared with the level implied by the cost of capital);

(b) at Gatwick the projected NPV of net revenue is zero in both Q4 and Q5, reflecting the assumptions set out above; and

(c) at Stansted our Q4 projections show a shortfall of revenue compared to costs amounting to an NPV at 31 March 2003 of £33 million, which is assumed to be recovered from Stansted's charges in Q5.

Any future price caps would need to take into account the implications of the CAA's eventual decision for Q4 revenue advancement at Heathrow and revenue deferment at Stansted.

TABLE 10.10 **NPV at 31 March 2003 of projected net revenue**

£ million (2000/01 prices)

	Q4	*Q5*	*Total*
Heathrow	300.4	−300.4	0.0
Gatwick	0.0	0.0	0.0
Stansted	−33.1	33.1	0.0
Total	267.3	−267.3	0.0

Source: CC estimates.

Note: NPV of net revenue is defined as: NPV (revenue − opex − capex) − NPV(opening RCV) + NPV(closing RCV) where NPVs are evaluated using our 7.75 per cent cost of capital; opex, capex and revenue are assumed to accrue for discounting purposes in the middle of the year.

11 Views of the CAA and the Department for Transport

Contents

Introduction

11.1. This chapter contains the views of the CAA, its panel of advisers and the DfT.

CAA

11.2. The CAA is the UK's specialist aviation regulator and, inter alia, has powers under the Airports Act and the Airports (Northern Ireland) Order 1994 for the economic regulation of airports in the UK. As described in Chapter 3, the Government has designated four airports (Heathrow, Gatwick, Manchester and Stansted) for detailed price control. This means that for these airports the CAA sets a price cap to limit the amount that can be levied by way of airport charges for a five-year period. The CAA has to refer the airports to the CC, which recommends a price cap and decides whether the airport operators have acted against the public interest over the previous five years. The CAA has to impose conditions if the CC finds that an airport has been acting against the public interest but the CAA takes the final decision on the price cap.

Background to the references

Introduction

11.3. The CAA in 1999 decided to embark on a fundamental review of the way in which airport charges were regulated. In a report published in July 2000 *Issues for the Airport Reviews—Consultation Paper*, the CAA identified a range of themes that, in the CAA's view, had emerged or intensified in the airports sector over the preceding years.

11.4. These themes were:

(a) demand for access to Heathrow and Gatwick increasingly exceeds available capacity;

(b) in the absence of an efficient market in take-off and landing slots, utilization of existing capacity may not be optimal;

(c) whether the incentives under the current regulatory framework for the promotion of appropriate investment in capacity are the best possible, consistent with achieving sustainable development in the industry;

(d) the role of unregulated commercial revenues and costs (for example, from the provision of retail, car parking and office facilities and services) in setting airport charges; and

(e) the importance of service quality for customers and consumers and the wide variation in quality that different users may require.

11.5. In addressing these issues, the CAA undertook its review of regulation within the existing framework of the Airports Act, but cautioned that the best approach to future airport regulation might differ from that taken in the past, and from the approaches adopted in other regulated industries. The CAA also warned that the various approaches that it could take were likely to involve trade-offs between its statutory objectives.

11.6. This was followed by a second consultation paper in October 2000 which commented on the response to the July 2000 paper and set out the line of work that the CAA intended to pursue. The CAA set out four fundamental principles to underlying its approach to economic regulation:

(a) Regulation should focus on monopoly behaviour which is likely to reduce economic efficiency via insufficient capacity, rather than distribution of non-monopoly rents.

(b) Regulation should be consistent with the CAA's obligation to impose minimum restrictions and encourage commercial solutions.

(c) The regulatory framework needed to be credible and sustainable over time.

(d) Regulation must be transparent and predictable.

11.7. The CAA said that it would focus initially on the key options to the approach adopted in previous price reviews. The initial work programme undertook to address seven issues; these are shown below:

(a) the possibility of the price cap acting as a 'default' that would provide a firm base for airports and customers; airport users could then contract for additional or reduced services outside the price cap (February 2001);

(b) the separation of the setting of the price cap from the airports' own costs by the use of techniques such as benchmarking or incremental cost estimates (December 2000);

(c) setting charges to reflect incremental costs (including for additional outputs rather than for current outputs) (February 2001 and November 2001);

(d) the treatment of capex (January 2001);

(e) the single till versus the dual till (December 2000);

(f) service quality (including contracting outside the price cap) (December 2000); and

(g) competition within airports and further tendering out of services (February 2001).

11.8. The pattern in each case was publication of a consultation paper by the CAA on its web site with an invitation for responses from interested parties. The CAA also arranged workshops for the industry, Government and research consultancies.

11.9. Further papers published by the CAA in 2001 were as follows:

(a) Price structures (March 2001).

(b) Cost of capital (June 2001).

(c) The performance of each of the four designated airports during their price control periods (August 2001).

11.10. In November 2001, the CAA produced its preliminary proposals for prices in the 2003 to 2008 quinquennium. These proposals were published on the CAA web site and were discussed with the airports and airlines and others. The CAA's final proposals to the CC on 28 February 2002 were a slightly modified and expanded version of the preliminary proposals. Details were placed on the CAA web site at www.caa.co.uk. We took full account of the CAA's submission, but, since that is publicly available, this summary is primarily based on Part 1 of that submission, the hearings held with the CAA, and other information provided during the inquiry; other CAA material, however, is reflected elsewhere in the report.

Statutory objectives and international obligations

11.11. The CAA said that the Airports Act required the CAA to set the price cap at regulated airports at a level which it considered was best calculated:

(a) to further the reasonable interests of users of airports within the UK;

(b) to promote the efficient, economic and profitable operations of such airports;

(c) to encourage investment in new facilities at airports in time to satisfy anticipated demands by the users of such airports; and

(d) to impose the minimum restrictions that are consistent with the performance by the CAA of its functions.

In addition, section 39 (3) of the Airports Act requires that:

> In performing those functions the CAA shall take into account such of the international obligations of the United Kingdom as may be notified to it by the Secretary of State for the purposes of this section.

The CAA said that it had to operate within the Airports Act objectives, but the CC did not have to do so. Therefore the CAA urged as much clarity as possible about the objectives the CC followed in coming to its recommendations. In particular, the CAA said that as there was no appeal against the final CAA decision under the Airports Act except judicial review, there could be human rights legislation problems. So the CAA told us it had said publicly that, unless it saw a problem in terms of its Airports Act duties, it would wish to implement the CC recommendations. The CAA added that it might be that new information became available very late in our process or early into the last part of the CAA's process which it would be rational to take into account, but its strong desire would be just to implement the CC's recommendations.

11.12. The CAA said that its recommendations best met its statutory objectives laid out in section 39(2) of the Airports Act and reproduced in paragraph 11.11.

- *Furthering the reasonable interests of users*

11.13. The CAA considered that this objective required it to provide adequate protection to users from monopoly pricing for access to infrastructure and services that were essential for the provision of passenger air travel and freight forwarding services. This was widely accepted as the primary motivation for price cap regulation. Setting prices to reflect the costs of these monopoly services provided for such protection. However, under the traditional single-till approach these costs were reduced for price cap purposes by the projected profits in excess of the regulatory cost of capital made on commercial activities. The result was that revenues from airport charges were lower than the costs of the aeronautical facilities. The CAA's view was that this went beyond the reasonable interests of users. In particular, the CAA did not consider that users' 'reasonable interests' amounted to an automatic claim to locational rents generated from commercial activities.

11.14. This was particularly so at Heathrow and Gatwick, where the consequence of the single till offset was simply a transfer of rents between the airports and airlines, with no current benefits for passengers and freight forwarders and probably net costs longer term as development was compromised. With the removal of the offset through a move to an RRCB, prices would still be well below long-run marginal costs, which would provide for a better benchmark for a 'competitive' price.

11.15. It was also relevant to consider competitive circumstances of the airports. In regulated utilities a key issue had been when price cap regulation could be loosened or dispensed with as competition grew. The CAA considered that this applied for commercial activities across the three airports. This argument was also relevant to Stansted where competitive constraints may be stronger than for Heathrow and Gatwick, and where a price cap set on the RRCB could be held to provide appropriate protection for users.

- *Promoting the efficient, economic and profitable operation of the airports*

11.16. The efficient operation of airports pointed to price caps that provided good incentives to deliver services cost-effectively and to appropriate standards. The CAA considered that this would be best met through a long-term commitment in relation to price caps, with less reliance on BAA's actual out-turn costs. The addition of a service quality factor assisted appropriate focus by airports.

11.17. At congested airports, the economic operation of airports was achieved (and net aggregate benefits to end users were also maximized) where scarce capacity was used by those that valued it most. In principle this objective, in the absence of an effective slot mechanism, would be better met by airport charges that were closer to market-clearing prices (or prices that reflect the opportunity costs of scarce capacity) although the distributional implications were significant and there would be adverse effects on investment incentives. At Heathrow and Gatwick it would point to higher charges than current levels, and also supported a move to peak pricing.

11.18. At Stansted, where there was spare capacity, this objective would be best met in the short term through lower charges that might encourage greater use of the airport. In the longer term, capacity was likely to become increasingly under pressure, particularly in peak periods, pointing to higher charges and peak pricing. However, the RRCB, by taking commercial activities out of the regulatory till, gave Stansted strong incentives to ensure that volumes remained high and continued to grow, since additional volumes would generate (higher) additional commercial revenues and profits.

11.19. The profitable operation of airports would be enhanced through lighter caps on charges and deregulation of non-monopoly activities. Where higher caps still ensured protection against monopoly power, this objective suggested that the CAA should not place greater weight on rents accruing to airlines as opposed to the airports.

- *Encouraging investment to satisfy demand*

11.20. The CAA said that this was a critical issue, especially at Heathrow and Gatwick where there was heavy demand for additional capacity and, given long lead times, government and BAA policy, might be a major development issue for Stansted in due course. This objective was central to the CAA's proposals, which placed heavy emphasis on incentivizing desirable capacity additions. The objective made clear that it was not investment per se that was to be encouraged, but investment offering net benefits to users. Investments that did not generate benefits that were greater than their costs should not be encouraged. This augured against, for example, charges at Heathrow and Gatwick being set to remunerate assets at Stansted, where users at Stansted did not value the facilities at a given time and scale in question to the extent that Stansted was expected to be able to cover its costs through charges at Stansted alone over the life cycle of the investment.

- *Impose minimum restrictions*

11.21. This gave a clear steer on the approach to regulation to be adopted. It pointed to incentives as the central means of achieving the objectives, as opposed to detailed intervention and attempts to impose detailed obligations on the airports.

- *International obligations*

11.22. The CAA had taken account of the UK's international obligations notified to it by the Government in developing its proposals. It believed that its proposals were consistent with these obligations.

- *Trade-offs between objectives*

11.23. The Airports Act did not provide any guidance on how trade-offs, if any, between the objectives should be judged. The CAA believed that trade-offs between the objectives should be judged against the criterion that where there were potential gainers and losers between airport users and airports from different regulatory options, the aim should be to choose the policy that was expected to maximize net gains to users and airports combined taking account of the costs of regulation. There was nothing in the objectives that suggested that the CAA should weigh the interests of different parties differently, or that ascribed to users de facto property rights over certain streams of profits outside regulated charges, such as commercial revenues.

CAA analytical framework

11.24. The CAA said that to meet the above statutory objectives the price cap was its only policy tool. There was, for example, unlike other utilities, no licence, and the public interest finding was the

CC's responsibility. A major development since the last review was the new Competition Act for dealing with abusive behaviour by dominant market players.

11.25. It had therefore adopted an evaluation framework of maximizing net benefits to customers, airlines and airports including minimizing regulatory costs—essentially a cost-benefit framework. The CAA had no environmental objective under the Airports Act. Its focus was on net benefits—a pound was a pound—and it argued that the distribution of this net benefit was of no concern to the regulator, since—as noted in paragraph 11.14—it was only a matter of the distribution of rents between airports and airlines.

11.26. The CAA said that the problems facing the BAA airports varied. At Heathrow and Gatwick, the key issues were excess demand for access to the airports' runways and peak hour terminal capacity, the implied demand for greater capacity and the inability of the airports to deliver capacity to meet demand. As capacity came under growing pressure, there was greater importance for good incentives to provide desired service quality while maintaining safety standards. Against this were important environmental issues concerning airport expansion. These environmental issues were primarily addressed under the town and country planning legislation, not by the CAA under the Airports Act.

11.27. At Heathrow excess demand was reflected primarily in slot values and to a lesser extent in runway queues. A 10-minute delay was programmed into the scheduling at Heathrow, and extra capacity had been obtained by taking more and more delays. However, the excess demand in terms of demand for slots at the airport was even greater than such delays implied, so the infrastructure was under tremendous pressure. In the short term, there was an option for some additional runway capacity which required effort by BAA, namely mixed mode: the runways operated in segregated mode at the moment.

11.28. The CAA believed that there were very large social costs of delays, which it did not think were fully internalized in the way the market was working. Fundamentally, however, the CAA said that the prices charged by the airport at the moment probably had no relationship with either the incremental costs or the incremental values of the airport capacity. The CAA estimated that the advantages of Heathrow had resulted in a premium—ie higher profit per passenger—of about £20 per passenger on short-haul routes and of up to £110 per passenger on long-haul services compared with services from the other London area airports. It also quoted transactions between airlines for slot rights—rights to a slot to arrive or depart at a congested airport at a particular time—implying a valuation of £16 million in one case in 1998 for four pairs of slots, equivalent to an annual valuation of £400,000 per slot; a more recent transaction implied a slightly higher valuation.

11.29. There was some off-peak capacity available at Heathrow, but it was operating in excess of planning standards at the peak periods. T5 was obviously the main issue for this review in terms of adding extra capacity, even though it would not actually be in operation until the next review period.

11.30. Partly because of excess demand, the CAA did not believe airlines had any countervailing power in their dealings with BAA, or that there was significant competition from overseas hubs as, even if any airline were to leave Heathrow, the runway capacity would soon be taken up. Prices, being so far below market-clearing prices or incremental costs, were not at the level where market power could be tested.

11.31. As to service quality, while the monitoring done by BAA did not indicate a problem, problems were evident to passengers: for example, holes in the floor and wires coming down from the ceilings, and a generally poorer experience on the aeronautical side than at other European airports. The problems suggested that the airport terminals were suffering from under-investment and cheap investment (for example, poor wear of carpets). This had become more of an issue as the existing terminals were trying to handle increased passenger numbers, and the pressures would continue over the next five years.

11.32. In the case of Gatwick, runway queues were likely to continue in spite of 11 September. The runway was always going to be at full capacity with ten-minute queuing built in, and slot bidding was well in excess of available slots. There was terminal capacity available at Gatwick off peak, but during the peaks it was under a lot of pressure: service quality as passenger numbers increased would be an issue. BAA in its investment programme was essentially trying to maintain an improved service quality, for example use of airbridges rather than coaching.

11.33. At Stansted there was less congestion but congestion might worsen in the future. Capacity was available at Stansted. The very high growth rate of the LFCs was one of the big changes since the last review, which those carriers expected to continue.

11.34. Stansted did not appear to have similar levels of market power as Heathrow and Gatwick. The cap had only been loosely binding at Stansted over the current quinquennium, as was expected when the cap was set: competition in the short to medium term, from Gatwick and Luton, was a relevant factor.

11.35. It was important to recognize the role played by airlines and other intermediate users of airports. Unlike some other regulated utilities, airlines formed an informed and resourced body of intermediaries that took an active interest in airport strategy and operations. This pointed to a relatively lighter-handed framework that provided for protection against monopoly and provided the clearest possible basis and encouragement for effective consultation and direct contracting between the parties.

11.36. Major capacity enhancements at airports could have very long lead times, and very long pay-back periods. Correspondingly, the regulatory framework should aim to provide for long-run regulatory stability and long-run incentives. Following from its statutory objectives, the price caps should be set to best achieve the following:

(a) protection against monopoly pricing, ensured through linking the caps to the costs of providing monopoly aeronautical infrastructure and services;

(b) incentives to meet demand at desired service quality cost-effectively;

(c) prices that better reflect market conditions at the airports to encourage economic operation of the airports including best use of available capacity;

(d) provide best possible incentives, in the long run, for investment in new capacity where it is demanded, reflecting the incremental costs and incremental valuation of new capacity;

(e) limit the scope of regulation to the provision of monopoly infrastructure and services to airlines and freight forwarders; and

(f) be sustainable over time.

11.37. The CAA's recommendations reflected this framework. All regulatory regimes had short-comings, however. Regulation could never fully overcome the problems of information asymmetry and the impossibility of perfect incentive design to the extent necessary to substitute for an effectively competitive and dynamic market. The best incentives to sharpen operational efficiency, provide desired service quality, and to invest in new capacity where there was demand for it, derived from the threat of competition. The CAA had not considered in depth the question of whether its statutory objectives would be better met through greater competition between the BAA London airports in its review since the issue was recently addressed by the Government and because the Airports Act did not appear to give latitude in this area. Ultimately, however, the central objectives of protection from monopoly abuse, efficient airport operation, high-powered incentives for well-directed investment, and minimizing the regulatory burden may be better achieved if there were greater competition in the South-East, even if runways were currently fully utilized at Heathrow and Gatwick.

11.38. The CAA told us that to best meet its statutory objectives, its proposals were therefore founded on a number of underlying principles, namely that:

(a) regulation should focus on the monopoly services provided by the airport to users;

(b) increased contracting and competition recognizing the strategic and operational interdependency between users and airports assisted by improved information disclosure could allow less intrusive economic regulation;

(c) congestion on Heathrow and Gatwick runways meant that increases in permitted airport charges were likely to result in better use of those airports with consequent benefits for passengers;

(d) users' high valuation of additional capacity, particularly at Heathrow, indicated that incentives to invest in new capacity were central;

(e) major investments had long lead times and long payback periods, both of which could be well beyond the statutory five-yearly reviews emphasizing the importance of long-term regulatory commitment;

(f) a greater focus on service quality was a core part of the regulatory framework at Heathrow and Gatwick; and

(g) Stansted would have more limited market power than Heathrow and Gatwick over the 2003 to 2008 period and would remain dependent on the success of the LFCs, pointing to a continuation of light-handed regulation.

11.39. The CAA told us there were four regulatory options. The first was the current system of regulation, which was a fairly standard RAB, cost-plus model but, in aviation, with the tradition of the single till whereby the expected excess profits from retail were used to reduce the aeronautical costs. A second option was to move away from that and focus on an RRCB, commonly called the dual till. A third option was to adopt incremental cost or incremental value-based pricing, and a fourth, to adopt market-clearing prices, where, particularly in the case of Heathrow, the gap between current charges and economic values looked to be very high. The use of incremental cost base prices (ie to charge all users prices equivalent to incremental costs) or market-clearing prices would result in large shifts of rent to the airports.

The CAA's proposals for all three airports

11.40. The following were the CAA's recommendations for all three airports.

- *That price caps be set in relation to the assets and costs of each airport on a stand-alone basis*

11.41. Separate price caps for each airport, based on the individual cost base for each airport, provided for a level playing field between Stansted and non-BAA airports in the South-East, removed the potential distortion whereby Stansted investments might be undertaken even though Stansted users did not value them sufficiently to pay for the life-cycle costs at that stage, and improved the transparency of regulation for each airport.

- *An RRCB, which should comprise only the costs of monopoly airport services excluding commercial costs and revenues or surface access infrastructure or activities*

11.42. This set regulated charges to reflect the costs of providing the monopoly aeronautical facilities and services (but not the costs of surface access provided to passengers). It provided for protection of users' interests from monopoly pricing while reducing the scope of regulation and the scope for regulatory distortions in other activities. It significantly increased airports' incentives to invest in new capacity. At Heathrow and Gatwick the higher charges gave incentives to better utilize available capacity and better reflect LRICs. They would improve the use of existing capacity. At Stansted it was likely to continue the current situation where the price caps had not been binding in practice.

- *Enhanced information disclosure and consultation between airports and airlines*

11.43. This should facilitate the integration of users into airport strategy and build on the commonality of interest between airports and users, assisting contracting.

- *Facilitating more direct contracting between airports and users;*

11.44. Individual users had different interests that might be better addressed through direct contracting than through the regulatory regime. The intention was that the regulatory regime would continue to provide protection to users, but would allow scope for 'win-win' contracts outside regulation where this was desired. All such contracts, of course, would be subject to competition law and section 41 of the Airports Act.

- *No automatic cost pass-throughs*

11.45. This should enhance the efficient operation of the airport by providing price cap incentives across the board. While there was greater uncertainty about increased security costs post-11 September the CAA considered that, seen in the context of the overall set of regulatory policies, BAA should be well able to manage this issue (unless it was demonstrated that the additional costs were likely to be very large and also very uncertain, where there might be a case for revisiting the question).

- *Retention of the revenue yield approach to setting the cap*

11.46. In the absence of substantive support for its preliminary proposal in November 2001 to move to a tariff basket at Heathrow and Gatwick, the CAA now recommended that the revenue yield approach be retained.

- *Removing revenue from non-passenger flights from the yield calculation and setting a separate condition for these flights*

11.47. The revenue yield approach with passenger numbers as the denominator meant that airports that priced up to the cap derived no additional airport charges revenue from flights that did not carry passengers. This was perverse and the CAA recommended extending the separate treatment of non-passenger flights at Manchester (agreed in March 2001) to the BAA London airports as well.

- *Calculating the revenue yield as if airlines which receive unpublished discounts pay the published tariff*

11.48. The revenue yield approach meant that airports could attract additional traffic through discounts and recoup any shortfall in revenue by raising charges to incumbent airlines. The CAA believed that airports should not be able to do this unless the discounts were published and transparent.

- *'Something to lose'*

11.49. In addition the strategic incentives of the framework—'something to lose'—gave BAA the prospects of higher returns over time than would have been the case if the single till were continued. While the CAA was committed to a stable long-run framework, if the airports were to simply sweat assets, provide poor service quality, and unreasonably fail to meet user demand, BAA would perceive a risk that the CAA would revisit the framework at subsequent reviews. The risk of 'something to lose' should focus BAA on delivering services and facilities to the satisfaction of users.

Additional recommendations for Heathrow

11.50. The CAA made the following additional recommendations for Heathrow.

- *A long-term PPC under which the real price cap for outputs delivered from current capacity and through T5 would be preset in real terms for a 20-year period, with a commitment not to reset the cap at future reviews*

11.51. While anchored in the RRCB cost base, the CAA believed that a long-run PPC would provide a superior basis for price cap setting than continuing a standard RAB framework on a number of counts. It directly addressed the long lead times and long payback periods for major capacity enhancements, and reintroduced the benefits of price cap incentives in relation to them. As an output-based framework it provided a more direct link between what users wanted and the investment necessary to accommodate them. It transferred the risk of new capacity from users to the airport; the CAA believed that it was appropriate for the airport to bear this risk, but had allowed for a higher cost of capital (8.5 per cent real pre-tax) to be applied to the costs of T5 to compensate. It made explicit the high incremental costs of additional capacity and therefore acted as a better signal for the costs of new capacity than under a standard asset-based approach. While providing sharper investment incentives, it provided for a simpler and less intrusive form of regulation than the standard RAB approach. The CAA believed that the commitment was no less credible than a standard RAB approach, and in many ways was more credible. It therefore provided for a stable basis for capacity investment.

- *Average revenue per passenger handled by existing capacity (passengers up to 60 million once T5 is opened) be set on an RRCB*

11.52.   The CAA had accepted the views of BA and BAA that 60 million passengers per annum was the appropriate benchmark. However, the CAA did propose profiling this part of the commitment with higher charges in 2003–08 and lower charges thereafter. The proposal was to set RPI+6 per cent as the cap over 2003–2008 (against actual charges in 2002/3) to signal the credibility of the regulatory commitment to BAA and its investors. This achieved a price profile for 2003 to 2008 that limited the speed of the move to the new regulatory framework, but did not fall below the prices that would have obtained under the single till (but allowing for prefunding of T5 under the single till).

- *Average revenue per passenger from T5, set at the estimated incremental costs of T5 of £18 per passenger. This was to be triggered by the opening of T5, but applied to the number of passengers at Heathrow as a whole above 60 million passengers a year*

11.53.   This provided for strong incentives to deliver T5 in a timely manner, and avoided the potential incentive simply to sweat existing assets.

- *An incentive linked to the opening of aircraft parking stands at the T5 site (expected in 2006/07) that would generate additional revenues of £10 million a year (in real terms) once the stands were operational*

11.54.   This would generate at Heathrow an additional £10 million a year (in real terms) once the T5 aircraft parking stands are opened (expected 2006/07).

- *An incentive to deliver additional ATMs in peak periods*

11.55.   Given the very high user valuation of additional slots at Heathrow, this measure would better align airport and user interests to maximize the efficient utilization of the existing runways.

- *A service quality term as part of the cap (the 'Q' term) including an element related to airport delays*

11.56.   There should be three components: quality dimensions of primary interest to airlines, those that were of primary interests to passengers, and a delay term. The airline component would be asymmetric in the sense that performance below par would result in a reduction in the cap, while outperformance would not be rewarded. The passenger and delay components would be symmetric. The total impact of the term should be limited to 3 per cent of aeronautical revenue a year.

- *A reduction of the starting RAB to reflect T5 prefinancing and prefunding in Q3*

11.57.   The CAA believed that this was consistent with the regulatory 'contract' implicit in the 1996 price cap decision and, as such, should enhance the credibility of the regulatory regime.

Additional recommendations for Gatwick

11.58.   The CAA made the following additional recommendations for Gatwick.

- *As for Heathrow, but with no reliance on incremental cost-based incentives for additional outputs for 2003 to 2008 given that no major capacity enhancements were planned, nor any additional incentive linked to ATMs*

11.59. This reflected the absence of any major capacity enhancements currently proposed for Gatwick (as opposed to service quality enhancements).

- *Profile of PPC allows gradual move to new price levels*

11.60. The limit over 2003 to 2008 should be RPI+5 per cent against actual charges in 2002/03.

Additional recommendations for Stansted

11.61. The following specific recommendations would apply to Stansted.

- *Retention of standard asset-based approach (based on RRCB)*

11.62. It was expected that the resulting price cap would not be tightly binding, that Stansted would choose to price below the cap to meet its commercial objectives, and these would drive its investment incentives. The CAA did not see a PPC as necessary at this stage.

- *No service quality term*

11.63. A service quality term would not have any direct value since the cap would not be binding. The CAA considered that Stansted should work with its users in the context of enhanced information disclosure to ensure that the desired service quality was provided cost-effectively.

- *Profile of introduction of RRCB occurred over ten years*

11.64. The CAA recommended a profile of prices over ten years that resulted in a gradual introduction of the RRCB price cap.

Impact of proposals on price caps

11.65. The CAA said that following 11 September 2001 there remained uncertainty as to the medium-term outlook for aviation and therefore for demand and capex requirements at the BAA airports. To address this the CAA had considered the implications of its policy recommendations for the price caps under three scenarios. The most optimistic of these was the CAA's projection for future demand. BAA had presented two scenarios, a 'high case' and a 'low case'. BAA's 'high case' was less optimistic than the CAA's projection and, given current information, the CAA considered that BAA's low case was particularly pessimistic. The table below shows the price caps implied by the CAA's proposals under the CAA's scenario. To provide a reference point actual average revenue per passenger from regulated charges levied in 2000/01 was £5.23 for Heathrow, £4.06 for Gatwick and £4.36 for Stansted.

TABLE 11.1 **Projected caps on average revenue per passenger under the CAA's recommendations**

£

2000 prices	Average, 2003–2008	Average 2008–2013
Heathrow	6.35	9.95
Gatwick	4.65	5.60
Stansted	5.40	7.40

Source: CAA.

Note: Figures rounded to nearest £0.05. Heathrow figures do not include any premium for delivery of ATMs. Based on CAA scenario projections. Adoption of BAA scenarios would give higher figures. Source: CAA modelling.

11.66.   While the projected price caps remained subject to caveats because the medium-term outlook for air transport in the UK remained uncertain, the basic trends presented were reasonably robust. The largest permitted charge increases would be at Heathrow. The main reason for this was the high cost of T5. Had the single till been continued, the cap at Heathrow would have risen at around RPI+6 per cent a year over 2003 to 2008 (equivalent to a rise of around £3.40 by 2008 if T5 opened as planned); the effect of the CAA's proposals in increasing this (to an increase per passenger of around £4.25 by 2008 if T5 opened as planned) would not be felt until 2008–13, and was linked to new capacity being delivered. The difference between the single till and the CAA's proposal was moderate in comparison to the value of Heathrow capacity and the incremental costs of new capacity.

11.67.   At Gatwick the price cap under the single till would have continued to decline. However, the impact of moving away from the single till at Gatwick was greater than for Heathrow, so the effect of the CAA recommendations was to increase the price caps there compared to the situation if the single till continued. Nonetheless, at Gatwick the price cap would increase by much less than Heathrow, reaching a plateau £1.60 per passenger higher than 2002/03 levels, and then only in 2010/11. At Stansted the single till would result in charges that were slightly higher than current levels. The CAA did not expect Stansted to price up to the cap so actual charges were likely to be lower than those presented in the table.

11.68.   The CAA considered that these recommendations would best meet its statutory objectives. They ensured that users' reasonable interests were met through capping charges at a level consistent with the costs of providing the monopoly aeronautical services. They created significantly stronger incentives for investment in aeronautical capacity where it was demanded. They would improve the efficient operation of Heathrow and Gatwick airports by allowing prices that better reflected market demand given an imperfect slot market. They continued to provide for a light-handed regime at Stansted that reflected its market position and, by the move to stand-alone regulation, would reduce the distortions created by the regulatory regime to date. By removing regulation from non-monopoly commercial activities this lightened the regulatory burden and allowed these activities to develop normally.

11.69.   The CAA recognized that its proposals would result in a transfer of rents from airlines to the airports, and expected the airports to respond with credible plans to deliver the desired improved service quality and investment that their customers wanted. If the airports failed to do so they would run the risk that the CAA would reconsider the appropriate regulatory framework at the next review.

Issues arising

11.70.   This section expands on the issues raised above. The CAA said that there was considerable common ground on the proposals such as enhanced information disclosure and service quality terms. But some proposals had raised particular controversy.

Airport charges and air fares

11.71.   The CAA's recommendations pointed to higher caps on airport charges than would have occurred if the single till were continued. Several airlines had argued that this would be passed on to passengers in the form of higher air fares. The debate on this point differed according to whether the airport was congested or not.

11.72. As noted above, at Heathrow and Gatwick there was virtually no spare runway capacity and considerable excess demand. At Heathrow there were also severe capacity constraints in relation to terminals across wide periods of most days (until T5 opened). It was widely acknowledged that there was large unmet demand for access to both airports, but especially at Heathrow. This was the source of the high value of access slots. It followed that airport charges were not the consideration in determining air fares. If airport charges rose, but remained below levels at which capacity and demand for access were in balance, air fares would continue to be determined by airline capacity permitted by (constrained) capacity, not by airport charges. The effect was instead to reduce the implicit value of slots at the airport.

11.73. This was standard economic analysis. Airlines' rebuttal tended to run along the lines that the rents implied by the CAA's analysis did not exist, as evidenced by the low operating margins of airlines, or did not accrue to airlines. Given these low operating margins any increase in costs must result either in higher charges or exit from the market. The CAA had not undertaken a detailed review of airline profitability, but made the following observations. First, if airlines' profitability was genuinely so marginal and below their cost of capital it would expect aggregate contraction in output. This was not consistent with the observation of continued, and large, excess demand at current levels of airport charges for both Heathrow and Gatwick capacity. There had been reports of BA and Virgin each seeking to acquire additional slots. Second, airline operating margins could fluctuate significantly over time and the relevant issue was airline decisions on the margin in a forward-looking framework. The current period of difficulty for the industry was not a good benchmark for operating margins in the longer term. Third, operating margins were not the only possible evidence of rents. High airline cost structures were an alternative and plausible source.

11.74. Finally, the CAA reiterated that regulated airport charges made up a small percentage of airline costs, and the difference in airport charges resulting from the CAA's revised framework were smaller still. An increase in airport charges of less than £2 per passenger (compared to continuing with the single till) would have minimal impact on fares that amounted to hundreds of pounds in many cases. While there may be some market segments with lower (implicit) fares than this (charter traffic at Gatwick for example), higher airport charges were more likely to lead to a shift in the use of scarce capacity if other types of service were more profitable, rather than higher fares.

11.75. Subsequently, the CAA acknowledged that fares were likely to go up on routes where frequency was reduced: but in that case the slots would be used more efficiently on another service, on which the fares would reduce. On balance there could be a net improvement, as a more efficient use of a slot replaced a less efficient one. The CAA believed that on average fares would not be changed, but, as they said, rents redistributed. A rise in charges might affect costs, but those costs did not determine prices, which were determined by the degree of capacity. Hence, the primary driver on, for example, BA fares at present was not changes in variable cost but competition from LFCs. Indeed, increased charges might have an effect on landing or parking charges, rather than passenger charges, which would not represent a change in marginal costs: restructuring following the dual till was likely to be on the former rather than the latter, to give incentives to maintain passenger numbers.

11.76. At Stansted the CAA accepted that higher airport charges were more likely to result in higher air fares. Stansted was less congested, and therefore there was less evidence that slots there had positive values (although it was possible that they may have in peak periods). Moreover, Stansted's low-fare/low-frill user base meant that airport charges made up a rather larger fraction of air fares. However, the CAA considered that the impact of a higher price cap would be moderated by the following. First, the cap at Stansted had not been binding to date. The CAA did not expect Stansted to price up to the recommended cap. Even under the single till the 2003–08 cap would be higher than current charges. Second, precisely because demand was more elastic and dependent on LFCs, themselves operating in a price elastic market, Stansted had every incentive to ensure that its pricing actions did not reduce demand growth. In part this would be reflected by not pricing up to the cap. It may also result in peak pricing. Finally, the move to the RRCB would increase the marginal profitability of generating higher volumes because higher commercial profits would no longer be 'taxed' away at a rate of 100 per cent as they would under the single till. This would enhance the incentive to set prices to maintain volume growth.

11.77. As to whether the effect at Gatwick or Stansted could primarily be on charter or LFCs, the CAA believed that if BA, for example, won the auction for spare capacity at Gatwick, it must be offering a higher net added-value product. This was not a matter of technical efficiency: the market mechanism was the best way of achieving best use. If the charter market was so competitive, this was in part because less value was placed on using Gatwick and passengers would be more prepared to use other airports.

11.78. If, on the other hand, there was particular concern about the effect on regional services, explicit subsidies would be the more transparent and accountable way of addressing the problem: but reduction in such services had happened anyway, and the real problem would be capacity constraints.

11.79. Fundamentally, airport charges were currently out of line with efficient marginal costs, including opportunity costs. The CAA's proposals, even in Q4, would move prices in the right direction (there was quite a substantial price increase in Q4 anyway, driven mainly by T5).

11.80. The incremental costs of substantial capacity additions at Heathrow and Gatwick were also well above current charges, which was very unusual in utility regulation. The single till was worsening that difference between price and incremental cost, contrary to the requirements of economic pricing.

Rent transfers

11.81. Airlines had argued an equity case that since commercial profits only existed because of airline passengers, they were entitled to a share of the locational commercial rents. This was an argument over rent distribution. The CAA did not accept that its statutory duties conferred upon airlines these rights, particularly when it also compromised achievement of these duties. In a wider context it was difficult to justify using regulation to give higher primacy to rents accruing to one set of corporate entities (the airlines) over another (the airports). Thus while the CAA understood that rent transfers between consumers and monopoly suppliers might be of legitimate concern for other regulators, it did not apply to the distribution of rents between airports and airlines. Moreover, the CAA's proposals only affected the locational rents from commercial activities. Airlines at Heathrow and Gatwick would continue to enjoy the bulk of the scarcity rents deriving from limited aviation capacity, via slot values.

Single till versus RRCB

11.82. The CAA said that this was the most controversial of its recommendations. The over-arching position, however, was that all users objected to any move away from the single till, while the airports supported it. If the move only had the effect of shifting rents, this split of views would be easy to comprehend. However, the CAA's view took investment incentives as central and considered that the RRCB gave significantly higher-powered incentives to develop new capacity. Airlines professed this to be in their interests, so the complete absence of support required further exploration.

- *Effect on investment*

11.83. In terms of investment, particularly at Heathrow and Gatwick where there were very large excess demands currently and therefore a very high valuation of additional capacity, under the single till the airport would expect, subject to a regulatory risk, to get 7/7.5 per cent on capacity additions, but those who were benefiting from them were valuing them at a much higher level. There was a significant mismatch between the airports' incentives and the travellers who would get huge value out of those additions if they were to come. There was no question that moving away from the single till would substantially increase the marginal incentives to get new capacity. The airport would not only earn its 7.5 per cent on aeronautical assets but the further commercial benefits of increasing its volumes: a very marked increase in incentives to increase capacity. Hence, the dual till both improved incentives to commercial investment by reducing the current distortion referred to above, and enhanced the approach to aeronautical investment, which would earn not only the cost of capital but also the benefits of additional commercial spend.

11.84. The CAA believed that there was a large economic cost of unsatisfied demand, and, in answer to our questions, was not sure that the failure to meet demand could be regarded merely as an external exogenous constraint of the planning system: it could think of few other utilities with so much unmet demand, and where users were willing to pay for additional capacity. There was no evidence that BAA was not responding optimally to its incentives, but the incentives were a price cap regulation based on costs, with very strong local dominance or regional dominance, and BAA would respond to more high-powered incentives. It was impossible to say whether this would have made a difference to introducing capacity more quickly: but in the CAA's view, had the dual till been in operation, BAA would have had the incentive to handle the T5 inquiry differently. Under the current regulatory system, there were advantages to BAA as a result of the delay to the T5 inquiry, and it would certainly have pushed for a new runway or mixed mode more quickly if faced with higher-powered incentives. But, the CAA said, it was not surprising that it was difficult to find evidence that higher airport charges would increase investment—if the policies and incentives were changed, the plans would emerge because it would be more profitable for BAA to search for them and put the effort in.

11.85. Stylized examples showed the single till led to sub-optimal incentives compared to the dual till on investment, but other benefits from the dual till were to increase the overall returns on investment, and to increase charges closer to incremental costs in situations where they were currently, on a single-till basis, below incremental cost.

11.86. As to concerns that the dual till could result in promotion of commercial activities to passengers at the expense of aeronautical facilities, the CAA did not believe the dual till would make much difference in this respect. Any problems could be addressed through service quality measures, or a code of conduct proposed by BAA.

11.87. The main argument put forward by airlines was that the single till provided adequate incentives to invest, and that the investment problem derived from the planning system and an absence of penalties on the airport for failure to invest. The CAA agreed that the single till provided incentives to generate asset additions, but considered that these incentives were weak and not well focused on optimal aeronautical capacity. The RRCB gave stronger incentives to invest, and the CAA's proposed PPC should serve to strengthen the direction of this investment. Of course, this did not guarantee new capacity, but it did provide a framework that was more likely to see it emerge. Moreover, the CAA found it hard to square the argument that the single till provided adequate investment incentives but at the same time penalties for failure to deliver were required.

11.88. As to whether it would not be preferable, as some airlines argued, to impose obligations on BAA to invest, the CAA could see no instrument to do so under the Airports Act. There would, for example, be huge problems in requiring any agreement on investment programmes, and for which permission might not subsequently be granted. The CAA believed 'ownership' of the business plan must stay with the airport—the risk of diffused responsibility must be avoided, but enhanced information disclosure was an important part of the regulatory solution including, in the longer-term, business planning framework, targets, performance, and plans to bridge the gap between the two (discussed further below).

11.89. The CAA therefore saw the trade-off at Heathrow and Gatwick between a modest shift in rents from airlines to the airports as being the price for a greater likelihood of new capacity as well as better utilization of current capacity. Since the CAA did not weight the rents of airlines higher than those of airports, and because there were other well-founded objections to the single till that carried their own merit in relation to the CAA's statutory objectives, the higher likelihood of new capacity and the high value that this would bring to passengers were the strongly preferred option. Airlines, however, would view the trade-off differently. Since they obviously did place considerable weight on the lower charges, currently particularly understandable, they were less likely to view the stronger investment incentives as an acceptable return for the rent transfer.

- *Do the airports have monopoly power in commercial activities?*

11.90. The CAA said that the single till took the projected net profits of commercial activities, particularly retailing, surface access etc, and used those to reduce the airport charges set to the airlines. This did not in any way prevent the airports from exploiting commercial activities; it was not providing any direct protection to users, but simply taking those profits away from the airports and using them to reduce charges to airlines.

11.91. The widely accepted objective of economic regulation was usually to provide protection against exploitation of monopoly power and to prevent monopoly pricing with consequent reductions in output and losses for consumers. Hence, the general trend in UK utility regulation had been to focus direct price cap regulation on those areas of utility activities which were genuinely monopolistic. The single till, on the other hand, went well beyond this, taking a very wide range of other activities which were not obviously monopolistic and using those to reduce charges to airlines well below the cost of providing those services.

11.92.   Commercial activities were major areas of economic activity in their own right, producing a situation where, even after the losses due to the withdrawal of some of the duty-free tax advantages that the airports have had, commercial revenues were still well above half of BAA's total revenues from its regulated airports: a very major part of their activity. Prior to the changes to duty-free revenues, commercial revenue was often even as high as 70 per cent of total revenue.

11.93.   As well as having an effect on the actual level of the airport charges, the single till extended the domain or the effect of the regulatory regime well beyond the monopoly services. Rather than considering whether or not to invest in a particular commercial project, an airport would expect to get its appropriate cost of capital on those assets, irrespective of the marginal value actually added by those activities. Regulation had distortions, and the single till extended those distortions across a very wide range of activities.

11.94.   A common objection to the move away from the single till was that the airports did not just earn 'locational' rents from their commercial activities, but that they had market power in relation to those activities. Thus the single till was a means of ensuring that they did not profit from that market power. The CAA did not accept this argument for two reasons.

11.95.   First, the CAA had seen no evidence that the airports had widespread market power in retailing activities beyond that associated with other desirable retail locations. The main benefit was simply that these were locations with larger numbers of consumers that were willing to spend and there were tax concessions.

11.96.   In retailing, BAA could be compared to supermarkets or Oxford Street or other well-located shopping centres, which were often protected by stringent planning restrictions. Yet, despite various inquiries into them, nobody was yet proposing price caps for supermarkets. In relation to meals or cups of coffee in the terminals, although customers in a terminal might be thought captive, this was little different from sellers of hamburgers under licence at a football match. There was no evidence that the airports had deliberately curtailed the extent of retail space and outlets, and anecdotal evidence from the airports and airlines was that the contrary was true. Thus the CAA did not believe that there was any more case for direct regulation of airport pricing or profits on commercial activities than existed for regulating profits at other desirable retail locations.

11.97.   Second, even if there were activities that did enjoy genuine market power, the single till was a very poor means of addressing this. The single till operated in effect as imposing a 100 per cent tax on projected commercial profits in excess of the regulated cost of capital, using the proceeds to reduce regulated airport charges. At Heathrow and Gatwick this would not have the effect of reducing air fares. It did not in any way give direct redress to any customer who might be overcharged, but simply meant that airlines were paying a little bit less for their rights to access the airport: given the excess demand, that was simply going to affect the implicit slot values of access to that airport, it was not going to result in lower ticket prices. At Stansted the effect was likely to be very indirect and would be non-existent if the single-till cap continued to be non-binding. Therefore consumers that lost out due to any 'monopoly' pricing of meals in the terminals, for example, did not see any benefits in terms of lower airfares; instead the benefits accrued primarily to the airlines. If there were serious monopoly problems in relation to a commercial activity this should be dealt with directly on a case by case basis, either through a public interest finding by the CC under the Airports Act, or through the CA98, or by addressing the remaining tax advantages that airports had. For example, the recent decision on appeal on *Napp Pharmaceuticals* appeared to have established some form of precedent that the CA98 could be used in practice against excessive pricing.

11.98.   The single till was also influencing the longer-term dynamics of retail developments at the airports. In terms of medium to long-term developments, the airports would receive a return of 7.5 per cent cost of capital irrespective of its commercial plans; in the short term airports would have the incentive to fill up the terminals as much as they could with retail space, as long as this was adding value, because that was the only way airports could outperform the immediate price cap. The longer-term effect could be significant: extending the regulatory system to this was both distorting and possibly dampening the incentives to maximize profit from these commercial activities, producing very strange incentives. It was quite possible that, over time, if a company was working in a system which was not single-till based and started to look at commercial developments on a commercial basis, it would start to make more profits over time out of them than otherwise. But this added to one of the useful incentives effects of moving away from the single till, which was that the airport would regard its profits in the commercial activities as largely determined both by its own actions and by the number of passengers coming through, giving a stronger incentive to increase the number of passengers. Hence, the CAA said, although in the short term a single till might have the effect of slightly increasing airport charges, in the long term some of those dynamic incentives would have a dampening effect: the last thing the airport would want would be a decrease of traffic through the terminals.

11.99. The effect of the dual till on commercial investment could go either way, given that the basis on which these facilities were currently established had been distorted by the regulatory regime. BAA could invest in less commercial facilities if the returns were less than the cost of capital or even turn them into seating areas. However, the areas where the two activities could be substituted were probably not that great. Much of the commercial investment at the moment was short term and insubstantial, reflecting the incentives under the single till and the taxing of commercial profits to cover the effective losses of aeronautical activities. If a dual till were introduced, the nature of that investment would change, with benefit to customers.

11.100. As to whether there could be more regulatory involvement under a dual till, the potential costs of investigation by, for example, the OFT, were basically internalized by BAA: it would have good incentives to be responsible and commercial.

- *Effect on resource allocation*

11.101. Given excess demand, both short term and long term, the single till also had the effect of reducing airport charges below the levels of alternative regimes and of the dual till. The CAA said that this had completely the opposite effect that any intuitive economic understanding of pricing would expect. If charges increased, this would at most simply affect implicit slot values; but at best would improve use of the capacity because some airlines which were currently fairly marginal operators, but could not easily sell their slots in the open market, may leave the airports or curtail their operations, and another airline would pick them up and make better use of them. It was difficult to find detailed evidence of price responsiveness of runway and terminal use; price elasticity was not very high at Heathrow—but was not zero and there clearly were some marginal airlines, which currently could not put slots up for sale because the slot allocation mechanism did not allow it—although it was very difficult to decide who would respond to what was still a fairly moderate price increase or what the impact would be, which was impossible to predict.

11.102. The slot mechanism at Heathrow was not totally ineffective, and implicitly the airlines knew there was a value they had to pay for operating at Heathrow, and to a lesser degree Gatwick. Airlines perceived that if they wished to get extra capacity, or keep capacity at Heathrow, there was a big opportunity cost of doing so. Hence, airlines were probably already internalizing the opportunity costs and there was already a marked changing pattern of usage at Heathrow, many destinations no longer being served that used to be. But, the CAA said, even BA acknowledged in its submission that it was likely that there was not optimal allocation of runway capacity at present. The CAA was pessimistic about the likelihood of the EC bringing in improvements to the slot allocation process over the next five years or so.

11.103. As to whether the CAA had powers under the Airports Act to promote efficient use of capacity, the CAA said that it did not rely on its objective to promote the efficient operation of the airports in this respect (although it did not believe that precluded its approach), but on the power to further the reasonable interests of users. Users, including customers, in aggregate were better off if slots were put to higher value use.

- *Effect on profitability*

11.104. As to whether the dual till involved a rewriting of the regulatory framework, albeit to the advantage of the regulated utility, the CAA put a lot of weight on regulatory sustainability and credibility. However, it had to judge that against its duties under the Airports Act and the problems it saw over the medium and longer term: compared with other regulated utilities, the issues in terms of excess demand were very stark, capacity being under a lot of pressure and service quality imposing social costs.

11.105. The package the CAA had designed almost minimized any potential windfall gain through the profiling it had adopted. (Indeed, the PPC increased the risk to BAA, for which the CAA had increased the cost of capital.) Other instruments were available to address any issue of windfall returns: this was more of a Treasury matter (whom the CAA said it had consulted) if there was an equity concern, although it was not possible to design a perfect windfall tax without adversely affecting incentives. But for Heathrow, the CAA was essentially continuing with the single-till numbers for Q4; at Stansted the proposals would not be binding; and for Gatwick, there would only be an increase in charges of £1 by the end of Q4, applied to some 35 million passengers, but then subject to corporation tax: the effects of the CAA's proposed new dual-till regulatory regime were therefore limited in Q4.

11.106. The CAA had not undertaken a full assessment of the value transfer between airlines and airports that could result from applying the dual till. The impact of the dual till would result in an increase in airport charges over time of between £1 to £2 per passenger compared with the single till, a small change in relation to air fares, and representing a moderate value transfer compared with the value of the aviation services being provided from the airports. Moreover, under the CAA's proposals the gains would mainly arise from 2008 onwards, not in the next control period. In the very long run this could have significant value for BAA although the scale of these would be subject to considerable uncertainty. A rough modelling calculation indicated that if the impact of the CAA's proposals were projected into perpetuity the present value of the higher revenues could be around £3.2 billion.[1] This was likely to be small in relation to the value of aviation services being provided from the airports over the same period. The scale of the price changes and the value transfer implicit in them would not affect air fares to passengers at Heathrow and Gatwick, and was likely to have only a moderate impact at Stansted.

11.107. At one stage, the CAA had suggested that the possibility of applying the dual till in such a way that any such extra accrued to BAA would be used for investment. This would have taken away the NPV of enhanced commercial revenues from the RAB, but was not consistent with regarding these existing assets as massively undervalued in economic terms. That would also apply to reducing the RRCB to offset windfall gains: hence it would be better to approach any such windfall gains as an issue of taxation (analogous to the APD).

- *International agreements and practice*

11.108. The CAA said that there were now a large number of explicit exceptions to the single-till policy—for example, Sydney, Frankfurt, Copenhagen and some US airports—although practice at individual airports was not always easy to establish. The CAA accepted the only singular and direct comparison, with a coherent and established regulatory regime where the dual till specifically applied, was in Australia, albeit it had not been operating very long. Ownership and property rights arrangements at some of the US airports were not comparable with the situation at the BAA airports. Regulatory regimes were different on the Continent. Hence, international experience could not prove the dual till produced the gains the CAA believed it would: but the CAA was not using the international experience as justification—its justification was limiting the regulatory domain and the consequential distortion. But the CAA said that international obligations did not constrain the UK from moving to the dual till.

RRCB till definition

11.109. The CAA believed that it was quite feasible to envisage separate aeronautical and commercial activities with separate outputs in separate markets. It fully accepted that commercial activities were at an airport only because passengers were there and there was a high level of dependency. But this was nowhere near enough to justify the current extension of the regulatory domain to non-monopoly activities, and implicitly to regulate in a distorting way the commercial activity. Arguments, for example, that airlines, by carrying passengers to the airport, should share in the commercial revenues generated, were only an issue of equity, the airlines currently receiving the bulk of scarcity rents, and continuing to do so under the dual till: the single till was causing serious problems against the overall development of the market in the longer term and was not a good way of setting maximum airport prices.

---

[1] We noted that the CAA model showed an upper estimate of £3.7 billion if dual till charges at Stansted were fully recovered.

11.110. Activities had to be both essential and monopolizable to be appropriate for regulation under the Airports Act. Commercial activities were separately priced and clearly substitutable.

11.111. The CAA said that several airlines had argued that the compliance costs of moving to a dual till were quite high. In response to this, the CAA said that there certainly were complexities in identifying costs, revenues, assets and capex that should be attributable to the monopoly services and not to the commercial activities. The CAA had spent a lot of time looking at this and its view was that these costs were largely one-off. In the case of Heathrow and Gatwick, it was suggesting a PPC of a dual till with no need to keep the split under review in the future: the costs of splitting the assets would be one-off. But even at Stansted the CAA thought the costs would be mainly one-off and it would not be too difficult, should a dual till actually be implemented there, to provide for a framework of regulatory accounts that would provide for a split of assets leading up to the next review.

- *Surface access*

11.112. Passengers had a choice of how to travel to an airport and the user-pays principle applied. They could use, for example, taxis, coaches, or rail. So the only monopoly service was the 'front door' to the airport—which was not currently priced at all. In the CAA's view, the only issue was the ability for one such mode, the Heathrow Express (wholly owned by BAA), to cover its costs, but the CAA saw no reason why the airlines should pay for the Heathrow Express. Environmental externalities should not be a problem for the airlines: and the effects of Heathrow Express on road congestion were extremely low. In the CAA's view, road pricing seemed a sensible response to the problems of congestion, but would need a separate regulatory regime to deal with possible monopoly abuse. Surface access could, though, be regarded as necessary for aeronautical activities, if a condition of planning consent, hence its inclusion in the aeronautical till in such a case.

11.113. The CAA's proposal to exclude surface access from the aeronautical till was strongly contested by the airports and largely supported by airlines. The DfT's view was that the proposal might undermine the use of airport charge revenue to support unprofitable surface access investments. The CAA's general position was that there was nothing in the CAA's statutory objectives to suggest that the cap on regulated charges should be set to encourage investment in unprofitable surface access infrastructure. If the expected demand for the infrastructure was insufficient to cover its costs over its project life then neither aviation users' interests or the need to encourage demanded investment pointed to its completion. If there were wider policy imperatives linked to the externalities created by airport access these should be dealt with transparently and directly. Relatedly, the CAA supported airports having the ability to impose road pricing for airport access within an appropriate regulatory framework.

11.114. However, where the development of some form of surface access was made a condition of expanding aeronautical capacity, there was a stronger case for including it in airport charges caps since it could be considered a direct cost of the capacity expansion. The CAA had included the Piccadilly Line and Heathrow Express extensions to T5 in the aeronautical till at Heathrow partly for this reason. Future cases would be also considered against the Airports Act duties via the CAA framework outlined above.

Price path commitment

11.115. The CAA said that the PPC had been less controversial than the dual till as far as airlines were concerned (except that they did not like it being based on an RRCB as opposed to a single till). However, it was probably the more radical of the proposals the CAA was putting forward, from a regulatory perspective.

11.116. The PPC identified three different categories of outputs at Heathrow: namely *(a)* those deliverable by existing capacity, *(b)* those deliverable by the major addition of T5, and *(c)* the delivery of stands prior to the completion of T5.

11.117. The PPC set a revenue per passenger that would be deliverable by each of those output categories. The existing outputs, defined as passengers up to 60 million a year, were what the CAA and the T5 planning inspector believed to be the capacity of the current terminal infrastructure without running down service quality. The CAA calculated capacity at 70 mppa which was the actual level of throughput expected when T5 opened, but—as noted above—the CAA had reduced this figure after both BAA and BA argued that the current capacity should be 60 million.

11.118. The CAA envisaged the PPC as follows. Passengers up to 60 million a year once T5 had opened (and prior to that all passengers) would for 20 years earn a prefixed revenue. This was currently about £5.37, but would rise up to about £7 towards the end of the quinquennium and then start to decline slightly. The cap for additional output was based on estimates by the CAA of the incremental costs of T5. This would apply to all passengers above 60 million once T5 was operational. The upper limit to that would be 90 million, which was, in the CAA's view, the upper level of the whole airport with T5 fully completed without serious deterioration in service quality. Hence, once T5 was opened, these passengers would generate their own average revenue of £18 a passenger which would be the same in every year for the next 20 years. When T5 opened, there would therefore be a fairly large jump in prices. The additional stands should begin to earn a revenue allowance of £10 million once completed, which was projected for 2006/07. Again, that was in response to the views of BAA and BA that there should be some milestones.

11.119. The PPC therefore fixed all these components for 20 years and implicitly beyond; the CAA had only set it up to 20 years because that was as far as it decided to project it. The CAA proposed no change at future reviews.

11.120. The recommendation of the PPC, as opposed to continuing with a RRCB-based RAB, was a balanced judgment, and there were arguments in favour of each. The RRCB-based RAB had the advantage of offering high-powered incentives for the airport to invest in aeronautical assets but gave limited direction for the focus of this investment. It also raised the traditional problem of prefunding expected capex (if such assets were prefunded, the marginal incentive actually to undertake the investment was reduced) and more generally did not directly address the mismatch between five-year price caps and investment projects with very long lead and construction times. It could also claw back efficiency gains, at five-yearly intervals, and give these to users.

11.121. The PPC, linked directly to output delivery, provided high-powered incentives to invest to deliver higher volumes, and in doing so explicitly signalled the high incremental costs of additional capacity to users. It bridged the gap between price caps which were set for five years and investment in very long lead-time projects such as T5. Under a single-till RAB system, T5 basically became a cost pass-through because, by the time it was built, the regulator knew what the costs actually were and these would be included in charges. The PPC, therefore, brought proper price cap incentives back into play for long-term investments, adding very high-powered incentives to the airport operator to be efficient as regards costs and to deliver capex projects efficiently. There were no benefits to gold plating or to deferring opex gains; this fitted in very well with one of the CAA's statutory objectives, and the general objective of regulation.

11.122. The link to outputs transferred the risks of capacity additions from users to the airports who, since they were accountable for the investment undertaken, should be exposed to this risk. It was not unreasonable BAA should be exposed to such risks: when deciding to build such projects, it should take into account the likelihood that actual usage would be less than predicted (although the CAA did not think this a big issue with T5). It would, also, however, maximize the incentive on BAA to increase volumes. The PPC put the risk in the best possible place, gave BAA the incentive to manage the risk, or share it with airlines or property companies. However, the CAA accepted that outputs could never be perfectly specified, particularly in relation to service quality. Since efficiency gains were not clawed back it also gave higher-powered incentives in this area. The fact that the gains were not passed back to users was unlikely to cause losses at Heathrow since marginal values to users exceeded the PPC cap. A standard criticism was the risks of adverse cost shocks compromising either regulatory policy or continued output delivery. Because in this case charges were well below marginal values and a more flexible price cap was proposed this risk was reduced. More generally the PPC was an attempt to bridge the divide between five-year price caps, and capacity enhancements with very long lead times and long pay-back periods. Ultimately, it also produced a simpler regulatory framework and a solid base for future investment incentives.

11.123. The PPC also had excellent properties in terms of regulatory commitment; for the first time, a regulator was stating over a very long period of time precisely what would occur at future reviews. Normally, regulatory commitment amounted to some form of either explicit or implicit agreement on how RABs would be rolled forward. Both approaches gave huge amounts of discretion ultimately to judgement on various factors but, with the risk under the RAB of a cost plus approach in the next regulatory review, much reducing incentives.

11.124. A further benefit of this framework was that it was wholly flexible to changes in government policy. If the Government were to agree that a new runway at Heathrow were acceptable, and BAA wished to proceed, a new set of outputs with a new revenue attached to them could simply be added on to the existing structure. Because the PPC was a very flexible framework, the CAA was proposing to introduce it at Gatwick where the situation was much simpler, namely only one set of outputs, of current capacity, but it would think about adding to this if the Government were to think about new runways as a possibility.

11.125. The drawback of the PPC was that future regulators might not agree to it and the framework might not survive. The CAA believed that, with endorsement from the CC and clear and transparent statements by the CAA in making the decision for the next five years, the PPC really would have a powerful commitment value and be likely to last. Any system was subject to regulatory risk, but the CAA was proposing that the standard cost-based approach would be replaced with an approach whereby, if the airport performed as it should, it would keep this framework: in combination, a very good incentive package.

11.126. Should BAA do better than expected, there would be no obvious gain from changing the cap: the dual till would simply result in a distribution of rent. Should the costs of T5 prove higher than expected, this would not be evident until they were largely sunk and remaining marginal costs would be low. The CAA's proposed service quality term (the Q factor) would safeguard the quality of the investment. Subsequent major increments in investment would be subject to a further incremental cost approach, maintaining incentives to invest.

11.127. As to whether the PPC was credible, therefore, the regulatory commitment could not be absolute, but formed part of a wider set of expectations, and would also be cushioned by the dual till. However, the Government's White Paper on the future of aviation had raised the possibility of a longer, say ten-year, regulatory period.

11.128. As to consistency of that approach with Bermuda 2 (see Chapter 3), the approach was cost-related in a forward-looking framework, just as with a five-year cap, but for longer. The CAA did not think there would be a particularly good case under Bermuda 2 for serious challenge: Bermuda 2 could itself soon be amended.

11.129. The CAA therefore believed that the PPC would provide a sounder base for the airports to deliver desired capacity enhancements, stronger efficiency incentives, and a simpler approach to regulation more generally. As such it was on balance more likely to meet the CAA's statutory objectives.

Assets in the course of construction

11.130. Under an RAB approach, the CAA believed that there would be a problem in not allowing for AICC, since prices would fall over Q4, and rise considerably in Q5. The PPC was the best solution to this. Under the CAA proposals, the price profile for Q4 was essentially based on the price that would have resulted under the single till, if T5 had been funded by AICC. Moreover, the £18 figure on opening of T5 included allowance for AICC within the overall discounted cash-flow calculation.

Separate regulation for the BAA London airports

11.131. BAA and three airlines based at Stansted had argued in favour of continuing the system approach, which in practical terms meant the assets invested at Stansted generated the allowed cost of capital via higher charges at Heathrow and Gatwick. Stansted airlines also appeared to be arguing for a system price cap whereby BAA might set lower charges at Stansted (which had spare capacity) and higher charges at Heathrow (which did not).

11.132. The CAA continued to recommend a move to stand-alone regulation on the grounds that it eliminated a regulatory distortion favouring Stansted against non-BAA airports in the South-East and because it provided a more transparent basis for regulation and for consultation between the different airports and their different respective user mixes. The CAA acknowledged that there was interdependence of demand between the three airports in the sense that demand at Gatwick and Stansted is probably higher because of constraints at Heathrow, but took the view that there were also distinct local markets.

The original concern about funding Stansted—which had been brought on stream too early—on a stand-alone basis, had changed now that Stansted was generating positive free cash flow due to the very rapid growth of the LFCs.

11.133. In relation to investment, the CAA considered that the system approach created a distortion in that BAA might be willing to fund new investment at Stansted even though the costs might be higher than the benefits to users of Stansted (including any who would prefer to be at Heathrow or Gatwick) over the life of the project, given the project in question proposed timing and scale, since this would count as an asset addition and be recovered through higher charges at Heathrow and Gatwick, to earn the allowed cost of capital. The result was investments that did not generate net value given their timing and scale being undertaken as a result of regulatory distortion.

11.134. Regulation should not mean that investment at Stansted should earn the required rate of return regardless of the business case for it. Investment in a new runway would have much greater value at Heathrow than at Stansted, and any new runway at Stansted should be viable on its own merits and might be relatively late, although this is a judgement for BAA: in the CAA's view, using Heathrow rents to subsidize the earlier development of another runway should be done transparently using the tax system, rather than by regulation. If a new runway at Stansted was not viable, that was because users did not value it highly.

11.135. The CAA also expected that if Stansted and Gatwick were operating independently of Heathrow under a different regulatory regime, there would be an incentive on separately-owned airports to be the first to propose to construct a new runway—an investment race: a dramatic change from the present position where BAA is standing back, leaving the running to the Government.

11.136. The CAA accepted that a system price cap that allowed BAA to set lower charges at Stansted and higher charges at Heathrow and Gatwick had attractions from the perspective of best use of capacity. It acknowledged that under separate caps for each airport, charges at Stansted could increase closer to market-clearing levels—while remaining far below them at Heathrow and Gatwick—and that this would be a distortion. However, the same argument could be made for Luton, London City airport, and any other UK airport that had unused capacity. The only real solution would be market-clearing prices at Heathrow, which would give rise to excessive rents and poor investment incentives. But in practice, Stansted's charges would be well below the cap since it was not in a position to charge at the level of the cap without losing business, and lower prices at Stansted would have little impact at Heathrow. Moreover, the CAA noted that BAA's position appeared to be not that Stansted's charges should be forced downwards, but that caps, which BAA did not price up to, should continue with the effect that the actual airport charges would continue to be based on what the market will bear. The CAA's proposals would allow BAA this greater flexibility.

Regulatory consistency and recovery of T5 prefunding

11.137. BAA argued that a number of the CAA's proposals were inconsistent with past regulatory practice in respect of airports, and that they therefore raised the spectre of inconsistency in the future that served to undermine the credibility of any PPC. Areas in question included inter alia the move away from the airport system, various changes to modelling practice, the exclusion of the Heathrow Express from the aeronautical till, the end to the security cost S factor, and the decision to claw back 50 per cent of the prefunding of T5 in the current quinquennium. The CAA did not accept that these changes seen as a package undermined regulatory credibility.

11.138. It noted that BAA's arguments did not extend to the replacement of the single till with the RRCB, which in terms of the level of the overall price cap was easily the largest change to the regime. If BAA were able to show that the CAA's proposals amounted to a loss of projected shareholder value compared with continuing with the single till, then there might be cause for concern and the CAA would wish to address this, but so far no evidence had been forthcoming, and the CAA was confident that its proposals did not amount to any regulatory renegement.

11.139. On the specific question of T5 prefunding, the CAA believed that its recommendation that part of the value generated by BAA should be recovered was entirely consistent with the spirit of the CAA decision in 1996 and was entirely consistent with the actions required by a regulator under an RAB approach where a large return on future capex was included in the price cap. If the airport was allowed to benefit from a higher price cap by pledging a large capex programme but faced no recovery when the programme failed to materialize, it would have very poor incentive effects by acting as a signal that higher returns could be expected by delaying major capex projects after price caps are set. The CAA believed that its recommendation was more likely to add to the credibility of the regulatory regime, rather than detract from it.

11.140. On the other hand, to clawback the full difference between projected and actual capex was very close to a cost plus regime. The CAA believed that it was reasonable for BAA to argue it had to invest in other projects because of the delay to T5, and hence, the CAA had allowed for that additional spend.

11.141. The amount of the clawback was calculated as the difference between projected and actual capex on a single-till basis. The CAA proposed that that would be taken off the single-till RAB, and also off the aeronautical asset base, rather than split between commercial and aeronautical tills, since aeronautical customers had paid 'up front' out of their charges.

11.142. On whether BAA should have sought an interim review because of the delay to T5, the CAA said that BAA was not obliged to seek such a review, given the wording of the CAA condition which accompanied the setting of charges for Q3. Such issues were anyway being picked up in the current review. BAA's argument that its actual returns in Q3 were similar to those projected, however, partly reflected its use of actual rather than projected depreciation; the CAA used projected depreciation in rolling forward the RAB in its model (see also Chapter 10).

ATM incentive and other triggers

11.143. The CAA was also proposing an incentive for extra ATMs. As noted above, initially it had proposed a payment for movements in excess of 480,000 a year at Heathrow, but in response to suggestions particularly by BA, it had focused the same amount of money only on additional movements at the peak periods. This would, for example, be an encouragement to mixed mode.

11.144. On the use of other possible triggers to relate charges to progress of T5, however, the CAA was nervous that future problems of specifying such triggers could arise, as with the experience in Q3: detailed specification would be necessary.

The Q term

11.145. The CAA said that the Q factor (see Chapter 6) was valuable, first, for the signalling effect and, second, to provide a focusing of incentives and management attention which was currently lacking. It acknowledged that the maximum 3 per cent of revenue it proposed would be far too small to internalize the probable benefit to the airport of under-providing or the extra costs of over-providing. On the other hand, because it did not have the outputs fully specified with prices against them, there were quite big risks of perverse and unintended outcomes. Hence, it was appropriate to have a very modest approach to start with and see whether the system was capable of taking financial incentives. It was a cautious first step, which it hoped, went in the right direction.

11.146. As far as the passenger elements were concerned, (QP), the CAA was well focused on the elements it would have in the term. On the criticisms made by airlines of the QSM, the CAA believed that the best solution was an audit to ensure it was working reliably and properly: any alternative would entail considerable costs. It recommended that the QSM term be continued in times of disruption.

11.147. A working group set up some time ago by BAA was well advanced on agreeing airline elements (Q_A), based on the SLAs that had already been devised, and giving a financial bite to them. Reliability of the measures was variable, being better for mechanical systems; a tightening of the definition on measuring security queues was particularly necessary. An independent survey, however, would be too expensive to set up. The CAA therefore accepted that it could have a role in ensuring the adequacy and fairness of the systems used by BAA. It also believed planned maintenance should be treated in the same way as any other 'down time', changing the standard if necessary.

11.148. The CAA continued to recommend a delay term at Heathrow and Gatwick, strongly supported by most airlines. The value of this was potentially very great and there were large sums of money in terms of the value of queuing time that might be involved. However, the CAA recognized that this was a source of major disagreement between airlines and BAA concerning accountability for airport delays and the mechanics of measuring delays. It also recognized that airports could not be held solely accountable for all delays. However, as negotiator of the contract with NATS for airport ATC, and as the party with the final say on the ten-minute average delay used to declare runway capacity at these airports, the CAA considered that it was reasonable to expose BAA to performance on delay, particularly where the term in the first instance was unlikely to be very large and BAA had incentives to facilitate additional traffic.

11.149. The question of measurement was more difficult. Work was continuing on how the data could be captured, and the CAA would only implement such a term if a robust system could be established. The CAA's advocacy of a term in the price cap (as opposed to information disclosure) was contingent on these problems being overcome. The main problem was information on queuing. There did not appear to be good, robust, data systems to capture the event of an aircraft being otherwise ready to push back power, except that it needed clearance from the tower, nor on actual take-off time or landing time or time back on stand. There was technology on its way in terms of secondary movement radar at Heathrow, which would collect data by aircraft with a tag that uniquely identified that aircraft and would provide a reasonably comprehensive data source. But BAA and NATS were unclear as to how long that was going to take. Hence, the CAA might not be at a stage where it could define exactly what the term should be when the review process came to an end, and might have to define something that might start after the beginning of the control period. Subsequently, however, the CAA thought that it might be possible to extend the current NATS sample information as a temporary measure until more comprehensive and continuous measurement systems were in place.

11.150. It did not believe it would be necessary to have a system of attribution, believing any variance from the ideal time at both ends of a flight would represent the responsibility of BAA and NATS; BAA should have taken a view ex ante on such causes, so any further variances would show it had made the wrong decision. Even if some delays were caused by other parties, BAA would have an incentive to sort these out, but over time the effect of such delay would tend to cancel out.

11.151. The CAA believed that FEGP should be included, since it was a sine qua non of using a stand given environmental concerns about use of auxiliary power units. Given the number of firms involved in baggage systems, on the other hand, the CAA did not think it was remotely close to having measurement systems; there would always be argument as to why a particular system broke down.

11.152. The CAA said that it would be quite happy to retain the remote stand rebate in its current form; if it was retained there might be some case for not having pier service as part of this structure of standards, although something based upon payment that was already in place might be of benefit. There was an issue about how the rebate was treated. At the moment it was treated as a negative revenue; to be consistent with the approach to standards being discussed it would be better to treat it as a cost that did not then have an impact upon the revenue yield formula. At the moment the airport was indifferent to off-pier service because it still received the same amount of revenue through the formula.

11.153. The passenger element would be symmetrical; the aerodrome congestion element would be symmetrical; the airline element (QA) would be penalty-only since this would provide a better base from which to move forward into individual contracting. The CAA agreed that the standards set should be such that a reasonable company making reasonable efforts should be able to avoid penalties, but disagreed with BAA where that standard should be. It did not incline to the view that where this was part of the price formula this should lead to standards that the airport should never fall below—to do so would take away a significant part of the incentives at least where the airport was operating normally. (In the event of an adverse public interest finding, however, a significantly lower standard might be appropriate.) Standards should be based on existing targets—but should not take account of changing traffic loads, or incorporate a 'dead band'. The charges condition should be based on reaching standards in SLAs in all months—the SLA standards already had a certain amount of slack built in.

11.154. The CAA had some fundamental problems with using planning standards as a basis for service quality, because the only instruments that BAA would have for many of these standards would be to provide more capacity which would take some considerable time (and T5 was a project to provide exactly that) or to restrict the declared capacity of the terminals. It also did not seem to the CAA that the planning standards based upon space per passenger etc were a good basis on a tactical level to assess quality of service.

11.155. The CAA was suspicious of any system which involved payments of penalties to individual airlines, since a lot of effort might then be put into chasing them. The effects of a few elements of service failure could, moreover, be attributed to particular airlines. Attribution to terminals, and payment of penalties to users of these terminals, may, however, be reasonable.

11.156. The CAA did not see a need for a Q term at Stansted. Given the costs that would be associated with it, and with a non-binding price cap, the benefits were not sufficient to justify the costs. It had, however, agreed enhanced information disclosure, to include service quality information.

11.157. Some of the service terms were negatively correlated with traffic, and some not correlated with traffic at all, so the CAA did not believe the Q term would affect the cost of capital. There might however be a case to allow for additional costs of achieving any targets that were higher than current performance; there could also be a cost at Heathrow as congestion increased before T5 opened.

The default price cap

11.158. The idea that the regulatory regime should provide for protection against monopoly abuse, but that voluntary arrangements outside of the cap should be permitted had received widespread support in principle, but mixed views on its likely impact. Two points were relevant to make here. First, the concept was one that facilitated direct contracting; it did not impose it or specify what contracts outside the cap could or could not be entered into. All such contracts would continue to be subject to competition law and potentially section 41 of the Airports Act, and this should guard against undue discrimination. Second, concern had been raised about the protection of those remaining in the cap if service levels for them were not adequately protected. The CAA believed that the service quality term should provide some protection in this regard and that if serious falls in service quality were occurring due to contracting, competition law and section 41 could, again, apply. The CAA saw no reason why it should prohibit contracting below a generic standard (as many respondents had argued) while accepting that there might not be large demand for contracts of this type at Heathrow.

11.159. The CAA said that the default price cap concept was more an extension of a practice that had gone on for some time rather than something completely new—bespoke business lounges, for example, already being on a direct commercial basis. The revenues did not count as airport charges. The difficulty came where something might count as an airport charge and therefore the CAA would have to put a cap on it, so if there was an agreement for a certain quality of product or for some bespoke area of the terminal, part of which counted as an airport charge, it would have to fall within the cap.

11.160. The CAA also believed that airlines should be able to contract for lower charges for less quality.

11.161. Subsequently, the CAA said that, whereas it had originally believed that a price cap should be applied to individually negotiated contracts where these involved the payment of airport charges separate from the cap applying to the payment of standard published charges, it now believed such special arrangements should merely be treated in the same way as non published discounts at Manchester: that is, when comparing out-turn yields with the price cap, it should be assumed the full published charges were levied. It also told us that where top-up charges were levied as discrete charges in addition to a basic charge, such payments would not count as airport charges.

S factor

11.162. On the S factor, the CAA believed it necessary that the airports should be 'owning' and taking responsibility for the management of the investments and costs associated with additional security requirements which at the moment were passed on to the airlines. As to whether the cost base should be adjusted for the future costs that might be incurred, BAA should be able to finance such costs as part of the overall regulatory settlement that the CAA was recommending: airports faced a lot of uncertainty in many areas of their activities, and those associated with security requirements were not significantly different. If there was a serious problem, there was always the possibility of an interim review.

Other aspects of the formula

11.163. We noted above that the CAA had been convinced by the industry to retain the revenue yield approach, the gains from the greater complexity of the tariff basket being more than offset by the costs. On a possible volume term, the CAA rejected this since it believed airports should have the incentive to take extra traffic.

11.164. On non-passenger flights, removing them from the cap was just a technical adjustment, so the revenues would not contribute to the calculation of whether or not the airports were complying with the average revenue per passenger cap. On whether that could encourage such flights at the airports, there were very strong mechanisms including the slot mechanism to deter such low-value flights from using Heathrow. Such flights would still be subject to their own cap; at Manchester, where the CAA introduced this two years ago, charges to non-passenger flights had to be no higher than the equivalent charges for passenger flights.

11.165. The CAA proposed a similar treatment for unpublished discounts as at Manchester, namely in calculating revenue against the price cap, it should be assumed users paid the full price. The CAA believed that this was not unreasonable, and that discounts should in some circumstances not be transparent, nor, in answer to our specifically raising this, would the CAA want to be informed of them, since it would not want to be seen as having endorsed them, as this might prejudice its decision in any complaint under section 41 of the Airports Act and it did not feel that the costs of mandatory notification would be justified.

Stansted charges

11.166. The proposals for Stansted were light-handed in not having a price cap that was binding, so its behaviour would be unaffected by the price cap. But the CAA could foresee a different situation in the future and the cap would start to bite if the airport was still designated. The CAA was trying to set a framework through information disclosure whereby BAA and its key users came to an arrangement and the Secretary of State might in the future be satisfied that Stansted could be dedesignated.

11.167. But BAA would have to make the case that it had dealt with the monopoly problem satisfactorily with the customers, and its information disclosure would be allied to it.

11.168. Users should be starting to negotiate long-term contracts with BAA to lock in what they thought was a reasonable relationship for five or ten years. Moreover, the LFCs emphasized the point that their market was very price elastic and, to a degree, that was signalling to BAA that it would be receiving customers who were very price responsive themselves. Since BAA was trying to fill up that facility, there would be bargaining power.

The value of X in Q4

11.169. As to the basis for the X in the next five years at Heathrow and Gatwick, the CAA was fixing a long-term framework and there was discretion about whether prices should be higher or lower early on. The CAA adopted two decision criteria. First, given this was a radical shift in the framework and there were obviously problems in aviation at the moment, a limit of RPI+6 at Heathrow and RPI+5 at Gatwick over the next five years would moderate the speed of introduction of the dual till. At Heathrow there would still be quite a large jump at the beginning of the next quinquennium, so there was a trade-off between how fast to allow prices to rise currently and how big the jump should be in future. The RPI+6 recommendation was therefore judgemental, but reasonable. At Gatwick 5 per cent maintained the differential growth in prices at Heathrow and Gatwick, which was attractive for other reasons. Second, the CAA had to take into account signals in the financial market concerning regulatory renegement. Its decision criteria was that prices over the next five years should not be lower than the levels that would have been achieved if the single till, including T5 prefunding, (ie a normal return on assets as the capex was spent) was adopted. The profiling at Stansted was not so important because the CAA did not think Stansted was going to price up to the cap, whatever profile was adopted: it had basically taken a ten-year profile there.

11.170. As noted above, after 2008/09, Heathrow charges would rise to a little over £10 and then effectively level out against current projections; at Gatwick they would do this at £5.69; and at Stansted they would carry on rising to the end of 2013, but that was unlikely to have any material effect on what actually happened at Stansted. The CAA believed that this was the best package to address the investment and service quality problems among the options available. It saw the enhanced information disclosure and consultation as building on BAA's current practice. It had been putting a lot of pressure on BAA to come to a strategic compact with the key airlines. The business plan was the basis of that.

Cost of capital

11.171. In line with standard practice, the CAA had based its cost of capital calculations on the framework provided by the CAPM. The CAPM could be seen as a highly simplified but 'industry standard' representation of efficient markets.

11.172. The CAA said that one of the main disadvantages of the CAPM approach was that it was based on several critical unobservable variables. The CAPM was based on expected returns but only past (that is realized) returns were observed. Therefore, the estimation of parameters such as beta was based on average past returns, the assumption being that past returns on average were the best available measure of expected returns.

11.173. Given the high volatility of stock returns, ie there was a lot of 'noise' in the data, the CAA warned against spurious precision. Statistically, there would be a 95 per cent probability that the true mean of the cost of equity lay between 2.75 and 12.65 per cent. The CAA therefore stressed the great level of uncertainty surrounding cost of capital calculations: a considerable degree of judgement was involved, bearing in mind the investment focus of the review.

11.174. With respect to the market parameters, the CAA examined recent academic research, empirical evidence and recent decisions made by other regulators and the CC. This had resulted in the CAA adopting a risk-free rate of 3 per cent and ERP of 4.0 per cent as adopted by the CC in the Water appeals.

11.175. With respect to firm-specific parameters the CAA distinguished between the different BAA airports and different regulatory regimes. Based on BAA market figures, the CAA adopted a debt premium of 90 basis points for Stansted, Gatwick and existing assets at Heathrow, all based on an actual gearing level of 25 per cent reflecting the current data. However, given that T5 was likely to be in part debt financed, BAA's gearing level was likely to increase. Considering the move to output-based pricing for new assets at Heathrow, with a projected gearing level of 45 per cent, the CAA assumed a debt premium for new assets at Heathrow of 160 basis points. Also, the move to output-based pricing was likely to expose BAA to greater levels of volume risk, which at least in part would be non-diversifiable, and hence be reflected in a higher equity beta. The CAA therefore assumed an equity beta of 0.8 for Gatwick and Stansted and of 0.7 for Heathrow existing assets and for new assets at Heathrow an equity beta of 1.3.

11.176. Given the above, the CAA determined the pre-tax real cost of capital for Gatwick and Stansted to be 7.5 per cent (both under single-till and RRCB pricing), for Heathrow existing assets 7 per cent and for Heathrow new assets (output-based pricing) 8.5 per cent.

Opex and capex

11.177. On opex, the CAA adopted a fairly standard regulatory approach of seeing what cost structure was revealed by BAA in the current quinquennium, and making sure what the numbers for the next quinquennium were. It did not think it was appropriate to be estimating the productivity growth rate BAA could achieve compared to the economy on average because that was inconsistent with the service quality objectives of this review. It had carried out a partial performance comparison with other airports: but given the caveats caution had to be exercised in interpreting the results.

11.178. On capex, the CAA relied quite heavily on the extensive information disclosure by BAA to the airlines, particularly BA and IATA and took a lot of comfort out of their involvement. The critical thing was BA's and IATA's reaction to the new programme.

Conclusion

11.179. The CAA said, therefore, that the increasing problems of excess demand, congestion and the failure of new capacity to emerge at Heathrow and Gatwick led it in July 2000 to embark on a 'fundamental review' of airport regulation policy that should be applied to set the price caps for the 2003–08 period. Its final recommendations reflected an exhaustive process of market consultation and investigation into the practicalities of alternative regulatory approaches. They were squarely based on the CAA's statutory objectives, within which the CAA believed that primacy should be given to providing high-powered incentives to expand capacity in the face of congestion and to accepting that market conditions increasingly pointed to higher airport charges to improve efficient use of the airports (not lower charges). That recognized the central importance of the role that airlines played in representing the requirements of their passengers.

11.180. The CAA did not believe that its conclusions would be a panacea. The external costs and benefits generated by airports would continue to impact on capacity growth, through planning constraints and otherwise. The high-powered incentives that the CAA was proposing were not a perfect substitute for the dynamic incentives that effective competition would bring. But given the current market structure in the South-East the CAA believed that its recommended approach would provide a sustainable basis for better investment in improved service quality and new capacity desired by users. It expected BAA to engage with its key customers, given this set of proposed regulatory policies, to reach a lasting strategic compact on airport development thus boosting regulatory certainty.

Public interest issues

11.181. The CAA had no specific comments on the public interest issues raised with the CC. It noted, however, that many of the issues raised related to investment, consultation or service quality. It believed concerns about investment were best remedied by a price cap which gave appropriate incentives to invest, its proposals for moving away from the single till and for a PPC being designed to sharpen these incentives. Concerns about consultation were addressed by the statement on advanced information disclosure and consultation in the exchange of letters with BAA; service quality by a Q term within the price cap at Heathrow and Gatwick. It was not aware of any particular problems with service quality at Stansted which would warrant regulatory action.

11.182. The advanced information disclosure and consultation requirements would be more comprehensive than the latest CIP, to include details on the market, demand, capacity, service quality and the capex plan as a way of closing any gaps. BAA would have to give options for the development of the airport around the central plan, including details of the cost and output trade-offs involved in each option, and the likely impact on user charges. The CAA believed that airports should give reasons for their decisions following consultation with users, explaining how the comments had been taken into account. By international standards BAA did an exemplary job on consultation; the CAA would like to build on that, but hoped to get agreement and had done so.

11.183. The CAA placed a lot of emphasis on the involvement of the airlines in developing these plans, but there were obvious difficulties with giving airlines an effective veto over them or over changes to them. There was the obvious problem of how to decide what the airlines' view actually was. Different airlines had different agendas and perhaps different weights in arguing their case with the airport, and there had been examples in the past where particular airlines had argued vociferously that they wanted certain things and then undertaken short-order strategy changes that largely removed the reasons for them.

11.184. As to whether the CAA could be more fully involved in the relationship between BAA and the airlines on disputes on capex, its broad framework was that it would like to see the airlines and the airports in proper consultation with proper information disclosure, allowing the various views to be properly taken into account, and that ultimately the airport should be accountable for what it did. But to have the CAA essentially acting as arbiter on details of capital investment carried obvious dangers. Its policy was that it should not be suggesting a particular element of the capex plan was good or bad.

11.185. On other public interest issues raised with the CC, the CAA was surprised at the number of complaints that had come forward, because it was not aware during the five-year period that these matters were simmering. The section 41 complaints procedure was hardly used at all by the airlines, and it was not aware of many of these matters even on an informal basis.

11.186. The CAA was trying to put in place a framework where at least it should become far more transparent that there were major disputes. The point of its information disclosure/consultation proposal was to enable consultation to move more effectively than it had done in the past, and as part of that it was looking for the airport to give good reasoning as to why it was not going along with the views of particular users or even users as a whole.

11.187. But the CAA was not prepared to commit itself to step in on individual cases and act as an arbiter, nor was it clear precisely what powers it would have, if it was not a formal complaint, to do so. Legal advice was that while it had the formal powers under section 41, it could not at the same time take on the more informal role airlines had suggested.

11.188. On peak pricing, BAA should be doing this anyway under the flexibility given by an average revenue cap and its being a profit maximizer. To impose it via a tariff basket etc, however, would be too heavy-handed.

11.189. On the definition of airport charges, since 1986 the CAA had followed the advice that the MMC had had from Mark Littman QC about what was included and excluded in the definition of airport charges, and that had tended to form the basis of subsequent reviews. It would, though, make sense to review the definition if there were a new Act.

11.190. On our raising a possible U factor to take account of increases in unregulated charges, it was not obvious there had been a huge problem, except there were some issues about the transparency of some overhead allocations. So in the absence of something having gone obviously wrong, the CAA was reasonably happy that obvious breaches would be coverable by section 41, which was the fall-back in such cases. It knew perfectly well what had been assumed in the regulatory settlement and it would be able to see easily if sudden increases in charges looked wholly unreasonable. It did not really see that it was necessary to bring in a kind of ex ante regulation in the absence of evidence of clear detriments in the past.

11.191. Finally, the CAA rejected the view of some airlines that the CAA should be a more hands-on type of regulator. Its role partly came from the legislative arrangements where the comparisons were usually made with utilities operating under a licensing regime. Those licences were usually quite prescriptive. Under the Airports Act the five-year cap could not be opened up by the CAA, only by the airport. It had a complaints procedure, but there were not the usual tools that the other regulators had for intervening. But the CAA did try to build on what it saw as the strengths of that legislative framework, by making sure that the ownership of the problem was clearly with BAA and that the regulator did not get in the way such as to diffuse accountability and control.

11.192. But the CAA had come up with a comprehensive package that in some ways could be argued as being quite intrusive, namely a service quality term, enhanced information disclosure, and splitting the cost base, a lot of which some of the key airlines agreed with.

11.193. Hence, the CAA was addressing the problems within the statute. It did not have powers to become an arbitrator or a dispute resolver. If it had those powers, it would obviously do its duty but it saw some risks about being sucked halfway in and of diffusing the accountability for solving the problems.

The CAA panel of advisers

11.194. The CAA panel of advisers (Professor Martin Cave, Mr Brian Pomeroy and Professor Ralph Turvey) stated that since 2000 it had acted as a panel of advisers to the CAA on the process, analysis and conclusions of the reviews of the regulated airports. It thought it useful to write to the CC independently.

11.195. The panel largely supported the CAA's approach and process. It considered the emphasis on economic efficiency with less concern about rent distribution to be sound.

The Department for Transport

11.196. The DTLR (subsequently the DfT) said that in the integrated transport White Paper, *A New Deal for Transport: Better for Everyone*, published in 1998, the Government had announced it would prepare a UK airports policy looking 30 years ahead and bring forward new policy on civil aviation that would reflect its commitment to sustainable development, integrated transport and regional growth. The Government intended to publish at the turn of the year an air transport White Paper that would provide a policy framework for the long-term future of aviation and airports in the UK.

11.197. The DfT said that the process of approving large airport investment projects had been difficult, time consuming and expensive as the experience of Heathrow T5 had illustrated. The Government believed that new measures were needed to modernize the planning system if major infrastructure projects such as new airports were to be delivered in a timely and cost-effective manner. The Secretary of State announced in July 2001 the intention to bring forward proposals aimed at streamlining the planning procedures and reducing unnecessary delay, whilst safeguarding and increasing public consultation and involvement. Detailed proposals were set out in consultation papers issued in December 2001. They included power for the Secretary of State to 'designate' major infrastructure projects, which would then be subject to new procedures, including Parliamentary scrutiny and approval to the principle, before detailed aspects were considered at a public inquiry. The consultation period ended in March and responses were now being considered. The Government's proposals if they were implemented, would be valuable in facilitating the provision of sustainable airport capacity, provided they were underpinned by a clear statement of government policy and a regulatory regime that gave adequate incentives to the airport operator concerned. Even so the task of securing authorization for major airport projects would not be straightforward.

11.198. The DfT confirmed that in general there were currently no objections from international obligations to moving away from the single till. As to ICAO guidance, the DfT said that while it was arguable that this was not formally part of the UK's international obligations notified for the purposes of section 39 of the Airports Act, the DfT's view was that consideration of such guidance was a relevant consideration for the purposes of making a decision. Although there was no express obligation for the CAA to take account of ICAO guidance, the DfT believed that the CAA should have regard to such guidance in reaching decisions, and would like the CAA to do so. The Government's general policy presumption was that ICAO guidance should be complied with and discharged seriously. The DfT also doubted that the proposal to move away from the single till on a wholesale basis was consistent with the ICAO principle of flexibility in the interpretation and application of this concept whereby it was recognized that a range of approaches might be appropriate given that circumstances differ between airports. This implied that the arguments at each airport should be considered on their own merits. As the CAA had recognized, the economic arguments for moving away from the single till were strongest at severely congested airports such as Heathrow and Gatwick and were more finely balanced at Stansted and Manchester. Once Stansted became congested, the arguments for moving away from the single till there would become stronger.

Security requirements and the S Factor

11.199. The DfT was concerned with the proposals to remove the S factor arrangements for the BAA London Airports and Manchester. Following the 11 September attacks in the USA, the aviation security regime in the UK had been reviewed and extra requirements had been laid upon airports in September 2001. Final costs, however, remained unclear but could be considerable, particularly for larger airports, as requirements such as additional criminal record checks for staff entry restricted zones, and better use of CCTV systems, could require several million pounds of expenditure. Further incidents could have considerable implications. In principle, TRANSEC (the DfT security arm) could be more involved in assessing whether the costs claimed were reasonable, as long as this was a matter within its professional capability.

11.200. Furthermore, following a separate review of security after the recent robberies at Heathrow Airport, the Secretary of State and the Home Secretary had announced on Thursday 28 March 2002 further enhancements to airport security. These included the introduction of improved access control systems, and management of passes; the extension of counter terrorist and criminal record checks; and the enhancement of CCTV coverage. Details of these improvements had yet to be worked up, so it was impossible to say now what the additional costs might be.

11.201. If the S factor arrangement was withdrawn, it could have the effect of the relevant airports doing the bare legal minimum to meet the security requirement, which could have serious consequences. The CAA had argued that airports would still be legally obliged to meet all security standards. This was true as regards security measures that were set down in directions under the Aviation Security Act 1982 (as amended). It was not true as regards the many other security recommended practices that were contained in the National Aviation Security Programme. A reaction to removal of the S factor might therefore be a reduction in airports' willingness to comply with recommended practice.

11.202. The DfT said that it was already subjected to regular representations from the industry about the Government not meeting additional costs of security arising from the 11 September attacks, when other governments (notably the USA) were funding at least some of the extra costs centrally. The DfT's counter to such arguments was to say that the aviation industry should bear its own running costs, and that such costs could be passed on to the end user (the passenger). If the S factor was removed this argument would fall in respect of the regulated airports. If the CC came to the view that the S factor was anomalous, the DfT would argue for a reduction as opposed to total removal. A compromise option might be for a reversion to the previous level of 75 per cent of costs being recoverable.

Single till

11.203. In its recommendations to the CC, the CAA had concluded that the single till was not the best basis for meeting its statutory objectives at the three BAA airports and Manchester, and had proposed an RRCB, effectively a dual till, which comprised only the costs of airport services, excluding commercial activities and surface access infrastructure.

11.204. The DfT believed the economic arguments were for moving away from the single till as capacity constraints and congestion became more severe, and to do with both investment incentives and the efficient allocation of scarce resources. The downward trend in charges had become difficult to reconcile with efficient allocation of an increasingly scarce resource. It shared the CAA's view that where there was substantial excess demand (such as at Heathrow and Gatwick), the single till did not promote the efficient use of existing capacity. Using proceeds from commercial activities to reduce regulated airport charges when an airport was congested did not encourage the best use of scarce capacity. The DfT agreed with the CAA that the objective of using scarce capacity by those who valued it most would be better met by allowing airport charges to move closer towards incremental costs and/or market-clearing prices with beneficial effects at the margin. It expected that the more competitive airlines would be less able to absorb higher charges; the smallest impact would be on profitable long-haul services where airport charges represented only a small proportion of costs. However, the effect on LFCs would be heavily blunted by Stansted continuing to price below the cap set; the effect on charters at Gatwick might be blunted since the fare was only one element of the costs of a holiday. There could, on the other hand, be a heavy impact on scheduled operations using small aircraft. Abolition of intra-EC duty-free had had a bigger impact, without causing any acceleration of movement of charter aircraft out of Gatwick.

11.205. Although changes to the slot allocation mechanism would be a better mechanism to improve efficient utilization of slots, which could not currently be relied upon to happen.

11.206. The DfT agreed with the CAA that the key considerations were the impact on investment incentives and the efficient use of existing capacity from raising the effective rate of return on regulated assets. However, it did not believe that the delays in T5 coming on stream were attributable to the lack of investment incentives and it would be hard pushed to find evidence of under-investment. But it saw addressing investment incentives as complementary to acceleration of the planning system.

11.207. The DfT did not see a problem of excessive returns on the aeronautical side, but would be concerned if any windfall profits tax effectively undid the benefits on investment incentives of moving away from the single till. However, it emphasized that the windfall tax on various utilities in 1997 had been firmly stated to be a one-off measure and not to be repeated. It also agreed with the CAA that whilst airports enjoyed locational rents from commercial activities, they did not enjoy significant market power, and that concerns over market power were better dealt with more directly by competition authorities than by maintaining the single till. Any rents currently, however, accrued mainly to airlines: airlines might have to give up a proportion of such rents to be more certain of investment.

11.208. As the CAA had acknowledged, the case for moving away from the single till at uncongested airports such as Stansted was weaker. In current circumstances the single till should perform better in terms of encouraging the use of spare capacity since this would result in price caps that were closest to low marginal costs. The DfT felt that the economic case for moving away from the single till at Stansted had not really been made.

11.209. The theoretical basis of the CAA's statement that the single till had no effect on reducing fares at Heathrow and Gatwick and that fares would not rise materially if it were removed was not disputed, but this was an extreme case which assumed airlines fully exploited the shortage of capacity, and all scarcity rents accrued to them, and none to passengers. This was not necessarily the case.

11.210. The DfT agreed with the CAA that the removal of the single till would strengthen investment incentives at Heathrow and Gatwick but it should be noted that the key element of the CAA proposals to encourage optimal aeronautical investment was the PPC, which was specifically limited to output delivery.

11.211. The DfT agreed with the CAA that its proposed RRCB approach was better placed to meet its statutory objectives at Heathrow and Gatwick than the single till because of its effect in increasing charges closer to market-clearing levels and restricting regulation to monopoly services. It was acknowledged that practical problems existed in the issue of splitting costs and revenues between aeronautical and commercial tills (for example, the case of common facilities).

Stand-alone price cap

11.212. The DfT expressed concern that the proposal to regulate airports on a stand-alone basis could make it difficult to finance investment in a new runway solely from charges at that airport.

11.213. The DfT wished to emphasize the distinction between the financial viability and economic justification of investments. The DfT was currently considering other options for financing economically worthwhile, but possible financially unviable, investments in the context of the forthcoming White Paper (for example, a transparent levy devoted to a particular project). A decision on possible options would not, however, be known by the time the price cap came into play in April 2003 and the capex would be largely incurred after the period being considered here.

11.214. The Government had recently issued a statement indicating it did not favour any splitting up of the ownership of the three BAA airports. The review that led up to that statement was essentially looking at the current position, in which against the background of severe capacity constraints, likely to continue in the future, it was unlikely there would be any real benefits from opening up competition.

Surface access

11.215. The DfT agreed with the CAA that airlines should not be asked to subsidize surface access projects where there was no clear evidence of benefits to users, but noted that there might be some schemes which were economically worthwhile, but possibly financially unviable as the net benefits could not be fully captured by users of the services provided. The DfT considered that there was a case for including surface access projects within the aeronautical till where, despite the fact that they were commercially unviable, they had the support of airlines.

Price path commitment

11.216. The DfT agreed with the CAA that the PPC would strengthen the incentives to deliver appropriate investment. In its response to the CAA consultation document, the DfT noted that the PPC proposals appeared 'not to have been adequately tested to ensure that the CAA is satisfied that it is able to comply with the UK's international obligations when it makes its decision'. However, the DfT subsequently accepted the CAA's assurances that the rate of return produced would not be excessive. The deferral of returns from adjusting the profile of charges could indeed increase the risks of the airport.

11.217. The DfT also noted that, although incremental costs of increasing capacity at Heathrow from 60 mppa to 90 mppa were estimated at £18 per passenger, the overall price cap would be much lower (around £10 per passenger). By reducing the threshold level for payments for additional passengers to 60 mppa when T5 opened (as compared with 70 mppa in their consultation document), the price cap would be higher earlier on, and the risk of more than reasonable accounting returns after 2013 should be reduced.

12 Views of airlines and airline representative bodies

Contents

Introduction

12.1. This chapter summarizes the views of airlines and airline representative bodies from whom we heard. As well as the evidence summarized here, many of these parties agreed for their initial submission to be put on the CC web site, http://www.competition-commission.org.uk/inquiries/baa, where, at the time of publication of this report, they remain available.

Airlines

Air 2000

12.2. See Charter Group.

Air France

12.3. Air France told us that it supported the continued economic regulation of the designated airports of Heathrow, Gatwick and Stansted as it believed that such regulation was necessary to protect the airlines, the main users, against possible abuse from monopolistic providers of essential services.

12.4. Air France supported separate price caps for the three London airports, elimination of automatic costs pass through (such as the S factor); and reduction in the starting asset bases at Heathrow and Gatwick to reflect the prefunding of T5. However, it did not support the proposed move to an RRCB. Rather, it argued for full adherence to the single-till principle, which in its view had never been an obstacle to new capacity. Air France argued that the single till enabled a reasonable price for the user and significant profits to the airports; a win-win situation which should be preserved. Air France rejected the proposal to set RPI+6 per cent as the cap over 2003 to 2008, which in its view would not meet users' interest. Instead, it requested continuation of the existing regulatory structure with RPI–X.

12.5. Air France indicated concern that the impact of these proposals on the price caps would result in significantly higher charges immediately, which was both unacceptable, and against the interests of users. This was considered to be especially unacceptable at a time when the industry was experiencing a crisis situation and there was no certainty that the adequate capacity and service levels would be achieved.

12.6. Air France was also concerned with the risk of increasing the competitive disadvantage of air travel versus rail. On the journeys operated by Eurostar (London–Paris, London–Brussels) it was crucial to ensure an even-levelled playing field, especially with regard to the financing of investment.

12.7. In Air France's view the main objective of economic regulation should be to achieve the lowest possible prices with an agreed standard of service and capacity. This would be best achieved using the single-till principle with RPI–X.

Air Transat

12.8. Air Transat told us that they were a Canadian-based passenger airline operating year-round scheduled and charter services between Canada and numerous points in the UK, including Gatwick. Its flights primarily served the holiday/leisure market, and it had been operating these services for the past 14 years, competing against major carriers such as BA and Air Canada.

12.9. As a result of the continuing fall out on worldwide air travel engendered by the events of 11 September 2001, Air Transat had undertaken a drastic cost-cutting programme designed to ensure its long-term viability. To this end, it had cut available capacity for the IATA summer 2002 season by approximately 25 per cent compared to the same period in the previous year and had reduced its labour force by the same percentage. It had also asked its major suppliers and airport authorities to assist it in its efforts to control and reduce its operating structure.

12.10. Gatwick represented Air Transat's second largest transatlantic destination in terms of passenger volume. It estimated that a return to pre-11 September transatlantic leisure traffic levels would take a minimum of two to three years at least. Consequently, it was Air Transat's view that relief from airport fee increases during this period would be highly beneficial and would ensure continued ability to offer competitive air services to the Canada–UK market. It therefore recommended that all fees and charges at Gatwick be frozen at current levels until at least 1 April 2004. Thereafter only cost of living or consumer price index increases should be allowed for the remaining portion of the five-year period.

12.11. Air Transat also told us that its ability to develop new and competitive services in the Canada-London market was directly dependant on its ability to secure slots at Gatwick for such flights. While it had generally been able to obtain necessary slots to operate its services over the last few years at Gatwick, it had nevertheless been required on numerous occasions to alter its proposed operating schedules in order to secure desired arrival and departure times. Air Transat expressed concern that Gatwick might not be able to accommodate any new significant increases in services by it, particularly in light of a potentially faster than expected recovery in international leisure travel demand.

12.12. Air Transat told us that it therefore believed that a pool of slots dedicated to the development of new long-haul intercontinental services (which were most affected by the terrorist attacks) should be created and made available at Gatwick over the next three years. It suggested that this slot pool should be established by having short- and medium-haul operators give up 20 per cent of their current peak morning arrival and late-morning/early-afternoon departure slots.

Airtours International Airways Ltd (My Travel)

12.13. Airtours International Ltd (Airtours), which during the inquiry changed its name to My Travel, told us it was the second largest UK non-scheduled airline, employing 2,200 staff in the UK and operating some 33 aircraft on the UK register. It carried approximately 7.25 mppa, serving almost all of the 28 largest designated commercial airports in the UK. According to Airtours, non-scheduled airlines carried more than 25 per cent of all international passengers from the UK. Airtours told us that it was a major user of both Gatwick and Stansted airports. It was also a member of the UK Charter Group (whose evidence is cited separately).

12.14. It was Airtours' belief that many of the CAA recommendations were fundamentally flawed, overly complex, and failed to recognize the efficiency, contributions and margins of the non-scheduled sector of the aviation business. Moreover, by its own admission, many of the CAA arguments were based on anecdotal, not hard evidence. Airtours told us it believed that the CAA's position was misguided and focussed more on theoretical economics than on attempting to understand the realities of the market-place in which the UK non-scheduled airlines operated. It believed that the concerns raised by Airtours and its colleagues in the Charter Group had been ignored by the CAA in the development of its proposals.

12.15. Determining the maximum level of airport charges should be based on a continuation of the existing single-till pricing mechanism with increases governed by an RPI–X factor. The CAA proposal to move to a dual-till mechanism was based on flawed analysis and was unproven. There should be no increase in charges without a proven improvement in service quality or addition in relevant capacity. Airtours urged the CC to give serious consideration to the implementation of an efficiency discount pricing option where an airport user delivered a high level of throughput per ATM utilized. This discount would be triggered where an operator achieved a loading per ATM that was 50 per cent greater than the average achieved at the relevant airport over the previous financial year.

12.16. Airtours cited a number of examples where BAA had operated against Airtours' best commercial interest, and where this had adversely impacted on its ability to serve its customers in the most effective manner. BAA's failure to increase the runway capacity at Gatwick, and its constant pressure to increase the runway movement rate on the existing runway, had increased Airtours' scheduling block times and associated costs by up to 20 per cent on its services to Mediterranean destinations, compared with when it had started operations in 1991. The pressure for BAA to maximize commercial retail income, particularly after the loss of duty-free operations had resulted in BAA making significant investment in additional retail and commercial facilities at Gatwick. Airtours believed that this was at the expense of additional facilities for passengers in operational areas, for example provision of adequate seating, toilets etc. Airtours also felt that the development of additional retail facilities in

358

'quiet terminals' could often lead to delays as passengers were distracted from making their way to the departure gates on time.

12.17. BAA's apparent inability adequately to resource staffing levels at security check points had led to excessive delays to its passengers. Airtours also felt that there was an apparent attitude at senior level within BAA that appeared to favour scheduled services over the non-scheduled operators.

12.18. Airtours suggested that the CC consider what the impending publication of the government White Paper on air transport would mean to the CC's assessment of the new charging regime for UK regulated airports.

12.19. In making its series of recommendations, it was Airtours' belief that the CAA might have breached its statutory objectives (as laid out in section 39 of the Airports Act). The proposed changes in price regulation, particularly from the single to dual till, would increase costs and do nothing to guarantee further investment. Instead, the dual till would work against achieving maximum efficiency of the airport that Airtours served in terms of maximizing passenger throughput per ATM. Non-scheduled airlines moved an average of 213 passengers per flight through Gatwick, compared with 106 on the scheduled airlines, yet it would be the non-scheduled airlines that would be further marginalized by the CAA recommendations. Airtours contended that this did not further its reasonable interests.

12.20. Airtours argued that BAA's lack of investment in new runways, in London and the South-East, had resulted in delays and congestion increasingly markedly, particularly at Gatwick. Airtours' average trip costs had increased by some 40 minutes extra block time over the last ten years, due in large part to an increase in the runway movements rate at Gatwick to between 45 and 50 ATMs an hour. The only way that such high levels of sustained movements could be achieved was by having aircraft queuing for take-off or in holding stacks waiting to land. As noted above, this resulted in Airtours requiring 20 per cent more resources to fly a typical series of flights to the Mediterranean than it had in 1991. Airtours claimed that this was almost entirely a function of inadequate investment in runway capacity by BAA. However, this could not be attributed to the single-till regime, as shown by Manchester Airport's development of a new runway under the single-till regime. Indeed, since the planning restriction at Gatwick prevented runway development, it could not be argued that higher prices could give an additional incentive to develop a second runway.

12.21. Airtours argued that in an ideal world there would be no need for economic regulation of airports as there would be adequate airport capacity, a choice of airports and airport operators, or at least a choice of independent terminals (as was the case in the USA). In the UK South-East, however, Airtours had no choice in using a BAA airport as the A330-200 aircraft that they operated ideally required a runway length of 3,000 metres in order to operate non-stop, maximum payload to destinations in the South-East of the USA and Mexico. Airtours told us that any airline whose aircraft type and operations required the use of a runway with length in excess of 2,200 metres was forced to use a BAA airport, assuming it could obtain a slot. It therefore argued that it had no choice but to use a BAA airport, but it felt that it was being increasingly penalized under the CAA proposals for doing so.

12.22. Airtours also took objection to any claim that there was inefficiency on the part of charter operators.

Britannia Airways

12.23. See Charter Group.

British Airways plc

12.24. We received extensive information and submissions from BA during the course of the inquiry, its initial submission also being made available on the CC's web site. BA said that Heathrow was its main base and it was strategically dependent on Heathrow for the growth and development of its core business. It was a network airline, and its competitive advantage hinged to a large degree on the ability to develop its Heathrow 'hub' in competition with other hub airports. It had previously attempted to develop a second hub at Gatwick, but now realized that was not feasible and it was moving a number of its long-haul international services (critical for its hubbing operation) back to Heathrow. Gatwick was still important to BA, however; this summer it had 250 daily departures from Heathrow to 103 destinations, and 119 daily departures from Gatwick to 77 destinations.

12.25. Direct charges from BAA to BA were about £250 million a year. But in addition, poor service quality and congestion added to the costs of operating at both Heathrow and Gatwick. Congestion reduced utilization of expensive assets, in particular crew and aircraft, increased fuel use and compromised BA's ability to offer an efficient and punctual service to passengers. BA estimated its costs of congestion at £67 million at Heathrow in 2000, and £29 million at Gatwick (based on the cost of five additional aircraft along with crew and fuel costs).

12.26. BA said that in a normal competitive industry, the setting of prices was left to market forces. The need for regulation of airport charges arose from the monopoly position of BAA as the supplier of airport services in London and the South-East of England. This monopoly position stemmed partly from BAA's control over Heathrow airport—the UK's pre-eminent aviation hub, which accounted for the majority of passenger movements in the London area. It was reinforced by control over two major airports in the London system—Gatwick and Stansted. BAA airports accounted for over 90 per cent of the passenger traffic in London and the South-East and over two-thirds of total UK passenger movements.

12.27. It was widely agreed that the need to deliver higher levels of investment was a key issue for this regulatory inquiry, as it was in the last. T5 was to be built at Heathrow over the next five years and additional investment in runway capacity was urgently needed to meet the needs of London and the South-East of England. The key challenge for setting the level of airport charges over the next five years was to establish a regime that ensured prompt and efficient delivery of the required infrastructure to meet the expanding demand for air services, at a reasonable cost to users.

CAA recommendations to the CC

12.28. BA said that a number of the CAA proposals addressed issues of concern to BA and other airlines and were welcome as far as they went:

(a) Separate price caps were recommended for the three London airports, reducing the scope for cross-subsidies that distorted airline competition and sharpening the incentive to invest where demand was strongest within the airport system. BA believed that this was a key means of strengthening the incentives on BAA to make investments that met the needs of the users at each airport. Each airport should be developed to meet the needs of its own users; a new runway at Stansted, for example, would do nothing to relieve the congestion at Heathrow and Gatwick. Separate caps should help to ensure that the airport developed capacity where it was financially sustainable. Cross-subsidies between airports might not be sustainable over the long term and might lead to airport capacity being developed where it was easiest to build rather than where it was valued and needed by users. (While separate tills would give safeguards to users of each airport, BA regarded separate ownership as irrelevant to solving the problems it identified.)

(b) Specific incentives were proposed for the addition of peak aircraft movements at Heathrow and the early delivery of Heathrow stands linked to the construction of T5.

(c) Improved consultation procedures were recommended on capital spending plans, though as discussed below BA proposed that a formal public interest finding should support this.

(d) Automatic cost pass-throughs—ie the S factor—were rejected, on the grounds that these blunted the incentives for efficient airport operation. BA said that it was also difficult to distinguish between the costs of additional security requirements and costs of other developments, such as refurbishing a pier, which may be carried out at the same time. In BA's view, abolition of automatic cost pass-throughs would give BAA an incentive to introduce security requirements in a cost-efficient manner and would encourage proper discussion with airlines; competitive tendering of the security function could be desirable. Clearly, there might be circumstances in which airlines would wish to contribute towards improvements, but BA did not believe that this should be automatic; BAA could also trigger a mid-term review if necessary.

(e) BA agreed with the CAA that price caps should be based on the full revenues, not taking account of any discounts. This was necessary otherwise the airlines paying the full price would be subsidizing other airlines that might be competitors. In addition, BA argued it was possible to challenge discriminatory treatment only if information on discounts was published. It therefore believed that BAA should be obliged to publish details of all discounts including the terms on which such discounts were given.

12.29. BA had argued in the past for a volume term to protect users from overpaying and giving the airports a windfall profit that they had not earned. However, BA agreed that it was important to preserve the airports' incentives to accommodate growth. At the same time, it was crucial to ensure that, if passenger growth was higher than expected, then the airport spent the additional revenue on projects that increased capacity, relieved congestion and maintained service quality. BA therefore regarded the use of a volume term as a fallback solution if there were inadequate incentives in the regulatory settlement, by providing lower charges if an airport was more congested. Its preferred solution was to see the introduction of financial mechanisms, such as a delay term in the price cap, the imposition of service standards with compensation arrangements, and improvements in the capex consultation arrangements (as discussed below). If, and only if, these improvements were made to the regulatory regime, then BA agreed with the CAA that there was no need for a volume term in the price cap formula.

12.30. The CAA had proposed to introduce a Q term to the price formula in recognition of the difficulties and expense caused to airlines, and inconvenience to passengers, by delays. BA welcomed the CAA's intention to act, but believed its proposal was much too weak as it currently stood and was capped at far too low a figure to align airport interests with those of its customers. It proposed an alternative framework containing more robust measures, discussed further below.

12.31. The CAA also accepted the argument that the benefits obtained by BAA from T5 prefunding needed to be taken into account in setting future charges, though the solution they were proposing was inadequate. BA believed a full credit of Q3 prefunding should be made to the Heathrow airport till to prevent charges rising in the next quinquennium, rather than the partial refund proposed by the CAA through an adjustment to the Heathrow and Gatwick asset base.

12.32. However, the CAA was also proposing a radical reshaping of the charges regime for BAA airports, which BA did not support. There were three key elements to the CAA's proposal:

(a) the abolition of the single till and its replacement with separate aeronautical and commercial tills, with the aeronautical till being used as the basis for airport charges;

(b) long-term price caps for Heathrow and Gatwick to provide stability in the returns that airport operators could expect in the future; and

(c) an explicit policy of allowing charges to rise in real terms to ration scarce capacity.

12.33. BA rejected all three proposals on the grounds of practicality and principle. It did not believe that they would achieve the benefits claimed by the CAA. There were serious practical difficulties with implementing the proposals. And they exposed airlines and passengers to increased risk of the abuse of monopoly power by BAA.

12.34. The CAA's proposed changes to the regulation of charges would increase further the real cost of operating at BAA airports to BA. On the basis of the CAA recommendations to the CC, including inflation at 2.5 per cent a year, there would be a 50 per cent increase in the aeronautical charges paid by BA at Heathrow and Gatwick over the next five years. Its regulated charges would rise from an estimated £175 million this year to around £260 million by 2007/08. Over the five years of Q4, it would be paying around £250 million extra in charges compared with the current level—with only one-quarter of this increase due to inflation.

12.35. BA's concerns on the issues of single till, under-investment and service quality are set out further below.

Regulatory approach

12.36.   As to the general regulatory approach of the CAA, BA said that in its proposals to the CC, the CAA placed great emphasis on investment incentives and downplayed the traditional role of economic regulation in containing market power. BA argued that:

(a) The primary purpose of regulation was to prevent abuse of a monopoly by simulating competitive pressures and by encouraging competition where possible.

(b) Firmer contractual commitments were needed to give BAA incentives to maintain and improve service quality. They also offered a route towards regulatory disengagement.

(c) Proposals to introduce congestion charging were beyond the regulator's remit, and higher airport charges would increase the fares paid by passengers.

12.37.   The first of the CAA's statutory objectives was 'to further the reasonable interests of users of airports'. The CAA acknowledged that the primary motivation for price cap regulation was widely accepted as being 'to provide adequate protection to users from monopoly pricing for access to infrastructure and services that were essential for the provision of air travel and freight forwarding services'. BA said that the risk of detriments from monopoly provision were of course wider than just that of higher prices which were the prime focus of many regulatory regimes. Regulation must guard against the risk that the monopolist offered lower output than would be attained in a competitive market, resulting from failure to invest in timely and adequate capacity in a timely manner. The third of the CAA's statutory objectives—'to encourage investment in new facilities at airports in time to satisfy anticipated demands by the users of such airports'—was specifically aimed at this problem. The lack of incentives to produce at lowest cost and the failure to innovate were also key failures in monopolies.

12.38.   BA said that the CAA acknowledged that, in the context of airport regulation, the regulatory regime had been somewhat more successful in restraint of price increases than in encouraging higher levels of output. It was the degree of failure in the latter respect, and the need to improve service quality and adherence to planning standards, that was rightly the focus of this review of airport charges.

12.39.   BA said there was nothing to indicate that the existing regulatory regime, despite its success in holding down charges, had been too severe. BAA appeared to have had no difficulty in meeting its expected rates of return, and arguably had exceeded them. Any shift in the regulatory regime that reduced the degree of effective price restraint should therefore be judged on its ability to redress the balance by improving the incentives for airports to invest in adequate and timely additions to airport capacity. The CAA was proposing an easing of the regime on price controls, thus raising airport charges, but without generating a significant improvement in the ability of infrastructure development to keep pace with demand, and without delivering a high-quality passenger experience at the airport.

12.40.   This approach relied heavily on positive economic incentives even though it was clear, because of BAA's market power that these could not be relied on. They held out the prospect of higher long-term returns on new major investment projects, while threatening a return to regulatory intervention if capacity did not materialize.

12.41.   This was an untried and high-risk approach. BA was not satisfied that high-powered incentives combined with unspecific and unenforceable threats of tightening up the regulatory settlement next time would prevent abuse of monopoly power in practice, with no safeguards provided. It was completely contrary to the approach that most other regulators had taken. The CAA themselves admitted that it was no panacea to the problems experienced by users at airports.

12.42.   The CAA appeared reluctant to follow a more interventionist approach as taken by other regulators, even though the Government had concluded that airport regulation should be brought more into line with standard utility regulation; and that airport competition issues should be dealt with by regulation rather than by breaking up BAA's monopoly.

12.43.   The CAA often argued that it lacked the powers necessary to be able to take a more interventionist approach as other regulators had done. Nonetheless, the CAA appeared to have considerable scope for discretion in the following areas:

(a) in recommending the price cap, the CAA had wide discretion and could make orders for compensation if specific service standards were not met;

(b) a wide range of assumptions made in setting the price cap would have strong incentive effects, for example on counting as revenue excess income from the previous quinquennium (whether from revenue advancement, capex shortfall or rental increases), on whether to remunerate assets in the course of construction, on the scope for achieving operating efficiencies etc;

(c) the CAA had powers to require disclosure of financial information. This could be used to ensure that there was much greater scrutiny of capital investment; and

(d) the CAA's powers under section 69 to take whatever steps were necessary to facilitate the provision of new airport capacity were wide ranging and so far untested, but could be very useful as a measure of last resort.

12.44. The CAA in its recommendations sought to emphasize that the regulatory regime under the Airports Act was intended to be less intrusive than other regimes, and to suggest that this was in part the consequence of the fact that users include corporations as well as individuals. BA rejected this distinction. Airlines operated in competitive markets and were accountable to their passengers, whereas BAA was a monopoly. The fact that airports had companies as customers, rather than the general public, did not mean that airlines were not entitled to the normal protections provided to users of monopoly utilities. Users of electricity and water and other utility services included corporation as well as individuals. All users under the differing regulatory regimes were entitled to expect a degree of regulatory protection against the exercise of market power by the company concerned. The Airports Act regime was no different from other regimes in this respect.

12.45. BA believed that further unilateral regulatory disengagement by the CAA was wholly inappropriate because there were few competitive pressures operating on BAA. Despite BAA's assertions about the strong bargaining power of airlines, even the largest airlines such as BA had found it difficult and sometimes impossible to negotiate with BAA because of their strong monopoly position.

12.46. Indeed, BA believed there was a case for extending the scope of regulation to a wider range of airport charges where BAA had a monopoly. Traditionally, charges for specified activities had not been regulated directly, partly because the single-till mechanism was thought to remove much of the incentive to exploit market power, but a transparency requirement was placed on BAA following a public interest finding in 1991. In practice, BA found there had been insufficient transparency and that BAA had loaded in high overhead costs and opportunity costs.

12.47. It was clear that the statutory objective to impose the minimum restrictions was subject to the CAA's ability to meet its other objectives. Even though there was little immediate prospect of competitive forces substituting for regulation, there did appear to be scope for introducing commercial mechanisms that would have similar effects. This was possible in the case of airports because the paying customers were a relatively few companies rather than the general public as in the case with other regulated utilities.

The dual till

12.48. BA argued that commercial revenues at an airport were a by-product and an inseparable part of the aeronautical business. This was especially true for many essential services provided to airlines and passengers that were not included in regulated charges (such as the provision of airside licenses, car parking, airport lounges, baggage systems etc). In these cases, airlines had no choice but to buy these services from the monopoly supplier. Even with the retail shops, passengers were a captive market and they did not choose to go to the airport to shop, but to catch a flight or to meet or greet a passenger.

12.49. In the case of commercial revenues that were dependent on the regulated business (as distinct from stand-alone businesses such as management of an overseas airport), there was a strong case for retaining them within a single till. Where demand complementarities existed in normal competitive businesses, single-till type arrangements operated even though this term was not used. This was the case with other transport services (for example, rail) as well as in publishing (advertising in magazines) and other sectors (for example, meat and wool production from sheep).

12.50. In the last review, the MMC concluded that the single till should be retained and BA believed that little or nothing had happened to change the arguments.

12.51. The single-till approach met the UK's international treaty obligations and was still standard practice worldwide. BA was not aware of any airport that had moved away from this except Sydney (an airport being prepared for privatization) where the move was justified partly on the basis that the CAA was proposing this change in the UK: a large part of the operation at Sydney, moreover, was domestic, and the domestic terminals were owned by the airlines. In Eire, the move was not implemented at Dublin following consultation. The US model was totally different, with the base of the airfield and land being owned by a type of municipal authority and airlines developing the terminals. Current ICAO guidance, while allowing for more flexibility over implementation, remained clear that aeronautical charges were entitled to be reduced by contributions from retail revenues. BA was also concerned about retaliation against it if there was a move away from cost-related charges in the UK.

12.52. The single till also provided a mechanism under which surface access infrastructure within the airport boundary could be funded.

12.53. BA said that airline users all supported the retention of the single till.

Effect on efficient allocation of capacity

12.54. The first argument in support of abolishing the single till was that at congested airports prices would rise towards (but not reaching) market-clearing levels and that this would be likely to lead to a more efficient allocation of resources.

12.55. BA rejected this argument wholeheartedly. Congestion charging could not be accepted in the context of monopoly regulation as it rewarded the monopolist for failure in delivering something over which they had significant control (the expansion of output and capacity). The problem that needed to be addressed was primarily one of inadequate supply. Heathrow and Gatwick's runways and terminals operated extremely efficiently by world standards. Heathrow and Gatwick had the highest peak hourly capacities in Europe, and exceptionally high annual runway capacity utilization, with more than 90 per cent of all possible movements through the whole year being used (and very high delays due to congestion). This was greater utilization than any other international airport in the world. There were already mechanisms promoting the efficient utilization of capacity; individual airlines and alliance groupings, being constrained in their use of slots, all looked to deploy their slots in the most efficient manner; and there was also some trading of slots. BA acknowledged that more efficient use could be made of capacity, due to the lack of transparency in the market for slots—but this should be achieved by improving existing mechanisms for slot allocation and transfer, and higher airport charges were not the right mechanism for addressing that issue. BA did not deny that under the dual till there could be some withdrawal of services and their replacement by more profitable services; but this would not be significant enough to justify such a large swing in the basis of airport charging.

12.56. The analysis underpinning the CAA's proposals seemed to rely on a fundamental misinterpretation of its second statutory objective—'to promote the efficient, economic and profitable operation of such airports'. This objective was designed to promote greater cost efficiency and to give a stronger incentive to innovate than might otherwise be pursued by a monopoly services provider. However, the CAA insisted on interpreting this objective as a requirement to deliver a more efficient use of airport infrastructure. In other words, a prime aim of the CAA's proposals was by its own admission to secure the best use of available capacity by encouraging the more efficient use of scarce take-off and landing slots by airlines.

12.57. This was an admirable objective, but the setting of airport charges was a blunt and inefficient mechanism for achieving this objective, one that was more effectively pursued by means of a fluid and transparent slot-trading system. Furthermore, BA did not believe that the CAA had the statutory powers to pursue such an objective.

12.58. The Airports Act did not require the CAA to promote the efficient 'use' of airports, but the efficient, economic and profitable 'operation' of airports. BA argued that this objective was designed to promote greater cost efficiency through relating charges to the reasonable costs of running an airport, and to give a stronger incentive to innovate than might otherwise be pursued by a monopoly service provider;

the setting of airport charges, on the other hand, was an inefficient mechanism for securing the best use, for example of slots, and the CAA did not have the statutory powers to pursue such an objective.

12.59. Airport resources were allocated by an independent co-coordinator under a clearly defined administrative slot allocation regulation that fell within the competence of the EC, and had broader objectives than simply ensuring the efficient use of slots. BA did not believe the CAA was entitled to try to pre-empt a change to the regulation unilaterally by using airport charges as a rationing mechanism, and in any case this was likely to create conflicting regulatory objectives. As noted above, moreover, the CAA's statutory duty under section 39 of the Airports Act was to ensure the efficient and profitable operation of the airport, as opposed to the efficient use of the airport. That section also stated that the CAA's general objectives under section 4 of the 1982 Civil Aviation Act, which referred to the CAA's other objectives and powers to look after passengers' interests in the way that air transport services were provided, should accordingly not apply in relation to performance by the CAA of those functions under part IV of the Airports Act. Hence, both the Council Regulation 95/93/EEC and section 39 of the Airports Act prevented the CAA from using its powers as an economic regulator of airports to deal with allocation of airport capacity between airlines.

12.60. The CAA also interpreted its duty as being 'to choose the policy that was expected to maximize net gains to users and airports combined taking account of the costs of regulation'. In other words, the CAA sought to achieve an improvement in economic welfare where the total benefits accruing to some stakeholders exceeded the total losses suffered by others.

12.61. But the regulator could not be indifferent to the distribution of benefits between the regulated party and its customers. A monopoly airport service provider had no incentive to compensate the losers, even if the CAA's proposals constituted an overall welfare gain. The whole point of regulation was to ensure that the benefits that might accrue unjustifiably to the monopoly supplier in its absence were distributed fairly between supplier and users of airport facilities. Only if the starting point for any change was obviously unfair, in that one party held an unduly large share of the benefits at the expense of the other, thereby representing a serious misallocation of scarce resources, could there be a case for transferring some of the benefits to the other party without compensation. Yet there was no suggestion that the existing regime had been unfair. In any changes to the regulatory regime, there should therefore be some mechanism to prevent an unwarranted transfer of the benefits from one party to another.

12.62. The CAA admitted that there would be a redistribution of income—which it described as scarcity rents, arising from specific airport locations and from the capacity constraints that were present at Heathrow airport in particular—from airlines to airports under its proposals. They justified this by arguing that airport users did not have an automatic right to any such rents.

12.63. BA strongly refuted the proposition that there were any rents accruing to airlines to be redistributed. The CAA argued that, because airlines earned higher revenues at Heathrow, they were willing to pay for Heathrow slots, and this demonstrated that they were earning scarcity rents. But this logic was flawed. The value of a slot reflected the use airlines could make of it to generate revenue, which would depend on their ability to establish a level of product, network and service at that hub in order to attract high-yielding business passengers. For instance, the fact that such networks had been long established at Heathrow had traditionally meant that a greater proportion of business travellers had been attracted to Heathrow, generating a bigger share of premium passengers, and hence higher average yields. This was nothing to do with capacity shortages or scarcity rent. It was the result of passenger choice based on the services offered at each airport.

12.64. BA had generated higher yields at Heathrow because it was its major base and it offered a better quality of service there than it was able to offer from a secondary base airport, ie a superior network product to a wide range of key business destinations. This was not scarcity rent; it was perfectly normal pricing behaviour that saw higher prices paid for higher-quality goods and services. It had nothing to do with the intrinsic value of locating services at Heathrow, but arose because BA had chosen, for efficiency and customer service reasons, to concentrate the provision of premium services in a single location. Such commercial and strategic decisions by airlines may add to the potential value of a slot at Heathrow, but this told us nothing about the scope for earning scarcity rents.

12.65. Even if airlines had been able to earn scarcity rents at some point in the past (which BA would dispute), any rents would have been eliminated since then, for a number of reasons:

(a) The introduction of air passenger duty, and subsequent restructuring to bear more heavily on long-haul and premium passengers, had in practice a greater impact on airlines and passengers based at Heathrow than at Gatwick or other UK airports because of a higher concentration of long-haul services based there, further reducing the ability of airlines to earn excess profits at Heathrow.

(b) LFCs had entered the UK market in force since the mid-1990s, developing services at other London airports very rapidly, and undermining the profitability of short-haul services operated by the main network carriers at both Heathrow and Gatwick.

(c) Greater competition from Continental European hubs, which suffered little from runway and slot limits and had therefore been able to expand their networks rapidly, had eliminated any long-haul premium at Heathrow.

(d) Capacity constraints had increased at both Heathrow and Gatwick, and the resulting congestion had considerably increased delays and the cost disadvantage of trying to operate a hub network at such airports.

12.66. The CAA was unable to point to convincing evidence of the existence of airline rents. A good pointer to scarcity rents was the existence of excess profits. The airline industry had a record of poor financial performance, with most network carriers struggling under pressure from strong competition and rising costs. This was no less true for carriers operating at Heathrow airport, including BA, where even in the good years profit margins had been sparse and capital investment had not been adequately remunerated. As to whether the rents were absorbed in an inefficient level of costs, all British carriers at Heathrow made little profit in the previous year, but it could not be argued that all three were uncompetitive. Cost comparisons also failed to allow for differences in the operations of airlines, particularly in comparing carriers such as BA with the LFCs, who operated smaller aircraft over shorter distances than BA.

12.67. The CAA argued that, because there was a transfer of rents from airlines to airports, air travellers would not pay. BA totally rejected this argument. The airline industry was a competitive industry and the evidence of falling real yields, declining unit costs and thin profit margins of all UK carriers at Heathrow supported this view. In a competitive industry with very low margins, or even experiencing losses, increases in costs from any source would have to be passed on to consumers in the long term. There had been many recent instances of airlines raising published fares in response to cost increases that affected all participants in the market rather than just a few. For instance, when fuel prices rose sharply during the second half of 2000, airlines worldwide imposed fuel surcharges; more recently, many carriers had added price surcharges to cover the extra costs of security and insurance following the terrorist attacks on September 2001. Whilst some costs may be absorbed in the short term as a result of competitive pressures and an ever-present focus among companies in competition to find efficiencies, any rise in airport charges, that affected all users at an airport, would eventually be passed through to passengers in the form of higher fares or lower service levels. Price increases of nearly £5 per passenger at Heathrow (hence BA's public statements of an increase in fares of £10 per departing passenger resulting from the CAA's proposals) could not simply be absorbed by BA when its average per passenger profit before tax over the last five years has been just over £4.70.

12.68. Passengers would therefore face increased charges, both because of the ability of BAA to exploit unregulated monopoly revenue streams under the dual till, and because of the changes to the regulatory regime that the CAA itself was proposing. Using the CAA's own estimates, the abolition of the single till and the move to the proposed long-term price caps would cost users an additional £1.8 billion over the next ten years—more than the amount they would be paying towards the costs of T5 over this period. Such significant charges increases were unjustified and unwarranted and the regulatory settlement needed to pay more attention to the need to keep down the cost of airport facilities to users at a time when charges were likely to rise in any case to fund T5 and other infrastructure developments.

12.69. The view that airlines would not pass on any increase in airport charges to passengers underpinned the CAA's entire approach to its price cap recommendations. The CAA accepted that its proposals would lead to significantly higher charges to airlines, and that higher prices would damage the airlines' interests. Clearly it was against airline interests to pay more for infrastructure than necessary. But it was also against passenger interests because either all airlines would put up prices, or if they could not because the market remained weak, they were likely to withdraw from marginally profitable routes leading to a loss of services and a loss of competition. The CAA's proposals therefore involved a transfer of income from users whom regulation was intended to protect to the monopoly airports.

The setting of fares and effect of higher airport charges

12.70. BA provided us with further evidence on the setting of fares and how this would be affected by airport charges. It told us that marginal cost per passenger was an important element in pricing decisions, both when the initial tariffs were set, and in adjusting pricing as seats were sold in the weeks and months before each flight, as airlines pursued marginal passengers who covered their short-run marginal costs. But it could not be the only consideration: BA aimed to offer value for money fares to a range of consumers, while achieving a return for its shareholders. So although it sought to increase marginal revenues up to the point where they continued to exceed or equal marginal costs, this was against the background of a wide range of demand and supply factors influencing price.

12.71. Frequencies and published fares were set some months before the flights took place—usually when the flight schedules for the following season were agreed and the slot requirements at various airports worldwide were confirmed. At this early stage, decisions had to be based on the best commercial judgements about the expected revenue and cost performance of each individual flight—including the impact of all airport charges—while offering the range of prices necessary to provide widespread access to BA's network of services. Once the schedule of flights had been fixed, pricing had to be flexible to adjust to sales performance. This meant that the price of empty seats, and the availability of flights in different fare categories, may be adjusted as each flight's departure date approached. For most flights, there was adequate leeway in terms of aircraft seat factors to continue this process to the point where the revenue so gained would exceed the short-run marginal costs of carrying an extra passenger. The latter would include any extra passenger charges levied by the airport operator, but not charges related to the number of landings or stands used.

12.72. Because BA operated in competitive markets, prices were strongly influenced by market conditions and competitor activity. In setting a price for a particular flight, BA took into account capacity on the route and the overall quality of its product offering relative to that of our competitors. The factors considered included its schedule and frequency relative to other carriers; relative capacity provision; and the quality of its capacity relative to that of other carriers. While competitors' prices did not by themselves determine BA's prices, BA could not afford to ignore them as significant price differences may in some cases lead to sub-optimal revenue performance. BA may also from time to time make strategic responses to competitors' behaviour. Thus the competition from the no-frills carriers generated a response in the form of BA's recent 'Future Size and Shape' exercise. But an increase in airport charges would still raise fares, simply resulting in the entire tariff being raised.

12.73. An increase in passenger-related airport charges would directly raise the amount paid by passengers, as it was identified as a separate item on the airline ticket. Unless BA chose consciously to cut fares to offset this—which was most unlikely—the absolute increase in charges would therefore be passed through equally to all customers. This would result in a larger proportionate increase for the vast majority of passengers—more than 80 per cent of BA's customers travelled in non-premium cabins—and a smaller increase in premium fares. Airport charges were also a larger proportion of short-haul air fares, which would thus rise proportionately more than long-haul fares.

12.74. An increase in airport charges per aircraft movement would have to be recovered from across all passengers on each flight. Airlines practiced differential pricing between different market segments, and thus there was some flexibility as to how cost recovery was allocated between passengers. But higher costs still needed to be recovered somehow from across the mix of passengers.

12.75. If the additional costs were faced equally by all competitors, then it should be possible to recover the higher costs equally from all passengers, as in the case of an increase in passenger-related charges. But if the cost increase did not affect all competitors, the higher price elasticity of demand among lower-fare passengers might prevent their contributing their full share of additional costs. In this case, fares for less price-sensitive passengers—typically time-sensitive travellers paying premium fares—may have to rise more than proportionately. The pass-through might take longer, as airlines could choose for tactical or administrative reasons whether to pass them on immediately: but this was only a matter of timing.

12.76. The speed with which many airlines passed on recent increases in security costs in fare surcharges demonstrated the difficult financial circumstances facing BA, and the rest of the airline industry. It was therefore almost certain that higher airport charges now would also be passed on immediately.

Effect on investment

12.77. Second, the CAA argued that a dual-till arrangement would provide better incentives for investment and would therefore benefit users through the delivery of improved airport facilities.

12.78. BA argued that in a regulated industry, the incentive to invest was provided by ensuring that the service provider was adequately remunerated for its cost of capital. This happened under a single till as applied in the UK and the CAA accepted this argument was valid both in principle and in practice. However, the CAA also noted that new runway proposals had not been forthcoming under the current regime at Heathrow and Gatwick—despite the pressure of demand on existing facilities. BA shared this concern about runway capacity, but the failure of BAA to advance proposals stemmed largely from the prolonged T5 inquiry and the absence of a clear government framework for airport capacity. The T5 inquiry was now completed and the Government had launched its proposals for consultations on runways in the South-East. The experience of the current quinquennium demonstrated that generous financial incentives provided by prefunding could not be relied on to achieve these results. BA also believed that there were better, more cost-effective and direct ways to address this problem. The fact that Manchester Airport was able to build a second runway also provided evidence that the single till itself does not prevent investment.

12.79. The CAA argued that runway proposals had not been brought forward because all investments were alike to BAA and there were incentives given to BAA to over-invest in short-term retail developments at the expense of aeronautical facilities. BA shared these concerns with the CAA, but it did not understand how the CAA had reached its conclusion that scrapping the single till would be either effective or proportionate. The chosen solution appeared to be nothing more than an experiment justified by economic theory. No precedents were cited. No protection was offered to users if the benefits were not forthcoming and, given BAA's market power, incentives alone could not be relied upon.

12.80. The problem of capacity shortage had more complex causes and included other factors, especially:

(a) the airport system approach which allowed BAA to make investments at any airport according to its own business priorities and not those of their users;

(b) the remuneration of the entire capex programme in advance without any discrimination between projects or any controls or checks that the developments had taken place;

(c) a lack of clarity on the costs and outputs of CIPs and on changes to the plan, which rendered the consultation process inadequate;

(d) the fact that airlines and passengers, but not BAA, bore the costs of congestion or lower service quality and that BAA may even benefit from increased dwell times, increased parking charges, improved opex etc; and

(e) external factors such as the prohibitively lengthy and unwieldy planning system (which the Government was now trying to change).

12.81. Financial mechanisms may have a part to play in ensuring that there were adequate incentives to add new runway capacity, but a wholesale rejection of the single till was not necessary to achieve this. Proposals elsewhere in the CAA's package appeared to deal with these problems much more directly, effectively and at a significantly lower cost to users than a move to an RRCB; if these measures proved to be insufficient, the CAA also had ultimate recourse to its wide-ranging powers under section 69. First, as the CAA was proposing, separate airport tills ensured that BAA was incentivized to provide capacity where excess demand was most in evidence. Second, runway capacity increases could be encouraged directly by providing a financial incentive to expand (peak-hour) runway movements—as indeed the CAA was proposing as an element of its proposals. Third, if a framework were established by which

BAA was encouraged to invest in useful things in consultation with users, and to get the cost of capital, over-incentivization would not be necessary. The dual-till approach was therefore poorly targeted and indirect in the way it related to investment incentives by merely deregulating commercial returns. Hence, BAA believed that the CAA's arguments on the effect of the dual till on investment were flawed, and the cost of moving to a dual till far outweighed any benefits, as also applied to the CAA's arguments for deregulation of commercial activities, which are now considered.

Deregulation of commercial activities

12.82. Third, the CAA argued that a dual till allowed deregulation of commercial activities (especially retail), which should not be regulated. In BA's view, the argument for regulatory disengagement was an even weaker one for moving to the single till. The current regulation was far from onerous, creating an incentive on BAA to do better than expected within each five-year period. By allowing for estimated profitability of the activities in setting charges, however, there was a contribution to the funding of aeronautical activities, that was particularly important with the construction of T5 and, possibly, other infrastructure investment.

12.83. The commercial revenue which airports generated was closely related to its monopoly of airport services and could add significantly to its profit stream. Many of these commercial activities were very closely linked with the running of the airport (for example, car parking, providing facilities for car hire, etc). Under the current arrangements, there was already an incentive for airport operators to drive up charges for these facilities, to generate a short-term profit gain—but the single till provided a backstop whereby these profits were taken into account in the five-year regulatory settlement. A dual till would remove this backstop and expose airlines and their passengers to much greater abuse of monopoly power (for example, the possibility of increases in car park charges). This problem was likely to be most acute where its market power was strongest—at Heathrow.

12.84. The general principle applied to support regulatory disengagement was where the introduction of new competition allowed the regulator to stand back. However, the CAA was not proposing any mechanism to increase competition to curb BAA monopoly power. Nor had it produced any evidence— by reference to affected markets—that adequate competition now justified a change in regulatory approach. By contrast, the evidence suggested there remained a problem of abuse of dominance from the current behaviour of BAA in its setting of unregulated charges. BA therefore believed that a dual till would result in significantly increased charges for airlines and their passengers without generating any noticeable benefit in terms of improved infrastructure delivery.

Practical difficulties in applying the dual till

12.85. In addition to these arguments of principle, BA saw great practical difficulties in applying a dual till.

12.86. This would require an arbitrary and artificial division of what was quite an integrated operation. The CAA had found it was impossible in practice to separate capex, space and management overheads of strictly aeronautical and commercial operations at a single airport in any fair and sustainable way. A choice would have to be made between an arbitrary division (that gave plenty of scope for abuse) or a huge amount of regulatory involvement. Therefore, any attempt to reduce the scope of the core monopoly would create serious problems and distortions. Use of space occupied was artificial (allocation of costs and revenues of the Heathrow T3 South Wing being put forward as one example: there was concern that the bulk of the costs but few of the revenues would be allocated to aeronautical, and conversely several million pounds of income but only a small share of cost would be allocated to commercial). It would be necessary to consider how a terminal would be constructed without such facilities. BA suggested that costs of particular aeronautical developments were also affected by the other facilities being provided: for example, the costs of the T1 baggage hall had increased significantly when the scheme was adapted to increase the departure lounge above. T5 costs were increased by devoting a whole floor to retail developments, with further costs of escalators etc, and inconvenience to passengers of having to change levels, in order to ensure they passed the retail areas.

12.87. Surface access illustrated the problem with the dual till, serving the airport as an entity and being extremely difficult to divide between commercial and aeronautical people coming to the airport both to travel and to shop. The CAA's proposals did not follow the logic of their own argument. Clearly, under a dual-till arrangement, all surface transport should fall squarely in the commercial till, since they were not part of the core aeronautical monopoly. The fact that particular projects were made planning conditions was irrelevant, especially as the two Heathrow projects concerned were offered by BAA during the inquiry. The assumption at that time was that the single till would be in operation. Any division of surface access projects between tills would also create uncertainty and complexity.

12.88. If the single till were abolished, all surface transport would have to be included within the commercial till. If subsidy were needed, BAA could use the proceeds of its short-term parking revenues for this purpose (because shopping centres did not charge for parking). However, BA did not support such a move and believed that the single-till arrangement avoided the surface transport problem.

12.89. Other serious allocation problems arise. For example, the capex programme would be based on certain assumptions about the split between commercial and aeronautical projects (or splits within a project). However, there was nothing to stop BAA from justifying higher airport charges on the basis of a programme that was subsequently changed significantly. Tracking actual spend was already very difficult. Other splits (for example, revenue and opex) did not appear to have been finalized and it was difficult for BA to comment on the details. In any case, BAA might resist full disclosure of information to airlines on grounds of commercial confidentiality, and this would make it difficult even to know whether or not BA was being overcharged.

Long-term price path

12.90. BA did not, therefore, see any justification for moving away from the single till. However, the CAA proposals went beyond a dual till and argued that it was desirable to set a long-term price path at Heathrow and Gatwick. At Heathrow, this took the form of a guaranteed return over 20 years of £18 per passenger in excess of a threshold of over 60 million. At Gatwick, the price path took the form of a guaranteed return on existing capital plans.

12.91. BA did not see these price paths as sustainable or credible regulatory commitments. The T5 prefunding problem had highlighted the difficulty created by changes in the circumstances that underpinned price commitments going beyond the current five-year period. A five-year period provided some reasonable stability for airports and airlines over the medium term but, by extending that, many of the assumptions that underpinned the formula could be invalidated.

12.92. BA did see the need for stability in the framework for airport charges, to provide airport operators with reassurance that long-term investments would be properly remunerated. It saw this re-assurance being provided by continuing with the approach to airport regulation that had served it reasonably well so far in the UK—five-year reviews, with a price cap being set to remunerate reasonable operating and capital costs. It believed that staying with this framework should provide more reassurance than a move to an untried and untested long-term commitment.

12.93. Other aspects of the long-term price path that were of concern to BA were:

(a) the assumption that a long-term price commitment generated extra risk to the airport operator, hence justifying a higher cost of capital. If credible, such a long-term commitment should help to reduce risk;

(b) inadequate support for the £18 per incremental passenger formula underpinning the Heathrow price path, and the wide range of estimates that had been produced for this;

(c) the failure to provide for efficiency improvements in the long-term price caps and the absence of any mechanism for reviewing this issue at future quinquennial reviews if excessive monopoly profits resulted from the proposed regulatory settlement;

(d) the proposed prices were excessively high and also took no account of the scope for operating efficiency improvements or the possibility of radical change in technology that could sig-nificantly lower airport costs;

(e) the trigger mechanisms were too loose and not sufficiently weighted towards completion (for example, too much depending on T5 opening and not enough on completion or linking T5 to other terminals), and geared solely to passenger transfers rather than, for example, quality. Runway incentives were too generous, but BA agreed with the structure;

(f) the methodology was not robust and the framework was unsustainable, given the uncertainty and volatility in the industry and the fact that the outcome of the government review of airport policy was unknown; and

(g) any commitment by the regulator to these price caps was contrary to the express provisions of the Airports Act (section 40) under which pricing must be reviewed every five years (or six if extended). Therefore there could be no firm commitment from the regulator beyond this period.

12.94. BA therefore believed that the focus in setting airport charges in Q4 should be on the conditions in Q4 alone. It did recognize that it was helpful to give the airport operator and users some clear signals about the charges that were likely to apply in Q5 as T5 infrastructure came on stream, especially as prices were likely to rise significantly. However, any such statements needed to make explicit any conditions (for example, about service quality and T5 being fully opened) and other factors that would be taken into account in return for any such assurances.

12.95. The T5 prefunding problems in the current quinquennium highlighted the problems that arose with arrangements that attempt to deal with future quinquennia. However, if the terms of a strategic compact could be agreed in a way that commanded broad user support and be endorsed by the regulator, it offered a possible way of allowing a longer-term view to be taken, which BA would welcome. It was difficult to envisage such a commitment extending beyond ten years given the uncertainty about future market and industry conditions. However, BA would be very willing to discuss this as an alternative to the PPC so as to provide longer-term stability for investment.

Terminal 5 and prefunding

12.96. The background to this review was the experience of airlines at the London area airports over the last five years. A key disappointment for BA and other Heathrow airlines over this period was the delay in the construction of T5. This undermined two key elements that formed the basis of the last regulatory settlement. Capex had been considerably lower than anticipated—some £914 million (and some £558 million for the south-east airports as whole)—and the revenue advancement—which resulted in a price cap of RPI–3 per cent instead of RPI–8 per cent was not required. Investment on retail projects or on projects at other airports such as Stansted did not provide compensating value to the users that paid for this.

12.97. At the end of the financial year 2000/2001, there were 13.7 million additional passengers above the level expected by the MMC in 1996 and they had generated £169 million in airport charges above the levels expected by the MMC. This revenue was therefore available to fund projects unforeseen at the last review. By allowing for the fact that monies scheduled to T5 were diverted to provide for these extra passengers, some of the T5 prefunding had, in BA's view, already been disallowed. Although BA was prepared to allow for the fact that money had been spent on other things, disallowing a further 50 per cent, as the CAA proposed, on the grounds that this represented capital efficiencies by BAA therefore went too far. BA did not accept BAA's argument that its overall rates of return were no higher than expected, since this was specific additional revenue relating to a specific project.

12.98. The understanding of the MMC, BA and other airlines at the time of the previous settlement was that significant delay to T5 would result in a reopening of the price cap and, indeed, BAA had given the MMC and the CAA informal undertakings to support this. BA had formally raised the possibility of an interim review in late 1999: but the suggestion that the basis on which the formula was set was invalidated by the delay to T5, and BAA should be adjusting its charges accordingly, had been raised earlier in the year in discussion of the April 1999 changes in charges. The failure of BAA to request a mid-term review in the last quinquennium was therefore a clear breach of the assurances provided by BAA during the last regulatory review and constituted a course of conduct contrary to the public interest. In the light of this, the appropriate remedy was to credit the prefunding of T5 (both through revenue advancement and charges levied to cover capital spending which did not take place) in full to Heathrow users in Q4.

12.99. In addition, the CC needed to safeguard against these problems recurring in the future. BA believed that this was best achieved by avoiding revenue advancement mechanisms altogether. In addition, it believed that it was in the public interest that consultation mechanisms on capex were improved both at the time of the regulatory review and between regulatory reviews so that projects, along with statements of their costs and outputs, were clearly specified, changes to capital plans were made transparent and airline approval was sought when major changes are being proposed. There should also be a mechanism whereby disputes over the deferment or cancellation of capex could be remitted by BAA or any user or group of users to the CAA to facilitate a resolution. (BA's proposals are expanded upon in the context of other public interest issues below.)

12.100. One way to strengthen investment incentives was not to inflate the asset base or remunerate assets in the course of construction but to remunerate assets only as and when benefits flowed to users. This had been rejected in the past because it increased regulatory risk and cost of capital and therefore the ultimate costs to users. However, the credibility of prefunding mechanisms had been seriously undermined by the absence of firm arrangements to protect user interests in the event that payment was made in advance for investments that did not take place. The experience of Q3 showed that it was difficult in practice to deal with prefunding problems at the end of a quinquennium, even when the regulatory decision made it perfectly clear that this would happen.

12.101. However, despite the problems that had arisen in Q3, BA would support a continuation of the policy of remunerating AICC in Q4 if the following action was taken to protect the interests of airlines:

(a) the full amount of prefunding (£500 million) was credited as revenue in Q4;

(b) separate price caps were set at each airport to prevent capex justified at one airport being spent at another;

(c) the single till was retained, so that there was little long-term gain to BAA from shifting its investment programme towards commercial projects at the expense of aeronautical ones after the price caps had been set;

(d) a binding undertaking was given by BAA—or a condition imposed by the regulator—that any shortfall in capex in Q4 that could not be justified by efficiency gains would not be remunerated again in Q5; and

(e) a clear definition of the Phase 1/Day 1 opening facilities of T5 was made part of the Q4 regulatory settlement.

Service quality

12.102. BA's views on service quality are partly set out in Chapter 6 on Quality of Service. More detail is given below. BA agreed with the CAA that there was a strong case for addressing quality of service explicitly as part of the regulatory framework, believing there should be a much better linkage between prices, service quality and also the benefits of the capex plan. Many dimensions of service quality were under the direct control of BAA—at least to the extent that any company was in control of the quality of service provided.

12.103. However, the CAA had adopted a very cautious approach which was unlikely to make very much difference in the forthcoming Quinquennium. The CAA said that they 'do not propose to introduce … high powered incentives immediately, but recognise that there may be considerable merit in moving towards this objective gradually.' Given that the CAA was proposing radical changes in some areas, BA was disappointed to see such timidity on their proposals in an area of great importance to airlines and passengers.

12.104. Hence, while welcoming the CAA's willingness to act, BA believed that the CAA proposals were inadequate to address the problem—there was a degree of 'tokenism' in the proposals that would give an impression of going forward, but to little effect. Clearly they had powers to introduce a more meaningful service quality term in the price cap. They also had powers to impose conditions in the

Licence ('Permission to Levy Charges'), which could be used to deal with some dimensions of quality, whereas a quality term in the price cap would prove unsatisfactory.

12.105. Among the problems BA saw in the CAA's proposed Q term, the CAA's basket approach to quality, which would apply to Q_A and Q_P, suffered from the drawback of averaging. Even a severe shortfall in one important area would have little effect on the price, because each dimension of quality was averaged across time (rather than concentrating on peak periods), and because the basket itself had the effect of averaging performance across all measures of quality. In normal commercial arrangements, compensation was provided for specific failures.

12.106. The second problem, which applied to the Q_A, Q_P and Q_D terms (see also Chapter 6), was that the CAA had limited the aggregated price cap terms (airline, passenger and delay) to a maximum of 3 per cent of aeronautical revenue. Therefore, even when there was a consistent long-term quality failing over one or more quality measure, BAA would find it financially advantageous to allow the service shortfalls to continue rather than making the investments necessary to meet the standards. A related problem was the lack of immediacy between performance and the financial consequences that flowed from it, by when the managers responsible may have changed.

Possible delay term

12:107. BA strongly supported the use of a stand-alone delay term for which the diluting effect of the basket did not apply. However, BA found it difficult to understand the CAA's proposal to limit the effect of this term to approximately 1 per cent of aeronautical revenue, while accepting that this, in the CAA's words, 'was nowhere near commensurate with its importance and impact on users' (see paragraph 11.77 of CAA Recommendations). Airlines and NATS were already legally accountable to their customers for delay and it was essential that BAA, which was responsible for what were expected to be two of the most congested pieces of aviation infrastructure in 38 European Civil Aviation Conference (ECAC) countries by 2005, was held accountable for its delays in a meaningful way during Q4.[1] A bigger delay term should also provide incentives for BAA to complete T5 as quickly as possible.

12.108. BA did not accept that the measurement of the delay term needed to be watertight, and it was important that an asymmetrical delay term was in place at Heathrow and Gatwick at the start of the quinquennium.

12.109. The Eurocontrol Performance Review Commission had also done a great deal of work to calculate the costs of delay if further evidence was needed. In the Year 2000, the latest published analysis, 8 per cent of all air transport departure delays were caused directly by airports. A further 23 per cent of delays were caused by ATFM delays which were broken down into en-route delays (the responsibility of air traffic management) and airport delays, which accounted for 23 per cent of the ATFM delays or 5 per cent of delays overall. Thus airport delays accounted for 13 per cent of direct delays. In addition to the direct delays, many delays were reactionary, ie the snowballing effect of a delay causing later delays because the incoming aircraft or crew was not available when it was needed. This accounted for 39 per cent of all delays. If this was apportioned in equal quantities to the direct delays, it could be assumed that airport delays accounted for a further 8 per cent of delays.

12.110. Therefore airports around Europe accounted for some 21 per cent of all air transport delays. However, delays were not evenly spread and several congested hot spots accounted for much of the problem. Looking only at the ATFM element, Eurocontrol found that seven airports generated 59 per cent of airport ATFM delays. Heathrow was in fourth place. This was likely to get considerably worse in Q4 before T5 opened. In the UK, airport delays at Heathrow in particular were likely to account for well over 20 per cent of all air transport delays.

12.111. The ECAC and Eurocontrol PRC reports both provided clear and independent evidence that a significant problem existed. Furthermore, delay was the most important measure of service quality in terms of costs for both airlines and passengers alike, as shown by BA's estimate of the financial costs of congestion referred to above. Eurocontrol have also commissioned independent evidence on the costs of

---

[1] Source: *Constraints to Growth*—ECAC March 2001.

delay from the Institut du Transport Aerien. Their research concluded that the costs of each minute of primary delay to airlines alone was €40–66.

The CAA's proposed Q_P term

12.112. BA was not opposed to the proposals for Q_P, although it did not believe they were likely to have much effect for the reasons given above. Any shortfall in the quality of service offered to passengers would affect airlines because many passengers expected their airline to take responsibility for the entire journey. However, it strongly supported the CAA's suggestion that BAA's QSM should be subject to independent audit to ensure that this provided a more objective measure of passenger service quality. Passenger perception was more difficult to measure than those aspects of performance relevant to airlines, but particular criticisms of the QSM included:

(a) The study was conducted by BAA themselves who benefited, so any conclusions drawn from the questionnaires were open to challenge. QSM should be owned and conducted by an impartial group that had no incentives attached to the results.

(b) Second, the QSM neither fully represented nor adequately captured the interviewee's opinions (which consequently implied bias). Different passenger segments may have different needs, hence the QSM methodology should ensure representative samples from each segment, but instead it relied on a random sample of passengers invited by the interviewer to participate. This would tend to exclude some segments such as delayed passengers, non-English-speaking passengers, and regular business passengers (for example, if likely to spend less time in departure lounges), and therefore introduce a bias into the results. The location and circumstances of the survey might also cause passengers to answer quickly, without giving adequate consideration, resulting in a tendency to give broadly favourable answers. In addition, passengers might be unable to answer accurately as several activities might have occurred since any incident and the interviewee might not fully remember what happened or distinguish between the different elements of the airport experience, nor understand the distinction between the responsibilities of the airport and the airline. The survey was also suspended during times of operational disruption, and measurement of passenger opinion during these unfavourable circumstances was excluded. Finally, having used a five-point scale, many people might have felt reluctant to choose either extreme, or prefered a neutral response (the error of central tendency). Hence bias was inherent in the results. The QSM surveys also did not measure the departure experience of passengers as the final method of reaching and boarding the aircraft could not be measured.

(c) They were designed for internal monitoring and decision-making, and hence were not appropriate for use as a tool to measure quality for presentation in a public forum.

The proposed Q_A term

12.113. Service quality terms should not be symmetrical and BA was pleased that the CAA had changed its view in relation to this. However, it believed the same logic applied to any price cap term, especially QD. Higher levels of service did not automatically create benefits to airlines if they had not been agreed in advance. Plans and schedules were set in advance, with contingency arrangements, on the basis of expected levels of performance. Therefore, symmetrical terms, which rewarded BAA in retrospect simply provided BAA with a means of increasing income, which may be unwarranted in terms of the benefits provided to users, and reduce the effectiveness of performance incentives by giving BAA the means to offset. BA believed that top-up quality measures needed to be the subject of contracts with users in advance. This problem would be especially acute if the CAA set low par values to begin with.

12.114. BA agreed with the CAA that there was no case for weakening service quality measures that depended on variations in traffic levels. It also agreed that the use of a dead band was unnecessary and a complication.

12.115. In BA's view, therefore, the proposed financial incentives were not direct and immediate enough, nor of a sufficient magnitude to align airport interests with the legitimate concerns of users. BA therefore concluded that an alternative approach would be better suited to the purpose, which is given in the context of its views on public interest issues below.

Unregulated charges

12.116. BA's experience was that BAA had used its position as monopoly supplier of various ancillary activities by making charges outside the price cap which were not cost reflective, sometimes arbitrary and often excessive. Currently, the single-till arrangement provided some safeguard for airlines and passengers by ensuring that these revenues were taken into account in the next price settlement and BA believed it was essential that the single till was retained for this purpose. BA believed that a number of additional elements ought to be brought within the scope of regulated charges to safeguard against excessive charging in future—notably air traffic and navigation control (ie ANS charges) and transfer baggage. It also proposed a regulatory formula for Gatwick rents in line with the arrangements in place at Heathrow. In addition, better mechanisms had to be found for appropriate scrutiny of the setting of unregulated charges to reduce the exposure of airport users to unwarranted price increases in the future. These points are expanded on in the section on public interest below.

BA proposals for BAA airport charges in Q4

12.117. BA supported a price cap for the next five years based on the following principles:

(a) retention of the single till, broadly as currently defined;

(b) T5 prefunding during Q3 to be used in full with interest to reduce Heathrow charges and offset increases due to T5 construction costs;

(c) remuneration of the BAA asset base (including AICC but to be tracked and credited towards revenue in the next quinquennium if the expenditure did not take place) at a reasonable cost of capital, which BA estimated at 6.6 per cent (pre-tax) in real terms. The basis of this estimate (which BA believed very similar to the 6.7 per cent in Q3 which MMC had previously suggested would be appropriate on the assumption of RPI–3 in Q3) is given in Table 12.1;

(d) separate airport tills;

(e) a quality term in the price cap (but different to the CAA's proposal) including a delay term;

(f) incentive for early delivery of T5 stands;

(g) full user consultation over the proposed capital programme;

(h) inclusion of excess rents at Gatwick and Heathrow as income in Q4 as recommended in paragraph 2.86 of the MMC report last time—over-recoveries were calculated as £57 million to date in the CAA's August 2001 report (see Table 2.3); and

(i) no revenue advancement into Q4 from Q5.

TABLE 12.1 **BA proposed WACC for BAA**

	LHR & LGW
Real risk-free rate	2.75
Equity risk premium	3.5
Equity beta (number)	0.75
Cost of equity (post-tax)	5.38
Taxation adjustment	30.0
Cost of equity (pre-tax)	7.69
Gearing	25.0
Debt premium	0.5
Cost of debt	3.25
Pre-tax WACC:	
Calculated figure	6.6

Source: BA.

12.118. BA broadly accepted the demand projections made by the CAA, but was concerned that the passenger number projections, even on the CAA's figures, appeared to drift a little below the BAA's own stated capacity limits. It expected underlying demand for air travel from Heathrow to rise steadily and to exceed the CAA forecasts in every year except 2003/04 (continuing after T5 opened): while capacity in the past had often turned out higher than declared capacity limits.

12.119. BA based its estimates on the capex figures provided by the CAA. It believed these may be slightly overstated in the near-term due to the size of the contingency being allocated to Phase 1 of T5. Although its involvement in the T5 baggage system was very good—and capital costs had reduced—BA had little influence on design and construction of other aspects of the project. BA had stated at the CAA hearings (held in January 2002, prior to the CC references) that costs of T5 were broadly acceptable at this stage of the design process but it fully expected them to come down as a result of incentivization and better procurement: it would expect £2.6 billion to translate into a target cost of £2.2 or £2.3 billion, a number which would be acceptable given the size and complexity of the terminal and the constraints of the site. This clearly did not imply that it regarded the increase in the cost estimates since the 2000 CIP as reasonable. A contingency of 20 per cent on £3 billion was high for a project that was only six months away from the start of construction. In practice, there would usually be a small contingency for those elements about to be built, and a much higher percentage for Phase 2 elements, but as an average, 20 per cent was high when the majority of the spend was in Phase 1. The baggage system in Phase 1 of the project was now being funded by BAA, not BA, but the airport operator would be reimbursed by BA or a third party once the system was fully operational. There was a short-term cash flow impact, but little long-term effect on the capital cost of T5. As very little of the capital cost would be met out of regulated charges, it did not appear appropriate to include it in the asset base during construction.

12.120. Within the current capex plan, BA also believed BAA should be committed to build and operate, by the time T5 opened, a passenger transit system and baggage transfer system between T5 and the CTA—specifically the terminal from which the balance of BA's services would operate. BAA's current concept and proposals for inter-terminal connectivity (with only buses linking the terminals) were flawed and unacceptable, being subject to unacceptable road delays and congestion and offering only a 75-minute minimum connection time, rather than the 60 minutes in BAA's planning standards (on which basis BA had been planning). The amounts currently allowed for CTA redevelopment should instead be used for connectivity. BA also suggested trigger points for price adjustments linked to the delivery of the capex programme, including opening of T5 early release stands in 2005/06, and of Phase 1, the baggage connection and passenger transit to CTA in 2008; and timely start of building of T5, and of passenger and baggage transit, and of Phase 2 of T5 the year after Heathrow demand reached 70 mppa. For Gatwick for Q4 it suggested timely start and opening of Pier 6, and start of building a mid-field satellite the year after demand reached 36 mppa.

12.121. BA did not, however, believe that the scale of the capex programme was sufficient to require higher airport charges: over the ten years 2003/04 to 2012/13, BAA's capex per passenger was lower in real terms than the equivalent plans set out at the last review over the ten-year period 1997/98 to 2006/07. Hence, if BAA believed charges had to rise, this was because it had not controlled costs or generated sufficient commercial income despite the commercial developments undertaken. (Square metre of retail space per passenger was also expected to double in T5 compared to T4.) BA was also concerned that there was almost £250 million of expenditure on projects relating to baggage handling, for which users could be charged twice—both through airport charges and through check-in desk rentals.

12.122. These points highlighted the need for full consultation with users over the capex plan. In the absence of such consultation and a reflection of its outcome in the costings being used by BAA, any regulatory settlement would be flawed. BA believed that:

(a) BAA's airport-by-airport capital programme needed to be agreed at the regulatory review, including major projects and deliverables;

(b) BAA should produce an improved annual review of capex in the autumn;

(c) subsequently, agreed changes should be incorporated through the annual capex review; and

(d) the annual capex review should also be an input to the annual charges round, with any disagreements referred to the regulator.

12.123. It was clear from the CAA's report that the CAA had not carried out a full independent scrutiny of projections of opex and commercial revenues either. This was most disappointing. BA's own financial modelling had been conducted on the basis that productivity improvements allowed BAA operating costs to fall by around 1.5 per cent a year in real terms and that commercial revenues per passenger grew at 2 per cent a year in real terms.

12.124. Under the above assumptions, however, BA estimated that the appropriate price caps for Heathrow and Gatwick, to give a pre-tax WACC of 6.6 per cent at each airport separately, were RPI–4.4 per cent at Heathrow and RPI–6 per cent at Gatwick.

12.125. BA recognized that Heathrow charges would need to rise in Q5 as the benefit of T5 prefunding came to an end and the full costs of T5 began to be reflected in the price formula. Stability in the regulatory framework for remunerating airport investment—which underpinned BA's proposals—should provide BAA and its investors with confidence that its investment would be remunerated over the lifetime of the project. BA believed that BAA should have no difficulty raising finance on that basis given the profits it had made, and it had had no difficulty raising finance in the past. There was no parallel with the difficulty of raising charges in Hong Kong when a new airport came on stream: opening additional facilities at Heathrow where there was strong demand for it was very different to trying to move to a very large new airport.

Public interest issues

Under-investment

12.126. We have referred above to BA's argument that BAA's failure to request a mid-term review following the delay to T5 was against the public interest. BA believed that cumulative capital under-expenditure at Heathrow, referred to above, was explicable only in part by delays in work on T5. It was unaware of any acceleration of other projects at Heathrow, but there had been delays or deferrals of a number of different planned projects. The following were among the examples.

12.127. BA complained about delays to the Iceberg project in T1, the completion date for which had been delayed from April 2001 to at least November 2003. This project would have helped to compensate for the T5 delay by providing additional long-haul capacity in T1. BAA had also unilaterally imposed scope reductions on the project (reducing baggage systems and cancelling the Europier extension) that impacted on baggage handling capacity and performance and pier service: these were examples of BAA's very poor track record in keeping to agreement. Performance on this project was symptomatic of consistently poor overall management of capital projects; it required the airline to underwrite the airport's development costs without providing any enforceable commitment in return, refusing to enter into binding agreement, preferring instead to provide non-binding heads of agreement.

12.128. BAA had also laid down unreasonable funding terms for that project, despite the huge underspend of capital at Heathrow and BA pressing for the project to provide alleviation of congestion whilst T5 was under construction. BAA had initially required compensation for loss of retail revenue in T4 when Iceberg was completed; and BAA sought to negotiate a further 'rescue contribution' when the project fell short of BAA's target return of 15 per cent, although all capital was funded through infra-structure charges. Since final project costs were remunerated by airlines, it left airlines to bear all price, performance and construction risk, but with no opportunity to directly manage or mitigate these risks. A further example of BAA's seeking to eliminate investment risk, or offset it to the airlines had been shown by its reluctance to invest in that T4 baggage structure, asserting that T4 would become a 'stranded asset'. BA said that such 'unreasonable funding terms' were not unique: BAA often broke projects down into component parts, and requested a contribution to some of them.

12.129. BAA had stopped the building of Pier 6 at Gatwick after 11 September 2001, despite this being the highest priority project of the airlines to continue, and pier service having been below the agreed planning standard for more than ten years. That project had an estimated cost of £70 million.

12.130. BAA had also failed to provide airbridge service to Heathrow Metro stands, initially intended to come online by July 2003, to redress imbalance in pier service between T3 (95 per cent) and T4 (85 per cent and declining). This deadline was unlikely to be met, BAA regarding this project as of low priority.

12.131. Delays to many of the above projects resulted from a reduction in BAA's investment programme after 11 September. BA believed that reduction in the investment programme, which occurred with very little consultation, and where passenger throughput was still above the level forecast at the last review, was against the public interest. Work was suspended before the review process announced by BAA was completed: BAA did not give users sufficient information to enable them to form a balanced view or understand how its proposals would impact airline development plans: BAA's response to the situation failed to take a longer-term view on capex requirement; and savings to BAA were not passed on to users.

12.132. BA also argued that the capex programme at Gatwick had been undelivered by £190 million in Q3 but through further analysis and meetings with BAA determined that the cause for such a large discrepancy was that BAA were quoting the original forecast of planned expenditure from the last review at 1996 prices and then quoting the out-turn expenditure at 2002 prices. They then quoted the difference between the two as indicating how much extra was spent at Gatwick. This created the impression of significantly higher than forecast spend at Gatwick but was not a comparison of two like figures. If the original amount of expenditure as forecast for Q3 had also been uprated to 2002 prices the level of underspend would be closer to the CAA's £90 million figure. BA also said that users were unable to track the expenditure BAA had claimed to have undertaken in that period, although recently BAA had offered to provide more detail on the spend between the capex plans of 2000 and 2002—this was something the users welcomed but had not yet received. BA believed that for all BAA's airports the capex programme should be executed as planned and agreed between the airports, the regulator and the users; any alternative should be subject to full consultation and agreement with users, and users should be rebated through airport charges for any capex underspend.

Absence of transparency and consultation on capex

12.133. BA said that the CAA recognized that there had been insufficient transparency and consultation over capex and the development process generally. The CAA had noted various failings:

(a) the ten-year CIP contained insufficient information to be an effective consultation tool. In particular, it had insufficient quantitative information addressing costs and outputs of different development options both at a macro (airport) and micro (individual project) level;

(b) much of the practical consultation was at local operational level, and did not consider project costs in detail; and

(c) in relation to Heathrow in particular, the CAA recommendation noted that 'it was some time since users have had the opportunity to comment on a full capital expenditure plan, and that BAA's current projections have not been the subject of full consultation'.

12.134. BA believed that this was a matter of particular concern since the capex plan was an essential input as part of the process leading to the setting of charges for Q4.

12.135. Particular and long-standing concerns about the inadequacies of the CIP, for BA and other airlines (as expressed at the LACC), had arisen from BAA's failure to provide quantitative information on development options, or a master plan for Heathrow or Gatwick airports over a number of years. At Heathrow this had:

(a) prevented users from considering and commenting on the longer-term vision for Heathrow, and left consideration of individual projects without the necessary context. This failed the test of transparency and proper consultation when a multi-billion-pound investment programme was at stake. It was not possible at present to get an overview of how individual projects were contributing in a balanced way to the development of Heathrow's infrastructure, or to have a proper debate about long-term options;

(b) failed to provide the integration of T5 with the other Heathrow terminals by producing timely evaluation of options for passengers, staff and baggage to transfer or travel efficiently between terminals (referred to also above). Work was only presented to airlines in February 2002, with a request airlines commit themselves to the preferred solution within weeks. There had also been

failure to consult on Heathrow runway development, BAA inviting the Inspector to rule out another Heathrow runway; and

(c) led to piecemeal development that was likely to be wasteful and would make future comprehensive development more costly and disruptive at Heathrow, as it had done at Gatwick.

12.136. At Gatwick, BA said that BAA had no master plan or development strategy until 2001. Gatwick was unprepared for the rapid growth in operations that it experienced in the second half of the 1990s. Piecemeal development had taken place on the western apron. This led to:

(a) initial BAA Gatwick development proposals to meet growth and to bring the standard of service up to the planning standards being driven by a desire of BAA to build piecemeal—with a series of remote satellites to be accessed by crossing live taxiways with passengers and baggage vehicles;

(b) protracted debate (eventually successful) on a development strategy that was acceptable—but that should have taken place in the early 1990s, to be ready for the development as required; and

(c) continuing failure to provide sufficient pier served stands—to provide a level of service agreed with the airlines more than ten years ago. Even now it would take the next quinquennium to reach the standard, following BAA's suspension of the first major capital project (Pier 6) to add pier-served stands.

12.137. In current circumstances, with the Government about to consult on future options for runway development across the UK, and especially in the South-East, BA said it was vital that BAA consulted fully and in a timely way with its users, the airlines, as the decisions would have decisive implications for their future. On the contrary, BAA had invited the T5 Inquiry Inspector to recommend to the Government that it should rule out another Heathrow runway 'once and for all': discussion with users was only invited after the announcement.

12.138. Absence of consultation and transparency over capex and development planning by BAA represented a course of conduct on its part which was against the public interest. It was fundamental to the effective operation of the regulatory regime, and the CAA recognized that it could only justify a light-handed approach to reviewing capital investment in circumstances where there was effective consultation with users. Failings in this regard accordingly operated against the public interest.

12.139. We referred in paragraph 12.132 to BA's view that there should be agreement on the capex plan at this and future regulatory reviews. BA proposed that there should be a condition imposed on BAA that would:

(a) require BAA to consult periodically with users on a development/capex plan for the South-East generally and for each airport concerned;

(b) enable the CAA to specify the information to be included in such a plan for consultation; and

(c) require the CAA at the request of BAA or any user or group of users to participate in any consultation forum.

12.140. We refer in Chapter 14 to the exchange of letters between BAA and the CAA on enhanced information disclosure. BA believed that no airline was involved in agreeing the content of the CAA's proposal, but welcomed a number of useful aspects of it. However, there still needed to be a commitment on BAA to produce a 30-year master plan once the SERAS decisions were announced. BA also believed that BAA should be required to forecast demand and capacity for ATMs, as well as passengers. References in capex plans to regulated and non-regulated tills should also be removed.

12.141. It was also essential that the capital plan for Q4 defined explicitly and unambiguously the Phase 1/Day 1 opening facilities of T5. BA had set out its understanding of the minimum requirement that should be fully functioning on that day (see Appendix 12.1). There could be no room left for doubt on these essential features, or the way would be left open for thrifting of the project to save capex and reduce Phase 1/Day 1 capacity or standards. This schedule of facilities should be put to BAA by the CC to secure its agreement and the adoption of the schedule should be a key condition of any charges settlement for Q4, which would begin to remunerate the capital investment for T5. Similarly, any future uplift in charges linked to the opening of T5 should meet the same conditions.

Service standards

12.142. We have noted above that BA did not regard the CAA's proposed Q term as sufficient. BA believed that there were many cases where service quality had been compromised by the behaviour of BAA. This should be partly remedied by linking the future price formula to the achievement of satisfactory planning standards, and by giving greater regulatory force to the obligations on BAA to maintain service quality through the licence.

12.143. BA said that the current regime failed properly to define the facilities and services that were covered by airport charges paid by users, or to specify the service standards to be delivered by BAA in respect of those facilities and services.

12.144. At the last quinquennial review, the MMC recognized that the absence of quality standards was a deficiency inherent in the regulatory regime, and that the adoption of formally agreed service standards was necessary to ensure no future deterioration of service. Believing SLAs between airlines and BAA to be the best way forward, the MMC had urged that these should be introduced in short order so as to be widely applicable. It also stated that the extent to which service standards were established, agreed and met should be taken into account in the next quinquennial review.

12.145. Despite the MMC's aspirations, users were still not given a clear and detailed statement of the services covered by airport charges, nor were they able to exert any influence over BAA to meet the minimum standards that airlines reasonably required in the provision of those services.

12.146. In the event, SLAs had not provided the solution to the problem. They had not been implemented to cover all key aspects of service provision. They had not been negotiated generally for the benefit of all airlines. In so far as concerned BA, it had only been able to negotiate some SLAs at Heathrow, but none at Gatwick. With those it had been able to negotiate, BA had faced the fundamental problem of being unable to use the mechanism of SLAs to identify and quantify the basic level of service to which it was entitled in return for regulated charges.

12.147. BA was therefore disappointed in the rate of progress achieved by SLAs, both in implementation and in improvement resulting from them. Where service standards had been agreed, BAA had consistently failed to meet them. Standards tended to be presentational rather than effective. This was to be ascribed to the lack of enforceability of SLAs, the lack of compensation in SLAs, other than relating to jetties (where it had been insufficient to make BAA stick to standards), and to the failure of SLAs to cover all key aspects of service provisions—for example, runway and taxiway availability, navigation services and terminal 'fabric' (for example, cleanliness and condition)—or any at Gatwick, or to meet standards set. QSMs were not a satisfactory alternative for reasons described above. One proof of this is that they had been established for many years but had failed to deliver the necessary service quality standards.

12.148. Incentivized SLAs had proved more successful in extracting improved levels of service and facilities. SLAs for baggage handling at Heathrow had been successful in improving services—but these were jointly managed. Service credit payments should take the form of asymmetric compensation and/or rebate payments to have sufficient bite to persuade BAA to meet the standards. Because of BAA's insistence on bonus payments, only less effective, best endeavours SLAs had been introduced for services provided to all airlines: airlines were unwilling to enter into arrangements whereby they may end up paying more to BAA for a level of service they did not want.

12.149. Many SLAs were flawed, for example not taking into account maintenance time and long-term outages, and use of manual measurements for security queuing, which may miss peak flows. Existing SLAs covering air-bridge availability and security queuing had little credibility with the front line operational areas, because of their design, measurement and exclusions. On the former, BA said that it had proved very difficult to adjust the measurements to include data on timing of dockings integrated with data on serviceability of equipment, and the trial ended in agreement to continue to use the existing jetty service ability measure.

12.150. On security, BA said that there was a target under the relevant SLA that no passenger should queue for more than ten minutes (but no compensation for failure to meet it). The target was too low—it should be no more than four minutes as laid down in BAA's planning standards—and it was poorly monitored by BAA itself, which had consistently failed to meet it. At Heathrow, carriers had to resort to funding separate Fast Track search facilities to meet expectations of premium passengers, and relieve congestion in the standard facility: they were effectively being charged twice, and with no apparent account taken of advertising revenue received in the Fast Track area—there was inadequate transparency in relation to the make up of charges to confirm this.

12.151. SLAs therefore fell short of being focused, clear, simple, easily measured, well reported and used as the springboard for action to correct poor performance: the goal of SLAs. Moreover, SLAs were only bilateral—there were no generic standards.

12.152. BA therefore proposed an adverse finding on failure to adopt and publicize the basic level of generic service standards covered by charges, or negotiate SLAs to cover all key aspects of services covered by charges. It said that there were many cases where (see below) service quality had been compromised by the behaviour of BAA. Its incentivization under the current framework was to limit the quality of services covered by regulated charges and sacrifice service quality in pursuit of commercial activities; this should be remedied by linking part of the future price control formula to achievement of satisfactory planning standards, and giving greater regulatory force to obligations on BAA to maintain service quality through the licence.

12.153. Among specific complaints about quality of service, airbridges on Victor 19 and 21 stands at T4 were unserviceable from 21 and 23 December respectively to 14 January. This level of service failure resulted in significant, additional, and avoidable costs to airlines, including costs of passenger dissatisfaction, and was completely unacceptable. The level of airbridge rebate given was far short of compensating for these costs (less than 40 per cent of the equipment and associated manpower costs alone); a similar situation occurred when the Victor pier was closed for structural repair. Hence, BAA engaged in a course of conduct in breaking its own service standard, offering inadequate levels of compensation which did not reflect costs to the airlines: this was also evidence that SLAs did not provide BAA with sufficient incentive to provide services to an agreed minimum standard.

12.154. BA told us that 69 stands had also been removed from service for five days at a time, causing significant operational disruption and inconvenience to passengers and cost to airlines (£62,000 estimated cost by one airline), to be painted with the HSBC logo as part of a £30 million advertising agreement. There was no compensation for this disruption. This also showed there was nothing to disincentivize BAA from sacrificing quality of service in pursuit of its own profit maximization objectives.

12.155. BA suggested way-finding was still worse in T1 than in T4—and told us that signage to one gate (Gate 24) had not kept in line with the horizontal segregation of the relevant pier, and the gate was now almost impossible to find.

12.156. Among other examples, users including BA suffered significant operational disruption as a result of BAA's implementation of a lucrative advertising deal with HSBC. Similarly, BAA's refusal to allow BA to provide a Fly-Through check-in facility unless it was compensated for dilution of its car parking income illustrated BAA's insistence on its own commercial activities over services that provide real benefits to passengers. Similarly, when BAA built the First Class check-in facilities in T4 for BA it could have, as requested by BA, provided a separate direct First Class route to the BA CIP lounge, but instead required passengers to be routed in such a way as to ensure they passed BAA's retail facilities.

12.157. BAA had exploited the lack of clarity in relation to the scope and quality of services covered by regulated charges to require airlines to pay separate charges for certain services or facilities which should rightfully be covered by regulated charges.

12.158. Examples were search facilities (where BAA had not invested sufficient revenue from regulated charges, forcing airlines to pay for additional services in order to relieve congestion), and BAA's recent notification of its unilateral decision to begin charging for waste management services which had hitherto been covered by regulated charges.

12.159. BAA had retained for itself extra revenue resulting from higher than forecast passenger numbers, rather than stepping up its capex plan to meet the greater demand for capacity. Since capex plans proposed by BAA were sufficient only to meet the needs of forecast passenger numbers, rather than actual numbers, investment in facilities was insufficient to satisfy user demands; infrastructure was therefore consistently inadequate to cope with levels of growth. As a result, users were faced with congestion costs and the costs of meeting demand in a constrained environment.

12.160. FEGP did not meet reasonable service quality standards; and there had been frequent outages causing considerable disruption and cost requiring ground power units (GPUs) and aircraft auxiliary power units (APUs) to be bought and maintained and used to make up for deficiencies in FEGP supply. This was a result of insufficient planning and investment by BAA. Where GPUs or APUs had to be used by airlines to remedy FEGP deficiencies, airlines were then also subject to noise related fines. Charges were based on blocks of 15 minutes, even when not connected to the system (for example, aircraft could still be taxiing or being towed). Metered charging would reduce costs, and would be more equitable. There should be no levy allowed to fund improvements. These facilities were paid for in user charges and should be reliably supplied.

12.161. BAA's planning standards should play an important role in ensuring that service quality was not compromised and should be given greater weight in assessing the performance of BAA. BAA had described its planning standards as 'the BAA contract with user airlines and the MMC' but the standards were not enforceable by users, nor was BAA incentivized to meet them. BAA had taken advantage of the absence of meaningful, enforceable standards to pursue commercial revenues and objectives at the expense of its provision of services and facilities to users.

12.162. An example of the above was the provision of airbridge services. BAA's Planning Standards included a target of pier service for 90 to 95 per cent of passengers, but BAA had not built an adequate number of jetty-served stands to meet this standard, nor was there any obligation on BAA to do so. For example:

(a) BA's SLA for T4 contained a target of 98 per cent jetty availability, which BAA consistently failed to meet by a significant margin. While BAA's Conditions of Use provided for a rebate to be paid to users where no jetty was available, this rebate did not adequately reflect the cost to users of service failure, nor was its impact on BAA sufficient to persuade it to invest to meet the target.

(b) Gatwick pier service recently averaged 78 per cent departures and 84 per cent arrivals, despite which, construction of Pier 6 had been delayed.

(c) In T4 in October 2002, BA was forced to accept 334 off-pier movements. Long-haul operations achieved only 78 per cent on-pier movements. Short-haul operations achieved only 60 per cent. These levels of failure by BAA constitute a serious degradation of the service quality that airlines and their passengers are entitled to receive.

12.163. For minimum connection times (MCTs), there was a planning standard of 60 minutes, which was a key aspect of performance. Heathrow had historically failed to meet that standard, with inter-terminal MCTs of 75 five minutes or more, and was still working on a 75-minute MCT between T5 and the CTA: to meet the planning standard would require a TTS which BAA was not prepared to invest in. In planning facilities, BAA was therefore seeking to lower its own standards.

12.164. BA said that BAA's failure to invest in facilities and projects to meet its own planning standards was a course of conduct that operated against the public interest. BAA should be required to produce an annual report for each terminal, detailing the extent of compliance with its planning standards, and should be financially incentivized through penalties for failures to meet them.

12.165. Additionally, the Conditions of Use document currently contained unreasonable disclaimers that destroyed normal, reasonable, accountability for services provided. In particular, BAA limited its liability to direct losses in those cases when it could be demonstrated that BAA did so 'with intent to cause damage, or recklessly, and with knowledge that damage would probably result'. In effect, that placed a prohibitively high barrier to any airline seeking a remedy—these should be withdrawn in the public interest. BAA should be liable for negligence, not just deliberate damage etc: the failure of main power supply was one instance in which airlines were unable to seek damages for negligence (of BAA's contractors).

12.166. In summary, therefore, BA argued that:

(a) users had no effective means of ensuring that BAA provided an adequate quality of service in return for airport charges; as a result, BAA's standard of service provision was lower than would otherwise be the case, which was clearly contrary to the reasonable interests of users;

(b) BAA had been incentivized by the current framework to limit the quality of services covered by regulated charges and to maximize revenues from other services—this imposed inequitable and unjustifiable additional costs on airlines and passengers;

(c) users had no means of determining whether they were in fact being charged twice (through regulated charges and through separate charges) for the same services and facilities; and

(d) BAA's retention of windfall revenues in lieu of capex had prejudiced investment in new facilities in time to satisfy demand, increasing congestion and driving down service quality.

12.167. Of particular concern was BAA's ability, absent penalties for failure to meet service standards, to sacrifice service quality to the pursuit of its commercial activities. It should be noted that the examples given above had occurred notwithstanding that the revenues generated by commercial activities went into the single till. If the single till was abandoned, then this issue raised even greater concern.

12.168. As a consequence of the continuing deficiency in the regime, BAA had been able to pursue courses of conduct, which BA considered operated against the public interest:

(a) BAA had failed to adopt and publicize the basic level of services covered by its airport charges.

(b) BAA had failed to negotiate with BA and others a series of SLAs covering all key aspects of the services covered by charges.

The resulting detriment to the public interest was identified by the MMC in its last report (see paragraph 2.39).

12.169. Since voluntary service standards had been shown not to deliver agreed levels of service or an adequate system of financial penalties for poor performance, a more radical approach was therefore required if service standards are to be given sufficient weight.

12.170. The remedy sought by BA would involve the following measures:

(a) a clear definition of the services covered by the regulated charges, so that there was no doubt as to users' entitlement;

(b) in place of the QA price cap term proposed by the CAA, explicit generic levels of service should be imposed on BAA through a public interest condition in the 'Permission to Levy Charges' under section 37 of the Airports Act. These standards would represent part of the description of the product that airlines were entitled to receive in return for the payment of airport charges (including charges for specified activities). These standards or par values had now been broadly agreed between airlines, and had been submitted in a separate document;

(c) these service standards should be established not only for activities covered by regulated airport charges, but also for other relevant activities in respect of which a de facto monopoly was enjoyed by BAA;

(d) they should include a delay term in the price cap, as proposed by the CAA, but without an upper limit, which would ensure that BAA put in place measures and investments to deal with the effects of higher than expected growth if necessary. This was perfectly equitable, because additional passenger revenues would be available to BAA;

(e) failure against any of these quality levels, not just the aggregate, should entitle users to a rebate and/or realistic compensation, which should be paid automatically by BAA. Where possible, pre-fixed rebates should be used to avoid lengthy disputes. The remote stand rebate (found in BAA's

Conditions of Use document) was a suitable model, albeit currently fixed at a wholly inadequate level; this provided for a rebate to flow automatically to airlines where an aircraft was not afforded pier service and had proved simple to administer and non-contentious. Great care would need to be taken, however, to ensure that rebates and/or recompense for inadequate performance were set at an appropriate level, ie a level that was at least fully compensatory, but preferably higher, in order to sharpen the incentive to BAA to meet standards;

(f) where an individual user wished to receive a service level above the generic level, this could be dealt with by way of bilateral top-up contracts between that user and BAA. The costs and value of such deals would be much clearer than at present, since the basic entitlement would have been spelt out;

(g) the CAA should establish a dispute resolution procedure (separate from, and less onerous than, the section 41 procedure), for resolving disputes relating to service standards within a reasonable time frame;

(h) there also should be in future a rebate should BAA fail to invest in proper infrastructure to meet a 60-minute MCT to/from T5, in the minimum range of £25 million to £50 million; and

(i) unreasonable disclaimers in Condition of Use should be withdrawn.

12.171. The above would, however, be part of a wider framework. While the price cap mechanism did not have the immediacy to address the shorter-term operational service quality outputs covered above, it was appropriate to the incentivization of terminal capacity provision, using the metrics already in place in Planning Standards. Regular audit against the standards could produce an accumulating penalty, which could be used to adjust a subsequent price cap, either through an interim process, or within the next quinquenniel review. For the longer term, it was essential to assure airlines that investment would be developed in a timely manner, by remunerating projects only on a 'pay-for-what-you-get' basis.

12.172. For the shorter-term operational service quality outputs, BA proposed generic standards of 100 per cent availability/ serviceability (consistent with the principle of rebating and/or compensating for denied service and to make the administration simple and practicable of runways) in respect of cancelled or delayed departure flights or diverted arrival flights, taxiways, stands, piers, airbridges, departure baggage system, people movers, arrivals reclaim, and FEGP; and that the security queues should not exceed four minutes on all occasions. It proposed a delay term based on minutes awaiting predeparture clearance; number of minutes flights take-off outside their slot window; minutes of stack delay; and minutes of slot delay attributed to the airport. (More detailed proposals relating to a delay term were also provided.) BA was more or less in agreement with the CAA's proposals, but not in the matter of the level of limitation of penalties.

12.173. Such a framework of measures would help to align the interests of BAA with airlines and passengers. They would also help to guide BAA's investment decisions without the need for detailed regulatory involvement by moving towards a more commercial approach.

Pricing of non-regulated charges

12.174. BA said that there existed a category of specified activities in respect of which the BAA was the de facto monopoly supplier to users: these included check-in desks, other desk licenses, staff car parking, staff ID cards, FEGP, hydrant refuelling, airside parking, airside licenses, cable routing, maintenance, heating and utility services and facilities for bus and coach operators.

12.175. The propensity of BAA to engage in a course of conduct contrary to the public interest in respect of charges and other terms of supply of these specified facilities had previously been recognized. Hitherto, attempts had been made to address these concerns in two ways. First, following the first quin-quennial review by the MMC, a transparency condition was introduced by the CAA. Where charges were not established in relation to cost, BAA was required to provide users with a statement of principles on the basis of which charges had been set, with full background information as to the calculation of such charges, including statements of any comparables used. Second, some very limited measures of protection may also have been available insofar as projected revenues from supply of these services were

384

taken into account under single-till charge control. But even that admittedly weak constraint disappeared if dual-till charging was introduced.

12.176. BA said that a pattern was observable in relation to charging for specified facilities, which showed that these charges were neither directly cost-reflective nor transparent. There was a lack of supporting information that would enable verification of apportionment of police costs, administrative overheads, maintenance costs of specified activities; and a lack of transparency in maintenance rents and service charges. BA believed that BAA had loaded in high overhead costs and opportunity costs on those services covered by the specified services condition: BAA did not present the information concerning the basis for charges in sufficient detail or with sufficient explanation to demonstrate that, for example, allocated costs were justified. Users were unable to satisfy themselves they were not being charged twice for services and management time, under allocated costs, which should already be funded from other sources. Hence, it was believed the charges were excessive and not related to costs. Charges outside the price cap that were not cost-reflective were against the public interest.

12.177. Hence, charges appeared to be non-cost-reflective, sometimes arbitrary and often excessive. Examples were as follows.

12.178. HAL charged £1.86 and GAL £1.90 per cubic metre for clean water and sewerage: where BA was able to purchase directly, it paid £1.00 from Three Valleys/Thames Water; £1.19 from East Sutton & Surrey/Thames Water. BAA ascribed the difference to infrastructure and allocated costs; BA believed the mark up was excessive and inflated by inclusion of allocated costs. Lack of transparency meant it was not possible to ascertain whether the capital charge was on assets included in the overall asset base of the airport in which BAA earned a return. Similar arguments applied to electricity where the actual electricity costs accounted for only just half of total costs to users, and rates charged by HAL and GAL were much more expensive than BA paid for its contract electricity. Recent price increases for BAA had been attributed to increases in infrastructure costs: recently, charges to users had increased by 4.4 per cent, whereas HAL had indicated it had achieved a supply saving of 6 per cent. (A consultation document had been described as 'purely explanatory'.) There was no transparent understanding, therefore, of BAA's overheads allocated costs or capex charges.

12.179. On staff car parking, no separate tariff or reduction was available for part-time or job share staff. There was a very large allocated cost—for example, £1 million for constabulary. There was also a recent 10 per cent increase in cost of Rover passes, without consultation, and an example of imposition of excessive charges without justification.

12.180. Fuel fees to BAA were substantial. Rental fees were established with no involvement of discussion with airlines. GAL had refused to provide a detailed cost justification of the rental fee—users believed GAL incurred almost zero ongoing costs. BAA was abusing its monopoly by levying fees that are not cost justified.

12.181. At Heathrow, other desks were priced on a similar basis to check-in desks but without a baggage hall fee; a similar arrangement had been sought at Gatwick but GAL had refused, asserting it made a market charge for the facilities. This was set by GAL without clear justification and was excessive: it should be based on cost (as once agreed by BAA) including amortization costs until fully amortized. GAL's charges were significantly higher than HAL's. BAA's course of conduct was against the public interest in that BAA was failing to satisfy its obligations under transparency conditions and was abusing its dominant positions in setting charges at the level it does.

12.182. There had been a 50 per cent increase in waste disposal charges. Refuse disposal was one of the items listed in Appendix 3.2 of the last MMC report as covered by airport charges, hence to the extent that waste management services were required in connection with the landing parking or taking-off of aircraft, these should be paid for through airport charges. As was the case with other services and facilities stated to be paid for through airport charges, however, users had no firm commitment as to the scope of services included within refuse disposal. BAA had stated it did not believe it had any obligation to provide a waste management service, but elected to provide a controlled waste contract which excluded special and clinical waste. Airport waste notices were often subject to unilateral change by BAA without consultation, which could exclude from the coverage of airport charges services and facilities previously included, without compensation to users. This policy was a clear attempt by BAA to push responsibility to deal with waste other than general mainstream waste onto contractors and airlines.

12.183. Recent recabling in Gatwick's North Terminal had resulted in the request for payment of £0.25 million a year in cable wayleave charges: cabling was necessary to carry on the business and there should be no charge over and above the rental paid. The charge was levied on cables in airlines' own trays and tubes as well as GAL's: the airline should be able to install cable trays and tubes and lay cables within them without paying a wayleave fee. There should also be no charge if cable was placed in GAL's cable trays, since they were part of terminal infrastructure, remunerated under airport or passenger charges. This was another example of BAA exploiting its position in relation to specified activities and lack of transparency for the basis of charges.

12.184. There was thus a course of conduct which consisted in the charging for specified activities (in respect of which BAA was the de facto monopoly supplier) otherwise than at cost. That practice produced results that operated against the public interest (as was found in 1991). The previously imposed transparency condition had proved inadequate as a remedy. Further, there had been no incentive to reduce costs on supply of these services.

12.185. The condition sought by BA by means of remedy would contain provisions that:

(a) required BAA to adopt cost-reflective pricing for all specified facilities;

(b) required (or at least encouraged) benchmarking of prices to provide an inducement to efficiency;

(c) established principles for cost allocation to the provision of specified facilities;

(d) required the BAA or its auditors to report to the CAA periodically on the operation of the condition, thereby reducing the need in the CAA directly to police its operation on a day-to-day basis; and

(e) provided a dispute resolution mechanism, in the form of a provision for the CAA to determine disputes over charges for specified facilities. Recourse would otherwise need to be made to section 41 of the Airports Act: this was too heavy-handed to be effective for the resolution of disputes between parties who for the most part needed to continue to cooperate with each other.

Rents at Gatwick

12.186. Following the last MMC review, BAA introduced a formula for the future setting of rental levels at Heathrow for certain guideline properties. Although not the result of a public interest finding, this formula was effectively approved by the MMC when it was proposed by BAA during the course of the last enquiry as a response to airline complaints concerning the level of, and increases in, rents at Heathrow. The formula was based on four equally weighted indices: the RPI, passenger growth, construction prices and changes in off-airport rents. BA considered that, on the whole, the formula at Heathrow had allowed airlines to achieve considerably better value for money and cost certainty than was the case before its introduction.

12.187. No similar formula was introduced at Gatwick, where flexible rental guidelines were unilaterally established by BAA. BAA then sought to conduct individual negotiations against its own established guidelines. Rent Guide prices had been introduced at Gatwick—but spot figures rather than a band, requiring negotiation for non-standard property. The guide prices had brought certainty—but annual review of rents by GAL was an abuse of its monopoly position. There was no explanation as to how GAL had reviewed its rental guidelines between 1 April 1997 and 1 April 2001. Increased rents had been selectively applied: in particular, operations in North Terminal had been penalized (offices in the North Terminal had a rent of £36 per square foot compared to between £32 and £34.50 in South Terminal; rents of pier accommodation of £20 to £21 per square foot in North Terminal compared with £19 to £21 in South Terminal). GAL rents had increased by between 7 and 67 per cent from 1995 to 2001. GAL argued that supply and demand were factors in it setting the rent, but by curtailing supply at a time of an increase in demand, GAL could obtain a higher price purely because of the increased demand. Under the Property Challenge, however, GAL was committed to providing an adequate supply to meet demand.

12.188. BAA's rental policy under the current arrangements at Gatwick had operated against the public interest in that:

(a) BAA had been selective in increasing rents, without justifying its actions: rents had not increased evenly across all types of accommodation and rents for certain accommodation in North Terminal had increased faster than in South Terminal (unfairly penalizing airlines operating out of North Terminal);

(b) while rents at Heathrow were rebased on the introduction of rent guide prices, no similar bench-marking exercise had been undertaken at Gatwick (again, certain airlines, including BA, have been unfairly penalized as a result); and

(c) it was not clear why BAA should award itself an increase in rents purely on the basis that it had met Property Challenge objectives that BAA itself had set.

12.189. The remedy sought by BA was the adoption at Gatwick of a similar formula to the one in place at Heathrow, in conjunction with a rebasing of rents. This should be imposed by way of a condition should BAA not agree to introduce it voluntarily.

12.190. BA also noted that, at the last review, the MMC remained concerned about BAA's ability to exploit its position by increasing rents in the future by more than the amount assumed in setting airport charges to the detriment of user airlines as a whole. The MMC recommended (see paragraph 2.86):

> If rental income rises above that assumed in the setting of airport charges for Q3, the regulator should consider recovery through the airport charges formula for Q4, unless this was due to BAA providing more accommodation than was currently planned. ... Monitoring by the CAA of rents and total rental income would, however, we think, assist the CAA... in the context of the next quinquennial review.

12.191. BA drew the CC's attention in that connection to the figures for BAA's actual rental income compared to MMC forecasts, set out in Appendix 9 to the August 2001 *Performance Report of BAA London Airports* (and, in particular, the 52.8 per cent variance for Gatwick for 2000/01).

Coverage of regulated charges

12.192. Subject to agreement on the inclusion of the T1–T4 tunnel, BA supported the rolling in of the TIFGAH asset base into the regulated cost base. This was to ensure consistency with the treatment of other operationally critical capex (in BAA's capex programme) from planning, consultative and incentivization perspectives. The transfer connectivity required for the T5 development and CTA expansion was of too great a magnitude to be dealt with by the current TIFGAH process and should rightly sit with the LACC (or its successors under its proposed consultation framework). Transfer infrastructure was integral to the operation of the airport and its ability to meet planning standards for MCTs and its planning and funding should be addressed in exactly the same way as all other generic airport capex projects. To do otherwise sent inconsistent signals to the regulated entity and may lead to gaming. The CAA were also minded to include TIFGAH assets into the RAB.

12.193. When NATS was privatized, DETR allowed services covered by terminal navigation charges (TNC, sometimes referred to as ANS) to pass into NSL, NATS unregulated business, as the Government believed TNC was a competitive market. In reality, TNC at the London airports was a de facto monopoly as it took two years to train a Heathrow tower controller and the likelihood of controllers in situ transferring to the alternative service provider was remote. NATS contracted with BAA to provide an approach and ground movement control service at the London airports but it was the airlines that paid for this service.

12.194. As this was a key operational service without which the airports could not operate and given that it was a de facto monopoly service which BAA contracted NATS to provide, there was a prima facie case for it to be included with the airports' regulated cost base and remunerated by the users through the landing charge. The precedent for this within the regulated airports regime already existed at Manchester, where the TNC was part of the RAB and charged through the landing fee. Transparency/cost-relatedness would be lost but given that transparency at London had not resulted in the users having any significantly greater involvement or control over the development of the charge (which was proposed to increase by 18 per cent in 2002), BA believed that the protection offered by economic regulation was preferable to the existing regime.

Aircraft parking charges

12.195. Within airport charges, BA also criticized airport parking charges which were based on block times with charges commencing a set number of minutes after aircraft touchdown to allow for average taxiing times to the terminals. However, the taxiing times varied within the airport and discriminated against users of T4 as often parking charges were levied on aircraft, which were in fact still taxiing to the terminal.

bmi british midland

12.196. bmi told us that it was greatly concerned over a number of the CAA recommendations, particularly as it felt that the CAA proposed regulatory regime would virtually double airport fees at Heathrow over the next ten years, with additional profits accruing to the BAA at the expense of the airlines. It was bmi's view that the CAA's proposals were fundamentally flawed and were not in the interests of the airlines or in the interests of passengers, who would suffer both in terms of price and choice of services.

12.197. bmi said that the CAA had focused its review on the regulatory framework and consequently there had been little opportunity for airlines to comment on the performance by BAA during the current quinquennium. It was bmi's opinion that performance issues should have formed a more integral part of the overall review, as price should be directly linked to the delivery of facilities and services to users.

12.198. bmi maintained that the single till represented a business partnership with trade-offs on both sides. It did not accept that the aeronautical and non-aeronautical aspects of an airport could be reasonably disengaged, as airlines had funded the development of the airport to date on the basis of a single till, and the airport business continued to be intrinsically linked. It therefore seemed to bmi, totally unreasonable to now split the assets, on what could only be a subjective basis, and effectively 'give' the non-aeronautical assets to the non-aeronautical till: it did not believe there was any proper way to disentangle the assets to provide a dual till. bmi argued that the current facilities far exceeded airlines' requirements, and similarly that the proposed T5 development was far more extensive and expensive than airlines required. Had the current facilities been subject to a dual-till regime, then airlines would never have agreed to fund the excessive scale of commercial terminal developments and would have strongly objected to the imposition of retail areas, especially where they adversely affected airline operations and passengers: without such facilities, space for airline operators, such as check-in areas, could be much expanded, and the efficiency of their operations improved. bmi said that it was solely because of the single till that airlines had accepted the trade-off of congestion and inconvenience versus cost. If retail areas were now removed from existing terminals, substantial additional terminal capacity would be created, alleviating current constraints, which would certainly reduce, and possibly negate, the need for further developments for many years.

12.199. The CAA had not provided supporting evidence to show that the single till had failed, except for citing that a new runway had not been built at Heathrow or Gatwick. The single till had, however, allowed BAA to make exceptional returns. The CAA had concluded that the single till was not the best basis for meeting its statutory objective of imposing minimum restrictions: but the CAA had taken a very limited interpretation of this objective and this should not be used as a reason for abolishing the single till.

12.200. bmi did not believe airport charges should be used to promote more efficient utilization of capacity: costs of operating at Heathrow were already so high that it had no incentive to be uneconomic with use of slots, but was focussed on maximizing their profitability. Unlike some airports, operations by smaller aircraft were already discouraged. Similarly, BAA had invested and was proposing to invest extensively under the single till: therefore there was sufficient incentive to do so under the single till.

12.201. Airport charges formed a significant part of bmi's cost base and consequently impacted the viability of routes and the airlines' business. The CAA's indicative pricing, using the PPC, resulted in a 81 per cent increase in charges over ten years. With competition from other airports, higher ticket prices were unlikely, and the increase in costs would have to be borne by airlines. This scale of increase would not be economically sustainable for base airlines and other operators, who would be forced to move away from Heathrow.

12.202. Based on the CAA statement that the proposed increase in charges arises mainly from the provision of T5, and the capital costs proposed in the BAA CIP, bmi believed that the scale of costs proposed for T5 indicated that the design was not economic for airlines. The costs needed to be supported by a good business case. BAA had not discussed any details, aside from connectivity, with the airline community, but they should be reviewed before commitments are made, since all airlines would be affected by the increased charges consequent on T5. Costings were based on specifications only agreed between BA and BAA—and had risen substantially. However, bmi also believed the CTA should be brought up to T5 standards before T5 opened to prevent competitive disadvantage (without which differential fees should apply). Only outline proposals for redevelopment of the CTA had yet been discussed: it was also unacceptable that the majority of such investments would be after the opening of T5, resulting in fundamental competitive discrimination between T5 and CTA carriers. Preliminary discussions were only just underway on T1–T5 connectivity which could result in loss of facilities, but bmi believed that the estimated costs of baggage tunnels and track transit connectivity to T5 far outweighed the benefits.

12.203. The regulatory regime proposed effectively meant airlines would continue to prefund T5 until it opened (at which point a premium would also become payable). bmi opposed the concept of prefunding, and there was no guarantee that future regulatory regimes would continue the PPC policy, or that monies would in effect be repaid over the longer term.

12.204. bmi also believed there should be separate price caps for the three airports, and saw no reason why they should be jointly owned: under separate ownership, each airport would be more concerned where airlines based their business and to attract new business. Runway development at any airport should be subject to the business case at that airport.

12.205. As to the S factor, bmi would be happy with abolishing it, and including the current security level and costs in the pricing formula. However, if significant new directives were introduced, bmi would consider accepting an additional fee, subject to thorough review of the project and costs by the CAA. There needed, however, to be more than a 5 per cent incentive borne by BAA: bmi suggested a 75:25 per cent split.

- *The setting of fares and effect of higher airport charges*

12.206. bmi also provided us with further evidence on the setting of fares and effect of higher airport charges.

12.207. bmi told us its business operated with a high level and value of fixed cost, and all fares needed to contribute. Specifically, marginal costs were taken into account when setting the lowest fares for each route to ensure that at least those costs are covered. Passenger-related airport fees at Heathrow generally accounted for more than half the value of marginal costs for a Heathrow sector.

12.208. Fares were always determined bearing in mind the prevailing competitive situation and state of the market, as bmi operated in a highly competitive environment and customers were extremely price sensitive.

12.209. An increase in passenger-related airport charges at Heathrow would have a significant impact on bmi. Consequently, bmi would find it extremely difficult to absorb cost increases at Heathrow due to its low margins and the scale of operation that would be affected. Clearly, bmi would seek to pass any increases onto the passenger through higher fares. Heathrow was strategically important to other UK routes, and it was important that services were retained and despite competition from operators at Luton and Stansted, and train, road and ferry services. Heathrow would otherwise lose its hub status. As Heathrow operators would be forced to increase prices, this would severely impact its passengers who would suffer both in terms of price and level of choice of services.

12.210. An increase in cost per movement would have the same impact as an increase in cost per passenger. Whilst some promotional fares were based on the marginal costs of carrying an additional passenger, and therefore not necessarily directly affected by an increase in cost per movement, clearly the overall cost of operation would be impacted, and fare levels would have to be increased, as airline margins were insufficient to absorb any substantial increases.

Service quality

12.211. bmi fully supported the inclusion of standards and targets with financial penalties for delays or non-compliance. However, the proposals only reflected part of BAA's deliverables, and the level of penalty was not sufficiently challenging—at most £0.33 per departing passenger. Normal commercial practice dictated that one paid for the agreed services and facilities received, and if quality was below standard or the facilities and service not delivered, appropriate compensation was provided. The customer would not expect to pay additional sums when targets were exceeded. It was also only reasonable that price should be linked to delivery of the capital programme, in full and on time, and to the provision of agreed facilities and services.

12.212. bmi told us that its only involvement in SLAs with BAA had been in relation to direct baggage, and discussions that had only recently started on transfer baggage.

12.213. It believed the following service standards should be implemented:

(a) airbridge availability—99.5 per cent of all airbridges to be available during airport operating hours 365 days a year; fault response time to be five minutes and 99 per cent of fixes to be within 30 minutes; planned maintenance to be agreed in advance with airlines/handlers and done during planned stand closures where possible; no more than one in ten jetties to be out of service for any reason at any time;

(b) stand availability—99 per cent of stands to be in service during any 24-hour period; the only exception to be major construction works and with airline/handler prior agreement; maintenance of all stand facilities, ie lines, cleaning to agreed standard; fault response for service (FEGP) 15 minutes and 99 per cent of return to service within one hour; 100 per cent of pier stands to have FEGP; no more than one in ten stands to be scheduled out of service at any time. Planned maintenance to be carried out outside operational hours;

(c) runway and taxiway availability—24-hour availability (emergency closures exempt). Two arrivals or departures and one crosswind runway. Maintenance 23.00 to 0.500 with one runway/alternative taxiways available;

(d) security search area—no queue dwell times to exceed four minutes in any 15-minute period at any time; facility to be available at all times during airport operational hours; all planned maintenance to be done outside operating hours;

(e) out of gauge—no queue dwell times to exceed four minutes in any 15-minute period at any time; facility to be available at all times during airport operational hours; all planned maintenance to be done outside operating hours;

(f) passenger travelators/escalators/lifts—99.5 per cent availability during airport operating hours; fault response time to be 15 minutes (unless people trapped in lift, in which case immediate) and 95 per cent of repairs to be completed in 30 minutes; planned maintenance to be carried out outside operational hours; no more than one in ten of each to be out of service for any reason at any time;

(g) baggage handling systems—system availability 99.5 per cent of airport operational hours; all faults to be responded to within five minutes and 99 per cent of repairs to be completed within 15 minutes; all planned maintenance to be done outside operational hours unless by prior agreement;

(h) HBS equipment—all HBS equipment to be available 99.5 per cent of operational hours; all faults to be responded to within five minutes and 99 per cent of repairs to be completed within 15 minutes; all planned maintenance to be outside operational hours; and

(i) heat, light and power—all areas of terminal buildings and facilities where either customers or staff are present to be maintained at temperatures within HSE guidelines, ie 16°C or 13°C minimum (the lower for industrial working environments) and 25°C maximum. All faults to be responded to within 15 minutes and 95 per cent of repairs within one hour. Any major planned outages of services to be agreed prior to works.

12.214. In bmi's view, the Q factor complicated matters by arbitrary weighting, which was not necessary. It was probably more appropriate for a value to be assigned directly to each item for levels of failure, be it for each 1 per cent short of target or bands of percentage shortfall. The value applied to target shortfalls might vary by item. A further review by airlines of items, targets and values of penalty was required to progress an appropriate generic scheme with the BAA. Clear, simplistic measures were essential to avoid subjectivity and administration, and therefore it might be that targets were measured monthly, but penalties applied by an annual adjustment to the revenue cap based on the preceding monthly results. The calculations should be transparent and automatic, as part of the regulatory structure. It was not appropriate to allow a bonus, should the BAA exceed a target. In line with normal commercial practice, standards were required for an agreed amount payable, with penalties for non-compliance.

12.215. A delay term should be incorporated—not only slot, taxi pushback and stack delay type measures, but other critical processes such as security queues, baggage belt failure, departure gate not available, broken flight information monitors at gate, or stand not available.

12.216. bmi paid little heed to BAA's QSM reports, the data being collected and measured by BAA, excluding situations of disruption and poor performance, and excluding planned maintenance, hence was generally unreliable. However, bmi had no objection to key perceived passenger interests being included, failure to achieve acceptable standards being penalized, but with no reward for over-achievement.

Public interest issues

12.217. bmi referred to undertakings given by BAA to request a mid-term review if there was significant delay to T5. Although the subsequent CAA conditions did not explicitly cover substantial delay, it believed that BAA had not operated within the spirit intended and had abused this goodwill of airlines: it should have reverted to RPI–8 or triggered a review when it became clear that T5 would be substantially delayed. There was, however, an asymmetry in arrangements for any mid-term review, which could only be sought by BAA, and BAA had subsequently not agreed to such a review. The airlines felt this undermined any similar provision for the future. bmi believed that the majority of projects undertaken in Q3 by BAA which were not part of the forecast investment programme in 1996 had nothing to do with delays to T5, and should not be viewed as offsetting the underspend on T5. The monies should be refunded by the end of the current quinquennium (Q3).

12.218. bmi referred to inadequate improvements to transfer baggage facilities in T1. BAA's proposed concept of a single baggage system for direct and transfer baggage in T1 was agreed in 1994, but with no mention of the T1–T4 tunnel which, with other problems, meant the new facility (B15 TBF) could not cope with the volume of BA and other carrier bags. Hence, bmi withdrew from the new facility to a building, A9, which contained no automation. BAA still tried to encourage airlines to use B15 TBF but it clearly could not cope without modification. bmi employed consultants to find a suitable location and draft proposed plans for a transfer facility at its own cost; BAA agreed to own the site and plans in early 1998, having earlier promised delivery in April 1998. Phase 1 of B139 was delivered in August 1998, and Phase 2 was originally to open by Spring 2000, to provide a transfer facility comparable with BA, but BAA were still suggesting B15 TBF be used although it did not provide early bag storage, reflight processing, out-of-gauge processing, nor was it cost-effective. BAA were told Phase 2 had to be ready for summer 2000. During summer 1999, bmi's costs were increased by having to relocate a reflight operation to B2, and employ additional contracted staff to guard and process bags there. Significant work only began in late 1999, with final designs agreed in January 2000 (a request was also made by BAA for underwriting some of the initial cost, but refused). Stage 1 was eventually delivered on 11 December 2000 and Stage 2 on 31 May 2001. In that period, performance suffered and costs were unfairly high through the lack of a reasonable facility: cost of mishandled baggage attributable to BAA was over £10 million. Even now, bags had to be processed from two locations, increasing handling costs, but with the opening of Phase 2, missing bag performance and costs had reduced dramatically.

12.219. bmi also complained about the general state of Heathrow T1 quoting lack of air conditioning in Gate 2, 8/12 and Pier 4A, poor quality of build of Pier 4 (including seating capacity, and long walk to the gate), leaking roofs, unsatisfactory provision of disability access facilities (including lack of lift from apron to gate room in gate room 2, although such a facility had been provided for BA in Gate 5).

12.220. bmi also referred to security screening facilities not opening until 0515 to 0530 although its own check-in facilities opened at 0500, causing delays, and late arrival of staff who provided random security checks; and Terminal Services delivery managers only working between 0700 and 1900. Appropriate procedures had also not been implemented for when there was a major baggage belt outage, with no alternative procedures for getting baggage airside, resulting in lengthy delays; the time taken to repair major operational systems, such as PA systems, unserviceable baggage belts at check-in, jetties, monitors etc could be unacceptable—for example, the monitors at Gates 36 and 38 were inoperable for four months. There had been recent short-notice requirement to close a succession of stands on a peak day for 'insurance inspection'.

12.221. bmi criticized encouraging passengers on Dublin and Republic of Ireland services at Heathrow to detour via retail outlets, increasing walking distances to gate by 400 metres and causing some passengers to miss flights. Its figures showed, for a six-month period, 62 flights were delayed as a consequence of passengers who failed to join and confirmed they had been delayed due to shopping. The majority of these delays resulted in passengers being offloaded, causing a total of 12 hours' delay to flights. In addition, bmi staff apply considerable effort in attempting to trace missing passengers and in the removal of bags belonging to offloaded passengers from the relevant baggage containers stacked in the hold of the aircraft prior to departure.

12.222. Some rents were excessive at Heathrow, for example £64 per square foot for CIP lounges—and new building and perimeter area and ground rents were not covered by the guide prices, resulting in high increases in rents for these areas. The rent formula, although an improvement on previous arrangements, did not take into account the worldwide nature of the airline industry and airline profitability.

12.223. bmi also maintained that the T1–T4 baggage tunnel should not be incorporated into airport charges prior to the expiry of the BAA/BA bilateral contract in 2008: this was a bilateral contract, with no consultation with other airlines, which should not now have to pay for it. The economic viability of the tunnel should be reviewed when T5 opened.

12.224. bmi also criticized the CAA's endorsement of peak pricing. Historically, this had had little effect on traffic patterns, as airline operations were primarily influenced by demand. The peak would have to be priced at such a high level to have any influence that operations would probably not be economically viable: hence peak pricing only served to increase revenues.

buzz

12.225. See KLM uk and LFCs.

BWIA West Indies Airways

12.226. BWIA West Indies Airways said that its input had been included in the submission from BAR UK.

Charter Group

12.227. The Charter Group refers to Air 2000, Airtours International, Britannia Airways, JMC Airlines and Monarch Airlines, who elected collectively to make a joint submission to the inquiry. Together, the Charter Group accounts for more than 90 per cent of passengers carried by UK non-scheduled airlines. In terms of passenger kilometres, the Charter Group's share of the UK aviation industry amounts to nearly 35 per cent.

12.228. In making a joint submission, the Charter Group sought to highlight its concern that the CAA's proposals had not given due consideration to the interests of the charter sector of the air transport industry or their passengers. The Charter Group criticized the CAA's proposals as lacking in practical experience, and warned that by pursuing its current proposals, the CAA risked not fulfilling its obligations as charged under the Airports Act (section 39(2)). It was the Charter Group's view that the CAA's apparent inability to engage regulatory problems mid-term and its increasingly laissez faire approach to regulation, threatened the level of protection that users could expect in the situation of monopolistic supply.

12.229. The Charter Group felt that it was unjust that airlines and their clients were forced to continue to prefund Heathrow's T5 project through the current quinquennium even after it had become clear that the project had slipped by a number of years. While the Charter Group accepted that to call for a mid-term review may not have been within the CAA's gift, it was of more concern that it did not appear that the CAA had taken any steps to support the airlines' attempts to seek alleviation from the burden of unwarranted prefunding.

12.230. Similarly, the Charter Group criticized the CAA for continuing to promote the dual till despite virtually the whole of the airline industry remaining in favour of retaining the single till. A move to the RRCB appeared to be fraught with difficulties and would rely on the regulator making a workable allocation of asset values between the commercial and aeronautical tills. The Charter Group doubted that the regulator, given its stated intention for a lighter hand, would provide the level of policing required in order to maintain the appropriate boundaries between the rival demands on infrastructure of the aeronautical and commercial camps. Aeronautical charges paid at Gatwick represented some 8 per cent of direct operating costs (DOCs) of a flight. The Charter Group argued that it was nonsensical to believe that airlines would be able to absorb the costs increases anticipated from the removal of the support of commercial revenues to aeronautical activities. With financial margins being so low in the majority of the airline industry, airlines would be forced to either increase fares or cease operations. If the latter happened, the gaps appearing at airports as low margin services were withdrawn would be filled by those routes which produce a greater margin; as a result the access that large numbers of the public currently enjoyed to a wide range of destinations would be significantly reduced.

12.231. Also doubted was the claim that the proposed changes to the regulatory system would result in investment benefits to the users. The Charter Group had seen no evidence that major infrastructure projects had been delayed as a result of failings with the current single-till regime. Indeed, it was under the single-till regime that Manchester airport had managed to build both an additional terminal and second runway. The Charter Group invited the CC to evaluate whether the CAA had adequately considered the external constraints on investment to meet the demand on capacity, citing the political rather than economic considerations that had delayed T5.

12.232. The Charter Group did not believe that the risk of the CAA reconsidering the regulatory framework would provide sufficient safeguard for users, if airports did not develop desired improvements to service quality and investment. There had been other examples—in particular T5—where the Charter Group had been disappointed in the CAA's approach to such matters.

12.233. It appeared to the Charter Group that the CAA's proposals were an attempt to use price manipulation as a form of demand management, which they viewed as inappropriate as a part of the economic review process. The Charter Group claimed it already operated perhaps more efficiently than any other sector, with relatively high-density aircraft, high load factors and high utilization. At Gatwick, their aircraft were both well above the average size and consistently carried passenger-load factors greater than average (frequently in excess of 90 per cent). Such operation also guaranteed high comercial revenues for BAA. Charter operators would be forced to increase fares, but the charter market was more price sensitive than other areas. Given that price increases would have a disproportionate effect in the charter market sector, the Charter Group strongly challenged the CAA's view that '...increases in permitted airport charges are likely to result in better use of airports with consequent benefits for passengers'. The Charter Group also believed peak pricing did not work given the constraints on airlines' operations, for example slot requirements at other airports: there were also few off-peak periods at Gatwick.

The setting of fares and effect of airport charges

12.234. The Charter Group also provided us with further information on the setting of fares and effect of airport charges. It emphasized that charter airlines did not set fares as such, but offered for sale to tour operators whole aircraft charters or occasionally part of an aircraft on a fully committed basis. Thus, from a charter airline's perspective the load factor risk did not arise as they enjoyed a 100 per cent guarantee on load. Clearly, in vertically integrated groups such as Thomas Cook, of which JMC Airlines was a part, this meant the load factor risk for package holidays (including the air travel) lay elsewhere in the group.

12.235. The direct operating cost of the aircraft, and thus the seat price as a guaranteed fraction of that, was taken into account when the charter price (or transfer price in vertically integrated airlines was concerned) was set. The airline's margin was added to the direct operating cost price per seat which then gave a contribution towards its fixed costs and eventual profit. The price thus arrived at additionally reflected the desirability of the day of the week or time of the charter, the size of the aircraft (risk and economy of scale) and the general competitive market position among other charter airlines.

12.236. Initially, in the first edition of seasonal brochures capacity would not be offered for sale where it was unlikely that either the fully committed cost of the charter flight and the corresponding beds in equivalent hotel(s) would not be filled at the price set. The price would vary around school holidays, including half-terms, and previous historic demand for the destination which may be affected by forecast weather as well as special events. Tour operators would hope to have set their price at the correct level to maximize sales through brochures, as the anticipation was that during the later period prices would fall in order to achieve maximum load factors on aircraft and in hotels. Marginal costs per passenger were a factor during late sales but were likely to be outweighed by a tour operator's commitment to the full price of the seat and possibly the hotel room.

12.237. Given the relatively low margins achieved by charter airlines (2 to 10 per cent) any increase in direct costs, whether marginal or otherwise, would be passed on to the charterer who would in any event be seeking to achieve 100 per cent occupancy of both seats and beds. Given that the charter contract would reflect a 100 per cent occupancy guarantee, any increase for aircraft movements would also be passed through as a direct fraction of aircraft capacity, ie divided by aircraft capacity. Given the 100 per cent occupancy guarantee, there should therefore be no difference in the effect of an increase in per passenger charge or per movement charge assuming the charges were comparable on a 100 per cent basis.

12.238. In the short term (within an operating season) it was difficult for tour operators to pass any increase in airport changes onto their customers as under the Package Travel Directive they were obliged to absorb the first 2 per cent of any increase and in any event they were already selling packages in the late period. In the longer term, increases in airport charges would be passed through to the consumer by being included in a charter airline charter price. There was far less scope in the charter sector for absorbing increases in costs by loading them onto certain categories of passenger.

Separate regulation of the airports

12.239. The Charter Group supported the recommendations that the London airports should be regulated on a stand-alone basis, and that there should be no automatic cost pass-throughs. Had BAA not been behaving from a systemic approach, it may not so easily have conceded the restriction on a second runway at Gatwick: separation of ownership may do more to promote investment than adoption of a dual till. Existing carriers should also not be burdened with in effect financially supporting an airport's marketing schemes.

Quality of service

12.240. The work on quality of service issues should be developed irrespective of whether the single till or dual till were to be applied. Airlines felt exposed under existing Conditions of Use and there was in effect no contractual requirement on the airport to perform consistently at a specified standard. Existing SLAs 'lacked teeth' with no true penalties attached to them and needed to be extended to include runway and taxiway availability, departure baggage, pier service, arrivals baggage and FEGP. There was some scepticism over QSM reports, since the data was recorded by the service provider; particularly if they drove financial calculations, they would need to be verified by a third party.

12.241. The Charter Group thought quality of service at Gatwick fell short of acceptable standards in a number of areas. Planned extensions to the South Terminal to improve service to arriving passengers and to departure lounges had not been delivered; there was a shortage of pier-served stands in the North Terminal, now also adversely affecting operation from the South Terminal; coach transfer times for remote stand operation impacted the ability to depart on time; and segregation was not being implemented in the optimal way (though external influences on this were recognized). Length of security queues at Gatwick also gave rise to public interest concerns. BAA had tended to put a higher priority on commercial development—such as the departure lounge—rather than the piers or baggage system.

12.242. Unusually in the modern world, therefore, there was no exact understanding of what customers' money should obtain for them, nor any mechanism to allow a refund if the customer received poor service: a mechanism should be put in place that would ensure the definition of proper, acceptable genuine standards and financial penalties in the event of failure to provide them. There should be no financial reciprocity against the basic standard: users wished only to receive value for money, not a gold-plated service. For airlines wishing to provide customers with higher than standard service, bilateral agreements should be used, provided it was not to the detriment of the wider community. Opting out to a lower level of service should not be permitted. Use of common areas in terminals should not permit great differences in per unit charges, and such opt-out could well be detrimental to other users paying the generic charges.

12.243. The Charter Group felt the CAA's proposed Q term was too weak, putting too little emphasis on items of greater operational importance: the Charter Group preferred a scheme focussed on rebates for shortfalls in service provision, rather than aggregating a whole range of different services. The 3 per cent maximum effect of the Q term was not severe enough. The Charter Group currently had no detailed view on the delay term, on which work had started later; although further investigation of it was welcomed, the QA element should be handled first. A scheme should also be put in place at Stansted.

12.244. The Charter Group preferred an adverse public interest approach, which would give an important difference in emphasis. On a strict interpretation, the fact that SLAs were not routinely used was operating in a manner adverse to the public interest.

Continental Airlines Inc

12.245. Continental Airlines Inc said that its response was being coordinated through BAR UK.

Delta Airlines

12.246. Delta Airlines' views were similar to those put forward by BAR UK.

Flybe–British European

12.247. Jersey European Airways (UK) Ltd, trading as Flybe–British European (Flybe), told us that it was not aware of any action carried out by Heathrow, Gatwick or Stansted Airports that could be considered to be against the public interest.

12.248. On the issue of the price cap, Flybe indicated that it would like to see any increases kept to a minimum, at or preferably below the rate of inflation. It stated that the previous 6 to 12 months had been very difficult times for most airlines, with passenger levels generally falling. Flybe told us that the best response to this had been to encourage more passengers to travel, by means of lower fares. However, it warned that this course of action would be unsustainable in many circumstances without charges being frozen or reduced.

Go Fly Ltd

12.249. See LFCs.

Helios Airways Ltd

12.250. Helios Airways Ltd (Helios) said that it only operated to Gatwick and did not have first-hand knowledge of all three London Airports, but it fully supported the general comments contained in the

IATA response to the CAA preliminary proposals of November 2001 on the Heathrow, Gatwick, Stansted and Manchester airports.

12.251. On the issue of service standards, Helios agreed with other airlines that QD should be asymmetrical (offering penalties against BAA but no bonus opportunity). However, Helios disagreed with the suggestion to start with a low weighting to the delay term, and capping BAA's exposure at 1 per cent.

JMC

12.252. See Charter Group.

KLM uk Limited

12.253. KLM uk Limited (KLM uk) is a wholly-owned subsidiary of KLM Royal Dutch airlines and operates under two brands: KLM uk, which operates from several UK airports (including Stansted and Manchester) into Amsterdam, and buzz, a low-fare operation launched in January 2000 which operates from Stansted to various European airports. KLM uk (in the name of buzz) made one submission jointly with Go and Ryanair; this evidence covers some of the remaining issues not covered by the joint LFCs' input.

12.254. KLM uk said that the CAA had recognized that capacity was the core issue in airport regulation and had focused on various ways in which investment could be incentivized. KLM uk agreed that capacity was indeed a core issue but rather than introduce changes at Stansted simply because they are being introduced at Heathrow and Gatwick, this Review should consider if capacity would really be an issue at Stansted during the next five-year period. Taking into account the projects which were already underway, if capacity would not be an issue, then Stansted should be considered on its own merit and changes being recommended for Heathrow and Gatwick should not be applied at Stansted if they are not appropriate.

12.255. The CC review should consider the relevance of conventional drivers which had historically been used by investors in airports. An issue which had not been covered specifically for Stansted was whether investors would be looking for the same conventional price signals of users' willingness to pay or whether they would be looking for different indicators, for example growth patterns, from an airport which was becoming an excellent success story in the low-fare, highly price-sensitive market.

12.256. The CAA had recommended changes to incentivize the airports to invest on the basis that if they chose to sweat assets and not invest, then they would have something to lose at the next regulatory review. On the basis that the outcome from one review was not binding on subsequent reviews, it was unsatisfactory for the regulator to assume that any adverse behaviour by the airport would necessarily be addressed at all. Stronger measures would therefore need to be put in place to ensure that the objectives were met.

12.257. There was merit in the principle of direct contracting between the airports and a user or users as long as this was carried out in accordance with CA98 etc as stated by the CAA. However, it was important that those users on standard terms did not cross-subsidize in any way those who had individual deals and transparency was desirable in this respect. It might be that such contracts, in practical terms, were difficult to apply on a non-discriminatory, non-anti-competitive basis and they might not work in reality.

Aspects of the formula

12.258. On the S factor, terrorist activities were a political issue and any security measures provided national protection. The provision of such measures should therefore be carried out by the Government and the cost incurred also borne by the Government.

12.259. If the Government insisted on imposing financial penalties on the aviation industry then TRANSEC should play a more active role in determining the appropriateness of the costs involved in implementing directives. This could work by setting up a working group to involve airlines, airports, the CAA and TRANSEC so that all views were made known to all interested parties. These meetings could take place on a local basis. The final decision on costs should remain with the CAA as an independent regulator.

12.260. The CAA had stated that if potential implications for security costs of the terrorist attacks on 11 September 2001 remained unclear when the price caps were finalized in 2002, they may revisit that particular issue. This was not possible without changes to the Airports Act which would allow the CAA to address this issue once the price caps had been fixed. Currently, only the airports were able to open up the price cap and this situation was unlikely to change in the short term. The CAA comments here therefore gave no comfort factor whatsoever. It would therefore be necessary to agree a one-off contingency arrangement at the time that the cap was set.

12.261. Although the Government should bear the cost of security, it was important that the costs of compliance remained totally transparent and that the meeting of any DfT security directives be carried out as efficiently as possible. The costs of security (including forecasts) which were used in the financial model to arrive at the final regulatory formula should be made transparent to users. Total transparency of costs should be provided by the airports on an ongoing basis and not simply during the year of introduction.

12.262. The danger of not allowing a cost pass-through for security-related charges was that conservative figures would be incorporated into the cost base used when arriving at the appropriate level of X. If this money was not spent, there was unlikely to be any claw back at the next regulatory review. If the allowance incorporated into the cost base was insufficient, the airport had the right to appeal to the regulator and open the formula to have the necessary changes made.

12.263. On balance, it would appear that the continuation of a cost pass-through for security-related charges would be the preferred way forward if such costs were still to be imposed on the industry by the Government. The pass-through should not be allowed at 100 per cent but should revert to 75 per cent on the basis that the airport also benefited from the security checks made and also that there should be an incentive for the airport to seek efficiency gains in this area. Full transparency on costs should be provided on an ongoing basis and not just for the year of introduction.

12.264. The revenue yield approach (as distinct from the tariff basket) should be retained as a basis for applying the cap.

12.265. On separate treatment of non-passenger flights (as proposed by the CAA), as Stansted had a relatively high proportion of cargo flights, the greatest impact of such a change would be there. Whilst understanding the logic for removing non-passenger flights from the revenue yield calculation, it was important that the calculations in arriving at the adjusted passenger yield were transparent and well understood by users. It was unclear from the yield figures given by the CAA in their recommendation paper whether cargo flights had been taken out of the calculation of the 2000/01 yield or not. This was important in determining the real impact which the CAA's recommendations could have on prices for carriers at Stansted.

12.266. The revenue for cargo flights would still need to be regulated and there would need to be clarity in the way cost allocations were made when determining the appropriate level of the cap applied. All users should be given transparency of both passenger and cargo flights on a regular basis.

12.267. On treatment of unpublished discounts, it was right and proper that, for the sake of calculating the allowable yield, all traffic should be treated as if it had been charged at the full-published price. It was important that all discounts were non-discriminatory and not anti-competitive. Such discounts would, in effect, be cross-subsidized by the airport from another area of its business. In the case of Stansted, such a cross subsidy would come from commercial revenues.

12.268. On rent transfers, it was well understood that airlines had no intrinsic rights as such to commercial revenues. To move to a dual-till scenario at Stansted which, in reality, would not be applied would add very unnecessary complications to charging at Stansted. Whilst the regulator stated that its statutory duties did not confer upon airlines any rights to commercial revenues, similarly it should not change a system for the sake of it when, in reality, there would be no change in what actually happened in real terms. There would be constant disagreements over the cost allocation applied between the two tills, and the trust which had built up between the airport and its users could be undermined.

12.269. If Stansted were to move to a dual-till scenario, KLM uk agreed with the regulator that surface access should not be included in an aeronautical pot on the basis that many of these investments were unprofitable. At Stansted much work was being carried out in improving the links from the M11 to the terminal—something which was needed for future growth but not really necessary for the market as it currently stood. Again, the continued application of the single-till concept at Stansted would resolve the issue here.

12.270. It was important that users at Stansted be advised by the airport of what service standards they should expect for the charges currently levied. Without this knowledge it was difficult to determine what standards should be considered as incremental. Airlines should not be allowed to contract for lower levels, only higher ones, and at Stansted the base should be lower than at the other airports to account for the low-frill nature of the bulk of the business there. Where contracting up occurs, users should be given full transparency to ensure that no other user was paying for the enhanced standards.

12.271. As it was only the regulated airport who could open the formula mid-term, it was imperative that users were protected or they would have to wait until the next review for action to be taken. Airlines at Stansted should be given more of a comfort factor with regard to the CAA's comments that BAA would not charge up to the allowable yield. There was no guarantee that the BAA would continue to price below the allowable yield and the CAA had not given any indication of how much it expected BAA to undercharge by. If users were forced to accept this situation and something went wrong then there would be no recourse until the next review and no guarantee even then that the situation would be remedied. Meanwhile, the low-fare market would have been adversely impacted.

12.272. KLM uk had considered the option of moving some of its operation to Luton. Whilst there appeared to be adequate capacity on the runway, overnight parking would appear to be a problem and something which would deter it from operating there. It could be possible that in the future it might operate one or two routes from there but if there was a shortage of capacity on the apron and it could not park, it would not see this as a viable alternative. For Stansted to be classified as being in a competitive environment, however, KLM uk would need to be able to move its whole operation to Luton and this it simply could not do even if it wanted to, not only due to the lack of capacity at Luton but also due to the property lease agreements which had been entered into with STAL. For this reason KLM uk considered Stansted to be in a relatively strong monopolistic position and recommended that the final decisions in the regulatory review should take this into account.

Low-fares carriers

12.273. The submission of the LFCs was reproduced on the CC's web site: the following summarizes the main points made.

12.274. Go, buzz (see KLM uk) and Ryanair told us that they were the three main operators at Stansted, and that jointly they represented over 80 per cent of the traffic there. They represented three of the four main European LFCs and although they competed vigorously against flag carriers, they also competed against each other. However, they shared common concerns over the CAA's views regarding the economic regulation at Stansted and particularly felt that the CAA had not given enough consideration to the changed circumstances at Stansted or to the particular needs of LFCs and their highly price-sensitive passengers.

12.275. The LFCs said that during Q3 Stansted had been transformed into one of the fastest growing airports in Europe with the current quinquennium seeing a revolution in air travel arising from significant competition in the low-fare sector. This had been of huge benefit to the traveling public as possibilities had been opened up to consumers previously restricted by monopoly level pricing. The phenomenal growth in passengers achieved at Stansted comprised a 'new market', ie consumers who otherwise could not afford to travel. Such growth and change in the traffic at Stansted was not envisaged at the time of the last regulatory review and served to illustrate the pace at which significant change could take place in the industry. It was envisaged that growth in the low-fare segment would continue as the number of new routes served continued to increase. An outcome from this regulatory process which allowed charges to increase would, however, have a serious detrimental impact on this future growth.

12.276. Airport charges currently accounted for as much as 30 per cent of total costs of the LFCs. Increases in airport costs could not be absorbed by LFCs and must be passed on to their passengers by way of increased fares, which was clearly not in the public's best interest. Such changes were immediate as the fares merely needed to be altered on the respective web sites. Such markets, however, were highly price sensitive, recent evidence of this being when fares were further decreased following 11 September, LFCs were actually able to increase their passenger volumes despite the perceived reluctance of the public to travel by air. Any decision which would result in an increase to charges at Stansted should only be made in the full knowledge of the immediate detrimental impact that such a change would have on what was currently a thriving segment of highly price-sensitive air travellers.

12.277. The objective of economic regulation was to act as a proxy for competition in an imperfect market where a monopoly supply existed. In the view of the LFCs, for such a proxy to be effective, the challenge it provided should increase over time if it was to fairly reflect the continued pressures in a competitive environment, were it to exist. The issue in relation to Stansted was the degree to which competition really did exist and therefore the additional degree of 'competition' required from economic regulation to simulate a reasonably competitive environment. If an appropriate level of 'competition' were not achieved so as to encourage the airport to act as if it were trading in a truly competitive environment, then economic regulation would have failed.

12.278. In reaching the decision to set up a base at Stansted, the LFCs had drawn up long-term business plans. Due to tight margins and a price-elastic market, such plans needed to take into account, inter alia, the impact of changes to aeronautical charges especially as fares included all taxes and charges and were set at low levels. As increases to charges had to be passed on to the passenger, consistency in the approach to regulation over time was extremely important in being able to continue to meet the needs of a continually growing low-fare market from which many parties benefited. Unforeseen price hikes brought about by significant changes in the way that charges were regulated could call into question the viability of some routes. Regulatory consistency was therefore important in enabling LFCs to maintain continued growth in their market.

The CAA's recommendations that Stansted should stand alone

12.279. The LFCs referred to the CAA's argument that with stand-alone regulation at Stansted the price cap would have been higher to allow it to make a normal return on its asset base. However, the LFCs said that both BAA and the CAA recognized at the last review that lower charges were important in being able to attract traffic to the airport. The airport would not have been able to charge any more than it had and the only difference would have been that the amount of undershoot on the allowable yield would have been greater.

12.280. The LFCs argued that a 'normal' level should be considered in light of the stage of development that Stansted had reached. BAA apparently considered that it was reasonable for new terminals/airports to make a return after a period of 10 to 15 years. Stansted was covering its operating costs after depreciation and making a contribution towards financing costs after 11 years. T5 was expected to reach the same position in a similar time frame and Gatwick took significantly longer. It would therefore seem reasonable to consider Stansted's return of 3.1 per cent after only 11 years as normal under the circumstances. Given the relative size of the airports, it was doubtful that the impact on the allowable yields at Heathrow and Gatwick had been any more than minor and that there would therefore have been any difference in the charges actually levied to users. It was difficult to see how any cross-subsidy could be considered to exist (or, if it did, in what way this differed from any cross-subsidy of new terminal developments at Heathrow or Gatwick) and the regulator had not illustrated that it did.

12.281. The CAA had also suggested that investment might have been lower than the spend over the past four years. But BAA had stated that it would consider capacity in the London area as a whole irrespective of the price caps in place. The LFCs said that it was doubtful therefore that the investment at Stansted would have been any different from what had actually taken place. Capacity would have been provided in the same manner to meet demands. The only difference might have been that the LFCs at Stansted could have prevented some development from taking place on the basis that they were not prepared to pay for it as it did not meet their requirements. In view of the fact that Stansted was used as a diversion as well as a hijack airport, this could have had a detrimental impact on the airline community as a whole. If the point the CAA was trying to make was that funds would not have been available for investment to take place, this was not true as any subsidy would have been generated from commercial revenues.

12.282. The CAA had also suggested that stand-alone price caps enhanced the timely delivery of commercially viable new capacity under future options arising from the Government's White Paper. The LFCs assumed that the CAA was referring to a potential new runway at Stansted. If the Government proposed that a new runway should be built at Stansted, it was not being proposed for the use of current users at Stansted alone but for the benefit of the airline community in general. Current users at Stansted alone could not afford to prefinance a new runway and it did not seem equitable to expect them to as they alone would not fill this capacity. That the construction of a runway providing much needed capacity in the South-East should be held back because current users did not need it and could not afford to pay for it would be a situation beyond belief.

12.283. The CAA had also suggested that the proposed PPC for Gatwick and Heathrow would be facilitated. The PPC was intended to provide investment incentives at these airports. The LFCs said that it appeared somewhat odd that the CAA should be considering such incentives in addition to the RRCB approach which was also intended to provide the incentive to invest. This also assumed that the BAA needed to be further incentivized to invest in a timely manner. In any event, changes should not be imposed on Stansted simply to make it easier to introduce schemes at Heathrow and Gatwick which had little or no real merit.

12.284. Finally, there was the suggestion that there would be a more balanced playing field between Stansted and other airports, particularly Luton. The CAA was referring here to the ability for investments to be supported from other areas of the business. Given that the cross-subsidization of new investments from other parts of a business was normal business practice, it was difficult to believe that Luton Airport did not benefit from similar treatment from within its own group. A balanced 'playing field' therefore currently existed and any change in the treatment of Stansted could be viewed as being anti-competitive against BAA.

12.285. Hence, the LFCs argued that the CAA's reasoning for Stansted to be treated on a stand-alone basis had been based on a totally academic approach to regulation and had failed to recognize commercial realities. No mention had been made by the CAA of the constraints which could arise as conditions of planning permission nor of the time which this process could take. No mention had been made of the fact that Stansted was used as a diversion airport for Heathrow and Gatwick and it was also the airport to be used in the unfortunate case of hijacks. The standby runway at Stansted had been enhanced beyond the requirements of current Stansted-based carriers at the request of Heathrow-based carriers. It was also perturbing that runway capacity in the South-East, primarily to meet the frustrated demand of Heathrow and Gatwick users, could be placed in jeopardy because current users alone at Stansted would not be prepared to pay for it. Hence the recommendations as they stood were against the public interest of not only highly price-sensitive passengers using the services who would be forced to pay more or be denied the possibility of travel, but also the airline community in general who could potentially be denied much needed runway capacity.

The single till

12.286. The issue of the single till was one which had been aired at every regulatory review which had taken place. At the last review of BAA London Airports the MMC endorsed the single-till approach, and in the light of the CAA's view that the joint and common costs characterized the economics of airport operation the LFCs concluded that meant that the single till was the right approach. It was difficult to see what had changed in this regard since the last review that would justify such a radical change in approach by the CAA.

12.287. Furthermore, the single till mirrored the situation in competitive markets. Airports operating in a competitive market offered below-cost aeronautical charges in order to increase traffic and the resulting commercial revenues. This approach was normal business practice and should continue to be encouraged at Stansted.

12.288. As to whether the CAA's proposals met its statutory obligations, the LFCs argued, first, that they did not further the reasonable interest of users. The CAA commented that it did not expect charges to increase to Stansted users as the airport had not been pricing up to the cap. The CAA had assumed that this would continue to be the case into the future. The commercial reality of the situation, however, was that the CAA would be proposing a higher cap as a result of the abolition of the single till and the airport would in theory be allowed to achieve this without any fear of action being taken against it. This could have a major effect on costs of LFCs leaving them with considerable uncertainty. Increased prices to consumers would result. The development of the vast network of low-fares services from Stansted had been and continued to be dependent on low costs. Without low costs, which could best be achieved under the single till, services would decrease and consumer choice and competition would suffer.

12.289. The LFCs also believed that the CAA had ignored the comments from all of the users who had participated in this consultation process that the single till had been an effective method of regulation and benefited the carriers, the consumers and the airports and must therefore be retained. Users had noted that the single till was a commercial partnership between airlines and the airport that worked not only because it resulted in lower costs and therefore lower prices to the consumer, but it was also easy to implement and monitor. The dual-till approach was complex and would lead to numerous disagreements between users and the airport as to the allocation of costs, for example, the cost of using airbridges where such airbridges were also being used for advertising purposes, and enormous animosity about the basis of allocating costs and charging. Without benefiting through the single-till approach, airlines would also not be prepared to put up with the inconvenience of commercial developments.

12.290. Second, the CAA's recommendations did not meet the objective of promoting efficient, economic and profitable operation of airports in the longer run and certainly achieved no more than could be achieved under the single-till approach.

12.291. The CAA had failed to provide any real evidence that the dual-till approach promoted any greater efficiency than the single-till approach. Indeed many users had expressed concern that the dual-till approach would incentivize an emphasis on commercial operations and therefore lead to inefficiency in aeronautical operations. Higher prices under the dual till would be likely to lead to stagnating or declining traffic at Stansted which would decrease profitability for both carriers and the airport. LFCs developed services on the basis of low cost and any increase in cost would force such carriers to re-evaluate their development plans at Stansted.

12.292. Third, the recommendation did not encourage timely investment satisfying user demands. The CAA had not provided any evidence that the dual till encouraged more timely investment than that achieved under the single-till approach. In fact the CAA had commented that the dual till gave higher-powered incentives for new capacity but that it only provided a framework—there was no guarantee. Vague references had been made to the fact that new capacity had not been forthcoming at Heathrow and Gatwick but the users had clarified that this was not related to any failure of the single till but related to exogenous planning constraints. The CAA was also recommending other incentives to invest, for example the PPC at Heathrow and Gatwick which cast doubt on whether the dual till would in fact incentivize investment as stated. Investment to date at Stansted under the single-till system had been timely. This had not been an issue there and the CAA itself acknowledged that Stansted had been keeping pace with growth. Indeed, Stansted had actually brought its development plans forward due to the phenomenal growth in the low-fares segment. The dual-till approach would lead to an emphasis on commercial development given that the airport would be entitled under the CAA's recommendations to retain all of the commercial revenues.

12.293. Fourth, the recommendations did not meet the objective of imposing the minimum restrictions consistent with the performance by the CAA of its functions. The CAA was charged with furthering the reasonable interests of users, not securing excessive profits for the airports, but restrictions proposed by the CAA did not provide adequate protection for users. If what the CAA was recommending was adopted and did not work, there was nothing the CAA or the users could do to rectify the situation unless the airport agreed to open the formula. Basically, users would be stuck in a situation until the next regulatory review. The recommendations did nothing to protect users against a lack of consultation, gold-plating and the exploitation of non-regulated revenue streams. The CAA stated in paragraph 3.17 of its proposals to the CC that: 'The ability of Stansted to provide terminal capacity in line with demand would depend on the planning process.' In the CAA's own words then, it was the planning process and not any incentives brought about by the application of the dual-till approach which would allow timely development to take place. If the dual till was applied, the CAA recognized that Stansted would probably not seek to recover the full allowable yield. In effect aeronautical charges at Stansted would be cross-subsidized in any event from commercial revenues thereby making a nonsense of any move to the dual-till concept. (In any event the recovery from aeronautical charges at Stansted was relatively higher at 46 per cent of total revenue compared to 38 per cent at Heathrow and 40 per cent at Gatwick.)

12.294. As there was less of a case for moving away from the single till at Stansted, it would appear that the only reason for such a move was to prevent a 'policy conundrum' for the CAA (the CAA's words). This should not be the driver for making such a radical change at Stansted and the single till should therefore be retained.

12.295. Hence, in summary, the LFCs said that the issues surrounding the single till had not changed. The CAA had stated that timely investment at Stansted depended on the planning process; although the allowable cap at Stansted would increase considerably, the CAA was relying on BAA not to price up to the cap, which was not a satisfactory situation; the CAA's recommendation did not meet its statutory obligations. As there was less of a case for change at Stansted, the single till should be retained there in line with previous decisions. This would provide a highly price-sensitive market with the regulatory consistency it needed to continue to grow. Low fares had added substantially to economic welfare and the CAA's recommendations as they stood would, without doubt, result in higher charges and ultimately higher air fares which would reduce economic welfare overall. Such a result would be against the reasonable interest of users.

Light-handed regulation at Stansted

12.296. According to the CAA, prospects for growth at Stansted would continue to rely on LFCs. Considerable inter-dependence therefore existed between the interests of the airport and its users and the situation was one of balance of power between users and the airport rather than overwhelming monopoly power on the part of Stansted. It was currently true to say that there was a degree of inter-dependence between the interests of Stansted and its major users, and that the main growth at Stansted would continue to come from the LFCs there in the foreseeable future. However, this situation would not necessarily continue for the duration of the next quinquennium or beyond. The CAA stated that Stansted's bargaining power might increase in the next decade if further capacity in the South-East did not emerge to meet demand. Although recognizing that the situation could change, the CAA's recommendations did not take this into account. It was therefore important that the regulation in place did not rely on the goodwill of the airport towards its users but sought to put some protection in place for users should circumstances change.

12.297. The CAA had claimed that the airlines' price elasticity at Stansted would mean that BAA would continue to adopt a market-driven approach to price setting as it had done to date. This assumption relied heavily on BAA actions and did not provide the regulatory 'stick' to ensure that this remained the case. The assumption was that LFCs would continue to provide all the growth at Stansted into the future. It was not certain that this would continue to be the case—even during the next five-year period. A change in traffic mix would mean that BAA was less dependent on low-fares operators and could therefore choose to increase charges to this segment. There was no guarantee that this would not happen. Meaningful protection for users was essential.

The level of the cap at Stansted

12.298. The CAA was recommending changes to regulation at Stansted which would result in a significant increase to the price cap. It recognized, however, that the airport would be unlikely to price up to the cap. The setting of a cap at a level in the knowledge that the airport would probably not go any where near to reaching it did nothing to incentivize efficiency and did not provide adequate challenge so as to simulate market competition. It should be recognized that the situation at Stansted had changed and that the cap should therefore be set at a level commensurate with the type of business the airport now found itself in. The cap should be set at a lower level, with pressure on the airport to reduce prices, so that it became meaningful and promoted real efficiency gains and would force Stansted to do what its users, primarily lower-cost carriers, were actually asking for in terms of services and facilities.

Public interest issues

Inadequate information disclosure and consultation

12.299. The consultation process at Stansted had been inadequate and consequently had resulted in the provision of some facilities which did not meet the requirements of LFCs. The process had not evolved to keep pace with the changes which had taken place at Stansted and the inadequate communication which had resulted had meant that the right people had not always been aware of issues at a time when their input was most needed. Whilst it was recognized that much of the early development of Stansted was predetermined and could not have foreseen the extent of growth in the low-fare services, certain recent developments had not reflected the demands of LFCs who were being forced to pay for facilities that were over-specified and more costly than necessary. In addition, the lack of consultation had meant that certain users had been denied the possibility to self-fund or co-fund facilities. However, there had been a meeting with the airport and agreement reached in principle on a revised consultation structure which would be more meaningful. (A written undertaking still had not been received on this issue by the end of October 2002 and was yet to be provided by airport.) The LFCs also acknowledged that Stansted had become more focused on the needs of LFCs; for example, the development of Satellite 3 need not be connected to the costly and inefficient transit system.

The fuel levy

12.300. The fuel levy at Stansted was very high and had been a major bone of contention for all users at Stansted for some time, as the airport had not provided any justification. Stansted was the only airport in the UK to provide the infrastructure for the delivery of fuel as this was usually provided by the fuel companies themselves. No evidence had been given as to whether provision of the infrastructure by the airport was good or bad, but it was costly. Fuel companies had indicated that they would be prepared to consider taking ownership of the facilities from BAA.

12.301. BAA had refused to address this issue until recently when it met with the LFCs and provided some transparency. The charge in question was originally for the purpose of recovering the capital costs of the infrastructure. The basis for recovery, however, was arrived at some years ago and assumptions made on the volume of uplift had been exceeded for several years resulting in what users considered to be a vast over-recovery.

12.302. BAA had said that the total levy broke down into 0.38p a litre for the concessions fee and 0.3p a litre towards the recovery of capital, ie the permitted amount at 8 per cent return. BAA argued that the fuel levy did not recover capex, LFCs, on the other hand, said that the capex was excessive. The throughput charge of £0.38 was high compared with £0.1877 at Heathrow, £0.33 at Manchester and £0.315 at Gatwick. However, the recovery of shortfalls from previous regulatory periods was also unreasonable, in that when the regulator considered the return actually made compared with that allowed, this presumably took into account the overall return, including any shortfalls or over recoveries. With BAA now seeking to recover for previous shortfalls there was a double recovery: it should only be allowed 8 per cent on an annual basis.

Quality of service

12.303. On quality of service, the LFCs said that unreliability of the baggage system had caused a lot of problems, partly due to poor maintenance. BAA had responded well to increased pressures on security by introducing more machines, but there was still scope for improvement. Reliability of the TTS was generally acceptable, but it was necessary to have coaches on standby in the event of failure. The airlines did not, however, know what service standard they were already paying for; there was, however, concern about standards being set too high for the requirements of LFCs unless there was scope to contract down as well as up.

Monarch Airlines

12.304. See Charter Group.

Qantas

12.305. Qantas described itself to us as having a small presence at Heathrow, but observed that together with its alliance partners, the One World alliance represented the single greatest input to BAA's revenues.

12.306. Because of the nature of its operations, Qantas limited its comments to Heathrow, but noted that its espoused principles of airport regulation applied equally to Gatwick and Stansted.

12.307. In Qantas's view, by not having three separate airport owners, the UK had missed an opportunity to introduce competition and market forces to airport pricing and behaviour for the majority of the UK's airline travellers.

12.308. Qantas expressed disappointment that over the past quinquennium, the delay in the construction of T5 had resulted in much lower capex than anticipated, and had therefore subsequently undermined the recommended pricing formula. Qantas felt that the combination of these circumstances has resulted in airlines at Heathrow and Gatwick effectively overpaying around £500 million (£300 million advanced revenue and £200 million prefinancing of capex that did not take place). It was therefore reasonable to expect an equitable arrangement to ensure that overpayment in the last quinquennium be remedied over the next quinquennium. It recommended that the prefunding and prefinancing be used to offset any real increase in charges at Heathrow due to costs of T5 construction in the period 2003 to 2008.

12.309. On other issues, Qantas said that it endorsed the CAA's proposal to eliminate the airport cross-subsidy and set separate tills for Heathrow, Stansted and Gatwick; the development of a clearer framework so that service quality is linked to a new price formula; a continuation of the traditional single-till approach to setting regulated charges; a more balanced contract between airport operators and users to replace the one-sided Conditions of Use; and a clear linkage between any increase in charges that are designed to pay for new infrastructure, and the delivery of benefits that flow from those services, for example T5.

12.310. Summarizing its view, Qantas said that it encouraged consideration of the following outcomes: retention of the single-till approach to airports; removal of any prefunding, as well as provision for the recovery of revenue already provided for T5 at Heathrow; separation of the Heathrow, Stansted and Gatwick tills; and replacement of the Conditions of Use documents.

RyanAir

12.311. See LFCs.

Saudi Arabian Airlines

12.312. Saudi Arabian Airlines said that its views were reflected in the submission from BAR UK.

Thai Airways International Public Company Limited

12.313. Thai Airways Public Company Limited told us that it was unable to provide detailed information on subjects related to the inquiry. However, with regard to the maximum level of airport charges, it recommended compliance with the ICAO Doc 9082/6, 'The ICAO's policies on charges for Airports and Air Navigation Services', Articles 15 and 22 accordingly (see Chapter 3).

Turkish Airlines

12.314. Turkish Airlines said that it welcomed the CAA's proposal to include service quality assessments allowing penalties for below-standard performance of the airports; that BAA was a monopoly operator made this point more valid. Turkish Airlines also welcomed the proposal for no automatic cost transfer, such as security costs. It was Turkish Airlines' view that aviation security costs should be borne by the state.

12.315. Turkish Airlines told us that it was concerned, however, with the proposed move from a single to a dual till, which it believed would increase its costs at a time when most carriers were facing financial problems. Airlines had already paid the airports more than they had to during the current review period: the prefunding for T5 was a case in point. Turkish Airlines felt that the CAA's proposition that BAA would invest less under a single till was unproven, and that therefore it should not be taken as an argument to move to a dual till.

Virgin Atlantic

12.316. Virgin believed that major revision of the CAA's recommendations was needed to avoid movement away from the goal of simulating a competitive environment where competition could not be introduced, and indeed movement was required to ensure that this goal could be achieved.

Introducing competition in the provision of airport services in London

12.317. First, Virgin argued that there should be further study of the issue of whether or not BAA should be broken up (via a transparent consultation process). The role of regulation was to simulate a competitive environment where competition could not be introduced. That is, regulation was only ever 'first-best' (in terms of producing outcomes similar to those that would result in a competitive environment) when it was not possible to introduce competition.

12.318. It was probably true that even if Heathrow, Gatwick and Stansted were under separate ownership, they would only compete with each other to a certain extent. This was because, from the airport users' point of view, these three airports were not effective substitutes for one another. In particular, Gatwick and Stansted were not effective substitutes for Heathrow (even though Heathrow may be an effective substitute for Gatwick or Stansted). Passengers, particularly time-sensitive passengers, strongly preferred Heathrow to the other airports given its closer proximity to the center of London and its greater range of flight connections: hence, there was a substantial difference in yield per passenger between the two airports. One study showed average fares per passenger 40 per cent higher from Heathrow to Newark than from Gatwick to Newark, although this may be higher than other routes.

12.319. Thus even if these airports were separately owned, they would still each enjoy substantial market power and hence needed to be regulated. Severe capacity constraints at Heathrow (at most times of the day) and Gatwick (during peak periods) increased the market power enjoyed by these airports. It would also always be the case that, regardless of ownership, airports would have a number of different ways to allocate funds given the large number of differentiated services produced at airports. A profit-maximizing airport would always be incentivized to allocate funds to those projects which generated the highest returns (and hence usually required the least capital outlay) and where it could fully capture these returns.

12.320. However, where airports were jointly owned, airport owners would also have the option of allocating funds at different airports. This would mean that where there were significant differences in the returns (and hence the level of capital outlay required) across airports, airport owners would invest at the airport where returns were highest, even though this may not be the same airport where returns were highest for users, and hence for passengers and the UK economy. A Heathrow consumer, for example, would be much more interested in pushing for runway and terminal development at Heathrow, whereas among the three airports, growth could be accommodated at lower cost at Stansted. Hence, BAA had asked the Government to rule out the possibility of a third runway, and invited the T5 Inquiry Inspector to recommend that a third runway be ruled out. BAA also proposed a number of measures—a freeze on the night flight quota, a cap on noise, and continuation of runway alternation (ie no 'mixed mode')—that would prevent an increase in runway movements at Heathrow. However, Virgin believed that it was in the public interest to have airports' interests aligned as closely as possible to passengers', and hence airport users' interests.

The regulatory price path

12.321. Second, the 'regulatory price path' recommended by the CAA would, in effect, allow a substantial increase in airport charges over the next quinquennium, prior to any delivery of desired improvements in service quality and investment on time, to budget, to the agreed specifications and at the airport where it was required. It would therefore continue to require airport users to prefund improvements in service quality and investment.

12.322. Virgin had consistently opposed prefunding, as it did not believe that airport users, rather than a monopolist, should bear the majority of the risk associated with the delivery of improvements in service quality and investment. Indeed, forcing airport users to bear this burden seemed inconsistent with outcomes that would occur in a competitive environment. It quoted academic studies that showed that where demand was growing over time, a price path under which airports bore the majority of the risk associated with the delivery of improvements in service quality and investment ensured financial viability of lumpy investment in the longer run, and that social welfare was higher than when airports were permitted to break even on an annual, or even short-run basis. Financial break-even would occur sooner, the greater the extent to which initial capacity levels were 'low'. It was difficult to see how this would not be true at Heathrow, given the magnitude of forecasts of the growth rate of demand for air transport services over the next two decades or so, even after the tragic events of 11 September 2001, and the low initial capacity levels.

12.323. Currently, it was also the case that airport users had absolutely no guarantee that desired improvements in service quality and investment would be delivered on time, to budget, and to the agreed specifications at the airport where they were needed. This was because airport users had no ability to enter into legally binding contracts with airports: certain clauses in airports' Conditions of Use effectively exempted airports from liability should delivery of service quality levels and investment desired by users not occur.

12.324. Virgin could not think of a single supplier that operated in a competitive market that was able to make its customers pay (substantial amounts) for goods or services prior to receiving them without customers having the legal ability to seek to be recompensed if what they paid for was not delivered (or was only delivered in part), they did not receive it when promised, they had to pay more for it than the originally agreed price, or it was delivered to someone else. Virgin therefore believed that the offending clauses in the Conditions of Use agreement should be removed in the public interest (this is discussed further below).

12.325. It was difficult to see how the threat that the regulator may force airports to pay back funds intended for improving service quality or investment should they not be spent, or be only partially spent, or be spent in ways not desired by airport users, or spent at a different airport, at the end of each five-year period, was likely to be much of a constraint on airports' behaviour in practice, as claimed by the CAA, if the CAA's proposal to reduce BAA's asset base in the next quinquennium by only 50 per cent of the amount prefunded over the current five-year period was implemented. This was because this would effectively set a precedent that airports need only assume a minimal amount of the risk associated with any government decision that led to delay, as they would be able to spend monies prefunded on other projects without consultation and without penalty (including the interest earned). Virgin argued that any increase in investment at Gatwick or Stansted was of no benefit to its operations at Heathrow and no other projects undertaken at Heathrow would compensate for the delay to T5. Virgin therefore believed that BAA should be required to pay back 100 per cent of the funds intended for delivery of T5 (on time, to budget, to the agreed specifications, at Heathrow) plus the interest earned by BAA on these funds.

12.326. At the moment, therefore, the regulatory price path proposed by the CAA, which continued to mandate prefunding, if implemented, would not lead to improvements in service quality levels or investment but simply allow BAA to capture further rents inherent in the provision of airport services. This was despite indications by the CAA that it supported slot auctioning (provided the correct regulatory framework was in place): implicit in the assertion that auctioning was optimal was the realization that the price elasticity of runway use and excess demand are at such low (in absolute value) and high levels respectively that using airport charges to ration demand would simply lead to further capture by airports of rents inherent in the provision of airport services.

Single till vs dual till

12.327. Third, as stated in Virgin's response to the CAA's Preliminary Proposals of November 2001, movement towards a dual till would decrease social welfare. An academic study showed that, compared to the situation where airports faced separate budget constraints on aeronautical and non-aeronautical operations, social welfare was higher when airports were subject to an overall break-even constraint and some cross-subsidy between non-aeronautical and aeronautical activities occurred. When a cross-subsidy was allowed, the profits earned on non-aeronautical activities relaxed the budget constraint on aeronautical activities and thereby reduced the mark-up on marginal costs on these activities. At the initial state of Ramsey pricing for aeronautical activities and marginal-cost pricing for non-aeronautical activities, the welfare gain on the former arising from a reduction in the mark-up outweighed the welfare loss on the latter arising from an increase in prices, and hence a subsidy from non-aeronautical services to aeronautical services was welfare-enhancing.

12.328. Unlike other regulated utilities, many different services were produced (horizontally) at airports, which could be broadly separated into two groups: those used in the provision of air transport services (aeronautical services) and those that were not (non-aeronautical services). On the supply side, there were common costs inherent in the provision of these two groups of services: an increase in the supply of terminal capacity also increased space available for retail outlets, for example. However, this only ran in one direction: an increase in the supply of retail outlets would not increase the space available for stands, gates etc. Similarly, on the demand side, an increase in demand for air transport services would increase the demand for goods and services sold by retail outlets, but the reverse did not hold.

12.329. If airports operated in a competitive environment, they would be expected to come to some sort of agreement with users on the sharing of gains arising from users bringing customers to airports' retail outlets and given users' contributions towards the cost of the facilities in which retail activities were carried out. This sort of agreement was implicit in the single-till regime. It was difficult to see how a similar agreement would be reached if the RRCB proposed by the CAA were adopted, given that airports would be in a far superior bargaining position than airport users, particularly at severely capacity-constrained airports such as Heathrow, and given that Gatwick was not an effective substitute for Heathrow.

12.330. As to whether the dual till, by increasing airport charges, could lead to a more efficient utilization of slots, Virgin believed that a change in slot allocation methods towards a more market-based approach such as auctioning, was more appropriate for that purpose. Given that airports were not effective substitutes for one another, and the extent of excess demand at Heathrow, the extent to which airlines would move in response to an increase in charges was very limited: they were aware of only one study on price elasticity of demand for use of runways which showed it to be very low (in absolute terms).

12.331. The move to the RRCB approach proposed by the CAA would therefore mean that charges under the proposed regulatory price path would be even higher and social welfare would be lower.

Relationship between airport charges and fares

12.332. Virgin agreed with an analysis we put to it by our consultants, NERA (see Appendix 2.2), showing that, in addition to indirect changes in price, increases in airport charges might also directly lead to increases in air fares where there were no or minimal scarcity rents inherent in the provision of air transport services. It strongly agreed with NERA's conclusion that this would be true at Heathrow, despite the severe runway constraints that existed at Heathrow at almost all times of the day. This was because there were only limited constraints on the size of aircraft with which slots could be operated. There were also only limited constraints on the number of frequencies that could be provided to each destination served from Heathrow by incumbent carriers with sizeable slot portfolios such as BA. There were thus only limits on the behaviour of non-incumbents in each city-pair market of which Heathrow was an end-point airport.

12.333. Virgin disagreed with the CAA's assertion that an increase in airport charges would lead to a reduction in airfares in some markets. Incumbents were unlikely to relinquish slots even if airport charges rose to such an extent that operating a particular route became unprofitable, as the loss associated with operating an unprofitable route was likely to be lower than that incurred if a competitor was able to enter new markets or add frequencies in markets already served. The market power incumbents enjoyed as a result of their substantial airport presence would enable them to sustain this sort of behaviour. Indeed, BA continued to operate services to UK domestic and continental European destinations, even though it had been making a loss on its short-haul network for years.

12.334. It was also the case that the carrier with the largest presence at an airport would generally be able to make use of any marginal slots that became available, by combining them with its existing sizeable slot portfolio. Any marginal slots that did become available were therefore likely to be used by incumbents to operate additional frequencies in markets they already served. It was difficult to see how this would lead to a reduction in air fares.

12.335. Virgin determined the fares it would offer in each city-pair market taking into account the fares offered by its competitors. It determined the number of seats to make available at each of these price points given market characteristics, and adjusted these in line with demand as the time of the departure of the flight became nearer, with the overall aim of maximizing the revenue accruing to it from each flight.

12.336. Virgin only entered a market or added capacity in a market it already served if it believed that, after an initial start-up period, it could at least cover the (route-specific) fixed costs associated with operating in this market. Of course, across its network as a whole, total revenue (from all services provided) must at least cover total costs, including common fixed costs, at least in the medium to longer term.

12.337. If, in any period, demand in any particular market was significantly higher than forecast such that it could not be accommodated on the capacity provided in that market, Virgin would examine the costs and benefits of increasing capacity in that market, taking the actions of its competitors into account. Given the severe runway constraints that existed at Heathrow at almost all times of the day, Virgin could usually only increase capacity by using a larger aircraft type (where it was not already using the largest) rather than by adding frequencies. However, an aircraft of the required type might not be available in the short term. Some rationing of capacity provided might therefore be required from time to time. In this instance, it would make a larger number of seats available at each of the higher price points. However, in practice it was at most only able to ration capacity on a short-term basis: in the year ending June 2002, load factors across Virgin's route network were approximately 77 per cent on average.

12.338. This was because whether or not rationing occurred in practice would also depend on the actions of Virgin's competitors. Incumbent carriers with sizeable slot portfolios and hence fleets such as BA would be able to more easily schedule additional frequencies in a given market, as well as redeploy aircraft. Where the increase in demand was perceived to be a trend (rather than a usual fluctuation in the economic cycle), Virgin would also examine increasing the capacity it provided in this market on a more permanent basis in the medium to long term.

12.339. Hence, if landing or parking fees increased such that rotational DOCs increased, a greater amount of revenue would be needed to break even. Similarly, if passenger fees increased, such that passenger DOCs increased, a greater amount of revenue would also be needed to break even. If a carrier was initially only just achieving break-even, it would need to reduce other costs, increase the number of passengers travelling at each price point (particularly the higher price points) or increase the revenue earned per passenger. Even if a carrier were more than breaking even, it would still need to achieve a certain profit margin in order to satisfy shareholders, other lenders, etc.

12.340. There was little that could be done to reduce costs in the short term. There was also only a limited amount that could be done to reduce these in the medium to longer term, given that the majority of these costs were attributable to using the goods and services of suppliers that did not face effective competition in the markets in which they operated (oil producers, airspace service providers, airports etc). Other costs were attributable to establishing and maintaining competitive advantage.

12.341. Virgin had, in the past, passed on increases in costs by increasing fares explicitly or levying a surcharge. For example, in response to the substantial increase in fuel prices in 1999, Virgin increased published fares in all cabins by several per cent across its route network in 2000. Virgin believed that other carriers increased their fares by similar amounts. In response to the substantial increase in insurance premiums and security costs after 11 September 2001, Virgin introduced a surcharge (ex-UK) of £2.50 per passenger per sector ($4 ex-US) on all tickets issued on or after 30 November 2001. Again, Virgin believed that other carriers increased their fares by similar amounts.

12.342. Virgin's increasing fares in response to the substantial increase in fuel prices in 1999 also suggested that Virgin would attempt to recover any increase in costs per aircraft from passengers at least in the medium to longer term, and might do so in a way that resulted in each passenger facing the same increase in percentage terms. The imposition of the surcharge in response to the substantial increase in insurance premiums and security costs after 11 September 2001 suggested that Virgin would attempt to recover any increase in costs per passenger from passengers, at least in the medium to longer term. Only if the increase in costs per passenger differed across categories of passengers would Virgin levy different charges on different passengers.

Service quality

12.343. Fourth, Virgin strongly believed that airport users were entitled to a specification of what they could expect to receive, including improvements in service quality and investment, in return for the charges they paid, as well as recompense when this was not delivered on time, to budget, to the agreed specifications at the airport where it was required. Virgin had therefore indicated its support in principle for the inclusion of a quality of service term within the price cap.

12.344. However, it was difficult to see how the service quality term proposed by the CAA would incentivize airports to deliver improvements in service quality and investment desired by airport users, for several reasons. First, the CAA had stated that it believed that 'soft standards' (such as toilet cleanliness) should be included in the generic standard. These outputs, which any company operating in a competitive environment could be expected to produce in the normal course of its business, and which had been prompted from parties that did not directly have to pay for these items (such that there was little link between 'wants' and 'prices'), made it easier for airports to meet the overall average should averaging be permitted. Second, the CAA had stated that it believed that 'bonuses' should be paid to BAA for exceeding the levels of service quality specified in the generic standard. Paying bonuses would mean that a monopolist was able to make airport users pay for levels of service quality higher than that actually needed to meet passenger demands, a clear misallocation of resources, and would make it easier for airports to meet the overall average should averaging be permitted. Third, it was unclear whether outputs which were not currently paid for via regulated charges could be included in the quality of service term. If not, some outputs critically important to departures and arrivals punctuality, such as baggage sortation, would not be covered by the quality of service standard. Fourth, the CAA had stated that it believed that penalties should be capped at 3 per cent of average yield. Setting penalties at such a low level would make it more attractive to BAA not to deliver and pay the penalty, maximizing the extent to which airport users were forced to contract privately. Penalties could be capped at 10 per cent of charges.

12.345. Virgin believed that airports should be incentivized to deliver service quality via the use of legally-binding agreements. There was already a precedent for this: BAA paid airport users a rebate of £1.50 per departing or arriving passenger whenever they did not receive pier service. However, this rebate, paid when airport users must use remote stands (and transport passengers to and from airport terminals by bus) would remain the only recompense received by airport users when desired levels of service quality were not delivered, unless the clauses in airports' Conditions of Use, which effectively exempted airports from liability when this occurs, were removed. Virgin therefore believed that the offending clauses in the Conditions of Use agreement should be removed in the public interest. Even if these clauses were removed, it would still be the case that airports would be in a far superior bargaining position than airport users, particularly at severely capacity-constrained airports such as Heathrow, given that, as stated above, Gatwick was not an effective substitute for Heathrow. Even if airports were willing to enter into contracts, it was difficult to see how these would not be on terms and conditions favourable to them. In spite of the MMC's findings at the time of the last quinquennial review, airport users (mostly BA) had only been successful in concluding (non-legally-binding) SLAs pertaining to inputs or to those output processes which required less capex on the part of airports to meet service quality levels desired by airport users, and they contained reciprocal payments.

12.346. Virgin therefore believed that what airport users were entitled to receive, including improvements in service quality, in return for the charges they paid, as well as recompense when this was not delivered on time, to budget, to the agreed specifications at the airport where it was required, should be determined by the regulator in consultation with airport users, and be made legally binding on BAA, in the public interest. This could be achieved by incorporating the service quality standard determined by the regulator in consultation with airport users in airports' Permission to Levy Charges.

Investment

12.347. Fifth, Virgin believed that shortages of investment (for example, in pier-serviced stands) could be attributed not to shortage of funds but lack of accountability of BAA. As in the case of service quality, airport users were entitled to a specification of what they could expect to receive in terms of investment in return for the charges they paid, as well as recompense when this was not delivered on time, to budget, to the agreed specifications at the airport where it was required. Virgin had therefore indicated its support in principle for the CAA's recommendation that there be greater information disclosure to facilitate greater contracting between airports and users.

12.348. However, it was unlikely that the CAA's proposal would incentivize airports to deliver desired investment unless the regulator set a precedent that making substantial changes to the CIP without consultation or payback of prefunded monies was acceptable, and given that the CAA believed that it only had the ability to assess airports' compliance with the terms of any regulatory settlement (and take action should airports have not acted accordingly) every five years.

12.349. Virgin believed that, while investment plans would need to be determined by airport users in conjunction with airports (with greater involvement of operational and user charges representatives than occurs currently under the LACC), airport users would need the regulator to be involved in their negotiations with airports over time and to resolve disputes when they occurred. Airport users would also require continual involvement of the regulator in order to ensure that those users with relatively greater bargaining power, vis-à-vis the airports, were not able to use this to exclude competitors with less bargaining power from the negotiation process or only include them on less favourable terms and conditions than they themselves enjoy.

12.350. The CAA continually stated that it believed that the only ability it had to resolve disputes was under section 41 of the Airports Act. It stated that airport users could also have disputes resolved by the OFT under CA98. However, complaints brought under section 41 required an enormous amount of resources and took at least six months to resolve; complaints brought under CA98 were likely to take even longer, particularly until substantial case law was built up. Indeed, the length of time taken to resolve disputes was why Virgin had not brought section 41 complaints against BAA recently. It was therefore difficult to see how the provisions of the Airports Act or CA98 alone could act as an effective constraint on airports' behaviour in practice.

12.351. If the CAA was correct, airport users needed the CAA to be given the ability (via a change in legislation) to resolve disputes between airports and users between regulatory reviews. It was difficult to see how there would be significant risk associated with empowering the regulator in this manner. In the case of disputes between airports and users, airport users would be given some degree of bargaining power against airports, which was what they would enjoy if airports operated in a competitive environment. Empowering the regulator would therefore help achieve the objectives of airport regulation. Of course, if the regulator decided in favour of the airport, no party was worse off than they would be if the CAA did not have the ability to resolve disputes. Similarly, in the case of disputes between airports and users, with relatively greater bargaining power vis-à-vis airports on the one hand and users with relatively less bargaining power on the other, the latter would be given some degree of bargaining power against the former.

12.352. Virgin also supported the submission of BA that higher airport charges were not necessary to fund BAA's capex programme; proposed new capex per passenger being below that assumed at the time of the last review.

12.353. It also criticized the 2002 CIP, which it found very difficult to comment on effectively due to insufficient information on the justification and costs of each project; the substantial risk projects would not be delivered on time or at all, because of BAA's behaviour during Q3; and the lack of separation of expenditure between that which would enhance the capacity of the airport and that which would improve quality of service for any particular airline or group of airlines. Additional detail needed to be provided, and regulatory authorities needed to set a precedent that making substantial changes to the CIP without consultation or payback of prefunded monies was unacceptable. To have sufficient detail on which to comment would be consistent with competitive market outcomes.

Role of the regulator

12.354. Finally, given airport users' need to have the regulator involved in their negotiations with airports over time and to resolve disputes quickly when they occur, Virgin was extremely concerned by the constant signalling of the regulator that it favoured regulatory disengagement. The fourth of the five duties of the CAA under the Airports Act was not 'to impose minimal restrictions' but 'to impose the minimum restrictions that are consistent with the performance by the CAA of its functions under [sections 40–56 of Part IV of the Airports Act]'.

Security costs

12.355. Virgin supported the principle of no-cost pass-through, even though this would reduce transparency. It was concerned that BAA currently had no reason to resist government demands for very significant new procedures, as illustrated by the Little America scheme referred to below. The current 5 per cent of costs borne by BAA was also nowhere near enough to incentivize BAA to keep its costs down.

Public interest issues

12.356. Virgin argued that given the many different factors on which airlines competed it was crucial that any new facilities which became available at airports were allocated in a transparent, non-discriminatory way, and that carriers using existing facilities had access to similar levels of technology as those inherent in the new facilities. It argued that this had not occurred in the case of T5; and that although several consultation papers had been issued, and BAA claimed to have consulted on how terminal space would be allocated among carriers once T5 came online, BAA had come to an agreement beforehand that T5 would be allocated to BA and its alliance partners on a preferential basis.

12.357. BAA was said to have told the airlines that BA would be in T5 and T1 and the Star Alliance in T3. It claimed that there had not yet been a transparent non-discriminatory consultation process on terminal allocation; nor concrete proposals on how BAA was to ensure a level playing field was established between carriers using T5 and carriers using existing terminals when phase 1 of T5 opens. BAA had recently referred only to the drawing up of some conceptual plans still at an early stage for the redevelopment of the whole central area.

12.358. Virgin also complained about lack of consultation post-11 September on changes in the BAA CIP—for example of Pier 6 at Gatwick, and of extension to Europier and Victor Pier at Heathrow—and with no corresponding reduction in charges.

12.359. There was also a lack of transparent non-discriminatory consultation on security-related issues post-11 September at Heathrow. Virgin claimed that on 19 February 2001, notice was given that gate room K16 on Pier 7 would be closed as a departure facility from Monday 22 October 2001 in order to create a 'Little America': an additional security screening area dedicated to US departures and arrivals. It said that concerns were raised at the time that this would reduce the number of piers available to all carriers and hence the capacity of T3; but also that only US airlines would use the facility and Little America would therefore discriminate against non-US carriers, first, by creating the impression that security measures were lower for these carriers' flights and, second, by increasing the extent to which they would need to coach passengers to aircraft parked on the remote stands. It said BAA subsequently estimated that the proposal would lead to a reduction in utilization of stands adjacent to piers of approximately 80 per cent even though this would mean that some airlines using T3 would be forced to coach passengers from remote stands when stands adjacent to piers were available. BAA claimed that the creation of Little America followed a directive from the DTLR almost a month before K16 was closed but later stated it was not the subject of a DTLR 'directive' as such. Only subsequently did BAA appear to ask the DTLR for a meeting to discuss issues associated with the implementation of Little America; or pursue with DTLR an agreement that it could be used by carriers other than just AA/UA. In the end, Little America was not implemented as proposed: but BAA was planning to horizontally segregate arriving and departing passengers on Pier 7 and the connector pier.

12.360. Virgin was also concerned about BAA's failures to promote competition in the supply of ground handling services at Gatwick. Virgin had suffered from poor service and little choice of ground handler: it believed BAA's policy of recovering the costs of check-in desks and departure baggage belts on a line-by-line basis contributed to this. Charges were higher for facilities for which demand was lower: which would not only not promote efficient use of existing facilities but also make it very difficult for a new entrant ground handling service provider to compete with incumbents. By assigning airlines to particular rows of check-in desks, if there were few airlines using a particular row, the charge per time period was higher on desks with low utilization and lower on those with higher utilization: the opposite of what would encourage efficient use of the desks. Hence, if a new ground handler was given permission to compete for airlines' business, and assigned a row of check-in desks where the charge was fairly high, it would not be able to attract new customers to those desks.

12.361. Virgin was currently lobbying for a fourth licence to be put out to tender, allowing a third ground handling service provider to commence operations at Gatwick's South Terminal, but was concerned both that BAA was 'dragging its feet', and that it was not seeking to ensure that this service provider would be required to offer services at reasonable cost.

12.362. Under a 'Power by the Hour' scheme, supposed to be implemented on 1 July 2002, the level of fees were to be determined by dividing the full costs of operating check-in desk and departure baggage facilities by timed desk usage with any overcharging or undercharging carried forward. Virgin suggested that GAL would have an incentive to under-forecast usage so that the level of charges per time period was set higher, hence the risk associated with under-recovery was lower: this would also enable GAL to earn interest on any over-recovery before crediting the amount of the over-recovery only to airlines in subsequent periods.

12.363. Virgin also complained that when it wished to share a CIP lounge with other airlines at Gatwick, BAA insisted on payment to compensate it for loss of retail income, and that direct lift access from the lounge to the pier be prevented, in order that passengers had to walk through the retail outlets. As a result of the delays, the scheme was not proceeded with.

12.364. Virgin also expressed concern about the costs of the T1 to T4 baggage tunnel being included in airport charges and passed on to other users at Heathrow. The bilateral agreement between BA and BAA had been entered into without other users having the ability to review the project, and to allow the agreement to be terminated before 2008 would set a precedent that bilateral agreements were meaningless.

Airline representative bodies

Aircraft Owners and Pilots Association

12.365. The Aircraft Owners and Pilots Association (AOPA) said that Stansted Airport had a poor reputation for its handling of, and attitude to, general aviation (ie light and private) aircraft. The AOPA argued that this was not in the public interest, as it increased the cost and complexity of operation for general aviation pilots, owners or operators by routing people around rather than through Stansted airspace. This was inappropriate, as in the AOPA's view, Stansted was not a very busy airport.

Airline Operators Committee—Heathrow Airport

12.366. The Airline Operators Committee—Heathrow Airport (HAOC) said that at the last MMC Review the comments on transfer baggage funding included 'with the prospect of this being consolidated in airport charges in Q4'. From that time onwards, the HAOC representing the airlines at Heathrow agreed to have as an objective the incorporation of the cost of baggage transfer as part of airport charges.

12.367. This was in line with the arrivals baggage system and the passenger transfer facility charges, which were already in airport charges at the time of construction of the Flight Connections Centre. Following the crisis of 1997, HAL commenced investment in the transfer baggage infrastructure. It was agreed, following considerable debate, that an overseeing steering group, consisting of the HAOC, airlines and HAL representatives, now called TIFGAH, would take on this role.

12.368. When the first 'per passenger charge' was agreed and the transfer baggage infrastructure identified, it was decided by TIFGAH that the baggage tunnel connecting T1 and T2 should not at that time be part of the charge as there was only one airline user. Currently, all airlines' transfer baggage are facilitated through this tunnel. At the TIFGAH forum it was agreed, supported by Heathrow and the airlines, that this charge, including a small percentage of the baggage tunnel T1 to T4 charge, should be incorporated into airport charges at this quinquennial review. The mandate and position of the airline community through the HAOC was that all transfer baggage infrastructure should be part of airport charges, which included the full cost of the T1 to T4 tunnel.

12.369. The HAOC said that it believed that Heathrow should be supporting the HAOC position for the future transfer infrastructure investment, to ensure operationally that connectivity was protected between terminals, including the proposed T5 connectivity. The HAOC position and mandate was not now supported by one of the main base carriers and one other airline of the TIFGAH Steering Group. The HAOC said that it had no option but to put on record its position and to ask the CAA to support the inclusion of the transfer baggage infrastructure at Heathrow into airport charges.

12.370. The airlines' concerns about the T1 common departure lounge was the passenger inconvenience caused by increased walking distances from check-in to aircraft, operational disruptions, and the possibility of departure delays due to passengers arriving late to the aircraft. The HAOC had received confirmation from Heathrow that the existing domestic security facility and the discreet route for domestic and Republic of Ireland connecting passengers would be retained. The T1 airlines accepted that this at least maintained the current level of service and the HAOC did not therefore propose to pursue the issue further at this time.

12.371. It was the HAOC's understanding that BAA were going to review the current list of airport charges with the intention of providing more detail to some of the product descriptions, delete any items that were no longer applicable and add new services and facilities as appropriate. To date the HAOC had not been consulted on an updated list of airport charges but understood it was to be reviewed.

12.372. The HAOC maintained the view that where buses were required to move passengers between aircraft and terminal buildings, due to the shortage of pier services, they should be provided by the airport operator and funded through airport charges. Heathrow had confirmed that it was willing to continue with the current arrangement of providing and managing the off-pier coaching and make it available to all interested airlines across the airport. The service was wholly funded, through the refund of 'Remote Stand Rebate' to HAL, by the airlines concerned. This arrangement was acceptable to those airlines requiring the provision of buses and the HAOC did not therefore propose to pursue this issue further at this time.

12.373. The provision of ambulances and high lifts to assist disabled passengers to get on and off aircraft were paid for by the Heathrow airlines, with a subvention from the London Ambulance Service. The HAOC had been concerned for some time that the London Ambulance Service might withdraw from this arrangement, making it impossible for the HAOC to continue to administer the provision of this service. This was an area which the HAOC believed should be provided by the airport operator and funded through airport charges. However, the latest indication from the London Ambulance Service was that it would continue to provide some financial support, which was fundamental to the HAOC's continued involvement in the provision of this service. Whilst this support remained, the service could be provided to a satisfactory level and the HAOC did not therefore propose to pursue this issue further at this time.

12.374. The HAOC considered that the airlines should benefit from retail commercial activity at Heathrow as the terminal infrastructure was paid for by airport charges levied on the airlines and others. The Heathrow Express and Piccadilly Line extensions should not be solely in the aeronautical till. With regard to the funding of T5 there was no clear explanation of how the CAA in February 2002 had arrived at a lower passenger figure of 60 million a year with regard to the incremental return; previously, in November 2001, this had been set at 70 million.

12.375. In answer to questions put by the CC about BAA's overall quality of service the HAOC said that Heathrow in general and the CTA in particular, suffered from major congestion due to lack of timely investment and current planning process constraints. Since the opening of T4 some 16 years ago, infrastructure improvements had been limited to upgrading some existing facilities, during which airline operations had had to continue in a 'building site' environment. In the meantime many airports around the world, such as Amsterdam, Frankfurt and Paris, had built new terminals providing better passenger facilities.

12.376. The introduction of SLAs in the last few years highlighted deficiencies in certain areas and resulted in some improvements to the availability of passenger-sensitive equipment. Since BAA assumed ownership of the transfer baggage system in 1999, improvements had been made to the infrastructure and operation, although more improvements were needed. In other areas airlines had had to provide resource to maintain standards at existing levels. For example, pier service levels, particularly in T3 and T4, relied on airlines increasing the number of aircraft required to tow off- and on-pier-served stands. In the coming years, prior to the opening of T5, it would become increasingly difficult to maintain service quality standards. It was therefore essential that standards were clearly defined and the airport operator was required to meet those standards through the regulatory framework.

12.377. Additional security requirements introduced since 11 September 2001 had resulted in the need for extra resources to process passengers through central search areas. Whilst the HAOC accepted that BAA continued to recruit additional security staff, security queuing was at times falling below acceptable levels. Parts of the general fabric of terminal buildings had fallen below acceptable standards. Walls, floors and ceilings, particularly in piers and gaterooms, need refurbishing. Leaking roofs exacerbate the problems. This situation needed to be rectified.

12.378. In answer to questions by the CC about the current position concerning SLAs at each airport the HAOC said that SLAs were in place with BAA for all four terminals at Heathrow, covering the availability of stands, jetties, escalators, conveyors, passenger lifts, goods lifts and security queuing. There was a separate agreement between BAA and BA covering the T1 departure baggage system.

12.379. The HAOC said SLAs or any alternative method of defining service quality standards should also include the availability of runways and taxiways, the performance of arrivals, departures and transfer baggage systems, the level of pier service and the availability of FEGP. The target for availability should be set to include planned maintenance in the calculation of downtime, as this could often be performed outside required operating times.

12.380. BAA published SLA performance monthly and distributed it to airlines by terminal, although for T3 the distribution was inconsistent. The content of the current SLA reports was satisfactory. The electronic 'back indication' system which showed faults on some of the equipment, should be extended to cover all SLA items, thereby eliminating the need to rely on manual fault reporting. The HAOC would like to see the introduction of CCTV to replace the current manual observations used in measuring security queuing.

12.381. The HAOC considered most of the current SLA target levels to be reasonable, but should include downtime for planned maintenance. The target for security queuing should be reviewed along with the method of measurement. Future SLAs should have target levels no lower than existing levels.

12.382. In answer to questions from the CC about the Q term and SLA rebates relating to airlines the HAOC said that none of the SLAs described above included price rebates or penalties for failure to achieve standard.

12.383. The HAOC believed that failure to deliver defined service standards should result in a financial penalty for the airport operator. An immediate rebate to the affected airline (similar to the remote stand rebate) was likely to be the preferred choice of the majority of airlines. However, a reduction in airport charges would also be acceptable.

12.384. The remote stand rebate was considered an effective way of compensating airlines for having to use a remote stand (this did not imply that the current level of rebate should remain unchanged).

12.385. In answer to questions from the CC about the Q term and SLA rebates relating to service to passengers the HAOC said that if a Q_P (passenger items) term were to be introduced, it believed it should operate in the same way as a Q_A (airline items) term. The performance standards for the passenger items should be defined with a financial penalty on BAA for failure to meet those standards. There should be no reward for performance above standard.

12.386. In answer to questions from the CC about the Q term and SLA rebates more generally, the HAOC said that if a Q-term approach was adopted, the elements for the QA components should be those outlined above. The airlines' main objective in having defined quality standards was to ensure that those standards were consistently met by the airport operator. The financial penalty for not achieving the standards must therefore be set at a high enough level to be a real incentive for the airport operator to deliver the required levels of service.

12.387. The HAOC said that with regard to airport congestion delays it agreed the principle of including a delay element as part of the defined service quality standards, whilst accepting that there were practical difficulties in implementation. The HAOC supported the initiatives from BA, and other airline industry representatives to find an acceptable method of implementing such a standard.

Air Transport Association of America Inc

12.388. The Air Transport Association of America Inc (ATA) told us it was the trade association for leading US airlines. ATA members transport over 95 per cent of all passenger and cargo traffic carried by US scheduled airlines. Speaking on behalf of its carriers with operations in the UK, as well as on behalf of its carriers operating at airports around the world, it wrote to us in response to our statement of current thinking on dual-till proposals.

12.389. The ATA told us that it supported the concept that airlines and airports existed and operated symbiotically. Their collective success or failure was ultimately determined by the manner in which they together served the transportation needs of the travelling and shipping public. For this reason, the ATA believed that business decisions made to enhance the relatively short-term returns of private investors, while running counter to the long-term needs of the larger public interest, were short-sighted and self-defeating. The ATA said that the commercial revenues flowed from, and were inextricably intertwined with, the aviation operations at the airports, and that as an economic and aviation policy matter, it was fair and appropriate for airlines to share in the commercial revenues.

12.390. The ATA said that some US airports did employ a dual-till system. However, it warned that it was important to note that under US federal law, these airports were required to retain all revenues—aeronautical and non-aeronautical alike—for reinvestment on the airport. Based on its experience with these airports, the ATA gave several key reasons why it believed the CAA proposals should be rejected. In the ATA's experience, a dual-till system (or 'compensatory system' as known in the USA):

(a) necessarily raised the charges airlines paid airports, with the result that these higher costs eventually were passed on to passengers in the form of higher fares;

(b) transferred revenue from airlines to airports;

(c) exacerbated the locational monopoly enjoyed by airports;

(d) did not lead to more efficient utilization of airports; and

(e) would not encourage new or greater investment in airport facilities.

12.391. The ATA said that the recent economic downturn, exacerbated by the tragic events of 11 September, had highlighted the fragile nature of the airline industry, which historically had existed on bare-bones profit margins of 0.5 per cent. Implementing a dual-till system would drive up airport costs for airlines, increases they could ill afford and, depending on the macro-economic situation, might not be able to recover. This would be unwise, especially if the increase in airport revenues returned nothing to the airport's aeronautical infrastructure in terms of greater capacity or efficiency.

12.392. The ATA told us that at the ICAO conference on the Economics of Airports and Air Navigation Services (ANSConf 2000), convened to revise ICAO Document 9082/6, the delegates from the signatory states had reaffirmed the principle that in sharing the costs of airport operations, allowance should be made for '… all aeronautical revenues plus contributions from non-aeronautical revenues accruing from the operation of the airport to its operators'. Recognizing and encouraging this partnership between airlines and airports was the best way to ensure that the public's increasing demand for a robust, efficient civil aviation system was met at reasonable cost and in a timely fashion.

12.393. The ATA concluded by saying that in this and other issues regarding the CAA Airports Review, it had originally allowed IATA to speak for it, since all ATA member carriers serving the UK were also members of IATA. However, at a later stage in the inquiry, the ATA's belief in the single-till principle was so strong that they chose in this instance to make their own submission as well.

BAR UK Ltd

12.394. BAR UK Ltd (BAR UK) is the trade association representing 90 scheduled airlines in the UK. It said it supported the CAA recommendation that the BAA London airports be regulated on a stand-alone basis. Separate price caps for each airport, based upon the individual airport's cost base, with no reference to the performance on cost or assets at the other two airports, should eliminate the possibility of cross-subsidy. Airlines operating at Heathrow and Gatwick also wanted to see developments at these two airports: greater use could be made of the existing runway at Heathrow through mixed mode. A new runway at Stansted would not therefore relieve pressure at Heathrow, nor should Heathrow users have to subsidize it.

12.395. BAR UK said that it did not support the proposal to move from a single to a dual till. The move would serve to increase its members' costs and came at a time when most of them were subject to severe financial pressures. BAR UK argued that prices under RRCB would be higher than under a single-till system, and that the CAA had attached greater importance to providing the monopoly operator, BAA, with an incentive to develop more capacity than it had to the interests of the airlines. At the time of the last MMC review in 1996 the CAA had assumed that T5 at Heathrow would have been built during the current quinquennial period. The price cap had reflected this assumption. BAR UK argued that the delay to the project could be ascribed to the planning procedures, and to a lesser extent to political concerns. BAA had indicated that it wanted to proceed with the project and had spent a vast amount of money in order to secure the planning permission. Therefore, the CAA's argument that the BAA's incentives to invest were weak under the single till ignored what had actually happened. BAR UK acknowledged that the Government was reviewing procedures for obtaining planning consent for major infrastructure projects and BAR UK hoped that the outcome would be a process that delivered in a reasonable time. However, its members had paid more than they should have during the current quinquennium and 50 per cent of the prefunding for T5 would not be refunded until the proposals for the next quinquennium were put into effect in April 2003. BAR UK felt that a full refund would be appropriate, as soon as possible.

12.396. Revenues generated from both aeronautical and other commercial activities occurred because of the passengers and shippers that patronized the airlines operating at the airports. It was reasonable that, as major stakeholders in the airports business, the airlines should continue to benefit from the success of retail sales in the terminals.

12.397. As to parallels with overseas airports applying the dual till, BAR UK noted that prime operators at major airports in the USA owned their terminals, and took the commercial revenues from them.

12.398. BAR UK regarded it as quite inconceivable that airlines would not have to raise fares if airport charges increased by about 70 per cent over ten years. The vast majority of its members currently made losses on their service out of Heathrow: if charges increased, all airlines would have to increase fares, and the benchmark for air fares would rise. As to whether efficient utilization of capacity would be improved if some airlines ceased operating out of Heathrow, BAR UK believed the natural market mechanisms were working anyway, with a number of short-haul services moving out of Heathrow.

12.399. BAR UK noted that the CAA commented that BAA would have 'something to lose' if it did not deliver outputs, in return for the higher revenues proposed, under RRCB. However, the review periods consisted of five years, and the airline industry could change significantly in such a period. In recent years competing airport systems in western Europe had built new runways and terminal buildings whilst the BAA London airports had had no such enhancements. Heathrow now served fewer destinations than it did ten years ago. BAR UK felt that the BAA shareholders were likely to act as a greater incentive to the company than the threat of having 'something to lose' over the five years from April 2003.

12.400. BAR UK believed prefunding of investment was undesirable, and was not a standard business practice: major companies would not normally be able to acquire revenues before new assets were brought into use. Although it acknowledged prices would have to rise because of the size of the infrastructure increases, it felt this could be offset by greater commercial revenues. As to consultation on investment, BAR UK acknowledged that BAA did consult on a regular basis: but often to little effect.

12.401. Service quality issues were of key importance to BAR UK and it welcomed the proposal to include them and an element relating to delays in the price cap. BAR UK was pleased to note that the

CAA had proposed that there should be a penalty for below-standard performance. Its members had no choice but to deal with BAA as the monopoly operator; however, the passengers and shippers who used its members' services did have a choice. If poor service quality from BAA resulted in business being lost, it was reasonable to expect that the regulator should afford carriers some protection.

12.402. BAR UK believed the 3 per cent limit on payments under the Q factor was too small; it also supported an asymmetric approach. It acknowledged that transfer baggage SLAs were currently working well—but would like to see such standards extended so it was clear what standards airlines could expect to receive for the charges paid. BAR UK was not seeking penalties as such however—but good service. It regarded a delay factor as important: although delays were caused by many reasons, its members were very clear about what caused delays and it was quite easy to establish how many could be attributed to the airport. A simple system could, in its view, be devised and shared with the airport.

12.403. BAR UK supported the proposal that there should be no automatic cost pass-throughs but felt that the current 95 per cent cost pass-through did not encourage the airport to be cost-conscious, and stated that staff were currently being inefficiently used. Security costs should be a responsibility of the state. BAR UK was pleased to note that the CAA was not pursuing its proposals to move to a tariff basket and wished to retain the revenue yield approach for the price cap. At Heathrow, BAR UK noted the CAA's intent to commit to 'a long run price path'. It understood the point made about long lead times and payback periods but questioned the credibility of the commitment when the review periods were of five years' duration. Furthermore, the present review could not make a commitment on behalf of the next review body.

12.404. At Stansted, BAR UK noted that the CAA thought a service quality term would be of no direct value. Like a long-term PPC, it might not be deliverable, but there ought to be an aspiration expressed at every airport in respect of service quality standards. The CAA should aim to have a service quality term built into the licences issued for all regulated airports. Airlines should know what they were getting for the charges they are required to pay.

British Air Transport Association

12.405. The BATA is the trade association for UK registered airlines. The BATA said it considered the CAA proposals overall to be counterproductive in their impact, serving to further enhance the powers of a sole monopoly service provider. It did not believe that the regulator was properly discharging its statutory duty to protect the reasonable interests of users. Accordingly, in the BATA's view, the CAA was not discharging its duties to the public interest.

12.406. The majority of the BATA members supported the recommendation that the price caps should be set in relation to the assets and costs of each airport on a stand-alone basis. Surface access infrastructure, within the airport boundary, could be included in these assets. There was only limited substitutability, from the airlines' point of view, between the three airports; the greatest demand was for travel through Heathrow, and investment at Heathrow; moreover, there was no longer any need for Stansted to be subsidized. The system approach merely encouraged BAA to invest where it was most comfortable rather than where the demand was greatest. Any new runway development at any airport should be paid for by users of that airport. The runways at Heathrow and Gatwick were already the most efficiently used in the world in operational terms, and operational efficiency was unlikely to be increased further by the CAA's approach, given also the low price elasticity of demand (in absolute terms) and the extent of capacity constraints. Even if there were to be a release of slots by some airlines, it would not necessarily be the case that the airline that acquired them would use them to provide services most valued by consumers: incumbents might be in a better position to operate the slots than new entrants.

12.407. Whilst the BATA supported the principle that the objective of a regulatory framework was to optimize the use of scarce airport resources and provide adequate financial incentives to provide additional capacity to meet increased demand, it did not accept that this objective could best be achieved by transfer to an RRCB with its requirements for ongoing and intrusive frontier policing and regular involvement of the regulator. The BATA therefore maintained that the standard RAB model, as presently used, was the best available option. To date the CAA had not provided detailed evidence on the conflicting benefits and disbenefits of the single-till versus dual-till proposals nor of the financial evaluation of alternative cost allocations between aeronautical and non-aeronautical facilities and services. The runways at Heathrow and Gatwick were already the most efficiently used in the world, and efficiency was unlikely to be increased further by the CAA's approach, given also the low price elasticity of demand and the extent of capacity constraints. Even if there were to be a release of slots by some airlines, it would not necessarily be the most efficient airline that acquired them: incumbents may still be in a better position to operate the slots than new entrants if earning monopoly rents.

12.408. Nor did the BATA believe the dual till would improve incentives for investment. It felt that incentives to invest in commercial facilities would be increased at the expense of investment in aeronautical facilities. It agreed with the CAA view that there was a wide commonality of interests between airports and users and a much greater degree of participation in the development of future airport strategy should be sought. However, BATA contended that it was not in the public interest for airports to undertake significant capex without holding prior discussions with appropriate user representatives. Airports should also seek agreement with users, rather than merely 'consulting' them; the results and consequences of consultation were uncertain.

12.409. The BATA said that the CAA's objective of establishing a stable long-run regulatory framework recognized that airports might opt to sweat assets, provide poor service quality and unreasonably fail to meet user demand. As a safeguard the CAA had warned it could revisit the framework at future reviews and BAA would therefore have 'something to lose'. The BATA considered that airports might well be prepared to take the risk of future revisions on the basis that the whole regulatory environment could well have significantly changed by the time of the next review. It would therefore prefer to see a system of penalties introduced for airports failing to provide capacity to match both increased traffic demand and capex plans agreed in prior consultations with the users.

12.410. The BATA supported the CAA's intention for the regulatory regime to provide suitable scope for 'win-win' contracts to be agreed outside regulation whilst continuing to provide adequate safeguards for the majority of users wishing to remain within the standard format. Under section 37 of the Airports Act any airport that was subject to economic regulation was only permitted to levy airport charges if the CAA had previously granted it permission by way of a specific licence. This could be used to incentivize service quality if it were to include service quality output standards, and the rebates that could flow automatically to users if such standards were not met. The Permission to Levy Charges should be used as the mechanism, to ensure adequate minimum levels of service since it had statutory force and was within the control of the regulator.

12.411. Recent examples of action taken without adequate consultation and of service charges that were not cost related were waste management; suspension of capex after 11 September; disruption when airbridges were repainted with advertising; poor TTS performance, with only one track running for several months, at Gatwick; and airport parking charges which include taxiing times which vary within the airport and discriminate against users of T4 (see paragraph 12.195). The conditions of use document contained unreasonable disclaimers that should be withdrawn. BAA should be liable for negligence, not just deliberate damage etc: the failure of main power supply was one instance in which airlines were unable to seek damages for negligence (of BAA's contractors).

12.412. The BATA considered that the current proposals to use price caps, explored in good faith by parties, had been critically weakened as operational service quality incentives by the CAA's decision to cap the risk to airports at an unrealistically low level. Price cap adjustments did not have the appropriate immediacy to be a good way of incentivizing on-the-day service quality outputs, but they could be useful in motivating airports to achieve planning standards. There should also be asymmetry in any system adopted: a supplier should not be able to charge for goods and services not requested. It also criticized unreasonable disclaimers in current conditions of use.

12.413. In the longer term, the BATA said that it remained essential to assure airlines that infrastructure would be developed in a timely fashion as described by the Airports Act. This had never so far been achieved, and this was undoubtedly to the public detriment. The BATA believed that prefunding should not be permitted unless specifically agreed by airlines: BAA would have no difficulty raising the finance required given the very low risk of projects particularly at Heathrow and at lower cost than if, in effect, funded by the airlines. Instead, projects should be phased, and remuneration should flow to the airport only when benefits flow to the passengers. There should be 100 per cent recovery of under-investment on T5.

12.414. Hence, the BATA suggested longer-term agreement on the investment programme; in the medium term a possible reopening of the price cap, subject to use of planning standards; and in the short term generic standards incorporated in the Permission to Levy Charges—details are given in Views of BA.

12.415. The BATA supported the recommendation that the structure of the price cap should be revised to eliminate automatic cost pass-throughs in order to encourage the airport to carry out security efficiently; requirements should be jointly managed between airlines and airport. There might be a need to revisit the whole issue of security costs (S factor) in the light of possible new government requirements post the attacks on 11 September 2001.

12.416. The BATA broadly accepted the recommendation that the well-proven and generally accepted revenue yield approach to the price cap should be retained. Non-passenger-carrying flights were already treated separately at Manchester and the BATA accepted the CAA recommendation that such flights at BAA London airports should be dealt with in a similar manner.

12.417. The BATA had been concerned for some time that the revenue yield approach provided an opportunity for airports to utilize unpublished discounts as a means of attracting new and/or additional traffic at the expense of existing carriers having to meet the cost burden of any resultant revenue shortfalls. It therefore fully supported the recommendation that all discounts should be transparent, published and available to all users of the airport.

Heathrow specific recommendations

12.418. The BATA supported the principle of transferring the risk of providing new capacity from users to the airport. The recommended price path approach would achieve the reverse and actually enhance the monopoly power that the regulator had a statutory duty to mitigate. The implication that assumptions could remain valid over such an extended time period was unrealistic and could not be said to be an emulation of competitive conditions. The CAA had been insistent that it could not bind the hands of future reviews.

12.419. The CAA proposed profiling the Heathrow price cap to enable higher charges in 2003–08 with lower charges subsequently. The CAA could not commit its successors to lower charges in the future. In addition, setting the price cap at RPI+6 per cent over the next five years effectively continued the policy of prefunding T5 which was totally opposed by all users.

12.420. The CAA had calculated that the incremental costs of increasing capacity from 60 mppa to 90 mppa was £18.00 per passenger a year (at 2000/01 prices). There had been no indication as to how this figure has been derived. The CAA's modelling assumptions forecast that the ART, and pre-phase 1 early release stands would be available in 2009/10 and thereafter provide BAA with a contribution to the overall price cap. The BATA had not had any opportunity to consider the programme nor any information as to what other items and assumptions were involved within the modelling and was therefore unable to comment on the issue.

12.421. The BATA could see no justification for introducing a stand-related incentive but reluctantly supported an incentive to deliver additional ATMs in peak periods.

12.422. The BATA supported the CAA view that there was a strong case for addressing quality of service explicitly as an integral part of the regulatory framework. However, the BATA believed that the whole subject was of such critical importance to both airlines and their customers as to warrant consideration as a public interest issue. It therefore supported BA's proposals on service standards. Users were seeking a clear specification of what their airport charges were paying for and believed that this could best be achieved by incorporation within an airport's licence to levy charges. This approach would not negate the ability of individual airlines, or groupings of airlines, to contract outside the generic level of charges for a higher level of service provision. The BATA were opposed to the principle of enabling airlines to contract for lower service levels. The generic service standards should be set at such a level as to meet the basic requirements of all users of the airport.

12.423. The BATA supported the application of an asymmetrical approach to the service quality term and strongly contended that the delay components should also be similarly treated. In addition it believed that the total impact of the quality term should be set at a higher level than the proposed limit of 3 per cent of aeronautical revenue a year to ensure that positive action was taken by BAA to both establish and maintain suitable service levels. It recognized there was still some way to go in developing a congestion term, but supported the CAA's proposals to do so; but it believed a delay term could be implemented based on Eurocontrol records.

12.424. The BATA was totally opposed to the whole principle of prefunding capital development. The CAA proposal to set the price cap for Heathrow at RPI+6 per cent over the period 2003/08 was in effect continuing with the policy of prefunding T5. The CAA's contentions that this would not lead to higher prices was theoretical rather than informed by business realities; airlines operated on low margins and there were a number of examples of recent cost burdens on the industry that it had to pass on to consumers, such as the additional insurance and security costs since 11 September; in such circumstances, an airline would match the reaction of its competitors.

Gatwick specific recommendations

12.425. The BATA accepted the CAA position that there were unlikely to be any major capacity enhancements at Gatwick during the period under review. The BATA was against a price-path approach at Gatwick for the same reasons as at Heathrow.

Stansted specific recommendations

12.426. The BATA was opposed to an RRCB approach but welcomed the recommendation to continue with the standard asset-based approach. The BATA had no strong views on whether a service quality term should be included for Stansted and considered that the issue could best be addressed by those airlines operating there.

Public interest

12.427. The BATA listed the following further matters of broad concern to the industry where it believed BAA's conduct had been against the public interest:

(a) BAA's refusal to seek an interim review given delays to T5 and higher than forecast passenger numbers.

(b) BAA's failure to produce a master plan for the London airports, together with a range of alternative options, detailed cost/benefit analysis of each project and full consultation with appropriate user representatives; which deprived users of the opportunity to adequately consider and make inputs on BAA's major approach. This resulted in piecemeal developments, impeding any subsequent longer-term redevelopment strategy.

(c) Lack of transparency on specified activities, in particular justification for allocation of costs.

12.428. BATA also criticized airport parking charges which included taxiing times which vary within the airport and discriminated against users of T4.

Business Aircraft Users Association Ltd

12.429. The Business Aircraft Users Association Ltd (BAUA) said that it was closely involved on a regular basis with the BAA airports on issues of access and costs. It also served on the CAA Finance Advisory Committee. If BAUA were to criticize charges at these airports after being involved in the work that produced them, it would seem illogical. However, for many years it had been concerned that these airports should not restrict access to their runways to only heavy airline equipment/scheduled carriers. That concern still existed.

International Air Transport Association

12.430. IATA said that it represented 275 members worldwide; some 130 of whom were using the London airports. IATA said it fully supported the proposal to establish separate price caps for each of the London airports. Although it recognized that it could be argued that operation of airport systems produced economies of scale, and allowed for capacity to be developed within that system if there were restrictions at particular airports, it was IATA's view that a system cap mostly led to unfair cross-subsidization and revenue diversion.

12.431. IATA did not believe that the RRCB incentivized appropriate or timely investment any more than the single till. While the CAA believed that the single till did not give the best use of available resources, IATA felt this was a theoretical view that had no practical effect. Additionally, the CAA stated that commercial revenues should not be regulated. IATA would like to see recognition of the relationship between aviation and commercial revenues. The airports enjoyed the same privileged monopoly on retail and on-site commercial revenues as they did on aeronautical revenues: the airport generated the profits by turning passengers into sales. Within the single-till policy there were sufficient incentives for the airports to increase profits from retail and commercial revenues, while minimizing the user charges.

12.432. IATA believed that the single till adequately and appropriately allowed for the sharing of commercial revenues between BAA and the airlines. It believed airports in a more competitive environment—as in the Gulf States—would use the single till in order to compete on airport charges. IATA was also concerned about the potential 'commercial creep' that would be encouraged through RRCB: airlines were currently prepared to put up with some inconvenience since they benefited from the commercial revenues, but given the finite amount of capital that would be available, it was concerned that preference could be given to commercial projects with higher returns.

12.433. IATA told us that airlines often owned the terminal buildings in the USA (and also Sydney) and commercial revenues were often shared as a result, depending on the terms negotiated. It also suggested that in the USA where airlines owned terminals, there was less element of shopping facilities. In IATA's view, the change from the single till at Sydney was clearly done to increase the value of the airport prior to its sale.

12.434. There was no reason to believe that the RRCB would be any better at incentivizing the airports to make appropriate or timely investments than the single till. Indeed, the CAA proposals recognized that the dual till actually increased the incentive for airports to invest in potentially higher yielding commercial projects than in aeronautical infrastructure. The main blockage to timely capacity investment had been political, planning and environmental reasons rather than the single till. The single till enabled lower airport charges to airlines and therefore lower prices to customers. A move to dual till took this benefit away from the airlines and their customers and put it in the hands of monopoly providers and their shareholders. Airlines and their customers faced significant price increases with no certainty or automatic improvement in capacity, congestion, delays or customer service. In the medium and longer term, fares would be affected by an increase in costs in a competitive market. IATA regarded the CAA's arguments that fares would not be increased as a result of the dual till as largely irrelevant.

12.435. In some areas users had been relatively undemanding on detailed transparency, justification and cost-allocation at the airports, against the background that the single till was beneficial to both parties. IATA warned that if the CAA proceeded with proposals to move towards dual till, however, with users paying full costs of aeronautical facilities, then the users would undoubtedly have more demanding and robust requirements for information and transparency. Dividing up properties between the two tills would also be difficult, for example for a new development such as T3 South Wing at Heathrow it would involve allocating the majority of the costs, but only a small proportion of revenues, to the aeronautical till.

12.436. IATA did not believe there was much credibility to the CAA's 'something to lose' argument, to the effect that if the airports failed to respond they would run the risk that the CAA would reconsider the appropriate regulatory framework. IATA felt that 'risk' and 'reconsider' were not indicative of any definite or robust action. Furthermore, IATA felt that in the event of any subsequent proposed changes BAA could presumably invoke protection of 'regulatory inconsistency'.

12.437. In general, IATA supported the possibility of direct contracting, provided there was an agreed robust price cap definition and adequate regulatory oversight to ensure no discriminatory or anti-competitive practices. The prerequisite was to first establish the agreed basic generic standards and levels.

12.438. IATA supported the elimination of automatic cost pass-throughs, or at least a reduction in the current 95 per cent cost recovery of additional security requirements which it felt gave inadequate incentive to provide the most cost-effective distributions, and as a separate cost base, with greater transparency: but it believed the cost of aviation security should be borne by the state and pointed to changes in arrangements in the USA, and the assistance given more generally to civil aviation in the USA after 11 September.

12.439. IATA supported the continued use of revenue yield and separate treatment of non-passenger flights.

12.440. IATA did not support any discounts or rebates that were not cost-related as these could be considered discriminatory or anti-competitive. It accepted start-up assistance for new routes providing these were for reasonable and clearly defined periods. However, there should be clearer transparency of discounts at Stansted.

12.441. With regard to Heathrow, IATA supported an output-based approach, and for the transfer of risk for new capacity, from the users to the airport. The CAA had frequently reminded IATA, however, that it was unable to bind conditions beyond the quinquennium under review. IATA was therefore surprised at the inconsistency with the proposal for a long-run price path. IATA felt it was unrealistic to expect that assumptions could remain valid over such an extended period of time. The adoption of a long-run price path would increase the monopoly powers of the airport that the CAA was supposed to be regulating.

12.442. IATA had not been consulted nor party to any discussion on the reduction of the target (beyond which the incremental cost of T5 would be charged) from 70 mppa to 60 mppa at Heathrow, and was unaware of any justification or reasons for this change from the CAA's preliminary proposals. It was concerned other terminals might not only handle far more passengers than that before T5 opened, but might also continue to do so after T5 opened. At any rate, IATA were not convinced that financial incentives were appropriate for addressing aviation capacity, nor for additional stand capacity.

12.443. IATA was extremely concerned at the significant impact on charges as a result of the proposed increase to RPI+6 over 2003 to 2008. As there was no guarantee that the CAA would be able to commit its successors to any subsequent lower charges after 2008, the RPI+6 level perpetuated the prefinancing of T5 to which IATA had consistently objected.

12.444. Further to IATA's belief that financial incentives were inappropriate for addressing aviation capacity, it felt that the provision of the necessary capacity was inherent in the statutory objectives or government policies, and should not be a choice between investment opportunities. Alternative and more cost-effective methods of financing terminal capacity should be investigated. Consideration should also be given to breaking the monopoly of airports' financing of terminal developments. Against this background the airlines should not be expected to bear the negative effects of obliging or motivating the airports to fulfil their responsibilities. The CAA recommendations were, in effect, asking the airlines to pay more to the airports for what they should already be providing. The proposed incentives for increasing passenger numbers and ATMs at Heathrow, together with the proposed move to RRCB, could be considered as being a combination of both incremental costing and prefinancing; IATA did not support this.

12.445. The proposed move to RRCB underestimated the ability of the airports and the airlines to agree on payment for genuinely demanded airport capacity to be delivered, independently from what was allowable by regulation. There was no evidence that airport charges had ever been an obstacle to additional capacity if airlines and airports had agreed demand. Capacity enhancement was highly valued by the airlines, but not at any price. In the longer term, it was essential for airlines to have assurance that the necessary capacity and facilities would be developed in time to meet demand, as described in the Airports Act.

12.446. IATA acknowledged that the general level of consultation with BAA compared well with other airports; in the USA, however, there tended to be negotiation rather than consultation, whereas there tended to be a presentation from BAA rather than negotiation or debate. It fully supported the

CAA's proposal that consultation should be more meaningful. IATA felt that appropriate bodies already existed for this. Consultation in relation to capital investments and strategic planning should be undertaken through the LACC, and through the User Charges Panel with regard to the impact on costs and charges. More detailed information in the CIP was necessary; issues of connectivity with T5 ought to have been developed earlier.

12.447. IATA welcomed the proposal to introduce quality terms in the price caps, together with the asymmetric application for those components that were of primary interest to the airlines. This would result in a reduction to the cap in the event of performance below par, while over-performance should not be rewarded; 'averaging' across output measures also weakened incentives. IATA was not aware of any other airport, which already had such standards. However, the CAA's proposal to limit the total impact of the Q term to 3 per cent of aeronautical revenue a year might be insufficient incentive to ensure that robust action was taken to establish and maintain appropriate service standards. Also, IATA did not find the customer surveys to be meaningful, as they were carried out by BAA and therefore potentially biased. It therefore only preferred 'hard' standards be included. IATA felt that a delay term must be considered for inclusion in service quality terms. Detailed statistics on causes of delay, standardized by IATA, were already collected by airlines but as an internal airline assessment for management to control delays. IATA recommended that this could, however, be extended and the data subject to independent verifications.

12.448. IATA supported SLAs as a means of ensuring airports delivered agreed service levels to airlines and passengers, but they were better suited to bilateral arrangements. It believed that generic standards should be included in the airports' Conditions of Use, and that such contracts should be linked to the charges (if these could not be used for legal reasons, consideration should be given to application through the licence or permission to levy charges). Airport charges should be for agreed basic facilities and service levels that the airlines needed and used. Agreement with users should be required on basic or generic levels. Those users who requested them should then be able to pay for additional facilities or services above this level, but contracting down for lower service standards could involve subsidy and therefore might be anti-competitive and discriminatory.

12.449. IATA supported BA's proposals for service standards. Planning standards were an essential part of service standards and should be linked to price caps as a means of ensuring service delivery in the medium term. Agreement on the investment programme through the regulatory settlement was the best way to achieve the required levels of service quality in the longer term.

12.450. IATA supported the proposal to reduce the starting asset bases at Heathrow and Gatwick to reflect T5 prefunding. During the previous review IATA had strongly objected to the proposal of RPI–3 that allowed for the prefinancing of T5. IATA had argued at the time that if capex were deferred the formula assumptions could be wrong. BAA also had the opportunity to subsequently spend either on projects that were not agreed airline priorities, or on commercial infrastructure at the expense of aeronautical facilities. IATA believed it was justified that the full amount be refunded to the users, and queried the CAA's preliminary proposal to only remove 50 per cent, rather than 100 per cent, of the estimated gains from the deferral. Rather than future prefunding, IATA's preference was for a factor to be included in the formula to allow for charges to be adjusted, as and when, major capital programmes such as T5 were actually brought into use. However, IATA acknowledged that some element of prefunding may be necessary for a development of the size and scale of T5, but subject to agreement between the airport and the airlines.

12.451. IATA welcomed the CAA's proposal to end the cross-subsidy of Stansted by Heathrow and Gatwick charges, but this would not come into effect until April 2003. IATA did not believe that the pricing structure would influence airlines to change airports—unless there were extreme differences—hence there was little cause for Stansted charges to be below those of Heathrow to reflect different pressure of demand.

12.452. IATA fully supported the recommendation to remove surface access infrastructure from the aeronautical till. Taking into consideration the economic benefits of the airports, financing should be done through the normal surface transport funding mechanisms. IATA were therefore concerned at the linkage of surface access infrastructure with planning permissions, and how this would be treated. It was particularly concerned at the possible diversion of aeronautical revenues to surface access infrastructure instead of essential aeronautical capacity and facilities.

13 Views of other third parties

Contents

Introduction

13.1. This chapter summarizes the views of other third parties. Two hearings were held with other third parties.

Concessionaires and licensees

Consignia

13.2. Consignia said it was the operator of the Royal Mail's universal postal service. Royal Mail had a statutory duty to provide a letter delivery service to every address in the UK at a uniform price irrespective of the distance. Consignia's parcels business, Parcelforce Worldwide, also made more limited use of air transport.

13.3. Consignia emphasized that, although it was a major and frequent user of aircraft facilities, it did not operate its own aircraft fleet but used the services of other operators. In the first instance then, it would be for those operators to comment directly on the effect of any proposed changes. Nevertheless, Consignia would ask the CC to bear in mind that Royal Mail's statutory obligations for provision of a major public service could be affected by any change that impacted adversely on either the time taken to deliver mail to its destination or any charges that added to the costs of providing mail services to the public.

Flightline International Ltd

13.4. Flightline International Ltd (Flightline) said that it had submitted to the previous inquiry that there was an argument for two travel outlets at Gatwick. BAA later decided to tender these separately as a flight-only outlet and a travel outlet that sold flights and holidays rather than allowing the two to compete.

13.5. Flightline said that it thought that the decline from two travel shops to one was caused by reasons that went back further than the current changes in the market and back to the original tendering process where the projections were inflated and which had resulted in unsustainable minimum fees and larger than required outlets. This had been repeated at Glasgow and Stansted.

13.6. Had the travel companies paid a rent rather than projected trading fees it would have been a different story. It was because Flightline was an airport specialist that it had been able to make it work while accepting the prestige of having an outlet at such an important international airport. Flightline said that its experience in the travel industry rather than of airlines at Gatwick had enabled it to operate reasonably successfully selling most flights right up to departure.

13.7. It was unfortunate that the criteria used to judge the other airport retail outlets (passenger throughput) had little bearing on the potential of the travel outlets. The fact that BAA retail staff knew little about the travel industry and the complications of requirements of the different licences in an instant travel environment had not helped and had resulted in travel shop failures. A number of regional airports had high-street travel outlets which on the whole operated successfully as the local population were able to pop in to make an inquiry and at the same time experienced the excitement of making what usually was a pleasant purchase.

13.8. Unfortunately there was a different story at a large international airport such as Gatwick where there was no such excitement, but rather more congestion, stress and expensive parking and food. Buying at Gatwick airport was expensive and with a large town locally with a range of high-street travel outlets the whole experience of visiting Gatwick became less appealing.

13.9. Flightline said that the growth of low-cost airlines who sold direct to passengers; the amount of discounted sales by airlines and tour operators; the increase in internet sales and other changes had effected the market. However, if an outlet was to be successful it had to have the right licences to match the point of sale and be able to provide one-stop shopping while complying with the CAA Air Travel Organiser's Licence regulations. Flightline believed this was the second major reason its competitors had failed rather than just the changing market conditions.

13.10. Gatwick Airport travel outlets needed to be airport specialists with the licences to sell on to all planes right up to departure and be able to evolve to sell on to the new carriers. Flightline said that because of the changing trading conditions one outlet was now sufficient.

Global Refund (UK) Limited

13.11. Global Refund (UK) Limited (Global Refund) said it wished to alert the CC to a course of conduct pursued by BAA in relation to the granting of exclusive concessions to operate VAT refund facilities at Heathrow and Gatwick airports. Many major airports in Europe operated with at least two operators authorized to offer cash refund services to travellers. Experience at these airports demonstrated that there were no significant problems as to queuing or customer confusion arising from there being more than one VAT refund concessionaire.

13.12. In 1999, Travelex was awarded the exclusive concession to operate VAT cash refund facilities on behalf of VAT refund operators such as Global Refund at Heathrow and Gatwick airports. The concessions expired in 2002 and Global Refund understood that BAA had decided unilaterally to extend them until 2006 without a tender exercise. The granting by BAA of exclusive rights to Travelex on an ongoing basis had resulted in a substantially higher level of fees being charged at Heathrow and Gatwick airports than at other major airports in Europe; a quality of service provided by Travelex which was not of a standard deemed satisfactory and a distortion of competition between Travelex and other bureaux de change not able to provide VAT refund services.

13.13. Global Refund requested the CC to investigate the issue and to recommend that BAA open up the market for VAT cash refund services by allowing other bureaux de change, and retail outlets approved by BAA, to provide this service at BAA-controlled airports on behalf of VAT refund companies including Global Refund.

Company A

13.14. Company A said that BAA operated in a manner which exploited their monopoly position as the airport authority. Company A said it was recognized by BAA that international car rental companies derived a substantial amount of their revenue from their airport businesses and that they were therefore dependent to a significant degree on their presence at the major airports. Car rental tariffs had remained static in real terms in general for the last five years. This in turn had resulted in profit margins in the car rental sector being extremely slim (at best) both as a percentage of revenue and as a percentage of investment made. Airport authorities imposed costs and trading conditions which were seldom negotiated effectively because the parties were not on a level playing field as a result of the authorities' monopoly position.

13.15. Company A paid a concession fee to BAA for being present on airport. The amount of the concession fee was calculated as the greater of a percentage of revenue or a minimum annual guarantee (MAG). The MAG was reduced if passenger numbers fell below a predetermined threshold. However, if this happened, the MAG was only reduced by the amount in excess of the threshold. As the fee was strongly influenced by the BAA's projections of passenger numbers, it would be apparent that both revenue and profitability were dependent upon those projections of passenger numbers issued by BAA. However, as the MAG was only reduced by the percentage, which exceeded the threshold figure, Company A was effectively penalized by the fact that it had to bear the extra expenditure up to the threshold. There could be no justification for this, but was an example of BAA exercising its monopoly powers. BAA should be required to reduce the MAG for the total fall in BAA's projected passenger numbers.

13.16. An example of a dramatic fall in passenger numbers arose following the terrorist activities on 11 September 2001. It would be appreciated that a fall in passenger numbers would inevitably have a damaging effect on the revenue of operators at the airport, not least because their fixed costs (in particular rents) remained the same. In addition, this inevitably also led to a loss of productivity and efficiency for the operators. There should, in addition, be a requirement upon the authority to also reduce the level of all fixed cost items payable to it. Unless this was done, BAA would increasingly move its revenue away from the variable items (ie the concession fee) to the non-variable items (for example rents).

13.17. The definition of revenue upon which the concession fee was calculated was crucial in determining the monetary amount of the fee. In other words the wider the definition, the higher the fee. BAA imposed its definition without recognition of whether the percentage, applied to any component in the make-up of the revenue, was economic or not. There was no effective negotiation of these components.

13.18. The Vehicle Licence and Registration Fee (VLF) referred to both the road fund licence and the charge imposed by the Government some four years ago to recover the cost of registering vehicles for the first time. BAA did not have regard to the fact that items such as VLF were charged to customers only to recover the cost of this charge. This fact was not recognized by BAA which nonetheless imposed the full concession fee rate. All attempts to negotiate this charge as not being within the definition of concessionable revenue had been turned down. BAA consequently benefited from a wider definition of concessionable revenue.

13.19. BAA required operators to set their charges on airport at a level which was equivalent or comparable to charges at its downtown locations. This inevitably meant that charges at some downtown locations were not determined by the usual market conditions, but by BAA using its monopoly position to dictate how an independent operator should set its charges. Charges at certain downtown locations could therefore be artificially higher, thereby distorting the market. The concession fee was expressed as a percentage of revenue. The fee for renewed concession periods was negotiated, but these negotiations were not characterized by the dynamics of normal free market negotiations. Negotiations regarding the concession fee were simply based on what BAA decided the fee should be. Company A currently paid the greater of a fee of 10 per cent of concessionable revenue or the MAG. Company A had no way of knowing whether the fee was fair given the monopoly position of BAA nor what relationship the fee bore to the operating costs of BAA, nor, whether in this monopoly environment the profit margins made by BAA were reasonable or not.

13.20. Fees could be fixed according to a determination being made after an economic analysis of what the reasonable operating costs of BAA should be, together with a RPI–X formula for any fee increased where X was determined by an external independent body. This should result in requiring BAA to leverage maximum efficiency and ultimately to lead to lower operating costs for on-airport operators. This would inevitably lead to benefits for customers in the form of lower tariffs and improved service. In addition, such a methodology would consequently require BAA to maximize the number of passengers using the airport, thereby increasing the revenue of operators.

13.21. As the concession fee payable to BAA was expressed as a percentage of the operator's revenue, BAA would consequently benefit from becoming more efficient by controlling its costs effectively and through any increase in passenger numbers. Alternatively, the initial fee should be based on the authorities' costs but BAA should not be allowed to increase the concession fee percentage thereafter. Any increase in its revenue should come from an increase in the operators' revenue.

13.22. The level of the service provided at Stansted for vehicle turnaround facilities was far from satisfactory. This had been the case for some ten years. It comprised the most basic washing facilities which not only adversely impacted upon the operator's efficiency and its service to customers, but also posed health and safety risks to the operator's employees. BAA for this airport had failed over a long period of time to correct these serious shortcomings and to make the necessary investment, despite numerous attempts to remedy this situation by the car rental operators.

13.23. Company A, in common with other operators, were required to make investments in the facilities provided to it by BAA. These investments could require significant expenditure costing several million pounds. The problem was that at the end of the concession period, BAA required (as a condition of the Concession Agreement) that the investment (for example, buildings, fuel tanks, plant and machinery etc) be acquired by BAA at no cost to BAA.

13.24. There was no recognition by BAA of this investment if the operator chose not to renew its concession, or if the operator failed to acquire a new concession. This effectively tied the operator to BAA and inevitably led to all incumbent operators who chose to renew their concessions offering higher and higher concession fees to BAA in order to assure themselves of their continued presence on airport and also to protect the investments made. Consequently, this led to higher charges to customers.

13.25. In addition, the operator was required to write down the investment over the relatively short life of the concession period. This led to artificially higher costs for customers because of the short period required to recover these costs. Under normal market conditions (ie off airport), one could expect to write down such investments over a much longer period in the region of 10 to 25 years. Further, at the end of the concession period when BAA acquired ownership of the capital item, the operator was required to pay a further amount for the use of that same capital item which it had already paid for itself during the earlier concession period. BAA should be required to compensate the operator for any unamortized capex items calculated reasonably and in accordance with a formula agreed with the operator. If, conversely, the operator did acquire a new concession, the operator should not have to pay for the use of that capital item in the new concession period.

13.26. In addition to paying the concession fee, the operator also had to pay rent for occupying premises on airport. As the operator was entirely dependent upon BAA, it was able to set the amount of the rent at levels which were substantially higher than properties in neighbouring areas. BAA should be required to set the amount of such rents reasonably taking account of rents in neighbouring areas and market conditions.

Ground handling agents

KLM Royal Dutch Airlines (ground services)

13.27. KLM Royal Dutch Airlines (ground services) said that the IATA response to the CC reflected its views. However, KLM explicitely stressed concerned with the CAA's recommendations to move away from the single-till concept, and also to introduce incentives linked to passenger numbers and ATMs, which would result in significantly higher charges without any certainty that the necessary capacity and service would be delivered.

13.28. Economic Reviews of UK airports had consistently endorsed the single-till approach as being reasonable and business plans for both KLM and KLM ground services had taken this into account. There were no new arguments to support a move away from the single till and it should be retained.

The Go-Ahead Group plc

13.29. The Go-Ahead Group plc operated at 17 UK airports through its various subsidiaries trading as Aviance. Airports served include those operated by BAA.

13.30. Aviance had a number of concerns about the operation of airports and the relationship between the airport operator, the airlines and other service providers, including ground handlers such as Aviance.

13.31. Aviance said that it had no opportunity to offer passenger handling services at Heathrow T4 because BA One World and KLM had self handling arrangements because of the BAA requirement that handlers must achieve a minimum threshold level of business (5 per cent) before being granted a licence. The transfer of airlines from the South Terminal to North Terminal at Gatwick was restricted until 2002 and was only allowed now because of the reduction of the BA programme. This meant that under-utilization of facilities including check-in desk operations, lounge business etc at individual terminals could not readily be dealt with. Equally, transfers to South Terminal from North Terminal resulted in similar under-utilization. Aviance said that economies of scale were therefore impossible to achieve.

13.32. Competition in both passenger and cargo handling was fierce, resulting in lower charges to airlines and difficulty in sustaining service levels and a reasonable return on capital. The market suffered from predatory pricing. At Heathrow, this enabled Globeground and Swissport to gain entry to T1 by underbidding for the handling contracts of South African Airways and Cyprus Airways. Similarly at Gatwick, Servisair underbid for Delta Air Lines and Emirates giving them access to North Terminal. Such bidding tactics further reduced margins for all ground handlers and resulted in an unsustainable price competition.

13.33. Gatwick had failed to police the business plans of new handling agents, allowing them to buy market share by offering below-cost handling, and therefore ultimately contributing to their failure. The lower charges were then cited by the airlines to be the market price and as a consequence were difficult to raise to sustainable levels. This increased competition and fall in revenues was not matched by a reduction in the cost of facilities.

13.34. The proposed introduction of a fourth handling agent at Gatwick was motivated by the airline community to increase competition and further reduce charges. This was being carried out despite the fact that BA had cut many of its Gatwick services and had re-entered the third party handling market to replace lost business. In order to make use of vacant space and underemployed staff BA had undercut Aviance for the Northwest cargo handling contract resulting in a loss of that business. Meanwhile, Aviance had been constrained by inadequate cargo facilities and had been unable to secure the improved facilities it had sought from BAA. A further handler would inevitably lead to further loss of business as the new entrant underbid to obtain market share. This would further reduce handling charges and profitability. Ultimately, this affected the handling agents ability to invest in the business, including airport equipment needed in order to meet the maximum age criteria determined by BAA.

13.35. Aviance said that at Heathrow, CTA rents were geared to an index of passenger numbers, RPI, Building Cost Information Service and the Investment Property Database Index (off-airport). At Gatwick and Stansted rental guidelines were produced annually, and purported to be based on the off-airport property market although no supporting information was provided. An example showed Gatwick guideline rents for cargo sheds growing by 13 per cent in the same year that cargo tonnages for the UK fell by between 15 and 20 per cent. The absurdity of this was compounded by the fact that the three component parts of the cargo sheds, warehouse, office and forecourt, were all listed as growing at different rates. Rental charges for accommodation such as business lounges were the same for airline and handling agents regardless of the airlines ability to charge for increased ticket prices compared to the handling agent charge per head, and the fact that business available to the latter was outside their control. As had recently happened at Gatwick, airlines often made the decision to open their own lounge. This resulted in an immediate loss of business without a reduction in rent.

13.36. Check-in desks were costed on the basis of full cost recovery as allowed by the CAA. Supporting information provided by the CAA was impossible for the handling agent to verify. Full cost recovery was expected regardless of whether the desks were fully utilized, ie the airport operator bore no risk in a downturn. At Gatwick and Stansted the charges were levied on the handling agent. It was therefore the handling agent who bore the burden of rent collection from the airline and the risk of airline failure. In the event of the failure of an airline the handling agent remained responsible through its occupational leases and licences for meeting the BAA overhead.

13.37. At Gatwick moves towards charging by the hour rather than an annual licence fee had been supported by Aviance but on the basis that the charge was levied on the airline and that a transparent charging mechanism was put in place which reflected any undercapacity in the terminal and that under-utilized desks were paid for by the airport operator rather than the handling agent. The current proposal, however, was that handling agents were still to be charged, despite the airport operator being responsible for allocation and the airline for choice of desks and the number of desks opened. The formula suggested that the optimum opening time for a desk was six hours a day and that any under-recovery was carried forward to be paid for by handling agents in the future by way of increased charges. Similarly, any over-recovery was put back into the pot to be spread across all desks in the future. This meant that the handling agent able to use a desk for more than six hours a day cross-subsidized airlines/handling agents who were less successful and also effectively paid for vacant desks. Aviance said that it believed this was anti-competitive.

13.38. Additionally, in the North Terminal at Gatwick, the calculation had been undertaken on third party handling lines only and without taking any account of BA as the majority occupier. Aviance believed that were this to be included the rate per hour would reduce and it was therefore both unfair and inconsistent with the approach at the South Terminal.

13.39. Maintenance rents and service charges on operational property in and around the terminals were not transparent. Maintenance rents were based on indexed uplifts of charges set many years ago and there was no reconciliation available to determine their accuracy.

13.40. At Heathrow in the last three years rents had risen on average by over 12 per cent, and at Gatwick and Stansted between 1998 and 2001 by between 10 and 30 per cent and 10 and 27 per cent respectively. Turnaround charges had not grown in the same way and in some cases had fallen. Rents were becoming an increasingly high percentage of turnover and therefore becoming significantly more important. The rental levels did not reflect the number of handling agents in any given terminal. Increased competition led to more competitive turnaround charges, handling contract movements and less business generally. Margins were therefore reduced and service levels more difficult to maintain at the level contracted between handling agent and airport authority.

13.41. The handling agents operated by virtue of a ground handling agreement, which among other things stipulated the service level to be provided and the penalties for non-compliance. However, achievement of the performance standards was often beyond the agent's control. It could be the case that an airline's own performance requirements differed from those through which the airport sought to maintain its own image and this could lead to penalties on the handling agents through no fault of their own. No-frill carriers were reluctant to open more than the bare minimum of check-in desks and this could lead to queuing times which contravened the service level requirement. There was an inconsistency in the policing of such service levels and new entrants had been given time to adapt to the different pressures that charter operations brought with their seasonal peaks and troughs.

13.42. Check-in desks were licensed direct to the handling agent whilst allocation to airlines and number of desks opened remained in the control of BAA and or the airline customer.

13.43. Despite its presence at all BAA airports including the three London airports and the Go-Ahead group's other significant transport operations in and around a number of these airports, BAA had been reluctant to enter into anything other than airport-by-airport relationships at a relatively low level. This was not the case with relationships between BAA and other transport operators or the airlines, placing ground handlers and other service providers at a significant disadvantage in understanding and contributing to the development of an airport strategy.

13.44. Aviance said that it was dissatisfied with the terms of the commercial approach BAA Airports had with their service providers. As an example, the terms and conditions of the ground handling licences at both Gatwick and Stansted were not concluded until well after initiation dates. Negotiations for properties at all three airports were not expedient and in most cases were concluded after occupancy. Aviance was also concerned that having identified business opportunities, confidentiality was not maintained and the opportunity was offered as a priority to the carriers first (for example, Gatwick arrival lounges) or implemented by BAA. It was not possible to have meaningful discussions on future development as a group. Recently, at Gatwick, meetings took place with the Managing Director of Gatwick to discuss the future cargo facility strategy. A request for purpose built facilities was made by Aviance. The initial response was that this would not be achievable as Gatwick would have to go through a tendering process (even though direct build for carriers had taken place without a tendering process). The topic was still unresolved a year later.

Local authorities

Mole Valley District Council

13.45. Mole Valley District Council (Mole Valley) said that it abutted Gatwick and experienced some of the environmental disbenefits of such close proximity, including air and ground noise, surface traffic and airport-related development pressures. The Mole Valley accepted the airport's growth within its existing single runway, two terminal configuration, but considered that more should be done through the application of economic instruments to ensure that the aviation industry met a greater proportion of its external environmental costs. This was an important matter which was raised in the Government's consultation paper on *The Future of Aviation*.

13.46. In this regard, it felt that the CAA policy of fixing price caps on airport charges was not making a sufficient contribution to this process. It was also part of a wider economic climate wherein current tax concessions gave the aviation industry an uncompetitive advantage. This whole issue should be examined by the CC, since these advantages helped fuel the increase in air travel without regard for the external environmental costs that this caused, including noise, pollution and the demand for more runway capacity.

13.47. While the CAA's proposal to end the single-till arrangement and the proposed increase in airport charges was welcomed, they would have only a minimal effect on reducing the environmental impact of the aviation industry and would not help align the price of slots to their true market value. This was something the CC should address since the current practice of price caps and slot allocation contributed to artificially holding down the cost incurred by airlines. The CC should give consideration to finding ways that would allow airport charges to reflect their true market value. This could include abandoning the practice of grandfather rights and include the auction of slots. This could have the potential to improve competition, help reduce the artificial distortion of the air travel market and go some way towards encouraging the aviation industry to meet its external environmental costs. It was appreciated that such an approach was outside the CAA's remit, but slot auctioning was under discussion within the EC and should be considered by the CC.

Reigate and Banstead Borough Council

13.48. Reigate and Banstead Borough Council (Reigate and Banstead) said that Gatwick immediately adjoined its southern boundary at Horley, which was the nearest town to the airport. Horley and the south of the borough therefore experienced some of the benefits and disbenefits of such close proximity. Reigate and Banstead were not in a position to specify a maximum level of airport charges for Gatwick. However, it supported the view that the charges should relate to the demand at the airport, as it was currently illogical for airlines using the busiest airports to be paying lower charges and thus inflating demand leading to environmental disbenefits.

13.49. The current CAA policy of fixing price caps on charges was not making sufficient contribution towards the government policy that aviation should meet its external costs. Reigate and Banstead therefore supported the end of the single-till principle which had resulted in price caps being driven down. If the single till was abandoned, it seemed that prices, and thus income, at the most congested airports should rise. Reigate and Banstead would be looking to ensure that this meant that additional money was available for an airport to meet its external costs, particularly public transport improvements at and to Gatwick and the amelioration of noise and air pollution locally. It was Reigate and Banstead's view that these external costs should include regular monitoring and reporting and would support the ring-fencing of a proportion of the charges to meet these external costs.

Surrey County Council

13.50. Surrey County Council said that it wished to endorse the comments made by the Aviation Environment Federation. It also supported the abolition of the single till to enable aviation to meet its external costs by charging more at congested airports.

Tandridge District Council

13.51. Tandridge District Council said that it did not wish to specify a maximum level of airport charges. However, it considered that airport charges should relate to the level of demand as it was not logical for airlines using the busiest airports to be paying lower charges and thus inflate demand. The regulatory regime should allow for inclusion of surface access/public transport requirements in the charges.

Waverley Borough Council

13.52. Waverley Borough Council said it considered that the proposals envisaged would adversely affect the borough by an increase of vehicular traffic relating to Gatwick on its eastern boundary.

National representative bodies

Airport Operators Association

13.53. The Airport Operators Association (AOA) said that it wished to confine its comments to three issues, namely the dual till, security costs and funding for ground transport.

13.54. The AOA noted that the CAA had recommended a move away from the single till as a basis for setting airport charges to a system based on an RRCB, or a dual till. This recognized the economic efficiency of ensuring that airport charges to airlines and passengers were based on the cost of providing the facilities which they actually used, and encouraged a more commercial approach to the provision of airport facilities as a whole. Such a move away from the single till was also consistent with the approach being adopted in other countries such as Australia, as recognized by IATA in recently revised guidelines to member states on the setting of airport charges which noted the move away from the single-till approach. The adoption of a dual-till approach to setting airport charges was of general application and was strongly supported by the airports industry worldwide. The change to a dual till would have wider application to other AOA member airports, which would assist them in developing their commercial approach to business opportunities. Thus the AOA urged the CC to adopt the CAA's broad recommendations in this area.

13.55. Particularly in the aftermath of 11 September, the funding of the costs of the required additional security measures had become a major issue for UK airports. It was clear that in many other countries, particularly the USA but also several in Europe, the costs of additional security measures were being met by member states, albeit that the costs were often passed on to users through taxes or security measures. This was in partial recognition of the fact that the threat was not specific to air transport but was actually a threat to national security. UK airports were very concerned that there were no equivalent proposals in the UK and the industry was being expected to fund the cost of additional measures directly. The AOA would thus strongly support the continuation of the use of an S factor to allow BAA airports to recover much of the cost of additional security measures imposed by the Government, consistent with the view that such costs were not directly related to airport operations but to national security.

13.56. It was thus, of general concern that the CAA had proposed that BAA and Manchester Airports should no longer be able to recover the majority of the costs of additional security measures, imposed by the state, from users via the S factor. This went beyond the UK Government's requirement that the airports paid the cost of additional security measures and recovered the costs from users to an expectation that airports should absorb the costs of additional security measures without any ability to recoup these from users. This further disadvantaged UK airports and set a precedent in relation to the responsibility of airports for funding the costs of additional security measures.

13.57. The AOA was aware that the UK Government placed great store on provision of improved surface, particularly public transport, links to UK airports. The AOA had been actively involved in the establishment of government guidelines for the airport transport forums. It was clear that airports and their users would be expected to meet a substantial proportion of the costs of the provision of improved links over time. The AOA had noted with some concern that the CAA had proposed that at the regulated airports such costs would not be included in the RRCB unless expressly required as a result of planning approval to a development proposal. This appeared to be directly contrary to the Government's intention to actively encourage airports to invest in public and other transport initiatives. Such investments were necessary to increase the proportion of passengers accessing airports by public transport, regardless of proposals for increasing airport capacity under the planning system. In many cases, such initiatives would not be commercially viable and, furthermore, funding would also need to recognize the extent to which there were wider network benefits to be obtained from the investment in improved transport links serving airports, as part of the urban infrastructure. The beneficiaries of such links would be the airlines, as it would be easier for passengers to access the airport by all modes, the passengers themselves and the wider community. Airports would seldom benefit directly from such links, particularly if they were not able to recover the costs through airport charges.

13.58. The AOA was concerned to ensure that its members were incentivized to invest in public and other transport links, consistent with the Government's policy objectives. Furthermore, the AOA supported the view that airlines and passengers benefited directly from investment in improved transport to airports, regardless of whether they used such links directly. It was unrealistic to expect that such improved links would be funded entirely by the state or wider local and regional transport interests, as the CAA suggested as an alternative. The AOA thus supported the inclusion of the costs of ground transport links funded by airports, within the RRCB, regardless of whether they arose as a direct planning condition or not. To do otherwise would result in a failure to invest, with consequent damage to the interests of users and the wider community.

13.59. The ATUC said that it had sought to identify where the consumer interest lay in the economic regulation of airports. It had accepted that changes in the price cap had little discernible impact on fares (not least because the per passenger charge to airlines from regulated airport charges reflected only a small proportion of the cost of providing the service) and had therefore sought to establish passengers' requirements of airports and to consider whether the regulatory regime might more effectively influence airports to meet those requirements. The ATUC had concluded that the passenger interest lay principally in the timely investment in additional facilities at the airports in line with increasing demand.

13.60. The CAA's statutory duty included the encouragement of investment, and such encouragement had been a feature of previous reviews. The ATUC welcomed the CAA's ongoing examination of whether the regime could be modified to pursue this goal more effectively. The ATUC felt that the current process appeared to be leading to a regime more closely tailored to passenger interests than those of the past.

13.61. The proposed move from single till to the RRCB would be a fundamental change in approach as seen from the perspectives of the airlines and the airports. A key issue for the ATUC was whether there was any consumer interest in which of the parties—airlines or airports—enjoyed the benefit of the economic rent arising from scarce capacity at Heathrow. The ATUC view was that if the greater proportion passed to the airports, and if the airports could be influenced to invest the rent in additional facilities, then a transfer from airlines to airports must be in the interest of consumers. The ATUC noted the CAA's caution that it had no powers to force airports to undertake capex, but were encouraged by the incentives for them to do so that the CAA was proposing. The threat of a return to the single till in future reviews if they fail to invest would no doubt provide further encouragement.

13.62. In specific terms, the ATUC believed that the proposed linkage of the price cap to outputs delivered was in the consumer interest. The recommendation in the T5 Inspector's report for a proposed cap on ATMs at Heathrow at precisely the level above which the CAA's proposals would reward additional movements was therefore highly regrettable. Such a limit would clearly militate against the CAA's objective of encouraging BAA to make maximum possible use of the airport's runway capacity. The ATUC took comfort, however, from the proposed incentives to increase passenger throughput and from the associated proposal for a service quality term in the price cap. The latter was essential to ensure that increased passenger throughput was not achieved by reducing standards and imposing greater levels of congestion and discomfort on passengers.

13.63. The introduction of a service quality term was of key importance for consumers. The ATUC noted the intention that the service quality factor would initially account for a small proportion of the regulated charges, and understood the CAA's reasons for wishing to proceed cautiously. From a consumer perspective, however, it was important that the proportion should nevertheless be of sufficient order to have a degree of influence over BAA's behaviour.

13.64. The ATUC appreciated the arguments against imposing service quality standards at Stansted for 2003 to 2008. However, the adoption of such standards for these airports would be consistent with the reasoning behind the CAA's cautious approach to introduction of service quality terms for Heathrow and Gatwick. The proposals started from a modest base, leaving open the possibility of modification in subsequent reviews. For Stansted, current conditions might not appear to warrant such a service quality term but this might not be the case by the next review. There might, therefore, be merit in introducing service standards now. This would go some way towards ensuring the maintenance of minimum standards during the full 2003 to 2008 period. And if, at the time of future reviews, more rigorous service quality terms were considered necessary, the principle would have been tried and tested in application.

13.65. In recent discussions with the CAA the ATUC indicated that it endorsed the list of service quality indicators proposed by BAA. It also took the view that the indicators which were measurable objectively through SLAs should be accorded greater weighting than those to be measured subjectively through passenger surveys. The ATUC noted, however, that subjective indicators nevertheless covered elements that were important to passengers. The ATUC therefore suggested that the weighting of subjective indicators should not be so low as to render them irrelevant in terms of their potential to influence the price cap.

13.66. On the issue of how to collect survey data, the ATUC's principal concern was that the assessment of BAA's performance should not be based unequivocally on the company's own QSM surveys. Nevertheless, there appeared to be sound practical reasons for making use of what was a well-established procedure. The ATUC would therefore support use of the QSM data with an external audit.

13.67. It would appear from the CAA's analysis that passengers using Stansted might have benefited in the past from investment in facilities before they were really needed, on the basis that the price cap regime facilitated cross-subsidy from charges at Heathrow and Gatwick. There did not appear to be any suggestion that this amounted to a diversion of funds away from higher-priority investments at the two larger airports. The system-wide arrangement might therefore be considered historically to have been marginally in the consumer interest. However, in the light of the long-term perspective behind the proposed incentive-based approach to airport regulation, there appeared to be no compelling consumer-interest grounds for dissent from the CAA's proposal for a stand-alone price cap for Stansted.

13.68. The ATUC responses to earlier consultations had supported CAA proposals to encourage contracting between airports and airlines, with the caveat that any such contracting should be underpinned by a default price cap associated with minimum levels of service. The ATUC noted the CAA comment that this implied a real increase in prices charged to airlines, but would not see this as a potential disbenefit to consumers. On the contrary, there was a clear indication that the CAA would encourage ring-fencing of revenues from higher charges for future investment. This could only be to the benefit of consumers.

13.69. The principal concern of the ATUC in respect of regulation of airport charges was that the regime should encourage the timely investment in additional facilities to meet growing demand. In the context of the limited powers of the CAA, it could be argued that some of the latest proposals for encouraging new investment implied an element of risk in that their success depended on the good faith of the airports. The ATUC considered that the measures proposed by the CAA not only considerably reduced any risks to passenger interests from the changes, but also offered considerable long-term advantages for consumers in terms both of timely investment in new facilities and of overall levels of service.

Aviation Environment Federation

13.70. The Aviation Environment Federation (AEF), writing on behalf of Friends of the Earth, Gatwick Area Conservation Campaign, the Heathrow Association for the control of Aircraft Noise/Clearskies and Transport 2000, said that it wished to draw the attention of the CC to an important omission in the CAA recommendations. The policy of auctioning slots, with the revenue accruing to the public purse, had now been accepted as official government policy, and was under negotiation with the EC. Yet nowhere in the 275 pages of the CAA recommendations did the CAA mention this matter. The AEF said it knew that to recommend such a policy would be outside the remit of the CAA, but since this policy would alter the competitive climate in which BAA would operate, it seemed curious not to mention it. The omission was all the more surprising in that the CAA document devoted considerable space to calculating the probable value of slots.

13.71. The AEF said that it was aware that the allocation of slots was controlled by an EC regulation, and that the British Government had started negotiations to amend it to permit auctions. The AEF had been told by the DTLR that other European countries were at present not showing much support, but suspected that the general lack of urgency was due to a desire to protect the aviation industry from the full impact of competition.

13.72. The CAA policy of fixing price caps on airport charges needed to be seen in a wider context. Various tax concessions gave the aviation industry an uncompetitive advantage over other industries. These concessions were as follows:

— no tax on aviation fuel;

— no VAT on air travel;

— no tax (or charge) to cover external costs; and

— duty-free sales.

435

These tax advantages, which amounted to over £7 billion a year (assuming aviation fuel was taxed at half the rate applied to motor fuel), were only counterbalanced in a small way by the air passenger duty (£1 billion). There was scope for much debate on the appropriate tax rates for aviation, especially in view of the fact that rail and sea travel enjoyed similar concessions. Nevertheless, it was the view of the AEF that the above concessions gave aviation a substantial anti-competitive advantage over most other goods and services. Because demand was skewed towards artificially cheap air travel, public welfare was diminished.

13.73.   The AEF said that its interest in the issue was that tax subsidies to aviation resulted in a high and rising level of demand, which was forecast to double in the next 20 years. If not controlled, this would have a serious effect on the world climate, would mean more noise and pollution, and would require the building of several new runways or a new airport, with massive environmental damage. This serious situation was made worse by the effect of the CAA price caps.

13.74.   The AEF said that it welcomed the proposed ending of the single till, and the small increases in airport charges recommended by the CAA. But the increases were small, would have only a minuscule effect on the environmental damage caused by aviation, and would still leave the price of slots far below their market value. The dilemma facing the CAA was how to keep down BAA profits while allowing airport charges to rise to market levels. This would only be achieved by the Treasury imposing a levy, or by auctioning slots.

13.75.   The CAA report gave interesting figures for the value of slots. It was stated that the NPV of additional landing slots at Heathrow was at minimum £2 million per slot (single slot, take-off or landing) and was likely to be higher than that. The value of existing slots may be higher than that of new slots. With over 600 slots a day it was clear that the revenue to the Exchequer would be substantial. A smaller, but still substantial revenue could be obtained by auctioning slots at Gatwick, and in future years as demand rose, at Stansted. If slots at Gatwick were auctioned the revenue from a Heathrow auction would tend to be higher.

13.76.   Similar figures were provided by the CAA for the estimated passenger preference for using Heathrow compared to other airports. This was estimated at £61. With over 60 mppa using Heathrow this suggested that up to £3.6 billion a year could be raised at Heathrow alone.

13.77.   The AEF believed that auctioning slots would have important advantages in improving competition. These included:

(a)   removing the present restrictive practice of grandfather rights whereby once an airline had a slot it had a permanent monopoly;

(b)   increasing competition between airlines, and increasing their efficiency;

(c)   ensuring the most efficient use of scarce airport capacity;

(d)   recouping to the Exchequer some of the revenue lost through tax concessions to aviation;

(e)   creating a more level playing field between aviation and other industries, thus improving public welfare; and

(f)   providing large sums for the improvement of health, education and other public services.

Auctioning slots would not alter the number of flights that would need to overflow from Heathrow and Gatwick to other airports, but it would ensure that the allocation of slots at various airports was done in an economically efficient way.

13.78.   If slots were auctioned, BAA would still need to charge for its services and some price control would be necessary to prevent it exploiting its monopoly position. The CAA had a narrowly defined remit to prevent BAA making excessive profits, and it had a statutory remit to protect the interests of the aviation industry. Its recommendations reflected these terms of reference. The CC, however, had wider terms of reference, and could look at the national interest. The AEF believed that, without slot auctions (or a levy), the effect of the proposed price caps would be to continue the artificial distortion of the market for air travel, add to the environmental problems caused by aviation, and diminish public welfare.

British Airline Pilots Association

13.79. The British Airline Pilots Association (BALPA) said that airlines, which faced a difficult cost environment, should not be penalized by the abolition of the single-till approach. The single-till method kept charges at a reasonable level for airlines ensuring that they shared in the revenues which their presence also generated, notably shopping, car parking, property rental etc. Whilst agreeing with the CAA that alternative measures could be found to distribute these costs and revenues, the single-till approach had worked well, and other methods would be less efficient. Any move towards a dual-till approach would lead to the airports reaping monopoly profits to an unacceptable extent, and would be directly harmful to the future of airlines, and indirectly would penalize passengers.

13.80. The BALPA welcomed the CAA's recommendation that London airports should be treated separately with the elimination of cross-subsidies and with the requirement to set separate price caps. It also welcomed the introduction of service quality standards and penalties for failure to meet these targets. However, the issue of capacity needed to be considered as many service delays were due to congested airspace. The BALPA would be concerned if pressure were put on the ATC system to deliver such benefits. It would urge caution, however, on punctuality targets and suggested that such targets should only relate to delays and failures wholly attributable to the airport operator. The airport ATC interface had to be taken into account in this regard.

13.81. The BALPA agreed on the need for improved consultation with airlines on capital spending plans to ensure that adequate resources were channelled into capacity and infrastructure enhancement. These questions could not be divorced from the wider question of capacity and infrastructure and that whilst scarce and valued resources should be regulated, especially where monopoly power was evident, the best solution overall was to allow more capacity to be provided.

The Association of British Travel Agents Ltd

13.82. The Association of British Travel Agents Ltd (ABTA) said that it represented the interests of over 1,700 travel agents trading out of some 6,800 high-street outlets and 800 tour operators who, between them, accounted for well over 90 per cent of the air holidays and 80 per cent of the air tickets sold in the UK. Members were part of groups themselves owning airlines. Changes in charges and other aspects impacted significantly upon the costs of air travel and package holidays sold by its members.

13.83. The ABTA said that it supported the CAA's recommendation that the three London airports should be regulated on a stand-alone basis. It could not support the CAA's recommendation to move from the current single till to a dual till or RRCB and suggested there was no evidence to suggest that investment had been inhibited as a result of the single till. Any delays to airport infrastructure had been due to political rather than economic considerations. A move to an RRCB was acknowledged by the CAA to result in higher prices. These could not be absorbed by the airlines and would have to be passed on to the travelling public. The ABTA wondered whether the CAA had adequately considered the external constraints on investment to meet the demand for capacity other than opting for a radical move away from single till.

13.84. The ABTA said that it was not in favour of prefunding and felt that services should be paid for as they were received. The ABTA considered that the work undertaken on quality of service issues should be developed. SLAs were important and should be introduced with the airports being made accountable for their delivery along with financial penalties.

Others

Adam Smith Institute

13.85. The Adam Smith Institute (the Institute) said that it believed the problem of competition in airports allied to the provision of additional capacity, particularly in the South-East of England, was largely about regulatory organization.

13.86. The Institute said that if a public monopoly was turned into a private monopoly, the disciplines of competition needed to be replaced by those of regulation. The Institute said that the regulating authority had not applied its powers sufficiently to turn the private monopoly into a competing airport system. It said that at a simple level this could be done by encouraging the separating out of the individual airport ownerships and at a more complex level by the separating out of the terminal ownership within the major airports. Either of these courses would increase the competition element and hence reduce the regulatory requirements of the current system. The Institute believed that the CC should expand its existing brief to consider this aspect.

13.87. With regard to airport charges the Institute considered that the regulator should not be concerned regarding the individual charges levied. It should concern itself with the costs against which these charges might be calculated and which the airport would seek to recover from the airlines. The costs against which the charges should be arrived at should cover the following aspects:

(a) the operating costs of the runway, aprons and taxiways including fire and rescue, ATC, maintenance etc;

(b) the depreciation of the runway and the upgrading and improvement works necessary for the runways, aprons and taxiways;

(c) the environmental costs based on the environmental impact of the runway on the adjacent community; and

(d) a security charge based on the actual costs of providing the appropriate level of security should be levied on a per passenger basis.

13.88. Because of the organization of the industry, the Institute believed that it was inevitable that neither the airport nor the regulator could accurately determine the public interest in the same way as market forces were able to do. The Institute urged the CC to review the ownership patterns and how these might be devolved into a competing system. The Institute recognized that it was unlikely that the South-East of England, for example, would ever produce a system of perfect competition as the number of runways would always be limited by environmental pressures. Therefore, the limited regulation of runways, aprons and taxiways would always be required. This should be cost based with air traffic charges being used as a model.

13.89. The Institute said that the other element which could distort the picture unless it was dealt with in an even-handed manner at government level, was the environmental impact. Every airport in the UK should therefore be subject to the same defined environmental standards as laid down by the Government. The New Towns policy developed by previous governments to overcome the environmental impact on existing countryside of major new developments would serve as a model.

13.90. Security and safety should not form part of the competitive environment. Security standards should be laid down, supervised and approved by Government, if necessary, licensing airports for appropriate traffic. Airports should be able to reimburse their costs for these services from passenger charges on a non-profit-making basis.

13.91. The Institute said that the nature of demand for aviation services was limitless. Equally there were no social issues involved in airports, which would normally be expected to distort the market. Every passenger who flew and everyone who worked at an airport was paid a fair price or was paid a fair wage. It was a classic case for market forces to be allowed to control the overall increase in activities of the aviation sector. The Government should stop worrying about the capacity of the system, as this should be provided by the market. It should, rather, concern itself with the definition of environmental standards and recompensing the community, together with establishing the security and safety standards which airports were required to meet.

Belfast City Airport

13.92. Belfast City Airport said that it wished to endorse the statement issued by the CC in July, indicating that the inquiry group were minded to exclude the dual-till approach proposed by the CAA for the purposes of price control at the BAA London airports. Belfast City Airport said Northern Ireland was geographically remote from other regions of the UK, and this was particularly the case in relation to the capital. Whereas other regions of the UK generally had the benefit of surface connections to London, in the case of Northern Ireland air services took the place of these key road and rail links. Whilst a large amount of this traffic—around 350,000 passengers a year—used Gatwick as the access point to London, a much greater number, around 1 million passengers annually, used Heathrow. In the case of Northern Ireland, the existence and continuation of air services to London, and in particular Heathrow, was vital to the economy of the region at a time of critical regeneration. Annually, some 434,000 foreign visitors arrived in Northern Ireland by air, to make their contribution to economic regeneration. Of these, over 60 per cent used Heathrow as their preferred means of accessing the region, a number which was eight times greater than those using Gatwick for the same purpose.

13.93. It was therefore of concern to Belfast City Airport that the CAA had come forward with proposals that could have a significant adverse impact upon airlines using Heathrow and Gatwick, which provide the lifelines essential to the economy of this region. Belfast City Airport's principal concerns centred on the proposals relating to Heathrow, firstly, with regard to the proposed move from single to dual till. The CAA believed this best met its objective 'to further the reasonable interests of users of airports', as higher prices would mean that only sufficiently profitable routes would be operated at Heathrow in future, which could absorb the higher price without increasing ticket prices, thus marginal routes would no longer be economically viable. Belfast City Airport said that these routes tended to be regional lifelines, like that to Belfast. Airlines tended to operate to extremely low margins, and could not continue operations at Heathrow if the current proposals were introduced. The impact of the increases on the shorter routes would be more dramatic, and it was unlikely that prices could be raised, particularly on domestic operations which faced competition from ferry, bus, rail and car. In addition, bmi at Heathrow were in direct competition with competing routes operated to Stansted and Luton which reduced considerably any scope for price increases. Without aeronautical activities, no profits would be generated from other operational activities, and such profits were properly used to offset the level of airport charges.

13.94. Second, the CAA had proposed a price profile with premiums attached to the opening of T5, based on the cost of delivering T5 and CTA developments. The cost was £18 per incremental passenger above 60 million, excluding inflation. Heathrow achieved 60 million passengers in 1998, and by 2008/09, when T5 was scheduled to open, traffic was forecast at 77.6 million passengers. At this point, the price cap would reflect 17.6 million passengers at £18 and 60 million passengers at £7. In addition, the CAA had proposed a T5 stand incentive of £10 million a year. This presented airlines supporting the T5 development with a serious issue as it resulted in a cost to the airlines of £18 per incremental passenger, compared to the current pricing level of £5.63 per passenger.

13.95. Belfast City Airport said that it had agreed extremely competitive charging structures for the airlines operating services from Belfast to Heathrow and Gatwick, in order to secure these services for the future. It would therefore be of grave concern if the CAA proposals were implemented to the extent that it caused airlines to seriously reappraise the economic viability of these routes. At a time when all airports and other service providers were under pressure to reduce or contain charges, it was inappropriate for the CAA to bring forward proposals to effectively increase the operating costs of airlines and call into question vital air services.

British Vehicle Rental and Leasing Association

13.96. The British Vehicle Rental and Leasing Association (BVRLA) said that it was concerned about the strong negotiating position held by BAA with regard to its ability to control property lease rents and to impose charges that could not be challenged by using comparables or by appeal. This led to a position whereby property rents within airport-owned land were artificially higher than the potential market rate rent elsewhere. The BVRLA considered that BAA should be governed by the same regulations on comparables and appeals that applied to property transactions outside airport boundaries.

County Ceilings Installations (Gatwick) Ltd

13.97. County Ceilings Installations (Gatwick) Ltd said that as contractors at Gatwick for the past 10 to 12 years it could not comment on what the maximum level of airport charges should be. It was sure that BAA would set charges which were fair and appropriate. However, it did not consider the use of a single major framework contractor over the last five to six years had provided value for money or was in the public interest.

Fidelity Investments

13.98. Fidelity Investments (Fidelity) said that the Fidelity group of companies, as at 6 August 2002, owned approximately 28.8 million shares in BAA representing some 2.7 per cent of the outstanding equity. Fidelity said that it had read the CC's statement of 11 July 2002 setting out its thinking on the CAA's proposal to introduce the dual-till approach to the setting of charges for the three BAA London airports. In particular, Fidelity noted that the CC recognized the CAA's concern that there must be adequate incentives for BAA to invest in the three London airports including T5 at Heathrow, and to maintain and improve quality of service to both airlines and passengers.

13.99. As shareholders of BAA this point was a critical one and the ability of BAA to make a commercial return on its invested capital was fundamental to the investment case. Capital was a scarce resource and Fidelity had many competing demands as to where it should best be allocated. Where companies were unable to make satisfactory returns this was a major disincentive to investment and could ultimately lead them to return capital to shareholders for reinvestment elsewhere.

13.100. Fidelity stressed that this was not its vision for the future of BAA but it would hope that the nature of the eventual pricing regime and the associated returns would reflect the increased level of risk in the aviation industry as well as construction risk. The events of September 2001 and the subsequent decline in passenger volumes had put some of these commercial risks into perspective. Fidelity believed that BAA differed from other utilities in this respect and it was worth noting that since the CC statement of 11 July the company's shares had fallen sharply to reflect concern about BAA's ability to generate adequate returns.

First Choice Holidays PLC

13.101. First Choice Holidays PLC (First Choice) said that its views were communicated to the CC under cover of a letter from Monarch Airlines on behalf of the Charter Group of which Air 2000 was a member and a wholly-owned subsidiary of First Choice.

Gatwick Airport Consultative Committee

13.102. The Gatwick Airport Consultative Committee (the Consultative Committee) said that it was comprised of representatives from local authorities, the aviation industry, passengers, business, environmental interests and other users of the airport. It provided a forum for discussion leading to the provision of advice to the Government, the airport operator, BAA and other organizations.

13.103. The Consultative Committee said that the airline industry's representatives serving on it did not support some of its comments. In particular they did not support the CAA's proposal to move away from a single till nor the proposed increase in charges.

13.104. The Consultative Committee had, over the past year, considered and commented upon the CAA's various consultation papers on the economic regulation of the three BAA London airports and was generally happy with the consultation process adopted by it. Given the projected growth in demand for air travel and the need to ensure airport infrastructure developments continued to be made, it was felt that the CAA's proposals focused on the best incentives for achieving the investment and service quality valued by users and passengers. However, some of the Consultative Committee's members were concerned about the level of landing fees at Gatwick. Because Gatwick's landing fees were among the lowest in the world, it meant that an artificial demand for capacity was created and the CAA's proposals did not address this.

13.105. The Consultative Committee was surprised that the CAA's submission gave the impression that BAA Gatwick had no plans to develop the airport. It was accepted that there were no major capacity enhancements or any additional incentives linked to air transport movements planned at Gatwick between 2003 and 2008. However, BAA Gatwick did have in place a Sustainable Development Strategy, which set out how Gatwick would develop to accommodate the growth of the airport from 31 mppa to 40 mppa over the next decade. This strategy was developed over a three-year period in close consultation with its airlines, users and the local community when views on how the airport might be developed and managed over the decade were sought. The Consultative Committee felt it important that this was taken into account by the CC.

13.106. The proposal to introduce a service quality term in the regulatory framework was of particular interest to the Consultative Committee and was much supported, especially the ability to reward for higher performance in the delivery of passenger service as well as the ability to reduce charges to airlines for below-target performance. It noted the distinctions drawn between the performance indicators of most interest to airlines and passengers but it felt that these did not tell the full story. The airline indicators such as people movers, pier service and security queues were also of major concern to passengers. The importance of the passenger in this respect should not therefore be overlooked and must be taken into account when measuring service quality. In addition to this, the provision of flight information (contained in the passenger indicators) relied heavily on the information provided by the airlines to their handling agent. The Consultative Committee had for some time been concerned about the provision of information from the airlines to the airport, particularly in respect of delayed flights. The provision of timely, up to date and accurate information was of vital importance to passengers. Responsibility for this should not therefore rest solely with the airport operator as the airlines had a crucial role in the provision of this information.

13.107. The Consultative Committee had noted the CAA's analysis on the question of including an element related to airport delays in the service quality term. The CAA was of the view that a framework to consider aerodrome congestion delay was a worthwhile feature of the charges formula. It was noted that a programme of joint working with BAA, NATS and the airlines was continuing in this area to develop robust measures and that BA had suggested that the delay term should go further to capture costly elements of delay arising at the terminal by using the airlines' reporting systems to identify the causes of delay. If the delay term was introduced relying on information from the airlines, the Consultative Committee would wish to be convinced that the system was even-handed, accurate, robust and properly audited.

13.108. The concerns about the use of BAA's QSM to measure performance were noted and the Consultative Committee fully supported the CAA's recommendation that the QSM should be subject to an external audit and checked to make sure there were no inherent biases. As regards the use of SLAs for measuring performance, the CAA had indicated that it was happy to accept par values agreed between the airlines and BAA. Where there was no agreement the CAA would be willing to accept the targets in existing SLAs. The problem with the use of existing SLAs was that they were perhaps disparate and not geared for this particular purpose. This needed to be taken into account by the CC.

13.109. The Consultative Committee was pleased that the CAA was not recommending enforced competition at the airports. Introducing competition between terminals would not be in the best interests of passengers, the airlines using the airport or the airport operator as it could create problems in the long-term planning of the airport and the timing of investment. It could also compromise the flexibility of the management of the airport to react effectively to changes in user airline operations and structures. A good example of this was the way in which BAA Gatwick was currently addressing the implications of major operational changes of its main airline users and the way in which it might impact on the timing of certain infrastructure investment at the airport. Also, introducing terminal competition could impede airport management in making best use of precious terminal capacity and could increase congestion within terminals in the short term when user airline business needs changed. There was also the risk that competitive advantage gained by an airline might be used to the detriment of other terminal users whether existing or potential.

13.110. As regards increasing competition for existing service provision, the Consultative Committee believed that the principle objective must be to provide a seamless service. From the passenger's viewpoint, transferring the operational rights of facilities could over-complicate the airport experience by the creation of differing levels of facilities and services. Passengers expected a seamless service from the beginning of their airport experience to the end. The introduction of more competition should therefore be treated cautiously. A good example of introducing unnecessary competition was in ground handling. BAA Gatwick was required by EC regulation to accommodate four handling agents at the airport. In the past the introduction of the fourth handling agent at Gatwick did not increase efficiency, reduce costs or improve service quality. There were proposals to reintroduce a fourth handling agent at Gatwick and the Consultative Committee would like to ensure that there were safeguards in place to prevent history from repeating itself. This was an issue which the CC might like to pursue further.

Heathrow Airport Consultative Committee

13.111. The HACC said that the most radical of the proposals was a move away from the present system of a single till to that of a dual till which would divide BAA revenues into those derived from aeronautical activities and those resulting from non-aeronautical activities with no cross-subsidy for Stansted. Given the trend to a substantial increase in traffic and capacity at that airport, with the increased income so generated, there seemed to be little argument to justify continuation of subsidy from the other BAA London airports.

13.112. With regard to a dual till, there was concern at the exclusion of retail income from the charging regime with some members expressing concern that this could encourage provision of shopping at Heathrow to the detriment of local shopping centres. Many members, in particular those representing local authorities, believed that single till exacerbated congestion due to the cross-subsidy of aeronautical activities by commercial activities and that aviation should meet its external costs which implied premium charges at congested airports. There was also concern at the extent of retail creep which occurred in some terminal areas to the detriment of space available for passenger movement in waiting areas.

13.113. The majority of members of the HACC supported the move to dual till but airline representatives expressed themselves as totally opposed to such a move and the increased costs that this would impose on their operations, that would need to be passed on in increased fares.

13.114. There were indications in the arguments advanced by the CAA that it favoured a break-up of the BAA monopoly of ownership of the three major London airports in the interest of securing greater competition although, as it acknowledged, it had no powers to achieve this. The HACC's policy had been consistent since the introduction of quinquennial reviews, it believed that there were benefits in those airports remaining under one ownership.

13.115. The HACC was opposed to the introduction of competition between terminals at Heathrow by way of sale, lease or contractual arrangements for their management. Given the extreme pressure on the available infrastructure of that airport, outside of the short-term influence of 11 September, and a need to be able to share or to move operations between terminals so as to use available capacity to the best effect, particularly with the trend to airline alliances, such divestment of responsibility would be to the disbenefit of airport users.

13.116. The proposal to provide for wider consultation with airport users (and this term needed to recognize that passengers and cargo shippers were the ultimate users) about airport investment and development plans was to be welcomed.

13.117. The proposals to reward BAA for extra movements generated at Heathrow to the extent of £300 each was a cause of concern to many of the HACC's members. The original CAA draft recommendation to reward movements above a level of 480,000 was, of course, overtaken by the decision of the Secretary of State to impose a cap of that same level as a condition of approving construction of T5 but this restriction would not be operative until the core terminal building was completed and would not prevent achievement of a greater number of movements in the interim period.

13.118. BAA Heathrow had explained to the HACC that it viewed this incentive as applying to the peak period of air traffic at the airport. However, at Heathrow the peak periods now extended over a substantial part of the operating day. The HACC was concerned that the encouragement being given to squeezing in extra movements in peak periods might be to the detriment of aircraft safety, the comfort of passengers in terminals and the environment.

13.119. The HACC noted the CAA reference to inclusion of a 'delay term' at Heathrow and that work was continuing on how the necessary data could be captured and whether a robust system could be established before such a term could be established in the price cap. The HACC would wish to be able to consider any proposal which would result in the inclusion of such a term.

13.120. The HACC did not feel it was competent, nor was it appropriate for it, to suggest what the actual level of the operational charges should be. The HACC supported the introduction of a service quality term in the price cap and was concerned that this quality should be adequately surveyed, analysed and reported. The HACC received regular reports from BAA Heathrow on the conclusions of its quality surveys. However, it believed that the five-point scale and the items to which these were applied needed to be reviewed so as to be more comprehensive.

13.121. The HACC monitored the quality of the services or infrastructure elements included in the SLA reports submitted to the CAA and were in favour, in principle, of that system continuing as a valuable tool in gauging performance. The design of the items to be subject to SLA in T5 needed to be considered at an early stage.

13.122. The HACC was concerned with regard to environmental issues that the CAA seemed to have overlooked the extent of the role played by the Secretary of State in Transport and Works Act Orders, airport policy making, in regulating aircraft operations at the BAA London airports in the interests of mitigating noise and, indeed, his 'Guidance' to the CAA on environmental matters in airspace policy, all of which had a part to play in airport operations and expansion matters and which were not affected by town and country planning legislation.

Leeds Bradford International Airport

13.123. Leeds Bradford International Airport (Leeds Bradford) said that it was opposed to any proposals that had the effect of threatening the viability of existing air services between Leeds Bradford and the London airports. Currently, bmi operated four daily flights to Heathrow and BAA CitiExpress operated three daily flights to Gatwick. These services provided vital connections for travellers from the Leeds area to London for both point-to-point travel and also for connecting flights. Passengers on the Heathrow service averaged around 200,000 a year, whilst the Gatwick service, which started in October 2001, would carry around 35,000 passengers a year. Together these services carried around 15 per cent of the Leeds Bradford total scheduled traffic.

13.124. Because of the shortage of suitable slots at both Heathrow and Gatwick, services to both these airports had been under pressure for some years. Indeed Leeds Bradford had no service to Gatwick between April 1998 and October 2001. In 2001, bmi made a public commitment to use their best endeavours to continue to operate a service between Leeds Bradford and Heathrow for at least five years. Clearly this commitment was subject to the economics of the service remaining favourable.

13.125. Leeds Bradford understood that the CAA's proposals for pricing at the London airports would have the effect of allowing significant increase in charges over and above inflation. It believed that such increases would seriously jeopardize the viability of existing services between Leeds Bradford and the London airports. The withdrawal of those services would have a serious detrimental impact on the economy in this region.

13.126. Leeds Bradford said the proposal to move from a single to dual till seemed to owe more to economic theory than to the economic realities of operating airline services. Airports operated as a single business, utilizing income from commercial activities to reduce their reliance upon revenues from airline operations. Leeds Bradford believed that there was nothing improper about the single-till approach and it should continue to apply. The alternative approach would have a particular damaging impact upon shorter sector flights and jeopardize the viability of Leeds Bradford's essential links to the London airports.

13.127. Leeds Bradford said that the CAA proposals for a price profile at Heathrow with premiums attached to the opening of T5 could also result in unacceptable costs to airlines, which in turn could threaten the viability of existing services.

13.128. Leeds Bradford said that the proposed increases for Heathrow and Gatwick, in the case of Heathrow of 81 per cent over a ten-year period, over and above any inflationary increases, were excessive and should not be allowed. Typically, services operating over shorter sectors had low margins. All the market pressure on fares was currently downward. Airlines' services over shorter sectors competed with other modes such as rail which did not face the prospect of similarly excessive cost increases. It was highly unlikely that airlines would be in a position to continue to operate 'marginal' services to regional airports under the pricing formula being proposed by the CAA.

13.129. Leeds Bradford said that it was strongly opposed to any proposals which had the effect of increasing charges to airlines at Heathrow or Gatwick on anything like the scale envisaged. In its view, if such increases were to be allowed, special provision should be made for services operating over shorter sector lengths so that they did not suffer the same impact. Leeds Bradford said that it could not overstate the effect on the regional economy if services to the London airports from Leeds Bradford were to become non-viable due to the proposals being advanced by the CAA.

Mr Peter Cannon

13.130. Mr Peter Cannon said he understood that London taxi driver George Duckling of Stevenage had been in contact with the CC to make a complaint against airport operator HAL. Mr Cannon said that he was also a taxi driver and would like to add to the information already provided by Mr Duckling.

13.131. Mr Cannon said that in February 2000, acting as litigant-in-person he commenced legal proceedings against HAL in the County Court with the intention of recovering £348 which represented the total amount he had been forced by HAL to pay to the HALT Friendly Society in 1999. His action against HAL was on the basis that, firstly, he was not a member of HALT and, secondly, the seven taxi drivers who described themselves as HALT 'executives' had no legal right to receive and control money collected from drivers by HAL.

13.132. In preparing the paperwork for a breach of contract claim, he was disadvantaged when dealing with HAL's lawyers Herbert Smith by the absence of documents covering HAL's commercial agreements with the HALT friendly society and with taxi drivers in general. Although the amount of his claim against HAL was only £348, the court decided the case was too complex to hear as a small claim. Rather than face the costs which would inevitably arise through not having copies of contract documents to refer to at a full trial, he discontinued his action. Mr Cannon said that the final result was that he was ordered by Uxbridge County Court to pay £12,700 in legal costs to HAL and leave to appeal was refused.

Mr George Duckling

13.133. Mr George Duckling said that he was a licensed London taxi driver and wished to make a complaint against HAL. He believed that HAL had pursued a course of conduct against the public interest as specified in section 41(3) of the Airports Act, in its commercial dealings with Heathrow taxi drivers. The substance of his complaint was that HAL unfairly used its bargaining position by refusing to produce a written commercial agreement setting out the terms and conditions under which self-employed taxi drivers were granted access to the airport's taxi ranks. In October 2001, HAL informed drivers that written terms and conditions covering the Heathrow Taxi System were about to be drawn up but nothing more on the matter had been heard.

13.134. Currently the rights and liabilities of Heathrow taxi drivers in their transactions with HAL were undocumented and were governed partly by common law and partly by the Heathrow Airport—London Byelaws, 1996. One of the unwritten rules for Heathrow taxi drivers enforced by HAL was that they had to make a payment of 49p to a taxi drivers' friendly society, known as HALT, each time they used the Taxi System. The payments made by drivers under this rule are collected by HAL and transferred to HALT on a monthly basis, less a 2.5 per cent handling fee. The airport byelaws were silent on the matter of payments to either HAL or HALT and although their wording could not be supplemented with extrinsic information, HAL insisted it could rely on airport byelaws to prevent a taxi driver from working at Heathrow should he/she refuse to make payments to HALT. Mr Duckling believed this particular use of the byelaws by HAL to influence the terms of a commercial agreement engaged the responsibility of the state on the basis that the airport byelaws were sanctioned by the Secretary of State when they came into force on 30 October 1996.

13.135. HALT was employed as a contractor by HAL to supply 'taxi support services' and one of HALT's main duties was to provide taxi information desks in the passenger terminals and to take bookings from taxi passengers travelling from Heathrow to London and vice versa. There were two fundamental questions concerning HALT's constitution that HAL refused to address. First, HALT registered as a friendly society in 1992, but had not elected an executive committee since 1994. Second, without exception HALT's executives were members of the T&G and yet in the London taxi trade taken as a whole, less than 1 per cent of drivers were union members. Therefore the T&G's taxi branch acquired, through its control of HALT, an unacceptably high degree of control over Heathrow taxi drivers which it would not have been able to acquire through the ballot box. Mr Duckling said that he found it repugnant to be obliged by HAL to contribute to funds which were controlled in effect by a union to which he did not belong.

13.136. On 25 April 2002, HALT held an AGM which was attended by only six of HALT's supposed 3,000 members and for the eighth year running the meeting was abandoned and declared inquorate due to lack of support. Despite what Mr Duckling described as blatant breaches of friendly society law covering procedures such as voting, issuing of proxy forms and passing of special resolutions, HAL continued to grant HALT's bogus 'executives' responsibility for the management and disposal of hundreds of thousands of pounds collected by HAL in subscriptions from Heathrow taxi drivers.

13.137. HAL had chosen to act as a collector of funds for HALT on the ground that the fruits of HALT's business activities should not enure to the benefit of drivers who made no financial contribution to HALT; but in making that choice HAL was not sufficiently competent to say exactly what benefits HALT produced for the taxi trade. Mr Duckling believed that HAL was wrong to claim that the serious constitutional malpractice, characterized by HALT's failure to elect an executive committee of drivers was not their problem. Mr Duckling said that, like all taxi drivers, he handed over £2.55 to HAL— including HALT's 49p—each time he picked up passengers at the airport and he believed this placed HAL under a non-delegable duty to ensure that HALT observed both friendly society and company law and had the legal capacity to manage funds collected from taxi drivers.

13.138. Mr Duckling said that he would like two conditions imposed on HAL:

— HAL should agree to publish the terms and conditions of the commercial agreement by which HAL and taxi drivers were bound in the Heathrow Taxi Systems, including terms covering compulsory payments to trade organizations.

— HAL should agree to publish the terms and conditions of the commercial agreement concluded by HAL and HALT in 1993, including the identity of parties represented during negotiations.

13.139. Following his initial submission Mr Duckling told us that he had received a copy of the commercial agreement published by HAL on 22 July 2002. He said that contrary to paragraph 2 of the agreement, copies of the airport byelaws were not displayed at the taxi feeder park; the new document did not stipulate that taxi drivers had to make five advance payments to HAL before access to the ranks was granted and nothing was stipulated about compulsory subscriptions to the HALT Friendly Society. Mr Duckling said the document was incomplete and would need to be rewritten.

Mr Michael Hasnip

13.140. Mr Michael Hasnip said that he was a frequent business traveller and passed through either T1 or T3 at Heathrow most weeks. The physical state of the two terminals could only be described as a disgrace. Both had been allowed to evolve over the years with little thought as to ease of use or sensible design. These problems were further compounded by a lack of maintenance and inadequate cleaning.

13.141. Mr Hasnip said that he had raised his concerns in writing with senior management at BAA on a number of occasions but they seemed to be unaware of their poor performance when compared to equivalent airports across Europe. As a monopoly supplier BAA was able to escape being held to account. BAA seemed to spend little on its day-to-day operations at Heathrow, hence the low levels of cleanliness and maintenance. It was not surprising that BAA was so profitable.

13.142. Mr Hasnip said he noted that the CC was investigating ways in which passenger perceptions of BAA performance might be taken into account. He said that he would be suspicious of any survey conducted by BAA. A better approach might be to select travellers from the major carriers' frequent flier programmes. The process should be managed and the questions for the survey selected by an independent organization, such as the Consumers' Association.

Mr H Hely-Hutchinson

13.143. Mr Henry Hely-Hutchinson said that arising from an experience upon landing at Gatwick in May 1997, when he had to walk 343 metres up a slight gradient to passport control, he had been advised by the CAA that it did not have power to regulate these matters. The CAA told him that the CC would be reviewing four airports in 2002.

13.144. Mr Hely-Hutchinson said that he considered it essential that some authority should have the power to regulate such matters.

Mr R J Hicks

13.145. Mr R J Hicks said that BAA did not allow him access to its intranet system. Mr Hicks said that it was used by BAA departments and by their contractors as a source of information. By not allowing him to advertise his services on the intranet but allowing his competitors to advertise Mr Hicks said that he was put at a disadvantage.

13.146. Mr Hicks said that his company, Streamline Airside Training, was set up to carry out airside driver training, and fire and evacuation at Stansted. He was issued with an airside licence to carry this out as a commercial venture. In respect of fire and evacuation training he had to follow the BAA guidelines as laid down in their directors notice. This took approximately three and a half hours, split between a classroom presentation and a physical walk round of the terminal and satellites, plus an examination and the issue of paperwork. For this training he charged £28 per person and trained no more than four at a time.

13.147. In August 2001, BAA issued a directors notice stating that BAA would now be carrying out fire and evacuation training. The cost would be £10 per person, there would be no need to book, and all training would be carried out in Enterprise House. Mr Hicks wrote to the person who signed the directors notice, a Mr Chris Butler, Operations Director. The substance of the reply was that BAA was not intending to take notice of his complaint but had noted it.

13.148. Mr Hicks said that as an ex-BAA fireman he knew the cost of a day's work and the cost of hiring a large room in Enterprise House. Mr Hicks said that it could not be done for £10 and BAA must therefore be subsidizing the cost. Mr Hicks said that Streamline Airside Training derived one-third of its income from fire and evacuation training; BAA had unfairly undercut him and the company had now ceased to trade.

Professor Stephen Littlechild

13.149. Professor Stephen Littlechild said that he was responding to the CC's statement on its initial thinking on the single/dual-till issue, for two reasons. First, in his experience the dual till was likely to be more conducive than the single till to effective regulation and management. Second, the overriding issue of the underpricing of the two main London airports was a further argument in favour of the dual till.

13.150. Professor Littlechild said the overriding issue was that the main London airport charges were seriously underpriced at present—certainly at Heathrow and also, though to a lesser extent, at Gatwick.

This caused or exacerbated numerous problems, and was likely to lead to inefficient investment on a large scale. The urgent need was to increase, and not reduce, these charges.

13.151. Underpricing led to demand being artificially stimulated. Airlines and therefore passengers were, at the margin, induced to fly to and from Heathrow and Gatwick instead of to and from other airports. At the same time, there was less incentive on the airport and airlines to increase the supply of capacity—for example, by providing for planes with larger passenger capacity. An important disadvantage of the present artificially low prices was that they provided less valuable information about customers' preferences regarding future investment decisions, for example, about expansion at Heathrow.

13.152. Increased airport charges would produce greater incentives on airlines to schedule flights to and from other airports. Passengers would have correspondingly greater ability to consider flying from other airports and better information would be available about customers' preferences and the case for increased capacity in the South-East.

13.153. One policy could be to set airport charges that would just equate the supply and demand for airport capacity at each airport. These would be market-clearing prices that would reflect opportunity costs. The main advantage of this short-run approach was that it would tend to allocate presently available capacity to the highest valued uses. However, while the level of a market-clearing charge would give an indication of what value passengers would place on a small increment of capacity, it might not be a valid indication of the value they would place on a large increment of capacity, such as a new terminal would provide.

13.154. An alternative policy would be to relate airport charges to the likely costs of expanding capacity. This would be a longer-run concept of costs. Such charges might not be sufficiently high to 'clear the market' in the immediate future. But they would provide better utilization of existing capacity, better incentives to passengers and airlines, and better information to inform future investment policies.

13.155. Professor Littlechild said that the present airport charges at Heathrow and also at Gatwick were significantly below market-clearing prices and the costs of expansion there. The implication of this was that there would be advantage if airport charges there were increased in real terms rather than held constant, let alone reduced.

13.156. Although other regulatory price controls in water and electricity had at times provided for increases in charges, nevertheless, higher charges were likely to be resisted by at least two sets of parties: the airlines and the passengers. There was also a third possible objection: that increased airport charges would reduce the incentives to internal efficiency at the airport.

13.157. Professor Littlechild said that experience had gradually been accumulating about the advantages and disadvantages, in a regulated context, of integrated business activities versus more separate business activities. This had particular relevance for the associated price controls on these activities.

13.158. Companies generally found that they could manage more effectively if they required each of their main activities to operate on a stand-alone basis. Individual managers were clearer as to their responsibilities, and could be held more effectively to account for their performance. Managers (and whole businesses) could no longer argue that their performance was not important since only the performance of the company as a whole was relevant. Companies also benefited from specialization and being able to give more attention to one activity rather than several.

13.159. The full application of all this to airports in general, and to BAA in particular, would require more detailed knowledge and it might not be entirely within the CC's present remit. Professor Littlechild said that he would not at this point urge the case for separating ownership of commercial activities from that of aeronautical activities. Nevertheless, the advantages of full accounting and management separation, and of separate price controls, were relevant to at least two issues that the CC had identified. First, it strengthened the case for a dual-till approach rather than a single till. The implicit blurring of responsibilities of a single-till approach could not be good either for regulation or management. It also involved the regulator in greater judgement of commercial issues than would seem to be desirable. Second, it strengthened the case for treating the three airports as separately as possible, and in particular for regulating them as quite separate stand-alone businesses. That would provide better signals to users, better information to regulators, better challenges to management and better performance for all.

13.160. Professor Littlechild said the assessment of the single till versus dual till needed to be seen in the context of all the above considerations. The CC's first observation, in the first paragraph of its statement of 11 July 2002 was that, other things being equal, airport charges were likely to be lower with a single till than with a dual till. If this was true, then for the reasons given above this was a significant disadvantage of the single till. It was a correspondingly significant advantage in favour of changing to a dual till. Professor Littlechild then commented in turn on the individual points made by the CC.

13.161. 'No evidence of aeronautical under-investment with single till or reason to expect it in future'. Professor Littlechild said neither approach properly applied should lead to under-investment. It was more likely that the single till led to over-investment insofar as the under-charging artificially stimulated demand and thereby led to more or earlier aeronautical investment than might otherwise have been needed. Moreover, the distortions implicit in under-charging might have led to less efficient types of investment. This would not necessarily be obvious.

13.162. 'Not clear that dual till would lead to better aeronautical investment in the future'. Professor Littlechild said that a dual till would indeed have this effect, because it would force airport management to look more closely at its airport investment policy and its operations in that area. Management could not assume that any aeronautical problems could be overcome by a little more effort or investment on the commercial side. The airport's customers, especially airlines but also passengers, could be expected to look more critically at the airport's investment plans, and this critical appraisal should have a positive effect on the design and implementation of investment. The dual till would enable the airport's allowed cost of capital to relate to its aeronautical activities rather than be a mixture of aeronautical and commercial, and this should make for more accurate assessments.

13.163. 'Dual till could benefit commercial activities at the expense of aeronautical, and the latter might not get funds or attention'. Professor Littlechild said that a disadvantage of the single till was that no one knew how present attention and funds were determined. The dual till would require due attention to both. There was no basis for suggesting that a properly set dual-till control would allow insufficient funds. The dual till would put greater pressure on the aeronautical management to make sure it delivered good performance.

13.164. 'Fares might be higher with dual till, and in the longer term represent a problematic transfer of income to airports'. Professor Littlechild said that he agreed that fares might be higher, but that would be an advantage at Heathrow and Gatwick. Without other provisions the transfer of income to the airport could be problematic, but his suggested airport charge for expansion could address this concern.

13.165. 'No benefits from any deregulation of commercial activities'. Professor Littlechild said regulation invariably introduced distortions of various kinds—for example, by reducing incentives to efficiency. Deregulation of commercial activities would tend to reduce such distortions in those activities. A second benefit would be in terms of regulatory effectiveness. The single till presumably required a responsible regulator to assess the potential revenues from commercial activities in order to decide what proportion of this should be used to offset aeronautical revenues in setting the control. That in turn presumably required a judgement as to what revenues an efficient commercial activity should yield. Reducing regulatory responsibilities here could enable better regulatory focus on the aeronautical activities, hence more effective regulation.

13.166. 'Insofar as airport charges affect fares, high profits from commercial activities benefit passengers, and the dual till might require increased regulation'. Professor Littlechild said that he had indicated that concerns about excessive profits in aeronautical activities could be addressed by means of an airport expansion charge. There might be similar concerns about excessive profits in commercial activities, especially if a dual till meant that such activities no longer had to contribute to airport charges. There seemed to be no reason why the commercial activities that benefited from the airport investments and traffic should not contribute to the airport expansion fund.

13.167. 'No beneficial effect of the dual till on efficiency in use of airport facilities'. Professor Littlechild said that a price control could generally be designed to encourage efficiency in particular areas. It would be surprising if this were not easier to do with a more focused control made possible by the dual-till approach, than with the blurred responsibilities of a single till.

13.168. 'Conceptually difficult to separate commercial and aeronautical activities'. Professor Littlechild said that regulators dealt with this sort of matter all the time.

13.169. 'Airlines should share in benefits'. Airlines benefited from the profits they made on the flights. They would benefit from the dual-till scheme proposed here insofar as the airport expansion charge would enable additional capacity to be financed and built sooner than otherwise. It would also enable lower airport charges to be imposed in future than would otherwise be necessary.

13.170. 'Arbitrary judgements could harm relations between airport and its users'. In so far as the single till may have induced a rather cosy relationship between airport and airlines, a more informed and pointed discussion about the need for and efficient use of airport investment would not be a bad thing.

13.171. 'Introducing dual till at all three airports on grounds of regulatory consistency not compatible with treating each airport on its merits'. The dual till at each airport should be in the context of a separate price control at each airport. Each component of each price control would be set to reflect the particular circumstances at each airport. The dual till would allow—indeed require—more attention to the merits of the charges at each airport. It was for consideration whether a price control was needed at Stansted.

13.172. 'Nothing to learn from overseas airports, as their circumstances are different'. Professor Littlechild said that this was remarkably complacent and almost certainly wrong on the first score. The Australian Productivity Commission's recent review of airport pricing policy in Australia and elsewhere was an informed contribution to debate. It seemed to be broadly in line with recent economic thinking internationally, as did the CAA's analysis. It was not obvious why the economic and regulatory issues addressed in the Australian report were sufficiently different from those in the UK to warrant their dismissal.

13.173. 'Dual till would not provide effective efficiency incentive to BAA via threat to revert to single till if it failed to do so'. The dual till should be introduced with every expectation of it being permanent. Properly calibrated it would provide the necessary efficiency incentives on BAA. If BAA nonetheless performed inadequately the solution was to take this into account in resetting the dual-till controls, rather than to revert to a single till.

13.174. Paragraph 4 of the CC's statement noted the importance of adequate incentives to invest. This was true, though it was equally important to ensure that the proposed level of investment was fully justified. Press comment referred to an £8 billion investment package. Whether all this would be fully justified if airport charges were to be set at a more economic level was something that the CC and the CAA would no doubt wish to consider.

13.175. As regards the CC's suggestion that there were more appropriate ways of ensuring investment, all the alternatives mentioned would seem appropriate regardless of whether there were a single or dual till.

13.176. Professor Littlechild drew attention to the view of the late Professor Michael Beesley, that the single-till approach had inhibited the development of effective regulation.

13.177. Professor Littlechild said that the single till versus dual till issue had been around for a long time. To date the restraints of international conventions, and the argument that it would produce lower charges for customers, had always prevailed. The argument in this submission was that these constraints no longer applied. There were serious disadvantages with the single-till approach. The costs in terms of excessive or distorted major investments in airport expansion seemed potentially very high. There would therefore be advantages in increasing airport charges to reflect congestion costs or future expansion costs. The dual-till approach would facilitate this. Quite independently it would bring additional benefits in terms of improved management focus and control, and improved regulation. However, it seemed helpful to accompany both these changes (higher airport charges and the switch to a dual till) by an 'airport expansion charge', or similar, that would prevent an unacceptable transfer of income from passengers and airlines to the airport.

Mr A J Lucking

13.178. Mr A J Lucking wrote to us as a travelling citizen who had studied air transport matters for some years. He told us that he had previously made submissions to the CAA on these matters. His comments to us were made in relation to the Issues Statement published by the CC on 5 June 2002.

13.179. With regard to passenger costs and benefits, Mr Lucking noted that in Tables 16.8 and 16.9 of the CAA's February 2002 recommendations, the figures indicated that between 2003 and 2013 the extra charge per passenger from the dual-till regulatory regime would range from 97p to £1.30 at Heathrow, and would increase by up to £1.85 at Gatwick, and £4.63 at Stansted. Mr Lucking compared these increases with other recent price impositions such as the segregation of the passenger service charges by the airlines, which he said had led the CAA to reduce the regulated Y2 economy fares, resulting in flights from London to New York being reduced from £422, via £413 to £404, ie a reduction of £18. The Chancellor had imposed an APD of between £5 and £40 per passenger, and it could also be anticipated that fare increases to cover insurance and security charges following 11 September were also likely. On demand fares had increased sharply—between 1994 and 2001, BA's business fare from London to New York had risen from £1,061 to £2,133. In comparison, however, the airline's cost increased over the same period from 32.45p per average tonne/km to 33.62p, though it should be noted that there had been some swing towards the cheaper long-haul operations at the same time, which would have reduced average costs. Mr Lucking noted that BAA was reported to be lobbying hard for the next South-East runway to be built at Stansted and questioned whether this could be because the ground acquisition and relocation costs there were assessed as £30 million by RUCATSE vs £1,162 million at Heathrow. Mr Lucking said that if the return on the operational assets was only about 4 per cent (see below), it was therefore the duty of the Directors to build at Stansted. Yet the resulting additional access costs to users—for time and travel—were estimated as £34.2 billion over 30 years.

13.180. Mr Lucking provided a number of quotations regarding the culture of privatized companies, focussing on the issue that for privatized companies, their first priority is their shareholders, and that in the case of the privatization of the BAA airports, this has led to under-investment in projects which were in the national interest as well as costly adversarial relations between airports and the regulator.

13.181. On the issue as to whether BAA had invested as needed, Mr Lucking suggested that the overcrowding, lengthy queues and lack of seating being endured by passengers, was not due entirely to the prolongation of the planning enquiry as generally believed, but that also the planning application had been made too late. The CAA February 2002 report showed the runways at Heathrow and Gatwick were already completely full, and Stansted full for either landings or take-offs during five peak hours. Many believed that Heathrow in particular was overfull. Since 1975, the average scheduled time from Paris had risen from 58 to 78 minutes, to allow 'recovery time', and average lateness in recent months had been an additional 12 to 18 minutes. It appeared that all south-east runway capacity would be utilized by 2005/06. Yet BAA had still not submitted a planning application for a new runway—even though its current estimate was that planning and construction would take until 2015. Mr Lucking also contrasted the two runway 'mini airport' that is the national hub at Heathrow, with the four- and five-runway airports that have been built up by Britain's three principal Continental competitors in recent years.

13.182. In concluding, Mr Lucking said that until 1995, BAA's annual reports had shown the breakdown between operational and non-operational profits—respectively £41.8 million and £231.4 million on total assets of £2,002 million (13.6 per cent). He estimated that half the assets were operational, a return of 4 per cent. The combined figure for 2001 was an operating profit of £345 million on assets of £2,771 million, a 12.5 per cent return.

13.183. Mr Lucking considered that the inadequate return on the operational airport assets under the single-till system had led to a failure to provide better facilities for passengers and could lead them to extra airport access costs far exceeding the higher charges resulting from a switch to the dual till. The impact on the national economy of the consequent lack of a competitive national air hub in an age of globalization should be evaluated as a matter of urgency before a final decision to reject the dual-till approach was taken.

13.184. Mr Lucking said that the combination of BA's public advocacy of an expensive third short runway at Heathrow, and its opposition to the dual till, was puzzling, for a company with a keen awareness of shareholder paramountcy. One factor could be the large sums BA had paid, upwards of £2 million each, for a considerable numbers of slots. An extra runway at Heathrow would undermine the profits generated by the current 'scarcity value' of slots there.

13.185. Mr Lucking said that a regulator might be uneasy about the large profits that could be made from the non-operational activities at an airport. It might be possible to regulate separately such activities as the letting of offices in the airport buildings, and car parking charges. On the other hand, spending in shops and at restaurants, pubs etc, was almost entirely optional.

Mr David Starkie

13.186. Mr David Starkie of Economics-Plus Limited said that he was responding to the invitation to comment on the statement by the CC on its current thinking regarding London airports.

13.187. The CC in its statement said that it remained unpersuaded that in practice there would be no effect on air fares at either congested or uncongested airports if airport charges were to be higher at the BAA London airports as a result of a switch to a dual-till regime. Commenting on these views, Mr Starkie said that, typically, airports combined provision of runway/terminal services with a retailing and property business. At large airports the latter accounted for a substantial turnover, which could exceed the turnover from aeronautical services. The two activities were complementary and consequently increases in air traffic volumes would usually produce significant increases in the profitability of the retailing/property activities. This provided an incentive for the airport to increase traffic volumes and had the effect of attenuating the normal downward pressure on profits that arose when prices for the use of runways, etc were lowered to attract more traffic.

13.188. Mr Starkie said that this practice was only worthwhile, however, so long as capacity existed to accommodate further air traffic. If the runways or terminals were operating at capacity then there would be little point in the airport business reducing aeronautical charges in the interests of the retailing business. At congested airports one might expect charges to rise to ration capacity notwithstanding the commercial sales. Consequently, airport businesses had an incentive to move the basic level of charges in a direction that was generally efficient. At uncongested airports there would be an incentive to keep charges low; at congested airports the incentive would be to increase charges to ration scarce capacity.

13.189. The CC, in its statement, said that there was no evidence that the single till had led to under-investment in aeronautical assets at the BAA London airports in the past, nor any expectation that it would do so over the next five years. The CC also said it was not clear that the dual, as opposed to the single, till would be likely to lead to better aeronautical investment in the future, and that the dual till could also risk unduly benefiting commercial activities, at the expense of aeronautical, which might not attract sufficient funds.

13.190. Commenting on these views, Mr Starkie said that for airport commercial activities to perform well required an increasing flow of passenger traffic. Therefore it would expect a dual till to encourage investment in aeronautical activities and, even if the dual till did not lead to better aeronautical investment in the future and, by implication, no worse investment, there would still be a gain in welfare if the dual till led to increased investment in commercial activities.

13.191. Mr Starkie said that he was also puzzled as to why the CC took the view that under a dual-till regime, aeronautical activities might not attract sufficient funds. This could only be as a result of regulatory failure; the return allowed on an aeronautical RAB (in a dual-till context), was determined by the regulator. Moreover, the parties could enter into an explicit regulatory contract that could secure increased investment in aeronautical activities as part of an agreement to adopt a dual till.

13.192. Similarly, the argument that there was no evidence that the single till had led to under-investment in aeronautical assets appeared to ignore the possibility that the single till might have led to under-investment by reducing the level of investment in commercial activities. Again, it was worth stressing that an increase in investment in commercial activities, was a welfare gain. The single till complicated the process of determining an appropriate cost of capital for the regulated airport; combining aeronautical and retailing activities meant that a view had to be taken on a composite cost of capital covering both activities. This added complication increased the risk that an inappropriate cost of capital might be chosen and that this might prejudice aeronautical investment, or commercial investment, or both.

13.193. The CC in its statement said that a move from the single to a dual till would in the longer term mean a substantial transfer of income to airports from airlines and/or their passengers. Mr Starkie said that the CC's comments appeared to be referring to a pure rent transfer from passengers and airlines to airport businesses. In this context, it was to be noted that a substantial proportion of aircraft movements at Heathrow were by aircraft on a foreign register. In efficiently operating capital markets, the distribution of rents would not really matter because ownership of the rents would be transferable. However, capital markets did not work efficiently in the aviation industry because of various institutional constraints. Shareholdings in BAA, for example, were limited to a single ownership of 15 per cent, but without any nationality restrictions; the latter restrictions did apply, however, in relation to airlines. Given the current use of Heathrow, for example, the effect of transferring rents from airport operator to airlines would be to transfer these rents from UK to overseas interests.

13.194. Mr Starkie said that he found it difficult to agree with the basic premise expressed in the quote from the CC. Because Heathrow and, to a lesser extent Gatwick, represented bottleneck facilities, an increase in demand for their use over time would have the effect of increasing the scarcity rents. Consequently, absent a dual till, the size of the scarcity rents captured by the airlines would continue to increase. Maintaining existing policies would see a continuing and increasing transfer of rents to users from suppliers which appeared to suggest that the CC was giving a preference to the former party (and, given the current structure of ownership of airlines and airports, was taking a benign view of the offshore transfer of rents).

13.195. The CC said that it was not convinced that the current profits of those (commercial) activities should be characterized as locational rather than monopoly rents. Mr Starkie said that he would argue that in the absence of deliberate attempts by the BAA to limit the quantity of commercial activities (as distinct from the limitations imposed by the lack of space or returns on capital), the profits accruing to BAA were of the nature of location rents. He was not aware that the BAA deliberately limited its commercial activities except perhaps in the interests of the quality of service having regard to its aeronautical activities.

13.196. The CC said that it was not clear that the dual till would have a significant beneficial effect on efficiency in the utilization of aeronautical facilities, in particular, of scarce runway capacity. The CC also said that it remained unpersuaded that in practice there would be no effect on air fares if airport charges were to be higher at the three BAA London airports as a result of a switch to a dual-till regime. Mr Starkie said that if the dual till did have an effect on air fares at congested airports, there would be beneficial effects on efficient utilization of scarce capacity. If, on the other hand, the dual till did not have an impact on utilization, this would be because it had no effect on air fares, in which case the shift of rents would be from airlines (with majority of foreign interest) to BAA (with a majority UK interest). However, it seemed likely that there would be a beneficial effect on utilization from an increase in charges at the congested airports. There would be more capacity available for high-value users at the expense of low-value users so that even if increased charges did not clear the market, they would at least have been some movement in the desired direction.

13.197. If the capacity of T5 was to be used effectively, there had to be a substantial increase in the number of passengers per movement. An increase in charges as a consequence of a move to a dual-till regime at a congested airport like Heathrow would facilitate this objective. In the absence of a dual till it would be more difficult for BAA to make effective use of its additional terminal capacity. Consequently, the CC's proclivity to maintain a single-till approach risked a less effective use of capacity and arguably reduced incentives for future investment.

13.198. The CC, in its statement, said that no useful parallels could be drawn at this time from overseas airports which used the dual till, as their circumstances were different from those of the BAA London airports. Mr Starkie said that the dual till had been used extensively in Australia. However, the CC did not explain why the circumstances were different. In a recent review of airport regulation in Australia by the Australian Productivity Commission, that Commission firmly supported a dual-till approach in the event of a continuation of price-cap regulation. In the event, the Australian Government chose to substitute price monitoring for price capping at all Australian airports including congested Sydney.

13.199. The CC said that each airport should be looked at on its merits. Mr Starkie agreed that this might lead to a different outcome for the congested airports, namely uncongested airports. For example, the single-till approach might be adopted only at uncongested airports where it would be consistent with incentives for efficient outcomes. Although Mr Starkie did not expect such an approach to act as a binding constraint (the airport business would have an incentive to keep aeronautical charges low), it would, nevertheless, provide the airlines with a degree of comfort. It was at the congested airports that the single-till approach had its most pernicious effects and it was at such airports that a move to a dual-till approach would be most beneficial.

13.200. Mr Starkie said that he wished to make two further observations. First, the CC did not directly address the point that the inevitable outcome of maintaining a single-till approach at a highly congested airport like Heathrow, was that it had the effect of placing downward pressure on charges (probably leading to their reduction in real terms) when common sense dictated that charges should be rising. It was perhaps not surprising that those US airlines not currently servicing Heathrow had lobbied to be allowed entry. In so doing, they were of course, seeking to transfer to themselves some of the scarcity rents. The CC, in appearing to support a single-till approach, increased those pressures, which might be argued to be having a detrimental effect on US/UK relationships. Second, the CC did not appear to address the general problem of capacity shortages in the south-east airport system. In view of the CC's concern with competition matters it might wish to pose the question: was a continuation of the single till likely to promote further competitive entry and thus provide competition to the current dominance of BAA in the South-East?

Mr J N Stevens

13.201. Mr J N Stevens described himself to us as a member of the public with a family interest in BAA shares, and with a concern for the environment. Mr Stevens said that on 4 July 2002 BAA officials had told members of the UK Shareholders Association that BAA were concerned at the possibility that the projected growth of air traffic might be curtailed by international government agreement in measures to curb global warming. Such a decision could make the planned expansion of Heathrow, Gatwick and Stansted airports' capacity at a cost of £8 billion in the next ten years redundant. Mr Stevens noted that the risk of this event had not been listed or discussed in BAA's submission to the CC; nor was it mentioned in the submission by CAA, which said that it had not been 'faced' with this issue.

13.202. This risk, however, raised public interest considerations relevant to the appropriate cost of capital and the use of a volume term for adjusting charges to compensate for unexpected changes in traffic. It would not be in the public interest if large investments were made and then found to be redundant. It was not just BAA airport investments that were at risk. The investments of other firms were involved and also that of associated infrastructure investments by government and local authorities. Mr Stevens said that the CC should try to ensure that the right price signals were conveyed by the industry to minimize the damage that would occur if the redundancy risk materialized. Compensating for the unexpected traffic changes suggested by the introduction of a volume term would give the wrong price signal since BAA would then be encouraged to ignore the risk.

13.203. It was Mr Stevens' view, that it should be possible for BAA to insure against this redundancy risk and to pass the cost to the users of its airports who were causing BAA to expand capacity. The greater the risk, the higher would be airport charges causing in turn less airport use and a consequent need for further investment.

13.204. Instead what was being proposed was the rewarding of prompt, even premature investment regardless of the risk of redundancy by international fiat. The CAA's submission concerning the proposed charges in respect of T5, stated that it 'provides for strong incentives to BAA to deliver T5 in a timely manner, and avoids giving BAA the potential incentive to simply sweat existing assets'. Mr Stevens did not think that one could rely just on the good sense of BAA managers to avoid the redundancy risk. Managers would be tempted to ignore this risk if, as was likely, their pay was geared to whatever 'strong incentives' were given to the company.

13.205. Insuring capital against its redundancy was a capital cost but Mr Stevens questioned whether it should be treated as part of the cost of capital. It should be part of BAA management's tasks to keep this cost down. Since this cost would be associated with how much investment flexibility there was in the airport expansions, BAA must be encouraged to sweat existing assets and to postpone new investment when it was sensible to do so. This suggested it should be treated as a cost to be deducted from profit rather than an element in the rate of return allowed on capital.

One NorthEast

13.206. One NorthEast said it appeared that the CAA's proposals comprised significant price profiling over the next 20 years to cover in part the capex programme for T5. These proposals would have a significant impact on domestic services bringing into question the sustainability of regional routes such as those serving the North-East of England.

13.207. The North-East hosted two airports, namely Newcastle and Teesside. Both airports offered scheduled services to Heathrow by BA and bmi respectively. These scheduled services provided essential and unreplaceable links to the capital, and crucially, wider global connections. This was an issue which had been stressed time and again through consultation with the DTLR in preparation of the UK air services White Paper.

13.208. The North-East had suffered from a prolonged decline of its traditional industries. One NorthEast along with its regional partners had embarked on an ambitious strategy to regenerate the North-East. Both its airports and the scheduled services they provided were integral to successfully meeting the economic objectives. They provide vital international links for many overseas companies based in the region and served to attract new investors. There was a concern that the CAA's pricing proposal could jeopardize these long-standing services, thereby eroding confidence and undermining aspirations in the North-East.

Strategic Aviation Special Interest Group

13.209. The Strategic Aviation Special Interest Group (SASIG) said that it was a local government association with over 70 local authorities in membership across the UK working together on aviation issues. It would not like to specify a maximum level of airport charges but would like to stress that airport charges should relate to the level of demand at the airport as it was illogical for airlines using the busiest airports to be paying lower charges and thus inflating demand.

13.210. The SASIG's understanding was that the CAA proposals sought to overturn this anomaly and the SASIG supported its proposals. However, the scope of those items included in the charges was too narrow. The regulatory regime should allow for the airports to include surface access/public transport requirements in the charges, some of which were a long way from the airport. Failure to do so might result in an excessive burden on the local authorities in the area surrounding the airport.

Tangney Tours

13.211. Tangney Tours said that it would like to take this opportunity to bring to the CC's attention a hidden cost being charged by the airports. This was a direct tax being levied against the handicapped traveller. Tangney Tours said that the handling and assistance of handicapped travellers at the BAA airports had been outsourced to private contractors. These contractors made a charge to the airlines for the handling and assistance of every handicapped traveller. The airline then reserved the right to pass on these charges directly to the purchaser of the air seat.

13.212. Tangney Tours said that in order to avoid discrimination to the handicapped traveller, these additional costs should be absorbed and the price charged should be the same for all travellers using the airport facilities.

Teesside International Airport Limited

13.213. Teesside International Airport Limited (Teesside Airport) said that it had grave concerns over the recommendations made by the CAA and their potential impact upon the current Teesside Airport–Heathrow service operated by bmi. The continuance of this vital connection to international flights at Heathrow was essential to the economic health of the Tees Valley Region. This service had operated for some 30 years during which time travellers from Teesside had contributed significant sums of money towards the development of Heathrow through the payment of passenger charges. Without such international connections, the business community within the Tees Valley region would be severely restricted in its travel options. Recent research by both the airport and the region had clearly identified the need for quality air service links to sustain the existing and future economic development of the Tees Valley.

13.214. The aviation market was becoming increasingly competitive and to ensure that the Teesside Airport–Heathrow service continued to prosper, the board of Teesside Airport had recently renegotiated the charging structure to bmi for a period of three years. Additional charge increases proposed over the next ten years by the CAA would further erode the profitability of this route and seriously threaten its continued operation. Teesside Airport had already contributed a significant sum of money through its revised deal, but was not in a position to provide further reductions to make up for these proposed Heathrow increases.

13.215. It was clear that the proposed increases would result in the termination of essential, but less profitable domestic feeder services from the regions. Not only from Teesside Airport but also many other regional airports. The profit maximization of Heathrow slots could not be used as the measure for the future operation of the airport if it was to play its required role as an international hub for the UK.

13.216. During the T5 enquiry it was not evident that such increases in the Heathrow charging structure would be required to finance the project. Had this been the case, then it would not have been supported by the Regional Airport Industry, if it had been understood that they would be the losers in the long run. If domestic feeder services were forced out of Heathrow, then Heathrow would inevitably lose its status as a hub—other than for European services feeding long-haul Atlantic routes. It was understood that T5 was required for the opposite reason—to ensure Heathrow could cope with forecast growth and retain its position as a premier international hub.

13.217. This charging strategy was not acceptable to both Regional Airports and the communities they served. Road and rail networks were unable to provide an acceptable, cost-effective alternative delivery mechanism to feeder services to Heathrow for the foreseeable future. The lifeblood of regional airports was their access to such hub airports. They had earned the right over the years to demand that these services were supported by the Government, without subsidy, to serve their respective communities. Teesside Airport urged the CC to reject the CAA recommendations and set a more realistic charging scheme for Heathrow.

TBI plc

13.218. TBI said that it provided services at 30 airports around the world and, in terms of passengers and ATMs, was the third largest operator of UK airports, after the BAA and Manchester Airport Group. TBI was the majority shareholder of Luton, and the owner of Belfast International and Cardiff International Airports in the UK. At Luton, it was conscious of its role as the only competition to the BAA monopoly of provision of airport capacity to serve London and the South-East of England.

13.219. TBI said that it did not believe that airport charges should be set as a maximum. Ideally it should be a range which reflected the cost of providing the services and associated infrastructure plus a reasonable profit margin for an efficient operator. TBI's concern was with ensuring that BAA did not establish a minimum level of charge at Stansted which was cross-subsidized by other BAA airports and allowed it to compete unfairly with Luton.

13.220. TBI believed that the existing RPI–X formula for pricing had kept BAA charges artificially low. This had had the effect of making the Luton cost base charges look high in relation to those of the BAA over the last six years. A strict comparison of airport charges was difficult because all airports had different approaches to setting charges and had specific costs that might or might not be included (for example, parking and navigation service). However, a basic comparison was Luton £11.50 (international) and £5 (domestic), while Stansted costs were £6.40 and £4.20. TBI said that it could not afford to reduce its charges to the levels charged by BAA Stansted, where capital investment was cross-subsidized by other airports within the BAA Group.

13.221. TBI said that it remained extremely concerned that BAA had made an application to Uttlesford District Council to expand Stansted to 25 mppa and 210,000 ATMs in advance of the government deliberations on a new Aviation White Paper and the SERAS consultations. Luton was the only real competition to BAA in the South-East of England. Because of the layout of airspace, geography and location of Luton and Stansted, any development of Stansted would potentially adversely affect capacity and development opportunities at Luton. Any planning permission for further development at Stansted could reinforce the already near BAA total monopoly in the South-East in that BAA should not in the future be able to cross-subsidize operations at, say, Stansted from the monopoly rents at Heathrow and Gatwick.

13.222. TBI believed that the CAA proposals for splitting airport operational and commercial income into different dual tills, was the right policy. It was appropriate that the cost of providing new operational infrastructure should be reflected in the price charged for using that facility and not cross-subsidized from receipts from commercial activity as at present. However, TBI believed that this policy should be taken further and rigorously policed, as proposed by the CAA.

13.223. With regard to the retention of standard asset-based approach, TBI said that the CAA suggested that 'the resulting price cap will not be tightly binding, and that Stansted will choose to price below the cap to meet its commercial objectives'. This situation was at the heart of TBI's concern. Even the CAA implied that lower prices would be used to meet commercial objectives. TBI asked that the CC set a minimum level of charges for BAA airports.

13.224. The CC was asked to examine whether the CAA had created a regime to meet its statutory objectives and enable operators such as TBI and Luton to compete on a level playing field with the BAA.

Other views

13.225. We were told that until February 2001, two private hire contractors provided the South Terminal and North Terminal of Gatwick with private hire services, colloquially referred to as 'taxi' services although there were no hackney carriage ranks on the airport. These contracts expired in 2001 and were the subject of a rigorous tendering process by BAA. BAA accepted tenders from two independent contractors, one to provide service at the South Terminal and another to provide the service at the North Terminal.

13.226. The tender and subsequent contract demanded a radical change to the operation, mainly in the ownership and standard of the vehicle fleet, previously exclusively provided by owner/drivers. The incumbent owner/drivers reacted violently to the proposed changes and BAA succumbed to considerable pressure from them resulting in the termination of the contract for the provision of the service at the North Terminal. The contractor providing the South Terminal service was appointed at the North Terminal also.

13.227. The situation at Gatwick is now that a single contractor provides the private hire service for the whole airport where as prior to February 2001, there had been two such contractors and thus an element of competition and alternative. The vehicle fleet was now provided solely by individual owner/drivers with the resultant compromise on vehicle standards and safety. The provision of private hire services at Gatwick prior to 2001 may have left much to be desired but there existed an element of competition and choice. This competition and choice no longer applied at Gatwick.

14 Views of BAA

Contents

Introduction

14.1. This chapter summarizes the views of BAA on the general approach to the setting of charges; the more specific factors relevant to the setting of X; and, finally, public interest issues with particular reference to complaints raised by other parties and summarized in Chapters 12 and 13. BAA's initial submission to the CC, on which parts of this chapter are based, is reproduced on the CC's web site. BAA also provided us with extensive information and attended a number of hearings, to which we refer in other chapters in this report.

The general approach

14.2. At the outset of the inquiry, BAA said that the CC was presented with a broad choice. It might adopt a narrow 'traditional' view of seeking the lowest possible prices consistent with providing a minimum incentive to invest and maintain service quality. This was the approach adopted most clearly in the transport sector for Railtrack and NATS; the results spoke for themselves. The adverse consequences of imposing the tightest possible controls were felt not just by the regulated company, but most critically by the end consumer.

14.3. There were particular reasons why this approach was too narrow for the airports industry. Planning restrictions and the slot allocation system meant that busy and well-located airports, such as Heathrow, possessed a unique economic value, or 'rent'. This rent may be shared between airlines and airports, but would not naturally flow to passengers so long as demand exceeded capacity. The general rule was that if airport charges were set low, so that airlines took all the rent, there was a real danger of lower airport investment, leading to lower capacity, resulting in higher fares and lower output. If charges were higher, the airport would have greater incentives to add capacity, facilitating a bigger and more competitive airline industry, leading to lower prices and to greater choice for passengers.

14.4. Higher airport charges (which were currently very low by international standards) may therefore serve consumers better than lower prices would. This issue was compounded by the fact that marginal costs at airports were on a sharply rising curve, and were already higher than average costs. Prices which gave an apparently reasonable return on existing assets were too low to give appropriate price signals for investment. The problems associated with narrow minimum-price regulation were exacerbated by the highly dynamic nature of the industry. Airline strategies and passenger preferences changed over short timescales, leading to continuous evolution of capital and operating programmes. A fixed minimum price effectively capped the ability of airports to respond to change of this kind.

14.5. BAA therefore supported the CAA's broader interpretation of its duties as best met by seeking maximum economic welfare overall. It agreed that this would be achieved by prices which:

(a) achieved dynamic efficiency, by encouraging additional investment when demand exceeds supply. Investment was currently the core issue for the business, with almost a united view among BAA and the airlines that more investment was needed;

(b) contributed to allocative efficiency by helping existing capacity to be taken up by those airlines which valued it most highly; and

(c) provided for productive efficiency by encouraging efficiency and innovation in management.

14.6. BAA also believed that the level of riskiness of investment it faced was now accelerating. Principle components were:

(a) T5 represented the commitment of almost £4 billion to an extremely complex and protracted project, combining engineering and construction risk, and major systems risk, all of which had historically led to major cost overruns and delays to infrastructure projects in the UK.

(b) In the case of T5, the risk was compounded by the heavily deferred nature of the returns, as the project was remunerated from gradual traffic build up after 2008. This in turn was dependent on airlines using sufficiently large aircraft to deliver sufficient passengers for the runway, given the 480,000 ATM limit which would bite on the opening of T5. These risks would be at their most acute in the period 2005 to 2008, when the major expenditure would have been committed, before the project was completed, and before the traffic base had emerged.

(c) BAA's other investments were also subject to major risk, including the vulnerability of Gatwick, and Stansted's continued growth being built on a base of only three airlines.

(d) Security was a continuing and growing risk, both in terms of its cost impact and the effect of security crises on passenger demand. This risk would be exacerbated by the CAA's proposal to remove the security element from the price formula. This was a change in regulatory risk which had not been captured in the cost of capital calculations.

(e) The increasing burden of compliance in other areas, including environmental controls, policing, fire cover and the like, also presented significant risk in an environment of fixed prices.

(f) The retail part of the business had its own, increasing risk, including the real threat that the World Health Organization would succeed in having duty-free sales of tobacco banned; bureau de change earnings being massively cut if the UK joined the Euro; and extension of the size of the EC further reducing the scope for duty- and tax-free sales.

(g) Regulatory risk overall had been significantly increased by the major changes to the regulatory environment proposed by the CAA. Key elements were the increased risk of assets being stranded at Stansted in particular; the risk to profits from the Q factor proposals; the vulnerability of the PPC to subsequent regulatory reviews; and the increased risk of a challenge under the International Obligations arising from the discontinuation of the system approach and the weakening of the long-term link between cost and prices.

Systems approach

14.7. BAA argued that, given the range of possible airport locations for new runways in the medium term, and the likelihood of annual fine tuning and rebalancing of the CIP between the airports as airline priorities changed in the short term, it was vital that any price formula did not create rigidity in the investment incentives at each airport. This was best achieved by the application of an overall system price formula, possibly in combination with overlapping individual airport sub-formulae, as the basis of control. This would allow the relative levels of airport charges at each airport to be set to reflect evolving relative levels of demand, and investment requirements, within a total revenue constraint. This would also eliminate the magnified forecasting error inherent in separately calculated values of X for each airport, since the variability of system-wide numbers was lower than that for individual airports.

14.8. An approach of this kind would avoid the economic pitfalls likely to result from the CAA's stand-alone approach. In simple terms, the use of a strict stand-alone approach, based on five-year returns linked to the cost of capital, would, in the long term, tend to produce the lowest charges at the most highly-valued, busiest, congested locations, with the greatest investment needs. This was the result of dividing fixed costs by large traffic volumes. Such an outcome would be perverse, leading to falling charges at Heathrow and rising charges at Stansted. It was only avoided in the CAA's proposals for Q4 by the judicious use of profiling devices. In the long term it was only prevented by the PPC, discussed below.

14.9. Underlying BAA's difficulty with a strict stand-alone approach was the market analysis (or absence of such an analysis) which underlay it. The CAA saw each airport as a separate market, and demand for each airport and the costs of expansion as being specific to that location. This was inherently inconsistent with its approach to demand forecasting, which, like BAA's, was driven by the allocation of overspill from Heathrow. This in turn was inconsistent with the CAA's discussion of slot valuation at Gatwick which failed to recognize that the value of slots at Gatwick was driven by the restriction of capacity at Heathrow. (The same omission applied to the CAA's analysis of Stansted.) The final paradox was then provided by the last paragraph of the CAA's overview (ie CAA proposals to us in February 2002), which hinted at the benefits of 'effective competition' between airports, a concept wholly at odds with the notion that each airport was a separate market, with a separate unique level of demand.

14.10. As to whether there were any detriments from the system approach, prices at Stansted were above marginal cost and below marginal cost at Heathrow; and so in economic terms cross-subsidy of Stansted did not currently arise. Indeed investment at Stansted up to between 30 mppa and 35 mppa was justified at Stansted's current level of charges given its low long-run marginal costs. The primary beneficiaries of that investment, however, were the airlines, which were paying below marginal cost at Heathrow since airlines were accommodated at Stansted which would have liked to compete with the Heathrow airlines but were excluded by the slot allocation system, enabling Heathrow airlines to keep the preferential access to slots at below market prices and providing extra capacity for them. It was also open to Heathrow airlines to move to Stansted to benefit from Stansted prices if they wished. Differences in rates of return, however, were to be expected given the different maturity of the airports. There had been a series of examinations by the CAA and the EC of the marketing of Stansted. BAA had shown this was to maximize profitability, but BAA also had to ensure its future investments were profitable, as a result of which it was careful not to invest too early, but 'nearly too late'. Hence, increases in the lounge and satellite at Stansted needed to handle between 8 mppa and 15 mppa only came on stream as through-put was about to exceed 15 mppa.

14.11. The real issue as BAA saw it was that the system cap maintained flexibility for Government in the longer term for location of a new runway at that location. The next runway would be designed to meet growth in demand for the London system as a whole: if the burden fell only on the consumer at, say, Stansted, that would be a significant disincentive to the provision of a new runway of that location. In effect it would require Stansted airlines to pay the price of not being at Heathrow, as well as the costs of developing Stansted. It would also be very difficult to reverse any decision that airports should be regulated on a stand-alone basis.

14.12. BAA said that its advocacy of an approach to pricing at the overall London airports level was not a mechanism for obtaining a more generous price formula; it was not asking the CC to recommend a formula more generous than the CAA's proposal for Q4. Its concern was to set out a basis for charging which was flexible and durable enough to continue to produce efficient and economic outcomes for the London area in the long term.

The single till or dual till

14.13. The CAA was to be credited in BAA's view for addressing the issue of the definition of the regulatory domain head on, from first principles, and taking account of developing international thinking and precedent. In 1996, the MMC had noted that the single till had perverse characteristics (see paragraph 2.22); the CAA had taken this forward, and had defined the domain more narrowly to encompass only those activities where the airport enjoyed market power and a capacity bottleneck existed. Subject to one important exception, and some technical concerns on the method of calculation, BAA supported the CAA's approach. The proposed domain (described by the CAA as the RRCB) had the following advantages:

(a) it eliminated the distortion to investment incentives for non-aeronautical activities inherent in the single till;

(b) it unbundled prices in accordance with sound economic principles and regulatory practice; and

(c) it allowed the airport operator to identify the returns associated with aeronautical investments, and incentivized such investment, even where there was no associated commercial income.

This would be in the interests of airport users, including those who may not yet exist, but may be important contributors to the competitive market in future, and whose prime interest was that there should be enough capacity for there to be a dynamic and competitive airline market. Air passengers were also best served by a large competitive dynamic industry: hence focusing on long-term investment needs was highly relevant to the reasonable interest of users.

14.14. In as much as, other things being equal, the RRCB might lead to higher average airport charges, it also brought two public welfare benefits:

(a) it increased the general incentive to invest in additions to capacity and service quality, which would in turn lead to more choice and lower prices for air passengers; and

(b) it contributed to improved allocation of existing scarce capacity (to the degree that demand elasticity was above zero), in the absence of an efficient slot market.

14.15. BAA believed that the dual till was compatible with international obligations. Many other international airports—for example, Sydney and other Australian airports, some seven of the top ten US airports (which adopted a compensatory basis, akin to the dual till) and certain European airports (Frankfurt, Zurich, Hamburg)—had also now gone down versions of the dual-till route, confirming the lack of international obligation to maintain the single-till approach. (It was, however, often difficult to say whether a particular approach was dual till or single till, since most airports in Europe did not have formal price control.) The use of the dual till by US airports was one reason the US Government would be unlikely to take action were the dual till to be adopted in the UK.

14.16. As to whether the dual-till approach should be applied to all three airports, BAA believed that to treat the airports as a single airport system within a dual-till framework was consistent with the ICAO and Bermuda 2. Within the revenue total, therefore, charges at individual airports should be set to reflect their individual role in the system, hence a dual-till approach could lead to charges at Stansted being capped nearer a single-till level. If the CC were to depart from the system approach, it should determine the dual-till question separately for each airport, including the exclusion of commercial activities provided in the competitive market and the high emphasis placed on investment incentives.

14.17. As to airline arguments that one could not at a conceptual level distinguish between the commercial and aeronautical activities, these could not be regarded as joint products; there was no fixed proportion between the two, and an airport could be produced with very little commercial activity or income. The bringing of passengers to the airport by airlines was a necessary, but not sufficient condition for the generation of commercial income: passengers themselves brought no commercial income, but what did so was BAA's ability to offer products and services which passengers wanted to buy. They were therefore an additional revenue stream, which BAA had maximized on the basis of its entrepreneurial skills. On this, many passengers regarded BAA airports as being among the best for commercial activity. At congested airports, the level of complementarity between the two activities was also low, because if airport charges were reduced, the number of passengers and commercial income would not be increased (indeed, if airport charges increased, the result could be operation by larger aircraft, increasing rather than reducing the number of passengers and commercial income—a negative complementarity). At uncongested airports on the other hand, if there was complementarity, it would be in the airport operators' interest to charge less than allowed under the dual till.

14.18. BAA acknowledged that in appraising investments in aeronautical facilities, likely commercial revenues would be taken into account and previously it had been possible to justify projects on that basis, even though any high commercial return would in effect be taken away at the next quinquennial review: but that approach was now more difficult with the increase in marginal costs. Hence—as discussed further below—BAA was now looking for an approach which increased the level of investment incentive, and allowed individual managers bringing forward aeronautical investments to identify the returns.

14.19. As to practicalities of the separation of commercial and aeronautical activities and cost allocation, which the CC in its July statement on the dual till (reproduced at Appendix 2.3) argued was difficult, the task was found possible when the Government required BAA to separate these activities for accounting purposes in 1967 and renewed the requirements in 1986. BAA auditors had found it possible to separate these activities, as had overseas administrations and airport authorities. Extensive work had also been carried out with the CAA on this. The CC itself found no difficulty in such separation when it imposed the requirement to report separately on the specified activities. As to the possible objection that there were common costs in the provision of aeronautical and retail facilities and that BAA would have an incentive to pass common costs through aeronautical facilities and to get revenues out of the retail side, this was the essence of ring-fencing in other utilities.

14.20. The CC's argument was also fallacious in principle, confusing joint goods, where cost allocation was indeed a problem, and related products. The key point was that whilst commercial activities could not be provided without aeronautical activities, the converse was not true and the cost could be identified separately; commercial activities were incremental and the incremental cost should be capable of identification. There would of course always be issues of overhead allocation, any answer would be approximate but robust, and the regulated company may expect to get the worst of any rough justice: but that was no reason for the CC to prefer to be absolutely wrong.

14.21. On arguments that, to estimate the appropriate division of costs, it would be necessary to consider how terminal buildings would be constructed with and without commercial facilities, BAA said that it had done work on that and the cost difference was quite small. The marginal cost of providing retail activities was low, retail floor space accounting for 8 to 10 per cent of T5, but the impact net of what circulation and seating would be required without retail would be a lower figure.

14.22. However, BAA disagreed with the CAA on the proposal to exclude surface access from the RRCB. The CAA excluded not just rail schemes, but also all roads, from the RRCB. The Heathrow Express project was excluded, despite the fact that the 1991 formula settlement from the CAA was heavily conditional on BAA pursuing this project and Heathrow Express was, in effect, a condition precedent to getting T5. The only projects included by the CAA were the Heathrow Express and Piccadilly Line extensions to T5, on the grounds that these were conditions of the T5 consent. To require projects to be planning conditions in order to be included in the aeronautical till would discourage the process of trying to reach accommodation with local authorities constructively on surface access schemes, rather than further protracting the more confrontational planning process. It appeared that the CAA envisaged that the solution lay in road pricing, although BAA was not currently legally empowered to road price, and a road-pricing technology had not yet been defined for airports. Until these problems were resolved, the exclusion of roads and railways from the RRCB removed from BAA the incentive to push forward with imaginative schemes to improve airport access capacity, reduce travellers' delays and add to service quality.

14.23. BAA therefore encouraged the CC to adopt the RRCB, but with surface access added until such time as road pricing was practically possible. This proposal was not a device for raising prices further in the next quinquennium, since it was not attempting to 'bid up' the CAA's formula proposal; its significance was in relation to the long-term investment climate it created for surface transport schemes. BAA believed that it would be inconsistent with previous regulatory practice to do otherwise. Consistent with this, BAA also suggested short-term car parks be included in the aeronautical till.

14.24. BAA also queried the CAA's assumption that all current liabilities should be deducted from aeronautical assets, rather than some allocated to commercial assets. It also argued that any adjustment for revenue advancement and under-investment should be allocated to both the commercial as well as to the aeronautical till. In consequence, BAA estimated regulatory fixed assets of aeronautical facilities of £3.1 billion compared with the CAA's estimate of £2.5 billion; of the difference, £410 million was attributed to advancement of revenue/capex adjustment, and £180 million to working capital.

14.25. BAA stressed, however, that while it wished to modify aspects of the CAA approach, it was not seeking higher revenue from airport charges than proposed by the CAA. Indeed, it was not seeking an immediate move to full dual-till prices, rather a lifting of the strict single-till cap and a clear signal of the move towards the dual till over a period of time. Although (as noted below) it also regarded smoothing of revenues between quinquennia as necessary, such 'money on the table' would have a much greater value if it was a demonstration of commitment to move to a dual till over the longer term, and to resolve the current perverse incentive of the single till in investment decisions, discussed further below. BAA did, however, see as feasible the CAA's suggestion that it could revert to the single till in future if BAA's performance was inadequate, although it was confident it would never operate in such a way as to bring that about.

14.26. BAA's main proposition was that the CC should no longer find itself bound strictly by the single till rate of return if other considerations, in particular the importance of investment, would otherwise lead us to a higher level of charges than under the single till: there could be a range of outcomes between the single till and dual till in the future. It also saw a strong argument that the cost of capital was not a fixed number, and no one knew quite what it was: alighting upon a single till cost of capital and setting charges to match that was as likely to give too low a level of charges as too high, with a 50 per cent risk of under-investment, whereas a priority for public welfare may be to ensure investment rather than minimize charges. The dual till provided a mechanism to reduce that risk by providing a cost base structure which demanded a higher level of charges.

14.27. Hence, BAA went along with the CAA's judgment in its February proposals to us, in recommending Heathrow's charges in Q4 be on a single-till rather than dual-till basis, in balancing off the ultimate level of charges and what was achievable in the shorter term: in practice, it believed it could not price fully up to the CAA's recommended cap at Gatwick or Stansted.

14.28. It acknowledged, however, that its main concern was to have the right level of airport charges—but the reasoning which underlay that was significant, and to set a price formula based on a dual till would send a clear message as to the future return and extent of regulation and provide a sounder and more sustainable basis than a single-till number which would be affected by future changes in commercial revenues. It would also tend to bring forward price increases so BAA was not as vulnerable to changes in capacity utilization.

Effect on resource allocation

14.29. BAA said that, although charges on aeronautical activities were lower under the single till than under the dual till, in the presence of capacity constraints and in the absence of auctioning of capacity, charges on aeronautical activities would have their main incidence on the profits of airlines, and it was unclear why they should be subsidized. (It showed us a number of papers on this point.) Indeed that would worsen allocative efficiency in the presence of capacity constraints.

14.30. Airlines were currently charging what the market would bear at Heathrow: not on the basis of their costs plus BAA's landing fees. Hence, the effect of an increase in charges (which would only be to European levels) would not be to increase fares at congested airports, but to weed out the least efficient, highest-cost providers. Slots operated on obscure short-haul markets may well then be operated by a more substantive long-haul market, raising consumer welfare. The biggest threat to air fares was insufficient airport capacity (as made clear in the Government's consultation on future capacity). The best way to prevent air fares rising was to provide more airport capacity; the incentive to do so was greater if airport charges were higher.

14.31. BAA agreed that it was difficult to assess the extent of the market's response to price changes, but to the degree that demand was not 100 per cent price inelastic (which would be exceptional) any move towards market-clearing prices would have some beneficial effect on efficiency which should be taken into account. There was ample evidence that the rises in runway charges on small aircraft at Heathrow from 1985 had an extremely beneficial effect on runway utilization of scarce capacity leading to significant increase in runway capacity. The dual till was likely at least to result in improved allocation of scarce runway resources at the margin, which would be of value: it was a reasonable assumption that some of the more marginal traffic at Heathrow would go to Gatwick. Airport charges at Heathrow were currently too low to clear the market: with the dual till, the gap between charges and market-clearing prices would be less, giving a higher incentive on BAA to increase capacity as well as on operators to make more considered decisions about the best use of capacity, to the degree that price elasticity was above zero. Since the process of trading in slots was likely to be made illegal by the European Commission, the differential in airport charges may be the only tool to improve efficient utilization of runway capacity: higher charges at Heathrow would help to manage the excess demand at Heathrow into other airports.

14.32. BAA also did not accept that the Airports Act confined the CAA's objective to promoting efficient 'operation', rather than 'use' of the airports as was argued by some airlines (see Chapter 12). Efficient operation encompassed efficient use; neither the Airports Act nor European regulation prevented the CAA having regard to the efficient use of airports. The CAA was merely making a contribution to a framework which provided for efficient allocation—not getting involved in the detailed allocation of individual slots.

14.33. As to whether higher charges at Heathrow resulting from the dual till could affect services to or from regional airports, BAA did not believe that it was in a position to make a value judgment about whether services to or from regional airports were of greater value than other services, for example long-haul services. Without any advice from the Government or the CAA on this point, the correct level of charges should be set, and the people who valued the capacity most would be those who used it. Low charges at Heathrow, moreover, discouraged direct services between the regions and overseas, contrary to Government strategy. Higher charges, on the other hand, could encourage higher investment in the London airports, and more capacity for regional services.

Effect on investment

14.34. BAA argued that it had invested adequately, subject only to the constraint of the T5 planning inquiry. However, whereas it had previously been possible to justify projects sensibly and credibly on a single-till basis, BAA argued that a move progressively towards dual-till based charges was now required by the rising marginal cost of investment, in order to discharge the regulatory duty to encourage investment, a factor that had changed within the last few years. However, an increasing number of projects were required to manage service quality, safety and security rather than generating revenues. The dual till would also allow an improved focus on aeronautical investments, the single till making it very difficult to justify such projects on their own and biasing managers to invest in projects with an element of commercial returns.

14.35. Hence, under the single till return to aeronautical projects depended on what they made on commercial revenues. (If, for example, there was investment in a jetty, but retailing did better than expected, airport charges would be lowered, and the jetty project would never make an adequate return because it had been cross-subsidized.) The fact that under rate of return regulation a rate of return was allowed on all investment, aeronautical or otherwise, was only true as a general principle: what mattered was how the revenues were attributed to the project; it was undesirable to assume a 7.5 per cent return on any investment merely because a rate of return would eventually be allowed on it, but necessary to prioritize projects. The dual till, by unbundling investments into their constituent parts, would give separate revenues and returns to aeronautical projects. On the commercial side it would also put BAA under a clearer discipline only to invest where there were true marginal revenues on capital costs, whereas currently the same return was guaranteed irrespective of merit. The dual-till mechanism would therefore lead to the most efficient use of capital. It would allow capital decisions to be made on a privatized commercial basis; whereas to assume all investment earned the permitted rate of return gave no incentive inside BAA to prioritize, use commercial thinking, or spend wisely.

14.36. BAA gave us a paper by Oxera which considered the effects of the single and dual till on investment in an airport taken as comprising two activities of retail and aeronautical.

14.37. First, the paper argued that the single till distorted investment in retail activities. By including retail revenues in the determination of the price cap on aeronautical, the single till would constrain anticipated returns on retail investment to be equal to the assumed cost of capital on aeronautical. Furthermore, by adjusting the aeronautical price cap at five-yearly intervals, the single till limited the period for which unanticipated excess returns on retail could be earned. It therefore reduced the incentive to undertake useful retail projects and deferred profitable projects until the start of a new five-year period; but in the long term there was no incentive on BAA to choose the most efficient (ie profitable) projects, as all retail projects would earn the same return. The dual till eliminated this distortion as regards retail investments (although aeronautical investments would remain subject to the permitted returns).

14.38. Second, the cost of capital used in the determination of price caps under the single till was not appropriate for providing incentives to invest in aeronautical facilities. To encourage investment in aeronautical facilities, anticipated rates of return should be equal to the marginal cost of capital on aeronautical alone. The cost of capital on T5 was quite different from that on retail facilities. Hence, the single till distorted incentives to invest in aeronautical facilities.

14.39. Third, the dual till provided stronger incentives to expand capacity during periods of capacity shortage. In a competitive market prices would rise in response to increases in demand, but under the single till total returns on aeronautical plus retail activities were fixed in the long run after a regulatory review. Under the dual till, retail returns would be higher and could rise in the long run in response to greater passenger throughput; hence incentives to invest in aeronautical activities rose under the dual till in relation to the single till.

14.40. Finally, the dual till provided less scope for regulatory failure than the single till. Under the single till, the regulator had to consider both aeronautical and retail activities, while under the dual till the regulator had only to examine the aeronautical till. Thus under the dual till the scope of regulation was reduced at the same time limiting the potential for regulatory failure. In addition there was little precedent for price regulation of commercial businesses (although implicit rather than explicit) and this would arguably increase the chance of inefficient regulation of retail activities.

14.41. BAA also commented on the following possible objections to implementation of the dual till in the context of investment:

(a) As to the objection that BAA had performed perfectly well and utilized capacity in full, BAA said that it was impossible to answer the counter factual of what would have happened if there had been a different regulatory system. But economic regulation was based on the premise that incentives mattered and the correct incentives yielded superior outcomes not incorrect ones (see also BAA's comments in paragraph 14.43).

(b) As to the objection that differential incentives on new investment and existing assets could be provided equally well under the single till and dual till, for example by the LRIC proposal, BAA said that in principle it was possible to have differential returns on existing assets and higher marginal returns on new investment. However, different marginal incentives would then be required for aeronautical and retail activities and regulated prices would not in general replicate the marginal incentives that retail activities faced and the competitive markets in which they operated. Regulation of retail activities created unnecessary complexity and incorrect investment incentives. If the CAA's LRIC approach was rejected, a move from single till to dual till was even more critical to provide correct investment incentives.

(c) As to the objection that there was a spill over from earnings on aeronautical into retail, ie when passenger numbers increased, BAA benefited from retail activities as well as aeronautical, and that the single till internalized this externality while the dual till did not, BAA said that this argument was precisely the wrong way round. The single till did not replicate a competitive market because marginal costs exceeded average cost. Hence the single till distorted investment in retail activities when no impact from aeronautical activities should be felt; and to the extent there was an externality the dual till offset some of the distorting effects of regulation on incentives to invest in aeronautical facilities.

(d) As to the objection that, by yielding a rate of return equal to the cost of capital on aeronautical and retail activities combined, the single till replicated competitive market conditions better than the dual till, BAA said that the single till set average returns equal to the cost of capital across the combination of aeronautical and retail activities, but not appropriate marginal incentives. The dual till ensured that marginal returns were equal to the cost of capital in each aeronautical and retail activity.

(e) As to the argument that, by raising returns on retail, the dual till would divert investment away from aeronautical, unless BAA was capital constrained raising the marginal incentives to invest in retail or aeronautical would increase investment in both activities. Under its planning guidelines, moreover, BAA must provide a minimum amount of aeronautical space per passenger, and the Q factor, if it were to be implemented, provided further incentives to invest in aeronautical facilities.

(f) As to the argument that planning constraints made investment incentives irrelevant and meant that, even if there were no financing constraints, raising returns on retail would lead to more space being allocated to retail rather than aeronautical facilities, the fact that there were serious planning and space constraints made it all the more important that BAA was adequately compensated for the risks and costs involved in planning applications and capacity expansions. The correct allocation of existing capacity was not obtained by artificially depressing returns on the competitive retail activity. The planning system itself reduced the relative amount of retail in any development as illustrated by the T5 planning decision in which the amount of landside retail space was restricted.

14.42. BAA also put forward the effects of the dual till on a number of illustrative projects:

(a) For entirely aeronautical projects which did not increase capacity, there would be no difference between the single till and dual till. (BAA subsequently qualified this point by adding that there were demand-side as well as supply-side considerations. Under a dual till the cost of adding to service quality was apparent and the price paid for it was apparent, hence airlines could trade-off the effects on price. But under the single till airlines in asking for capacity and service quality projects assumed there were no cost implications, since they would be lost in commercial revenues.)

(b) For entirely aeronautical projects which did increase capacity, the dual till would provide stronger incentives than the single till through greater retail spend.

(c) For projects which were a mix of aeronautical and retail, in fixed proportions, and which increased capacity, moving from the single till to the dual till had an ambiguous effect on the size of investment but brought incentives closer in line with costs.

(d) For projects which were a mix of aeronautical and retail in variable proportions, and which increased capacity, moving from the single till to the dual till would strengthen incentives, by increasing the returns to the project overall.

(e) For projects which were entirely retail, but which increased capacity, the incentive effect of moving from the single till to the dual till was ambiguous, but projects which had higher returns would be more highly incentivized under the dual till than under the single till, and the ranking of projects would be more efficient.

(f) For projects which were entirely retail, and which did not increase capacity, incentives would be higher for efficient projects and lower for inefficient projects under the dual till than they would have been under the single till.

14.43. In our July statement of current thinking on the dual till, we argued there was no evidence that the single till had led to under-investment in the past. BAA argued that if there had been under-investment then there were only two explanations: poor incentives under an RPI–X structure or the level of charges being too low. As to the former, the RPI–X structure did not in itself discourage investment, but would incentivize an investment rush at the end of the control period, for which there was no evidence. But if the level of charges was too low, either the cost of capital had been set too low or the formula had unreasonably credited investment for too low costs or too high income. BAA argued that there had not been systematic under-investment to date, because the unit costs of investment had been low and steady enough for investment to be remunerated under a single till. But this did not hold good for the future in which the unit costs of capacity were rising sharply. Hence lack of Q3 underspend did not in itself support a single-till regime, nor did the presence of overspend necessarily support a dual till. As to future under-investment, the CC's argument that there was no evidence that the single till would lead to under-investment in the future was not substantiated: there would be under-investment if charges were too low, ie if the cost of capital was too low or the unit cost of future investment was higher than of past investment and charges were set on the basis of past investment. This was the case under the single till and, although BAA acknowledged prices based on full marginal cost would not be a sustainable regulatory approach, the dual till provided a vehicle for moving charges towards marginal cost.

14.44. As to the CC's 'alternative proposition' that if prices were always set simply to remunerate past investment, then eventually all investment would be remunerated, this was not what would happen in a competitive market and it exposed the company to abnormal long-term regulatory and business risk, since returns were artificially deferred where marginal costs were rising. Single-till RCV therefore was inherently disincentivizing under this approach, and could only be corrected for by artificial adjustments which were by their nature unstable as they could be reversed by legal challenge or regulatory 'volte-face'.

Commercial activities

14.45. BAA argued that it was completely fallacious to suggest the single till represented sharing of common costs or profits: all benefits went to the airlines. It did not accept that its investment in commercial activities should, as with any regulation of monopolies, be subject every five years to being limited to the cost of capital: its commercial activities were not monopoly activities, but equivalent to the competitive activities of other utilities which were ring-fenced and unregulated. Nor did it accept the argument that competing airports would lead to a single-till environment: the Australian authorities had considered this argument, and concluded otherwise.

14.46. BAA broadly agreed with the CAA's view that its commercial activities were conducted in contestable markets but acknowledged there were degrees of market power, and some commercial activities for which there was more of a market than others. It argued that none of the retail products sold at BAA's London airports could be regarded as intrinsic to the travel product but were sold via competing branded operators at prices linked to their high-street stores. Even for duty- and tax-free sales, there were plentiful alternative buying opportunities of which regular travellers would be aware—on the aircraft, from the non-EC departure airport on the return leg and on the high street overseas where lower duty/VAT may apply—so market power was by no means complete. The same conclusions were reached by the Australian Productivity Commission. For catering, alternatives included eating before arrival at the airport or on the aircraft, passengers bringing their own food, or buying food from retail outlets such as Boots. Even if, for passengers with long check-in times and lack of catering on some flights, these were not realistic alternatives, this was merely a question of locational versus monopoly rent. Car parking was acknowledged as more contentious, BAA taking the view that short-term parking should remain in the aeronautical till. Market power in relation to long-term car parking was extremely low, this being a highly competitive market around the airport, and also with choice of different modes of travel (such as rail and buses) available in travelling to or from the airport

14.47. High rates of return on assets were primarily a function of asset valuation: off-airport market businesses would value the assets on a market asset valuation basis. The excess of market valuation over indexed historic cost, as in investment properties, effectively reflected a difference in valuation of the retail site, a reflection of the locational advantage enjoyed by airport retailing—ie a form of locational rental. The RAB made no allowance for locational rent in capital value. The historical expansion of airport retail and property space plus the BAA policy for most retail activities to price at or below high-street levels were also both evidence of lack of monopoly rent with regard to commercial space. A degree of locational rent was also at least partially due to entrepreneurial and development activity by BAA resulting in growing revenues over time. Even if there was market power, as the CAA argued, this was not an argument to use it to cross-subsidize airlines; but BAA ensured there was no abuse by requiring concessionaires not to price above high-street levels and in benchmarking prices against other locations.

14.48. In response to our July statement on the dual till, BAA said that we should consider the extent of the regulatory domain on a systematic basis, looking at each activity on its own merits. As noted above, certain activities, being clearly provided in competition with off-airport providers, should fall outside the domain: this was the only approach which was consistent with ICAO policy. They included inter alia long-term car parking and landside retailing where BAA's only strength lay in the location of its activities and consumers have clear alternatives. There was no reason in law, economics or regulatory best practice why the net proceeds of the sale of goods landside should be handed to airlines in their entirety. Although the CC's statement used the language of 'sharing' there had been no discussion of intermediate situations in which the proceeds of commercial activities (above the cost of capital) were shared on a continuing basis. Use of arguments against a full till to justify a full single till were particularly regrettable since BAA's proposition was never that a full dual till should be used, but only that the rigid single-till cap should be lifted.

14.49. The CC's statement also appeared to argue that the dual till would both deregulate and increase regulation of commercial activities, neither of which was accurate. Such activities were already regulated under normal competition and fair-trading law, duty-free and car park charges having been already investigated. The 14 per cent HCA return on commercial activities (including Heathrow Express) was well within the range of normal business. But the argument that the profits of commercial activities were monopoly rather than commercial rent were remarkable, not tested in any way. The profitability of retail or car parking was invariably driven heavily by location. BAA had shown evidence of significant additional retail space and property brought on stream in Q3; and highlighted its voluntary price code linking prices to those on the high street, neither of which were consistent with the concept of monopoly rents where supplies would be constrained and prices increased. Even NERA[1] admitted to the likelihood of some locational rent: to the degree the CC could accept this, it would provide a basis for an intermediate position between the dual and single tills.

- *The balance between aeronautical and commercial activities*

14.50. We also raised the issue of whether BAA's development of commercial activities had to date been at the expense of aeronautical activities, or whether this would be the case, or would be to greater extent under the dual till. We noted that BAA already performed better in IATA surveys for commercial than for aeronautical activities.

---

[1] NERA provided a paper to us arguing that the commercial activities at the airports earned returns beyond the cost of capital.

14.51. BAA disagreed with our interpretation of the IATA survey. It was not the case, it said, that for non-retail elements of service quality ratings tended to be significantly lower than average: the complaint only cited Heathrow, and Gatwick was generally better. BAA did, however, acknowledge that there were two areas where this could be claimed, notably ease of way-findings/signposting and 'connections'. The first of these was, if the CAA proposals were adopted, to be incorporated into a Q factor; the second was a joint responsibility and BAA believed that great strides had been made to improve performance. On comfort of waiting at gate areas, Gatwick was above average and Heathrow slightly below average. On a further possible example put to BAA—that in T3 customers had to enter the departure lounge through the duty-free shop—BAA argued that the shop could be bypassed by fast track customers and regulars, with no material increase in walking distances; there had also been very little negative customer feedback on the arrangement. (We had also noted low QSM ratings of landside and airside seating availability in T3. BAA told us that there was a need to reduce landside congestion and it was clear passengers were not aware of the facilities airside. A number of landside seats had been removed, to encourage passengers to go airside: ratings should, however, much improve when the current expansion of the T3 International Departure Lounge is completed.)

14.52. As to whether commercial activities would benefit from the dual till at the expense of aeronautical activities, BAA believed that there was already a risk under the single till, for the reasons outlined above, of it being more attracted to projects with a commercial rate of return, since it was not certain that, for example, customer service projects would be adequately remunerated. Hence projects that did not have an aeronautical return in their own right needed cross-subsidization from commercial revenues. However, it aimed to get a balance between customer service and retail revenues. Under the dual till, however, the argument was not about incentivizing a fixed level of investment but increasing the total quantity of investment: aeronautical projects would now earn their cost of capital, while investment in general and especially mixed investment would be more highly incentivized and the cake would be bigger for all investment. Second, the presumption there would be more commercial investment did not necessarily hold: it was a clear weakness of the single till that it did not disincentivize poor excessive commercial investments since any losses were submerged within the till; rather, the dual till provided a much superior, normal commercial basis for determining what commercial project should be undertaken.

14.53. Third, BAA put forward comprehensive measures of protection offered in the form of a Q factor and a code of conduct, in addition to the safeguards provided by law and regulation. Under its proposed code BAA would commit to collection and distribution of data on space utilization in common user terminal areas; maintain aeronautical space levels to meet Q factor standards; and consult on development proposals in common user terminal areas. Local approaches could supplement Q measurements at the airport level to alleviate specific airline concerns and provide additional information on other areas as required. For example, an airport would wish to share its late-to-gate surveys with airlines and handling agents. BAA acknowledged that some improvement in its space data would be necessary.

14.54. Hence, even if the proportion of space occupied by commercial activities were to increase—which was not necessarily the case—that did not imply the amount of space occupied by aeronautical activities would reduce. Inadequate aeronautical facilities (for example, seating) would indeed themselves damage retail sales.

Effect on BAA's overall profitability and regulatory consistency

14.55. As to the application of the single till from privatization, BAA said that its prospectus included an indication from Government that it expected commercial income to be taken into account by the MMC in the five-yearly price reviews, but this was not mandated. The requirement to account separately for the profits and losses of aeronautical activities signified and established dual-till information as relevant regulatory information. Custom and practice had since swung sharply towards the dual till. A move progressively towards dual-till-based charges was, moreover, now required by the rising marginal cost of new investment in order to discharge the regulator's duty to encourage investment; the CA98 would remedy the absence noted in our previous report of any method of regulating commercial activities.

14.56. BAA believed that the dual till would not therefore be a departure from the basis on which it was privatized, and would not represent any windfall to its shareholders. Much of its current commercial revenue was, moreover, due to entrepreneurial activity on top of the locational advantage of airports. However, there were precedents of unanticipated windfall gains made by privatized companies, which they had retained in whole or part, for example NGC's stake in Energis; Transco's properties windfall and Railtrack's property windfall. The effect of any windfall tax on the additional profits if a dual-till approach were adopted, moreover, would be to reduce the net level of charges to the point where investment was no longer attractive and/or severely weaken BAA's ability to finance investment: BAA was not asking for anything more than it thought necessary to incentivize and finance investment.

14.57. BAA was also asked about an alternative approach, of valuing aeronautical and commercial assets on the basis of profitability rather than cost. It thought that this would, in effect, require a one-off write down of the depreciated replacement cost of the aeronautical asset: but the end effect on charges would be much the same as the single till.

14.58. As regards income transfers and regulatory credibility, the CAA's estimate of a rent transfer of £3 billion to £4 billion—a figure BAA thought too high—was in BAA's view from airlines, not passengers: the transfer to BAA would take place over a very long time, with little in Q4, and the charge increase would merely take Heathrow's charges to the average level of European airports where airlines were all currently surviving and competing. It said that the CC was understandably concerned but did not reflect on the scale of the sums involved: only £2 per passenger in the next five years, equivalent to a transfer from airlines of approximately £200 million a year by 2007/08 at Heathrow. No individual airline would suffer a transfer of more than £80 million a year. This in turn would facilitate an £8 billion investment programme. The suggestion that such a regime would in principle be unsustainable or non-credible was not borne out by experience elsewhere, the CAA believing it could sustain the regime, and other regimes had been successfully sustained with significant activities excluded. The real danger was in the opposite direction: as the experience of NATS had shown. Although BAA accepted the importance of regulatory consistency, in this case the benefits of change would be greater than the cost of maintaining the current regulatory approach.

14.59. Also, however, in considering the objection that dual till could increase total returns and yield a windfall, BAA had noted, above, that in the presence of capacity constraints there were strong allocative as well as dynamic efficient reasons for raising prices. But, if only dynamic efficiency factors were thought relevant, the opening RAB could be adjusted to leave total expected returns unchanged. This would, however, create a perverse price movement in the short term—reducing prices now to raise them later—and amount to a sequestration of assets, with severe consequences for the reliability of the regulatory structure and attitudes of investors. A further option, which BAA put forward at a relatively late stage, would be to confine the dual till to new investment, with the single till maintained for existing assets.

Incentives under the single till

14.60. In a final comment on our statement on the dual till, BAA said that it may be true, as the CC argued, that adequate incentives could be provided under the single till, but only if the single till was implemented in such a way that it produced the right level of prices in a sustainable way, which was inherently more difficult than under a dual till. This would be more difficult if BAA's charges were capped on a rigid single-till ROCV basis. Satisfactory resolution of the review would require the CC to continue to apply the system approach; apply a cost of capital which fully reflected BAA's growing riskiness; incorporate AICC in the asset base; accept the importance of providing BAA with a financial margin or cushion to avoid a crisis in the event of any further disruptions; and resist the temptation to claw back or underspend indiscriminately.

Price path commitment

14.61. BAA said that the CAA had rightly recognized the particular problems of setting a five-year price formula in an industry which was exceptionally 'lumpy', extremely capital intensive and experiencing rising marginal costs. These factors tended to exacerbate the difficulties of prices based on five-year returns tending to vary wildly around a long-term trend; and for prices to lag behind cost increases, thereby disincentivizing timely investment. The CAA's proposed solution for this was the PPC, under which BAA received a significant uplift in charges per passenger after T5 opened, and guaranteed to apply for 20 years. The price signal set out in the PPC at £18 per marginal passenger after

T5 opened was very helpful in informing the industry of the likely long-term price path. BAA did not, however, give it the value of a true commitment, since the CAA had no power to commit its successors. Indeed airlines would almost inevitably and entirely rationally wish to avoid paying for what BAA had already built. It was also concerned that the consistency of this approach with Article 10(3) of the Bermuda 2 agreement had not been properly addressed by the CAA to date.

14.62. Hence, while BAA believed the notion of trying to achieve a long-term price signal was absolutely valid, it was not satisfied that under the current legislation there could be any commitment as to the appropriate level of prices in future reviews and attached very little significance to it. Indeed, BAA believed the CAA approach would lead to prices in Q5 being reopened on a single-till rather than dual-till basis. Lower costs, and higher profits than expected, would be liable to legal challenge—but not vice versa, resulting in asymmetry of risk. Hence, smoothing between quinquennia was also important, to give lenders a degree of certainty, rather than running the risks of any hike in prices, which airlines may be unable or unwilling to pay at the time. An alternative (discussed below), however, was the use of specific triggers for specific outputs.

Recovery of under-investment

14.63. BAA believed that the principle of claw back of net capital underspend was legitimate in principle where there had been deliberate underspending. However, it regretted the CAA's adoption of a 50 per cent level for claw back without any evidence that any of the 'underspending' to date had been contrived by BAA rather than externally imposed. (Indeed, BAA's returns had been in line with those projected in 1996.)

14.64. BAA objected to any implication of automatic recovery of underspend, since inter alia it believed such an approach would be a disincentive to efficient investment, and its rate of return had been broadly as projected. Hence there were no windfall gains—factors it believed were recognized in the CAA's 50:50 approach. Claw back of underspend should only be considered if underspend had been to some degree engineered by the company or it had made a windfall gain. Total returns, however, were very close to forecast because of high operating-cost depreciation due to the need to manage terminal congestion: high depreciation was partially caused by the purchase of shorter-life assets. Reduction of RAB would be arbitrary and mere punishment with no regulatory precedent and a very poor incentive for future capital projects.

14.65. BAA also noted the additional investment undertaken instead of T5, although it conceded that this was difficult to itemize. £500 million had been spent on T5 or T5-related projects including Heathrow Express, £200 million had been spent on additional non-T5 capex at Heathrow, £87 million at Gatwick and £186 million at Stansted: optimizing the use for existing capacity at Gatwick and Stansted and additional investment at those two airports was in its view a way of meeting unfulfilled demand at Heathrow; Stansted indeed had handled 60 per cent more passengers than forecast in MMC4. (Some £20 million at Gatwick probably could not be attributed to not building T5.) However, BAA believed another £100 million fixed expenditure on minor projects had occurred to replace worn out assets and deal with congestion conditions. It believed that this was conservative, as it excluded some additional expenditure on CIP lounges and the flight reporting centre. Changes in project scope were included within the additional £100 million element. (Such investment had been undertaken because BAA was confident it would be allowed a 7.5 or 7.75 per cent rate of return, since the airlines wanted it and BAA believed it right to provide additional capacity and quality of service before T5.) There had been increased depreciation on this investment, and there had also been some under-recovery of permitted revenues over the period. It was also now expecting to increase investment in 2002/03 by £70 million compared to its original forecast for the year: which, after allowing for the additional depreciation and under-recovery, reduced the amount of claw back to zero. Indeed, allowing for under-recovery of permitted airport charges, greater than expected loss of duty-free revenues, the CAA's allowance of £100 million for capital efficiency in its proposed recovery of under-investment (for which BAA could identify a number of specific efficiency savings) and centralized costs associated with capex but expensed, BAA could be regarded as overspending rather than underspending.

14.66. We have also noted above BAA's argument that any correction for under-investment should be applied not just to aeronautical charges under any dual till, but also to commercial activities.

14.67. On whether any claw back should be in Q4, rather than, as the CAA proposed, being incorporated in the RCV and spread over 20 years, claw back in Q4 would weaken the company financially at a point where it was already extremely weak due to the major capex taking place before revenues were on stream; it would also push prices down at a point where capacity utilization was highest, so prices should be at their highest. BAA drew attention to paragraph 182 of CAA 664 (the CAA's final report following the last review) as implying that, if there were other reasons, particularly to do with the trajectory of charges over the next ten years, return of that advancement may need to be over a period longer than five years.

Assets in the course of construction

14.68. BAA argued that to increase charges only when a project was on stream, rather than during the period of excess demand before that occurred, was inappropriate and could not be relied upon to happen. It referred to the 'Hong Kong experience', where airlines prevented increases in charges when the new airport opened. Without AICC, a project the size of T5 would be hopeless.

14.69. However, it recognized that the five-year control period presented the problem that some capex could be deferred without penalty. The CAA's proposal addressed this by the incorporation of price triggers linked to the delivery of specified capacity (namely ART and the T5 advanced stands). BAA supported the use of this device, and believed that it could be extended to other parts of the Heathrow programme in place of the PPC.

14.70. In response to our request for suggestions on airport charge increases linked to output and/or progress of a project by means of triggers, BAA suggested that only one project, T5, met the required criteria for such an approach of being financially significant; having an established scope of the project with confidence over timing; having the support of the airline community as a whole and providing aeronautical outputs; and for the airport concerned to be one where charging was based around the maximum cap and not determined by marketplace factors. Significant scope changes were also unlikely on T5 since they would be likely to be in breach of planning conditions. It proposed specific triggers of completion of the diversion of the twin rivers in 2004/05; completion of early release stands in the same year; the handing over of the visual control room to NATS in 2005/06; and the core terminal building being weather proof in 2006/07. These triggers variously represented important milestones in T5's completion; produced significant immediate outputs to airlines; provided a business partner facility without which T5 could not function and were all easily measurable and auditable. BAA had no objection in principle to a trigger for the opening of T5, probably at the beginning of Q5. The more detailed specification of facilities to be available on opening of T5—as put forward by BA—was, however, likely to change over the next five years. Some arbitration committee may therefore need to be involved but this was more an issue for the next quinquennial review: progress in constructing T5 was likely to be one of the focal points of the next review, and could directly effect the prices to be allowed in the first year of Q5. Triggers at Gatwick were less appropriate given the need for flexibility and the uncertainty of traffic patterns between Heathrow and Gatwick.

14.71. BAA proposed that where an event was expected to take place in a particular year but did not do so, one point be taken off the value of X in the subsequent year; the value of X would then be recovered to its base level if the projects were completed the next year. (BAA's subsequent views on this are included in Chapter 2.)

14.72. If the trigger was too large, on the other hand, highly adverse incentive effects could be created. It was more likely that there would be short delays with limited impact on the overall scale of a project rather than the total programme being delayed by a year: a large trigger could reduce BAA's ability to finance such a project.

14.73. The concept of triggers also mitigated the problem of how to deal with overspend or underspend at subsequent reviews, since it would give a significant incentive to deliver.

14.74. The CAA had also proposed an additional allowance of £300 per additional peak hour movement. BAA did not object to this, but did not regard it as particularly relevant given it already had every incentive to increase peak hour capacity if it could. An alternative approach put to BAA—of a penalty if total movements fell below a target figure—was legally more difficult given the limit on number of ATMs at Heathrow.

S factor

14.75. BAA argued that security costs following the events of 11 September were highly uncertain and that if there was to be any abandonment of the cost pass through mechanism, it would be necessary to include a possible allowance for the costs of any additional security requirements, which would itself be subject to considerable uncertainty. Safety and security were BAA's first priorities and should be the first priorities of everyone in a position of responsibility in the industry. The CAA had rightly focused on the incentive properties of regulation, but it had consistently disregarded the incentive effects of putting airports in a situation where they received no compensation for any additional costs of meeting enhanced levels of security imposed by the DfT.

14.76. The S factor had worked well over the past 15 years. It had not produced any cost inefficiencies. In practice it had not led to major cost rises to airlines, but it had provided airports with the reassurance that most of any additional costs would ultimately be met. The percentage of recovery may be debatable, but the principle of recovery should be retained.

14.77. The limitation of the CAA's thinking on this issue was demonstrated by the financial analysis in the reference:

(a) The CAA argued that the removal of the S factor would not alter the cost of capital because the risk was diversifiable, but made no attempt to demonstrate how it could be diversified. Neither did the CAA recognize the effect of risk, diversifiable or not, on the cost of capital.

(b) The CAA proposed to eliminate the S factor without making any attempt to allow for the likely future level of increased security costs on the cost base. This was casually justified on the basis that sufficient headroom was built into the CAA's proposals for the Q4 settlement. However, the proposal actually contained no headroom above a 7 per cent single-till return at Heathrow. By definition no one could know what costs would be incurred; the zero cost assumption was therefore 100 per cent asymmetric downside risk.

The CAA suggested (see paragraph 13.24) in its proposals to the CC that 'some form of alternative arrangement' may be needed to deal with major costs arising from 11 September but did not suggest what this arrangement may be, although it would need to be incorporated in the price formula determination. A mechanism allowing for the recovery of a percentage of the additional costs was presumably what was intended; in effect, some form of S factor.

14.78. BAA gave further details on the additional requirements that could be imposed. Since 11 September 2001, a greater number of passengers and their hand baggage had been subject to a search by hand at central search areas; were BAA to adopt best practice as recommended by the DfT and subject passengers selected for hand search to routine screening for explosives, there would be a need to purchase a substantial number of additional trace detection equipment (estimated at 60 machines at £19,000 each). Additional operating costs and staff numbers resulting from such enhanced measures required by direction had not been budgeted for within current business plans, nor the investment cost for buying additional trace detection equipment should this be required by future direction. Temporary solutions were currently being implemented for segregation of arriving and departing passengers during 2002: achieving full segregation would take five to six years at significant capital cost. Development work was also being undertaken on measures relating to identification of suspect passengers; subject to successful airport trials, it was likely that new processes would lead to the installation of new communication networks, redesign of check-in desks, and purchase and installation of new equipment, potentially involving passport scanning equipment, biometric solutions and CCTV: the outcome of the trials was unlikely to be known until 2003, and no provision for this development work had been made in current business plans. On screening of passengers and their possessions, BAA had been relatively early in introducing HBS, so could be required to introduce latest technology (including, for example, an explosive-sniffing machine). Should any of the various technologies lead to increased detection capability airports would be required to implement them. The outcome of development work and evaluation was not likely for two to three years, and no provision for the development work or the procurement of new equipment had been made in current business plans. Hence it was currently exceptionally difficult to forecast at this time exactly what processes and technologies would be required during the next two years and given the uncertainty in government requirements it was essential that some mechanism remained available to airports to pass on what could be significant capital and revenue costs.

Q factor

14.79. BAA believed that detailed service monitoring linked to the price formula was not necessary for BAA and may be counter productive. However, it acknowledged service quality was a legitimate area of concern for regulation, and had actively led the debate on the introduction of a Q factor that might achieve benefits while minimizing disadvantages. However, proper calibration of the model was very important if it was not to create its own distortions. It was also necessary to target those aspects of service important to the passenger, those for which BAA was wholly or mainly responsible, and those which were measurable without requiring a large bureaucracy to do so.

14.80. In this context it believed that the CAA's current thinking as set out in its proposals to us needed further refinement. It had the following areas of concern:

(a) The 3 per cent ceiling proposed by the CAA, although an apparently small number, amounted to exposure of £15 million a year at current price levels. This was a very material sum for an approach which was intended to be an initial experimental testing of the concept. Figures of 1 to 2 per cent were used in utilities.

(b) The major component of the Q factor, airline service, was structured on a penalty-only basis. That is, the airport could not be rewarded for service above the standard, it could only be punished for failure. Apart from the inequity of this approach, this created an asymmetric risk to the business, and had poor motivational characteristics for airport management: equalization of risk was important. Even a symmetrical approach, however, could have asymmetric effect, since marginal improvements in serviceability were increasingly difficult and costly as performance level got closer to 100 per cent.

(c) The proposed Q factor contained an aircraft delay term, although delay was effectively outside BAA's control, being largely in the hands of other parties. This approach created moral hazards for airlines. There was also, at present, no reliable data on which to base such a coefficient or on attributing causes of delay and BAA would be concerned if the calibration of the factors were to be left unknown when the formula was set. It would be inappropriate to base any delay term on information gleaned from the subjective and simplified attribution of delays by airline or handling agent staff. However, BAA did not object to a delay term in principle as long as the measure reasonably reflected BAA and NATS airport navigation service performance, accurate data could be collected, and there was sufficient understanding and experience of the measure to allow appropriate targets to be set: it believed that the CAA's proposals failed to pass these tests, but if a measurement system could be developed that would do so, then it would be willing for a delay term to be incorporated by mutual consent into a Q factor midway through the next quinquennium.

(d) BAA also objected to the inclusion of FEGP since this was not paid for through the airport charges covered by the RPI–X formula. It recognized, however, that FEGP was a high operational requirement and there were only limited alternatives should it be unavailable. BAA therefore conceded that it might be appropriate to include FEGP in a Q factor scheme.

(e) BAA also argued against inclusion of pier service where it did not carry out the day-to-day stand allocation: the scale of infrastructure was the primary driver of pier service levels, but the way the stands were allocated led to significant variations around these levels (plus or minus some 5 per cent). There were also practical difficulties in predicting appropriate target values given that level of performance depended critically on the nature of demand and provision of pier service stands.

(f) It also argued that departures baggage system performance should be excluded since increasingly bespoke financially incentivized agreements would be developed for individual baggage systems.

14.81. There were, however, alternatives to the Q term, namely additional transparency of service quality performance, without any airport charges; or a minimum service quality protection system, where penalties would be incurred only if performance fell below prescribed minimum levels.

14.82. BAA suggested equal weighting of the 12 elements it proposed: namely availability of runways, taxiways, stands, jetties, people movers (passenger lifts, goods lifts, escalators, passenger conveyors and in Gatwick's case TTS) and baggage reclaim facilities; queuing time for departures security process, and passengers perceptions of departures lounge seating availability, way-finding, flight information and cleanliness. It suggested a maximum impact of 1.5 per cent of regulated airport charges, which would be reached for very poor performance across the entire range of performance indicators. It also proposed revised measurement definitions, including a reduction in scope of the down time that would not count against the serviceability targets (for example, the scope would be limited to such items as equipment taken out of service for major refurbishment work) and revised target levels to accompany these new definitions. It firmly believed that any form of service quality regulation should reflect issues of importance to passengers which would often only be measurable through opinion surveys. Although it did not accept criticism of its QSM surveys, it had no objection to a further external audit of the QSM. Par values should be based on existing target levels where they existed, but may need to change to take account of changing traffic levels or circumstances over five years. Initially, runway and taxiway availability would be measured, to inform decisions on appropriate targets by late 2003, which may have to be by 'mutual consent'.

14.83.   The Q factor could, however, affect non-diversifiable risk, hence BETA, and BAA's cost of capital.

Default price cap, treatment of discounts and non-passenger flight and volume term

14.84.   BAA was not strongly for or against the CAA's default price cap proposal. However, BAA submitted that arrangements to provide exclusive use of facilities would probably be discriminatory at congested airports.

14.85.   BAA agreed treatment of discounts be changed as proposed by the CAA. As to whether discounts should be transparent, BAA preferred to apply these on a one-to-one, non-transparent basis, but with any operator on the same route having broadly the same discount (this did not necessarily imply exactly the same charge, but a contractual arrangement which had a comparable effect; this had been the position at Stansted). Since the discounts were geared to individual airline strategies on individual routes, it would be an unreasonable burden on airlines to disclose what their strategy was by revealing the nature of the negotiation with them. Since BAA was obliged to operate under a general principle of non-discrimination, however, it submitted that a halfway house would be to file the terms of discounts with the CAA.

14.86.   As to the CAA suggestion that non-passenger flights should be excluded from the charging formula, BAA questioned whether it was desirable to signal an implied regulatory incentive to non-passenger flights at Heathrow and Gatwick or indeed Stansted which was likely to be congested in the short to medium term. Nonetheless, it felt the respecification of the pricing formula would have no practical incentive effect: it would only allow theoretically slightly higher charges for passenger aircraft if each airport was close to the maximum allowable yield. Competition with other airports with cargo facilities would deter charging increases at airports where there was capacity, and non discrimination provisions would ensure that charges for cargo aircraft at airports with limited capacity could not be increased to deter cargo aircraft. The effect on yield was less than 1 per cent at Heathrow and Gatwick, but 7 per cent at Stansted.

14.87.   BAA agreed that since Stansted was not likely to charge up to its price cap, it should not be subject to a Q factor or default price cap.

14.88.   BAA continued to maintain that a volume term was not appropriate; it would require higher charges when airlines were in difficulty, but also only worked with a time lag.

Specific issues relevant to setting of X

Passenger forecasts

14.89.   BAA objected to the CAA's suggestion that BAA had taken a too cautious view of economic growth and of recovery from 11 September. Comparing the BAA and CAA forecasts, the differences were minimal as a whole, but some 3 per cent in the first year. BAA also objected to the CAA's suggestion that its assumed growth in average passenger per aircraft at Heathrow was conservative (0.4 per cent a year), believing the CAA ignored the fact that average loads at Heathrow had been in constant decline since February 2001 because of BA's decision to reduce average seating capacities and improve average yields. (For example, average seats on BA 747 aircrafts had dropped from 398 to 368 and on European services from 186 to 157.) BAA believed that its assumed Heathrow load looked optimistic.

14.90. Differences between the forecasts were greater at Gatwick, where BAA believed that the CAA short-term forecast looked untenable. Aggregate seat capacity this summer had fallen by 7 per cent: the CAA forecast would require growth of 3 per cent (for the remainder of this year), an implausibly high leap in load factor. If this year continued to decline by 10 per cent on two years ago, the CAA's forecast required a 20 per cent increase in 2003/04, way beyond any reasonable expectation of growth and unsupportable by the airports runway capacity without a massive unforeseeable growth in aircraft size. BA's process of gradually unwinding its Gatwick services had not yet been completed, although it was doing so in manner which was not making available slots for others to use in a pro rata fashion. It had given up 35 per cent of its seats, carried 35 per cent fewer passengers but only surrendered 25 per cent of its slots, most at already off-peak times.

14.91. BAA also criticized the CAA's assumption that traffic growth at Stansted would decelerate as the lost cost market matured and new route opportunities diminished. Such growth had declined from an excess of 30 per cent to close to single figures in the space of three years. BAA believed there were parallels with the charter growth in the early 1960s and 1970s.

14.92. BAA's main arguments in support of its latest forecast were therefore evidence of worldwide sluggish and in some cases non-existent recovery from 11 September in terms of air travel demands; the faltering nature of economic recovery; and airline strategies of cutting capacity never seen before. It also believed our initial assumption (put to BA when we were at the initial modelling stage)—of adopting BAA's forecasts at Heathrow and Gatwick but the higher CAA forecasts for Stansted—were high and with no buffer for likely downturns during the period, which BAA believed there should be. The assumed high traffic growth at Stansted could well be at risk if discounts were phased out and/or charges rapidly increased to the levels of Gatwick as we had also assumed. There was also an inconsistency between these traffic forecasts and the capex plan for further terminal development at Stansted, which, with higher traffic, would have to be brought forward from Q6 to Q5.

Cost of capital

14.93. BAA said that the level of charges overall needed to be set to provide BAA with a more than 50 per cent prospect of achieving returns in excess of the cost of capital. As the CAA had recognized, the welfare loss from setting charges too low may be greater than the loss from setting them too high, and a degree of headroom was therefore appropriate.

14.94. The cost of capital needed to capture all the risks described above was certainly higher than the 7 per cent proposed by the CAA for Heathrow's existing assets. It may also be expected to increase as it undertook the very substantial and risky investment in T5 to above the 8.5 per cent proposed for new projects such as T5. The cost of capital of 6.6 per cent put forward by BA was not a reasonable basis for BAA to pursue its investment programme.

14.95. In response to the CAA consultation document BAA had said that 'the cost of capital for the aeronautical till should be set at at least 8 per cent for the airports taken together. The use of the 8 per cent dual till should provide sufficient headroom to allow BAA to proceed with investment with confidence'. However, the figure would be higher if other aspects of the CAA proposals were adopted, for example: individual airport regulation; PPC; 3 per cent Q factor; and no S-term.

14.96. BAA subsequently submitted to us a paper by Oxera suggesting a pre-tax cost of capital of 7.4 to 11.3 per cent (a mid-point of 9.3 per cent) without T5—see Table 14.1 (see also Chapter 4).

TABLE 14.1 **Proposed WACCs for BAA**

per cent

	BAA	
	Low	*High*
Real risk-free rate	2.75	3.25
Equity risk premium	4.0	6.0
Equity beta (number)	0.86	0.96
Asset beta (number)	0.66	0.77
Cost of equity (post tax)	6.19	9.01
Taxation adjustment	30.0	30.0
Cost of equity (pre-tax)*	8.84	12.91
Gearing	30.0	20.0
Debt premium	1.2	1.4
Cost of debt	3.95	4.65
Pre-tax WACC:		
Calculated figure	7.38	11.23
Mid-point	9.31	

Source: BAA.

14.97.   However, BAA also believed that there would be a major increase in riskiness with the T5 project, given the scale of the fixed costs and the irreversible nature of investment with no second-hand value, the massive scope for cost overrun as shown by other major construction projects, and the dependence on increase in passengers and passengers per ATM. There was also a regulatory risk associated with a project dependent on 50 years of cash flow, and whether users would in future be prepared to pay for it. The events of 11 September 2001 had also changed the perception of riskiness of the industry.

14.98.   Oxera estimated a cost of capital of 7.70 to 11.6 per cent (a mid-point of 9.66 per cent) for BAA including T5 on an RAB basis. It would be higher (a mid-point of 11.21 per cent) on the LRIC basis proposed by the CAA (applying the estimated LRIC of £18 per passenger to passengers above 60 mppa) given the deferment of revenue and the additional variability of income to passenger growth and higher risk that would be implied. This estimated higher cost of capital of BAA with T5 primarily reflected the additional operational and financial gearing that BAA would face as a result of the construction of T5. However, on top of this must be added the extra risk imposed by the regulatory structure that the CAA had proposed. These proposals could add around 25 per cent to the asset beta of BAA, due to the inherently higher volatility of returns under a system for which the marginal impact of an additional passenger could be more than twice the average revenues per passenger. The estimated cost of capital also omitted such factors as the possibility of regulatory renegement, and the small possibility that BAA might have to turn to the equity markets for finance in the event of very adverse circumstances, hence might be expected to lie towards the low side of the true cost of capital that BAA faces.

14.99.   BAA commented on our own provisional views of cost of capital (which were of a range of 5.15 to 9.43 per cent, a mid-point of 7.31 per cent), being particularly concerned at low level of the mid-point estimate. It believed that if the estimate was too low, it would prejudice the investment programme—but if too high the consequence would merely be a small increase in cost borne by the airlines (and which would not necessarily be passed through to passengers), hence the greater public interest in this case lay in a high probability of a cost of capital adequately able to remunerate investment.

14.100.   On components of the cost of capital, the risk-free rate we proposed was below previous estimates due to recent trends: BAA, however, believed the effects of MFR were still being worked through, putting upward pressure on yields, as would the move of government finances from surplus to deficit; if anything, the tendency was above the 3 per cent previously used by the MMC. There was also an implication from our proposal that whatever cost of capital was given now would not be achieved, because the recent downward process would continue. Rather than revising the rate as new information came along, it would be better for the CC to try to stabilize the rate, and form a judgment of a reasonable long-term view. Over the long term, the rate in the UK had been over 3 per cent: as it still was in many other countries.

14.101. As to the equity risk premium, BAA argued that there was an immense degree of uncertainty, studies giving a range of estimates of 3 to 8 per cent. BAA was concerned about putting more weight on a recent study, which suggested a lower range of 2.5 to 4.7 per cent. Another recent study, for example, suggested 3.9 to 6 per cent; and while there was little evidence of an ERP below 2.5 per cent, there was quite a lot of evidence of it being above 5 per cent. (An assumption of a long-term rate of return on equities made by BAA's pension fund of 5 per cent, implying a risk premium of about 2.5 per cent, reflected the need to be fairly conservative in that specific context.) Given current volatility of stock return, there was a prospect of increases in the ERP.

14.102. On the beta, this had been about 0.8 since 1997: but this would increase due to the scale of expenditure in T5, in effect a fixed cost, an expenditure that had to be undertaken irrespective of performance (like debt, as if BAA had geared itself up). The full impact of T5 had yet to come through, but an increase was also consistent with the recent greater volatility of BAA's share price. There were elements of the Q factor that would reduce beta, others that would not affect it, and others that would increase beta: for example, BAA would be exposed under the Q term to 'cost shocks' in the economy as a whole, since the Q term would require it to make expenditures to maintain quality even if cost pressures increased. It was far from clear which way the balance would go.

14.103. As to the debt premium, there had been a lot of fluctuation, and undue weight should not be put on most recent evidence (spot rates having recently been between 0.65 and 1.06 per cent): the three-year average had been about 1.35 per cent and one-year average 1.15 per cent.

14.104. Closely related to the question of cost of capital was the issue of financing, which BAA said that the CAA had not addressed. BAA's medium- to long-term regulatory forecasts of June 2002, based on RPI+2 in Q4 (as indicated in our last report as a possible price control for Q4) and RPI thereafter, projected return on capital value in Q4 declining from 6.9 to 5.1 per cent (below the 6.7 per cent (after smoothing) put forward in the last report). It also projected interest cover of [✂] by the end of Q4, but below [✂] by 2008/09 and for the rest of Q4, compared to covenant requirements of [✂]; and gearing (debt: equity) of [✂] per cent by 2007/08 rising to over [✂] per cent by the end of Q5. The decline in interest cover was regarded as more serious by putting its covenants and investment grade credit rating at risk. Such projections took no account of a possible share issue: BAA believed that such an option should be held in reserve for expenditure on any new runway, or should there be any further major disruption to the civil aviation industry.

14.105. On BAA's current estimate the development programme, as a whole, was financeable from internal resources and debt by the airports taken together, at the level of prices proposed. However:

(a) The programme would be more difficult to finance from the equity base of each airport, taken separately, on a stand-alone basis. This was because the programme was inherently more lumpy at the individual airport level. It was difficult to imagine how Stansted—a £400 million investment followed by ten years of cash outflows—could have been funded under this approach. If the airport had not been developed, travellers would not have enjoyed the lower fares and greater choice the airport has brought.

(b) The programme would be progressively more difficult to finance if the price control formula were to be tightened, and any more aggressive proposals would need to be tested against gearing and interest cover effects. It was particularly important to maintain interest cover of over [✂] given default clauses if breached.

Regulatory asset base

14.106. BAA argued that the CAA had adopted a method of valuation of the RAB inconsistent with the previous report and the CAA comments when setting the current charges. BAA believed that the RAB should be based on accounting concepts, including actual depreciation using actual asset lives, and be estimated in a consistent way at each review, and on the same basis as used in the regulatory accounts. BAA was also concerned about what it regarded as the CC's failure in figures we put to them to take into account a significant shift in the amount of net current assets and liabilities, although BAA had produced its regulatory accounts including net current assets/liabilities since the last review. That would also be consistent with a financial capital maintenance approach. Not to include working capital would be an exproportion of financial capital. This is discussed further in Chapter 10.

Investment programme

14.107. BAA said that its projects were keenly costed, with little scope for cost saving. Commenting on points made by our consultants, BAA agreed with the need to have an independent review of T5 costs. BAA believed that its approach of partnering was preferable to one of fixed-price contracts, which had often not worked well in the UK: airport specifications were unlike other projects, and firms which had done the same job before were able to do so again at lower costs by introducing innovative methodologies. The rest of the construction industry was moving in that direction. As to benchmarking, BAA recognized it was far from an exact science, but did not consider benchmarking exercises were invalidated, as long as the limitations were understood and adjusted for wherever possible. Its current study represented the best effort at benchmarking T5 that the comparator data would allow. BAA also noted that the CAA's consultants had regarded its capex control and cost effectiveness as excellent.

14.108. On the contingency element of T5, BAA had started with £400 million contingency, which it regarded as not unreasonable for a project of this size, and the need for which had been validated by consultants. Some £150 million of this amount was left: just about enough to bring the project in on plan. Some of the £250 million could be accounted for by the cost of increased planning conditions BAA had not expected. The vast majority of T5 costs were not the terminal building which only accounted for £600 million to £700 million (£500 million excluding the baggage systems), but included buying the land from Thames Water and the cost of alternative waste treatment, and road and rail access.

14.109. BAA's comments on complaints about the capital programme, in particular about arrangements for consultation, are given in the section on public interest below. BAA said that it would have liked to have agreement with airlines on the investment programme—but had received few comments on whether the quantum, timing and distribution between airports was reasonable.

Operating costs

14.110. BAA also commented on a number of points raised by the CC on opex (see also Chapter 7). First, it believed there was little scope for real wages to increase less than assumed. It had already achieved everything achievable on pay in Q3, including lower pay rates for starters, and was now having genuine problems in recruiting the right quality of people for security, and there were increasing pay pressures in other areas. The job content in a number of activities was changing dramatically, much of which was dictated by Government. To meet these requirements it needed a good employee relation environment, a high-quality workforce, greater investment in training (including government statutory training) and low staff turnover. It believed its current pay levels were at the right level.

14.111. On productivity, BAA believed that it had taken all of the easy productivity gains over the last ten years or so: it believed it could not obtain further improvements without putting customer service at risk, particularly given government requirements. Productivity trends partly reflected lower traffic growth; but inter-company transfers also complicated comparisons of past and projected productivity improvements. Nonetheless, significant productivity improvements were built into BAA's forecasts, against a background of increasing requirements, particularly on security, and to cope with increased congestion before the opening of T5.

14.112. BAA believed absence levels were similar to comparable employees elsewhere, but had got slightly worse due to the increased stress on, for example, security staff: there was scope to make minor improvements. The degree of overtime was a direct corollary of efficiency in coping with peaking of passenger flows, but broadly in line with industry norms. BAA was, however, investing in a roster management system, which should result in some reduction in overtime, but which was already built into its projections. Central contingencies resulted from managers being set targets in the knowledge there was more chance of not meeting them than meeting them: the contingency balanced that to a more realistic target.

14.113. On pensions, there had been a five-year pension holiday with a zero contribution for Q3 (a 14 per cent funding rate had been assumed for that period), largely resulting from the performance of the stock market generally over that period. However, there was also at the last valuation a surplus associated with BAA's outperforming the market and similar schemes. In the financial projections there was allowance for a 7 per cent contribution, assessed taking the surplus into account, but there was a further 15 per cent centrally to take it up to a figure of 22 per cent which was assessed assuming the surplus did not exist. (The accounts also previously contained a 3 per cent allowance for a separate fund for firemen.) The size of the surplus was, however, likely to have reduced due to falls in stock market prices and the 7 per cent figure would need to be increased. BAA did not, however, believe that the surplus should be expropriated to give to airlines. This was a one-off gain, due to outperformance over a defined period of time (unlike permanent staff savings which BAA would expect to be reflected subsequently in charges). To reduce airport charges as a result of the surplus would effectively confiscate the gains that resulted from the schemes' managers outperforming the market. Such an approach would mean that BAA could not take any risk in its schemes but merely cover the liabilities, since it would not get the benefit of any return on that risk. This would mean closing the existing scheme and switching to a defined contribution basis. Alternatively, if excess returns were to be taken away in such a way, the CC must be equally prepared to compensate for underperformance.

Proposed value of X

14.114. BAA supported continuing with a ten-year analysis since it was strongly against significant oscillations in inter-quinquennial charges levels. It believed a strong price signal was needed in particular for T5 so current users started to pay earlier in Q4 for the costs of a terminal expansion which the airline community had been requesting. As apparent above, BAA disagreed with any allowance for capex underspend; any revenue claw back should be deducted from the RAB to avoid a huge price increase in Q5.

14.115. Overall charges should therefore be set by reference to the long-term financial needs of the London airports overall, translated into individual airport formulae which reflected the relative levels of demand and capacity at each airport and such that:

(a) BAA's airports had a reasonable expectation of achieving their overall cost of capital over the ten-year period, with recognition that this would rise as it became more committed to T5;

(b) the cost of capital could be achieved without reliance on steep increases in charges in T5. Smoothing of returns between Q4 and Q5 and allowance for AICC was essential if BAA was to be able to raise capital for T5, since the likelihood of getting a very substantial price increase in six years' time was so debatable and uncertain the risk would be very high;

(c) BAA could finance its £8.1 billion investment programme without any presumption of new equity and taking into account the need to allow for downturns from forecast in the event of repetition of 11-September-type incidents;

(d) BAA could maintain an investment grade rating; and

(e) BAA would have a reasonable platform to start work on a new runway, at whatever location the Government chose and take into account the initial capex on runway work required in Q4. This may require the raising of new equity.

14.116. The CAA had said that it would not accept proposals in excess of RPI+6 at Heathrow and RPI+5 at Gatwick and Stansted: hence BAA needed a formula at least equivalent to the CAA's proposals overall, constructed to reflect the relative pressures on each airport. Hence BAA proposed formulae of RPI+7 at Heathrow, RPI+3 at Gatwick and RPI+1 at Stansted: its priority, however, was the overall revenue requirement, rather than the balance between the airports. (The Stansted and Gatwick proposals did not increase the differential between the airports since in practice Stansted charges would rise as introductory rebates expired, whilst it may well be that the full RPI+3 was not taken at Gatwick.)

14.117. The formula should include trigger components, on the line suggested by the CAA, in which an extra £10 million a year in revenue was allowed on completion of the ART and ERS. The proposals assumed substantial increases in charges in Q5 would be required, but BAA would commit to set out on the capital programme on this basis. It could not, however, give an absolute assurance that the programme could be completed at this level of charges, especially if any of the forecasts turned out to be optimistic. It also proposed the formula would be subject to a Q factor accounting for not more than 2 per cent of revenues, symmetrically balanced, with half the total accounted for by airline-related elements and half by passenger-related elements, and an S factor with 95 per cent recovery.

14.118. BAA also proposed that we ratify the CAA's proposals for enhanced consultation, including spelling out clearly the responsibilities on airlines for effective participation in consultation; BAA would also be consulting airlines on proposals to implement a structured formal dispute procedure so that ongoing operational and capital issues were fully addressed between reviews. (These points are spelt out below.)

14.119. BAA also said that the CC needed to set out the criteria which would be used at future reviews for the treatment for overspend and underspend of capital. It should distinguish efficiency gains/losses, which should be kept or borne by the airport in their entirety; savings from a deliberate avoidance of spending obligations, which could be clawed back in full; and exogenous or windfall changes such as the delay to T5 which may be shared, but not less than 50 per cent being borne or kept by the airport. (Subsequently, however, it suggested that adoption of the trigger mechanism spelt out in paragraph 14.70 et seq would reduce the need for such an approach.)

14.120. BAA also commented on provisional proposals of the value of X we put to them based on a 7.25 per cent rate return. It said that, being on an IRR basis, this was effectively 7 per cent on a conventional basis, compared with the 7.75 per cent it had had, and which it believed was the absolute minimum in order to embark on such a large investment programme, when the aviation industry was in such turmoil. (It had previously regarded below 8 per cent as unacceptable.) If it did not get the IRR on which its own proposals were based, with no allowance for such a contingency, it would have three years of interest cover under [✂], and one year of [✂]. Moreover, in an industry investing for returns over 50 years' uncertainty about what the regulator was going to do at each review given such a change of policy and the prospect of [✂] interest cover did not provide a basis for such an investment programme. Risk on the other hand had increased since the previous review. Adoption of a lower return would also increase regulatory risk, BAA having been encouraged to invest over £2 billion in the current quinquennium on the understanding it would get a 7.5 per cent return on capital value: if it was now to get less than that, there was a significant problem in terms of further risk. No normal company, moreover, would financially plan on the basis of a mid-point estimate of interest cover of [✂], particularly if it was getting signals from its regulators about the unreliability of its long-term returns. Some of its covenants would be breached at [✂], so it would be in default, and there would immediately be a significant credit problem if it were to plan on the basis of a lower figure. It would therefore have to reconsider aspects of its investment programme—for example, to introduce T5 in many more phases.

14.121. BAA also believed that its own proposals were necessary to provide an appropriate profiling of price increases, before T5 opened. There may be scope to bring forward price increases from the end to the beginning of Q5, should there be problems of interest cover and an indication from the CC that price increases would be necessary in Q5 was important. But it could not rely on investing money now on the prospect of more significant price increases in Q5 than in Q4. One-off price increases were also extremely difficult to achieve since the airlines might not be in a position to pay them at the time. It could not therefore be in a position of needing, for example, a 25 per cent price increase on opening of T5; hence any deferring of increases from Q4 to Q5 would be unacceptable.

14.122. BAA also noted that the need to advance income from Q5 to Q4 was because we proposed that the advancement of revenue to Q3 be recovered in Q4 rather than later: as noted above, the CAA had not said there would be an automatic return of the advancement in Q4, but left open the possibility that there might need to be some consideration of the rate at which it was dealt with. Events had, moreover, changed, particularly BAA's substantially raising its levels of investment.

14.123. BAA also noted that its model did not allow for the effect of higher gearing on interest rates, which could affect the financial ratios; that there was no allowance for expenditure on a new runway in our preliminary projections, nor for any asymmetric Q factor and the payments that would result; nor for payment under the possible 'triggers' being considered to relate charges to progress on capex, which also involved downside asymmetric risk.

14.124. We suggested that, even if the maximum level of charges at Stansted were set to earn the cost of capital, for modelling purposes Stansted charges should be assumed to be no higher than Gatwick. BAA said that published prices at Stansted above those at Gatwick would make no commercial sense. A lot of the low-cost airlines flying out of Stansted had an approach quite different from any other in aviation, and were quite capable of deciding against adding service, or moving to another airport. A one-off increase in prices at the beginning of Q4 was also not possible given the two- and three-year deals based on volumes. Some discount on Gatwick prices would therefore be logical, with an assumption that charges moved towards those of Gatwick given BAA's intention to reduce current discounts.

Public interest issues

14.125. In commenting generally on public interest issues, BAA said that many complaints were unsubstantiated or subject to ongoing negotiations or to negotiations that had been successfully concluded. Some were seriously inaccurate; several had never previously been brought to the attention of BAA, and in some circumstances actually contradicted previous feedback from other parts of the same airline; many attempted to contrast quality of aeronautical and retail areas etc, possibly an attempt to undermine the dual-till approach, which presumably could be put to one side if the single till were retained; several referred to projects being stopped/altered without recognizing the fact that the primary driver for this was often a change in airline strategy which BAA was seeking to respond to; many allegations were 'naked self interest'; and others were merely 'fishing expeditions'.

Investment

Interim review

14.126. We referred above to under-investment in T5. Some airlines believed that BAA's failure to request an interim review, or further adjust charges because of under-investment, was against the public interest. BAA argued that none of the triggers mentioned in CAP 664 (see Chapter 5) had been activated; it itself gave no assurance that a review would be triggered merely by delay in receipt of planning consent. It argued that timing fluctuations were and are a part of the risk of running the business; if the decision had been earlier rather than later it would have honoured its commitment. In maintaining this view it was reassured by the fact that its returns on capital value were almost exactly as the MMC had intended. Hence it regarded the view it had taken as true to the concept of RPI–X regulation, which envisaged that once fixed, the maximum price should not be variable at each turn of events but be reviewed at the end of the control period, taking account of the evolution of all aspects of business environment in the meantime.

14.127. When a mid-term review was sought by BA in late 1999, it was already too late to incorporate it in the regulatory cycle. Airlines had previously requested mitigation of charges as part of the annual charges negotiations but not a mid-term review. A review could not have started before January 2000; its scope would have been controversial and possibly wide ranging (for example, BA also wished it to deal with traffic forecasts, but it would also have had to consider substitution projects); and in all probability the process would not have been finalized before charges were in place for 2001. Moreover, at the time BA made its request, the CAA had just extended the existing formula for one year, to 2002/03; to have opened a mid-term review at the same time would have been perverse. The scale of the airline demands was indeed disproportionate to the delay to T5 expected at the time; the length of the delay, however, was also uncertain at that time.

Specific complaints

- *Runway developments*

14.128. We note in Chapter 12 criticisms by BA and others of BAA's asking the T5 Inspector to rule out a third runway at Heathrow. BAA argued that much of the massive local opposition to T5 was based on the fear of the third runway; it had become apparent the Inspector understood this fear and found it difficult to find a way to recommend the approval of any development without trying to close the door to such a runway. It also argued that BA had not linked T5 with a third runway either privately or in public. BAA argued that it could not have consulted airlines publicly on the statement since that would have invited massive criticism. Indeed it had to be able to say to the Inspector the disposition had not been driven by airline views. However, BAA was in no doubt that BA did not wish it to make the statement but it felt it was the price which had to be paid to secure the T5 consent.

14.129. Airlines also complained about BAA's failure, as they saw it, to push for mixed mode to increase the capacity of existing runways at Heathrow. BAA told us that mixed mode would require approval by the Secretary of State and planning approval for associated developments. The ATM limit to be introduced on opening of T5 would also much reduce the benefits of mixed mode, although this was an option being considered in the SERAS process. BAA argued that at Heathrow its objective had been to get T5 agreed and it had not wanted to do anything to undermine this.

14.130. As to criticisms of lack of runway development at Gatwick, BAA said that there had been improvements in Gatwick single runway capacity and the level of delays had declined, and any suggestion of another runway at Gatwick was subject to the role of Government in approving construction of any new runway: the Government had rejected all of the options of RUCATSE including one at Gatwick. It was not practical for BAA to bring forward proposals for another runway other than in the context of government policy, and given the government approach the question was one of runway capacity for south-east London as a whole, not for Gatwick in particular.

- *Iceberg*

14.131. We refer in Chapter 12 to criticism of delays to and other aspects of the 'Iceberg' project to provide additional long-haul capacity in T1. BAA said that the original target completion date of April 2001 alleged by BA was not one which any normal supplier would have committed to contractually because BA had not specified the project at that stage and BAA always had reservations about its achievability. (It had been accepted as a target only before the project scale had been defined.) The project was substantially delayed by the failure of the BA board to approve its financial contribution for some months, the ongoing operation requirements and by the very reasonable requirements of other T1 users to understand the impacts of changes on their operations and costs. BA's own Board of Directors did not approve the project until October 2000 because of its complexity. The project was also complicated by renewed pressure for Open Skies. As to BA's complaint of poor project management (see Chapter 12), the project was massively complex. Indeed BA staff had been appointed to the BAA project management board, and to that degree shared accountability for the project. BA had also not noted that the major victim of the post-11 September review had been that part of the project that provided enhanced retail space.

14.132. The project board had members from the principal T1 airlines, and consequently the airlines had full access to the development and delivery process. BAA also had the support of BA operational management in developing project timings and mechanisms which were compatible with the need to obtain satisfactory day-to-day operational capability. The need for a schedule which met the needs of both BA operational and BA project groups had been a major challenge and was one of the principal reasons why BAA had been unwilling to offer any guarantee of a delivery date in advance of such an agreement.

14.133. On other aspects of complaints about Iceberg, BAA said that it never sought to make a total 15 per cent IRR on the project, its current forecast overall IRR being a negative 2.7 per cent without the IDL extension, 2.8 per cent once the IDL extension was completed. This was associated with an increment in capacity of around 200,000 passengers a year. BAA's decision to proceed on this basis should reassure the CC that it did not use IRR's wilfully to evade its capital responsibilities. However, being less than the MMC's last cost of capital benchmark, this should alert us to the fact that projects of this kind would lead to rises in price over time.

14.134. As initially proposed, any capacity gain was modest and incidental: BA wished to take passengers from other airlines, BAA providing BA with new and altered facilities to allow it to shift long-haul routes into T1 and short-haul into T4, and to collocate routes with high connecting passenger flows, a facility not available to other airlines. It was also to provide a premium check-in area occupied exclusively by BA and capable of providing powerful branding: an exclusive facility not, for example, available to bmi (a scheme acceptable to bmi was subsequently achieved, but not pursued when bmi deferred its long-haul plans). It also provided other ancillary exclusive use facilities needed for long haul such as arrivals and CIP lounges.

14.135. BAA said that it did not and should not oppose projects of such a kind, recognizing it was a pursuit of competitive advantage which took forward the industry generally. However, it could not offer bespoke projects to all airlines at the same time for reasons of space if nothing else. Hence such projects could either be funded through inclusion in the RAB, which might be unreasonably discriminatory; or be separately appraised and a separate charge levied on the client airline, including the cost of capital.

(Failure to recover the full return from the client airline would mean other airlines would be paying for their capital.) This approach was of no lasting financial gain to BAA, since the revenue from specific charges offset general user charges. Given such competition concerns and the provisions of the Airports Act and CA98, BAA believed that it had to adopt this second approach.

14.136. However, it regarded key aspects of BA's initial scheme as ill-thought through and developed the project into a more worthwhile scheme which combined both specific elements for BA and general purpose user benefits to the airline community at large. Only as a result of such changes did any increase in capacity now result and the new facilities were likely to handle fewer passengers as BA reduced the number of seats per aircraft.

14.137. The project was therefore now divided into two parts: the bespoke elements to be separately remunerated under a bilateral agreement and the common elements to be remunerated by airport charges. The 15 per cent number related primarily to those elements of the project which were not general-user airport capacity, but bespoke provision for the improvement of BA's competition advantage, such as improving BA's check-in area. The 15 per cent was a nominal ex ante hurdle rate, likely to exceed the ex-post out-turn; and offset by much lower rates for other elements of the project such as bespoke baggage systems. A rescue contribution was directed only at CIP lounges, without that contribution these lounges were forecast not to make an adequate return. BA already had extensive CIP lounge facilities and its need for additional space arose only because of its wish to reorganize services between terminals to its own advantage; since 1987 BA had indeed provided CIP lounges as separate commercial projects which the MMC in 1991 and 1996 had not faulted. Hence, it would be unreasonable for BA to expect CIP lounges not to be fully remunerated including their cost of capital, through separate charges to BA. BAA was now content to receive the remuneration through rentals rather than through a capital sum.

14.138. After 11 September, there had been cuts to retail facilities, the baggage system (subsequently reinstated) and Europier: BAA said that it had accorded Europier high priority in the expectation of Open Skies which did not happen. It was still open to reinstating the project if airlines could establish it represented one which gave appropriate benefits (evidence on the value of pier service which it had asked for from BA would have been helpful). Consultation post-11 September had produced a clear level of emotional commitment to the scheme from BA, but little clarity on its strategy or business case.

14.139. As to the complaint that BAA had originally required BA to compensate for the loss of retail revenue in T4, this was simply a complaint that there was a single till at Heathrow: ie about the way the MMC had regulated BAA. Either all users would have borne the cost of lost commercial income; or BA through a separate arrangement. There was at the very least a case for this latter approach, but in the end it was not pursued.

14.140. BAA also argued that BA could have pursued any complaints either under the detailed dispute resolution procedure in the heads of agreement or with the CAA. BAA inferred that BA had effectively committed BAA to the investment and was now trying to evade the cost. The reality was, according to BAA, that BAA had sought to develop a cooperative, inclusive, team-based stance with BA throughout the project development, where a large number of contentious and difficult issues had been constructively addressed and resolved by the operational and project management of both parties.

- *T4 baggage*

14.141. There were also complaints about BAA's reluctance to invest in T4 baggage facilities. BAA said its problem was that BA sought a baggage systems specification which it believed would not be required by any other airline: hence after T5 opened and BA moved out of T4, any incoming airline may reasonably decline to pay for the higher specification, in which case all airlines would pay for it under the single till. BA had never denied it approached baggage operations differently from many other carriers, and hence that its facilities were often more automated and more complex.

- *Gatwick Pier 6*

14.142. Several airlines complained about delays to the Pier 6 project at Gatwick. BAA described Gatwick Pier 6 as a project which did not add to airport capacity significantly but simply provided pier service to additional stands. It was originally conceived by BA and agreed with BAA as part of the BA strategy to develop Gatwick as a second major hub (although initially BA had pressed for construction of a major satellite costing several hundred million pounds and a row of B747 hangars); BAA was subsequently concerned that the cost of Pier 6 alone could exceed the benefits accruing to airlines and asked BA repeatedly for assistance in identifying and quantifying the benefits, but no useful information was forthcoming. BA had subsequently rested on the argument that the project must be completed regardless of its cost and benefits to meet the 90 per cent pier standard. BAA, however, pushed ahead with the work, the stage 1 reconfiguration of stands being completed shortly after 11 September.

14.143. After 11 September, however, Gatwick traffic collapsed, BA abandoned the Gatwick hub strategy and began lobbying for Open Skies at Heathrow and was also gearing up for its own 'size and shape' strategy review, telling BAA its own financial situation was desperate and asking for massive reductions and waivers for landing charges among other things. Other supporters of the project included the US airlines who had also given notice of an intention to shift service from Gatwick to Heathrow if they won open skies. Any airlines transferring into North Terminal to replace BA or other airlines may either use the existing piers more efficiently than BA for which there was considerable scope or attach a lower priority to pier service. BA was not revealing its intentions to release slots at Gatwick, while BAA was aware the airline most likely to want to pick up any unused slots was easyJet, which was currently in South Terminal and had a lower priority for jetty service than BA. Hence BAA decided to delay the project. BAA believed its judgement had been vindicated, because of BA's massive cut in its services at Gatwick and release of slots in tranches, while easyJet grew its operation in the South Terminal. Completion of Pier 6 was included in the capital programme, however, since other airlines supported it and it would be restarted as and when the prospects justified it. BAA did not, however, want to execute the project primarily for use by an airline which then left Gatwick leaving others to pay for it. Airlines needed to engage with BAA on the issues raised about the real benefits of pier service. (See also paragraph 14.183.)

● *Metro stands*

14.144. We also received complaints about delays to a project to provide pier service to the Metro stands in T4. BAA said that the decision to pause the project was taken at a time when Heathrow's traffic was down by 20 per cent, and following BA's announcement of massive staff and service cuts, and demand for emergency relief. BAA was also 'bleeding cash': hence, temporarily pausing non-essential projects was a sensible step. BAA also said that BA's response to consultation did not give BAA confidence that BA had a clear strategic priority for the project, since it was entering its major size and shape review, with uncertainty as to the restructuring of its activity in the Heathrow short-haul market, which would have made the Metro stands redundant before being opened. When BA decided to transfer-in services from Gatwick, the scheme was reinstated in a draft CIP provisionally to start in 2003, but still subject to consultation: if users attached high priority to the scheme, BAA would be sympathetic to bringing it forward. (Further comments by BAA on this scheme in the context of quality of service are in paragraph 14.182.)

● *Transfer baggage facilities*

14.145. We refer in Chapter 12 to complaints about the time taken to improve transfer baggage facilities for bmi in T1. BAA said that construction was originally scheduled for April 1998 and Phase 2 by summer 1999. The construction of Phase 1 was delayed by the time taken for decant of BA ramp handling from that building. It was therefore complete by only August 1998; however, the actual processing capacity of the facilities did not meet the original design specification, and extensive analysis and monitoring was implemented to determine why. The processing and bag profiles were found to be different from the original brief in relation to messaging and reconciliation. Discussions took place during 1999; and the final design brief for Phase 2 in the light of those shortcomings was not agreed and signed off until December 1999, when both parties were convinced it was robust.

14.146. BAA acknowledged that the redesign of the original T1 baggage works and implementation of the tunnel did create disruption for bmi, hence in 1997 BA made a concession on the rent of the bmi hangar to include a waiver of the up-coming rent review in part to offset the costs to bmi of disruption. In February 1999, it agreed to give bmi a credit of £[✂] against its invoices, as ex gratia compensation for the disruption. The payment was an agreed settlement of all bmi claims relating to Phase 1. As part of that settlement it undertook to complete Phase 2 as soon as possible with an initial target date of early 2000. In the event the final design brief took longer to complete, as well as the delay in reclaiming occupation of the site from its previous tenant: hence the project was not fully completed until May 2001. In August 2001, bmi submitted an additional claim against BAA for losses resulting from this delay (for £5.4 million); BAA did not have a legal obligation to meet the claim but it was prepared to consider a further ex gratia payment. bmi admitted that the calculations were subjective and were based on the arbitrary and unexplained assumption that the delay to the project was responsible for 62.5 per cent of missed bags during the period. BAA, on the other hand, examined the records held in the data warehouse, collected automatically from the system installed in response to exhortations in the 1996 review; this established that no more than 5.4 per cent or less of total missed bags could be attributed to inadequacies within the building. By contrast, a significant proportion was attributable to the sale by bmi of tickets allowing insufficient connection time. The quality of the data had not been challenged, but notwithstanding this BAA made a goodwill offer of a package of measures worth [✂]. BAA had also indicated its willingness to consider an increased package of compensation measures, although it did not accept that the evidence supported a larger settlement. BAA subsequently told us that it had agreed with bmi a full settlement of bmi's claims, and that bmi was now happy with its facilities.

- *Stansted*

14.147. We refer in Chapter 12 to criticism of investment at Stansted not reflecting the needs of lower-cost carriers for inexpensive facilities. BAA referred to Satellite 3 at Stansted being developed as a two- rather than three-storey building and without provision of airbridges, at significantly lower cost, as an example of the flexibility it needed to embrace the needs of current operations and potential future users (provision had been made to add airbridges at a later stage should circumstances alter). It also said that amendments and additions to Stansted had to be in line with the terms of original permission. BAA did safeguard the TTS station box in Satellite 3 in order to allow future extension of the TTS to Satellite 3 and 4 if required: this aspect did not meet with the universal approval of the low-cost airlines, but BAA believed this to be the most appropriate design to protect the airports' long-term flexibility.

- *Gatwick*

14.148. BAA also commented on BA's claim that there had been less investment at Gatwick than projected at the time that the formula for Q3 was set. It said that Gatwick investment had exceeded that previously projected, the figures showing this being available in each years CIP.

Systemic under-investment

14.149. Airlines, including BA, argued, based in part on the above project, that there had been systematic under-investment in Q3. BAA argued there was no evidence to support this, referring to investments on projects other than T5 exceeding the 1996 assumptions, and projects added to the programmes of all three airports in response to the T5 delay. Net underspend of £435 million was itself less than 15 per cent of total capex. BAA's willingness to commit £250 million to T1 future concepts (previously called Iceberg—see paragraph 14.131), which was not in the 1996 programme and which had a weak financial case, was strong evidence against systematic underspend. Neither had BA acknowledged that at each year's capex consultation BAA asked airlines to identify additional projects to compensate T5 delay, but airlines had failed to do so. Two of the projects cited, Pier 6 and Metro stands, were both based on the events of 11 September. BAA also argued that BA failed to address the consequences of its own swings in strategy and its shortcomings in providing information and explanation for its proposals.

Response to 11 September 2001

14.150. Some of the specific complaints raised related to BAA's failure, as airlines saw it, to consult on reductions to capex after the events of 11 September, or to lower airport charges following those reductions. BAA argued that such assertions were incorrect. In the two months after 11 September, traffic was so volatile and so depressed it was impossible to forecast, especially as it was unclear whether further acts of terrorism would follow. Traffic was 20 per cent down at Heathrow, 12 per cent at

Gatwick; airlines were in deep distress and using the uncertainty of future demand to justify major reductions in capex and other expenditure; BAA was still spending over £10 million a week on capital projects; but was also experiencing monthly revenue shortfalls against budget at a rate equivalent to over £150 million a year.

14.151. For BAA to have proceeded without at the very least taking stock of the situation would have been irresponsible. Indeed had it continued spending unabated, accumulating the cost into the RAB would have exposed airlines to the greatest infrastructure risk.

14.152. BAA had indeed written to all airlines inviting their views; and consulted the AOC and arranged a meeting with some of the airlines, and also had discussions with LACC and SEAG.

14.153. As to consultation with BA, BAA said that in its view exchange of correspondence was merely a vehicle for BA to game in front of the regulator. Correspondence with BA at the time was focused almost entirely on demand for charges reductions.

14.154. As to the BA argument that BAA did not cut its airport charges in line with its capital expenditure cuts, BAA was not considering changes to the capex programme simply to give airlines cuts in airport charges. Airlines were already paying charges below the maximum allowable, and were separately demanding major rescue cuts. BAA in reviewing its programme had in mind that if the collapse in traffic was prolonged, its own finances could be severely tested; and that 11 September was likely to presage major structural changes in the industry which were likely to affect the level of demand and distribution between airports (as subsequently proved true, demand being lost at Gatwick and gained at Stansted). This would affect the priority between projects; airlines themselves were likely to change the balance of their priorities after these events, for example by deferring aircraft purchases such as the A380; 11 September was likely to create demand for new security-related projects, the cost of which was unknown, but which would have to be financed out of existing resources; and it was most critical to focus efforts and spending on those projects which contributed most value to airlines and passengers.

14.155. BAA said that it had raised all these issues in the consultation; the first was simply ignored, little insight was provided on changes in the structure of demand, and not much was said on priorities.

14.156. In practice, the capex programme was not halted immediately after 11 September; the largest projects continued on site; some projects were temporarily paused, mainly Pier 6 at Gatwick, now reinstated for start in 12 months, and Metro stands at T4, also now reinstated. New projects were added to the programme, most notably the accelerated segregation of piers to meet security requirements. Actual spend in 2001/2 was £525 million, a shortfall of 10 per cent: the effect of any reduction in airport charges to reflect that amount would have only been one-fifth of 1 per cent (about £0.01 per passenger).

Consultation

14.157. BAA said that the CAA rightly identified effective transparency and consultation as an essential part of the regulatory contract. BAA supported this view and was continuing to improve its own consultation processes independent from any regulatory requirement. It also welcomed the CAA's acknowledgement that future consultation processes may be subject to some issues of price sensitivity and delicacy in relation to planning negotiations.

14.158. A number of real world limitations needed to be recognized in specifying the content of consultations, namely:

(a) The views of today's airlines did not necessarily represent the long-term interest of the public. The CAA recognized this in its October 2000 paper. Indeed there were circumstances where users may wish to frustrate the development of new competition, or gain competitive advantage. Airports must not therefore be put under an obligation simply to do 'as asked' in consultations, although they may legitimately be expected to justify their decisions where they differed from airline preferences.

(b) The consultation process should not inject undue rigidity into planning. A fixed fully specified ten-year master plan would represent a kind of mechanistic, deterministic thinking dating back to the 1970s, which had now been superseded by broader long-term strategies, with detailed plans for the short term.

(c) Excessive information and publication demands would create an 'intrusive cottage industry', aimed at satisfying the regulator in a 'gaming' process, rather than genuinely improving consultation.

(d) More generally on BA's suggestion that the capital programme be established as part of the regulatory decision and executed as set out and only altered with full airline agreement in writing, BAA believed it highly improbable that airlines would ever reach a full consensus on major aspects of the CIP which affected their commercial objectives.

14.159. Of course consultation would only be effective if all parties resisted the temptation to 'game', and came to the table constructively. BAA had made the proposal that the obligations of both airports and airlines should be the subject of a code of conduct, and encouraged the CC and CAA to consider this possibility further.

14.160. BAA referred to over 80 'main ways' of consultation at Heathrow over the last six months. It told us that it had made great efforts to improve consultation arrangements on its investment programme, with very positive feedback from recipients. It was used as an example of best practice by airlines.

14.161. Its broad ten-year development strategy was set out in the 2002 CIP. This represented another step forward in providing airlines with information on which to review the overall programme, and was almost certainly the most comprehensive consultation document produced by any airport operator in the world. A number of airlines found it too detailed and were unable to digest the amount of information provided. The CAA's requirements had only emerged during the course of this review and the 2002 CIP was BAA's best effort to moving towards meeting them in the time available, but it envisaged further improvements next year. The CIP was not meant, however, to be the main vehicle to discuss in detail the changes and configuration of individual projects. Quantification of outputs was normally provided in separate specific consultations, and the same was true of options which were discussed with airlines at great length. To include all these individual project details in the CIP would make the document extremely voluminous and unwieldy and divert readers from the broader issues into detail. Precise quantification of outputs of projects in the medium to long term, moreover, was more problematic: they were by definition not fully designed and in some cases simply represented provisions of money to deal with anticipated issues. Even if specified, the outputs would depend on major forecasting assumptions

14.162. To the degree that BA's version of a masterplan was not reflected, BAA took this to mean a fixed and fully specified programme for each individual investment comprising the total development of the infrastructure. To produce a fully specified single plan would also require an assumption on if, where and when a third runway would be built. The Government had made no decision on this. BAA would also have to make an assumption about segregated mode and the ATM limit; Open Skies; and which airline would occupy which terminal in future; and other external issues including, for example, prospects for Crossrail, powers to road charge, future environmental policies and constraints; and finally about future airline alliances. These were all good reasons for BAA to operate a broad development strategy which could accommodate evolving conditions rather than work to an original masterplan. Had a masterplan previously been adopted, there would have been considerable expenditure at Gatwick related to BA's development there of a separate hub, a strategy that subsequently changed but would have left other airlines to pay significantly higher charges had that investment gone ahead.

14.163. On criticisms that the absence of a masterplan resulted in piecemeal development, BAA said that it did not believe there was a material risk of projects currently in the programme needing to be demolished in the foreseeable future: over 15 years it only had to mothball one project (a small scheme to provide domestic facilities at Gatwick North Terminal, specifically demanded by BA to meet its urgent need to transfer services from the South Terminal). It also did not envisage any need to demolish the Virgin hangar at Heathrow, about which BA complained, which would only be required if the most grandiose scheme for the development of the Eastern Apron were implemented. This would only be contemplated if there were a third runway and there was no prospect of it happening in the next 10 to 15 years. The Eastern Apron development was not included in this capital programme and if it were it would have a major effect on charges.

Connectivity

14.164. As noted in Chapter 12, we received particular criticism of lack of consultation on connectivity between T5 and the CTA. BAA said that studies had been undertaken into connectivity as part of the design concept work for T5 which identified road-based solutions as the best way forward. The airline community had expressed a strong interest in the TTS with both passengers and baggage; at their request, BAA had investigated such a solution and sought views on it. The core issue was whether a TTS would be a cost-effective solution: BAA had been determined to ensure a careful consideration of costs and benefits. It was recognized in the planning objectives that overall benefits should outweigh overall costs.

14.165. A minimization of the need to transfer bags and passengers was one of the criteria adopted in the original T5 occupancy discussions, at which time BA envisaged moving all its service into T5 and T4 and connectivity requirements would have been low. Subsequently, BA's vision of its operations had changed and it now envisaged keeping operations in T1 and subsequently in T3 or T1. But the number of passengers using the system would still be relatively small, and at high cost per passenger.

14.166. A development of initial cost estimates for connectivity, an outline programme, and outline charges implications were presented to the London AOC in October 2001 when the airlines were asked to consider the implications of the potential charges and advise on their wish to proceed or not. Neither was forthcoming but in February 2002, BAA were asked to proceed with the next stage of planning against an understanding of an airline commitment to consider and debate charges implications, with feedback anticipated this coming autumn. BAA was now focusing on the incremental benefits and costs that would arise from a change from the current plans for a road-based solution to a TTS for passengers and a more automated transfer baggage system. However, the work continued to be complicated by the continuing uncertainty over terminal occupancy post-T5s opening.

14.167. BAA recognized, however, that efficient and effective connectivity was essential; any nervousness was a product of uncertainty over whether incremental benefits exceeded incremental costs. However, it had responded constructively and its CIP assumed the first phase of an automated transfer baggage system at the opening of T5 between that terminal and T3; Phase 2 would then extend the system to T1 and Phase 3 to T4. There were a number of options for further elements of connectivity, including road-based, automated and mixed system: airlines had been provided with cost data and asked to advise their preferences. The possibility of a third runway further complicated the issue since different schemes would be appropriate with/without the runway. There would also be significant disruption problems if the project was to be completed to make the T5 Phase 1 opening: and the need for land acquisition from Thames Water may prevent that timing. It was also not feasible to extend the TTS until Satellite 2 was in operation; Satellite 2 itself could not be built until the new Thames Water sewerage works was in operation. But when Satellite 2 was open and more BA services could move to T5, the case for the TTS was even weaker.

14.168. BAA argued that BA had pressed for early implementation of a fully automated option with no regard to its costs or who would pay for it. The cost of additional tunnelling schemes put to it approached £1 billion, of which little material on the benefits to airlines had been made available. The project was linked to BA's promotion and development of the Eastern Apron, which would also cost well in excess of £1 billion (major remodelling of the apron, the closing of the crosswind runway, and the construction of two satellites). BA's proposals for an Eastern Apron scheme that would provide very substantial increase of total aircraft parking capacity were very difficult to reconcile with the 480,000 movement limit cap. BAA also felt the BA proposal for a T1 to T5 tunnel inconsistent with its wish for T3 airlines to move into T1 and for itself and its partners to co-locate to T3 and T5. The optimum design of a TTS system also depended on whether BA was successful in promoting the third runway at Heathrow; if so, any scheme which failed to take that development into account would be very suboptimal or even a major constraint on third runway or terminal design. Increased construction work in the CTA would also have major implications for airline disruption and passenger service, but BAA had received no clear guidance from airlines whether they would be prepared to contemplate such disruption: without such guidance, its view was that such a scheme could not be implemented in full before around 2010.

14.169. Hence, when T5 opened, BAA would have provided for a workable, flexible, low capital cost, road-based solution to connectivity with an automated baggage link: BA had not yet made a compelling case for its fully automated TTS option, but if it could do so and users generally were prepared to commit to paying the high charges and land purchase could be resolved, BAA could move to a decision to move forward. (One option could be for the TTS to go halfway into the CTA rather than all the way around.)

T5 occupancy

14.170. We also refer in Chapter 12 to complaints of inadequate consultation on which airlines would occupy T5. BAA told us that it sought to establish the likely occupiers of T5 at an early stage so it could work with them to develop the details of the scheme most effectively. To help make that decision it established, in consultation with the industry, three criteria for terminal allocation generally and T5 specifically, namely to allow for best use to be made of the airport, terminal and apron capacity overall; to maximize the number of passenger transfers able to take place without changing terminals (and connectivity issues were still best satisfied with the current plan); and to minimize the number of airlines required to shift between terminals. It employed consultants to build a complex computer model to test options under the criteria which demonstrated that BA was the occupant best able to fit them. The community overall was consulted thoroughly in 1996 and again 1998. Having established the preferred occupancy BAA was addressing the subsequent issues. It was important to ensure that the appropriate infrastructure was in place to allow airlines remaining in the CTA to have appropriate facilities: hence, the CIP included £510 million expenditure over five years at T1 and T3, plus minor projects at T2, T4 and between CTA terminals. However, BAA had not yet committed to a specific long-term allocation of airlines between terminals but wanted to discuss the needs of each airline individually, and then to consult further about the occupancy paths for all five terminals when T5 was open: no airline had yet been firmly committed to any particular location. There was also provision for a further £600 million expenditure on CTA post-T5 opening.

- *T5 costs*

14.171. We raised the issue as to whether there had been adequate consultation about T5 with those airlines unlikely to occupy it, but who would nonetheless pay higher charges as a result. BAA said that there had been consultation at varying levels over the years, including all airlines on the broad issues at the early stages. Subsequently, consultation on detail had been primarily with BA (but with major consultation on the TTS). All airlines were given details on the overall shape and structure of the project and its cost, and there were six-months of discussion with them about this; and LACC met frequently and could raise any issues on it. BAA was quite happy if airlines wanted to look over the detailed changes, but none had not yet wished to do so.

Little America

14.172. We also note in Chapter 12 criticisms of inadequate consultation on changes in security arrangements in T3 after 11 September—a scheme referred to as Little America. BAA said that a directive was issued by the DTLR in January 2001 requiring all non-segregated terminals to become segregated and until such time as segregation had been implemented, non-compliant terminals were required to carry out additional security measures. Following 11 September, there was a requirement that in all non-segregated terminals, passengers were to be subject to 20 per cent search at the departure gate and, in addition, continuous searches of passengers' cabin baggage and items carried were to be conducted in respect of all North Atlantic departure flights. This was later formalized as a direction. To achieve economies of scale, HAL attempted to consolidate gate search: hence the possibility of using Gate 16. Planning exercises, however, identified resulting problems of stand utilization and loss of pier service, and the gate room was also found not to be physically large enough. It was also identified that there was insufficient capacity to accommodate all the non-European flag carriers on Pier 7, placing these carriers at a competitive disadvantage as their flights would require searching in the departure gate. There would be a significant decrease in pier service for these and other T3 carriers not flying to the USA. The DTLR also failed to give definitive answers as to the acceptability or otherwise of Little America: but stated that an alternative partition solution on Pier 7 offered a better all round product. Final notification from the DTLR that the Transport Security Administration (successors to the Federal Aviation Administration) had rejected the UK proposals for Little America was received 22 April 2002: the DTLR were stressing that physical segregation of Pier 7 must be given immediate priority. This had recently commenced.

Alternative approaches to investment and consultation

14.173. During the course of our inquiry, BAA and the CAA agreed the contents of an enhanced information disclosure and consultation document. The document would allow users to understand the principal business drivers; forecast demand capacity (including implications for quality of service); options for the development of the airport around the central plan; resourcing implications; cost estimates of individual projects; and expected outputs. It would be provided on an annual basis and include an account of how the plan had changed and an explanation. It would act as a basis for consultation only and would not represent a mandatory investment programme. BAA noted the CAA's statement that 'demonstration that BAA has consistently ignored the reasonable request of users in the consultation process without good reason and contrary to the interests of local users generally would jeopardize the sustainability of the regulatory framework'; also that airlines would need to cooperate in the provision of information on the costs and benefits to them, and allocate sufficient resources to engage in the process.

14.174. We note in Chapter 12 suggestions that there should be legally binding agreements between BAA and the airlines, and/or mandatory investment programmes. BAA believed that there were several problems to this approach to capital planning:

(a) There was no evidence the current approach with an annual CIP is in any way flawed. Users did not seem to have claimed there had been projects undertaken which were not required or projects not undertaken which should have been and which were within BAA's power to instigate.

(b) Such an approach would be completely inflexible as BAA would be uncertain how to proceed with mandatory investments which might no longer be required (for example, due to airline moves).

(c) It was unclear how agreements which were legal/mandatory in nature would deal with projects delayed by planning or governmental issues.

(d) As a result the process would continually be stuck with either the CAA or lawyers to resolve leading to more intrusion, higher costs and delays.

(e) Incentives would be very poor—BAA would only proceed under conditions of complete certainty and there would be no incentive to be cost-efficient.

(f) Agreements that obligated BAA to carry out investment projects which airlines were free to use or not would be one-sided.

(g) It was by no means certain the current legislative framework supported such an approach.

(h) As a result, not surprisingly, the CAA rejected this form of capital planning and investment.

14.175. BAA therefore agreed with the CAA approach which focused on customer specified outputs rather than levels of expenditure. If airlines specified throughput levels and quality of service, BAA's performance should judged on these. The CIP consultation should be positioned within this framework allowing BAA to judge how best to meet user needs.

14.176. However, BAA was sympathetic to airlines' views that charges should in some way be linked to delivery. This could comprise either airports simply undertaking to provide any given level of throughput at a certain level of service standards (with the incentive provided by its Q factor proposals); or charges linked to the provision of certain predefined outputs; or charges contingent on major project milestones throughout Q4. These would have to be for projects already well defined where there was a high probability this would still match airline requirements: see BAA's specific proposals in Q4 in paragraph 14.70.

14.177. In the context of complaints more generally, BAA said that it was surprised and disappointed by submissions regarding its conduct. Few of the issues put before the CC had been raised at meetings with the Chief Executives of major airlines. No complaints, moreover, had been made in the last six years under section 41 of the Airports Act.

14.178. BAA was therefore intending to consult with airlines and other interested parties on the creation of a formal complaints procedure, to provide its business partners with a mechanism to challenge actions which BAA had taken after those business partners had exhausted the usual means of communication. Subject to a positive response from consultees, BAA would launch this procedure in April 2003, and review the trial later that year.

14.179. It thought that there should be a two-stage process. In the first stage the complainant would submit a written formal complaint to the relevant airport, indicating whether or not it wished to have a meeting; the recipient would then have a specific period within which to arrange any meeting and to respond. If the complainant was not satisfied with the response, it would have one month in which to decide whether to submit an appeal, to be made in writing to the member of BAA's Executive Committee with responsibility for the airport. Again the submission would indicate whether or not the complainant would wish to have a meeting with that member; that person would then have a specific period within which to arrange any meeting and to respond. Before responding, the member of the executive committee would be required to review the complaint with a senior BAA executive not employed at the airport concerned, to enhance the degree of independence in considering the appeal. BAA had considered creating a role for an independent third party, but believed the risk of a third party making recommendations based on limited knowledge of the subject outweighed the potential benefits of a fresh view. This would though be an issue to raise in the consultation. This mechanism would not be used for individual passenger complaints, but for complaints by aircraft operators and handling agents. BAA would expect any complainants to agree to suspend or not initiate litigation action or Airports Act section 41 complaint while the formal complaints procedure was underway. Suggested time scales should enable a relatively rapid response to any complaint made, but it would be prudent to allow for them to be shortened or extended if necessary by mutual consent.

14.180. The main advantage of this approach was that the procedure could provide an additional mechanism for resolving issues about which business partners felt strongly, thereby reducing the danger of issues festering. There might also be fewer complaints made at the next regulatory review. The main disadvantage was that it could harm the generally successful relationships that BAA enjoys with its business partners, or add costs and possible delay to the resolution of any disagreements.

Service standards

14.181. We referred in paragraph 14.79 et seq to BAA's views on the Q factor proposed by the CAA, and in Chapter 12 to complaints by airlines both about service standards in general, and particular aspects of service.

Specific complaints

- *Pier service*

14.182. There were criticisms of pier service levels, particularly at T4 at Heathrow, and North Terminal at Gatwick (partly associated with complaints about the Metro stand and Pier 6 investments referred to above).

14.183. BAA acknowledged that T4 pier service levels had dipped below 90 per cent. However, pier service levels were determined by a combination of infrastructure, operating practice of airlines, and commercial and operational priorities adopted by airlines and handlers in operating aircraft stands: BA's choices regarding its aircraft maintenance regime had a tendency to lengthen aircraft turnaround and on stand time, thereby reducing pier service levels. BAA had been determined with the support of airlines to provide additional aircraft parking stands whether pier served or not to minimize the impact of this capacity constraint. The opening of T5 in 2008 implied the benefit of any new pier development would be negated in six years' time. Nonetheless, extension to the Victor Pier into the Metro Stands would increase the level of pier service by between 6 and 10 per cent; this project had faced a number of practical difficulties in addition to these operational and strategic difficulties. The recovery of Heathrow's traffic subsequently had been more rapid than expected and BAA would entertain positively a suggestion from BA that the project should be brought forward, although BAA subsequently told us this also offered the only ability in T4 to provide capacity for A-380 aircraft operated by Qantas (which would presumably in turn free up stands for BA). The move of BA from Gatwick to T4 was itself likely to lead to a reduction of around 4 per cent in pier service levels this year. It would be prohibitively expensive to provide pier service to some stands, which BA had accepted. With the benefit of hindsight

BAA recognized that it was possible that it could have progressed more speedily on extension of the Victor Pier: but BAA was confident that at each stage of the process it had taken the appropriate decisions.

14.184. BAA said that the overall pier service level at Gatwick was not as low as quoted: in 2000/01, the figures were 96 per cent for South Terminal and 79 per cent for North Terminal (the latter figure, however, probably underestimates the true level of pier service as it excludes for example aircraft that depart from a pier served stand but were held on a remote stand). BAA did not believe it appropriate to reduce runway and terminal capacity to improve pier service: and BA had been aware of pier service limitations when it moved from Heathrow to Gatwick and subsequently co-located its operations in North Terminal, worsening the pier service level. Subsequently, studies with BA into a wide variety of options took time to complete. Pier 6 was the more obvious example. Were BAA to have leapt forward with more radical pier service options, the airport would currently be in an extremely difficult position.

14.185. There were also complaints about BAA's failure to achieve the T4 jetty service availability target for two months. BAA said that this resulted from two unforeseen and serious faults with the air-bridges which involved the acquisition of spares that were not normally stock items for Heathrow or the manufacturer. However, except for those two months the target had been reached, and had been reached over the year as a whole. BAA also said that as a goodwill payment it had voluntarily made the standard airbridge rebate in circumstances where an airbridge was unserviceable but the stand could still be used, although coaching costs would not normally apply.

14.186. On the adequacy of the remote stand rebate, BAA said that it was intended to recognize the service offered to passengers on remote stands as less attractive. Airlines in recent years had raised concerns that the rebate did not reflect the cost of coaching and BAA had responded by increasing its size to £3.00 per departing passenger. The purpose of the rebate was never to compensate fully for any increase in costs to airlines or reduction in services to passengers: but it was also a very substantial proportion of the total charge per terminal departing passenger. However, the coaching service at Gatwick had recently been tendered with the supplier currently charging £0.93 per passenger—hence it was surprising to see the suggestion that rebate was insufficient to cover costs. That benchmark of £0.93 per passenger suggested the rebate more than covered coaching costs and, therefore, probably met or exceeded any additional costs arising from coaching (handling staff were clearly required to operate a jetty and these costs should be deducted to arrive at the incremental costs in any assessment). It was difficult to envisage an airline losing business as a result of passengers being bussed or walking up and down stairs: BAA's survey of passengers in 1999 showed use of jetties to be the 33rd most important contributor to a good airport experience out of 38 items listed. BAA had also asked BA for information on the value of pier service: no such information had been forthcoming which made it difficult for BAA to take account of airlines' costs and any marketing loss in evaluating pier service projects and judging how to set the remote stand rebate.

● *T1 complaints*

14.187. We note in Chapter 12 a series of complaints about service standards in T1. BAA told us that during holiday periods bmi operated some charter flights which check in earlier than usual: on some of these occasions HAL was asked to open the security combs earlier to accommodate these passengers and to allow for the increase in security processing time. Where possible it tried to respond positively to these requests by bringing in staff early, but on the last occasion this was done the facility was not well used, which led to a discussion with bmi explaining that HAL would be reluctant to do this in the future if bmi was not able to confirm expected flows in advance. BAA was not aware that these opening times had been the cause of delays to departures. In the immediate aftermath of 11 September, however, and with new security requirements implying secondary searches at gate rooms, HAL did not have sufficient staff to cover simultaneous flight departures and at times staff were rushing from one gate to another: it was possible that staff were delayed to the gate sometimes. Additional staff had since been recruited.

14.188. As to hours of manager service delivery (MSD teams) although they were as stated by bmi, these were supported by a team of customer service duty managers who covered across the full 24-hour period. The MSD teams were in addition extremely flexible and altered their hours to suit local needs. HAL did not believe the MSD teams' rostered hours impacted on the level of customer service or operational management.

14.189. On contingency arrangements for baggage system failures, the T1 baggage system had built in contingency and redundancy and most failures could be addressed by redirecting bags on the system. Serviceability of the system was good and in most eventualities BAA could alter the process in a secure manner and secure the operation. Prior to 11 September a major departure baggage belt outage could be addressed by sending hold baggage directly to the gate via the main passenger security comb. A change in the security requirements since 11 September had meant that a major baggage belt failure had a more serious impact on the main passenger security comb since all sharp items must be removed and due to the increased search imposed by the DTLR. As a consequence HAL was actively exploring options to give further redundancy contingency to the system on the very rare occasions when hold bags needed to be taken to departure gates. The airline community would be involved once the contingency arrangements are sufficiently developed.

14.190. On time taken to repair major operational systems, the individual PCs used to run the system to the monitors at Gates 36 and 38 had failed and required rebuilding with new main component parts. Once this had been completed the systems were reinstated, but subsequently the monitors themselves failed and had to be replaced. The accumulation of these activities led to the delay in repair which was regretted. HAL planned an investment project to replace these entire systems, which was under development.

14.191. As to short notice closure of stand for insurance inspections, HAL was aware there had been some difficulties. Its aim was to communicate with airlines by notifying them four weeks in advance, but there were occasions when inspection staff arrived at the stand at the planned time to find the stand in use preventing the inspection from taking place. HAL did receive and respond positively where possible to request from airlines to change these times. However, a more carefully planned approach was now being undertaken with regard to insurance inspections on all passenger sensitive equipment: the appointment of a statutory insurance planner within the HAL engineering department and the integration of this activity with planned maintenance had already improved performance.

14.192. On roof leaks, roof repair had been part of the general airport building and civil engineering contract. Following some concerns about work undertaken and the complexity of other repairs leading to unacceptable periods of disruption, a specialist roofing contractor had been appointed, and he had a planned schedule of surveys and maintenance. Any minor repairs identified were rectified immediately, more detailed work was raised with the project/planning department. Blocked gullies and roof outlets had already been identified as a major contributory factor to roof leaks and the planned maintenance of these items had been included in the role of the roofing contractor.

14.193. On air conditioning, poor performance of air handling units serving Gate 2 and 8/12 was identified last summer and the original manufacturer was repairing and enhancing the performance due to the inability of the existing contractor to rectify the faults. At Pier 4A the units had also been identified as performing badly and these were currently being replaced.

14.194. As to Pier 4 a programme of repainting and replacing significant areas of carpet was underway; seating was provided throughout the gate rooms totalling approximately 1,000 seats.

14.195. On specialist assistance facilities, the pier was built over 30 years ago and was not as wide as more recently designed piers which could provide travellator assistance. Special need assistance to the apron level was provided via a lift at Gate 6; provision of a lift in Gate 5 was part of a recent scheme to extend the gate room in partnership with BA.

14.196. We put to BAA a complaint that passengers on Dublin and Republic of Ireland services at Heathrow were encouraged to divert via retail outlets. BAA commented that a retail unit on Pier 4A did not require passengers to divert; rather, they walked past a shop and catering outlet on their route. BAA further commented that they could not identify any situation where passengers were required to divert significantly from their route to go through retail outlets.

- *Pier repainting*

14.197. A number of airlines, including BA, complained about closures of stands for repainting with advertising logos. BAA said that BA supported the project in principle, which comprised not only external repainting but some internal redecoration, improvements sought by airlines which enhanced passenger service. It could not be undertaken without some outage but yielded significant benefits.

14.198. The programme for the jetty painting was developed and implemented to cause the minimal disruption to the normal airport operation. For scheduling purposes each terminal apron stand declaration assumed an allowance for stands which had to be closed for maintenance, to ensure that both planned and unplanned maintenance could be accommodated without impacting on the operation. All the stand closures required for the jetty painting were carried out within these allowances. A maximum of one bridge was taken out of service in each terminal at one time and every effort was made to coordinate other maintenance activities with the jetty painting closures. The programme was finalized and agreed at the weekly works programming meetings and was attended by BA's stand planning representative from T1 and T4, and amended to suit particular airline requirements. The work was carried out from July 2000 to May 2001 and protective tents purchased so that it could continue seven days a week throughout the winter. Preparatory work was undertaken at night. Stands were normally repainted on a four-day cycle and in all 136 jetties on 115 stands were painted. In general the work proceeded very smoothly and the only issue that was raised at the time concerned T4 in spring 2001 when it became clear BA had stand planning problems and could not accommodate its summer schedule. HAL agreed to assist by only having a single stand closed and indeed suspended the work over Easter 2001.

14.199. As to whether the closure times were extended to allow for logos to be painted, BAA said that it was a multi-purpose project which brought some refurbishment benefits alongside the income gains, and it was therefore difficult to separate the time required for each element.

- *Way-finding*

14.200. BAA said that it was not yet satisfied with the way-finding and signage particularly at Heathrow. Indeed in its 1999 survey, half of the top six aspects about which passengers were asked in terms of relative importance, related to way-finding or signage. Hence, it had been placing increasing efforts into improving way-finding, including appointing a group way-finding manager; developing a tool kit, a guidance methodology which could be applied in a variety of situations generally to improve way-finding; appointing a way-finding consultant (uniquely in the world), and on-the-ground improvements. Though not satisfied with way-finding, the results of its QSM survey were generally satisfactory.

14.201. On specific complaints about signage of Gate 24 in T2, signage had been complicated by segregation requirements; BAA had reviewed the issue and implemented some changes to reflect a clear understanding for the route to Gate 24. BA had been advised of the changes and appeared satisfied with the response. BAA also noted that its proposed Q factor would include way-finding measures because of its importance to passengers. Hence, airport charges would be dependent in part on its performance in way-finding.

- *Security*

14.202. BAA said that BA had only recently, and informally suggested that the target that 95 per cent of the time, security queue lengths should be no more than ten minutes should be tightened. It believed the current target to be a reasonable balance. There were, however, problems in the time taken to recruit staff to meet the additional requirements following 11 September; and shortage of space for the additional equipment required. On monitoring of performance against this target, BAA said that it was going to move to a CCTV-based system.

14.203. As to complaints about charges for Fast Track, BAA said that Fast Track was a marketing product which airlines at Heathrow chose to ask BAA to provide as a specific facility to support their product differentiation requirements. BAA responded positively to this request. Agreement was reached on how it would be funded: in essence BAA charged for the security manpower resource required to operate the channel plus a charge to fund the equipment in that channel. Advertising was visible from both the fast track and the standard track. The advertising visible by passengers in the fast track channel would have been located there whether or not a separate channel existed. Income from this source was not therefore included in fast track charging calculations. Charging arrangements were based on BAA proposals for the hourly cost rate for security staff. These rates had been discounted by BAA Heathrow in recognition of passengers using fast track and not using standard channel; discussions were under way into future charging calculations. It was possible fast track arrangements would not be sustainable in the longer term as resourcing implications of government requirements remain onerous.

- *Gatwick*

14.204. On criticism of poor service standards at Gatwick, BAA did not believe that this allegation was consistent with SLA performance. There had been some problems with transit system availability but this was far from being a course of conduct against the public interest.

Service level agreements

14.205. We received complaints of poor progress in development of SLAs. In response, BAA said that airlines had not raised such concerns with BAA to date. Other than BA, airlines had shown no particular interest in extending the scope of SLAs to new areas. Nor had BA consistently argued in favour of financial incentives. SLAs had been in place at Gatwick for several years.

14.206. BAA referred to the conclusions of MMC 4 as suggesting any compensation under SLAs should be reciprocal. BAA had followed this lead and suggested the best approach would be for any compensation to be on a reciprocal basis. It also noted the reference in MMC 4 to reciprocal arrangements 'where the trials show compensation to be feasible': this was possible with bilateral agreements but significantly more difficult for any multilateral agreements. Hence the Q factor proposals circumvented the difficulty of creating a payment mechanism separate to airport charges. BAA added that in reality there had been little or no interest from airlines on even penalty-only SLAs. Even for baggage systems, detailed work by BAA and BA had led to the development of carefully considered measures; the initial ideas for measures had been shown to be inappropriate.

14.207. BAA's view was also that any mechanism for regulating service quality did not need to be financially compensatory to form an effective incentive; incentivization included the personal distress to BAA senior managers on publishing poor results at AOC meetings, and incorporation of SLA performance into incentive schemes.

Generic standards

14.208. On the suggestion that there should be generic service standards, BAA told us that it had undertaken an initial piece of work which it had thought would clarify the service quality level that airlines might expect to achieve in each of the areas covered by airport charges: the results of the exercise were shared with BA. However, the exercise highlighted how difficult it was to quantify the expected level of service in many of the areas and that BAA's performance in a number of areas was covered by safety regulation. It therefore did not believe it was possible to develop a statement quantifying the level of service which airport users could expect for each area covered by airport charges. Partly as a result of the difficulties inherent in that approach, BAA and the airlines had developed SLAs, and BAA had more recently developed the Q factor concept.

14.209. We noted in paragraph 14.81, however, that BAA did itself suggest shortfall from minimum standards as an alternative to a Q factor. It suggested that a minimum service level approach with action only taken when particularly poor performance was observed might be a simpler scheme to administer than a Q factor but subject to the same level of complexity in developing a workable scheme which avoided perverse incentives.

14.210. BAA were supportive of bilateral top-up contracts if an airline wished to receive service above the generic level—but a number of issues related to extensive use of them in general would need to be considered.

- *Public interest consideration and possible remedies*

14.211. We note in Chapter 12 that a number of airlines argued that the absence of standards was against the public interest, hence standards should be included in airport charging conditions, rather than as a Q factor. BAA acknowledged that there was a public interest concern in a system where BAA provided a set of services without any defined standards. However, BAA did not believe the absence of service level standards could be a public interest issue of itself: if all services were being carried out to appropriate levels then the fact there were no service targets was of no concern. It was, for example, difficult to see how an adverse finding could relate to runway availability, where performance was 100 per cent. Rather any public interest issue would have to be related to a service failure and proper thought needed to be given as to how that failing might be remedied or prevented.

14.212. Moreover, as noted in the MMC's previous report, the concern related to a structural problem with the system of regulation in that it did not capture the issue of service standards rather than conduct on the part of BAA. (BAA believed that the MMC's statements at the time of the previous review and BAA's actions in the light of them, had a strong bearing on whether it had carried out a course of conduct against the public interest. BAA acknowledged, however, that this might not determine the CC's conclusions on this public interest issue.) The MMC, in the previous report, had said that BAA should try and mitigate the structural failure in regulation by introducing SLAs—which BAA did—and by introducing compensation in those SLAs where the principle of reciprocity was recognized, but most airlines refused to recognize that principle, so it could not do so. Nonetheless, BAA had worked closely with airlines on improving the very poor performance on baggage, one of the most important factors for passengers and airlines, as a result of which performance was now among the best in Europe. It had also introduced four two-way SLAs on baggage where there were opportunities for both bonuses and penalties to BAA, with two more on offer to airlines. It had introduced 52 non-financial SLAs that it monitored regularly. It also went beyond that, in deriving Q to go into the price control formula. This was therefore a structural problem which could be dealt with in the formula.

14.213. Moreover, although there was no formal tariff under which prices paid reflect levels of service, there was a variety of situations where BAA did indeed adjust prices when the service quality was worse than expected, for example:

(a) Contractually binding SLAs with BA for a number of baggage systems at Heathrow, with two-way financial incentives—referred to above. This opportunity had been offered to other airlines who had so far declined to participate.

(b) The remote stand rebate.

(c) A rebate at Heathrow and Gatwick when airbridges were not serviceable. At Heathrow, this was at a rate of the original air jetty charge (when invoiced in its own right about ten years ago) uplifted by inflation.

(d) Rebate of the FEGP charge on application when the supply was not serviceable.

(e) Well-defined rebate structures of BAA Heathrow's property management where facilities were unsatisfactory, such as heating, ventilation and air conditioning equipment.

(f) At Gatwick, different check-in desk charges for each line of desks in South Terminal, reflecting the differing quality of the check-in area and the associated baggage systems; information on these different charges are publicly available.

(g) In some instances agreement not to fully recover specified activity costs where there were service quality issues. (For example, BAA Heathrow had recently put additional temporary staff into the ID unit to deal with a backlog in applications, but had agreed not to increase charges as a result.)

(h) Examples of other ad hoc price adjustments which tend to be on an individual negotiated basis, for example with bmi relating to their transfer baggage facilities; and where BAA Heathrow rebated aircraft parking charges when there was operational disruption caused by a major fire in T1 and when there was an explosion in an electrical sub-station resulting in delays to aircraft movements.

14.214. BAA did not believe that there were other alternatives available which it could have implemented.

(a) Further airline rebates or discounts around particular SLA failures would have not only been very rare but also complex to administer (even impossible in some cases). This was essentially because of difficulties of establishing which airlines were disadvantaged—either because the SLAs related more to passengers or because it would be difficult to recreate what would have happened had a specific facility been available.

(b) A much more promising approach was via the Q factor which could only be implemented as part of the regulatory review. BAA had therefore been working on this concept for the last two years.

14.215. Moreover, BAA also believed its priority was to help the airlines optimize the throughput of its scarce facilities at Heathrow: this might require reductions in, for example, pier service, by helping BA move flights from Gatwick to Heathrow, for which it was not right that BAA should suffer financially. Such trade-offs were also relevant in considering the public interest.

14.216. BAA believed the suggestion of the CC that a quality company operating in a competitive market would make a standard trade-off between service quality and price was not clear cut. Suppliers often tried to raise their overall level of service to match their overall level of price—which was inherent in the price formula setting itself—but without compensation for specific service failures.

14.217. BAA said that, although it might be difficult for us to crystallize a Q factor before the end of the review, nevertheless it believed that if we gave the CAA clear guidance as to what we thought needed to be in a Q factor, the CAA could put that into the price formula either at the start of the quinquennium or during it, on the back of a commitment by BAA that it would accept the price control formula which met the criteria we set out. There were three dimensions to its commitment:

(a) BAA's commitment that it did not expect, nor did it believe it was required legally, a fully defined and detailed Q factor scheme, to be contained in the CC's recommendations to the CAA; it was important, however, for the CC to give general recommendations.

(b) BAA's commitment on developing runway and taxiway performance measures. Namely it could:

   (i)   develop, with airlines and the CAA, well-defined measures of hours of unserviceability of runways and taxiways;

   (ii) collect data on actual hours of unserviceability during 2003/04;

   (iii) propose to the CAA targets and a bonus/penalty structure for unserviceability from 2004/05 onwards;

   (iv) either, at the appropriate point in time, agree voluntarily with a CAA proposal to make an amendment to the price control formula to accommodate this specific element in the Q factor at Heathrow and Gatwick, if the proposal was in line with the CC's general recommendations on a Q factor; or

   (v)   create a separate stand-alone method of rebating airlines for poor serviceability performance of our runways and taxiways at Heathrow and Gatwick.

(c) BAA's commitment on developing measures of delay. Namely it would:

   (i)   use its best endeavours to work closely with NATS, airlines, handling agents, and the CAA, to research existing and new measures of delay and its contributory factors;

   (ii) gather data on these measures to understand their robustness and degree of attribution to an airport operator's performance;

   (iii) conclude by September 2004, for review by the CAA, whether it was possible to measure satisfactorily an airport's contribution to delay and, if it was possible, what the appropriate measures and targets would be; and

   (iv) if it did prove possible, agree voluntarily to a CAA proposal to make an amendment to the price control formula to accommodate this specific element in the Q factor at Heathrow and Gatwick, if the proposal was in line with the CC's general recommendations on a Q factor. (The amendment may need to include adjustments to other aspects of the Q factor such as the removal of runway and taxiway measures and/or changes to the financial impact of other elements to allow for the inclusion of a delay measure.)

14.218. The formula could capture separate terminal differences (although BAA said that would be creating a fairly large compliance mechanism for what would be relatively small sums of money) and provide for the payment of sums monthly (although BAA suggested monthly reporting, to be aggregated to a yearly total for payment), and apply across a range of elements.

14.219. BAA also commented on proposals from ourselves, that would be based on the standard of service for some facilities provided to specific airlines, and with compensation paid to the specific airlines affected. BAA preferred a Q factor, applied generally, to attempting to identify exactly which airline was affected by any particular equipment not being available. First, the latter approach would require a lot of staff to work out; and second, BAA did not actually know which airline might have been affected or not affected had the equipment been available—for example, which airline would have occupied a stand had it been available and given that it was not BAA that did the allocation. A payment spread across all airlines would be equally effective in providing an incentive to BAA to ensure systems worked. BAA (as noted above in the context of Q) believed it was almost impossible to do anything about delays at this stage: but would be happy to work with others to research the data on delays and their attribution. BAA was also concerned there was likely to be decline in standards before the opening of T5 (by when up to 73 mppa could be handled in the existing terminals). It believed it in the public interest to maximize throughput as long as it did not breach safety and security standards; hence the risk referred to above that, if an airline wished to move from Gatwick to Heathrow, BAA would be penalized if quality of service declined as a result.

14.220. Many airport processes, moreover, were shared processes, where the attribution of service quality was very difficult. Legally, it was difficult for BAA to impose standards on others, for example ground handlers or airlines; all it could do was threaten to terminate a licence which would cause enormous disruption. Practical problems of attribution would lead to an increasingly litigious climate and airlines would be strongly opposed to being contractually obliged to deliver their part of service quality, just as they had refused to address reciprocity in SLAs. Problems with ground handlers often resulted from the poor terms they received from airlines.

Planning standards

14.221. A number of airlines suggested service standards should include BAA's planning standards. In response, BAA said that the purpose of its planning standards and more recently planning objectives had been to help its managers in assessing the capacity of existing facilities and in identifying the appropriate size of future facilities: it had never been BAA's understanding that such standards or the planning objectives were an immediate and blanket obligation and there was no regulatory obligation around them. While it gave careful weight to its planning objectives in considering future airport developments, it did not and should not give excessive weight to any individual planning assumption in determining the best overall solution. There was no less importance attached to the planning objectives than to the previous planning standards: rather, the new terminology better reflected their longstanding purpose. The reference to other factors was an overt recognition of the way that these targets and guidelines have been used in planning.

14.222. BAA saw three difficulties with linking the regulatory regime to the planning standards:

(a) the role of planning objectives was not to create an operational performance monitoring tool; SLAs had been developed for this purpose;

(b) operational performance in many of the areas covered by the planning objectives was a shared responsibility; and

(c) there were practical difficulties associated with assessing whether a planning standard/objective was being measured, for example the cost of monitoring queue times against a planning standard/objective for areas such as check-in, security or immigration. Calculation of space per passenger was highly dependent on assumptions as to traffic mix or dwell time, the latter of which was very difficult to measure in its own right.

BAA could reduce an airport's runway and terminal capacity to reduce demand so that the planning objectives were met but it did not believe this to be in the best interest of the airlines, consumers or themselves.

14.223. Service quality output was more important than any input figures—hence BAA's Q factor concept and why it did not believe planning objectives should have greater force.

14.224. Facilities in existing terminals were not, therefore, systematically compared to BAA's planning objectives since they were not and were never designed to be measures of operational performance: other operational performance measures such as SLAs and QSM had been developed for this purpose. It was also unclear whether such comparison would be helpful: for example, if passengers queued longer than the current objectives, this might be due to airline/handler check-in desk resourcing rather than to the number of desks.

14.225. The practical difficulties in developing a cost-effective performance measurement system were shown by the costs of obtaining even a reasonable sample of queuing times. There would also be difficulty in measuring the number of passengers on the concourse at any one time should BAA wish to compare space per passenger with a planning objective. Planning objectives were applied only to typical busy hours which did not occur in a controlled manner at airports, making a proper comparison of actual performance with planning objectives virtually impossible. Hence, it was more appropriate to use other performance output measures such as QSM. Passengers' views of departure lounge overcrowding or seat availability were more telling than the amount of space or number of the seats provided.

14.226. However, recognizing issues of competitive advantage as well as BAA's desire to provide the right level of facilities in each terminal to meet predicted passenger flows, BAA did undertake periodic capacity assessments which required as inputs its planning objectives and other assumptions such as traffic mix, process times etc. The output was an hourly passenger-flow rate which airport managers used to inform their decisions over the declared scheduling limits used in the slot allocation process, and the information was also used to inform investment plans.

14.227. BAA did not believe that it would be appropriate to attempt to generate a comparison of facilities in terminals with its planning objectives and include this within the improved CIP consultation process. It may, however, be possible to supplement the information in future investment programme consultations by setting out where it believed its analysis was showing additional capacity was required and where investment would need to be made.

14.228. We raised the issue of whether, unless planning standards were applied to existing as well as new assets, users of existing facilities (for example, the CTA) would be disadvantaged compared to new facilities (for example, T5) where they would be applied. BAA acknowledged that older facilities were never going to match newer facilities, but it tried to upgrade the old facilities as best as it could, for example converting the unacceptable in T2 to something that was tolerable: but, despite that, T2 (unless it was demolished and rebuilt) could never be of the same standard as T5. BAA would, however, maximize the possibilities of redevelopment and upgrading of all existing facilities at Heathrow—and where possible seek to offer airlines a degree of choice regarding space per passenger or location next to their alliance partners. Consultation was a necessary part of this process.

Comments on BA's detailed proposals

14.229. BAA also commented on BA's criticisms of the proposed Q factor and on BA's proposals for service standards. BAA said that it recognized the concerns about a scheme whereby service quality performance did not affect airport charges until between 13 and 24 months later; however, it said that operational managers would be focused on performance from the very start of the scheme as they would be very well aware it would have a financial impact, albeit deferred. As to averaging, BAA said that it was important to have a basket of measures in any Q factor to reflect the range of BAA's outputs: having set the maximum impact of a Q factor it would be inappropriate for performance of individual elements to give rise to penalties representing a large proportion of the maximum impact. It added there was a clear rationale for a symmetrical structure. The combination of a basket of measures, capping of individual elements and symmetry necessarily resulted in an averaging effect. BAA had sought to reduce the impact of averaging by retaining monthly rather than annual targets for many parts of the Q factor.

14.230. BAA said that it was disappointed and surprised to see the reference to tokenism by BA: BAA had taken a very constructive stance to developing a ground-breaking, practical and effective mechanism, which put at risk over 5 per cent of its post-tax profits. It certainly would not put airlines in a worse position: if they truly believed this was the case, it would withdraw its Q proposal.

14.231. It saw one further problem with BA's proposal, namely the need for a year's data for many of the elements listed (for example, number of monthly targets achieved for people movers). An approach whereby monthly airport charges invoices were adjusted using monthly service quality performance results would be very complex and administratively burdensome. BAA also regarded BA's proposal of targets of 100 per cent in some areas as unreasonable, and creating a very poor management incentive. The current infrastructure, for example, made a pier service target of 100 per cent unachievable, and an extremely large level of investment would be required to achieve it. Elsewhere, BA had proposed retaining existing percentage targets but changing the measurement definition to include planned maintenance: such a change in definition would require targets to be reduced. BA also referred to a six-minute generic standard, compared to the existing ten-minute queuing target of the SLA, also with significant resource implications. BA had also argued for inclusion of baggage systems and FEGP. BAA said that these should be excluded as they were not covered by core airport charges, and a single serviceability target contrasted with the range of measures which the joint working of BAA and BA concluded was necessary to judge the effectiveness of a particular baggage system. Were baggage system performance to be incorporated in a Q factor, then BAA would be forced to remove the financial incentives from the existing Heathrow baggage system SLAs to avoid double jeopardy.

14.232. The suggestion of a delay term was also surprising given the flaws in the quality of data and the degree to which BAA was responsible for performance. A sample survey showed that some 35 per cent of BA aircraft pushed back more than 10 minutes after schedule time of departure; but the time between a push-back request and actual time of push-back was very much smaller: 92 per cent of flights had no delay and only 2.7 per cent had delays of more than three to four minutes. Variability in push-back request time itself caused delay in granting a push-back request. Peaking of the demand on the system imposed by airlines who would not forgo their grandfather rights also caused such delays with more flights being scheduled at times than could be handled. Similarly, delays in the stack would be caused if the rate of arrival exceeded service rate of the airport system, but stack delay was not a true measure of delay as flights could be rerouted or slowed as an alternative to circling in the stack. The stack also made it possible for controllers to pack aircraft on the approach path because the controller could select an aircraft sequence to maximize the flow rate on to the runway. NATS had a tendency to prefer stack management rather than inbound capacity restrictions: hence slot delay was not an appropriate measure of BAA's performance or influence.

14.233. As to BA's medium-term proposals, BAA said that it already had an incentive to increase airport capacity if the demand existed as this would result in increased income. However, it had to take a realistic view as to the individual projects. As to the longer term, BAA referred to its previous proposals that charges should in some way be linked to delivery.

Conditions of use

14.234. We refer in Chapter 12 to complaints about the disclaimer in BAA's Conditions of Use. BAA said that the identical sentence was examined by the high court in the case of Monarch Airlines versus London Luton Airport in 1998. It was held that the exclusion clause was a fair and reasonable term to include, it being generally accepted in the market including the insurance market in that it had a clear meaning and that the insurance arrangements of the parties could be made on the basis of the contract. As regards the second sentence, BAA asserted that it was standard practice in commercial contracts to exclude economic loss arising as a result of negligence and breach of contract. Both parties would make their insurance arrangements on the basis of this condition. Under the law of negligence, it was not possible to cover for economic loss unless physical damage had been caused by the defendants negligence. Accordingly the airlines would not have been able to claim against the electricity company in the example referred to. The purpose of the conditions of use had been to promulgate charges information and operational requirements and restrictions with mutual rights and obligations. They were more appropriately considered as a licence setting out the terms on which an airline may use the airport. They were therefore more akin to the conditions of use for a public car park than to a contract for the supply of particular services. Where particular services were being provided, these were supplied by separate contracts for the reciprocal contracts and obligations.

Airport charging issues

Peak pricing

14.235. We raised the issue with BAA of whether the limited degree of peak pricing could adversely affect the public interest. BAA said that there were peak- and off-peak charges for both runway and parking elements; and Stansted had a seasonal peak- and off-peak component to its runway charge. But peak international passenger charges were precluded at Heathrow until T5 opens. However, introduction of peak passenger charges only at Stansted and Gatwick would pose several problems. Given the ban on peak passenger charges at Heathrow there would be increased risk of legal challenge to any extension of this principal to Gatwick and Stansted; having a peak passenger charge at Gatwick and Stansted but not Heathrow would lead to perverse pricing differentials with higher peak prices at those two airports than at Heathrow; and peak passenger charges were very unpopular with airlines who usually claimed they had little choice but to operate at peak times.

Aircraft parking charges

14.236. We note in Chapter 12 complaints about the basis of aircraft parking charges, based on average taxiing times. BAA said that an average had to be used because of poor data. If the average was too high, short-haul operators would benefit as a greater proportion of their parking time would be free. It was not apparent that T4 airlines would be systematically disbenefited, T3 airlines having longer taxi times when departing towards the West on R27L. T4 was also well placed for BA's maintenance area which would reduce fuel burn. Hence, there was little evidence average taxi times were discriminatory against T4 as this could only be established by looking at long- versus short-haul operators; different runway usage patterns; and other factors. It suspected that BA's estimate of its savings were actual times to be used also did not assume the yield equalization required for any change to the taxiing allowance and the savings were therefore miscalculated.

Pricing at Stansted

14.237. We note in Chapter 12 complaints about charges at Stansted. BAA commented that predatory pricing had been investigated several times by the CAA, the MMC and the DGIV and no evidence ever found. The fact that Stansted's tariffs and average revenue yield had both increased since these investigations was in itself substantial evidence that predatory pricing was unlikely. However, BAA had a policy decision never to charge below variable costs and indeed in a single-till environment short-run variable costs net of retail revenues were extremely low. Stansted airport as a whole now met its full operating costs and was forecast to be making real pre-tax returns of 7.5 per cent by around 2010.

Non-regulated charges

14.238. In Chapters 12 and 13 we summarized a number of detailed complaints about activities not included in airport charges.

Ground handling

14.239. We refer in Chapters 12 and 13 to a number of complaints concerning ground handling, first, the requirement, to be allowed to provide services at Heathrow in any terminal, for a minimum percentage of business in that terminal. BAA stated that this condition was intended as a protection against operational difficulty at Heathrow, arguably the most congested airport in the world, to avoid the unworkable congestion and safety risks that could arise from a plethora of small handling agents operating in a confined space. The condition was effectively waived if the new handler was able to demonstrate that taking over an airline's ground handling operation at a terminal would not add to congestion on the ramp or the baggage operation. It had only been cited in one case, where the existing airlines conveyed the very strong view that the proposed new handler would indeed worsen congestion.

14.240. On a number of other issues raised, BAA noted there had been a number of factors which had affected the overall size and shape of the market for third party handling, including BA's acquisition of Cityflier, which had led to its operations being absorbed into the BA operation; the takeover of Virgin Sun by Air 2000 and the general downturn in traffic following 11 September. The loss of economies of scale whilst regrettable was a reflection largely of airline market conditions which BAA had little or no control over. GAL had worked with and in partnership with the airport users committee which had a formal consultative role under EC legislation. The selection criteria used had been agreed with the Airport Users Committee (AUC) who also played a significant part in the process, for example organizational standing, resources and training, relevant experience, financial etc. Following an initial assessment against these criteria the AUC had been asked to indicate which of the organizations they would wish to see appointed. The eventual appointment was made taking account of the AUC's views and the results of the initial assessment. GAL was, however, concerned that financial arrangements could have a broader impact on the operation of the airport and level of service, and was currently attempting to facilitate a debate with the airline community aimed at addressing this. However, it was not possible for GAL to police the business plans of ground handling companies, but reviews were undertaken on service and operational issues. It had no jurisdiction over issues of predatory pricing. As to the fourth ground handler, the selection process was now close to completion. The CAA had previously rejected GAL's proposals to limit the number of handlers to three.

14.241. On suggestions BAA would only deal with ground handlers on an individual airport basis, BAA said that the approach taken at individual airports towards ground handling and a wide range of other matters sought to strike a healthy balance between following group-wide policies while taking local circumstances into account. BA said it recognized handling agents had a critical role to play and they were already involved in discussions about airport development and operation. It believed it had adopted the correct general approach.

14.242. On the setting of service standards in ground handling licences, BAA said that it was important to set service standards at its airports to help ensure service provision to passengers was maintained at appropriate levels. These were encompassed within agreements each handling company was required to sign, and covered issues such as baggage delivery performance, check-in queuing etc. Handlers should refer to these minimum standards acceptable to BAA before entering into contracts. There were no specific financial penalties within the agreements relating to poor performance, although there was an escalation process which could ultimately lead to termination of a contract. The escalation process was intended to ensure specific issues of performance difficulties could be identified and plans put in place to resolve them. As noted above, however, BAA could not impose penalties if there was failure to meet the standards: merely threaten withdrawal of a licence, with adverse consequences for the airlines and risk of action in the European courts.

14.243. On delays in finalizing ground handling licences, BAA acknowledged that the agreement and signing of handling licences had been a slow and arduous process for the main ramp and baggage handlers, including BA and Virgin and at Gatwick GHI and Service Air. The latter were largely due to the fact that both handlers were already operating at Gatwick and there was no pressing need to conclude documentation. A further complication was stripping out of property elements which were placed under separate agreements, the work on which was largely complete.

14.244. On the conditions for rent of check-in desks, BAA said that operational accommodation such as desks was often on a one-month notice period. However, the terms of occupancy were subject to individual negotiation and agreement: it was important the handling agent advised the airport management team on its particular requirements bearing in mind its own contractual arrangements with airlines.

14.245. On rents for cargo facilities, BAA said that it was not the case that cargo tonnages at Gatwick had fallen: rather, they rose by 9 per cent in 2001/02 and 24 per cent over Q2 as a whole. It also noted there had been no significant deterioration in demand for transit shed warehouse accommodation, nor had it experienced any voids. However, cargo volumes had been affected by 11 September and guide prices had been reduced from £12.50 to £12 reflecting the difficulties experienced by this sector (guideline rents for warehouses had increased from £9 to £12 over seven years, a compound growth rate of 4 per cent a year).

14.246. Rents for business lounges were also subject to the same approach of published prices, but again each was subject to individual negotiations; BAA tried to operate a level playing field and did not distinguish between airlines and handling agents. Rent reviews were negotiated individually in line with open market rental value; all reviews had been agreed by negotiation.

Check-in desk charges

14.247. On cost recovery of check-in desks, BAA said that the operator bore the risk. GAL had never fully recovered costs although cost recovery remained its long-term intention. Whatever BAA's charging policy on desks, the agent had to charge the airline; if the agent structured his agreement to pass through desk charges this was entirely a matter of his choice.

14.248. As to the North Terminal check-in desk used by BA, BA had its own systems and these desks were incapable of common use by other handling agents. Other desks in the North Terminal benefited from common user terminal equipment and were capable of common use. The total cost to be recovered had therefore been split equally to arrive at a cost per desk across the terminals; only the costs associated with desks on A and B had gone into the calculation of the hourly charge in the North Terminal.

14.249. BAA acknowledged that with the present charging by row, variation in utilization of different rows resulted in higher charges on relatively under-utilized rows and lower charges on more highly utilized rows. Under-utilization had been recognized in certain circumstances with reductions in liability agreed with users. The issue had been addressed through rebate/reduced charges agreed with handling agents to account for low utilization.

14.250. However, the hourly charges it was proposing to introduce would reflect only the differences in the types of check-in desks depending whether they were fully mechanical or semi-mechanical, location and queuing depths etc. Otherwise, recovery of costs would be dependent on actual use: only if one desk was used for a greater number of hours would the cost recovered be higher. BAA said that it was recognized that hourly charging was the fairest means of charging. BAA believed that hourly charging would assist new entrant ground handlers by creating a level playing field on charges for check in. This did alter the balance of charges, hence, while some of the Gatwick community had welcomed the proposal, others had objected. BAA had, however, now deferred hourly charging until winter 2002.

14.251. BAA acknowledged a number of assumptions that had gone into the hourly charging calculations which had been openly communicated to airlines and handling agents alike, and for this reason made provision that revised hourly charges could be introduced on one month's notice in the circumstances of significant over- or under-recovery. If not significant it would be carried forward to subsequent years: hence there was no incentive to understate usage and over-recover revenues.

14.252. BAA told us that it had historically charged handling agents for the use of check-in desks; in the most recent consultation with airlines, the AOC confirmed it wanted this arrangement to continue. It was unaware of any approach from an airline wishing to be charged direct for check in desks on zone A.

14.253. BAA said the principle of lower rates of charges when amortization had expired was agreed and would be the basis on which charges were levied. The discussion with BA on lines E and F were ongoing and transparency would be provided as part of the process of concluding this discussion with BA. On the issue of transparency generally, GAL produced annual pricing statements on specified activities. Further evidence on the consultation process included several examples where GAL had invited further discussion; hence, it was not clear to BAA where it had moved away from previous transparent arrangements. It was not aware of any outstanding requests for information.

14.254. BAA said that it was correct to say that the different basis of calculating non-check-in desk licence fees had applied at Heathrow relative to Gatwick and Stansted: Heathrow using a site fee plus amortization plus outgoings, and the latter a market rate forming part of rental guidelines. BAA said that non-check-in desks could be described as both relevant and specified activities, hence, there was a requirement to be transparent and the inclusion in the rental guidelines at GAL and of STAL with revisions in accordance with Property Challenge criteria, ie market-based. These also formed part of the annual consultation process for specified facility charges. BAA believed that the market rate approach was the correct one, especially since desks were in many cases used for commercial purposes and customers had a degree of choice: at Gatwick the charging on non-check-in desks had been market-based since at least privatization. Discussions had been taking place with a view to changing the Heathrow approach to market rates, with transitional relief where this resulted in any increased charges and incorporation of increases into the rental formula.

Rents

14.255. BAA said that overall rents had grown by 1 to 3 per cent a year for offices, 3 to 6 per cent a year for apron accommodation, 2 to 6 per cent a year for industrial/cargo and 5 to 6 per cent a year for CIP facilities; applying Heathrow guidelines to Gatwick would have produced mostly higher rentals for a range of projections. The criteria on which BAA's rental policy was based needed to be market related—it was inappropriate to review it only in line with the handling agents profitability, it must reflect the climate across all business types. There was no evidence to support any allegation of curtailing supply: it was also not clear how BAA was failing to meet its transparency obligations.

14.256. As to lack of explanation of how GAL had reviewed its rental levels, BAA said that revised rental guidelines had been produced at Gatwick annually and new guideline rents openly communicated to main customers. It had recently circulated a customer report supporting its approach to the April 2002 guidelines, in response to requests for greater explanation on the basis of setting guide price rents. However, it re-emphasized that all rents at Gatwick were subject to individual negotiation and published guide prices were merely a guideline to assist the negotiation process.

14.257. BAA said that the 53 per cent increase in rents at Gatwick related to the quantum of rents rather than individual rentals, and was in the main due to the supply of new infrastructure and buildings not allowed for in the projections. Growth by asset varied from property to property but all were significantly below 53 per cent. The trend in rentals would have been no different if the Heathrow formula had been applied.

14.258. BAA said that CIP lounge rents at Heathrow were covered in their entirety by the formula: an approach which had been maintained throughout Q3 and applied to virtually all accommodation within the terminals. Perimeter properties were mainly on an open market rental basis; where these leases included provision for rent reviews, such reviews were generally to open market rental value and required agreement between the parties or in absence, reference for independent determination: it did not believe any reviews had been referred to arbitration other than in the instance of HAL and bmi jointly agreeing to refer the value of a stand to expert opinion upon a new letting.

14.259. On Virgin's complaint about the conditions BAA sought to negotiate when Virgin wished to share a CIP facility, BAA said that it was entitled to negotiate to reach agreement to realize some of the increased value to Virgin for itself: the likely loss of retailing, particularly if the direct lift were used, was pointed out as an opening negotiating position, which it believed was understood by the airline. It would not be fair or reasonable for BAA to be forced to accept changes to its financial detriment, which would ultimately be passed on to other airlines, while other parties made additional profit. However, it agreed to moderate its claim, but negotiations lapsed for other reasons.

14.260. On complaints about access via retail outlets to CIP facilities in T4, BAA said that this complaint related to designs 14 to 22 years ago. The design of the extension, developed shortly after the terminal was open, would not have permitted a direct route through to the CIP lounge. At the time the extension was designed, passengers were also still subject to outbound passport controls, hence it was not in BAA's gift to provide a short cut security route. The point currently made by BA was not raised in 1991 or 1996 reviews.

14.261. BA controlled most of the check-in desks at T4 and if it wished to reduce the walking distances experienced by its first class passengers it could simply reallocate the economy desks closest to the central zone to first class.

14.262. BAA had, however, considered requests from BA for direct access to the CIP lounge, in the light of additional capital operating costs, the option of relocating the first class desks to meet BA's needs, and what BAA appeared to acknowledge were legitimate concerns over loss of retail income, which would work through to higher charges under the single till. It noted a similar issue had arisen in the context of the current T1 future concept project and BAA had incorporated a separate route from the new premium check-in area to the international departures lounge close to the CIP lounge.

Waste

14.263. There were complaints about arrangements and charges for waste disposal. Refuse disposal was one of the items listed by BAA in Appendix 3.2 of the last MMC report as covered by airport charges but BAA argued that did not cover airlines' waste oils and lubrication or waste food off aircraft. It was fairly normal practice for tenants to pay for their own waste disposal. To the degree this had been free in the UK and charged elsewhere, BAA had experienced tankering of waste—waste for an outbound flight being brought back to the UK to avoid controls elsewhere.

14.264. BAA said that it wished to undertake a review of its current waste management policy and charging methodologies. The overall aim would be to establish a uniform operating and consultation procedure; a data monitoring system; and a charging policy to facilitate cost recovery and provide incentives under a polluter pays principle.

14.265. At HAL prior to 1997 the airport provided a foreign object debris (FOD) and pollutants, oil and lubricants (POL) bins for all aircraft stands, which was continually abused by users who refused to segregate their wastes at source and led to duty of care issues. New procedures were introduced in 1997 and POL bins removed, empty oil cans being placed in the FOD bins and part full oil bins to be disposed of by the producer.

14.266. At Gatwick, GALs waste contractor in 2001 received a prohibition notice for transporting waste oils in an unacceptable manner. Attempts to address the issue by introducing systems which separated the oil from the can failed due to misuse by users. When the prohibition notice was served, GAL worked with the waste contractor to identify a compliant method of collection and disposal. The solution adopted was relocation to a single managed airport waste collection site, for oil waste to be deposited at that site in a compliant manner whence GAL's waste contract managed and disposed of it at no direct additional cost to the user, and GAL taking responsibility for legal compliance for the airport waste collection site. A consultation meeting was arranged to communicate this, all airlines and aircraft maintenance companies agreeing in principle to the proposal and accepting the marginal increase in travelling time to the site. At no time was the waste collection service suspended.

14.267. Subsequently, BA asked GAL to consider the possibility of installing a dedicated facility within BA's waste areas at stand 59, BA not wishing to use the centralized facility due to additional travelling time. GAL agreed to do so for the sole use of BA (at no additional direct charge) provided facilities were used in the manner that was compliant with GAL's requirements. This was not an attempt to shift responsibility for compliance to BA since the airline already had a responsibility under the duty of care to ensure it disposed of any waste in a safe and compliant manner. The conditions were an attempt by GAL to ensure the site was used in such a manner. BA had raised a number of issues; a trial arrangement had been agreed and the equipment was due to be installed shortly. GAL's waste contractor would collect the oil waste from the site and transport to it to the airport waste collection site for disposal. It would also monitor the use of the site to ensure it conformed with GAL's instructions. If the trial was successful BA would formally agree to GAL's conditions.

14.268. On increase in terminal waste charges, a review of HAL's waste contracts showed that cost was being under-recovered by approximately £200,000, and rates needed to be increased by some 50 per cent. Some seven weeks' notice was given on that. As part of the waste management review undertaking, BAA was prepared to include review of the consultation process on waste charging issues to ensure users had adequate time to adapt to any new proposals. It would undertake to provide transparency on the charges if it had not already done so. However, the element of check-in charges associated with waste/refuge collection was identifiable with the check-in desk charge calculations.

14.269. It was BAA's policy to ensure that it delivered a value for money service to all airport users, which had meant charging the users the cost to BAA and not a commercial rate which would be significantly higher. The rates were based on direct costs apportioned to each business area in a transparent manner and charged according to the amount of waste collected from each source.

14.270. BAA's view therefore was that separate charges for aircraft waste disposal should now be instigated to provide incentives to minimize waste; assist with safety FOD issues; provide fairness to users (user pays principle); and help with its general neighbourhood obligations on environmental issues. Hence it had been signalling to users for some time the desirability of a waste disposal charge, and had proposed amending the airports charges definition correspondingly. A question of compensation did not arise. It subsequently added that its charging strategy had not yet been fully developed. It would support a defined list of operating procedures for waste collection on airports; where there was no choice for the customer but to use BAA's managed collection services, it would undertake to provide full transparency for any direct charges levied.

Staff car parking

14.271. On complaints about charges for staff car parking, BAA said that BA's analysis of staff car parking was simplistic given the dynamics of staff car parking; charges were not levied on a per diem basis and were not time-related. Charges were based on total cost divided by the total estimated consumption, ie the number of passes. BA recently raised the issue of reduced charges for part time staff, but BAA explained that within the pricing mechanisms the consequence of this would be lower charges for some passes, but higher charges for others.

14.272. The nature of the aviation business was of peaks by both hour of day and seasonally; HAL needed to provide sufficient spaces to satisfy peak demand and to allow for overlaps of staff levels as shifts changed. Hence the main cost driver was not time parked, but the need for space to be available when required. Hence part-time employees put exactly the same demands on the provision of space as full time employees. Significant proportions of cost were also incurred in provision of coaching services to and from car parks. Differential time-based charges would also require suitable control mechanisms, which could cost £1.5 million plus annual operating costs: the community had been very reluctant to accept further increases in parking charges. Hence, the present method of charging was, administratively, reasonably cost-effective and gave the customer greater flexibility.

14.273. Heathrow was significantly under-recovered, £4 million over five years; airlines had full flexibility to apply for or return passes to match seasonal or business demands. Allocated costs included rates. Allocation of constabulary costs was based on rateable value: it has been discussed with the AOC pricing committee at Heathrow and to include all police costs within airport charges would mean the whole burden of these costs would fall on airlines rather than be spread across all airport users. Heathrow prices compared favourably against other local car parks. The comparison of annual car parking costs showed Heathrow to be some 10 per cent of Brewer Street, and below or comparable with areas around Heathrow. Consultation on recent charge increases did take place with the AOC Secretary who should have communicated the price increase to users; users did have the opportunity to return rover passes and not incur the increase. Rover passes were for public car park facilities and therefore separate from staff car park permits. Their prices were set on a more market-based approach and reflected the very high demand for public car parking within the Heathrow CTA.

FEGP

14.274. On complaints about the basis of charging for FEGP, BAA said that the time-based system had been in operation at Heathrow for ten years; moving to a meter-charging basis would be possible but expensive and in overall terms increase cost per unit in the order of 8 per cent. Charging would be more accurate but costs merely be moved around between airlines: there had to date been no response from the AOC pricing committee who had been asked for their views on metering. The example quoted by BA was not representative. The current method of charging came about partly because of practicality and cost, but also charging for time acted as a direct incentive for the airlines to use more environmentally friendly services. BA senior operations personnel had agreed this point in previous pricing consultations. It took the total cost and divided it by total estimated aircraft parking units to derive an average cost per time unit: it had not therefore taken account of the consumption characteristics of different aircraft types. BA's point as regards taxiing time applied equally to charging for parking. A move to more accurate time-based charging would simply lead to a reduction in the denominator and an increase in average cost per time unit. It also required the upgrade of HAL ground systems and that aircraft be fitted with aircraft communications and reporting system equipment (ACARS). Even for metering, the majority of equipment in use recorded the time FEGP was being used and not the power consumed: hence operators of larger aircraft would still be favoured. BA's calculations on savings also needed to be treated with a very high degree of caution, being based on a sample period of one day.

Water and sewerage

14.275. On complaints about charges for water and sewerage, BAA said that in BA-solely-occupied areas, BA could provide its own infrastructure if it wished. It further argued that water and sewerage charges were cost-based, and were under-recovered against the fully costed charge. It was the case that the assets were also included in the base on which the airport earned an overall return, but that did not mean users were being charged twice, only that the income earned and costs associated with water and other activities was taken into account when deriving the residual allowable charges income.

Wayleaves

14.276. On complaints about introduction of new charges for wayleaves, BAA said that it was perfectly normal practice for any landlord to charge a wayleave for running cabling across his property. Tenants had a choice between using the BAA infrastructure product, or their own.

14.277. BAA was, however, examining the viability of establishing an improved charging strategy for wayleaves. BAA said that rampant cable installations by airport occupants/tenants had led to changes to the fabric of the building and non-removal of redundant and life-expired cabling which may not comply with fire, health and safety instructions, and increasingly poor documentation and housekeeping arrangements. BAA claimed it must improve on this situation, to incentivize occupants to be more efficient and responsible with the increasingly limited cable-storage space available and most importantly to be compliant with fire, health and safety guidelines. It believed that installation and removal of cabling with accommodation which was specially demised to its property tenants was adequately covered within its existing agreements, but it was reviewing its policy on the installation and removal of cables in BAA cable trays within ceiling voids and ducts outside demised premises and was considering whether to have a consistent approach across its airports. Use of common infrastructure would allow customers to use existing circuits within the ceiling voids and ducts without the need for laying their own cables.

14.278. It also noted that a charge of £1 per metre run a year had been in existence for some considerable time. This policy was supported through GAL's rental policy, ie where a tenant required additional rights beyond those granted within its existing leases, it should pay a market consideration for the grant of such rights; GAL regarded it as fair and reasonable to negotiate an appropriate consideration for the grant of such rights. Its charges covered the granting of rights over land owned and maintained by GAL; a management fee to cover documentation, monitoring, access requirements and space; provision of sufficient cable trays and other infrastructure; security arrangements and controls in respect of contractors and health and safety, protective and preventative measures.

14.279. BA had asked to lay significant amounts of cabling to floodwire the North Terminal and provide BA with an Ethernet network: BAA said it appeared that BA was arguing for free installation rights, contrary to established and accepted principles of land ownership. The right should not be treated as a free good. Finally, BA was seeking rights in addition to its granted 'standard lease' rights by wanting to lay entirely new infrastructure outside areas demised to it at Gatwick: GAL's view was that standard leases would not grant a tenant automatic rights to lay new infrastructure across large areas which were not defined or specified in any way: any other view could lead to an unsustainable conclusion that any third party tenant could expect or demand rights over land not in its ownership or defined.

Fuel fees

14.280. On complaints about fuel levies BAA said that Gatwick Airport Service Hydrant Company Ltd (GASHCO) was formed in 1994 to facilitate the raising of external finance for new development on airport. It owned and operated the storage and hydrant facilities of the airport and was obliged to allow a supplier to use the facilities. Its fees and GAL's throughput levy were shown separately on invoices to customers to ensure transparency. Changes to the throughput levy were advised to the airlines annually through the specified activities consultation process: BAA did not therefore accept there had been no involvement or discussion with airlines. Although not a cost-based charge in the sense of being directly derived from actual annual costs, it said the levy took into account both actual costs and opportunity costs. The latter included rental forgone from land including underground pipelines and loss of revenues from GALs inability to build aircraft and commercial facilities at or near storage facilities.

14.281. Subsequently, however, it told us that there were very few costs associated with the levy: the levy was on a turnover basis, in effect a commercial rent, not related to costs; it could be justified by reference to opportunity costs, but that had not been done. This was, however, no different to practice at the time of the previous report (or before that); meterage charges were custom and practice at virtually every airport worldwide. Prices had been established by reference to annual increase in RPI for several years at Gatwick. BAA therefore believed that the throughput fee represented a fair charge for the facilities provided. In a single-till environment, if the fuel levy did not exist, BAA's income short fall would be met by an increase in airport charges, which would be borne by all airlines using the airport, rather than those who used the fuel system. This would disadvantage those airlines who chose to fuel their aircraft elsewhere. BAA believed that this would be less efficient than the current arrangement, transferring cost burden to airlines not using the facilities and resulting in airlines who did not take fuel subsidizing those that do. The levying of fuel charges on the throughput basis was standard at airports throughout the world.

14.282. The current transparent charging structure had served the industry well. London airports had some of the lowest fuel prices in the world: Gatwick and Heathrow were about the 11th and 12th cheapest airports for jet fuel prices out of about 130 or so airports compared. Gatwick also had one of the highest levels of competition and one of the best developed and most efficient fuel infrastructures.

14.283. As regards Stansted, BAA invested in infrastructure as necessary to support the growing business at Stansted: it was the only one of BAA's three south-east airports that owned the infrastructure and it was entirely appropriate and fair that this was recovered via the throughput charge. Stansted had consulted fully with its airline customers on this issue: there was no evidence to support the allegation of excessive capex on the fuel infrastructure. It had said to the airlines that the annuity rate per litre would be reduced once the shortfall (£3.1 million in March 2001) had been recovered. It did not accept the argument that under-recovery of the capital element of the fee for prior periods should not be carried forward. Its formula did not work on the basis the rates of return were applied strictly to each year or indeed to any five-year period, rather they were smoothed over five- to ten-year periods. Such smoothing was necessary to increase prices gradually, especially when assets were under-utilized in early years. Recovery in later years was therefore required, otherwise the asset would never be fully remunerated. BAA also noted that Stansted did not achieve breakeven for specified activities as a whole in any of the five years to 2000/01; the all-in price of fuel at Stansted was among the cheapest in the world; this was a competitive market and airlines had the option of tankering and could choose to take up fuel at the most competitive end airport—hence, Ryanair had started to take up fuel equally at Dublin and Stansted as a result of suppliers giving the airlines substantial reductions on fuel costs and would do so elsewhere; and in a single-till environment it was Stansted's total income from chargeable activities which underlay its price cap. Airlines would naturally try to cherry-pick charges to reduce costs, but in order to achieve its allowable income the airport would need to recover any shortfall from other activities, in the event of the fuel levy being reduced. BAA believed that it was appropriate for Stansted to earn a reasonable rate of return on its investment and infrastructure within the single till. BAA's regulated business performance had not demonstrated profits systematically exceeding allowable returns over any regulatory period.

Extending the scope of regulated charges

14.284. BAA said that it had always been clear about what was charged for separately, and this policy had been unchanged since privatization.

14.285. Seeking to include all operational activities in airport charges, on the other hand, would be difficult to implement and incorrect from an economic standpoint. Many were for activities which airlines had differing requirements for, so to have a common charge could be discriminatory; BAA would find it impossible to react to airline needs on some of these services and facilities if they were defined as airport charges and had no separate revenue stream. This was particularly the case where the requirements were not anticipated or anticipated but not costed at the time of the quinquennial review, for example additional check-in desks or baggage enhancements. This could also conflict with ground handling legislation and destroy the competitive market in baggage handling, since only the airport operator could levy such charges. Hence, BAA took the view that separate charges were appropriate, but usually checked with the CAA.

14.286. Following discussions with IATA, which concluded that Heathrow transfer baggage was the main change of scope for airport charges, BAA undertook to review the scope of facilities and services covered by airport charges. The position on inclusion of local ANS was being dealt with separately by the CAA who, it was believed, was consulting with the industry to establish if there was a common viewpoint. By the time this was finished and the matter determined by the DfT, it was likely the current regulatory review would already have set airport charges for 2003–08: hence, there was little scope to change the current arrangement. However, BAA said that should users wish to change the scope of activities covered by airport charges BAA was always willing to consider these provided that there was a clear majority airline view requesting any change; that airport charges were adjusted to take account of any lost revenue or additional costs (hence this could only be done as part of the quinquennial review); that no perverse incentives were introduced; that other stakeholders were not comprised by any changes (for example, abolishing utility charges would clearly be perverse in economic terms as well as being environmentally unfriendly); and that the expansion of BAA responsibility did not tend to reduce competition and the provision of services (for example, baggage handling).

14.287. On including ANS within charges, BAA thought it relevant to note that NATS itself was 46 per cent owned by a consortium of UK airlines, led by a former BA director. The consortium had a management control of NATS. They and not BAA had direct responsibility for the effective management of airport ATC. To put BAA in the position where it was paying airlines for airport ATC delays, while airlines were responsible for the company that provided the ATC would create a structural moral hazard. This would simply be compounded if airport ATC provided by NATS was incorporated in BAA's cost base.

- *Transfer baggage systems*

14.288. Since our last report, BAA said that it had significantly improved Heathrow transfer baggage systems and introduced a per passenger TSC. However, BAA claimed that management of this process took excessive amounts of management time for both the airlines and the airport.

14.289. BAA agreed with the general airline view that transfer baggage infrastructure should be included within the scope of airport charges. There were varying views among the airlines, however, as to how much of the infrastructure (particularly the transfer baggage system (TBS) tunnel) should be dealt with in this way.

14.290. BAA would like to move to a per bag charge for all transfer baggage infrastructure at Heathrow (including the TBS tunnel) from 1 April 2008, to deal with remuneration of all baggage infrastructure in an integrated manner.

14.291. Following the TIFGAH agreement on 27 May, BAA intended to incorporate TSC within airport charges from 1 April 2003 onwards with limited transparency available via an apportionment of the passenger charge. However, BAA also believed that BA should continue to meet its rental obligations on the TBS tunnel until migration to T5 in 2008.

14.292. BAA believed that the TIFGAH group had been driven too much on cost and not on transfer baggage performance. BAA advocated the revision of the governance of the transfer product at Heathrow to a group whose members were drawn from an airline/airport operational or customer service.

14.293. The remuneration of direct baggage systems would form the subject of separate discussions with airlines with the aim of implementing and changes as part of the next regulatory review.

Specified activities

14.294. We noted in paragraph 14.19 that BAA was currently required to produce annual statements on the cost, revenues and basis of charges of a number of specified services. BAA agreed with a CAA suggestion that the CC consider whether disclosure of information be best handled by the current arrangement, or through an enhanced information disclosure and consultation commitment. It listed a number of additional charges outside of airport charges which had been informally outlined to users. (Revenue from specified activities amounted to £126 million, from other charges to airlines excluded from this requirement £77 million in 2000/01.) It stated that for all new charging activities it would ensure there was full consultation and transparency on the pricing methodology, and for market-based charges they were fair and reasonable and linked to recognized external market benchmarks. It was also willing to undertake that the total revenues from all specified activities and other similar charging activities were capped in real terms on a per passenger basis.

14.295. BAA proposed categorization into cost base and market-based charges; the former either using PCR or simpler direct cost plus percentage overhead. Cost-based charges would be retained for financially significant activities such as check-in desks and utilities including FEGP; and could include charges for transfer of baggage (TIFGAH) if agreement was not reached to include this activity within airport charges. The market-based approach would be used for charges for which a competitive rate could be readily obtained (benchmarked where possible), and other charges which could be increased in line with RPI. This was subject to consultation with the CAA and IATA. It would ring-fence the forecast revenues from these activities with a revenue cap based on passenger yield linked to inflation. (The approach was similar to that of our proposed U factor, except the U factor would have linked the cost to airport charges, the BAA proposal to a separate form of price control.)

14.296. As to whether there was adequate transparency in the information it provided on specified activities, BAA said that its PCR cost allocation system was introduced to deal with the conditions, and ensured that costs were allocated on a consistent basis for activities and prevented double counting of cost to more than one activity. Considerable time had been spent going through the specified activities statements with the airlines and explaining all the numbers with them. BAA was, therefore, disappointed about users complaining about the extent of information. It was not aware of any instance where reasonable request for further information or clarification has been denied. It believed that confusion of users about the PCR cost allocation system and how this related to the single till formula for airport charges and overall rates of return for the regulated airports could be explained by staff changes within the consultative committees. It had offered individual coaching sessions for new members to explain pricing methodology and how the single till operated: if a user wanted to see the full apportionment of overheads, this would in theory be possible. The PCR system, as had been explained to users, was fully reconciled with the statutory accounts and independently audited, particularly recently in the context of its use in the dual till. There was certainly no question of double counting: under the single till all revenues from these other charges were credited against airport charges anyway.

14.297. It believed information provided to users was sufficient to discharge its responsibilities under the specified facilities conditions, and the CAA had never queried the quality, accuracy or sufficiency of the data provided. It believed queries by users had always been dealt with in a timely fashion and as comprehensively as possible, within the bounds of commercial confidentiality.

14.298. It believed airlines (and BA in particular) would always try and cherry pick charges to challenge on the basis that too much cost was allocated. They would always take the view that was most beneficial to themselves, which may not be in the interest of the airport community in total, however, which was BAA's interest. Within the single-till framework, and with a cost-allocation system which was independently audited and based on consistently applied allocation bases, if costs were taken out of charging for one activity they would reappear in another: as all activities were taken into account in the single till there was no overall gain to be had by forcing costs into one or other activity. Recent reviews of the system on behalf of the CAA confirmed this was the case.

14.299. However, the CAA conditions did not require charges to be set with regard to costs. Where charges were not established in relation to costs, BAA was obliged to provide a statement of principles on the basis of which the charges had been set, with which it believed it fully complied. Where an external market for any product or service could be established, a market-based price competition was therefore theoretically superior to a cost base.

Other complaints

Charges to disabled passengers

14.300. BAA shared the concern in Chapter 13 about any instances where passengers with reduced mobility were directly charged: it did not believe this was an acceptable practice. This was made clear in the European airports' voluntary commitment on passenger service. However, a very small number of airlines persisted in directly charging passenger of reduced mobility, which led to the suggestion a better approach would be for airports to organize the assistance services to these passengers. A trial at Gatwick, however, had failed; a sufficient proportion of airlines when faced with higher charges resulting from a better specified assistance service indicated they would prefer to continue with their existing arrangements. BAA remained concerned about a centrally organized approach, as the assistance service had always formed part of ground handling services procured by airlines. Airlines were always going to be in the best position to determine the appropriate assistance required as they had the initial contact with those passengers. However, such an approach could not prevent individual airlines from adopting their own arrangements for the assistance service and continuing to charge directly should they wish to. This was also a matter on which the European Commission had been consulting. In conclusion, although understanding the concerns expressed, BA did not believe that a centrally organized service was necessarily the appropriate solution.

Car hire

14.301. A number of complaints were made about arrangements for car hire (see Chapter 13). BAA said that all car hire contracts were tendered on the open market or sometimes negotiated individually. This process ensured that the market assessed the value of the on-airport rental locations. The only additional costs imposed were for backup areas, concession fee and utility charges. The MAG was based on 80 per cent of the concessionaire's own forecast; with a predetermined threshold relating to the passenger clause of 15 per cent: so if the threshold was met there was still a 5 per cent gain for the concessionaire on their original forecasts.

14.302. Historically, most concession fees were payable on gross turnover, including fuel, which was stated at the outset as a contractual stipulation and should have been taken account of by the bidder (more recently fuel had been excluded). Similarly, car rental companies had always been responsible for road fund licence fees. In 1998 the Government announced this fee would be charged based on the fuel efficiency of the car, this was an additional cost to the operators which they chose to pass on to the customer, and then included in the concessionable sales, and the car rentals company paid their concession fees on this.

14.303. As regards pricing, BAA's policy was designed to ensure the customer was charged no more than a comparable downtown location. The requirement only applied to walk-up prices, a small part of the market, the rest being highly competitive. It was nonsense to suggest BAA was artificially holding prices high. BAA only set maximum prices, allowing companies to discount from that price if they risk.

14.304. As to Stansted, BAA had gained planning permission for a new car rental turnaround facility, designed with input from the car rental companies and to be complete by spring 2003. The car rental companies were responsible for managing the health and safety of their employees and BAA tried in every way to assist.

14.305. As to the basis of the concession fee, historically car rental companies preferred negotiating, although BAA insisted on tenders from time to time and tenders still made up the majority of contracts awarded. It provided a clear indication of market forces. Tenders allowed access to the market and in a fair and transparent way. Tenders on the basis of price were the most suitable way of rationing scarce resource of land, and if higher than elsewhere this could only be because of desirability of airport locations. There were also many off-airport operators. Profitability to BAA was bound to be high, since the assets and costs involved were low; if charges were set only to cover costs, there would be a rent acquisition by the companies with no benefit to users (the same principle applied to other retail facilities), and—under the single till—higher airport charges.

14.306. BAA provided the basic facilities required to fulfil the car rental products, but companies may invest in improving the product to suit their customer requirements. The contracts were tendered or negotiated based on their investment being written off over the period of the contract to ensure their writing off investment met their own accounting requirements. It expected the concessionaire to write off all capex over the life of the contract. If concessionaires had a sizeable investment then the contract period may be extended. If an operator went bankrupt, the current provision allowed for BAA to get hold of the site for a nominal sum rapidly; the value of any assets would be offset by outstanding tender fees. These terms were included in the tender, but BAA sometimes took a pragmatic view, allowing the assets to be recovered.

14.307. The concession agreement was made up of a fixed element and a variable element; the fixed element was broken out of the total concession income according to a split agreed between concessionaires and BAA. This element was not directly related to property rents: some concessionaires preferred a higher level of fixed costs than variable and others vice versa.

General aviation

14.308. On complaints about facilities for GA, ie international business, private and air taxi traffic, BAA said that Stansted had arguably the best dedicated GA facilities of any major south-east airport. There were two fixed base operators whose primary business was to supply facilities and services to general aviation. BAA did not actively market the airport to GA, preferring to rely on the fixed-base operators to do so, but it did ensure that both operators could develop their facilities in line with growing demand. In most cases GA operators were required to file for runway slots, for which regular commercial services took precedence. If Stansted became busier, particularly at certain times of the day, it was likely that GA taxi operators would find it more difficult than previously to gain runway access at peak times. However, at other times they had full and open access to the airport.

Taxis

14.309. On complaints about recent changes in arrangements for taxi services at Gatwick, BAA said that up to February 2001 there were two taxi operators at each terminal. However, it became apparent that this did not work in the best interest of the customer. The drivers of one operator being self employed and being licensed by the local authority had been able to derive their livelihood from a mix of journeys both local and longer distance; appointing two operators operating side by side had created an imbalance in the job mix and confusion for the customer. Controllers from both operators were under some pressure to allocate work evenly between the drivers and competition was effectively abandoned, in order to ensure drivers were retained at Gatwick. Service declined as drivers were supplementing Gatwick work with local work, often resulting in drivers being unavailable at peak times. Hence, when the contract was retendered in February 2001, tenders were sought on the basis of a single operator in both terminals, and one operator at each. Contracts were awarded on the basis of one operator per terminal. However, the uneven and seasonal split of passenger numbers between the terminals and the very different profile/mix led to a similar situation and the drivers working solely from the North Terminal were disadvantaged in their earning capabilities. It became apparent that one operator with one pool of drivers serving both terminals was the best option providing flexibility and better service to the customer. The incumbent operator now operated under a very comprehensive SLA ensuring standards were kept to a high level from cleanliness and appearance through to safety of vehicles. Every private hire vehicle was also subject to stringent checks by the local licensing authority. The most significant improvement had been the prequoting of fares prior to boarding the taxi. Customer research showed that 70 per cent of customers preferred this. This afforded the customer the real choice before getting in the taxi between using the airport taxi service, telephoning off-airport companies, using public transport or alternative means. Gatwick airport now received only about ten complaints per 10,000 journeys a month with regard to taxis, a significant reduction on complaints under the previous contractual regime. Both operators and drivers were also now able to invest in the phased introduction of new vehicles and a computerized booking facility.

14.310. Commenting on the complaint about taxi services at Heathrow, BAA confirmed the present charge was now £2.55, comprising the operation cost of the system of £1.75, the HALT levy of £0.49, and VAT. The increase was discussed with trade bodies and published when due. HAL had not made any profits from the collection of its fee, and currently under-recovered by approximately 50 per cent. As there were 7,500 current individual taxi users registered to go through the taxi feeder bar, HAL met only representatives at the trade quarterly meetings to discuss policy, improvements, management issues and increases of use for the taxi feeder. This was done to establish formal communications with taxi drivers and to do so on an individual basis would lead to nothing being agreed. A number of trade bodies were invited which were recognized as the major taxi representative bodies, and also the joint radio taxi association, public carriage office and the metropolitan police. All minutes were published and placed on the taxi notice board.

14.311. HALT had received funding from the Heathrow taxi drivers since the early 1990s. This was primarily to fund the taxi information desk in the terminals and was in response to an original request from the taxi trade. It was agreed that HALT would be set up as a company formed by the trade as a registered friendly society. All of the original documentation went missing in the Heathrow tunnel collapse. Although there had been no contractual documents entered, the system had worked well for many years and only two of the registered users had complained. Legal proceedings had been issued by one or more of this group against HALT which BAA believed were unsuccessful.

14.312. HALT had informed HAL that all drivers received the same service and benefits from HALT whether they were HALT members or not: the only difference was the opportunity to vote at the AGM. It was HAL's understanding that all trade organizations agreed the desks were of benefit to the trade as a whole; if the majority view changed or circumstances altered then HAL had said it would review the HALT funding but at present HAL had no evidence to this effect. BAA had asked for proof of the allegations of corruption and malpractice within HALT: this would clearly concern HAL who would obviously investigate this in conjunction with the police. This had not been forthcoming. HAL had made representations to the register of friendly societies concerning the management of HALT following allegations about HALT's AGM, but had been advised there was no statutory regulatory function to intervene or make an interpretation of the rules of society. In the event of a dispute to the rules HALT members could enforce under County Court; HAL had no knowledge of any action taken.

14.313. BAA was of the opinion that the operation of the taxi feeder park and the charges made were legal; no other documentation existed; individual taxi drivers had the choice of plying for hire outside of the airport, but by entering the taxi feeder park accepted the terms and conditions of use and this had been accepted by one driver in his withdrawal of his legal action.

VAT refunds

14.314. On complaints about arrangements for VAT refund operators, BAA referred to a special arrangement now in operation for over two years at T3, in which Travelex staff had manned the HM customs desk. Hence, the second check at the cash refund desk was not required and the customer could be given the cash refund straightaway, reducing queuing time; and the landside customs desks was being consistently staffed, which was not the case before, also improving customer service. This had also allowed HM Customs to redeploy staff to focus on more important issues. This arrangement was dependent on an independent company processing the cash refunds, since HM Customs were not able to work with that company directly involved in the business due to concerns over confidentiality. It also required only one company to process all the cash refunds.

14.315. The Travelex contract had recently been extended due to the successful operation of the business over the term of the previous contract. BAA said that it was under no obligation to retender the contract, its code of practice stating it was acceptable to negotiate an extension if criteria such as good service were satisfied. A further reason for extension was the exceptional circumstances of the contract, Travelex being the sole bureau operator present at every terminal at Heathrow and Gatwick, and able to provide the service in a more cost-efficient manner than any other operator and without the requirement for additional space, and having a working relationship with HM Customs.

14.316. BAA believed that having more than one refund point would substantially detract from customer service as customers with vouchers from different operators would have to queue at three different desks (HM Customs, Global Refund and VatBack). There would be potential customer confusion; and the arrangements with T3 would no longer be viable. BAA currently subsidized the current operation at T3 landside because of the implications for customer service.

14.317. Customers did not pay extra for the current service because there was only one operator; it was irrelevant to the customer who they obtained their cash refund from, hence to provide the customer service it was important simply to ensure the process was as simple as possible, which was best achieved with one location rather than multiple locations; if dedicated VAT refund operators were to be provided space, this would also take up valuable space that could be better utilized for other services. BAA also insisted no surcharges be made for cash refunds although this was a higher cost than post or credit card: hence there was no detriment to the customer from the current arrangements.

14.318. There was also no obligation for VAT refund operators to provide a cash refund service; if charges were too high, neither Global Refund nor its competitors would agree to do business with Travelex or BAA. The fee structure for all VAT refund operators was the same to ensure those who wished to offer the service could do so on a level playing field; the level of the fees charged to Global Refund by Travelex was also similar to the level of fees charged to Vatback when Global Refund held the contract at Gatwick to provide cash refunds on behalf of itself and other operators. It was also similar to the amount that Global Refund proposed charging its competitors when it tendered for the Heathrow business. The cost of doing business was also probably no higher than when Global Refund operated the cash refund desk itself, as the fee it paid to Travelex should be the equivalent of the cost of building, fitting out and staffing and managing a unit and paying a concession fee to BAA.

14.319. Quality of customer service in T3 had also improved substantially since BAA commenced provision of VAT cash refund service from an independent operator, queuing time being reduced and goods being able to be checked landside and stored in hold luggage rather than taken airside as hand luggage.

14.320. Hence, BAA believed that the current method of providing the VAT cash refund service did not operate against the public interest, as there was no increase in cost to customers; quality of service was improved; having one VAT cash refund point was a simpler solution for a customer and was the most efficient and cost-effective solution; and operation of the service through an independent operator meant all those refund operators who wished to offer their customers the option of receiving their VAT refund in cash were able to do so on a level playing field. Hence, BAA believed that the provision of the service by a sole operator was essential to derive and develop the substantial customer service benefits arising from the close working relationship that had been developed with HM Customs.

Fire training

14.321. On complaints about fire training arrangements at Stansted, BAA said that the training of BAA staff was previously undertaken by various trained facilitators on a departmental basis. In order to improve efficiency, enhance consistency and effectively increase the number of fire training sessions available to staff it was concluded that all such training should be led by BAA fire service personnel. The number of airlines, concessionaries and tenant staff was increasing as the airport grew, and BAA was keen to ensure that they undertook the appropriate legally required training. Given the courses being run for BAA staff, the offer was made to third parties to book their staff on these two-hour courses at £10 a head if spare places exist. This had the effect of ensuring that frequent courses accommodating around 40 people were available on predetermined dates throughout the year, thereby assisting all occupants of the airport by providing opportunities for the many new staff being recruited. As a result the marginal costs of providing third party training were very low and therefore there could be no question of cross-subsidy. The course was not obligatory for non BAA staff: indeed BAA also offered a 'train the trainer' course to enable other organizations to undertake the regular annual training themselves in future. The primary objective had been to approve BAA processes and take the opportunity of contributing positively to fire safety at Stansted. Since the new procedure for fire training commenced in September 2001, STAL had billed £9,050 to external companies for attendance at the regular session and £6,400 for train the trainer courses. One other company offered fire and evacuation training, charging more than STAL but more flexible as to dates and days and providing a full tour of the terminal which STAL did not.

Travel agent outlets

14.322. BAA asked the CC to recommend to the CAA that the formal conditions from the previous report relating to travel agents at Gatwick be revoked. One agent terminated the contract two months before it was due to expire in March 2002; the other contract was due to expire on 31 May 2002. Sales were down 21 per cent in 2000, and a further 45 per cent in 2001. Various factors were mentioned for this, including rapid growth of LFCs selling direct to passengers, the amount of discounted sales by airlines through affiliated tour operators, the very significant increase in internet sales, tour operators improving their own late sales systems, use by tour operators of large call centres, and airlines paying lower levels of commission. The remaining agent wanted the guaranteed minimum payment to be reduced by 50 per cent for it to extend the contract.

14.323. BAA explained that the concessionaire paid the higher of the agreed minimum fee or an agreed percentage of sales as the concession fee: the figure for the guaranteed minimum was calculated as a percentage of expected income to BAA (less than 100 per cent) based on the concessionaire's sales forecast. BAA had not considered the rental of desks alone for these contracts: when the two travel shops were open the concessionaire requirements were for space for four to six staff who could both deal face to face and answer phone calls. However, methods of booking holidays had dramatically changed. A change to rental of a desk would not offer any financial advantage to a travel shop operator—Flightlines current minimum guarantee payment was less than the amount they would pay using the rate applied to airline or handling agent ticket sales desks—even if the existing frontage was reduced by 25 per cent and did not have any office behind the desk. BAA would, however, consider a change in the form of space requirement, subject to availability of desk space. The old operator did not have an ATOL licence but did have other licences enabling it to offer travel products.

14.324. BAA's strong preference was for the condition requiring it to have two outlets to be removed; but it believed the market for the service had changed to such an extent there should be no condition at all governing the number of travel outlets at Gatwick. Its intention was to tender the existing FIL unit as a travel outlet concession but it would have to review this plan if there was a disappointing level of interest in the tender; or if the concession proved uneconomic for the concessionaire. At the end of the three-year contract it would review the market and identify whether a further contract was appropriate both in terms of the demand for airport-based outlets and the potential alternative uses for the site. If the demand was similar to that today, its intention would remain to retender a single unit for this purpose.

Separation of ownership of the three airports

14.325. BAA said that this had been reviewed many times by third parties who had all concluded in favour of the current system framework. Hence, it said that there was little to be gained in giving further consideration to this topic, but acknowledged that if it did not operate in the national interest, or blatantly did not carry out what it had agreed to do, there was always a threat of being broken up.

14.326. As to not allowing third parties to invest, BAA said that this was incorrect in fact and in policy terms, and there were numerous examples of such investment such as maintenance hangars, cargo sheds, transfer baggage facilities; furthermore it was unaware of any cases where airlines had required investment and the company had been unprepared to undertake this. However, it would seek to build to its planning guidelines and in a manner which complied with its sustainability objectives.

D J MORRIS *(Chairman)*

R HOLROYD

P MOIZER

J A REES

J RICKFORD

R FOSTER *(Secretary)*

31 October 2002

Printed in the UK by The Stationery Office Limited
12/02 800736 19585